Mayor Helen Boosalis

MAYOR
HELEN
BOOSALIS

My Mother's Life in Politics

BETH BOOSALIS DAVIS

University of Nebraska Press
LINCOLN AND LONDON

Library of Congress Cataloging-in-Publication Data

Davis, Beth Boosalis.

Mayor Helen Boosalis : my mother's life in politics /
Beth Boosalis Davis.

p. cm.

Includes bibliographical references and index.

ISBN 978-0-8032-1740-9 (cloth : alk. paper)

1. Boosalis, Helen.

2. Mayors—Nebraska—Lincoln—Biography.

3. Lincoln (Neb.)—Politics and government—20th century.

4. Politicians—Nebraska—Biography.

5. Lincoln (Neb.)—Biography. I. Title.

F674.L7D39 2008   978.2'293033092—dc22

[B]

2007050927

Set in Dante MT.

Designed by Ashley Muehlbauer.

To the magnificent men in my life . . .
my dad, Mike
my husband, Max
my sons, Mike and Chris

Contents

List of Illustrations   ix

Note on Sources and Structure   xiii

Acknowledgments   xv

Introduction   xix

Flash Forward: Calling Me Home   1

1. Call to Action   12

   Flash Forward: Down to Two   43

2. Madame Mayor   54

   Flash Forward: May the Best Woman . . .   87

3. This Is Not Your Father's City Hall   99

   Flash Forward: Money Talks   134

4. Roll Up Her Sleeves   146

   Flash Backward: Roots—All Greek to Me   174

5. Expect the Unexpected   206

   Flash Forward: Getting to Know You   248

6. Everything Old Is New Again   259

   Flash Forward: One False Move and . . .   290

7. Mayors' Mayor   307

   *Flash Forward: Issues, Debates, Polls,
   and Other Irrelevancies   340*

8. Another Time Around   351

   Flash Forward: Trail's End   383

9. Life After Is Politics   398

Afterword   423

Photo Acknowledgments   425

Appendixes: Biography Timeline, City Councils   429

Notes   431

Interviews   509

Bibliography   513

Index   515

Illustrations

1. Helen, the seamstress   18
2. Helen, the homemaker   19
3. 1959 Boosalis for City Council campaign card   28
4. Boosalis family campaigns in Helen's 1959
   city council race   29
5. Helen Boosalis, city council chair, 1974   40
6. Mike Boosalis in his university lab, 1975   41
7. 1986 Boosalis for Governor campaign sticker   44
8. Helen shares Mother's Day with family
   during governor's race   45
9. Helen accepts Democratic primary election
   nomination for governor   46
10. Helen's supporters celebrate her gubernatorial
    primary win   47
11. Democratic unity event after the
    gubernatorial primary   48
12. 1975 Boosalis for Mayor campaign brochure   70
13. 1975 mayor's race: Schwartzkopf v. Boosalis   71
14. Helen stakes her own yard signs in 1975
    mayoral campaign   72
15. Democrat Helen Boosalis and Republican
    Kay Orr   91
16. Helen takes oath of office as mayor, 1975   100
17. Mayor Boosalis appoints Police Chief
    George Hansen   115
18. Bill Bradley comes to Nebraska for
    governor's campaign   137
19. Maynard Jackson touts Helen's national
    reputation as mayor   138
20. Gary Hart rallies Boosalis voters at press
    conference   139

21. The mayor takes the bus to work   148
22. Helen's parents, Bertha and George Geankoplis   177
23. Helen Geankoplis at age three   178
24. Helen and her siblings   179
25. Helen's 1937 high school graduation photo   191
26. Helen Geankoplis dates Mike Boosalis, 1942   195
27. Helen Geankoplis, engaged, 1944   196
28. Mike Boosalis, U.S. Army Air Forces   197
29. Mike Boosalis with B-24 flight crew   199
30. "Just Married"—Mike and Helen Boosalis, 1945   201
31. "Win Amazes Mayor" reads the headline   241
32. Helen and family celebrate 1979 mayoral
    reelection   242
33. Helen's grandsons and daughter campaign
    for Helen for governor   251
34. Helen takes her campaign for governor
    across the state   254
35. The mayor's door is always open   267
36. "Take Off the Gloves" editorial cartoon of
    governor's race   305
37. President Carter meets with U.S. Conference
    of Mayors executive committee   311
38. Mayor Boosalis applauds President Carter at
    U.S. Conference of Mayors   316
39. U.S. Conference of Mayors president Boosalis
    meets with President Reagan   324
40. Governor Kerrey and former governor
    Morrison join Helen's campaign   343
41. Helen prepares to fly in 1926 Swallow biplane   364
42. Helen prepares for an ostrich race   365
43. Helen "copilots" an F-4 fighter
    reconnaissance jet   366
44. Lincoln's first woman mayor and portraits of her
    forty-three male predecessors   368
45. The mayor greets five thousand well-wishers
    as she leaves office   380

46. The mayor's farewell appreciation party   381

47. Mike and Helen cast their votes for governor,
    November 4, 1986   389

48. Helen Boosalis delivers concession speech   392

49. Helen and Mike at home, post–governor's race   397

50. Senator Exon meets with AARP National
    Legislative Council member Helen Boosalis, 1989   405

51. Vice President Gore meets with AARP board
    chair Helen Boosalis, 1998   406

52. Helen, Mike, and Beth at Helen Boosalis Trail
    dedication in 2005   411

53. Jan Gauger and Helen are honored in 2007 as founders of the
    Lincoln–Lancaster Commission on the Status of Women   414

54. Helen Boosalis in Lincoln, 1999   420

55. Helen and Beth, mother and daughter   421

This book relies on personal memory, newspaper clippings, research on contextual history, and interviews. Chapter 1 begins with my childhood memories of my mother's first run for local elected office; chapters 2–8 rely extensively on newspaper clippings my father cataloged during Mom's mayoral years, after I moved away from home; and chapter 9 relates to my mother's post-electoral life. The chapters move chronologically from 1959 to the present.

Distinct from the chapters are Flash Forwards, which are interspersed among the chapters and focus entirely on Mom's 1986 campaign for governor. I call these "flash forwards" because they transport the reader forward in time to moments in my mother's race for governor. The Flash Forwards include my snapshot memories after I joined her campaign for governor. After each Flash Forward the reader returns again to a chapter account of an earlier chronology along Mom's political path. The one exception to the Flash Forward sequence is the Flash Backward ("Roots—All Greek to Me"), which appears between chapters 4 and 5; as its name suggests, the Flash Backward goes back in time to my parents' family roots rather than forward in time to the 1986 governor's race. The specific time periods covered in the chapters, Flash Forwards, and Flash Backward are noted as each begins.

Asterisks (*) within the text indicate further explanation or commentary that can be found by locating corresponding page numbers and asterisks in the Notes section at the end of the book. The Notes section contains both the explanatory notes (marked with asterisks) and the sources for quotations or information in the book.

I interviewed, both locally and nationally, thirty-five people with a range of personal perspectives on my mother's political life, and their interview quotations are spread throughout the book. And, of course, I interviewed my mom and dad for their reflections and insights in framing the story to add to my view as a daughter.

Acknowledgments

My number one thank you goes to my dad, whose monumental efforts more than twenty-five years ago were invaluable and essential for writing this book. I asked Dad what possessed him to collect meticulously the sixty-five volumes of newspaper clippings that documented nearly every day of my mother's years as mayor and provided me the historical window into Mom's political leadership. Dad says he has no idea why he kept such careful records, but I recognize his devoted efforts sprang from love and admiration, as this book springs from a like source.

Thanks to Dad, too, for connecting me to Mary Pipher, who gave me the tools and confidence as a writer in her class, Writing to Change the World, at the Nebraska Summer Writers' Conference. Thanks also to my University of Iowa Summer Writing Festival instructors: Stephen Bloom, who set me on the path to publication; Marc Niesen, who helped me find my voice as daughter, not biographer; and Kate Gleeson, who encouraged my project's earliest glimmer. I also thank Carleton's Harriet Sheridan and Owen Jenkins, Southeast's Mary Commers, and Holmes's Joan Dumpert for their dedication to teaching writing.

I am greatly indebted to University of Nebraska Press associate director and editor Ladette Randolph, who believed in my telling my story my way, helped me cut the chaff, and guided this first-time author through the labyrinth; thanks also to Margie Rine for her enthusiasm and valuable perspective on Mom's political history; and to Ann Baker, Kate Salem, Kristen Rowley, and the entire University of Nebraska Press team.

I am grateful for the thoughtful reading and constructive suggestions of Ethlyn Bond, Barbara Bonner, Charles Cullen, Elizabeth Demers, Michael Dukakis, Janie Gabbett, Dona Gerson, Nikki Heidepriem, Martha Lavey, Wendy Bay Lewis, Margaret Lurie, Diana Nielander, Bonny Roth, Dixie Watterson, and the University of Nebraska Press readers who reviewed my manuscript, and for the fine copyediting of Jonathan Lawrence. Bonny Roth somehow tamed the book's voluminous citations through dozens of hours, at all hours, of painstaking work in my red dining room.

My thanks to the *Lincoln Journal Star* and to former editor Kathleen Rutledge for permission to use the many photographs from the paper's archives as a courtesy; and to Denise Matulka, *Journal Star* news librarian, who generously contributed her expertise in locating and identifying the photos. Special acknowledgment to former editorial pages editors Bob Schrepf (*Lincoln Star*) and Dick Herman (*Lincoln Journal*), whose editorial insights and analysis during my mother's mayoral years added enormously to my view of Mom and the times; thanks, too, to all the other journalists upon whose work I so depended.

Also expanding my perspective were personal interviews with thirty-five of Mom's local and national political colleagues and others (identified in "Interviews"), who graciously permitted inclusion of their comments and whom I thank for their generosity, warmth, and recollections. Thanks also to DiAnna Schimek and Frank Daly, who filled in research on the governor's campaign; and to Linda Garrison, Ed Sobel, and Tim Evans for publication advice.

No effort as all-consuming as writing a book is possible without unflagging support from dear friends who have been so important in my life: my walking group—Shirley Cullen, Jackie Crihfield, and Donna Zupancic; law compatriots Sandy Balick, Nikki Heidepriem, Sheli Rosenberg, Susan Wise, and Sarah Wolff; Evanston City Council colleagues Sue Brady, Ned (and Albe) Lauterbach, Maxine Lange, Dona Gerson, Betty Papangelis, Don Borah, Sandy Gross, Bob Romain, Dave Ream, Marge Collens, Marge Wold, and Cheryl Wollin; National League of Cities cohorts Ruth Messinger, Andrew Lachman, Jim Scheibel, Mary Pat Lee, Margaret Barrett, Al Simon, and Alice Wolfe; Carleton friends past and present; longtime Steppenwolf friends; my thirty-year-old book group, especially founder and friend Susie Alberts; the Gripper Girls; Danuta Sadzewicz; Evanstonians Tasha Deutsch, Ingrid Stafford, my kind neighbor Mary Finnegan, and forever considerate sister-in-law Annie Boyle Davis; friends at Evanston Community Foundation, First Bank and Trust, Leadership Greater Chicago, Legal Assistance Foundation of Chicago, Schiff Hardin and Waite, Ross and Hardies, and Centel; Greek Orthodox congregations in Lincoln and Minneapolis, and our First United Methodist Church of Evanston community. Thanks, too, for cheers from my siblings-in-law Peter, Paul, Karen, and Diana Davis and Mary Lynn and Michael Beasley, and from my incomparably terrific "Big Fat Greek" extended family.

Thanks to new friends I made along this journey—the Benedictine Sisters of Chicago, who welcomed me to a peaceful refuge at a critical writing point; and to Drs. Rhonda Stein, Rima Nasser, and Jennifer Schneider, who literally kept me moving.

My deepest appreciation, beyond words, is for my parents, my sons, Mike and Chris, and especially my husband, Max, with whom I've shared thirty-five precious years and whose understanding never wavers, whose support sustains, whose courage inspires, whose love endures.

Traveler, there is no path. The path is made by walking.
—ANTONIO MACHADO Y RUIZ

I have known my mom for fifty-nine years. Perhaps I should subtract two or three of those that I cannot now remember, but I knew my mother even during those years. I knew her in the way most children, even grown ones, know their mothers—as a being whose purpose is my well-being.

Granted, as children mature we develop a slightly less egocentric, one-dimensional view of our mothers, but my appreciation of my mother remained skewed by her devotion to me. How can you be objective about the person who is your ultimate cheerleader, who loves you unconditionally, who believes you can do no wrong? The short answer is, you can't.

I knew when I set out to write this book about my mother that attaining objectivity about her would not be possible. But that was not my goal. My quest sprang from a desire to know more of the whole woman, not only the mother parts.

Familiar to me were Mom's political accomplishments, unusual for a woman of her era: elected city council member in Lincoln, Nebraska, my hometown; mayor and chief executive of Lincoln; first woman president of the U.S. Conference of Mayors; and Democratic nominee for governor of Nebraska in the country's first two-woman gubernatorial election. But I wanted to walk that path alongside her—to grasp more fully the twists and turns of struggle, joy, disappointment, satisfaction, frustration, and triumph that she encountered along her way.

And I wanted to understand what kept her going on the path that was not a path before she walked it. What illuminated her next uncharted steps, renewed her strength after falling, nourished her determination? Was she graced with a special set of qualities, or did she learn what she needed along the way? Is she unique, or one of us? Can one not only admire her example but also find the same within? Can I?

You see, I wrote the book for myself. I chose the moments that most intrigued me, my own cups of tea. My mother's own story, were she telling it, would be different. For one thing, Mom will undoubtedly think the book is too much about her and not enough about those who supported her, especially my dad.

But this is my story, my version of one woman's remarkable journey—a woman who is also my mother.

Calling Me Home
March 1986

An unfamiliar voice at the other end of the phone asked, "Is this Mary Beth?" Immediately the question engaged my Nebraska self—Nebraska, where I was known for eighteen years as Mary Beth before going off to college, where I was M.B., and eventually dropping Mary altogether by the time I married. Mary Beth had always sounded southern to me anyway, though I liked being named after my grandmothers, Mary and Bertha (Beth and Bertha are the same in Greek: Panayiota).

This disembodied phone voice was calling me by my familial, familiar, Nebraska name—and not my grown-up name, Beth. Who was it? "You don't know me. My name is Neil Oxman and I'm working with your mother's campaign."

"Oh hi," I managed to interrupt the increasingly emphatic, eastern-accented caller.

"Look, you don't know me. I don't know you. But everyone I've talked to here in Nebraska agrees that you need to come home. Your mom needs your help and people say you'll know what to do. Besides, you're the only child, so it's up to you."

I sat at the kitchen table, surrounded by stacks of unread memos for my Evanston City Council meeting that evening, feeling both assaulted by and drawn to this stranger's insistent tone. I don't remember the rest of the conversation, just that I hung up with a vague promise that I'd see what was possible at my end.

A week later, I stepped off the United plane in Lincoln with Christopher and all the baby paraphernalia that accompanies a two-year-old.

Christopher's older brother, Michael, stayed home with his dad to go to kindergarten. As Chris and I heaved ourselves out of the jetway into the waiting arms of my dad, I didn't know that this would be the first of many commuting trips between Chicago and Lincoln, and that my life for the next seven months would be bifurcated.

As we arrived in Lincoln that blustery March day in 1986, I still felt torn about leaving home but clung to my husband Max's parting words: "Of course you have to do this for your mom . . . it's one of those once-in-a-lifetime things . . . you don't question, you just do it."

In Lincoln I had to race to catch up with the status of the governor's race. Mom hadn't had a moment to fill me in on her campaign. All I knew was that it had ejected from the launch pad at the eleventh hour, just like all her earlier campaigns.

But this time the lateness of my mother's decision to run for elected office was not of her making. Nebraska Democrats were in disarray when the popular governor Bob Kerrey stunned the state by announcing his decision not to seek a second term. In late October 1985, a year before the end of his first term, Governor Kerrey made his surprise announcement, saying he no longer had any desire to hold the office. One reporter speculated that Kerrey's absence from the race would be good for the Democratic Party because he had been "indifferent" to the party—his party affiliation had not appeared to be important to him or to play a significant role in his administrative appointments. Some political leaders thought the absence of the "charismatic and sometimes controversial bachelor" from the governor's race would drain excitement from the contest.

Not long after Governor Kerrey's bowing out, speculation about likely gubernatorial primary candidates began. On the Democratic side, Omaha mayor Mike Boyle and state Game and Parks director Gene Mahoney were viewed as banner carriers for conservative Omaha Democrats, including organized labor. Lincoln liberals hoped to persuade Lincoln's former mayor Helen Boosalis—my mother—to enter the race, although state senators Chris Beutler (Lincoln) and Vard Johnson (Omaha) were also potentially acceptable to Lincoln Democrats. On the Republican side, early speculation identified state GOP chairman Kermit Brashear, who had been busy bashing Kerrey after studying his record and vulnerabilities; Nancy Hoch, an unsuccessful U.S. Senate candidate the year before; U.S. representative Hal Daub; and state treasurer Kay Orr.

In the wake of Kerrey's unexpected October announcement, the cast of potential candidates shifted throughout the fall. Mayor Boyle removed himself from consideration early. My mother responded to pressure to run by saying that she would probably not decide until January 1986 to allow time to judge her depth of support and ability to raise money. Several other Democrats were quick to fill the vacuum and jumped in the race early, including Norfolk attorney David Domina and state senators Chris Beutler and Marge Higgins (Omaha).

In December 1985 Mom and Dad flew to Chicago to spend the holidays with us, and Mom "did all the motherly and grandmotherly things—baked cookies, played in the snow." As always, she jazzed our boys' bedtime with her elaborate and hilarious stories. She let them cover themselves and the kitchen in flour as they clumsily used the rolling pin and sprinkled colored sugar on Christmas cookies.

During their holiday visit I don't remember Mom agonizing or even mulling over her decision to run for Nebraska's top elected office. I wonder if self-absorption with my own hectic life as a parent and a first-term city alderman obscured my view of the magnitude of her imminent decision. Perhaps she deliberately kept her own counsel and used the geographic distance from the roiling political waters of Nebraska's wide-open governor's contest to take a break and just enjoy her family. In any event, my mother returned to Nebraska ready to resign her cabinet position in the Kerrey administration—she had decided to run to succeed him as governor.

On February 3, 1986, Mom made her formal announcement to enter the Democratic gubernatorial primary race. She had planned to launch her campaign in Lexington in rural Dawson County to emphasize the importance of the state's farm communities, then fly to communities across the state—Omaha, South Sioux City, Grand Island, Kearney, North Platte, and Scottsbluff—on a whirlwind two-day announcement trip. But thick fog blanketed the Lincoln area that morning, and the pilot of the twin-engine plane nixed the day's plans. Undaunted, Mom and her campaign group piled in a van before dawn to cover as much of her original announcement tour as possible.

In the rush of changing plans and the excitement of the mission, no one had eaten breakfast. About thirty miles southeast of Lincoln the van stopped in Unadilla, population 291. The fog may have thwarted the travel plans of the eager campaign group, but they lucked into breakfast at Horstman's Café, where the special was sausage gravy and biscuits— $1.25 for a huge plate, and a half order for 75 cents. While others in her group worked their way through their bountiful half orders, Mom worked her way with exuberance through the café's Formica-top tables, shaking hands and receiving a warm welcome from Otoe County farmers and a solitary banker. Although unplanned and unscripted, the breakfast in Unadilla proved an inspiring start to my mother's campaign for governor.

On home turf in Lincoln later that day after campaign stops in Omaha and South Sioux City, Mom announced her gubernatorial candidacy at Isco, a homegrown scientific instruments company founded by family friend Bob Allington, who grew the business from his garage and basement into a global enterprise. Then, after two days of news conferences and appearances across the state by the newest Democratic primary candidate, the nascent Boosalis for Governor campaign held a large rally on February 5 at Lincoln's Cornhusker Hotel. My mother told the jubilant crowd jammed in the ballroom, "You are going to give Nebraska its first woman governor, Helen Boosalis!" Coincidentally, attending the annual dinner of the Association of Commerce and Industry that same evening in the hotel's adjoining banquet room were two other women who also had hopes of becoming the state's first woman governor—Republican primary candidates Nancy Hoch and Kay Orr.

With the primary only three months away, pundits predicted the winners to be Republican Nancy Hoch and Democrat Helen Boosalis and anticipated their parties' campaign strategies. Prevailing views were that Democratic candidates would be forced to concentrate their campaigns in Omaha, Lincoln, and larger Platte Valley towns where the most Democratic votes lay, with Omaha being the major battleground. Because Republican voters were not as concentrated in population centers and major news media markets, Republican candidates were predicted to fan out into heavily Republican rural areas without relying as much on media coverage in the primary.

A month after her announcement, Mom named campaign co-chairs to expand her bases of geographic and political support: Omaha attorney Ben Nelson, former state insurance director and Nebraska co-chair of President Carter's reelection campaign; and Maurine Biegert of Shickley, former Democratic National Committeewoman in the Third Congressional District (rural western Nebraska) and active in the successful campaigns of Democratic governors Frank Morrison, J. J. Exon, and Bob Kerrey.

By the primary filing deadline in mid-March 1986, seven Democrats and eight Republicans had filed to run for governor, setting a gubernatorial primary record of fifteen candidates and surpassing the previous state record of fourteen in 1934. In most non-presidential primaries fewer than 50 percent of registered voters go to the polls. Nebraska had a total of only 850,000 registered voters (42 percent Democrats and 51 percent Republicans), and state law allowed election of primary nominees by a plurality of votes rather than a majority. The fifteen candidates for governor would surely have to scour the state for every vote if they hoped to emerge as primary winners.

Such a crowded field made it difficult to distinguish singular voices from the chorus of candidates putting forth their programs for economic development, agricultural assistance, school financing, streamlined government, and a host of other state issues. One reporter viewed the primary campaign as a "performance overflowing with actors and actresses all trying to play the lead."

How to pull away from the pack was each candidate's dilemma. An *Omaha World-Herald* poll at the end of March, only six weeks before the primary election, showed both parties facing close three-way races. On the Republican side, Nancy Hoch led with 26 percent of those polled, but Kermit Brashear and Kay Orr were in a close fight for second with 17 and 16 percent, respectively. The Democrats were even more closely grouped, with my mother and Chris Beutler tied at 17 percent and David Domina at 12 percent. Although Mom may have enjoyed strong name recognition and an early lead, some questioned whether her campaign was being too cautious given that the largest percentage of Democratic voters seemed to be undecided and that her Democratic support in Omaha—the Second Congressional District battleground and must-win for any Democratic gubernatorial hopeful—appeared to be weaker than in the other two congressional districts.

In the crowded primary field, endorsements played some role in distinguishing one candidate from another. As sitting governor, Bob Kerrey declined to choose publicly his favored candidate among the seven Democrats running in the party primary. Former governor Frank Morrison eagerly endorsed my mother, saying, "The Democratic Party has several candidates who are competent, but none has the experience that Helen has." On the Republican side, former state governor Nobby Tiemann endorsed Nancy Hoch in the primary and suggested that "voters take the opportunity to retire Kay Orr, an 'againster,' from politics"— leading some to speculate that a rift between the conservative and more progressive wings of the Republican party was reemerging.

In its endorsement of my mother, the *Lincoln Journal* noted that the former Lincoln mayor had "earned . . . permanent foes" for "her insistence on putting public concerns before individual private interests, as a councilperson and as mayor" and praised her for her "amazing store of personal energy and an astonishing empathy with and for people." Somewhat inconsistently, the *Journal* admitted that its "single greatest concern about Helen Boosalis is her age. Being governor is an energy-draining, non-stop job."

While none of the candidates blatantly focused on the age issue, news stories often referenced Democrat David Domina, age thirty-five, as potentially the youngest Nebraska governor to be elected in seventy years, and Helen Boosalis, who would be sixty-seven before the general election, as potentially the oldest governor to take office. My mother's response: "I know people who are old at 30 and young at 85." Had anyone asked, I would have told them of my dream to catch up someday to Mom's energy level; instead, I had to accept her ability to run circles around me when I was eighteen, twenty-eight, thirty-eight (my age when she ran for governor). Even now her stamina confounds me.

With tight races in both parties heading into the home stretch before the May primary, statewide advertising became critical. "This may be more of a contest between ad agencies or shoe leather than a struggle of ideas," one reporter said of the crowded field of primary candidates. "Voters may be left to choose . . . the one with the most, or the best,

TV ads." Prior to the close *Omaha World-Herald* poll results published on March 30, only Democrat Domina and Republicans Brashear and Orr had run television ads; my mother and Republican front-runner Nancy Hoch had yet to advertise on TV, with only six weeks to go before the primary election on May 13.

Before my hasty last-minute trip to Lincoln, toddler in tow, I was in the dark about most of these campaign details that had transpired in the period after my folks' Christmas visit, Mom's announcement of her candidacy in February, and the heating up of the crowded primary campaign in March. The phone call from Neil Oxman had interrupted my self-absorbed young adult life of marriage, family, and career and persuasively commanded my attention to Mom's campaign for governor. Now I was stepping off the plane and into the fray.

On the short drive to my parents' home from the Lincoln airport, my dad seemed distracted and somewhat edgy. We didn't even play our usual game from my childhood: when returning from annual family trips to Minnesota, the three of us—Mom, Dad, and I—strained to be the first to glimpse Lincoln's majestic capitol building rising from the plains, thereby winning a nickel from the other two. Instead, Dad spoke of the tightening primary race for governor and his concern for Mom's well-being and her stressful campaign schedule.

After settling Christopher with a babysitter that afternoon, I headed for Mom's campaign headquarters in downtown Lincoln, a warren of small offices and cubicles in a good location off O Street. Once inside I was bombarded by the boisterous buttons, banners, posters and signs, all screaming the name—my name—BOOSALIS. People were cordial but busy—no, frantic—with the May primary election less than two months away.

An imposing, chain-smoking woman commandeered the under-sized reception desk, managing to give me a fragmented welcome between incessant rings of the multi-button phone, "Boosalis for Governor. Please hold. . . . Boosalis for Governor. One moment." Between rings I took in the room, seeking signs of order in the chaos. Boxes and placards and pamphlets were stacked in corners, under tables, behind doors. At one end of a long table a woman instructed volunteers on the fine points of stuffing envelopes. Glancing down the hallway of offices leading from this circus ring, I heard the receptionist tell someone I had arrived.

Then I met the voice—the voice from my kitchen phone call a week earlier. Neil Oxman came striding out of one of the offices down the hall. Big, I mean really huge, with black curly hair and an intensity in his gaze and his movements that made you feel like you'd been caught taking an afternoon nap. I knew little about him—I'd picked up only scraps of information in the nanosecond conversations with my mom as I rushed to make preparations to leave Illinois and answer this stranger's siren song.

Before getting Neil's call, I knew almost nothing about the hectic weeks after my mother's announcement of her candidacy—nothing about assembling from scratch a full-blown campaign viable enough to defeat the other six Democratic candidates in the primary: prepping for candidate forums, outlining issues, leasing office space, organizing volunteers, scheduling speeches, choosing colors and logos and slogans to sling, finding and hiring professionals who knew how to run a statewide, not local, campaign—and, of course, raising the money to make this overwhelming challenge somehow attainable.

On that March day I arrived in Lincoln, all I knew about Neil Oxman was that his firm, the Campaign Group, was the Boosalis campaign's "media consultant," but I had almost no idea what media consultants do. I had some vague notion that they are the ones who make political ads for TV, some kind of thirty-second-spot producers. I was right, but only about a portion of Neil's broad-ranging role in the campaign.

I was to learn, painfully, that in a statewide campaign, unlike local, grassroots efforts, the ability to get the candidate's message on TV effectively and frequently—to feed the voracious, insatiable media monster—is the campaign's major driving force. Sometimes you can feed the monster table scraps of news stories with hopes of getting free media coverage, but that won't satisfy the beast's relentless hunger for large wads of cash in exchange for ridiculously little advertising airtime. And that was Neil's job—to feed the media monster.

I didn't know all this at the moment of my introduction to the campaign, when Neil strode in. All I knew was that Mom and her campaign manager, Marg Badura, after a few harried days of interviewing, had hired Neil and ruffled more than a few Nebraska feathers by going out of state for talent. Even worse, they had hired someone from Philadelphia—an easterner, most of whom think Nebraska is a long, boring, flat, driving endurance test to see how much they want to get to California or Colorado. From even my brief phone conversation with Neil, I suspected that Mom had been drawn to his potent, powerful intensity.

Here was Neil now, larger than life, exuding a fierce and ferocious presence towering over me. I was scared. He took me back to his office, sat me down, and, dispensing with social niceties, proceeded to lay it on the line. "Your mother's a great lady, a great candidate—one of the best I've worked with. But the primary is May 13 and unless she gets on TV by next week, this election is over. We have to raise $60,000 in new money in the next week to make our first media buys, or she's never gonna get her shot at governor."

I was stunned . . . $60,000 in a few days. How in the world was that supposed to happen? And why was my help so critical? What about the campaign staff, the organization? Neil dismissed that line of inquiry, barking that the campaign had gotten a late start. The staff was still getting organized and had strong capabilities, but they couldn't turn it around fast enough for the first media buys. They needed someone with personal connections and knowledge of whom to go to quickly to help raise the money in time. "So I guess that's you, kiddo. Let me know how it's going tomorrow morning."

I was shocked. I'd raised a few thousand dollars over several months for my city council campaign at home with lots of help from volunteers and old neighborhood political warhorses. But this—this was the big time, and the timing seemed impossible. Neil handed me a short list of potential contributors, many of whom I recognized, and said it was a starting point.

After leaving Neil's office, I crumpled into my chair at the little desk in the back office where someone told me to sit. Worried and dejected, I thought about how much easier it would be if my family had come from wealth and had wealthy friends, but my dad was a university professor and my mom had been a lifelong community volunteer. Their friends were by and large salt-of-the-earth people of modest means.

With the campaign clock ticking and my fear palpable at having nothing to report to Neil by the next morning, I picked up the phone and started down the A's on the list:

- Mike Alesio—owner of Valentino's, whose pizzas were the favorite of all my high school friends
- Bob Allington—brilliant son of my dad's former colleague and founder of Isco, the scientific instruments business that he built from his wheelchair after contracting polio as a graduate student at MIT (my mind wandered to the backseat of our car during family trips in the 1950s when I was told to roll up the windows as we passed through Iowa towns with reported polio outbreaks)
- John and Catherine Angle—parents of my childhood friend Margaret, who were then living in New York City where John was CEO of Guardian Life Insurance

And on it went. Although I dreaded and nearly died before making each call, the responses were overwhelmingly positive: "I really respect your mother. . . . This state needs her. . . . I'd love to help. . . . How do I make out the check?"

The $60,000 was raised in time, and Neil made the all-important first media buys to air the campaign spots he produced.

Whether as a result of her television advertising or a combination of the ads and the coalescing and shifting into high gear of the Boosalis campaign, my mom's poll numbers rose dramatically in the remaining month before the May primary election. I will never know if Neil was right—that without the timing of those first media buys, one or both of Mom's major opponents could have seized the opportunity to get out in front and stay there—but Neil seemed so sure about most campaign matters, it was difficult to doubt him.

I had never worked with anyone like him. His energy was boundless, his patience nonexistent. Neil once said to me that every time he got off the plane in Lincoln from Philadelphia, he felt like he had stepped into a world where people moved and talked at molasses speed. Of Hungarian and Russian descent, he had the zeal and commitment, I later mused, to fuel a revolution, not a mere campaign.

Several weeks after I joined Mom's campaign for governor, Neil thrust out an epithet that haunts me to this day. I had been trying to manage a reasonable commute between Chicago and Lincoln to keep up with my responsibilities on the city council, shuffle care of the boys, and give the "Hi" sign to my husband, Max, once in awhile. But my Herculean effort was not enough for Neil.

One afternoon he burst into my office. In typical Neil style, he shunned the chair in favor of looming over my desk, barking and punctuating the air to make a point. Had we been outside, he would have blocked the midday sun. Here in my office, his words were dark enough. In a tone defying contradiction, he challenged my commitment to my mother and the campaign, which he said needed much more of my time. In this intense battle to win, he said, my effectiveness was limited by my commuting schedule and divided loyalties.

"Look, Beth, do you really want your mother to win? It sure doesn't seem like it, the way you're shuttling between your lives, like you can somehow give them equal time. Are you just dabbling at this campaign thing? Are you just some kind of dilettante?"

At the word "dilettante" I became enraged. I picked up pens and pencils on my desk and hurled them at Neil. How dare he accuse me of being a dilettante when I was killing myself to keep all the balls I was juggling from crashing to earth? I cannot recall ever throwing things at anyone before or since, so why did his accusation undo me? Was I, in fact, a dilettante—not just in the context of the campaign but also in my life? True, I had wide-ranging interests and a zigzagging career: teaching English, law school, legal aid, corporate law, government law, city council, nonprofit work. Add to this mix my commitment to motherhood and marriage. Was Neil right? Is that why I threw pencils?

I don't know. I still sometimes ask myself the same question that Neil confronted me with that spring day in 1986. What I do know is that shortly after picking those pencils off the floor I took a leave from my Illinois life, arranged to put both boys in day care in Lincoln, assumed permanent residence in my cubbyhole at Boosalis for Governor campaign headquarters, and learned to survive on four or five hours' sleep a night for the duration of Mom's campaign for governor.

Chapter One

Call to Action
1959–1975

"Your mother thinks democracy. She always thinks of people at the bottom of the totem pole and wants to make sure their problems are being dealt with. She's democratic, with a small 'd'."—SUE BAILEY JACKSON, Lincoln City Council member, 1973–77

"The important traits Helen had for public office were her integrity, her willingness to listen to both sides, her ability to work with people—to let them know where she stood and to give them counsel. She also knew how to mix humor with serious issues to diffuse tension."—LLOYD D. HINKLEY, Lincoln City Council member, 1961–69

1959: A VERY GOOD YEAR

At age ten I knew for sure that my mom wasn't just my mother. She was also a person of the people, a person of the world beyond my neighborhood—and most shocking, the person for whom I was suddenly asking strangers to vote.

My astonishment at this unexpected morphing of my mother was understandable. At age ten my sense of the world was strictly confined to my neighborhood where my mom and all the other mothers seemed to share the same purpose: to love, protect, and feed us kids and occasionally ruin our good times. My world was the neighborhood surrounding 1932 South Forty-eighth Street in Lincoln, Nebraska. The west side of the street wasn't part of my neighborhood, because none of the kids who lived on the east side was allowed to cross Forty-eighth Street traffic.

So Forty-eighth Street was the western boundary of my world. I would sit with Ronnie Pfeifer, two years my senior, under the tree that dropped little orange berries in my front yard. We closely monitored the busy Forty-eighth Street traffic for our favorite car models and colors, and for excitement we sometimes fired the orange berries at particularly ugly cars that whizzed by. That was until the day one of the undesirables screeched to a stop after a direct hit by a berry barrage. Before the driver had slammed the car door and started walking toward us, I scrambled into the house and hid under my bed until the coast was clear. We never mentioned the incident to our parents, but we never threw berries again either.

Ronnie lived two doors down, and I looked up to him as I would an older brother. His dad bought the very first television set in the neighborhood. Watching *I Love Lucy* and *Queen for a Day* every Monday night at Ronnie's house was my biggest treat of the week. One Monday my mother wouldn't let me stay at Ronnie's for our favorite shows, so the two of us composed a vengeful note to her ("You are the meanest mom in the whole world and we hate you"), which I surreptitiously dropped on her bedroom floor when I got home.

Later I skulked by my mother's room to sneak a peek whether she had found the note. She was sitting at her dressing table, my favorite place in her room. I had often explored the glass-topped, brocade-skirted oval table to examine its treasures: my mother's White Shoulders perfume, a sterling brush and comb set given to her by her mother (my Gram), and an oversize wooden jewelry box containing a bracelet packed with delicate little charms, each with its own story from my mother's life.

I could see Mom slightly bent over the dressing table, and as I looked closer I saw that she was holding the note and crying. I was dumbstruck. It was the first time I remember seeing Mom cry, and even worse, it was because of me. I ran into her arms, sobbing and saying over and over that I didn't mean it—it was all Ronnie's idea. She comforted and held me, but I've never forgotten the burning shame and guilt I felt for making my strong, beautiful mother cry.

Ronnie was an only child just like me. Being the oldest and also the coolest, he ruled as the anointed leader of our neighborhood pack: the four Ebeling kids, whose backyard house and toys and parents I shared interchangeably with my own; the three Shelley kids, who lived in the next block on Forty-ninth Street; Jimmy Kelly, who lived next door and liked to be tied up like a dog; Jacky Jackson, always in full cowboy attire; Nancy Bornemeier, terrified of tornadoes; Stevie Sankey, who died in third grade when he fell out of an unlocked car door during a family road trip in the days before seatbelts; Teri Brady, whose dad let us X-ray our feet at his children's shoe store.

Ronnie ran a tight ship. He chose the games we played and at whose house we played them. One of his favorites was "The Roundy Round Creature." He would lead the gang down my basement stairs in the dark and scare all us younger kids with frightening tales of the Roundy Round Creature, who Ronnie swore lived in our basement. One day as his story reached the scary climax we all heard a deep, threatening voice: "I am the Roundy Round Creature. What do you want with me?"

Ronnie froze, mid-story, and pushed us aside as he ran screaming for the stairs. Just then my mother appeared, laughing and hugging us. She had stuck her head down the clothes chute only a few feet from where we gathered around our storyteller, so her disguised voice seemed to surround us. After that day Ronnie was never quite the same invincible general of the neighborhood troops—we had seen his feet of clay. Today in his sixties, Ron recounts with great amusement the day Mrs. Boo became the Roundy Round Creature incarnate.

Other than the Roundy Round Creature, we had only a few fears to mar our otherwise carefree childhood: air-raid warnings signaling either tornadoes or Soviet nuclear bombs (I always assumed the latter), and Charles Starkweather, who in January 1958 went on a killing spree in Lincoln and eluded capture for several days, during which time Lincoln was on high alert. The sheriff deputized one hundred men as a posse, some fathers even showing up at my elementary school to collect their children in pickup trucks, with deer rifles and shotguns ready. That convinced me that Charlie was going to crawl in my first-floor bedroom window facing Forty-eighth Street, which I kept imagining right up until he was executed in 1959.

But neither real nor imagined bogeymen interfered with our elaborate neighborhood hide-and-seek games and butterfly safaris. We spent most of one summer catching live flies to feed my praying mantis, George, who drowned when we left his jar on the back porch during a rainstorm. Bobby Ebeling and I once found several cocoons, and he kept them in his attic bedroom until huge cecropia moths emerged and laid hundreds of eggs everywhere, much to his mom's horror.

The Ebeling and Shelley kids and Ronnie were my closest neighborhood friends, probably because our mothers were such close friends, and we spent a great deal of time at each others' houses. Although my mother had lots of other friends from the League of Women Voters, university faculty wives, bridge clubs, Girl Scouts, and all her other community volunteer work, the women from our neighborhood were her closest friends and remained so all their lives.

These neighborhood friends and their husbands would get together for grand parties in our black-tiled, low-ceilinged basement rec room, adjacent to the cement-floored, dimly lit furnace and laundry room. I would sit on the basement steps (a reasonable distance from the Roundy Round Creature's abode) and watch the grown-ups talk and laugh and smoke. The women wore fancy, full-skirted dresses with cinched-in waists and spiked high heels; they looked much more glamorous than they did as mothers in their kitchens fixing us tomato soup and peanut butter sandwiches. I wanted to be just like them—above all, like my mom—except I planned to be dressed up and glamorous all the time, not just for parties.

All the mothers in the neighborhood stayed home in those days and had time for coffees and bridge and long chats over the back fence. My mom's morning ritual was to ring up Sue Shelley, even before we kids got off to school. It was like the two women needed to touch base and touch lives before they could officially begin the day. They talked about kids and home and their everyday lives, but they also talked about local and national politics—bond issues, Bryan Hospital expansion into the neighborhood, zoning changes, Eisenhower and Stevenson.

Sue and my mom shared a boundless energy and enthusiasm for life. The two were infamous bargain hunters and would show up for big sales at Gold's department store downtown on O Street before the opening bell. I hated being dragged along for those sales because all the women jammed between the inner and outer doors before the ringing of the opening bell and then sprinted to the sales tables en masse, squishing small children like me in their wake. Once Mom brought home a "pair" of shoes, one size 7A and the other size 9AAA, because they were such a good bargain—a dollar for the pair. She wore them once.

My mother and Sue were the most fun of all our Brownie leaders because they laughed and were silly and made our dopey projects seem like adventures. Every year Sue's daughter Nancy and I stayed a week at Camp Catron in Nebraska City with other Brownies and Girl Scouts from around the state. The first year we were required to get special Brownie camp uniforms. Sue and Mom, ever the economizers, went downtown to the Girl Scout office to buy secondhand camp outfits.

When I tried on the bargain outfit at home, the shorts' hems hung to my ankles and the crotch to my knees. My dad took one look and turned accusingly to my mother, "Can't you buy the poor girl a decent new uniform?" As my mom worked frantically to pin up hems and take in seams, I cried while assuring them both that the used camp uniform was just fine, in fact I loved it. Although it was a rare occasion, I couldn't stand for my dad to be angry with my mom.

My father worried every summer that Nancy and I would be washed away in our Camp Catron tents by storms and the flooding Platte River. So I worried about that, too. I'm not sure whether Mom was as cavalier about my trying new adventures as she seemed to be, or whether she was trying to counterbalance my dad's anxious, expect-the-worst nature. Even now I try to adopt her positive, accepting attitude toward life, but more times than not I end up worrying about most everything like my dad.

My classmates from Holmes Elementary School loved being around my mother. When kids came home with me after school she often baked chocolate chip cookies and let us eat mounds of dough by the spoonful. (Decades later she would warn me of the dangers of this practice with my own kids because of salmonella poisoning, as documented in one of the hundreds of health and household tips she regularly clipped and mailed me.) Other schoolmates came to our house for help on their 4-H projects because my mom was the best seamstress, the best carpenter, and the best chef of all the mothers around.

My dad's tastes in food were pretty pedestrian, so our dinners were typically midwestern meat and potatoes with a few traditional Greek dishes for variety. Every time Mom had a chance to entertain, though, her culinary gifts shone. In the days before cleaning help was common, our house was spick-and-span and orderly. My job was to dust the whole house every day before going to school, which my mother now denies making me do.

Mom made all of my clothes as well as hers and I always had a pretty neat wardrobe, although I sometimes envied other girls' matching store-bought sweater-and-skirt sets. One Christmas I think she nearly went blind sewing a complete miniature wardrobe—coats, hats, the works—for my six-inch Muffy dolls. When I went away to college she sewed an entire coed wardrobe, including a gold brocade party dress from a fabric remnant she bought for a nickel and a zipper for which she reluctantly paid sixty-five cents. But the coordinated ensembles hung mostly untouched in my dorm closet in favor of the 1960s jeans uniform. Years later my mother and Gram together made my wedding dress patterned from a newspaper picture I clipped. Unfortunately, their fine seamstress skills abruptly ended with my generation.

Neither did I inherit my mother's handiness for an amazing array of household projects: upholstering furniture, rewiring lamps and fixtures and switches, building shelves, refinishing house sale furniture, sewing draperies and bedspreads, laying linoleum, and wallpapering. Mom said she inherited her mother's energy and her father's handiness. Watching TV was not a pastime of Mom's unless she was also hemming pants, wiring a switch, or constructing a picture frame.

While everything inside the house was my mom's domain, my dad was in charge of maintaining the car and the outside of the house. With help from other neighborhood fathers, he chopped down a huge elm tree in our backyard. That evening my plant pathologist dad taught me the cycles of Dutch elm disease, and for my fourth grade project I made a dandy poster to illustrate the fate of poor infected elm trees. The tree's absence made it so much easier to play our cutthroat croquet games, which often ended in tears (mine) since Dad never let me win.

My father must have had hopes of my becoming a scientific inquirer,

1. Helen, the seamstress

since he took me with him every Saturday morning to his plant pathology lab at the University of Nebraska. I wonder if my professor dad knew that my eagerness to accompany him was not sparked by the lab and Bunsen burners and petri dishes full of fuzzy fungi, but rather by the root beer floats we got on the way home at the fountain in the back of the College View drugstore where they always called me Little Miss Root Beer.

If childhood in my house and neighborhood sounds idyllic, it's because it probably was. It was the 1950s and everybody's role was pretty clear, at least from a child's view. Moms were home, dads worked, kids played—at home or down the block.

Life at our house was the same as everyone else's in the neighborhood, except that my mother frequently went to League of Women Voters meetings. When I was eight or nine I eavesdropped on a meeting at our house. It seemed to be all about making hats, so I reasonably concluded that the League of Women Voters was a hatmaking group. That made sense to me because in addition to making all my clothes and her own, my mom loved making and wearing hats. She had a hat block that

2. Helen, the homemaker

was just the size of her head so she could work with her hat creations, stretching the felt or sewing on feathers or beads.

Using her hat block, my mother designed a goofy-looking hat that showcased Nebraska's products and industries—cows, corn, motor scooters, sorghum—to be worn in a hat parade at the League of Women Voters national convention in Atlantic City to dramatize the importance of foreign trade. This unusual hatmaking was the subject of the league meeting that I had overheard. I thought the finished hat looked dopey, even on my mom, who wore her original creations with flair, but after the meeting she told me the hat was not for looks. It was to show the people at the league convention what we grew and made in Nebraska. I got it—like show-and-tell at school.

Soon after I began fifth grade in 1958, it seemed there were lots more League of Women Voters meetings at our house. All I could surmise from listening in the wings was that the meetings had something to do with government and nothing at all to do with hats. It wasn't until many years later that I learned how these meetings were the first steps toward enormous change in our lives.

CITY CHARTER BATTLE

My mother became president of the Lincoln League of Women Voters in 1957, her term to expire in March 1959. During her last several months as president and under her leadership, the league mounted a major public education effort to urge defeat of a proposed amendment to Lincoln's home rule charter.

Lincoln's charter, adopted in 1917, established the city's form of government: a "weak-mayor" system in which the part-time mayor has few powers that the city council does not also possess. In the mid-1950s the city council appointed a Charter Revision Committee to study and recommend changes to Lincoln's charter and its weak-mayor form of government. After months of study, the committee recommended thirty-three charter amendments, most just cleanup measures.

However, one charter amendment—the fourteenth amendment—proposed to change the entire form of city government from a "weak-mayor" to a "strong-mayor" form. Under the latter there would be a clear division of powers between the mayor and city council. The full-time elected mayor would be the city's chief executive officer—responsible for administration of city government and preparation of the budget—and would have powers to veto city council legislative action and to appoint and remove administrative department heads. The seven city council members, elected at large, would exclusively hold the legislative powers of the city but would not share in administrative power as they had in the past.

The charter amendments were to be the subject of a special election to be held on March 3, 1959. The League of Women Voters, led by my mother as president, supported the proposed amendments recommended by the Charter Revision Committee and strongly backed the switch to the strong mayor form of government.

However, when the city council made revisions to the fourteenth amendment as proposed by its own appointed Charter Revision Committee, the league withdrew its support. The modifications were billed by the council as "minor": the mayor's power both to appoint and to remove administrative department heads and the assistant to the mayor would be subject to city council approval. The council's altered version of this amendment would be the one to appear on the special charter election ballot.

The league took great exception to the city council's "minor" modifications. As league president, my mother appeared before the city council on January 26, 1959, and charged that the council had "robbed with a few strokes of the pen" the essential elements of the strong-mayor plan as recommended by the Charter Revision Committee. In so doing, she argued, the city council had deprived the voters of the chance to vote on a conversion to the true strong-mayor form of city government.

A front-page headline that evening read: "Charter Bombshell Dropped, Women Voters Unit Threatens Fight." My mother explained to the city council that the league had looked forward to supporting the "blueprint for good government" reflected in the Charter Revision Committee's proposal, but the council's weakening of the hiring and firing powers of the mayor would blur the clear separation between the executive functions of the mayor and the legislative functions of the council—and thus dilute the mayor's chief executive role.

The city council was "quite surprised with the action of the League" but stood behind its version of the proposed fourteenth amendment to be placed on the ballot. Pointing at my mother, one councilman angrily attacked the league's position: "You are uninformed. You are taking a lot of theory out of books and trying to apply it to Lincoln where it doesn't apply." Mayor Bennett "Abe" Martin also defended the city council version. "The plan still strengthens the position of the mayor's office," he said, "but perhaps not as much as the Charter Committee wanted. But it makes for better harmony between the mayor and the council."

The league was not against harmony, but it believed that a mayor's responsibility and authority would be only nominal without full powers to remove and appoint department heads. Moreover, such divided and diffuse responsibility between mayor and council would undercut the clear and separate accountability of the executive and legislative functions that was envisioned by the Charter Revision Committee.

The battle lines were drawn. In the remaining weeks before the March special charter election, the league launched an extensive public education campaign to provide information for voters and urge defeat of the council's watered-down charter amendment proposal. The league membership was unified in its opposition to the council's weakened version of the strong-mayor form of government, but the issue became more and more controversial as the bigwigs in town began to counter more vocally the league's position. Even a few league members grew lukewarm about the issue in the face of such powerful opposition, but the league leadership under my mother's direction held firm.

The charter fight over Lincoln's form of government was the reason I had noticed so many more league meetings at our house, and why my mom so frequently dressed up and headed out the door, donning one of her stylish hats. My mother kept a full schedule as speaker at dozens of informal neighborhood coffees sponsored by the league throughout the city and at debates and formal panels discussing the special charter election. At home I often found her in the basement, pounding away at our old Underwood typewriter, working on speeches. I was amazed how fast her fingers flew over the keyboard. She told me she had lots of practice typing all my dad's papers in grad school.

I didn't know this sudden flurry of league meetings and typing speeches was about to change her life. But then, neither did she.

At the special charter election on March 3, 1959, voters defeated the fourteenth charter amendment as proposed by the city council. The League of Women Voters' position had prevailed. My mom and her league cohorts were ecstatic. They had stopped a change in the form of city government that fell short of the best form of that change. Their next step would be to work for the passage of the true strong-mayor form of government. But that was for another day. First, they would celebrate their accomplishment.

On March 11, eight days after the special charter election, my mother was getting dressed for her last official meeting as president of the Lincoln League of Women Voters. Although still high from the election outcome and greater visibility than the league had enjoyed in years, she also was somewhat relieved to be turning over the presidency after leading the intense battle over the city charter amendments. Mom couldn't dwell on these mixed emotions in her usual last-minute hurry to get out the door. The phone rang. Afraid of being late for the meeting, she almost didn't answer it but decided at the last moment to pick up and tell the caller she would call back later.

The caller was Abe Martin, the mayor and the league's chief adversary in the charter amendment election just eight days earlier. Mayor Martin's voice on the phone was friendly and didn't reflect their fresh disagreement or the electoral defeat of his position on the amendment. Despite their many political differences, my mother had always found Abe an affable fellow. "You know, Helen, the league has been active on issues of city government for so many years," Mayor Martin began. "Isn't there someone in the group interested in running for city council? The primary's coming up in early April and the general election's a month later, so anybody interested would have to jump in quickly."

At first incredulous, my mom felt a rush of pride—the league had not only won on the issues in the charter amendment election but had won the respect of the prominent opposition leader. Already running late, she now was even more eager to get to the league meeting to relay the mayor's surprising message. She thanked Abe for his call and his confidence in the league, threw on her hat, jumped in our 1950 Plymouth, and raced to the meeting. Mom couldn't wait to see the faces of her fellow leaguers when she told them of the mayor's call. She and Dad had lived in Lincoln only eight years, but she knew that the league old-timers would be thrilled after spending years fighting for good government issues, with few victories and little recognition.

My mother was right. The election victory, the mayor's call, the satisfaction of a job well done—all fueled the ebullience of the league meeting that day. With such a sweet ending to her tenure, my mother turned over the league's presidency to her successor with satisfaction and savored the league's achievement on her drive home.

The phone was ringing as she walked in the door, and it didn't stop ringing until late that evening. In the time it took Mom to drive home from the meeting and make a quick stop at the grocery store for dinner supplies, the energized leaguers had arrived at instantaneous consensus on a city council candidate from their ranks. Helen Boosalis was their unanimous choice. The League of Women Voters, which doesn't endorse candidates for elected office, could not officially back a Boosalis candidacy, but surely every breathing league member was ready to sign up as a private citizen to do whatever was necessary to organize an eleventh-hour, whirlwind campaign to elect my mother to the Lincoln City Council.

The leaguers' candidate of choice seems obvious in hindsight, but it was not to my mother. She never imagined herself as a candidate for elected office. She had always loved politics—from her childhood fascination with the boisterous political arguments among her Greek relatives, to her deep admiration for Franklin and Eleanor Roosevelt, to her own volunteer civic involvement as a young wife and mother committed to giving back to her community—but nothing in her background suggested an inclination to run for public office. She wasn't sure she was cut out for that. She hadn't finished college after leaving the University of Minnesota to work for the Minnesota Department of Employment Security to help her parents support the family. After marrying she continued to work while my dad finished his master's and PhD, and soon motherhood came. Her lack of a college degree sometimes made my exceptionally competent mother question her preparation for certain roles, and this call to run for public office at age thirty-nine undoubtedly was one of those times.

Yet when I asked Mom if she felt scared in making the decision to run, she shrugged, "No, I really don't scare easily. There's something in my makeup that's always encouraged me to try. So what if I don't make it? Besides, after preaching citizen involvement at every opportunity as league president, I had to ask myself, 'How about practicing what you preach?'" She did, on the other hand, admit to being scared to death of public speaking, which induced a pounding heart and blood rushing to her head. Nevertheless, there was no time to agonize over the decision, and once she accepted the unexpected challenge, she found campaigning fun, as it drew on her natural gifts for connecting with people.

The day after the league meeting and the mayor's phone call, my mother approached some key community people whose support she would need to run a credible city council campaign in such a short time frame. She figured their responses to her potential candidacy would provide a good barometer of possible support outside her own circles of influence. She scheduled meetings that day with Jack Thompson, CEO of a large downtown company, who had an interest in good government; Jack Wells, the Campbells, and Nate Gold, owners of prominent downtown retail department stores; and Breta Dow, who was appointed to the city council for a short time during the war (and replaced in 1946 by Fern Hubbard Orme). After my mother presented reasons for considering her candidacy, each one of them encouraged her to run. And Mom already had the wholehearted support of my father. "Your dad has always urged me to do more than I think I can."

DOOR KNOCKING

I was unaware of this turn of events, but I did begin to notice that our kitchen breakfast nook (behind which I had for years systematically dumped peas, carrots, broccoli—essentially all vegetables served at dinner except corn) had become the hub for meetings lasting late into the night. These unusual late-night kitchen soirees included mostly our neighbors—the Ebelings, the Shelleys, the Pfeifers—and a few of my mom's league friends, like Sue Bailey and Helen Porter.

After several of these meetings I learned that Mom and Dad and their neighborhood friends were rushing to plan a last-minute campaign for my mother's run for the city council. In short order, she had decided to run, circulated and filed the required petitions to get on the ballot, and assembled the grassroots neighborhood campaign of "just us greenhorns" whom I heard strategizing and laughing in our kitchen late at night.

I wasn't quite sure what running for the city council meant, but Mom explained that everybody in Lincoln got to elect seven people they wanted to represent them on the city council to make laws and help keep Lincoln a good place to live. Every two years there was an election to choose about half the city council—three council members would be elected in this election and four the next time. She said there would be a primary election first, and the top six vote-getters would then run in the general election one month later. Out of those six, the top three would be elected to the city council for a four-year term. She drew pictures of stick-figure candidates for me.

It sounded easy to me—why wouldn't everyone vote for my mom? She had to be the best one. Mom explained that not every voter would know who she was or why she would do a good job. That's why we had to go out and tell as many people as we could about her and give them papers to read about why she was the best candidate. Because she hadn't decided to run until very late, Mom said we would have to work really hard to try to reach everyone in Lincoln before the primary election—only three weeks away.

My Forty-eighth Street neighborhood and the blocks surrounding Holmes Elementary School constituted my everyday community, but I knew from going downtown shopping with Mom and to the university with Dad that the whole city of Lincoln was much, much bigger than my neighborhood. (Lincoln's population in 1959 was about 130,000; today it's about 240,000.) Then I started to worry. How would Mom be able to find all the voters in the whole city to show them how good she would be on the city council?

Mom opened a big map on the kitchen table that had millions of lines and boxes showing all the streets and blocks in Lincoln. She showed me 1932 South Forty-eighth Street, our house, on the map. Her eyes were all sparkly and her voice bubbly as she told me the campaign plan. Lots of our friends—like the Shelleys and Pfeifers and Ebelings and Blomgrens and their kids and friends of their kids and my school friends and basically everybody we knew—would go out together with leaflets to campaign every night after dinner and on weekends in different neighborhoods all over Lincoln. Dick Ebeling would get the leaflets printed because he knew about printing from his job. Ronnie's mom, Betty, would have a coffee to get the volunteers organized. The plan was to knock on every door in Lincoln.

Mom showed me the sketches of her first "campaign piece" created by our neighbors at those late-night meetings in our breakfast nook. The front had drawings of children's blocks: "The ABC's of Good Government." On the inside it read, "Always vote . . . Be informed . . . Check the candidates." There was a picture of my mom's face circled by "Helen Boosalis for City Council," then more ABC's: "A Vote . . . For Helen B . . . Means Greater EfficienCy."

Dad, always the comedian, had suggested joke slogans for the brochure like "Make Lincoln a Palace—Vote for Boosalis" and "Don't Be Useless—Vote for Boos-lis." That must be why I heard so much laughter coming from the kitchen as I lay in bed late at night. On the back of the little pamphlet was a list of all the great things my mom had done:

- Resident of Lincoln since 1951
- Native of Minneapolis—attended University of Minnesota
- Married to Michael G. Boosalis, Univ. of Nebr. Professor
- Past President, Lincoln League of Women Voters
- Family Service Association Board
- Bryan Hospital Service League
- Lincoln/Lancaster County Mental Health Association Board
- Leader of Girl Scout and Campfire Groups

And wow, there was even something about me:

- One child, 10 years old

I've seen campaign materials for student council elections in my own children's schools that were more sophisticated than this little piece that my mother so excitedly showed me, but at the time I just knew this would make her win. All we had to do was give one of the leaflets to every person in Lincoln—they would read it and then for sure vote for my mom.

So one minute my mother was like everyone else's, and the next minute she was doing what nobody else's mother was doing—running for city council.

When Mom transformed overnight from being a League of Women Voters volunteer to a candidate for public office, everything changed. I started having nightly adventures. Every evening after our 5:15 dinner, Mom, Dad, and I, along with neighborhood kids and parents, would pile into a caravan of cars. The kids wore white fake-straw hats banded in red, white, and blue, like out of *The Music Man*. Each team of adults and kids was assigned an intersection of four blocks to knock on every door, leaflets in hand and spiels ready. "Hi, my name is Mary Beth Boosalis. My mother, Helen Boosalis, is running for city council. I hope you will read this and vote for her."

At first I was so scared and shy that I secretly hoped people wouldn't be home so I could leave the pamphlet and not have to talk to them. But after a few nights I was swept up in the excitement. I felt so proud of my smart, brave mom that I was sure every single person in the city would vote for her.

3. 1959 Boosalis for City Council campaign card

4. Boosalis family campaigns in Helen's 1959 city council race

After door knocking, we piled back in the cars and gathered at our house for cookies and stories about the strangers behind the doors. My father described one "geezer" who said he would never vote for a woman. When Dad asked why, the fellow nodded toward his house and barked, "I've got one in there I can't control. I don't want to encourage any more of that!"

My neighborhood pals and I were giddy from the novelty of the nightly party and adventure and rally all rolled into one; yet even the youngest among us felt a part of something serious and important. We had a cause, a David-and-Goliath mission. No one involved was famous or influential or powerful. It was my first exposure to grassroots politics.

In addition to our nightly door-to-door campaigning, the candidate's "visibility" campaign was launched—not with TV or even newspaper ads, which my mom's campaign coffers couldn't support, but with yard signs. Mom herself went scouting for the best locations and in the process got acquainted with scores of businesspeople and homeowners who later, as voters, remembered meeting the candidate. She even made a point of taking a hammer along on these location safaris so that along busier streets with high volumes of traffic, drivers would see her staking her own yard signs. That sight in itself probably picked up more than a few votes.

The primary campaign, only three weeks long in my mother's case, went by in a doorbell-ringing, sign-pounding flash. Still passing out leaflets on the day of the primary election (April 6, 1959), my mother's supporters were tireless, but no more so than the candidate. All gathered at our house for the biggest party I'd ever seen and waited for the election results. Even though it was a school night, I got to stay up with all the grown-ups until the final results were in. Everyone was cheering and hugging and some were even crying.

Mom placed third out of nine primary candidates—behind two city council incumbents, Del Tyrrell and Pat Ash, and ahead of the third incumbent, Ken Lewis. In just three weeks the "housewife and past president of the Lincoln League of Women Voters" (as the newspapers often identified her) had organized and executed a campaign in a field of eight businessmen candidates, managed to score in the top three vote-getters, and pulled ahead of one of the three incumbents. We were ecstatic.

But my mom warned, even on that joyous evening, that with the general election only one month away the situation could change quickly, especially when supporters of the three incumbents realized that their candidates might not be automatic shoo-ins for the three open council seats.

The four weeks leading to the general election were a blur of frenzied door-to-door campaigning. With her surprising third-place finish in the primary, my mother and her campaign troops of mostly neighborhood folks were energized beyond belief. Caught up in the excitement, I no longer wished for no-answers to my doorbell ringing. I was eager and proud to tell people why they should vote for my mom.

My mother, too, grew more comfortable with public speaking at candidate forums. She relied on typed-out note cards for speeches but really shone in question-and-answer sessions. She even squeezed in a few Toastmaster classes at the YWCA, one of which ended when her speech instructor was demonstrating relaxation techniques to use before public speaking and somehow relaxed his vocal cords so much that he lost his voice.

After the primary election, an unexpected development in the race for mayor took shape. The one-term incumbent, Abe Martin, found himself battling a primary election write-in candidate to retain his mayoral seat. The challenger, E. Bartlett "Pat" Boyles, campaigned hard for a "new look in city government" and "return of city affairs to the people." He attacked the holding of closed pre-council meetings prior to the open meetings in the city council chambers and called for dissolution of the "hierarchy succession" of mayors and council members. Boyles's surprise write-in candidacy and my mother's strong showing in the primary suggested swirling winds of political change in Lincoln's centennial-year election.

And change there was. Clouds and thunderstorms rolled in for the May 5 general election but did not discourage the largest voter turnout in ten years. I squirmed in my desk and felt butterflies all day in Mrs. Powell's fifth grade class. Mrs. Powell and the kids in my class were excited about the election because for the first time they actually knew somebody on the ballot, or at least knew the daughter of that somebody.

Public opinion polls were not used to predict the outcome of Mom's campaign, both because the election was local and because it was 1959, long before the proliferation of polling that we take for granted today. On election night my mother's friends gathered at our house to await the outcome of their weeks of campaigning. The length of time it took for the manual vote count after poll closing heightened the suspense. My dad and I were nervous, as usual, but my mother seemed to float through our house greeting everyone as naturally as if she were entertaining guests at one of her festive dinner parties.

The results came in by phone, and the cheers were deafening. Helen Boosalis—the newcomer, the non-incumbent—not only captured one of the three open city council seats but also received the second-highest vote count among the three victors. She looked much taller to me than her pre-election five-foot, four-inch height as her voice carried above the applause of the elated crowd: "I feel privileged to have been given this opportunity to serve the people of this wonderful city. Needless to say, this victory would have been impossible without the faith and tireless support of all of you, my friends."

The Forty-eighth Street neighborhood gang, the core of the Boosalis for City Council campaign machine, and scores of other volunteers from all over the city somehow squeezed into our basement rec room. My band of young campaign compatriots jumped around, grabbing and tossing each other's red, white, and blue hats from our nightly door-knocking campaign uniforms. We fed off the energy of the adults, who acted more like kids than we did—they kept cheering and clapping and laughing and hugging my mom, their new city councilwoman.

Two of the city council incumbents, Del Tyrrell and Kenneth Lewis, were reelected, but in a major upset Helen Boosalis unseated the third incumbent, Pat Ash, who had come in a strong second in the April primary just a month earlier and had been a top vote-getter in his previous council elections.

Mayor Abe Martin was undoubtedly as shocked by the election results as vanquished Councilman Pat Ash. In a "Cinderella finish," mayoral write-in candidate Pat Boyles unseated the incumbent by a margin of 3–2 and became the first write-in nominee in Lincoln's history to become mayor. Shell-shocked, his voice breaking, Mayor Martin expressed dismay at his ouster: "It was a surprise to me. You tell me what happened. I guess the voters wanted a change in City Hall."

And change they would get. In Lincoln's centennial year, fresh city leadership emerged seemingly out of nowhere: a new mayor was carried in on the wings of a most unusual write-in effort, and a new woman city council member was elected, with enthusiastic support from lots of just plain folks.

The breathtaking victories of these two political novices—both champions of open government—shared the front pages with other stories of the times: a visit by Sir Winston Churchill and President Eisenhower to ailing John Foster Dulles and General George Marshall at Walter Reed Army Hospital; President Eisenhower's warning to negotiating management and steelworkers to avert an industry-wide strike; Nikita Khrushchev's anticipated meeting in San Francisco with Eisenhower, Charles de Gaulle and Harold Macmillan; and the death of Henry Ford's younger brother at eighty-seven. But the biggest and boldest headlines on the front page of the *Lincoln Star* were reserved for "Pat Boyles Elected Mayor" and "Council Seat to Mrs. Boosalis."

I woke up the morning after the election aware that a mere eight weeks earlier my mother was just my mother—an active community volunteer, but in my eyes first and foremost my mother. Now she also belonged to all those people celebrating in our house the night before, and to the thousands of people who voted for her, and even to those who hadn't bothered to vote. I looked across the breakfast table at this woman who was and was not my mom. I had no idea of all the lessons I was yet to learn from her as she entered this new arena.

And I'm quite sure Mom could not comprehend the great adventure on which she had embarked or the changes she would inspire—both in herself and the city.

DOGS, POOLS, AND FALLOUT

I was a celebrity in school for two or three days after the election. The teachers spoke with excitement about my mom in class, and the kids asked me lots of questions about the election and the city council. Soon the hoopla died down and things went back to normal, except that our phone at home never stopped ringing. Night and day, callers wanted to talk to Mom about city issues, but that produced a benefit for me—a private line to replace our party line, which I had always hated because the other party could listen to my phone calls with friends.

I could overhear Mom's conversations because our only phone sat in a wall alcove in the short hallway between my parents' bedroom and mine. Despite my eavesdropping and my parents' talk of city council issues at the dinner table, I couldn't fathom most of Mom's phone calls about city matters. I understood that not everyone agreed with her because some callers didn't try to mask their anger even when I—a little kid—answered the phone first.

Once, a few months after her election, I answered and the caller screamed that my mother was a dog hater and should be ashamed of herself, then hung up. The stranger's angry voice frightened me, and I started crying. Comforting me, my mom explained that she had introduced an ordinance (like a law or rule, she said) requiring that dogs get rabies shots before being licensed. Many dog owners (and the Cornhusker Kennel Club) opposed the city's compulsory rabies shots, and some were quite emotional about it, as I had experienced.

"There will be lots of times when people will disagree with me," Mom explained, "but it's part of my new job to listen to all kinds of opinions. It's OK if some people want to tell me how upset they are, but it's not OK for anyone to yell at my little girl. That woman was wrong, and I'm sorry that happened to you." I sniffed and said I was fine, never realizing I had just grown the first veneer of the thicker skin I would need for my mother's rugged political road ahead.

Besides dog vaccinations, another issue even I could understand as a kid was building new swimming pools. Living in a state where bodies of water are scarce, my friends and I loved spending summer days at Muni, one of three municipal swimming pools. I had a love-hate relationship with Muni—hated it when I had to take swimming lessons early in the morning when my teeth chattered and lips turned blue; loved it when I could go with my friends, talk on beach towels for hours, and take a cool dip when the Nebraska sun began to fry. But even we noticed the pool was too crowded, and kids constantly crashed into each other when diving or jumping off the side.

Because of overcrowded existing pools and lack of access to pools in some areas of the city, my mom advocated the construction of new swimming facilities. She expressed disappointment that no new pools were included in the 1960–61 proposed budget, and she pushed for new swimming pools during council budget deliberations. "I guess the only way people are going to get more pools is to appear before the council and speak for them," she said. With some guidance from their newest elected representative, proponents of new pools did exactly that.

In fact, during one morning council budget session, Mayor Boyles's secretary brought him a flood of phone messages, taken just minutes apart and each dated July 26, 1960, from constituents all registering their support for "an additional mill levy for another swimming pool." In response to the raft of messages—showing callers' addresses all within a block or two of each other—Mayor Boyles good-naturedly passed them to my mother. "I see we have a large number of people supporting new swimming pools who all live within a block of you, Helen, and who all coincidentally decided to call this morning."

By the end of council deliberations on the 1960–61 budget, two new swimming pools were added, one in northeast Lincoln, favored by veteran Councilman Del Tyrrell, and the other in southeast Lincoln, where my mother's neighborhood supporters had organized their phone campaign. The two neighborhood pools plus an Olympic-size pool—along with improvements to eighteen parks, two new parks, a golf course, skating slabs, tennis and basketball courts, softball fields, two new recreation centers, Children's Zoo, picnic shelters, play equipment, park lighting—all were rolled into a twenty-year bond issue that accelerated Lincoln's parks and recreation program by ninety years compared to the slow route through the park department's annual budget appropriation. Parks and recreation were a top priority of the new councilwoman, who devoted much energy in her first term to ensure their adequate funding.

I agreed with my mom's push for more money for swimming pools, parks, and recreation, but we parted company on a matter related to my personal safety: construction of a community civil defense fallout shelter through conversion of an abandoned underground water reservoir. My mom's was the only dissent in the 6–1 council vote; she questioned the future value of this model structure to accommodate fifteen hundred people, regardless of the availability of federal funds to build it.

I waged my own protest against my mother's stand on the fallout shelter. After all, my parents had already vetoed my plans to build our own fallout shelter in the backyard. I had even identified which possessions I would take with me to the shelter. If only my mom had been in school with me when we went through all the duck-and-cover drills, crouching under our desks and along hallway walls, remembering not to look directly at the nuclear blast—if she had, then she would have been more aware of the Communist threat to Lincoln (an obvious target because of the Strategic Air Command base in Omaha). Maybe then she wouldn't have voted against the municipal civil defense shelter.

Perhaps I would have felt safer from nuclear annihilation if I had gone with my mother and twenty-seven other women from the Lincoln-Omaha area (teachers, civic leaders, news media) invited to get a firsthand look at the army's training and air defense systems through "Operation Understanding." They saw Nike air defense missile systems and training of Army Missilemen at Fort Bliss in El Paso, Texas; Nike Ajax and Hercules missiles at McGregor Range and the White Sands Missile Range in New Mexico; continental air defense systems at the

North American Air Defense Command; and U.S. Air Force Academy training in Colorado Springs. Maybe if I had gone on that tour with Mom, I would not have lain awake worrying every time the civil defense sirens went off that we were being attacked—I could have confined my worries to Nebraska tornadoes.

Another city council controversy that I could comprehend was over a proposed ordinance to force businesses to close one day a week, either Saturday or Sunday. It was the first time I heard the term "blue laws." Lots of phone calls and mail tried to convince Mom that her opposition to the ordinance was or was not the right thing. Most who agreed with her were individuals or small businesses who saw the mandatory closing ordinance as "overreaching government restriction on personal liberties." Many who supported Saturday-Sunday closings were those who argued on religious or moral grounds or were large downtown retailers who already closed their stores on Sundays and did not want smaller competitors open seven days a week. My mom patiently listened to all the calls, read all the letters, and voted no on the ordinance.

These bits and pieces of issues I picked up during her early city council days helped define my child's perception of my mother's entry into the rough-and-tumble political world. Still, I was sometimes confused by Mom's unconventional role compared to other mothers and, at the same time, comforted by her being the same old mother I had always had.

I wasn't the only one confused. Media accounts of the new councilwoman vacillated between reports on the effectiveness of her council work and soft articles on her personal style. The jarring juxtaposition reflected a changing and often contradictory attitude of the public at large toward women entering the political arena. For example, one editorial highlighted the serious work undertaken by the new councilwoman: "Under Mayor Boyles, and with the aid of a very determined woman member, Mrs. Helen Boosalis, the entire City Council is facing up to Lincoln's problems in parks, sewers, fire, police and lighting." In contrast, a feature article emphasized the traditional profile of the council's new woman member: "The newest member of Lincoln's City Council prefers hats to cigars, she would rather refinish a piece of antique furniture than play golf, and she begins her day's activities not by dictating to a secretary, but by ironing a shirt for her husband, preparing breakfast, and assisting Dr. Boosalis (a University of Nebraska faculty member) and their daughter off for classes and school while the telephone jangles incessantly."

My mother soon resurrected the issue that had propelled her from housewife and community volunteer to running for city council—a charter amendment to provide for a true strong-mayor form of government. With her advocacy now as a city council member, the council approved the original strong-mayor plan supported by the League of Women Voters and the Charter Revision Committee, with clear separation between the executive function of the mayor and legislative function of the council.

The first strong mayor under the new form of government would be elected in the 1963 municipal election. Pat Boyles, the successful write-in mayoral candidate in 1959, would not have the opportunity to test the strong-mayor powers because he resigned before the end of his term to accept a judgeship—a disappointment to my mother, who believed he would have made a good model as Lincoln's first strong mayor.

When Mayor Boyles resigned, Councilman Del Tyrrell asked his fellow council members to support his appointment as acting mayor until the 1963 municipal election. My mother agreed to support Tyrrell's appointment as acting mayor only if he would agree not to run for mayor in the upcoming election. She felt that Lincoln's first strong mayor should be a strong leader who would set the standard for using the considerable mayoral powers under the new form of government. Although Tyrrell was fine as a member of the council, he did not fulfill her aspirations for the city's first strong mayor.

My mother was shocked when Tyrrell agreed to her terms of support, and equally shocked that she had the guts to play political hardball. Mom had developed more confidence in her political skills during three years on the council than even she realized.

AND A DOZEN MORE

As her first city council term ended, Mom decided rather easily to run for a second term. She loved what she was doing. In the 1963 city election, my mother and Del Tyrrell were the only incumbents in a field of thirteen candidates for four vacant city council seats, and both won reelection handily. Also elected was the city's first mayor under the new strong-mayor form of government—Dean Peterson, president of a milk transportation company.

I don't have the same vivid recollections of Mom's second city council campaign as I do of her first, but she organized her same door-to-door effort with the cadre of friends and volunteers from her whirlwind campaign four years earlier. No longer a ten-year-old kid of the Forty-eighth Street gang, in 1963 I was a teenager with grown-up junior high friends like Christie Reed, Gail Tupper, and Judy Wright. None of us would have been caught dead wearing those red, white, and blue fake-straw hats that my neighborhood cohorts and I had gladly donned every night after dinner in my mother's first campaign. I did go door knocking again with Mom and Dad, only this time almost everyone who answered knew very well who my mom was. Most liked Helen Boosalis and were nice to me; only a few slammed their doors.

By the time Mom ran for a third council term (in 1967) and a fourth (in 1971), she had become a revered figure at city hall with a reputation for openness and integrity. An editorial endorsing her third term election almost sounded like a campaign piece:

> Of the many candidates for City Council, one stands out. . . . For eight years now Mrs. Boosalis has served with distinction in city government. . . . She has always shown concern over the ability of taxpayers to support public programs but has taken equal cognizance of the need of the city to progress. Citizens have found her to be a public official to whom they could easily talk, even though her final decision might or might not be in agreement with them. And she has been a public official with whom other members of city government have had no difficulty in working. Her influence has been toward good, honest and progressive public programs and policies.

One of my mother's city council colleagues, Lloyd Hinkley, reflected on serving with her: "One great thing about working with Helen is that she didn't have to have, or take credit for, the idea. She recognized others' good ideas and would work hard on them without needing any personal recognition. Philosophically and politically—I'm a Republican—we had a lot of differences, but that didn't get in the way of our working well together."

In all four of her city council campaigns, my mother faced large numbers of opponents. Had voters been displeased with her performance, they had ample alternative ballot choices; but voters seemed to agree with a *Lincoln Evening Journal* editorial opinion that she was "an exceptionally intelligent, capable and dedicated member of the Council, who steadfastly has placed the interest of the public above all other in her official actions." In her fourth primary (1971), in a field of seventeen candidates seeking four city council seats, Mom racked up nearly 60 percent of the votes. Handily winning the general election, she was joined by three newcomers—Steve Cook, Bob Sikyta, and Dick Baker—whom she would come to know well in years to come.

With the implementation of the strong-mayor form of government, the city council had been freed of administrative duties and now served as a strictly legislative body, akin to the federal system. As a result, the council had taken on a meatier legislative agenda. It would be some time, however, until the strong-mayor side of the equation would be fully realized by a forceful, independent chief executive.

The city's first mayor elected under the strong-mayor plan, Dean Peterson, was defeated after one term by Sam Schwartzkopf in 1967. During his administration Mayor Schwartzkopf sought Mom's advice on important city matters because of her valuable experience, her political instincts, and their agreement on many issues. She played a dual role of councilor and counselor—her official city council legislative role and her behind-the-scenes role counseling the mayor on how best to exert executive leadership to achieve positive results for the city. But the considerable strong-mayor powers under the charter amendment had yet to be fully tested.

In 1973, midway through her fourth term, Mom welcomed another woman to the council: her old League of Women Voters colleague Sue Bailey. The two made a terrific team—Sue Bailey with her studious, thorough approach to issues, and Helen Boosalis with her practical leadership and powers of persuasion.

Before one city council meeting, Sue Bailey overheard a conversation that may have changed the course of my mom's political career. Bai-

5. Helen Boosalis, city council chair, 1974

ley was in the city hall women's room when she heard voices through the ventilation grate: the male council members in the adjacent men's room were agreeing on a scheme to elect their choice for city council chairman. Bailey immediately informed my mother, who then pulled her own surprise maneuver at the council meeting that day by throwing her name in the ring for chairman. The councilmen were so caught off guard that Mom was elected city council chair, much to the delight of Councilwoman Sue Bailey, men's room snitch.

My mother had wielded the gavel as city council chair for only five months when it appeared she would have to relinquish it and her council seat. In October 1973 my dad accepted the department chairmanship of botany and plant pathology at Michigan State University. As I was growing up, my parents periodically discussed job offers my dad received from other universities. Dad hadn't pursued earlier nibbles or offers, but this one presented an opportunity in a preeminent department in his field—the kind of chance that was unlikely to come again. His job decision would not affect me, as I had by then left home and had recently married. The impact would be on Mom's political life, but when reporters asked her about vacating her council seat to move to Michigan, she replied simply, "He's my husband." Even without the move,

6. Mike Boosalis in his university lab, 1975

she said, she probably would not have run again after four terms on the council. Dad said his wife was enthusiastic about the Michigan move and "a heck of a lot more adventurous than I am in these things." Anticipating my parents' departure, editorials in the *Lincoln Star* sounded like obituaries:

> It is a rarity to find someone of her particular combination of assets. Through the years, her guidance has been significant in the orderly and efficient growth of the city. . . . Mrs. Boosalis, to our knowledge, has never made an enemy while serving on the

council. This is a tribute to her good humor and pleasant manner, even when in strong disagreement with someone. She has always respected the opinions of others, even though a firm defender of her own position.

Helen Boosalis has been, simply, a towering example of integrity and dedication in city government. If there is such a thing as statesmanship in municipal affairs, she personifies it. . . . Mrs. Boosalis has been controversial. She has been stubborn; holding tenaciously to her own view of what this city should be. It has been her insistence on taking the long view, of regarding each action in terms of its lasting effect on the community as a whole that has frustrated those who would criticize her service on the council.

But the ink was barely dry when suddenly everything changed. Mom and Dad were taking a walk on one of those perfect fall days when the clear Nebraska sky is a dazzling blue. My dad was having second thoughts. "Look at that beautiful Nebraska sky, Helen. I just don't want to leave this great state, this great city where we've been so happy." And that was it—what had been done was undone. Dad's reversal of his job acceptance honored what he truly valued rather than grasping for the next rung of the ladder. And my mother, ready to support her husband either way, retained her city council chairmanship for the remainder of her fourth term instead of starting a new life in East Lansing.

During the last half of that fourth term, Mom's prominence and visibility increased as local-access cable television began televising weekly council meetings. Her role as council chair dominated the coverage, so much so that she was recognized almost everywhere she went. By the end of her fourth city council term in 1975, after sixteen years as legislator, Helen Boosalis had perhaps become "an institution unto herself," in the words of one of her last city council primary opponents, Richard Hanson. My mother's seasoned experience in office, her close rapport with citizens, and her effective leadership (observed on home televisions every week) combined to form the conditions for a positive version of the perfect storm—powerful, sweeping, and welcome as the rains after a long drought. That storm—her storm—it was a-brewin'.

Down to Two

April and May 1986

Growing up, I loved having two Easters—Greek Orthodox Easter and what Gram called "American" Easter—mostly because it meant I got two Easter baskets. Also, the music and spectacle of Easter services in Lincoln's Greek Orthodox church made it the most beautiful service of the year. With a church membership of only thirty families, I played the organ for Sunday services from age ten, my mom directed the tiny choir of six or seven, and my dad kept the candles going.

American Easter fell on March 30 in the spring of the 1986 governor's race, and Mom took a rare day's break from the campaign. Even so, she couldn't escape thinking about the upcoming election—that day the *Sunday World-Herald* published the results of its first gubernatorial primary campaign poll. The poll showed Helen Boosalis and Chris Beutler tied at 17 percent for first place on the Democratic side, with lots of undecided voters. However nerve-racking it was to read the poll results in the Sunday paper, it would be the last time before the primary that the Democratic race would look so close. April would see Mom pulling further and further ahead.

The next *World-Herald* poll, in late April, showed Boosalis at 27 percent, Beutler at 19 percent, and David Domina at 13 percent. Then, just a few days before the May 13 primary election, Mom's polling numbers shot ahead to 37 percent, more than doubling her polling numbers in six weeks and leaving her competitors far behind at 17 percent (Domina) and 15 percent (Beutler). The Republican race appeared tighter according to the same poll, with Kay Orr ahead at 29 percent, Nancy Hoch at 19 percent, and Kermit Brashear at 16 percent.

7. 1986 Boosalis for Governor campaign sticker

By Mother's Day, May 11, just two days before the gubernatorial primary election, we were all feeling pretty good—nervous, but good. Mom, Dad, Max, the boys, and I went in high spirits to the Cornhusker Hotel for a Mother's Day brunch. The boys exhibited their best behavior, as if they knew how the grandsons of a potential governor ought to behave.

The night of the primary election was an extravaganza of joy. Mom raced to Omaha soon after the polls closed, and the first returns were so strongly in her favor that supporters at the Omaha party confidently celebrated victory from the moment they arrived. She told the group at the Omaha Field Club that she had seen signs three weeks earlier that her visibility and support in Omaha had increased. In fact, her visibility that evening could not have been higher as she wove her way through the crowd, receiving hugs and handshakes and pats on the back, her signature pure white hair accentuated by her white suit, bright red blouse, and several strands of Gram's long white pearls. Mom looked, well— positively gubernatorial.

By the time she got back to Lincoln, the hometown crowd had swelled and sweltered in the banquet room next to the steamy Holiday Inn swimming pool. As she buoyantly entered the throng of ecstatic supporters, they broke into choruses of "Hello, Helen" to the tune

8. Flanked by her grandsons, Helen shares Mother's Day with her family during governor's race

of "Hello, Dolly." They didn't seem to mind the interminable time it took her to get to the podium as one TV reporter after another stopped her for interviews. Governor Bob Kerrey's arrival delayed her victory speech a bit longer as he embraced her and greeted the giddy group. As the crowd continued chanting "Helen, Helen," I barely heard Kerrey say, "I could not be happier being able to introduce an exceptional public servant and leader, one whom I hold in the highest regard and whom I will be proud to serve as a citizen."

Eyes brimming, I strained to see Mom take the podium but I heard her loud and clear. "Governor Kerrey will be a tough act to follow. But I will, won't I!" The laughter and cheers and clapping continued for several minutes. Mom spoke a bit about the issues that her general election campaign would address, but the night belonged to jubilant celebration. For the first time, I truly realized that my mother could be the next governor.

As focused as our family and the Boosalis campaign were on Mom's

9. Helen Boosalis accepts Democratic primary election nomination for Nebraska governor

victory, the national interest in her election came from the combined win of Democrat Helen Boosalis and Kay Orr, the winning Republican nominee. It was the first time in U.S. history that two women had won their parties' nominations and would go head-to-head in a general-election campaign for the governorship.

After just a few hours of sleep, the two women gubernatorial candidates from Nebraska ("of all places") made countless appearances on morning talk shows and gave reporters interview after interview, patiently answering the same questions about how it felt to be in a two-woman race for governor, and why this phenomenon happened in Nebraska. Only a few reporters resisted being sucked into the two-woman story "hook" of the primary outcome, but one Lincoln journalist overtly downplayed its importance. "While this contest between two women has captured national attention, it is more than that," said a *Lincoln Star* reporter. "It is also a contest between two very competent politicians, probably as strong a pair of individuals as Nebraskans have ever nominated for the governorship in the same year. Tough dudes. It's going to be a rousing campaign."

The primary vote outcome was far better than we had dared hope: in a field of seven Democrats, Helen Boosalis received 44 percent of

10. Helen Boosalis supporters celebrate her gubernatorial primary win, May 13, 1986

the vote, David Domina 27 percent, and Chris Beutler 22 percent. Because registered Republicans so outnumbered Democrats statewide, the typical "unity" gathering to demonstrate Democratic Party unity behind the primary winner would need to be more than symbolic. If the Democrats were to pull off a win in the general election, they had to be staunchly unified, which Mom's decisive primary victory made possible.

When the Democratic Party scheduled a unity session for the day after the primary election, my mother was at first skeptical about the timing. She knew it had been the toughest fight of her political career and thought the losing candidates would "hurt too much" without a little time to heal. But she was convinced to go forward less than twenty-four hours after the primary to express gratitude to her former rivals in a Democratic unity news conference at party headquarters near the governor's mansion.

There Governor Kerrey described the new Democratic nominee for governor as a friend and supporter and also his former mayor. As a businessman, Kerrey said, he found out firsthand that Helen Boosalis had the ability to say no, even to supporters, and as a result she built a quality of life in Lincoln that is "the envy of the country." That put

11. Helen at Democratic unity event after the gubernatorial primary with (*from left*) David Domina, Robert Prokop, Governor Bob Kerrey, and Chris Beutler.

to rest my question of whether Kerrey held a grudge for Mom's op-posing a zoning change he requested for his business when she was mayor. I should have already known the answer, given his appointment of my mother as director of the state's Department on Aging three years earlier. In any event, on this day of unity all past quarrels among Democrats were pushed aside in their single-focused desire to keep the governor's office in Democratic hands.

Other party leaders chimed in the unity chorus. Tom Monaghan, chairman of the Nebraska Democratic Party, expressed confidence that my mother would get support from all parts of the state because she "has proven experience, she has a (political) base, she has an organi-zation and she captured the imagination of Democrats." Even Chris Beutler's campaign manager, Jim Crounse, said just hours after his candidate was defeated, "Everyone likes Helen." At a later Democratic unity event in Omaha, former U.S. congressman John Cavanaugh, a Domina supporter in the primary, said, "Every Democrat is comfort-able with her [Helen] and confident she can do the job." Terry Moore,

Omaha Federation of Labor president and also a supporter of Domina in the primary, proclaimed, "I've never seen another candidate mend the fences so well."

The primary results demonstrated that "Mrs. Boosalis had a much easier time winning the primary than Mrs. Orr," who more narrowly defeated her leading Republican opponent, Omaha attorney Kermit Brashear: Orr received 39 percent of the vote, Brashear 32 percent, and Hoch 22 percent. The closeness of the Republican primary reinforced speculation that the Republican Party was split between its conservative and moderate wings and might have difficulty uniting behind its nominee, Kay Orr, who was firmly entrenched in the conservative camp.

When Neil Oxman called me home to Lincoln in March to help in Mom's primary campaign, I was unfamiliar with Nebraska's recent gubernatorial and political party history. I had left the state twenty years earlier, in 1966, to go to college, eventually moving to Chicago, where the Republican Party barely exists. Because Kay Orr had come from behind so late in the primary campaign, I was even less familiar with her political background and where it fit with Nebraska Republican history. It was time to catch up.

Orr had worked her way up Republican Party ranks to become co-manager of Charles Thone's successful campaign for governor in 1978. Governor Thone appointed Orr as his chief of staff and then appointed her state treasurer in 1981 to fill the unexpired term of Frank Marsh, who had resigned. Orr then ran for the treasurer's office in 1982, defeating state senator Shirley Marsh in the primary. Until Governor Kerrey made his surprise decision in the fall of 1985 not to seek reelection, Orr was planning to run for reelection as state treasurer, not run for governor.

In the gubernatorial primary, Orr won Omaha while her closest primary competitor, Brashear, won Lincoln. Therefore, Orr's primary victory edge came from voters in the western, rural Third Congressional District, the state's traditional Republican heartland. Orr, observed *Lincoln Star* reporter Don Walton, appealed to "GOP loyalists as perhaps the most clearly certified doctrinaire conservative in the field, closely tied to the politics and the political friends of President Reagan." Orr applied her skills as former governor Thone's campaign manager to her own campaign. Organization was her political strength, Walton said, and might have been the most important ingredient in her campaign victory, even more than her conservative message.

In the political equivalent of Monday-morning quarterbacking, my mother's relative ease in winning the Democratic primary by such a convincing margin was hashed and rehashed. Her strength among Democrats in western Nebraska was attributed in part to extensive local TV coverage of her performance as mayor of Lincoln and her later visits to more than 150 senior groups during her state directorship of the Department on Aging. It was no surprise that she garnered high vote counts in Lincoln after serving so many years in elected office, but even in Omaha, where she was least known and her support was thinnest at the campaign's outset, she ended up winning by a comfortable margin.

Of Mom's Democratic primary win, retired University of Nebraska–Lincoln (UNL) political science professor Robert Sittig reflected, "Helen's gubernatorial primary win was a really big deal. First, she had never been a party activist, a rank and file partisan. In addition, her major opponents were a campaign consultant's dream—two all-American boys who were good Democrats. Chris Beutler was young, a Yale graduate, title company owner, state legislator, family man; and Dave Domina was a similar version of Beutler. For Helen to beat both of them and without being a party activist was really big." Former St. Paul mayor George Latimer similarly observed, "Helen had never been a real party, partisan person. She ran for governor more as an extension of her public service—here are the issues, here's what needs to be done—than as a party chief."

Some post-primary news analysis bought the notion that Boosalis's planned winning strategy was to ride on her name recognition until the final weeks before the primary and then unleash a media campaign with a blitz of TV ads. I smiled when Mom's campaign chair, Marg Badura, made it sound for reporters as if the Boosalis late media advertising were an intentional strategy for peaking at just the right time—"saving money for a late, sustained media blitz"—rather than the absolute scramble to raise the money to make that first media buy, and then the next, and then the next. No, holding back was not the strategy—*being held back* by lack of money was the reality.

By today's comparison the money raised by the gubernatorial primary candidates seems paltry, but raising and spending the most money clearly did not dictate the primary victors. Brashear and Domina raised $365,000 and $309,000, respectively (each with large personal loans), while primary winners Orr and Boosalis raised $307,000 and $278,000, respectively.

Soon, political analysis of the primary outcome gave way to predictions on the upcoming Orr-Boosalis battle in the general election. I poured over a *Lincoln Journal* post-primary editorial—liking some parts, hating others, heeding its warnings. I hated the part that picked Orr as the favorite in the general election, even though I couldn't argue with the reasoning that Orr was the "certified champion of the state's largest political party"; that the GOP wanted to "reclaim the prize . . . lost four years ago when Bob Kerrey upset Charles Thone"; and that Orr could "tap into great national support" (i.e., President Reagan).

I liked the part of the editorial acknowledging that if anyone could appeal across party lines it surely would be Helen Boosalis. "Tuesday, Boosalis showed a statewide strength. The only surprise was how easily she vanquished a pair of attractive male opponents. She came close to a simple majority in an eight-candidate [seven, actually] field." And then came the warning: "Extremely important to Boosalis is the willingness of the Douglas County [Omaha] Democratic establishment to work enthusiastically for her—its leadership as well as precinct troops. . . . Boosalis won the Douglas County rank and file Tuesday, but not the warlords and chieftains."

Warlords? Chieftains? I had a lot to learn about Omaha politics—and, I suspected, so did my mom. It would definitely take more than the symbolic post-primary Democratic unity event to bring warlords and chieftains to the table. In the primary campaign, Domina had "played most of his cards in Omaha. There he won the endorsement of several Democratic leaders who often serve as kingmakers in Douglas County," said a Lincoln newspaper. As the campaign marched toward the November general election, I would come up with my own name for the Omaha warlords-chieftains-kingmakers: I came to call them, in my head, the "Omaha Big Boys."

Media interviews dominated May 14, 1986, the day after the primary election. Outside her campaign headquarters in downtown Lincoln, my mother answered questions about why she liked campaigning for public office. "It's an opportunity to be with people," she said, "to see what they are thinking and what they want. That's what democracy is all about." When asked why she was seeking the governorship when troubled times were clearly ahead and she had already achieved the age and accomplishments on which many would retire, Mom seemed centered and ready to take on the general election campaign. "Well, it sounds like campaign rhetoric, I know, but . . . I have my health, and my life has been dedicated to public service and I have the experience Nebraska is going to need. That's really it." Orr, also besieged by reporters that day, received a congratulatory phone call from President Reagan, who promised support for her campaign ahead.

Although Orr and Boosalis had a combined fifty years of political involvement, they were barely acquainted and had belonged to only one organization in common—Women Executives in State Government (wesg)—Boosalis as director of the state Department on Aging and Orr as state treasurer. The day after the primary—the first day of the general election campaign—Mom told reporters that she had dropped her wesg membership more than a year earlier to save money in her state agency budget. "Fiscal conservative, you know." *Omaha World-Herald* reporter David Kotok characterized the comment as "the first dig of the campaign."

To launch her campaign for the general election, my mother planned to fly around the state for a few days to thank voters in Lexington, Scottsbluff, North Platte, and Grand Island for helping her win the primary. But in a repeat of her attempt to kick off the primary campaign three months earlier, her plane was grounded because of bad weather. No matter, the Democratic nominee for governor would crisscross the state relentlessly over the next six months.

After Mom's rousing victory party on May 13, Max and I took the boys home to Evanston, where Michael could tell kindergarten friends about his Grami winning the primary election for governor. I flew on to Washington DC for my National League of Cities meeting with other city council members and mayors, where the victory of Lincoln's former mayor in the Nebraska gubernatorial primary was big news.

Once school let out a few weeks later, both boys and I would return to Nebraska for the long campaign summer ahead.

Chapter Two

Madame Mayor

Spring 1975

"Helen knew who she was and what she wanted to accomplish. I believe we owe people we represent an honest answer. I've been surprised that more people in politics don't conduct themselves in that manner. I'm not afraid, and I don't think your mother was afraid. If you're not afraid, you can be who you are."
—CHUCK HAGEL, U.S. senator (Nebraska)

"Women are good at coalition building because growing up we were continually admonished to play well and to learn to play well with others. We know how to share the sandbox or the tables of power."—BARBARA A. MIKULSKI, U.S. senator (Maryland)

I missed my mother's third and fourth campaigns for city council in 1967 and 1971. The late 1960s and early 1970s took me far from Lincoln and my folks, geographically and mentally. I graduated from college in June 1970, wearing a white armband over my graduation robe along with my classmates in protest of the Vietnam War, the recent invasion of Cambodia, and the killing of Kent State student protesters just a month earlier. Following the ceremony on the campus lawn I overheard my mother trying to explain to my grandmother and other members of my dad's Minnesota family just "why Mary Beth had to spoil her graduation robe with that white rag on her arm." Later that day at the family graduation party in Faribault, Minnesota, just down the highway from the Carleton campus, one of my dad's brothers stormed out of Grandma's house after a heated argument with my mother over Vietnam, and Mom chased after him to apologize. Undoubtedly, the same scene was repeating itself in divided families all over the country.

After spending half my senior year of college student-teaching in two inner-city high schools on Chicago's South Side, and much of the other half "on strike" in the student protest movement to end the war, I left the ivory tower for the world beyond college and my Nebraska home. After a year teaching in the Chicago area, I went to law school and clerked in a Chicago law firm, where I met by far the smartest man I've ever known. I married him in 1973 at the beginning of my last year of law school.

Max reminded me a lot of my dad—modest and understated, with a quick sense of humor and supportive of whatever I chose to do with my life. Because my mother had stepped beyond traditional women's roles into politics, I'd grown up thinking women had unlimited choices for world engagement. When I looked around my law school class in 1973, however, I was tangibly aware how few women filled the seats—27 out of 180, or 15 percent of my class. The numbers were even smaller at the law firms where I clerked and eventually worked. I realized my dad was way ahead of his time in supporting my mom's atypical political life outside the home; and although the women's movement had opened more doors for me by the early 1970s, Max's support—like my dad's for Mom—bolstered my confidence to walk through them.

NOT SUCH A LONG WAY, BABY

Just how far by the early 1970s had women progressed on the political front? Back in 1961, during my mother's first city council term, President Kennedy had created the President's Commission on the Status of Women, chaired by Eleanor Roosevelt—a "tacit admission that there was indeed a 'problem' regarding women's position in American society, that the democratic vision of equal opportunity had somehow left them out." The commission's 1963 report acknowledged women's family roles as primary but also examined inequities in their lives, employment discrimination they faced, and their need for child care. With the women's movement in the 1970s came an even greater recognition how far behind women lagged in holding positions of influence—in business, in academics, in the professions, in politics.

Throughout American history, women's movements have mobilized and transformed how women view themselves and their relationship to each and to their government," wrote Denise Baer in an article on women's political interests, even if their efforts were not recognized as "movements" at the *time. According to Baer, historians recognize three distinct women's movements: "the *Equal Rights Movement*, arising from the 1848 Seneca Falls Declaration of Sentiments; the *Suffrage Movement*, developing in 1890 out of the merger of the two rival woman suffrage groups; and the contemporary *Women's Rights Movement*, originating in 1966 when the National Organization for Women was formed to lobby the Equal Employment Opportunity Commission."

Women have also long engaged in wide-ranging community activism for social change through such national efforts as the Women's Peace Party (1914–15), temperance and settlement house movements, workers and trade unions (e.g., International Workers of the World), Women Strike for Peace to protest American and Soviet nuclear politics (1961), and the civil rights movement. Women's community activism has included a spectrum of grassroots efforts to improve conditions in their own neighborhoods and cities, such as calls for higher-quality education, opening health clinics, gaining access to neighborhood services.

Through these political movements and social and grassroots community activism, great numbers of women developed strong leadership skills. Unfortunately, the process of translating successful movements and community activism into correspondingly greater numbers of women elected to public office has been *slow, especially at the national level. As recently as January 2007, women held only 16 percent of the 535 seats in the 110th Congress: 16 women in the Senate and 71 in the House of *Representatives.

By the early 1970s and my mother's fourth election to the city council, more women had been elected to municipal office than when Mom ran for office the first time, in 1959, but gains were not dramatic. Although data on women elected to municipal office are scarce for these early years, records of women mayors in 1989 show that 12 percent of mayors of the one hundred largest cities were women, and that percentage remained unchanged in 2006. Data on numbers of women state legislators show greater increases (from 4.5 percent in 1971 to 23 percent in 2006), but the numbers still do not reflect a proportional representation of women. While the 1970s women's movement insisted that more women could and must be elected to public office, the numbers of elected women have fallen far short of those aspirations.

Back in those early 1970s, my mother and I were operating in our separate spheres of politics and law—both underpopulated by women. While we shared with one another little of our respective struggles, I suspect each of us then was at least encouraged by the promise of the 1970s women's movement that times were changing. Mom's early entry into politics had already proved she was not one to wait for times to change, but neither of us knew then how much more change she herself was yet to initiate.

SURPRISING NEWS, LATE DECISION

Max and I spent much of our first year of marriage (1973–74) glued to the TV watching the Watergate hearings. Between following Watergate and the end of the Vietnam War, taking the bar exam, adjusting to marriage, and working long hours as a law firm associate, my attention was not on Mom's sixteenth year of city council service in Lincoln, five hundred miles away.

What a shock, then, when I answered the phone one Sunday afternoon in late February 1975. My parents had important news to tell us—my mother was running for mayor! I was speechless. Listening to my mother talk about her city council work through the years, I'd grown accustomed to her legislative role. But being one member of a legislative body and being the sole chief executive of the city seemed two entirely different ball games. Regardless of the slow but positive effect of the women's movement on the numbers of women candidates for elected office, my mother was taking a gigantic, overwhelming step.

I had a thousand questions: Whom was she running against? When was the election? Who would run her campaign? What did Dad think? What were hot issues? Who was supporting her? Was she ready for the stress of such a demanding job? My mother laughed and told me not to be such a worrywart. She said I sounded like Gram, whom she had called minutes before calling us. Gram worried that the stress of being mayor would take a toll on her daughter's health.

Neither Gram nor I, however, had time to dwell on our personal worries about the well-being of our daughter/mother. The decision had been made, and my mom's compressed, intensive campaign for mayor was about to begin. We jumped aboard a train that had not only left the station but was steaming down the track. If my dad, a virtual worry factory, was 100 percent behind my mother's decision to run for mayor, that was enough assurance for me.

Later, Mom told me that shortly before her decision to run for mayor she had shared a cab with a young man from Denver who was attending meetings with her of the Association of Comprehensive Health Planners in Washington DC. She expressed doubts about her pending decision, to which he responded, "Sometimes the brass ring on the merry-go-round comes around only once—you have one chance to grab it and then it's gone." My mother listened.

My mother announced her decision to run for mayor of Lincoln only five weeks before the primary election on April 8, 1975. When I asked why she waited so long to make such a critical move, she responded simply, "I didn't decide until then." But Mom was no longer the political novice she had been in 1959, at the time of her first city council race. Running for mayor after serving sixteen years on the council surely did not occur to her out of the blue.

So why did she wait until the eleventh hour to make the decision to run, when a decision so late in the process was bound to put her campaign at a disadvantage? This isn't the kind of question my mother ponders. She's not prone to that kind of introspection. She is a woman of action: define the issue, seek input, take action, reach resolution, move on. She doesn't dwell on whys and wherefores after the fact. So I can only speculate from years of observation why her pattern of last-minute candidacies may have developed.

One likely reason lies in my mother's motivation for running for office. No matter how great her popularity in office grew, Mom was never enticed to run by the prospect of personal power. Her decisions to run for office were less a reflection of her individual will than of those whom she had inspired to get involved in their city. Since the electorate is slow to focus on the next election ahead of time, Mom's last-minute decisions likely came at the point when a critical mass of citizens urged her to run.

In addition to a particularly persuasive visit from a citizen watchdog group concerned with local justice issues, a "flood of mail and calls" ultimately swayed Mom's decision, she told the press, to run for mayor—perhaps like the call she received from UNL professor Robert Sittig, who was driving "home from work when I heard on the radio that Helen Boosalis was not running for another term on the council. I realized then that I had come to rely on her being there and to do the right thing for the city. As long as someone like that was in local government, I didn't have to worry too much about the city. But that announcement really shocked me. When I got home, I called to urge her to reconsider. Maybe she got enough calls like that and they helped her decide to run for mayor."

Another reason for my mom's late candidacies may have been total commitment to whatever was her current office. An early decision to run, especially for a higher office, would have detracted from meeting present responsibilities and making decisions free from electoral concerns. On a tough vote during my own city council tenure, Mom counseled me to determine what was right for that issue without considering its impact on my future elections; she surely applied the same standard herself.

I also wonder if my mother felt, as I did, the insecurities of sitting way out on that limb of running for office. Did her eleventh-hour candidacies offer a subconscious excuse for losing? As confident a figure as my mother presented publicly, she nonetheless seemed privately surprised at her own electoral success. Having only weeks instead of months to organize a campaign could have explained a potential election defeat.

Perhaps my mom's reluctance to declare her early candidacy had its roots in women's historical aversion to being perceived as ambitious. In *Closing the Leadership Gap*, Marie Wilson describes the expectation of ambition in men, who "anoint themselves for positions of power . . . [and] act with bald certainty of the right to ask, if not the right to win. And they get taken seriously." In contrast, Wilson says, women feel the need to mask and "soft-sell their ambition with self-deprecation and a nurturing style" in order to be accepted as political leaders. For example, when asked about her rise to congressional power, Nancy Pelosi described her reluctant transformation from invisible party functionary to high-profile politician, a job she said she loves but never craved.

Wilson cites research showing that women who run for office are less likely than men to be "self-starters" politically and seek office only after receiving encouragement from others. In a 2001 political science study, 37 percent of male candidates polled said it was their own idea to run for office, compared to only 11 percent of women candidates; similarly, 37 percent of women said they had not considered running until someone else brought it up, in contrast to only 18 percent of men. To jump in a race early may seem to women like an unacceptable show of ambition, but masking that ambition by waiting for "the call" can put their late-starting campaigns at a disadvantage.

The specific nature of the 1975 mayoral race may also have played a role in my mother's hesitancy to throw her hat in the ring. Rather than running for a vacant office, Mom was taking on a fairly popular two-term incumbent, Sam Schwartzkopf, who had been mayor during half of my mother's sixteen years on the city council. The incumbent was an amiable fellow, a businessman with an avid interest in golf, and a former varsity football player at the University of *Nebraska. Schwartzkopf easily won his first two terms in office and expected to have another four years to complete a number of projects.

Unseating an incumbent is nearly always daunting, but at least my mother had an insider's knowledge of the incumbent based on eight years of working with him from her city council seat. She had used her leadership role as council chair to guide and push priority issues, which equipped her with a thorough understanding of the city's executive branch. Behind the scenes my mother had helped the mayor take the lead by doing the homework and organizing necessary support for him. City council member Sue Bailey said to me, "I told your mother she had to stop making Sam look good when she was the one doing the work. 'You're doing Sam a great favor, but you're not doing the public a favor. Why don't *you* run for mayor, Helen?' She told me it didn't matter—it was for the good of the city. But I think what I said eventually made her stop and think about her own leadership in relation to the Mayor's."

Even though her prospects for winning the mayor's race did not seem great in 1975, Mom was determined to make the incumbent accountable for using (or failing to use) his strong-mayor powers to benefit the city. Once she was in the race, however, she realized that she really did want to win.

In addition to the difficulty of challenging incumbency, the scope of the mayor's job may have given my mother pause. Although she had fought as a member of the League of Women Voters to change Lincoln's form of government to the strong-mayor type, it must have been somewhat intimidating to contemplate *being* that strong mayor—the city's chief executive—herself. As mayor, my mother would hold all executive powers of the city's administrative branch, including appointment and removal of department heads, preparation of the budget, and power to veto legislation. She would be administrative chief of all city departments: police, fire, planning, finance, public works, urban development, health, and more—the whole works.

There would be no professional city manager responsible for the day-to-day administration of city operations, as in a council-manager form of government. Reflecting the much greater level of responsibility, the mayor's position was full time with a salary of $28,000. My mom would be earning nearly as much as my dad, a huge increase over her wages on the city council, which had started at ten dollars per attended weekly meeting.

Perhaps pieces of all my conjectures played some part in my mother's late decision to run for mayor, or perhaps none of them did and she really just "didn't decide until then." For whatever reason, my mother did not announce her candidacy for mayor until March 3, 1975, just five weeks before the primary election. One newspaper editorial expressed "surprise . . . that the 16-year council veteran finally agreed to a proposal (that she run for mayor) that she heretofore resisted."

READY FOR A WOMAN?

My mother's announcement raised a thorny question: "Is Lincoln ready for a woman mayor?" The question was posed editorially, along with its answer—the hope that "this city is too enlightened . . . to have that crop up as an issue in the upcoming campaign."

By 1975 gender as a political issue had gained the spotlight. The women's movement had spawned significant new legislation affecting women. Congress passed the Equal Rights Amendment in 1972 (first introduced in Congress in 1923) and sent it to the states for *ratification. The Equal Employment Opportunity Act, which enabled federal court enforcement of Title VII of the Civil Rights Act, was passed that same year, as was Title IX, which granted women equal access to federally funded education programs. A year later the U.S. Supreme Court ruled on *Roe v. Wade*. After Bella Abzug, Betty Friedan, and Representative Shirley Chisholm formed the National Women's Political Caucus in 1971, more women attended the 1972 national party conventions, and Shirley Chisholm became the first black woman to campaign for a presidential nomination.

At the municipal level, prior to 1975 only one woman had been elected chief executive of a major U.S. city (population over 100,000): Bertha Knight Landes, mayor of Seattle from 1926 to *1928. In Landes's campaign for mayor, "the issue of her gender, although seldom addressed directly by her opponents or the press, was an ever-constant presence affecting the conduct of the election." Would gender play a similar role a half century later in my mother's campaign for election as chief executive of a second major U.S. city, this time in the *Midwest?

Even now, many question a woman's suitability for the role of chief executive. Studies have shown that the nature of the office determines how much a candidate's gender influences public perception of that candidate. People often make distinctions between legislative and executive leadership that mirror their beliefs about gender: legislative leadership tends to be associated with the feminine stereotype, while executive leadership is associated with the masculine stereotype. Assuming that similar attitudes about gender and executive leadership were even more prevalent during the 1975 mayoral race, how would my mother steer the public's long acceptance of her as a consensus-building, caretaking "feminine" legislator to perception of her as a strong, decisive "masculine" executive?

And how did my mom feel about being a woman *candidate? In making her decision to run, did she feel pressure as a woman political pioneer seeking the office of chief executive? Mom predicted that being female would be a neutral factor in the mayor's race and that men and women would vote for her because she had done a good job on the city council. In her eyes, the electorate's readiness for a woman mayor was not the biggest issue. Her motivation to run was the need for "dynamic, positive leadership in the office [of mayor]," given the critical decisions facing the community in the next four years.

My mother's notion of leadership is not some set of top-down skills—the individual out ahead of the pack, somehow persuading others to adopt the leader's point of view. She has always instinctively understood that it is followers who make a leader. (As Garry Wills wrote, "The leader needs to understand followers far more than they need to understand him.") Mom believed the sole reason for her to run for public office was to give voice to the people: "I strongly feel that government is there to serve the people. Whether I'm a councilperson or a mayor I want to serve the people. I'll be responsive. I'll have an open ear and an open mind. It doesn't mean I'd do anything people say, but I'll listen."

My mother planned to deploy her brand of leadership to address the issues she highlighted in her announcement of candidacy: revitalization of the downtown business district, neighborhood development, updating the city's Comprehensive Plan (governing land use and zoning), police-community relations, affordable housing for seniors and lower-income families, consolidation of city and county governments, fiscal planning and accountability, and making city hall responsive to citizens. Citing the Schwartzkopf administration's overemphasis on "brick and mortar" improvements, she also said that addressing human service needs required a new form of municipal leadership. Today the importance of city-funded human services seems obvious, but in 1975 the role of cities was to provide traditional services such as police and fire protection, sewer and garbage services, water, streets, and lighting. My mother's call for a commitment of city expenditures to meet human services needs was ahead of her time but reflected her motivation in running for office: to serve the people.

PLACE YOUR BETS: THE RACE IS ON

In the one day between her candidacy announcement and her first mayoral campaign committee meeting, my mother paid a visit to Bailey
Lewis, a marketing and communications firm fairly new to Lincoln.
She found their work a creative and exciting alternative to that of some
better-known, traditional advertising pundits in town. After the meeting Mom hired the young partners on the spot, convinced they would
bring fresh insight to a campaign that in itself would be startling in
character—a woman running for mayor. Rich Bailey, founder of Bailey
Lewis and its successor firm, Bailey Lauerman, told me that "because
of the times, she stood out as a candidate. Being the only woman was
both a blessing and a curse—a blessing because she gained more attention from being different than expectations, and a curse because when
you're different in any environment, people are suspicious."

Upon her announcement the editorial press began speculating
whether she could garner the votes needed to beat the two-term incumbent. The *Lincoln Star* speculated that my mother would be "facing
an acknowledged uphill battle to unseat Mayor Sam Schwartzkopf."
A poll taken six months before the mayoral primary—long before my
mother's formal candidacy—showed support for "likely" mayoral candidates: Schwartzkopf led the field with 42 percent, Boosalis a distant
second at 15 percent, and other possible candidates scored in the single
digits.

"If not wildly popular," wrote the *Lincoln Evening Journal*, "Schwartzkopf has not been especially unpopular, either. He's pretty much kept
his head down . . . while either the council or city department heads
have called leadership shots." Also noted was the financial soundness
of Schwartzkopf's administration, primarily due to the city council's
enactment of a 1 percent sales tax and to generous federal revenue sharing. Despite my mom's "record of extraordinary dedication to Lincoln"
and the "tide of grassroots support," the *Evening Journal* predicted that
"as of now, it's doubtful local bookies would make Mrs. Boosalis as
much as an even-money bet."

Wherever the smart bets lay, the race was on.

A few weeks into my mother's truncated campaign, her candidacy received a boost that changed the betting odds for those skeptical local bookies. The Lancaster County Democratic Party endorsed Helen Boosalis over the incumbent Mayor Schwartzkopf, also a Democrat. Although from a family of FDR Democrats, my mother had not been active in partisan politics during her years as leader in the nonpartisan League of Women Voters. She characterized her own city council voting record as moderate and viewed issues of city governance as nonpartisan. While the political parties played no formal role in Lincoln's nonpartisan municipal elections, a party's endorsement of one candidate over another of the same party could certainly have some effect on *voters.

In response to this slap in the face from his own party, Mayor Schwartzkopf charged that the Democratic Party endorsement of Boosalis was the work of the party's Central Committee, which Schwartzkopf characterized as "a small faction representing the very 'ultra-liberal' side of the Democratic Party." Using the "ultra-liberal" label surely rallied those who wanted to preserve the city's status quo leadership—the old guard, insiders, chamber of commerce, business-as-usual establishment interests.

Given my mom's history of nonpartisanship in her public service career, an editorial in the *Star* called the mayor's charge "ultra-ridiculous" and claimed that my mother was actually the *conservative* candidate in the sense that "few people have worked as hard over the past years as Mrs. Boosalis in efforts to CONSERVE Lincoln's unique character and quality of life." Variations of this "ultra-liberal" label shadowed my mother for a long time.

A few days after the dustup over the party's endorsement of my mother, a *Sunday Journal and Star* poll showed her and the incumbent neck and neck in the primary race: 42 percent Schwartzkopf, 41 percent Boosalis, 5 percent Bragg, and 12 percent undecided. Since the primary election would not be a party primary, the top two mayoral vote-getters would run against each other in the general election. Not surprisingly, Schwartzkopf and Boosalis were the likely primary winners. Surprising was how quickly the odds were shifting, the race tightening.

As the campaign progressed, poll numbers weren't the only numbers of interest. My mother voluntarily reported all campaign contributions of a dollar or more and limited individual contributions to her campaign to one hundred dollars, saying, "I just don't believe it's necessary to have big contributions to win an election in Lincoln." Yet even with her voluntary restrictions on contributions, she was raising more money while spending less on her campaign than the incumbent. Schwartzkopf hadn't yet raised enough in contributions to cover the loan to finance his primary campaign, but so far he had spent one and a half times as much as the Boosalis campaign.

Following the poll showing a dead heat with the primary election only a few days away, city hall observers were not laying odds that the mayor would come out the decisive winner as he had in his first two elections. My mother appeared to be one of the few who could defeat him. "She is popular, has made herself available to citizens and has the reputation of being one of the toughest campaigners around," wrote a *Star* reporter. Four days before the primary, an editorial in the *Evening Journal* speculated that the post-primary matchup between the incumbent (whose second term had been "generally trouble-free") and Helen Boosalis ("the dynamic city council president") could become "the most spirited race for mayor in many, many years."

"Spirited" didn't come close to describing my mother's campaign style. Campaign volunteers, who tried in vain to keep up with her, described her as an "energy freak," but this was just one of her secret weapons. My father stood right beside her, urging her on, telling her she could do it, calling on her Spartan blood when the going got tough, telling a joke when campaign intensity called for levity.

Meeting both his responsibilities as a UNL professor and the crazy demands of the campaign, my father still found time to keep me informed by mail of the campaign's progress. Almost daily he sent me the latest news article, often with a little index card attached and a note in his small, cramped handwriting. I pictured Dad writing the notes, tired at the end of very long days, sitting at the kidney-shaped desk in the living room where he had been a fixture throughout my childhood as he drafted and redrafted lab results or research articles.

The little index card notes were my window to the campaign, and also to a husband's support for his nontraditional wife:

Mary Beth, I was out ringing doorbells all afternoon yesterday. And last night I helped assemble yard signs—and guess what— your old friend Judy was helping with the signs as were her mother and father—slogan: there are no big shots in the Boosalis campaign. Daddio.

Max and Beth, I was out ringing doorbells again last night. One chauvinist came to the door and said, "Save your breath. I'm not registered to vote, but even if I were I would not vote for a woman for mayor. I strongly believe that women should not hold leadership jobs." One woman said, "No way can I vote for her because she is not a native Nebraskan." Another "sawed-off runt," shorter than my dad, was working on his yard, and when I approached him and stated I was campaigning for Helen, he practically shoved the literature down my throat without saying a word. However, most people were very nice—even though I did not detect a "ground swell." Take care, M.G.B.

Max and Mary Beth, H is more relaxed and is enjoying every min-ute of the campaign. Telephone rings constantly. I hope all the support is representative of a wide-based ground swell. H awak-ened this morning at 5:00 and went downstairs to enter some ideas in her campaign book—she dreamed about them. Dad/Mike.

I loved getting my father's scribbled notes and news articles. Little did I know then that he was also keeping a full set of articles about the campaign and every city issue related to it. As a scientist, he used me-thodical care as if he were documenting the steps in a laboratory experi-ment. In a way, I guess he was—electing a woman mayor was certainly a social experiment at that time. He carefully clipped the news articles, taped them on heavy paper, and assembled them by date in binders. My telescopic vision into my mother's mayoral campaign began with my father's copiously detailed clippings notebooks.

Even with my dad's frequent updates, I was frustrated watching my mother's gutsy run for mayor from distant sidelines in Chicago. I didn't miss the stress of campaigning that I'd endured from the age of ten, but I did miss being part of something that felt big—much bigger than my mother's earlier campaigns for city council. This time I cheered for her to win not only because she was my mother but also because the stakes seemed so much higher—for her and for other qualified women to reach higher levels of elected office.

The election commissioner predicted a voter turnout of only 25 percent for the municipal primary, in part due to the Watergate-induced political turnoff of voters. But disillusioned or not by the national scandal, voters turned out in higher numbers than predicted, perhaps because of their interest in the prospect that Lincoln could have its first woman mayor.

And with the April 8, 1975, primary results that prospect grew more likely. Helen Boosalis came in a strong first out of the three mayoral candidates, getting 53.4 percent of the vote and beating the incumbent by almost *13 percent. Just as in her first city council primary election, sixteen years earlier, news coverage used words like "surprise" and "unexpected" in describing my mother's decisive showing. "The council president's commanding performance came as a surprise to most observers," wrote one reporter, "because Schwartzkopf, with eight years under his belt, was considered tough to beat."

Monday-morning quarterbacks (who abound in Nebraska football country) were quick to analyze the election results. Election officials attributed the win to a better voter turnout due to "Mrs. Boosalis' grassroots campaign, compared to Schwartzkopf's more media-oriented efforts." Because the candidates agreed on a wide range of issues, a *Star* editorial cited the issue of leadership and voters' perceptions of who could best exert it: "Mrs. Boosalis has grabbed the leadership issue and it is a legitimate one." Even given the times and the unusual nature of the race, an *Evening Journal* reporter opined that "Boosalis' strong showing reinforces the belief held by many that a woman candidate here isn't handicapped by her sex."

Mom's campaign volunteers were less surprised than reporters by her strong primary showing. Robert Sittig recalled his volunteer precinct work in the Boosalis for Mayor campaign:

> I was assigned a precinct to leaflet in northeast Lincoln where we had always lived. I had a whole spiel memorized to convince

people, since I know so many people are confused or apathetic about local candidates. Out of my first eight to ten houses, residents interrupted me to say, "Oh, I know Helen. She's great. We've watched her on the city council." Pretty soon I junked my spiel and just handed people a leaflet, saying Helen was running for mayor. I remember thinking, "How can this woman have this kind of rapport all the way across town? If she's got this kind of standing with rank-and-file folks, she's really going to go places." I'd been involved in twenty to twenty-five campaigns and I had never seen that before. I realized that folks were responding to her graciousness, her sincerity. With Helen there's no backslapping—she's a person before she's a candidate for public office.

Although Mom's powerful performance in what was expected to be a nip-and-tuck mayoral primary surprised many, editorials cautioned against presuming a Boosalis victory in the general election. One stated that Mayor Schwartzkopf "can be expected to pull into play all the political resources at his command and if anyone thinks the mayor's office is signed, sealed and delivered to Mrs. Boosalis without another whale of a fight, they are dead wrong."

Editorial writers could not have known, as my dad and I did, that Mom takes almost nothing for granted. Preparation, even overpreparation, is the hallmark of her work. Whether cooking for a sit-down dinner for twenty or running for office, my mother, the strategist, prepares for all contingencies. There was no chance that she'd take her 13 percent winning primary margin and ease up. Before the primary votes could even be counted, she was full throttle toward the general election only a month away, and on the night of the primary election she whipped up her supporters for the critical battle ahead.

In a different part of town on primary election night, the trailing incumbent, Mayor Schwartzkopf, again lashed out at "ultra-liberal" Democrats. Publicly he said he wasn't surprised at the election results, but privately he seemed "dismayed at having lost the race." He credited my mother's 13 percent lead to the aid of Democratic Party workers following the party's endorsement and also to her campaign workers— perhaps a bid to rally his own workers for the general election only a

Make
a good
city
better.

Helen
Boosalis
for mayor

12. 1975 Boosalis for Mayor campaign brochure

13. 1975 mayor's race: Schwartzkopf v. Boosalis

14. Helen stakes her own yard signs in 1975 mayoral campaign

month away. The mayor was "rather snappy with some news reporters election night and appeared uptight," conceding he would have a tough fight to stay in office. Yet he was hardly defeatist about his primary election showing, hearkening to his former football days: "This is just the first half. The ball game is not over. A lot of games are won in the second half."

With no halftime show, no locker-room pep talk, and no marching bands, the campaign teams squared off on the field for the second half. Every play, every moment would count—for the previously favored incumbent mayor running down field for his political life, and for his upstart challenger energized by her primary win and the potential for upset.

DESPERATE TIMES: THE MAYORAL GENERAL ELECTION CAMPAIGN

With two candidates facing off in the general election, the press scrutinized the candidates' public profiles and campaign styles. One political reporter observed that Schwartzkopf had maintained a low public profile as mayor—preferring to operate behind the scenes, saying little in public meetings, letting his department heads do the talking. He was guarded with the press and could ruffle feathers in dealing with his staff and even the public. In contrast, my mom's more public profile was noted. As presiding officer of the city council, she actively participated in public meetings and was viewed as more accessible to both the press and the public.

In the final month's sprint before the general election, my mother hammered away at the leadership question. She pointed to a host of initiatives that were undertaken by the city council because of the leadership void on the executive side of city hall, such as initiatives addressing housing needs of the elderly, solid waste management, energy conservation, rehabilitation of shopping areas, human services planning, investigation of police procedures, transportation, and services for the disabled. Although the two mayoral candidates did not take wildly divergent positions on the substance of these issues, they often disagreed on the means and necessary leadership to address them.

Of broader campaign interest was the current debate over three al-

ternatives for guiding the future growth of Lincoln that had been proposed to update the city's Comprehensive Plan: first, concentric city
growth to the north, south, and west; second, expansion of the city to
the east into the undeveloped Stevens Creek watershed; or third, high-
density development in the central city requiring more reliance on mass
transit. The Goals and Policies Committee (a large citizens' advisory
group charged with recommending updates to the Comprehensive
Plan) favored concentric growth, with a focus on a strong central business district and redevelopment of existing neighborhoods.

My mother unequivocally opposed eastward development in the
foreseeable future in Stevens Creek. "Stevens Creek is the hidden issue
in the election," she warned a mayoral debate audience. "I still support radial growth to the west, south and north as the most efficient
and most economical growth approach." Mayor Schwartzkopf also
declared his preference for the concentric development alternative, yet
he forecast that the final Comprehensive Plan could well be a blend of
strategies, including development in the Stevens Creek watershed.

While the Comprehensive Plan did not come to a city council vote
during the mayoral race—and so was not a "watershed" campaign issue—it was clear that development in Stevens Creek would remain a
central debate for years to come. Developers and others whose business
interests would benefit by planning policies allowing development in
the Stevens Creek watershed used my mother's opposition as their symbol of her anti-business bias, providing yet another reason they didn't
support her for mayor.

To astute observers, the Stevens Creek debate was just one reflection
of the struggle for control of power that was at stake in the mayoral
election. The difference in campaign strategy, the inequality of campaign resources, the contrast in candidate styles, and even the novelty
of a woman running for the city's highest-level executive office—none
of these factors could account for the intense heat of battle preceding
the general election.

No, the white-hot flame in the final month's head-to-head campaign
came from one source: my mother's threat to wrest control from the
city's old-guard power brokers who had wielded unchallenged influence over civic affairs for decades. With her decisive primary victory,

this threat had been elevated to red alert. An *Evening Journal* editorial summed it up: "There's a real struggle going on in Lincoln. . . . Some might simplistically reduce the question to this: Who is going to run the town? A like-thinking cadre more or less dominant calling or significantly influencing the governmental-civic shots in this city for a long time seems to seriously feel imperiled" by bold new forces wanting to share in local government power, observed the editorial. "All of this has shaken some 'movers.' It appears to have threatened some egos, not infrequently male egos."

With only one month to reverse my mother's strong showing in the primary, the incumbent's supporters turned to advertising to redirect voter opinion against my mother. By today's norm of blistering negative advertising in many national, state, and local campaigns, the 1975 campaign ads suggesting that electing Helen Boosalis would pave the way for ultra-liberals to grab the reins of local government may seem relatively tame, but it was something new for Lincoln's electorate in 1975.

One newspaper campaign ad, paid for by "Citizens for Concerned Government," ran every day throughout the last week preceding the May 6 general election. It asked, "Is this the majority you want to govern Lincoln and Lancaster County?" The ad targeted Helen Boosalis, City Councilwoman Sue Bailey, and County Commissioner Jan Gauger—"three wives of University of Nebraska professors" whose "tax-supported" university salaries (including my father's) were listed by specific amount. The ad warned against takeover of the city by "people who are already being supported by our tax dollars." The ad also linked the three women candidates with "two activist lawyers aligned with liberal causes, an activist minister, [and] a former campus activist," and it raised the specter of handing over city and county government to "these seven liberally-oriented people, . . . a power bloc that could side-track Lincoln's growth plans, undermine the effectiveness of our police force and turn an acknowledged good city administration into a giveaway government."

Evening Journal reporter Warren Weber pointed out the new twist in the mayoral race, with Schwartzkopf's campaign unleashing "an advertising blitz which personally attacks his opponent, Helen Boosalis."

Mayor Schwartzkopf's campaign committee, wrote *Star* reporter Lynn Zerschling, "took a more personal approach in attacks against Mrs. Boosalis" by financing a series of print ads formatted as personal citizen letters of criticism addressed to my mother; some of the ads "contained half truths, some questioned Mrs. Boosalis' motives, another attempted to label her as a dangerous liberal." For example, one ad in the series echoed the university spouse innuendo:

Dear Mrs. Boosalis:

As a council member, you voted to raise the mayor's salary to $28,000. Then you and your husband decided to turn down his offer from another university so you could stay in Lincoln. I don't blame you, now that your combined salaries could be almost $60,000.

> [Signed by a resident, with address]
> *Paid for by Schwartzkopf for Mayor Committee*

The mayor defended his use of "anti-Boosalis tactics in his campaign," saying that his campaign committee "felt this was the only way to get our message across" since his press releases had been "distorted" by reporters.

Editorial criticism of this new advertising direction was unequivocal. The *Star* expressed hope that the low-road campaigning represented by the negative ads would be nipped in the bud before setting a standard for future elections. "Never, it seems, have the politics of desperation and distortion been so prevalent in Lincoln politics than in this city election," chided the editorial. "The ads in question include the personal types directed against Mrs. Boosalis and one curious, hysterical ad which made much of the labels 'activist' and 'liberal' and found candidates or officeholders guilty by association of marriage. . . . Inaccurate, broadbrush labeling, innuendoes, half-truths, provocative suggestions lacking any real basis in truth or fact—all these are part of such campaigning. It is something we hadn't seen in Lincoln before."

Despite editorials and several outraged letters to the editor denouncing the negative advertising attack on my mother, the ads continued unabated until election day. The ads infuriated Mom's campaign volunteers, and none more than my dad. After all, his university association was being used to taint my mother as a member of the ultra-liberal, radical left and as a double dipper in the public trough. My mother, although typically slow to anger, was equally incensed by the ads but mostly held private her view that the incumbent's advertising constituted a smear campaign.

But even more attacks were launched. "Citizens for Balanced Representation," working with a partner in the advertising firm handling the mayor's reelection campaign publicity, generated a paid half-hour television show to air the week preceding election day. Citizens for Balanced Representation ("a group closely associated with the Schwartzkopf campaign") brought to Lincoln Doug Christenson, a former city councilman from Madison, Wisconsin, to appear in the paid political infomercial. Christenson warned Lincoln voters of the dangers when a "liberal/radical regime" takes over a city, implying parallels to the current threat to Lincoln posed by "liberal" candidates. Stressing Madison's comparability to Lincoln in population, economic structure, and demographics, the former councilman blamed "radical" Madison mayor Paul Soglin and the liberal majority of the Madison City Council for driving out and stifling expansion of business interests through a no-growth policy and for the skyrocketing crime rate following the hiring of a "new breed of police chief." Also appearing in the thirty-minute paid program, which aired three times the week before the general election, was a city alderman from Boulder, Colorado—presumably another hotbed of radical politics and, coincidentally, another university city.

With the election just days away, Mom's campaign committee deliberated an appropriate response to the opposition's attacks. Many in the group struggled with their instinctive desire to retaliate with equally hard-hitting ads. Mom's communications consultant recommended against responding to the negative ads, and although my mother shared her supporters' anger and frustration, she was reluctant to veer from the positive course she had maintained throughout the campaign. Her volunteer committee came up with a middle course: an ad showing mud hurled and hitting a Boosalis campaign sign to focus voter attention on her opposition's mudslinging tactics. Still not comfortable even with this response, my mother reluctantly approved the mudslinging ad.

The ad had run only once when she received a call from Don Endicott, member of her campaign committee, asking to see her. My mother remembers his advice: "Helen, you're a lady and you know that ad isn't you. If you let the ad continue, you're playing just like them. It's negative. It doesn't reflect you or the campaign you've run." The words were barely out of his mouth when my mother agreed, relieved. She made a phone call and immediately pulled the ad.

This wouldn't be the last time Mom would be the object of negative advertising and face the dilemma of how to respond, but for now she had settled the issue. She would refrain from responding to the opposition's eleventh-hour negative ads and would hope they would not sway the election. My mother directed her volunteers to continue a positive, issue-oriented campaign while she pounded away on her campaign's central issue: leadership.

The question remained, though: Would Lincoln voters buy the ultra-liberal/radical labeling of my mother? Would the advertised specter of liberals at the helm of a declining city—inhospitable to business and victimized by no-growth policies and lax policing—scare enough voters away from voting for my pinko-by-way-of-marriage, radical mother?

Lincoln's old-guard business leaders who wanted to maintain the status quo with the reelection of their incumbent mayor were running scared. "Helen's business opponents were reluctant to give up their long-standing power in the city," reflected Coleen Seng, a later Lincoln mayor. "They didn't think anyone who did not have a business or meet a payroll could understand their interests."

Yet the Lincoln business community could not be painted with a broad brush, nor was it monolithic in opposition to my mother's candidacy. While downtown businessmen provided the nucleus of Schwartzkopf's campaign financing "because they fear his opponent is more concerned with social services than brick and mortar improvements for the city," some of Mom's strongest supporters had been downtown retailer giants Nate Gold and Robert E. Campbell, and her bipartisan campaign committee included businessmen, developers, and lawyers. Even among the mayor's own business supporters, not all bought into the negative advertising image of Mom as a university-connected, anti-business radical but viewed her simply as a stereotypically softhearted, spendthrift Democrat.

The Lincoln Chamber of Commerce could not directly oppose my mother's candidacy, but it did issue a transparent warning to the "People of Lincoln" in a newspaper ad signed by chamber president Paul Amen four days before the *election. The message was, if not loud and clear, then subtle and clear: since taxpayers foot the bill, they should vote for those candidates who "will not only promise the fulfillment of [social] needs, but who will enhance the abilities of the community to pay for them."

Some speculated that the impetus for the Schwartzkopf campaign's turn to negative attacks came from the published poll results late in the campaign. On April 27, 1975, just a few days before the negative ads began and nine days before the general election, a *Sunday Journal and Star* poll showed Boosalis with 56 percent of the vote, Schwartzkopf with 34 percent. My mother's strong bipartisan support (59 percent of Republicans polled, 53 percent of Democrats) diluted the incumbent's claim that the Democratic Party's endorsement of Boosalis had come from the "ultra-liberal" wing of the Democratic Party. Compounding the Schwartzkopf campaign's frustration with both the poll results and earlier labor endorsements were Boosalis endorsements by both morning and evening *newspapers. The mayor's negative ads began to roll out just two days later.

And with that negative turn, our newborn euphoria evaporated, our doubts multiplied as each excruciating day marched toward the election. Even with positive poll results and endorsements by the Democratic Party, unions, and both newspapers, we agonized over whether my mom's apparent lead would hold given the repetitive drumbeat of negative ads, the steady chant of "ultra-liberal" and "radical" and all that those terms connoted.

E DAY

Max and I flew to Lincoln from Chicago the week before the May 6 election. Max had never witnessed a campaign up close, particularly in its final, high-pitch days. He was stunned—within hours of our arrival, he became and remained a nervous wreck. I urged him to keep his hysteria under wraps and maintain a low profile, especially around my dad, who was as tense as I had ever seen him. I wasn't exactly a sea of calm myself, but I could release at least some of the tension by helping with the myriad last-minute campaign tasks. Mom seemed to be the only one in sight who was upbeat in her usual energized-by-people mode. I did notice darkened half moons under her eyes, and I suspected her normal five or six hours of sleep a night had been cut in half for quite some time.

Gram arrived by bus from Minneapolis for the election. She had taken the bus to visit us in Lincoln ever since we moved away from my parents' Greek clans in Minnesota when I was three years old. Her visits were celebrations as I was growing up. At bedtime she took down the braids she wrapped around her head and let me brush her long, silvery hair. Gram was visiting when President Kennedy was assassinated, and I remember the two of us sitting for hours, watching TV and crying.

By the time my mother ran for mayor in 1975, at age fifty-five, Gram was seventy-five and just beginning to slow down a bit. My dad called her the "angel of mercy" because she often delivered by public bus her hand-sewn flannel bathrobes and home-cooked meals to ailing friends and family. She was yet a vigilant watchdog of current news and held strong political opinions, which she kept to herself when among her few Republican family members.

After her initial concern about her daughter's running for mayor, Gram grew excited about the campaign and eagerly awaited my dad's frequent update notes with clippings, similar to those he sent to me in Chicago. Gram and I both arrived in Lincoln that pre-election week from our respective homes and generations to cheer on daughter and mother.

The morning of the general election, before my parents cast their ballots, I went with Mom, Dad, and several campaign volunteers to the 6:30 a.m. shift change at the Burlington rail yards and then to the Goodyear plant. We handed out don't-forget-to-vote-Boosalis-for-Mayor leaflets as workers headed from enormous parking lots to begin their shift in the plants, a migration transpiring over a fifteen- to twenty-minute period so that we could actually get a leaflet into most hands.

The harder task was to intercept at shift's end the stampede of exiting workers whose only desire was to reach their cars, unimpeded, within

nanoseconds of the piercing horn announcing their liberation. I pictured cartoon images of hordes of buffalo/horses/muskrats swarming
past, leaving puffs of smoke in their wake. A similar scene was repeated
that afternoon when Mom passed out flyers to Nebraska Department
of Roads employees as they ended their workday. However ineffective
these exercises may have been in producing more Boosalis votes, we felt
comforted in knowing we had turned all possible stones.

As we got dressed to go to the election-night party at the Knolls, a
restaurant owned by my Uncle John, I tried distracting Max with "remember when" tales of our Lincoln wedding reception at the Knolls
almost two years earlier. Growing up in crazed Nebraska football country, I had carefully chosen a non-football-game September Saturday for
our 4:00 wedding. Two weeks before the wedding, the date of Nebraska's opening football game against usc was changed so the game could
be televised. That would have put our wedding in the middle of the
opening game, in which case no one but our Minnesota and Florida
relatives would attend.

We changed the church ceremony to a postgame time of 7:00 p.m.
and, because my dad's brother owned the Knolls, we were able to delay
the reception. Max's parents and four siblings (Peter, Mary Lynn, Paul,
and Diana) were flabbergasted by the town's football frenzy. Our wedding pictures show many guests still in their "Go Big Red" garb, one of
whom was Mayor Schwartzkopf wearing a bright red blazer. All the
non-Greek wedding guests wanted to learn to Greek dance. Our best
man's fiancée fell during one such attempt and broke her arm. Max and
I were having such a great time that we stayed at the reception until
2:00 a.m., by which time the hotel had given our wedding-night room
to some lucky Nebraska football fan. We drove miles outside the city to
find another hotel, with me in tears, still in my wedding dress.

Now, almost two years later, Mom, Dad, Gram, Max, and I piled in
the car to head to the Knolls for a very different sort of party. I hoped
this night would not also end in tears. The place was packed when we
arrived, and somehow it kept accommodating more and more jubilant bodies as the night advanced. Everyone seemed to anticipate my
mother's victory and each wanted to hug, squeeze, or slap her on the
back. Even my dad emerged from his wary mood as he moved among

the energized crowd. Gram sparkled with pride for her daughter. Max adjourned outside to pace fidgety circles in the parking lot.

After the polls closed, the first ten precincts came in: Boosalis was leading Schwartzkopf by *eight* votes. The keyed-up crowd reacted as if the lead were eighty thousand. More campaign volunteers called in or arrived with a stream of positive vote results. Several party clusters were getting their own numbers from transistor radios and shouted periodically in chorus. The throng cheered with each new posting of poll results. The siren sounds of victory even lured Max back inside.

And victory came—deliciously decisive. When one radio station declared my mother the winner with 55 percent of the vote, her supporters demanded a victory speech. Mom stood on a platform above the crowd but could not speak over the joyous tumult for quite some time. She had little voice left anyway, having used most of it that day, talking to any last prospective voters before the polls closed.

The new mayor began by thanking all the volunteers who had carried to nearly every household in Lincoln the message of the city's need for stronger, more positive leadership. Then she introduced my dad: "This is the guy who started the whole thing. 'Of course you can do it. Of course you can,' he'd tell me. And he finally convinced me." The cheers for my beaming dad were nearly as great as for my mother. She continued, "People were staying out of the mayoral race because they felt the incumbent couldn't be beaten, but fortunately women don't always believe what they're told!"

If I close my eyes I can taste and smell the euphoria of those who believed that ordinary people committed to community could unite for change. Their newly elected leader was clearly the agent of change the people wanted. It was more than the joy of victory I witnessed that night—it was the thrill of *empowerment.

I wish I could have peeked inside my mother's head on election night—and my grandmother's, too, for that matter. Gram's journey in steerage class from Greece to America sixty-five years earlier, her brief public school stint in Brooklyn, her full-time job stitching baseball covers at a Spalding factory from age twelve—none of that could have prepared Gram for the road in her new country that would lead to this night celebrating her firstborn's election as mayor.

And in my mother's head? Beneath her gracious thanks to all those who worked so hard on her campaign and now looked with excitement to the future, my mother also must have harbored disbelief. She had certainly surprised herself in 1959 with her unanticipated run for city council when she was part civic activist/part traditional 1950s housewife. How much more amazed she must have felt that May night in 1975 to have made history by her election as mayor of Lincoln.

Surely she reveled in her electoral victory after such a hard-fought campaign. But knowing my mother, I would wager that after leaving her ecstatic supporters at the Knolls and after the rest of our family had fallen into bed, she probably stayed up writing notes for her first days in office, just two weeks away. As I told one reporter on election night, my mother "is not the kind that needs to go off for two weeks to recuperate. Give her about 10 minutes and snap! She'll be off again."

The phones started ringing close to dawn the next morning—first reporters, then hoards of personal well-wishers. Before driving Max and me to the airport for our flight back to Chicago, my mother had already done several live radio and television interviews. I smiled when I overheard her response to one interviewer who asked what she would be bringing to the mayor's office: "What I'll bring is my belief, as corny as it may sound, that government exists to serve the people."

Predictably, many post-election news stories focused on the historic election of Lincoln's first woman mayor. Mom denied that being a woman had been a handicap in the race. "I've always felt that if any community was ready to elect a woman mayor, Lincoln was it. Some will never accept a woman in politics, but I think my 16 years of service [on the city council] diffused that issue." She disagreed with any notion that support for women comes primarily from liberal voters, saying that "labels are preposterous. People are what's important, and people voted for me because they thought I could do the best job." Indeed, the day after the election the *Evening Journal* observed, "If the citizens of Lincoln ever elected as their mayor a person more qualified by frontline experience than Helen Boosalis, that rare episode must be buried in history . . . Mrs. Boosalis has the stuff to make the right and the tough decisions."

Analysis of the meaning of the election came from all quarters. A

Star editorial emphasized the failure of the incumbent's last-minute negative advertising campaign: "It is safe to say that this beautiful, mellow city rejected the slur and the slam, the distortion and the desperate tactics. . . . A solid majority bought the proposition—put straightforward and honestly—that City Hall could use some executive leadership. The mayor-elect did not have to hide her record behind a smoke screen. Her people did not have to make accusatory, provocative campaign statements or suggestions. Hers was the good, clean fight."

A congratulatory telegram arrived from Mayor Soglin, whose Madison "radical-liberal" regime had been linked by negative ads to Lincoln's likely fate under a Boosalis administration: "It's good to know that elections are still determined on the basis of issues and not emotional scare tactics." An editorial urged, "The next time a study is done and comparable cities are mentioned, it should be noted that the majority of voters in both Madison, Wis., and Lincoln, Neb., don't respond favorably to nonsense campaigning."

Voters in 1975 had yet to become inured to the "slur and the slam" and to slash-and-burn advertising. It was not common then for candidates to mouth a desire to conduct positive campaigns and then inevitably turn to negative advertising in response to opponents' jabs or to sliding poll numbers or, more often, just because they know it works.

If Lincoln voters in 1975 had not "known" Mom so well from her city council years and had relied instead on a version of today's thirty-second TV attack ads, would she still have been elected mayor? Is it even possible to stay on the high road in today's political free-for-all campaign arena? Don't choices about negative campaigning almost always involve trade-offs between integrity and expediency, winning ends and questionable means? Was the choice so different for my mother than it would be today? It couldn't have been easy even thirty years ago to refrain from defensively slugging back when attacked.

And what of her opponent's choice to proceed down the negative road? The same editorial that decried the "slur and slam" tactics suggested that the incumbent had been led astray by his campaign advisers: "If he had been left alone, his own natural decency would have dictated a far different campaign than the one that led him to defeat. He might have lost anyway, but it wouldn't have left such a bitter taste.

It is his tragedy that the bad advice was heeded." In assessing his loss, Schwartzkopf claimed that his advertising campaign, which aroused so much controversy the week before the election, was misunderstood and explained it as merely an attempt to get voters to see the differences between candidates.

Another focus of post-election media commentary was the impact of Mom's victory on Lincoln's business community. Because the bulk of the incumbent's support came from those with business interests, one reporter concluded that Schwartzkopf's defeat "signal[ed] a demise in the business community's political clout." Another observed that "what apparently has been taking place in Lincoln and other American communities is the replacement or counterbalance of the political clout of businessmen by other competing groups which have emerged on the political scene."

Responding to reporter questions about business as a political force, UNL political science professor A. B. Winter said that business began losing influence in the 1960s when other economic, ethnic, and social groups began paying attention to local government candidates who offered something new beyond the status quo. In the wake of the election, Winter concluded, "the 'O Street *gang' as an organized pressure group in Lincoln is dead." County Board commissioner Bruce Hamilton viewed the erosion of the business community's dominance in local elections as a result of neighborhood and grassroots groups becoming more active.

The power struggle between business and neighborhoods had begun years earlier when the long-standing political and civic power of business interests began to erode in the face of greater citizen participation in Lyndon Johnson's Great Society programs, organization of neighborhoods under Richard Nixon's Community Development Block Grant programs, and local grassroots political efforts over issues of land use. In his analysis of the shift in Lincoln's political power structure, *Star* reporter George Hendrix found that neighborhoods had organized to protect themselves against rapid growth and development favored by business forces, and "the rift took on definition." The sides criticized each other as believers in either "no growth" or "growth at any cost."

The election of my mother as mayor may have added to the growing polarization between business and neighborhoods, as many in the old-guard business community viewed her as an outsider—a perception she found hard to *shake despite her record of efforts to bridge business and neighborhood interests, both vital to the city's health, she believed. In its endorsement of Boosalis for mayor, the *Star* wrote: "Her record during 16 years of the City Council completely refutes the irresponsible assertions that have floated about during the campaign that she is 'anti business' or 'anti growth.' She has been a respecter of and has cooperated with business interests downtown and elsewhere and she has assiduously worked for orderly growth and the record will bear her out on that."

City Councilman Max Denney, who became council chairman when my mother was elected mayor, attributed the erosion of business influence to voters' "waking up to the fact that you can beat City Hall if you are organized." My mother would probably not agree that she had "beaten city hall"; after all, she had been in city hall for sixteen years. No matter which way they had voted, all in town seemed to know that city hall and the city would never be the same after my mother moved from the city council chambers to the mayor's office.

Ecstatic and exhausted the morning after the election, I took to show my Chicago friends the early newspaper, its headline screaming "Boosalis Is Elected Mayor" in ninety-point type. The half-page election story shared the front page with another news event. A tornado had roared through metropolitan Omaha on election day. Rereading the paper on the plane, Max and I agreed that my mother's election as mayor was another tornado simultaneously sweeping through Omaha's neighbor to the south—but Lincoln's tornado was one bringing change, not destruction.

May the Best Woman . . .
May–September 1986

Back in my cubbyhole at Boosalis for Governor headquarters I was rid-ing the wave, along with campaign staff and volunteers, of Mom's stun-ning primary win over six Democratic opponents. With the clearing of the primary field came the campaign's sharpened focus on the single obstacle to my mother's election as governor—her Republican oppo-nent, Kay Orr.

The media's obsession with the curiosity of two women running against each other for governor began at dawn on the morning after the primary election when Helen Boosalis and Kay Orr were interviewed on the CBS *Morning News* and ABC's *Good Morning America*. Front-page articles, photos, and editorials ran in newspapers across the country: L.A., Tampa, Baltimore, Miami, Richmond, Denver, New York, Wash-ington DC, Minneapolis, St. Louis, Philadelphia, Salt Lake City, Anchor-age, Chicago, Lexington, San Jose, Nashville, Kansas City, Atlanta, Paris, Manchester, on and on. In Nebraska, headlines and front pages of newspapers showed a wide variation of reaction to the Boosalis-Orr primary wins. My favorite small-town Nebraska headline appeared in the *Dodge Criterion*: "Gals Vie for Gov. First Ever in U.S."

On the heels of Geraldine Ferraro's presence on the Mondale presi-dential ticket in 1984, the simultaneous primary victories on May 13, 1986, of two women gubernatorial primary winners (first-time ever) in Nebraska as well as two women U.S. Senate primary winners (second-time ever) in Maryland prompted many to call 1986 "The Year of the Woman." That promising yet premature label has been applied to other election years as well, but we have yet to see an election year where women sweep into office in numbers approximating their percentage of the population. Still, 1986 seemed to represent an encouraging move forward.

The two-woman governor's race in Nebraska and the concurrent U.S. Senate race in Maryland between Democrat Barbara Mikulski and Republican Linda Chavez prompted a flurry of media background pieces reciting the slim history of women elected to statewide office. I gobbled them up, first because they were about Mom but also because I was like many other women who were eager for a crash course on the historical entry of women into the political arena as candidates. After all, the country may have been over two hundred years old by then, but women had only had the right to vote for sixty-six years—exactly my mother's *age when she won the primary.

By 1986 seven women (all Democrats) had been elected governor. The first three had succeeded their husbands in office—Miriam "Ma" Ferguson in Texas and Nellie Tayloe Ross in Wyoming (both in 1925) and Lurleen Wallace in Alabama (in 1967). In 1974, Ella Grasso in Connecticut became the first woman governor to be elected in her own right, followed two years later by Dixie Lee Ray in Washington. Two women were serving as governor at the time of my mother's historic race: Kentucky's Martha Layne Collins and Vermont's Madeleine Kunin. With absolute certainty, the Nebraska governor's election would add one more woman to that short list.

On the congressional front, in 1986 there were two women sitting U.S. senators—Kansas's Nancy Kassebaum and Florida's Paula Hawkins, the latter of whom was running in a tough reelection bid against Governor Bob Graham—and 23 women out of 435 U.S. representatives. The National Women's Political Caucus reported a record number of women running for congressional offices in November 1986: seven for Senate seats (including the two-woman race in Maryland) and fifty for House seats (including former congresswoman Bella Abzug). However, a *Christian Science Monitor* reporter noted the still-long road to equality, given the modest gains between 1971, when women comprised 3 percent of Congress, and 1986, when the number rose to 5 percent; the day after the Nebraska primary, a woman on Capitol Hill said, "At that rate, it will take us 400 years to achieve parity."

Women state legislators fared a bit better, increasing their hold on state legislative seats from 4 percent in 1971 (362 seats) to 15 percent in 1986 (1,103 seats). Women mayors, too, bettered their numbers from just 1 percent in cities over 30,000 in 1971 to almost 10 percent in 1980. (Few were chief executives/"strong mayors.") The *Monitor* article cited reasons for greater gains in electing women to local and state legislative office. First, far less money is required to run for local and state legislative office. "Many federal races have become million dollar campaigns and women find it difficult to raise that kind of cash." Second, the power of incumbency makes unseating male incumbents an uphill battle for women challengers. Most federal offices are already held by men who, as incumbents, generally have party support and support from other officeholders, who are mostly *men.

Harrison Hickman of Hickman-Maslin Research in Washington DC, my mother's pollster in the governor's race, was also advising the statewide campaigns of two other Democratic women candidates in 1986—Barbara Mikulski for the U.S. Senate in Maryland, and Carolyn Warner for governor in Arizona—and Hickman had also been pollster for Governor Martha Layne Collins of Kentucky. He had more opportunities than many professional campaign consultants at the time to observe electorate reaction to women candidates for statewide office. In a *New York Times* interview before the 1986 fall general elections, Hickman said that what works for a male candidate might not work for a woman. He had observed common perceptions of women candidates among voters:

- Voters are more at ease with women in legislative positions than executive roles. Why? The perception seems to apply to all "newcomers" to elective office (women and minorities). Voters are also more accustomed to women on city councils and school boards and in state legislatures.
- Women can't handle "issues of force" as well as men—for example, crime and military issues—but women are better on education and environment.
- Younger women and older men support women candidates in greater numbers than younger men and older women do.

- The better known a woman candidate is, the less dominated
  by stereotype she is. Voters are then more likely to consider
  voting for "this woman" rather than "a woman."

If these were, indeed, common voter perceptions, why were women
candidates on the move in *1986? "It's the absolute natural progression
of the women's movement. If you say it takes 15 years to build up to
the top positions in government, you take it back to when the women's
movement was starting to move forward in 1970," offered Peter Hart,
another leading Democratic pollster. "To me it's not surprising when
you see what's happening in Nebraska or Maryland. These are the people who make it through . . . because they're the best candidates the
parties have to offer."

And the *New York Times* weighed in: "The interesting thing about
women running in 1986 is you don't have women aged 30 and 40.
They're women aged 50 and 60. They're serious and professional candidates. They have their names at the top of the ticket because the party
is looking for proven vote getters." Celinda Lake of the Women's Campaign Fund told the *Washington Post* that the breakthrough of the Nebraska and Maryland all-woman races had been a long time coming
and that those races were "the fruits of the third wave of recruitment."
Lake reviewed the waves, or stages, of the history of women as elected
officeholders.

- *First wave* (accounting for almost all women's electoral victories before the 1970s): Women who won as wives or widows of
  male politicians.
- *Second wave* (dominating the 1970s): Women who shifted energies from volunteer work in civic groups to politics.
- *Third wave* (beginning with the 1980s): Women who succeeded
  in lower political office and set their sights higher, just as men
  had always done.

Kay Orr and Helen Boosalis were, indeed, riding a wave. The surge
of national interest in the Nebraska governor's race became a tidal roar
that threatened to drown out the candidates' own voices and to blur the
real differences between them. The cacophony of words and messages

15. Democrat Helen Boosalis and Republican Kay Orr in front of the state capitol

of the fifteen candidates who ran in Nebraska's gubernatorial primary finally died down when only two survived as the primary victors. But for weeks after the primary and again in the fall before the general election, the two Nebraska nominees had to shout to be heard above the media uproar over their historic achievement as the first two women in the nation to face off in a gubernatorial election.

"During the 1986 gubernatorial race in Nebraska between Kay Orr and Helen Boosalis," wrote political science professor Sara Weir in an essay on women as governors, "the candidates struggled to overcome the national media's unwillingness to view the race in conventional political terms. Although both candidates had extensive experience in state and local elective positions and although they debated the hard issues, such as taxes and the economy, it was mid-September before national newspapers were able to stop talking about the 'historic race' between two women."

Every tiny newspaper in every small town in Nebraska, every major national media outlet in every city hammered home the same story: two women for governor—two women nominated—first time two women—two women—two women. Their differing philosophies, disparate experience, and contrasting styles were submerged in a whirling eddy where two indistinguishable women were spinning. The two-woman phenomenon didn't dominate the entire campaign, but it did consume valuable chunks of campaign time where neither issues nor ideas were covered or heard.

I asked U.S. senator Barbara Mikulski if she had faced the same uproar in her race for the Senate that year. "The two-woman aspect of my 1986 Senate campaign against Linda Chavez did get a lot of national attention," she said. "The national media made a big deal out of two women running against each other. They wanted to turn us into novelties and celebrities. I was just trying to become senator. I wanted to do exactly what your mother wanted to do in her campaign against Orr: stick to the issues and talk about what I wanted to do for the state."

My mother tried to minimize the laser focus on the two-woman aspect of the race in a guest column in USA *Today* on May 20, 1986, less than a week after the primary. She wrote, in part:

> My state is making history. It is presenting its voters with a choice between two women as major-party candidates for governor. I am not surprised; women increasingly are viewing political involvement as absolutely necessary to their future and the future of their children.
>
> Women get into politics for the same reasons that motivate men: To work in a policy-making position where they can use their abilities and skills to influence their environment and to have a voice in governmental matters that affect their lives. . . .
>
> A woman candidate's success depends on her character, motivation, experience and competency—the same characteristics that apply to a man. . . . Women truly will have achieved equality when a victorious woman candidate is no longer news.

Two days later, a *New York Times* editorial voiced similar views: "Why did their [Boosalis's and Orr's] victories make headlines? Because they're both women. Politics is coming of age. Their race will be the first ever to offer the voters of any state a choice between two female candidates for governor—and the chance to make this the last celebration of their gender. . . . Steadily American politics approaches the welcome next stage in which women candidates are judged not on their gender but on their records."

A twist to the national media emphasis on two women was a not-so-subtle undercurrent: how could such a significant event in women's political history have possibly occurred in Nebraska? The *Atlanta Journal and Constitution* posed the question this way: "Who would have thought it would happen here first, in the middle of America's cholesterol kingdom, where men are men and now a woman is going to be governor? . . . And all of this in Nebraska?" An AP story found that "hard hit Nebraska, where the farm depression is approached only by Cornhuskers football as chief topic of many conversations, may seem an unlikely setting for a groundbreaking assault on the political gender gap." *U.S. News and World Report* asked the question: "Why such a first in a state reputedly so conservative?" And the *Philadelphia Inquirer* chimed in, "Nebraska, of all places, has taken the female office-holder a bit more seriously than most other states." One of *Newsweek's* quotes of the week on its "Perspectives" page came from Lynn Cutler, vice-chairman of the Democratic National Committee: "Let's face it, there was shock coming from this terribly provincial eastern seaboard. People are going around saying 'Nebraska?'"

The Nebraska governor's race challenged the assumption that political progress for women would likely occur in larger, more liberal states such as New York, California, and Massachusetts. Carol Bellamy, former New York City Council president and Ed Koch's mayoral opponent the year before my mother's campaign for governor, explained why Nebraska was more likely than New York to produce the country's first two-woman race for governor: "Everybody says New York is this big liberal showcase. And that's wrong. This is a very traditional, male-dominated political environment. . . . In addition, the bigger the state or city, the more important it is to raise lots of money to get a fast start in a significant race, and fund-raising is an area we're [women] just beginning to get good at."

The *New York Times* recognized that "outsiders seemed more struck with the [election] result than Nebraskans, when the conservative but populist farm state became the first to nominate women as the candidates of both major political parties." Nebraskans, too, confirmed their lack of astonishment at the choice they had produced. "Nebraska is not all that conservative," remarked former Nebraska congressman John Cavanaugh. "You don't find people in Nebraska looking on this as any sort of anomaly. They see two very capable candidates who happen to be women. If Nebraska is anything in demographics it's Western. It focuses on the worth and integrity of individuals."

On the "Why Nebraska" question, Francis Moul, a Nebraska journalist whose wife, Maxine, would later become lieutenant governor, said, "Nebraska will defy the historians of the future who will attempt to understand why this conservative, rural Midwestern state became the first to have an all-woman election. Could it be because the two are the best representatives of their party, regardless of sex?" To Robert Knoll, UNL emeritus English professor, "It is not surprising that two women were nominated for governor in Nebraska, as eastern reporters seemed to find it. There is a long tradition of prominent women in Nebraska, such as Willa Cather and Louise Pound. Pioneer women worked every bit as hard as men, and the men knew it. It was the spirit of the frontier. Helen was the modern version of these earlier pioneering women."

The candidates voiced their own opinions on the question. My mother spoke of the "myth of Nebraska conservatism" and said that "Nebraskans are independent people and far more progressive than many outsiders give them credit for." Orr claimed that the state's depressed agricultural economy made voters more willing to accept a woman, as expressed in a letter from a supporter who thought, Orr said, that Nebraska needed a mother—"someone to give us a hot bowl of soup, put on a pair of warm mittens and convey that kind of caring."

With so much attention on gender in the governor's race, some journalists noted that those who expected the campaign to be a forum for women's issues were probably disappointed. "Only Boosalis brings women's issues up with any regularity," one wrote in *USA Today*. Instead, the major issues in the primary campaign had been education, economic development, agriculture, fiscal management, and the candidates' experience.

The "big two" women's issues—ERA and choice—were not prominent in the primary campaign, but they would come more into play during the general election campaign. In a *Boston Globe* piece titled

"Ferraro's Legacy," reporter Thomas Oliphant noted that "on two key women's issues, Orr is anti-abortion and anti–equal rights amendment," while "Helen Boosalis . . . is pro-ERA and opposed to a constitutional amendment outlawing abortions."

Although Mom and I did not discuss the issue at length, I disagreed with her decision to supplement her position with a statement of her personal views on abortion—that she was *personally* opposed to abortion except in the case of incest, rape, or to save the life of the mother. She felt compelled to be open and express her full set of beliefs that acknowledged the complexity of the issue. I felt, on the other hand, that my mother's personal beliefs were not relevant to her governorship and that her declared opposition to a constitutional amendment banning abortions spoke directly to her public policy role as governor—end of story.

I suppose I didn't fully understand the conflicted nature of Democratic politics on the issue of choice in religiously conservative Nebraska. Most Democrats elected to statewide office in Nebraska were pro-life; some had managed to finesse the issue with some version of a middle-ground position. But as seen in many state and national elections since then, there seems to be little room for grey on the black-and-white abortion issue, even in states far more liberal than *Nebraska.

Her personal views on abortion notwithstanding, my mother was regarded as pro-choice by many in Nebraska—particularly by conservative Democrats in South *Omaha, who were led by a longtime activist in the anti-abortion movement, state senator Bernice Labedz. Labedz, Democrat and chair of South Omaha Christians for Life, said that Boosalis's position on abortion could "force me to simply stay out of the governor's race." Other Democrats felt the abortion issue could be overcome. An Omaha City Councilman and congressional candidate "who also opposes abortion, said Mrs. Boosalis's stance on abortion is similar to Governor Kerrey's [and] Kerrey won South Omaha in his successful run for governor in 1982." What I most remember from the campaign on this issue is an anti-Boosalis demonstration outside a South Omaha cathedral where Mom spoke in the final weeks of the campaign—children, parents, grandparents all protesting against Boosalis, waving signs with graphic pictures of fetuses and chanting slogans of the pro-life movement.

Orr's pro-life and anti-ERA campaign positions in the governor's race were unequivocal, but they hadn't always been so. Orr had modified her position on both abortion and the ERA through the years. As Kathleen Rutledge reported in the *Sunday Journal and Star*, Orr had been interviewed in June 1976 as a representative on the Republican national platform committee and had taken a middle-ground stance on abortion. Orr said then, "I do not believe in whole scale abortion, but I do believe the decision should be made between a doctor and his patient." Rutledge noted that "Orr also supported the ERA at one time but after the Nebraska Legislature ratified the amendment in 1972, she was among those who worked to get that action reversed. She said she supports equal rights for women, but not through a constitutional amendment." By 1986 Orr was in tune with the growing national effort to engage evangelical Christians in politics (including Pat Robertson's Freedom Council seminars in Nebraska), which was expected to result in their control of 20 percent of delegates to the state Republican Party convention where pro-life was the only acceptable position.

National women's groups such as the Women's Campaign Fund and National Women's Political Caucus were enthusiastic about Nebraska's two-woman race because it seemed to bode well for more women running for elected office in the *future. Their enthusiasm was tempered, however, because neither Nebraska woman candidate met the groups' strict litmus tests on choice. So Mom received no support from the national women's groups because she was not *sufficiently* pro-choice and, simultaneously, received no support or votes from Nebraska pro-life Democrats (and Republicans) because she *was* pro-choice. A *no-(wo)man's-land.

The attention to the two-woman nature of the governor's race had its lighter moments. Two women volunteers—one an Orr supporter and the other a supporter of Boosalis—were distributing campaign materials on the same corner in Omaha. As their campaign supplies diminished, one said to the other, "This will be a historic event if both major parties nominate a woman. These handbills will be collectors' items. How about one of mine for one of yours?" After making sure no one was looking, they quickly made the exchange.

The national media did not have far to look for local color on the subject of women running for governor. The chairman of the Madison County Democratic Party said, "There are probably some cowboy types out here in western Nebraska who still won't vote for a woman. But the fact that you've got so many candidates in the race probably offsets that, and anyway, none of these women comes across as a Geraldine Ferraro-type—you know, the so-called 'uppity female.'" A barber from Lincoln insisted, "I won't vote for any women for governor, and you know why? Because I'm prejudiced, I guess."

Even a few high-profile public figures made over-the-top comments about two women candidates. Nebraska state senator John DeCamp, a "flamboyant but powerful lawmaker," tried mounting a write-in campaign for governor after the primary on the platform that "Nebraska is running a state prom queen contest and calling it a governor's race." And the Reverend Everett Sileven, a Baptist pastor in Louisville, Nebraska, who had finished a distant fourth in his bid for the GOP nomination for governor, spouted his opposition to women candidates based on religious beliefs. "The nominations of [Orr and Boosalis] are a sign of God's curse," he said. "Selection of a woman leader indicates that a society has become degenerate. . . . In the study of history only in the decline and fall of a nation are women accepted as leaders and rulers. . . . God gives us women to rule over us when we are not living right."

On his own for the summer with his wife and boys in Nebraska on the campaign trail, my husband, Max, read about Reverend Sileven in his favorite *Chicago Tribune* column by Mike Royko:

> Most people took the nomination of two women to be an encouraging sign that sexism was declining and that voters could be swayed by merit—or at least by the more clever TV commercials—and not by anatomy.
>
> But not Preacher Sileven. He saw it as a clear sign from above that Nebraska and the rest of the nation were in deep trouble with the Lord. . . . I called Preacher Sileven, intending to ask him what other forms he thought "God's curse" would take in Nebraska. Would there be an increase in husband-beating? . . . [H]is wife, a grim sounding woman, said the preacher was on the road, going from town to town and spreading the word of God's curse, and could not be interviewed.

Regardless of the surprise, celebration, condescension, matter-of-factness, euphoria, or outrage prompted by two women winning the Nebraska gubernatorial primary election, one conclusion on which all Nebraskans *and* outside observers could agree—come November 4, 1986, a woman was sure to be elected Nebraska's governor.

Chapter Three

This Is Not Your Father's City Hall

1975–1979

"Helen always understood the power of the office—that she had it temporarily and would do the most she could with it."—BOB KERREY, U.S. senator (Nebraska), 1989–2001, governor of Nebraska, 1983–87

"Helen truly was the prime example of what strong-mayor leadership could do for the city. She fought that battle for the rest of us [mayors]. Lincoln is Lincoln in large part, in my judgment, because of its decision to enact a strong-mayor form of government and because of the decision of voters to elect Helen Boosalis. Much of how the city operates today is because of her vision."
—MIKE JOHANNS, governor of Nebraska, 1999–2005, mayor of Lincoln, 1991–98

Today as I read and reread the voluminous notebooks of newspaper clippings that my father cut, dated, taped, and assembled starting more than thirty years ago, I wonder if the notebooks may have been Dad's way to harness the cyclone of activity that immediately engulfed my parents' lives with my mother's 1975 election as mayor. The notebooks transform what used to be for me a golden glow of proud yet hazy memories of Mom's years as mayor into the black-and-white reality of what she faced in running a city, day after challenging day. I sometimes lose myself in the unfolding drama spun by the clippings. I become a time traveler with tenuous ties to the present me, hunched over my father's notebooks.

16. Helen takes oath of office as mayor, 1975

I read the unfolding tale of my mother's challenges as mayor with a knowing familiarity of the story's chief protagonist. Yet I am jarred by the intrusion of time, whispering, "How can it be that your mom, this mayoral dynamo in the clippings, was younger than you are now when she became Lincoln's chief executive, the boss of the city?"

I've had over thirty more years of knowing Mom after her election as mayor, thirty years to become inured to her role as leader. But reading now of a woman close to my own age who assumed a role that is still relatively unusual—and almost inconceivable for the times—stretches my ability even as her daughter to imagine my mother's fears, excitement, and disbelief on May 19, 1975, as she took the oath and strode into the office of mayor.

OUT FRONT, UP FRONT

The mayoral race and surprising victory over the two-term incumbent now behind her, my mother embraced the even tougher job of governing. After serving sixteen years on the city council, Mom's transformation from legislator to chief executive would require far more than a move to the second-floor mayor's office, and so would establishing her new role with old council colleagues.

In the same election the voters elected Helen Boosalis mayor in 1975, they also elected four city council *members, including three incumbents—Steve Cook, Bob Sikyta, and Dick Baker. That brought the total number of sitting council members with whom my mother had already served on the council to six, counting Sue Bailey, John Robinson, and Max Denney, whose terms had not yet expired. The only new council member elected in 1975 was Bob Jeambey, a Presbyterian minister and newcomer to city politics, who joined the three victorious incumbents by winning the only open council seat—the one vacated by Helen Boosalis. To her advantage, my mother could draw on her council history with six out of seven council members. She knew their philosophies, styles, hot buttons, strengths, and weaknesses. But how would this group—particularly those with whom she had regularly sparred—accept her new, separate, visible, and more powerful role as mayor?

Mom's break from the past was immediate, not only in vacating her former seat at the city council table but also in reversing Mayor Schwartzkopf's traditional absence from council meetings. Under the weak-mayor form of government—before 1963—the mayor chaired the city council sessions; but with the separation of administrative and legislative functions under the strong-mayor plan in 1963, the mayor's presence at council meetings was no longer mandatory. The first two mayors to serve under the strong-mayor plan (Dean Peterson and Sam Schwartzkopf) had rarely attended city council sessions.

Mayor Boosalis, however, took an audience front-row seat at the first post-election city council meeting and declared that she planned to be present at every subsequent council meeting. There she could better gauge firsthand the exchange between citizens and public officials, hear unfiltered council debate on issues, and respond to council members' questions about executive branch actions rather than let her department heads "fly either blind or unprotected." Since she held the veto power over council actions, she wanted to learn firsthand "all the facts on why a decision was made."

Many welcomed and some even lauded the mayor's demonstrated visibility. "That's accountability in our book," noted one editorial shortly after she took office. "Such is what we always seek in elected public officials, but never always get." About her visibility at city council meetings, one reporter observed that "during those long and often boring sessions, she's bobbing up and down, talking with department heads, chatting with citizens in the hall, jotting down a note to herself or hopping up to the Council microphone to tell lawmakers something or other about this or that program. At times she seems to steal the show from the Council."

Perhaps "stealing the show" was one reason why my mother's presence and participation at city council meetings more than irritated some of her former council colleagues. From her first days as mayor, this irritation would continue to fester and periodically erupt with charges that she was overstepping her bounds of authority. One of her most frequent critics, Councilman Bob Sikyta, often complained that the mayor's presence at council meetings inhibited the remarks of other city officials in her administration when they knew that the mayor—their boss—was present. Mom disagreed, arguing that she directed her department heads to answer all council inquiries with candor, but she also reminded the council that "there is only one administrative policy and that is set by the mayor."

"Before Helen was mayor, the directors were used to going to city council meetings and having their heads taken off," said administrative aide Mike Merwick. "The council was infuriated when the new mayor sat in the front row at council meetings to set the record straight or defend her directors when necessary. The council wanted her to stay upstairs." The dispute over the mayor's attending council meetings would not be settled for two years, when some council members asked City Attorney Charles Humble for a legal opinion on the mayor's authority. Humble's opinion clarified that the Lincoln City Charter gave the mayor the right to address council meetings, speak on any issue before the council, and suggest legislation.

The opposition by some council members to my mother's use of her strong-mayor authority began with her election and continued unabated. Shortly before Humble gave his opinion, a *Journal* editorial identified a "restiveness by a council majority about Mayor Boosalis' alleged over-involvement on the council's side of the governmental bed" and speculated about its source:

Is the mayor drafting ordinances and slipping them onto the council's agenda? Is the mayor voting in the council meeting? Has the mayor approved spending for departments above council appropriations? Not so far as we can tell.

What the mayor is doing, however, is attending council meetings, unlike her predecessors. There, Mrs. Boosalis—not subordinate department heads—is immediately available to attempt to justify actions of her administration or explain her position. Responsibility of the executive is quite clear and focused. That course of conduct ought to be cheered. We have had too many weasel executives in national, state and local office.

FIRST TEST: POLICE CHIEF

While her presence at council meetings signaled my mother's vision of mayoral leadership, the first real test of her strong-mayor powers proved to be a watershed for much that followed: her appointment of a new police *chief. More than thirty years later, my mother tells the story as if it happened yesterday. She speaks of it in almost reverential tones, as if her entire future as mayor had depended on the outcome of that single, early challenge to her administration. "My ability to be an effective leader for the next four years was on the line."

By 1975, for more than three decades Lincoln's police chief had been Joe Carroll, an old-school and old-time law enforcement officer who ran his department with a no-nonsense, autocratic hand. Carroll had the loyal support of the city's old-guard business establishment who wanted perpetuation of the status quo at city hall, including a new chief in Joe Carroll's mold when he retired.

Chief Carroll's style had worked just fine as Lincoln grew from a mostly tranquil prairie town at the start of his long tenure, but by 1975 even Lincoln had experienced some of the 1960s urban turbulence and faced more complex policing problems, including growing civil unrest among its small but increasingly vocal minority population. Chief Carroll retired in early 1975, just two months before the end of Mayor Schwarzkopf's second term. Schwarzkopf had conducted a nominal national search to replace the retiring chief, but it was common knowledge that Chief Carroll had handpicked his successor. Dale Adams, a capable, long-serving officer and police department administrator, would serve as acting chief until his anticipated appointment as police chief.

Apparently, the prior administration's national search was merely window dressing for the predetermined choice that would continue the status quo in the police department. This plan, of course, did not contemplate my mother's victory in the mayoral election. Suddenly the predictable outcome of the search for a new chief became as unpredictable as the path of one of Nebraska's summer tornadoes.

In keeping with her commitment to citizen involvement in government, one of Mom's first actions after being sworn in as mayor was to establish a process by which appointed citizens would review police chief candidates and make recommendations to the mayor. She would appoint a preliminary screening committee to narrow the field from the initial pool of ninety applicants, and later she would appoint a second committee to recommend up to ten finalists for interviews. City personnel director Walt Mitchell advised her on proper search procedures, which gave her confidence in the process.

Seeking a range of community and professional viewpoints, the new mayor set out to recruit for the first screening committee. She called Lela Shanks, a homemaker who she had heard from many sources was a woman of intelligence and integrity. My mother explained the screening committee's purpose and why she wanted broader citizen input for her police chief appointment. Though regretfully, Shanks declined Mom's invitation, explaining that she and her husband, Hughes, had moved to Lincoln from Kansas City, where they had been active in the civil rights movement and were jailed as a result. She was unwilling to expose herself to that level of controversy again. She knew about the growing unrest over police treatment of citizens in minority areas of Lincoln and the strong feelings surrounding appointment of a new chief—enough to know that the selection of a new police chief would take place in a highly charged atmosphere.

My mother hung up the phone disappointed and somewhat discouraged. Later that evening, however, Shanks called back after her husband had argued, "How can you turn the mayor down? Here she is, trying to turn things around in this community. That's why she wants to appoint

you to the committee, so you can help her do that. You should do it."
Renewed by Lela Shanks's acceptance, my mother continued to recruit
her other police chief screening advisers.

As the two-part process unfolded, Lela Shanks was the only member
to serve both on the preliminary screening committee and the finalist
selection committee. The screening committee weighed the large pool
of candidates' qualifications and their responses to a questionnaire that
posed hypothetical problems facing a new chief, and then reduced the
candidate field from ninety to twenty-two. In late July, two months after
her election, the mayor appointed the finalist selection committee to
further winnow the field and conduct interviews: Lela Shanks; Pierce
Brooks, director of Public Safety in Lakewood, Colorado; R. D. Anderson, president of Norden Laboratories; Fred Holbert, vice chairman of
the UNL Department of Criminal Justice; and newly elected City Councilman Bob Jeambey.

Members of the finalist selection panel could be characterized by
their open-mindedness and sense of civic responsibility, not by their political loyalties. Yet, outside the deliberation rooms a highly charged political pot was boiling, fomented by some who still could not accept the
outcome of the mayoral race or their subsequent personal and collective loss of power. The appointment of a new police chief was the first
and perhaps most important arena where the old guard was ready to
wage a bitter fight to retain some measure of control over civic affairs.
The new mayor, on the other hand, recognized that changing times demanded a major change in policing policies and administration as well
as the appointment of a new chief who could rise to that challenge.

As the selection panel deliberated during the sweltering Nebraska
summer, the mayor sought to insulate the panelists from the mounting pressures and political heat. Until the interviewing stage of the selection process, the applicants and their written questionnaire answers
were known to the panelists only by social security numbers, not by
name. Later, interviews were held at hotels throughout the city, not in
city hall, where speculation and rumor wildly circulated. The mayor
ordered these measures to maximize the finalist selection committee's
potential for objectivity in deliberations and to protect committee
members from efforts to lobby or pressure them.

Pressed to make her police chief preferences known, Mayor Boosalis would say only that she wanted someone with a "good, sound background in law enforcement who is not wedded to the old traditional approach to law enforcement," someone who "will initiate and encourage new ideas, seek new ways and approaches to reducing crime and maintaining peace and serve the community." She knew the appointment was a make-or-break-it demonstration of her ability to lead the city to make the changes she felt necessary—the reasons she wanted the mayor's job. If my mother failed in this first test of leadership, it would no doubt set back her agenda for change, if not undermine it altogether.

That summer, as the selection process ground on, the city council was enmeshed in its own struggle over a proposal for a citizens police review board. The measure had been put forward by the council's sole black member, John Robinson, in response to increasingly vocal complaints of police harassment and unfair treatment of minorities. Reports of morale problems in the police department surfaced during the council debate on the need for a citizens review board to monitor police actions. To complicate matters within the department, two internal candidates (including the acting chief) were vying for the position of police chief in a process that had become the subject of intense community debate and division.

While feeling the heat of the police chief search, my mother was by no means paralyzed in her first months in office. She organized changes to open wide the doors of local government for increased participation of its citizens—the core of her campaign promises and personal beliefs. From her first days in office, she expected much from her staff and department heads, who put in longer and longer hours but could not match her frenzied fourteen-hour days. The new mayor knew she had been elected to make changes, and she was anxious to deliver—so much so that her administrative aide, Mike Merwick, pulled her aside and said, "Whoa, Helen, slow down a little. Everybody's with you, but you've got to give folks a little breathing space."

Mom's early months in the mayor's chair flew by, charged with the committed drive for change. Yet, the weight of the police chief decision hung heavily over the fledgling mayor.

By August 1975 a citizen group favoring the appointment of Acting Chief Adams had launched a petition effort to bring further pressure on the mayor. A few days after announcing the finalist selection panel, Mom received petitions with twelve hundred signatures supporting the appointment of Dale Adams as chief. Petitions had been circulated in order to "help Mayor Boosalis make an appointment that satisfies the Lincoln citizens." Petition organizers insisted that they could have easily obtained thousands of signatures had they conducted a door-to-door petition drive, but they knew the acting chief "would take a dim view of any type of pressure being applied to your [the mayor's] office on his behalf."

Through the swirling controversy, the selection committee continued to scrutinize the twenty-two candidates screened by the initial panel. By late August, still using only social security numbers to identify the candidates, the committee pared the list to six finalists for interviews. During the week of candidate interviews, the police department officially announced the formation of a union. Clearly, the new chief would face a number of challenges from the start.

The six finalists—two internal candidates (including Acting Chief Adams), a retiree from the New York City Police Department, and three others from Minnesota, Colorado, and California—were interviewed over two days, the last interview ending after midnight on September 3. The exhausted but elated selection committee called the mayor with their unanimous recommendation. One candidate stood out in meeting all the mayor's requirements of extensive law enforcement experience, progressive leadership abilities, sensitivity to community needs, and ability to manage a multimillion-dollar operation. The panel did not even rank order the other five candidates interviewed.

Mom convened members of the city council at a closed-door breakfast meeting to inform them of her choice for police chief—George Hansen, director of Public Safety in Sunnyvale, California. His credentials included police chief positions in Connecticut and Illinois, and he had been director of the U.S. Army Military Police School. An added bonus, both Hansen and his wife were born and raised in Nebraska, and his wife and children had attended the University of Nebraska–Lincoln.

The suspense but not the intrigue ended with my mother's announcement. The reaction was swift. Emerging from the breakfast meeting, some council members implied a 3–3 council split—Councilmen Sikyta, Cook, and Baker opposed the mayor's choice in favor of Acting Chief Adams. Council Chairman Max Denney was out of town and did not attend the mayor's breakfast meeting announcing her appointment. Meanwhile, the acting chief, whom the mayor contacted the night before and encouraged to remain on the force, said he had been counting on the nomination and would probably not stay with the police department. The leader of the newly formed police union indicated support for the mayor's choice by rank-and-file patrol officers, who preferred an outside chief with no allegiance to anyone, but the command ranks of lieutenant and above supported Acting Chief Adams.

My mother might have been a neophyte mayor at this point, but as a seasoned political strategist she knew she could give the balky city council no wiggle room. Both at the closed breakfast meeting with city council members and later that morning at a press conference announcing her police chief choice, she made it clear that if the city council did not confirm George Hansen, the search would begin anew. She would not put forward any alternate finalists, nor would she offer Acting Chief Adams as a second choice for council confirmation.

The pro-Adams forces objected to the mayor's plan. Councilman Cook contended that my mother had maneuvered the council into having only one choice—to accept or reject Hansen—thereby blocking the pro-Adams councilmen from pushing the acting chief as a second choice if Hansen's nomination were defeated. Retired Chief Carroll broadcast his continued opposition to the mayor's choice: "I think it's quite a blow to the police department personnel."

The battle lines were drawn; the fight would continue. The pressure to which my mother had been subjected for weeks, both publicly and behind the scenes, had now transformed into a most public battle between the two sides on the city council. The day after my mother's appointment of Hansen as chief, editorials in the Lincoln morning and evening newspapers focused on the controversy. Agreeing with the mayor that no appointment she would make during the four years of her term would be more important than that of police chief and recognizing the vocal segment of the community who preferred Acting Chief Adams, the *Evening Journal* wrote: "A fair guess is that many of those people favored incumbent Mayor Sam Schwarzkopf in the last mayoral contest, won by Mrs. Boosalis." The editorial continued, "Yet, if there are dozens and dozens of pro-Adams, anti-anybody-else citizens, there is only one elected mayor of the City of Lincoln . . . [who] has authority to appoint department heads and, if those appointments are confirmed, finally be held responsible by the electorate."

Adams's supporters hastily called a meeting on September 6, three days after the mayor's appointment announcement and two days before the scheduled city council confirmation hearings. Thirty or so prominent citizens, most from the supporter ranks of defeated Mayor Schwartzkopf, met to solidify their opposition to the mayor's appointment and plan their presentation for the upcoming city council meeting. Included in the group were retired police chief Carroll, former governor Robert Crosby, former city Community Development director Leo Scherer, former city attorney Dick Wood, a school board member, several businessmen, and the three self-identified pro-Adams city council members—Sikyta, Cook, and Baker.

Angry attendees of the Saturday soiree charged that the mayor's appointment showed a lack of confidence in the police department, and they railed against the mayor's closing the door on other candidates. Rumors were aired, such as an alleged comment by Hansen's son, supposedly overheard during the mayoral campaign, that if Boosalis were elected his dad would have a good chance of becoming police* chief. The possibility of even seeking a recall election of the new mayor was floated at the incendiary meeting as well, but the group took no "official" action on that subject.

The three city council members who met that Saturday with other Adams supporters went on to form a solid anti-Boosalis bloc on the city council. "If they could have knocked me off the top of the Empire State Building," Mom told me, "nothing would have made them happier. If they could do anything to thwart me, they did. When they voted for one of my positions, it was because the public was so vocally and overwhelmingly with me on the issue, they had to."

But what about the seventh member of the city council, the one who

had been out of town on the day of the mayor's announcement breakfast with the other six council members? What about Max Denney, the
crucial fourth vote, the tie-breaking vote? Certain that she had the support of council members Sue Bailey, John Robinson, and Bob Jeambey,
the mayor was not content to wait for Councilman Denney to return to
Lincoln, where she knew the pressures on him would be enormous the
moment he set foot back in town. Mom placed a call to his son in Ohio,
where Denney had been visiting, and learned that he was driving back
to Lincoln and planned to stop overnight at a hotel en route.

With no cellular phone technology providing 24–7 communication,
my mother waited anxiously to call Denney at his predetermined hotel
stop. With first crack at him on the issue, she painstakingly described
Hansen's background and qualifications for police chief. When she
finished, Denney responded, "He sounds like an excellent candidate,
Helen. Besides, I believe in our form of government and it's the mayor's
prerogative to make the appointment. If you make a mistake on this,
it's on your shoulders."

Although mightily relieved, Mom hung up the phone knowing full
well that Councilman Denney would have to stand up to great pressure
on his return. Most knowledgeable sources speculated that his personal
preference was for Acting Chief Adams, but no one knew if he would
advance that preference to buck the new mayor's first critical test in
office. When reporters caught up to him later that evening, Denney signaled his intended vote in the upcoming council confirmation meeting:
"I have great respect for Dale Adams and I was kind of hoping that he
would get the job. But I'm also a firm believer in the fact that the mayor
should have the right to make her own appointments. . . . the council
shouldn't try to make these appointments."

Denney returned to a firestorm, with pro-Adams forces bent on recruiting his vote. He received more calls urging him to support Adams
in those few days leading up to the city council meeting than he had
received about any other issue coming before the council since he had
been elected. The pressure was, indeed, enormous. He received promises of support in a run for mayor at the end of my mother's term; his
loyalties to the police department in general and to Acting Chief Adams
in particular were called into question; he was pushed about as hard as
an elected officeholder can be pushed.

The day of reckoning arrived. The mayor presented her police chief appointment to the council in the packed city council chambers and in a clear and steady voice enumerated the reasons why she believed that Hansen was the best choice for the community. She reminded the council that when she ran for mayor she said repeatedly that she intended to seek the best police chief for the city, whether inside or outside the police department. "If the [citizen] committee hadn't been that strongly convinced," she said, "I wouldn't be here sticking my neck out."

Next, the chairman of the finalist selection committee, R. D. Anderson, summarized their selection process and why they had recommended Hansen. Then, "speaking emotionally, his hands trembling," he described Acting Chief Adams as a fine man but not yet qualified to be chief; Adams needed additional development that he had not received under past leadership in the police department. Anderson speculated that with further training and development, Adams could one day be police chief.

In the overflowing council chambers, two and a half hours of public testimony—most in opposition to Hansen's appointment—included statements by many of those who had gathered the previous Saturday to find the means to end-run the mayor's choice and install Adams as chief. Some were blunt in their comments: "Don't screw up what good we've already got in this town. The people of Lincoln don't want this guy," urged the manager of a local hotel. The vice president of a large insurance company claimed that the appointment of an outsider was a vote of no confidence in the police force. During the ensuing council debate, my mother stood leaning against the doorjamb to the council chambers. She said many years later, "My hair was already gray, but that afternoon I swear it turned white."

The vote was taken: 4–3 confirming the mayor's choice, George Hansen, with Max Denney standing firm and casting the deciding vote. Upon voting, he expressed his pain: "I think this is the hardest decision I'll ever have to make. I wish I could go away some place and not have to make a decision. But my decision is one I believe is right."

The excruciating battle ended. Minutes after the council decision, my mother told reporters that confirmation of her choice was "the end of a very difficult and trying period." But with characteristic spunk and humor, she added, "I am going to go home and lie down five minutes before getting supper."

In the wake of the climactic vote, editorials in both local newspapers supported the Hansen confirmation. The *Evening Journal* noted the emotional testimony at the confirmation hearing and surmised that "some citizens still are not convinced Helen Boosalis was elected mayor and, being mayor, is legally responsible for management of the municipal government's executive affairs." The *Star* focused on the positive selection process and highlighted the roles of the key players:

- Mayor Helen Boosalis' courage and determination to search for a person whom she would consider the best police chief she could find, regardless of political pressures. It was altogether a gutsy performance, not calculated to win her a whole bunch of new friends.

- The Lincoln City Council majority vote to sustain and confirm the Mayor's nomination in a firestorm of controversy . . . [and] Council Chairman Max Denney, who might have made another choice had he been mayor, but who recognized the executive's right of appointment of competent nominees, cast a surpassingly crucial vote.

- The good, hard work of the citizens' selection committee. . . . It was not an easy chore. The members have to live with themselves and their *neighbors. The entire community owes them a debt of gratitude. When passions subside, it will be remembered, hopefully, that they performed a lasting service to their city.

The editorial identified the factors and feelings that ran the gamut throughout the selection process: "tradition, loyalty, friendship, suspicion, apprehension, manipulation, politics, courage, professionalism, municipal pride." Many of these would play supporting roles in future productions during my mother's mayoral tenure, but they would not converge to deliver as dramatic a performance and denouement as in this first critical test of the new mayor's mettle. "I think the hardest thing Helen had to do was replacing the police chief," reflected former Lancaster County commissioner Jan Gauger. "She faced the most bitter controversy and major furor I'd ever seen. It's one thing to look back now and know what a good decision it was, but another thing to actually make that difficult decision without knowing how it would turn out. She was very brave."

My mom knew, even as it played out, that this decision was a defining moment. If her nomination had gone down in defeat, her ability to lead and govern over the next four years would have been seriously impaired.

The mayor could hardly wait until her newly confirmed police chief arrived in Lincoln. The "five-minute rest" she craved following the nerve-racking culmination of the police chief search was barely over when an array of pressing police issues fomented new community concerns. As if to underscore the appointment controversy, several serious law enforcement challenges arose during the three weeks between the council's 4–3 vote to confirm the mayor's appointment and Hansen's swearing in as police chief.

After months of emotional debate and testimony recounting police abuse, the city council approved formation of a citizens police review board just prior to Hansen's arrival. The newly formed police union opposed the review board formation and, instead, favored the department's policing of itself. How would the new chief respond? The week before Hansen's installation as chief, the shooting of a black man, Sherdell Lewis, by a county deputy sheriff demonstrated "a substantial racial credibility gap in Lincoln, especially in matters regarding law enforcement," said an editorial. Lewis had been shot through his front door and killed when a dozen law enforcement personnel (state troopers, sheriff's deputies, and city police officers) went to his home with a search warrant during a drug raid.

In the middle of the night that Lewis was shot, my mother received a call at home from a woman who identified herself only as a resident of the Malone community, an area with Lincoln's most concentrated minority population. "Mayor, did you know that a black man has been shot by the police?" My mother had not received word of the shooting from the police department, which was still administered by Acting Chief Adams. She dressed and drove to the police department, where the young lieutenant manning the desk was shocked to see the mayor before dawn. As sketchy details of the shooting emerged throughout

the next day, a group of demonstrators, mostly black, gathered down-
town with placards reading "Police or Killers?" "Who's the next victim?
And Why?" "There was a killing last night in Lincoln, a Black man" and
"Is your screen door bullet proof?"

The day following the shooting, the mayor got news of a huge explosion near the Malone area, a possible bombing. The explosion gave
rise to rumors of arson stemming from the Sherdell Lewis shooting the
night before. And later that same day, the police reported to the mayor
that a cache of twenty handguns had been stolen from a downtown
pawnshop. The three events seemed ominously linked, but it was later
determined that the explosion and the gun thefts were unrelated to the
shooting. The massive explosion—killing one, critically injuring four,
and causing millions of dollars in damage—was caused by machinery
sparks igniting dust in a grain elevator.

But the tensions from the shooting of Lewis, the second of two black
men killed by officers within a year, remained high for weeks as law
enforcement investigations proceeded. City and county officials committed to undertake a comprehensive review of all law enforcement
policies and procedures, and the Civil Rights Division of the U.S. Justice
Department was asked to investigate. The mayor also called for mediators from the Justice Department's Community Relations Division to
help relieve community racial tensions.

Police Chief Hansen, installed just three days after these high-profile
events, would be called upon to justify every bit of faith that his new
boss had placed in him. Much to my mother's relief and satisfaction,
Chief Hansen would prove to shine and to meet far greater tests of his
abilities than required during the grueling selection process that he and
the brand-new mayor had so adeptly survived.

NEW ADMINISTRATION: DEPARTMENTS, BUDGETING

Although tame in comparison to the battle royal over her police chief
appointment, my mother's appointments to fill other city department
director vacancies and her plans for departmental restructuring also
stimulated major council debate in her early months as mayor. Many of
her opponents expected—and some supporters urged—that the mayor

17. Mayor Boosalis appoints Police Chief George Hansen

clean house and build from scratch her own administrative team of city department directors the minute she took the helm—that is, to fire all city department heads to demonstrate who's in charge.

Mom never considered that approach. She had observed the department heads during her years on the city council and had developed respect for their professionalism and expertise. She wanted the opportunity to work with them as an administrative team first before making changes. Also, she wanted to revamp departmental structures before deciding on her administrative team. For example, she envisioned restructuring a new Department of Urban Development for economic/community development and transportation; however, Councilmen Sikyta and Cook wanted a separate transportation department and held up for months the mayor's appointment of Urban Development director George Chick.

The mayor's departmental restructuring was not about administrative power games but rather her vision for aligning administrative priorities to meet the needs of the city. When Public Utilities director Lee Blocker resigned after her election, the mayor restructured the Public Works Department to include Public Utilities and took immediate steps to redirect the city's water policy to secure Lincoln's long-term water supply. Mom had been frustrated as a council member with the previous administration's opposition to acquiring more land for water wells because it would mean unpopular water rate increases; now she could use her mayoral leadership and administrative powers to reverse that policy.

During the high-pressure search for a new police chief, the balance of day-to-day city business also pressed for the mayor's attention. Taking office in late May 1975 left my mother only six weeks of hectic number crunching and analysis before proposing her $100 million 1975–76 *budget to the city council for budget deliberations in July and August and approval of a final budget by September 1, the start of the city's fiscal year. Fortunately, my mother's sixteen years of reviewing budgets as a council member were invaluable in preparing in a matter of weeks her first budget as mayor.

My mother's election as mayor came at a time when the city's economic outlook was less than bright, or as one headline put it: "Economic Storm Clouds Gather as Mrs. Boosalis Begins Mayoralty." During the previous administration, expanding city revenues from federal revenue sharing and a new city sales tax (1 percent) made budgeting for operations and capital expenditures fairly painless, even for a growing city. Because of "what amounted to extra money pouring in from the city sales tax and federal revenue sharing funds," the city was able to pay for new programs and even to reduce its property tax mill levy. An editorial assessment of the city's changing revenue picture in the next four years was pessimistic:

> Lincoln's governmental progress the past four years was largely fueled by a set of fortuitous circumstances never likely to be repeated. Because of the city council's adoption of a municipal sales tax . . . ; because of the introduction of federal revenue sharing; because of the availability of tons of categorical federal aid

dollars for transportation, for the police function, for community development, money truly was not a terrible problem during the Schwarzkopf second term.

But revenue is apt to be an awful problem in the next four years. The salad days of municipal revenue growth and ever-expanding resources are over.

Indeed, the salad days were over by 1975—the city budget picture was discouraging in the face of high *inflation, dropping sales tax revenues, and the threat that the federal General Revenue Sharing Act would not be renewed. With high inflation, the increased costs of providing existing city services greatly outstripped current city revenue levels.

Tempers flared as the city council worked to trim my mother's first proposed budget as mayor. Councilman Sikyta proposed 5 percent blanket budget cuts, alleging that every budget has 5 percent fat and departments can get along with less money. Calling Sikyta's proposed cuts to salaries a meat-ax approach to budgeting, the mayor pointed out that her budget eliminated many city jobs because she had directed department heads not to fill vacant positions unless they were absolutely vital. Councilman Sikyta blew up, shouting at the mayor, "If I don't have the right [to cut the budget], then to hell with you." To her former sparring mate on the council, my mother coolly retorted, "You are the policy making body and what you decide, we [the administration] will carry out."

The city council—usually on 4–3 votes—made across-the-board cuts in departmental budgets (water system, sanitary sewer, municipal court, parks/recreation, library, etc.), but a majority acceded to the mayor's request for a new administrative director position to assist her in long-term fiscal planning, revamping the budgeting process, and managing thirteen city departments headed by directors who all reported to the mayor. Even Councilman Sikyta voted to fund the new position, although he felt that "Mrs. Boosalis had the stamina to get things done" on her own. To this day Mom is grateful for Councilman Sikyta's support for her administrative director position.

To fill that position, in December 1975 the mayor hired Reid Charles and directed him to convert the budgeting process by April 1976 to "program budgeting," one of my mother's cherished goals. She had grown weary, after sixteen years of council budget sessions, of being unable to decipher from the budget the total cost of a service or program. By the spring of 1976 the financial transparency that she had long desired as a legislator was accomplished.

Mom credited Reid Charles's financial acumen for achieving in months what other finance experts told her would take years to do, and also credited her department heads for working killer hours to change completely the way they had always budgeted. During my mother's entire first year as mayor, the department directors were simultaneously exhausted by the pace and invigorated by the results—a state not uncommon to those working with my mother. The mayor's administrative aide and later administrative director, Mike Merwick, recalls those hectic days: "Helen made the city staff into overachievers. She created a team that lasted twenty years in government, not just the years she was mayor. She inspired, she demanded, she led by example. She was always there working right along with staff and didn't ask anyone to do what she was unwilling to do."

On the other hand, Merwick recounts, the mayor recognized when the pressure on her staff became too intense: "If things were going badly and we were going nuts trying to bail out the boat, she would stop and tell me to come into her office. She'd take off her shoes, put her feet up and say, 'Well, how do you think things are going? What do you think? We're kind of in a pickle.' Then we'd kick things around for a few minutes, talk about other matters or tell a few jokes. Then she'd put her shoes back on and say, 'Let's get back to it. We needed a little break.' It was her way of getting us to unwind, letting off the pressure valve." And how did my mother deal with her own stress in this pressure cooker? Her mayoral campaign coordinator and confidante, Beatty Brasch, observed that "Helen was able to handle a lot of stress because she seems able to let go of things. She comes to conclusions and is a good decision maker."

Budget pressures were to become even more intense. By the end of her first year, the mayor proposed another hold-the-line budget in the continuing era of rapidly rising costs and inflation. "The mayor's budget represents a conservative approach to spending in the new year and ought to earn a few plaudits from weary taxpayers," an editorial noted. The 1976–77 budget as approved by the council eliminated thirteen federally financed positions and forty-eight city positions, including ten firefighters—the only layoff of municipal employees my mother could remember in her seventeen-year tenure in city government.

NATIONAL RECESSION—IMPACT ON CITIES

The mid-1970s were challenging economic times, and Lincoln was not alone among cities nationwide cutting budgets to cope with high inflation and shrinking revenues. The first long and deep recession in the post–World War II period, the recession of 1973–75, "is remembered primarily for its simultaneous rise in both the inflation rate and the unemployment rate—typically these two measures are expected to move in opposite directions."

The economic conditions of this recession—continued inflation and stagnant business activity, together with an increasing unemployment rate—gave rise to the term "stagflation" and to what Morgan Stanley economist Stephen Roach considered "the darkest period in modern financial market history." Much of the blame for the 1970s recession was placed on the 1973 Arab oil embargo triggered by the Arab-Israeli conflict (Yom Kippur War), which drove oil prices sky-high. "The explosion in oil prices ushered in a decade of 'stagflation' in which inflation soared while economies stagnated. By the end of the decade, the United States experienced double-digit unemployment, double-digit inflation and double-digit interest rates."

In those difficult economic times the collective voice of cities needed to be heard in the federal domestic policy debate. Just as Mom believed that citizens should participate in local decisions affecting their lives, so too did she believe that cities should have a voice in making federal municipal policy. She had a choice between two national organizations of member cities, both with missions to voice cities' concerns to federal policymakers—the U.S. Conference of Mayors and the National League of Cities. Knowing she would not have the time to participate in both organizations, Lincoln's new mayor chose to join the U.S. Conference of Mayors because it represented larger cities (populations greater than thirty thousand) and the participants all were mayors.

In addition to being part of a national municipal policy effort, Lincoln's mayor was eager to learn how other cities addressed common problems and how other mayors performed their *jobs. Mom attended her first U.S. Conference of Mayors meeting in Boston two months after her 1975 election. The attending mayors voiced urgent concerns over recession-pinched city budgets that were further threatened by federal policies. With the specter of a garbage-strewn New York City teetering on the edge of *bankruptcy, the mayors called for $2 billion in emergency federal urban aid. Although the Ford administration had declared that "the urban crisis is over," Mayor Joseph Alioto of San Francisco, then president of the U.S. Conference of Mayors, declared that "the recession hits the cities first and leaves them last."

My mother was a sponge at her first U.S. Conference of Mayors meeting, in 1975, learning both from her mayor colleagues and from speakers, including David Rockefeller, board chair of Chase Manhattan Bank; Leonard Woodcock, president of the United Auto Workers; HUD secretary Carla Hills; and U.S. senator Hubert Humphrey. In a speech eerily reminiscent of words he might speak today, Senator Ted Kennedy urged President Ford to pay as much attention to the problems of cities and voices of mayors as he did to the Pentagon. "Our cities have borne the burden of a decade's preoccupation with Vietnam," he said, "and after Vietnam, there was Watergate. You mayors are at the edge of a hurricane."

Although the economy and gloomy fiscal condition of cities nationwide dominated the U.S. Conference of Mayors meeting that year, other issues that surfaced in Boston reveal a roadmap of the times. Boston City Councilwoman Louise Day Hicks took over Boston mayor Kevin White's hotel suite and vowed to stay until White agreed to place on the U.S. Conference of Mayors agenda the issue of busing to achieve school desegregation. Boston had just gone through its first year of court-ordered desegregation as had Denver and Pontiac, Michigan, a few years earlier.

With the country still raw from the Watergate scandal, the public's loss of confidence in government was another U.S. Conference of Mayors theme. Pollster Lou Harris delivered sobering news to the mayors that only 14 percent of the population had any confidence in them and their old style of politics. In the wake of Watergate, the country had reached a record depth of demoralization with 67 percent of the nation feeling that "what they think doesn't count any more." Only two institutions rated as low in people's confidence as city government: the oil industry and the advertising industry. One of the few rays of hope reflected in the polls was that 90 percent still believed government *could* be made to work.

Like a revivalist, Lou Harris challenged the mayors to provide the kind of leadership the demoralized populace was seeking. "The public wants men of hope and genuine humanity," he said, "with compassion for the less privileged, but with a realism about the complexities of modern society. . . . Above all, people want leaders who have the courage to welcome the governed into the political process." Except for his call for *"men* of hope and genuine humanity," Harris could have been describing the two-month-tenured woman mayor from Lincoln, Nebraska.

At the time, my mother's unique position as the only woman mayor and chief executive of a city with a population greater than 100,000 made her a logical target for the U.S Conference of Mayors to groom for organizational leadership and as a spokesperson for cities on Capitol Hill. She might have been the new kid on the block, but she and several big-city *mayors went straight from their Boston conference to the White House to meet with President Ford and Vice President Nelson Rockefeller to discuss federal revenue sharing set to expire in 1976.

Federal funds then made up about 10 percent of Lincoln's total budget for such expenditures as street construction, buses, law enforcement, health care, and urban development in older neighborhoods. Like most other mayors, Lincoln's mayor was a strong proponent of continued federal revenue sharing as long as federal dollars did not mean federal control of local government. "As long as the major decisions are made at the local level, the red tape connected with the federal funds is worth fighting through," the mayor told a Lincoln reporter.

Mom eagerly joined her more experienced mayor colleagues to make the case at the White House for continued federal revenue sharing. It hadn't taken Lincoln's mayor long to step up from the plains of Nebraska to raise her voice in the national arena.

INVOLVING CITIZENS: COUNCIL RIFT

With the approval of her first budget, her administrative team in place, her police chief search resolved, and her introductory role on the stage of national municipal policy, the mayor had begun to define the distinctive changes she was bringing to her job of governing. As mayor, my mother could accelerate by miles her resolute campaign to open up government to its citizens and engage them in decision making. From the moment she became mayor and passed the city council gavel to Councilman Max Denney, she worked to fulfill her pledge that "an open administration was 'not idle campaign rhetoric.'" Mom's first months in office were proof that she would "lend the same receptive ear that has listened to citizen grievances and proposals during several council terms," as an early editorial predicted she would.

The difference was, as mayor, she could open many more paths to citizen involvement, amplify their voices, and solicit their diverse opinions. "Helen was a master in building networks and pulling folks together to work on their community long before social scientists ever thought about 'network analysis' and 'overlap groups,'" reflected UNL economics professor Greg Hayden. Mom worked hard to make herself accessible, believing that if people felt a personal connection to their mayor they were more likely to take ownership of their city.

Engaging with the public had been a hallmark of her city council service—meeting with citizens at every opportunity and responding in person to their questions and complaints—and she was determined to retain that close contact as mayor. The door to her office was always open, with or without appointment, and sometimes she arrived at city hall at 6:30 a.m. to find some folks waiting in the hallway to see her. Former Lincoln mayor and Nebraska governor Mike Johanns recalls that "Helen never forgot who put her in office—the people. She always served in their best interest."

The mayor ordered simple logistical changes to ease citizen communication with city hall, such as the installation of city hall telephone-answering equipment to tape citizens' non-emergency calls during non-office hours. She created an accelerated administration-wide system for handling citizen complaints and inquiries, requiring their response within five days rather than languishing indefinitely on someone's city hall desk.

My mother did not wait for citizens to seek out help from the city— she made local government more accessible by taking the city to the people. She scheduled city-neighborhood forums in the evenings at local schools throughout the city, often in conjunction with all-neighborhood events such as spring cleanup campaigns. With her she brought city council members and city administrators of planning, public works and utilities, urban development, parks and recreation, police and fire, personnel, finance and law, health, library, transportation, aging, human rights, Lincoln Electric System, and the housing authority. She also invited banks to explain home improvement loan programs. Rather than boring one-way presentations, most of the neighborhood forum time was devoted to questions and answers in small groups so that people could discuss issues of importance to them.

The mayor was determined that citizens understand and voice opinions on how the city spent their money. With each city budget cycle she conducted popular citizen forums on the budget ("Sound Off to City Hall") in each quadrant of the city. As the economy grew worse she explained that the city had managed to operate with hold-the-line budgets, hiring freezes, and layoffs but that current service levels could not continue in the face of increasing inflation. She asked for the public's views on spending priorities and cuts. Some citizens suggested spending reductions such as fewer street-widening projects, but many more suggested where to spend than where to cut.

Mom further encouraged residents to take ownership of their neighborhoods through a program developed by the city's Urban Development Department that sought input from neighborhood organizations on the use of federal funds for neighborhood redevelopment projects. Neighborhood activist Jacquelyn Herman related, "Helen had a lasting influence on the community through empowering people who had been shut out of public policy making. Neighborhood groups were strengthened during her era and became pretty good watch dogs over city councils and mayors." With an increased sense of ownership in their neighborhoods and city, citizens demanded more and more involvement in city decision making—an outcome that delighted the mayor but provoked some on the city council who feared that nourishing an awakening citizen interest in city programs and policies had created a "Frankenstein monster."

The new woman mayor was in great demand to speak to groups of all kinds, and she used the neighborhood forums to solicit names of people willing to serve as volunteers on governmental boards and commissions. She broadened her solicitation efforts by inviting people to join a Citizen Resource Bank by submitting their areas of talent, experience, or interest and willingness to be appointed to a city advisory committee. Mom then used the resource bank in making her numerous mayoral appointments to city volunteer boards and committees. A disgruntled letter to the editor (signed "Concerned Citizen") complained that the mayor's invitation to citizen service would add bookkeeping expense and only be answered by citizen friends of the mayor and those who saw things her way. On the contrary, through the Citizens Resource Bank my mom learned of scores of qualified, talented people willing to serve the city who she would not otherwise have known were good candidates for boards and committees.

The mayor's appointment of citizens to city advisory bodies provoked ongoing, heated disputes with her opponents on the city council. While Mom had prevailed in her choice for a new police chief, that fierce battle demonstrated the depth of resistance to change in the decades-old power structure in Lincoln. Mayoral appointments to city boards did not carry the same weight as the all-important, symbolic police chief appointment, but over time the cumulative effect of council member objections to several of my mother's key board appointments created a permanent council-mayor battleground.

An early citizen appointment skirmish arose several months into my mother's first term. The board of Lincoln Electric Service (LES), the city-owned and -operated electric power utility, had four vacancies to be filled by mayoral appointment subject to council confirmation. An increasingly hardened 4–3 split had formed on the council, with Bailey, Robinson, and Jeambey generally supporting my mother's positions; Sikyta, Cook, and Baker in general opposition; and Denney the increasingly opposing swing vote. As a result, the mayor began previewing her proposed appointments with the council before subjecting her nominees to uncomfortable public debate. At a council lunch session a week before the formal vote on the four LES appointments, she previewed her intent to reappoint two out of the three LES board members whose terms had expired and to appoint two new nominees to the board. The makeup of the LES board was particularly sensitive at that point because of a potential nuclear power generation issue.

During a dozen straw-vote stalemates on various combinations of potential appointees previewed by the mayor, the council majority consistently pressed the mayor to appoint all three veteran board members and those with business or engineering backgrounds. My mother explained that she was opposed to reappointing all three veteran members because new faces were needed to ensure a cross section of citizens on the board. At that, Councilman Sikyta exploded in opposition to the mayor's new-blood appointments: "Well, I'll probably be committing political suicide by saying it, but I don't care. I'm tired of being surrounded by college professors, their wives and members of the League of Women Voters."

Councilman Sikyta's candid outburst foreshadowed the continued struggle between my mother and the council majority over appointments threatening the political power structure that had historically excluded and ignored numerous segments of Lincoln's citizenry. The mayor shot back a challenge: "Look at the record, Mr. Sikyta. Prove what you say. Check them [my appointments] since last May." Later she said that if the council chose to limit the number of appointees from any one organization (such as the League of Women Voters), then the limitation should apply to all organizations, including the Chamber of Commerce.

Who knows if Councilman Sikyta took my mother's challenge to check the record, but after another year of repeated council tussles over her appointments, including claims that she appointed more women than men, a reporter did check her record. In her first twenty-one months as mayor, she had appointed 86 women and 115 men to the city's 48 task forces, boards, and commissions. To vacancies on the six most visible advisory bodies—City-County Planning Commission, Lincoln General Hospital, Lincoln Electric System, Park Board, Lincoln Transportation System, and Lincoln Housing Authority—she had appointed six women and eight men.

Refuting additional council claims made six months later that the mayor refused to reappoint veteran committee members, statistics showed that in just over two years my mother had reappointed 76 committee members, appointed new people to replace 19 existing members, filled 17 vacancies, and made 101 selections for newly created committees. Those numbers hardly supported charges of wholesale housecleaning.

The mayor said her goal was not to appoint equal numbers of men and women to every board but rather to appoint members who represented diversity in the community—geographic residence, sex, socioeconomic background, ethnicity, and age. Any one factor might play a more important role in appointments to particular boards. For example, ethnicity could be a higher consideration in appointments to the Police Review Board because minority citizens had filed many of the complaints against police, and the Lincoln Transportation System Board should have some appointees who actually rode city buses. Twelve-year-old bike rider Valerie Christy responded to the mayor's request that she serve on the city's Bicycle Safety Committee, "Wow! Yes!"

Mayoral appointments to boards that wielded power over the city's growth, land use, and development generated the most opposition among council members who were intent on retaining power over those matters. For example, my mother appointed Hughes Shanks, a retired federal administrator, to the City-County Planning Commission. The commission's zoning and land-use decisions had tremendous impact on developers and property owners. Shanks was rejected by the usual 4–3 council majority ostensibly because he lacked sufficient "professional expertise," even though the nine-member commission already had the expertise of a builder-developer, an architect, and an electrical engineer. A *Star* editorial blasted the council's rejection of the mayor's appointment of Shanks:

> True, Shanks, educated as a lawyer and now a retired government worker, has not been a land speculator, contractor or lender or anything else that might be deemed worthy by the councilmen who rejected him. But the mayor thought him qualified, competent and interested in serving. If he had been approved, Shanks,

a black, would have been the first minority member ever to serve on the planning commission. . . . The argument favoring more technical knowledge or professional expertise on the commission is a bunch of garbage anyway. The prime requisite for a planning commissioner or member of any other advisory group is common sense—and a willingness to listen. . . . As for the council majority, there is no doubting what they want: middle-aged, middle or upper income white males with pro-developer biases: mirror-images of themselves. It would appear that the rest of the city just might as well forget it. No diversity, no broad representation, no differing viewpoints.

When interviewed after his humiliating rejection by the city council, Shanks said that he did not believe race was an issue, that he bore no hard feelings, and that he would serve the community in any capacity that Mayor Boosalis asked. "Mrs. Boosalis asked me if I would serve and I said yes. Just about anything Helen Boosalis would ask me to serve on, I would say yes. That's the way I feel about Helen Boosalis." Perhaps out of shame, the council eight months later approved the mayor's appointment of Shanks to the Water Advisory Board.

The least-diverse boards were those of the city-run "businesses"— Lincoln Electric System and Lincoln General Hospital—their members coming almost exclusively from business and finance. My mother's appointments to those boards almost always generated the most controversy among the council. The ongoing wrangle over appointments to the board of Lincoln General Hospital was so bitter that in a spirit of compromise the mayor agreed to make appointments from three names submitted to her by the hospital board nominating committee. However, in October 1977, when she chose Fred Kauffman, an attorney and one of the three deemed acceptable to Lincoln General, Councilman Sikyta attacked the mayor's choice in favor of one of the other two—a banker.

Even worse, the chairman of the hospital board nominating committee that had submitted all three names to the mayor was none other than Councilman Sikyta himself. Denouncing the council's pattern of obstructionism over mayoral appointments, the *Star* wrote: "Now

Kauffman joins a growing list of Lincoln residents who somehow don't measure up in the eyes of a number of City Council members; a list of people interested in serving the city who are deemed expendable by some councilmen in this political war they are carrying on. One wonders to what depths of pettiness Sikyta and some of his colleagues will plummet in their childish vendetta against Mrs. Boosalis." Councilman Sikyta later apologized to the Lincoln General Hospital board and to Fred Kauffman for "making him look bad."

But the tug-of-war over my mother's appointments continued and intensified throughout her term as mayor. Clearly, more was at stake than her unfortunate board appointees who were caught in the cross-fire. The appointment battles symbolized the power struggle for control of the city and the test of strength of the new mayor's authority. The extremes some councilmen embraced in bucking the mayor's choices prompted some of the harshest editorial criticism of my mother's rivals and some of the strongest support for her during her entire mayoral tenure.

[Mayor Boosalis] has encouraged participation in city government from a broad spectrum of Lincoln citizenry. She has tried
especially hard to accommodate those who opposed her election.
That she has not strictly confined her appointments to the traditional ruling class, however, rankles and frightens some members
of the city council. (*Lincoln Star*)

What in the world can be wrong with a policy which holds that
men (usually) and women (now and then) appointed to city government administrative or advisory groups be genuinely representative of the whole community? What is so subversive about
an appointments policy which blows some life in the supposedly desired characteristics of diversity and reasonable turnover?
Those have been Helen Boosalis' appointment guidelines . . . Yet
the fleshing out of her policy seems to stick in the throats, if not
stab at the hearts, of several City Council members. Are they
really as insecure as they appear? . . . A strong mayor rankles a
City Council comfortably used to being the dominant local government power. Sharing of power always comes hard. That the

mayor is a woman probably ticks off the boys in the locker room even more. (*Lincoln Journal*)

What are the councilmen trying to accomplish with regard to appointments? They are trying to pack the city advisory panels so that they reflect only the council majority's own narrow perspective on municipal affairs. . . . This butts heads, of course, with Mayor Boosalis' attempts to obtain broad-based representation on advisory commissions and boards. . . . If those council members want to be mayor so badly, why don't they run for the office? (*Lincoln Star*)

Whether or not any council members aspired to be mayor, they all felt qualified to evaluate the performance of the new mayor. My mother received mixed reviews from the city council at the end of her first year as mayor. As might be expected, she got critical marks from Councilmen Sikyta and Cook, neutral comments from Baker, mildly positive remarks from Denney, and positive grades from Jeambey, Bailey, and Robinson. The critics focused on her adversarial relationship with some council members, her hesitancy to take a stand on controversial issues, and her reliance on advisers and advisory committees. Her supporters applauded her outspoken and vigorous execution of her strong-mayor powers and credited both sides of the council for developing adversarial relationships. "I think it's healthy that we disagree," offered council member Sue Bailey.

Media assessment of the mayor's first year was largely positive. Mom had a history of good relations with the press during her city council service because she was open to scrutiny. When the media complained that they had not had access to the mayor's office in previous administrations, she gladly set up regular press conferences. In one wide-ranging press conference late in her first year as mayor, she apologized to reporters who had criticized her in prior weeks for being less than candid. With unusual frankness from a politician, she responded, "I'll be the first to admit I've hedged a bit. It's one of the pitfalls of this office—you get a little defensive and guarded. But I realize that and I have an obligation to be candid."

One city hall reporter observed that the mayor had made significant changes by creating a more open mayor's office for the press and the public, by being "rather candid for a politician," and by taking a highly visible role with the city council. At the same time, the reporter criticized the mayor for avoiding controversy—her appointment of the police chief a notable exception—using as an example her conciliatory process of previewing with the council her intended appointments. Judging from the council fights over her appointments, however, the mayor did not succeed in avoiding controversy—if, indeed, that was her intent.

The council-mayor discord continued unabated. In the spring of 1977 Councilman Sikyta even called a press conference—a tool seldom used by council members and his first since being elected to the council six years earlier—to say that the council and Mayor Boosalis seemed unable to cooperate to settle an issue. He blamed the mayor and council members Bailey and Jeambey for concentrating on personalities rather than issues. A *Star* editorial identified a different reason for the split: "The genesis of the problem in our opinion is in the election of 1975. Piqued that Mrs. Boosalis actually defeated the incumbent, a group of three councilmen of which Sikyta is one has been in a snit ever since. That faction has never allowed a decent relationship to develop between it and the administrative branch."

Almost from the outset of my mother's mayoral term, the seemingly intractable city council schism and the resultant rift between council and mayor surfaced in nearly every council debate on significant issues facing the city. In this rancorous environment, Mom faced a true leadership challenge.

A WOMAN'S PLACE IS IN THE . . . MAYOR'S OFFICE

What is of more importance to leadership—if the leader is a woman—than one's hair? A profile of the mayor at the end of her first year was headlined, "Mayor's Hair, Office Operation Alike: Everything Smooth, in Place." And the press attention to Mom's hair continued through her mayoral years. One article about the city's comprehensive planning process noted that "Mayor Boosalis, not a hair out of place, seemed to be on top of things." The caption for a photo of her being dunked to raise funds for muscular dystrophy described a "bathing cap snapped over her usually perfect hairdo." Another headline read, "Under Mayor Boosalis' Immaculate Coiffure Is Person Ranked First in Lincoln Power Poll" (ahead of Governor Exon and the University of Nebraska football coach).

True, my mother's white hair was rarely out of place and, like many women of her generation, she had a standing appointment with her hairdresser, Laurie Hauder, to set and spray her hair into place until the next appointment. To preserve the "do" required wearing rollers and a bonnet to bed. But receiving so much press attention seemed less a comment on Mom's immovable hairstyle than on her being a woman. Presidential primary candidate Hillary Clinton pointed out three decades later at Rutger's Center for the American Woman and Politics, "My hairstyles and fashion choices provide endless fodder for public discussion and dissection."

Although my mother laughed, and still laughs, at all the press comments on her hair, she recognized that her overall appearance received far more public notice than did the looks of her male counterparts. Often when walking down a street or shopping, people would approach her and say, "Mayor, I saw you on TV last night." Mom would then ask, "Oh, what was I talking about?" and invariably the response would be, "Oh, I don't know, but you sure had on a good-looking outfit!"

Her frugal mother had insisted after the election that her daughter the mayor buy some new clothes at Schlampp's, a high-end women's clothing store in Minneapolis, even though both of them had always sewn their own clothes for a fraction of the price. "Now that you're mayor," Gram said, "you have to look the part." Gram's extravagant advice was prescient, given all the attention to the woman mayor's appearance and the absence of time Mom had as mayor for sewing.

A woman in the mayor's office heightened interest in women's issues of more substance than hairdos and appearance, and Mom used her visibility to advance women's issues and support the involvement of more women in electoral politics. Shortly after her election, during her speech at a League of Women Voters event celebrating the ninth anniversary of the National Organization for Women, she announced her decision to establish a Mayor's Commission on the Status of Women.

Bobby McGinn, later the commission's chair, had worked with Mom when she was on the council in a four-year unsuccessful effort to interest the previous mayor in starting a women's commission.

My mother planned to establish the Mayor's Commission on the Status of Women by executive order rather than risk a city council vote. County Commissioner Jan Gauger proposed that the commission be enlarged to Lancaster County, and the order creating the city-county commission was executed on the last day of 1975, the International Year of the Woman. In addition to twenty-seven appointed commission members (including two men), more than one hundred citizens worked on committees focused on problems faced by women in such areas as credit and insurance, employment, health, education, and social services. Nationally, each state had formed a statewide women's commission, but the Lincoln-Lancaster Commission on the Status of Women was one of only two such local women's commissions in the United States, the other in San Francisco.

In addition to addressing problems confronting women communitywide, Mom was committed to helping women reach their full potential, one woman at a time, by supporting the work of talented women and extending her hand to bring other women along. For example, within her administration she identified women who had been kept in clerical positions but were performing at much higher levels, and she promoted their professional advancement. On the political front she solicited, encouraged, and supported women to run for elected office, never forgetting how much encouragement and support she had needed every time she ran for office. She was astonished to discover during her political career a few women elected to office who acted as if they had achieved success single-handedly, without recognizing the path painfully carved by many women before them. My mother never forgot how she got where she was, and she made certain to extend a hand to other women.

These kinds of efforts, which women may take for granted now, were critically important in the 1970s. With great expectations and enthusiasm, the women's movement had been launched and had gained traction in some quarters, but the political arena was slow to show gains. After the national elections in the fall of 1976, not one woman sat in the U.S. Senate, the number of U.S. House of Representatives seats held by women declined by one, to eighteen, and the only woman to chair a House committee retired.

In daily life at Lincoln's city hall, the external interest in the novelty of a woman mayor was of little relevance to the challenges my mother faced in governing the city. Compelling issues—energy consumption and conservation, the Comprehensive Plan governing future land use and growth of the city, downtown and neighborhood redevelopment, human services, and human rights—required time, effort, and leadership from the mayor's office, regardless of the occupant's gender.

Money Talks
Summer and Fall 1986

After my mother's gubernatorial primary win in May 1986, I finally felt myself in the swing of the campaign. I had come a long way from my first frightening day at headquarters when Neil Oxman gave me a week to raise money to feed the voracious TV advertising monster. That agonizing trial by fire strengthened my gut for the remaining months of the campaign.

Swept aside were my naive illusions that issues are the driving force of campaigns. This was no local race for mayor or city council; there would be no kitchen-table strategy sessions. This was the big time. Statewide races mean advertising, and advertising means money—big money.

Our Boosalis for Governor campaign fund-raising machine was geared up almost around the clock to crank out funds for the purchase of pricey TV airtime (media-buys), so that Neil's thirty-second ads could convey to voters throughout the state the compelling leadership of Helen Boosalis that Lincoln voters knew so well. Although Mom's campaign faced a relentless fund-raising challenge to pay the steep advertising costs, at least Neil knew he had the quality product—the quality candidate—to sell. "Compared to other candidates, Helen was *sui generis*," Neil recalls. "She wasn't one of the cookie-cutter guys in their dark suits and red ties who all look and sound alike. She was a legitimate, unique, serious person who stood out in a real way. She's one of our half-dozen favorite clients over all the years."

My mother's campaign co-chair Ben Nelson (later Nebraska gover-

nor and now U.S. senator) said he hoped that the total costs of the Orr
and Boosalis campaigns would not exceed the $2 million total spent
by Bob Kerrey and Republican opponent Charles Thone in their 1982
race for governor. (Thone then held the Nebraska campaign fund-raising record of $1.1 million.) The increased costs of campaigning in the
four years since 1982 made it likely that the Boosalis and Orr campaigns
would each spend more than $1 million. With the help of three popular
statewide Democrats—outgoing governor Bob Kerrey and U.S. senators Jim Exon and Ed Zorinsky—the Boosalis campaign hoped to wring
as many Democratic dollars from the state as possible.

With Nebraska's small population and weak farm economy, however, the need to raise funds out of state was evident. Ben Nelson cautioned that the campaign would decide whose help to accept nationally: "We have to keep the perspective on what Nebraska needs. We
will take all the help we can get, but we are not interested in making
this a national election. This is still going to be a Nebraska race . . .
decided on Nebraska's issues and Nebraska's future." Nelson's admonition notwithstanding, widespread media attention to the two-woman
feature of the race had already brought a national focus to the election.
Moreover, with only 1.6 million people in the entire state of Nebraska
and the pressing need to raise at least $1 million—peanuts compared
to current campaign war chests but overwhelming to us in 1986—the
Boosalis campaign knew it would have to go outside the state to raise
the serious money needed.

The fund-raising team organized targeted events in New York City,
Los Angeles, Boston, Washington, Miami, Detroit, Baltimore, Minneapolis—any place where loyal Boosalis supporters and other national
supporters of outstanding candidates were willing to host a fund-raiser
and identify lists of invitees. For example, Carol Bellamy—then a principal at Morgan Stanley after serving as president of the New York City
Council and running unsuccessfully against Ed Koch for mayor of New
York—helped us with New York women and Wall Street fund-raising
efforts; and Governor Mario Cuomo was honorary host of a New York
reception hosted by former Nebraskans.

National party officials took a heightened interest in the high-profile
two-woman race for the governorship of an otherwise less important

midwestern state. Lynn Cutler, vice-chair of the Democratic National Committee, promised that the Democratic Party would raise as much as it could for Helen Boosalis but warned, "The trouble is, you will see the Republican National Committee put big, big dollars in this race."

It was true that the Republican Party badly wanted to help elect the country's first woman Republican governor. In addition to a $65,000 contribution to Orr by the Republican National Committee, visits to Nebraska by President Reagan and Vice-President Bush poured $200,000 and $100,000, respectively, into Orr's campaign coffers. President Reagan's September 1986 appearance at a $1,000-per-ticket fund-raiser in Omaha was one of only two campaign appearances for gubernatorial candidates he made that fall—highlighting the importance of the Nebraska race to the Republican Party.

Some thought Reagan's September visit was timed to give Orr the early benefits of major media coverage and funds yet still provide a safe distance between his appearance and the election. The strategy proved wise as Reagan made a gaffe during his two-hour visit to Omaha for Orr when he said, "Times have begun to get better for Nebraska farmers"—no doubt a great surprise to farmers. Democratic U.S. senator Jim Exon thought Reagan's visit might have actually hurt Orr: "I've felt for some time that Reagan didn't understand the farm bill completely, but after hearing what he said in Omaha today, I am convinced that he is totally uninformed or else he doesn't give a damn. . . . Reagan has presided over six years of total tragedy in rural America, not just farmers and ranchers, but small town USA." No matter—the huge chunk of change raised by Reagan's visit fueled Orr's campaign and television advertising in the critical early phase of her fall campaign.

Mom would have to spend valuable time away from campaigning in Nebraska to travel out of state to raise funds if she was going to match the hefty amounts raised for Orr by Reagan's and Bush's Nebraska visits. "Money's always a problem for Democrats in this state," noted Boosalis co-campaign manager Marg Badura. Some opined that if money wins a race, then Orr had the advantage since the prospect of the first Republican female governor would continue to bring heavy national financial support. On the other hand, "if the natural ability to make people feel comfortable and important wins an election, Helen Boosalis

18. Senator Bill Bradley (NJ) (*center*) comes to Nebraska for Boosalis for Governor campaign

will be the victor in November." But the Boosalis campaign was not naive in counting on their candidate's personal strengths to overcome a gap in funding to support adequate campaign staffing, field operations, and most importantly, advertising—and we were not about to concede the fund-raising advantage to Orr.

One advantage resulting from the national attention on the two-woman race in Nebraska accrued to both candidates: most Republican and Democratic contenders with an eye on the 1988 presidential race were eager to appear in the spotlight of the high-profile Nebraska campaign. Following the lead of Reagan and Bush, Majority Leader Bob Dole, Congressman Jack Kemp, Secretary of Transportation Elizabeth Dole, and former Delaware governor Pierre du Pont came to Nebraska to stump for Orr.

The Boosalis campaign planned events around the likes of U.S. senator Bill Bradley of New Jersey, who touted my mother's ability to use her U.S. Conference of Mayors contacts to attract industry to Nebraska and organize a farm state coalition to lobby federal agricultural policy. "I like Helen because she's a no-nonsense person," Bradley said. (My high-level job was to secure a basketball signed by Bradley for auction-

19. Former Atlanta mayor Maynard Jackson touts Helen's national reputation as mayor during governor's campaign

20. Senator Gary Hart (CO) (*right*) rallies Boosalis voters at press conference

ing at his fund-raiser for Mom.) Although hardly matching the fund-raising appearances of the Republican president and vice-president, national Democratic politicos in addition to Bradley who came to Nebraska to stump for Mom included U.S. senator Gary Hart of Colorado, Kentucky governor Martha Layne Collins, former Virginia governor Charles Robb, and Missouri congressman Richard Gephardt.

My mother's mayor pals from her leadership days in the U.S. Conference of Mayors were also keen to help in her fund-raising efforts. Mayor Coleman Young hosted a fund-raiser in Detroit, and George Latimer, mayor of St. Paul and also candidate for governor of Minnesota, came to Nebraska as "Helen's fan and supporter." As mayor she had "displayed a blend of toughness and openness," he said. "As a Democrat I like the way she is tough on budgets and money. She's a fiscal conservative." Mayor Latimer stumped for my mother at an Omaha fund-raiser, then boarded a small plane with her to attend a second event in Lincoln. A thunderstorm tossed their plane so much that when Latimer and Mom made their late entrance at the Lincoln event, Latimer's aide was the color of the Nebraska sky right before a tornado—grayish green.

When former Atlanta mayor Maynard Jackson was scheduled to participate in Omaha's Operation Big Vote, which was aimed at registering more African American voters, he insisted that his schedule include events to support his mayoral ally, Helen Boosalis. In praising my mother's effective leadership as mayor and urging her election as governor, Jackson said, "The truth is that being mayor is probably the toughest job in politics. During those years [when Helen Boosalis was mayor], mayors all across the country were faced with . . . meeting demands for services without raising taxes while at the same time coping with three national recessions. If there was ever a worst time to be mayor, that was it!"

While I assisted in almost all the campaign's national fund-raising efforts, I was solely responsible for planning and implementing a series of fund-raising events in Chicago. I worked and worried for weeks arranging events to maximize the money raised and minimize Mom's time away from Nebraska.

An event hosted by Chicago-area public affairs and government relations executives and a corporate breakfast in the Sears Tower went without a hitch. I thought perhaps this fund-raising stuff was not so intimidating after all. Afterward Mom and I headed up to the Sears executive suite with one of the breakfast hosts, Dean Swift, who had gotten to know my mother during Sears' sponsorship of the national Junior Olympics Games in Lincoln. A fan of Mom's when she was mayor and now a supporter of her candidacy for governor, he had arranged for her to meet with Edward Brennan, the new CEO of Sears.

We were feeling upbeat as we left the Sears Tower and made our way to the next appointment I had arranged, with a Greek American executive at AT&T who was similarly encouraging and supportive. We continued making calls on several other Chicago corporate executives, some of whom must have privately wondered what possible advantage to them would be gained from participating in this Nebraska governor's race, interesting as it was with two women running.

Finally, we gamely ascended to the corporate offices of Quaker Oats, where we met with the head of government relations. As my mother answered question after increasingly hostile question, I wracked my brain trying to remember the connection to this man and why on earth I had scheduled the meeting with him. I never did figure that out, but I was later horrified to discover that I had delivered my mother into the jaws of Tom Roeser, former member of the Nixon administration, Republican activist for decades in Illinois (later conservative political columnist and media personality). Little Miss Campaign Fund-raiser had really messed up. Afterward my mother just laughed it off as a *Candid Camera*–type experience.

My big Chicago fund-raising event was born of the "Greek connection" from which the Boosalis campaign had already greatly benefited. I knew that Greeks, like many other ethnic groups of recent immigrants, are a clannish bunch with fierce loyalties to their fellow Greeks, even those whom they have not met and especially those whose accomplishments shine favorable light on the group. Even so, I was floored by the enthusiastic support of the national Greek American network for the fiery Greek woman mayor from Nebraska.

Mike Dukakis, not yet a presidential candidate but then governor of Massachusetts, was the leading political standard-bearer for Greek Americans (along with U.S. senator Paul Sarbanes). Governor Dukakis wrote a fund-raising letter in support of Mom's candidacy that was mailed to voters of Greek descent across the country and said in part: "If I have anything to say about it, Helen Boosalis soon will stand next to me in the ranks of Greek-American governors. . . . [Helen's parents] brought with them not only the traditions of our proud heritage, but also the values we hold dear: integrity, courage, enterprising hard work, education and family. . . . Just as a Greek family would, [as mayor] she protected the public's money and made it go a long way." Dukakis's letter brought in many thousands of dollars from all over the country and paved the way for several Greek American fund-raising events outside Nebraska, including those in Miami, New York, Washington DC, Baltimore, and Los Angeles, and also the one I helped organize for Mom's Chicago trip to raise money.

The fund-raiser for Chicago Greek Americans at the Knickerbocker Hotel was hosted by Andy Athens (yes, his real name), president of Chicago's Metron Steel Corporation and national Greek American leader. When Mom and I met with Andy about the Chicago event, I kept thinking how he would have blended right in with the Greek men at my wedding—short, round, bald, and smoking a big cigar. He was all business and produced a top-notch crowd of Greek loyalists who proudly and significantly added to the already large sum from Greek Americans in the Boosalis campaign coffers.

While I no longer recall the substantial amount raised that evening, I remember with stunning clarity the call from the school nurse the afternoon of the Greek event in Chicago, announcing a head-lice epidemic at Lincoln School in Evanston and requesting my retrieval of Michael for immediate anti-lice measures. I was harried in last-minute preparations for the Andy Athens event. Horrified, having had no experience with lice—head or otherwise—I was ashamed to tell my mother the result of what I assumed were my own obvious mothering lapses.

I dashed home to Evanston from downtown Chicago, stopping at a drugstore to buy "Rid" to launch the anti-lice campaign. I had less than an hour to strip all the bedsheets and wash them in hot/hot water, remove all stuffed animals from the boys' bedrooms and slipcovers from the furniture, and apply the horrible liquid to their potentially infested heads. The boys sat side by side, two little naked bodies on the edge of the bathtub, screaming and crying while I pulled the tiny-toothed nit comb through their thick, curly (Greek) hair.

I felt like screaming and crying myself—maybe I did—as I looked at my watch and hoped I could make it back downtown in time for Andy Athens's introduction of Senator Sarbanes, who had flown in from Maryland for the event, and the senator's introduction of the Greek American candidate for governor of Nebraska. I did make it just in time; the boys recovered from their outrage at my inflictions; and I later learned that head lice invade entire schools and do not constitute grounds for bad-mother-of-the-year award.

The next Chicago fund-raising event under my care was a party at the home of Dawn Clark Netsch, longtime Democratic Illinois legislator (and later state comptroller and candidate for governor). Dawn told me she had not opened her house for a political event since hosting a party for Adlai Stevenson at which someone broke a priceless art piece. Dawn and her husband, famed architect Walter Netsch, lived in an ultramodern house he designed to showcase their extensive art collection. The large crowd that showed up for the fund-raiser was undoubtedly there as much to see Dawn Clark Netsch's house as they were to support a candidate for Nebraska governor.

The Netsch event was a thrilling evening, complete with Chicago TV news coverage. The invitees included many prominent Chicago Democratic women who were practiced in the art of contributing to good women candidates for public office, no matter where they lived. One invitee did not attend the party but sent a contribution check to the Boosalis campaign in Nebraska for $1,000. The check was from Christie Hefner, then president and later chairman and CEO of her father's Playboy Enterprises.

I returned to Nebraska after the Chicago fund-raising events feeling proud of our efforts, maybe even a little bit smug about the trip's success despite the Roeser debacle. I should have known better—pride goeth . . .

No sooner had I walked into Boosalis headquarters in Lincoln than the campaign co-manager called me into his office. He was holding the check from Christie Hefner. I innocently remarked how great it was to get that substantial check as well as all the rest we had raised in Chicago. Visibly uncomfortable, he said that we couldn't keep the check. He asked if I knew what hay the Republicans would make of a check from a Hefner connected to Playboy. This was Bible-stomping country, and we couldn't afford to stir up a religious moral controversy that would put my mother on the defensive. He told me this might fly in Chicago, but not in Nebraska.

I was stunned. After all, this wasn't a check from Playboy, but from an individual woman who wanted to support an outstanding woman candidate in another state. I asked if Mom knew about the check, and he said no—that I could decide whether or not to tell her. In the meantime we had to return the check.

My heart was thumping. "Just a minute. I feel responsible for this situation. Dawn Clark Netsch is a well-known elected official in Illinois, a woman respected for her integrity, and she did me a great favor in hosting the fund-raiser. I'm sure she invited Christie Hefner because Hefner supports all kinds of worthy causes and candidates in Illinois. I don't agree that we should return the check. But if you're insisting on it, then I should return it personally on my next trip back to Chicago. To just mail it back is tacky and an even bigger slap in her face.

"I don't want to have to do this, but I also don't want my mother distracted at this critical point in the campaign. I'm pretty sure she would feel as I do, but I'm not going to put her in the position of having to make a decision that her opponent could blow up into a nasty issue. The check came from an event I arranged, so it's my job to make the whole thing go away, as much as I disagree with this route and dread the prospect of meeting with Christie Hefner."

He thanked me quietly and said I should trust him that this course of action was necessary. "This is Nebraska."

I walked back to my cubbyhole, my hands shaking. This wasn't the first time I'd chosen to keep a campaign problem from my mother so as not to pile on additional stress in an increasingly stressful campaign, but those earlier problems were just operational, typical glitches that happen in any organization. This was different because it involved principles. I wasn't at all sure I should keep the issue from my mother, but I did.

On my next trip home I packed the tainted check in my purse. I made an appointment with Christie Hefner at the Playboy offices in downtown Chicago. On the commuter train my stomach hurt all the way to the Loop. I tried to calm down by telling myself that Christie Hefner would probably understand my predicament and not make it too difficult for me.

But I was wrong. From the moment I was ushered into her palatial office with a desk the size of a Mercedes, Christie was cold and reproachful. I tried to convey the concerns of the campaign, but she was having none of it. She raised her voice several decibels.

She told me this was just the kind of action that threatens free speech in our society and intimidates minority views. She said we'd lose the protections of our Constitution not by legislation but by the gradual, insidious erosion precipitated by this kind of sheeplike behavior. Then she blasted me, accusing me of bowing to the right-wingers who want nothing more than conformity to their definition of family values and who don't care if they have to sacrifice free speech and other fundamental rights in the process. Her final shot—shame on you and shame on your mother.

My face was burning hot, and all I wanted was to get out of there without crying. By trying to save my mother from a hard decision

that would have consequences—the kind of decision Mom had cou-
rageously made all her life—I had actually sold her down the river. By
attempting to make the issue go away, I deprived her of choice. I was
wrong. And now this crushing humiliation was my punishment.

I got up to leave and meekly muttered, "My mother doesn't know
about the check." As I slunk through Hefner's office door, I could feel
her disgust trailing me like a bad detective. My mother, Nebraska, me—
Christie Hefner had contempt for us all. As I write this, I have yet to tell
my mother.

Chapter Four

Roll Up Her Sleeves

1975–1979

"Key to Helen's effectiveness was her sense of humor about herself; she did not take herself so seriously and had a sense of proportion about who she was and what she was doing. Those who are driven by a sense of their own importance make the worst public servants."—JAN GAUGER, Lancaster County commissioner, 1972–88

"Helen was energetic, empathetic, positive. She created an atmosphere of activism. Helen was anything but a caretaker officeholder—she had great vision and worked to accomplish something together with citizens. The lasting changes that I associate with Helen are the open environment she created for people to become active and involved in their city, and her downtown beautification and tree planting. She also greatly advanced a coordinated city planning effort."—JERRY L. PETR, retired professor of economics, University of Nebraska–Lincoln

Mom's 1975 election as mayor was dramatic, even thrilling, but the drama didn't end with her election. I assumed that reading about the hand-to-hand combat of her campaign for mayor was the dramatic part, but as I poured over Dad's old clippings I found plenty of drama after the election as well. I never dreamed I'd get so caught up in the conflicts my mother faced as mayor over issues that seemed, on the surface, mundane.

That may be why politics often makes good theater and may explain why I love both. In theater and politics, we are invited as community to bear witness to storytelling, action, conflict. But because electoral campaigns present such high drama on the political stage, the audience often mistakes the conclusion of a campaign—the election—for the end of the play, the resolution of the drama; and so the audience leaves the theater to go back to real lives.

But a campaign's culmination in election is only the end of the first act, perhaps just the first scene. The deceptively lower-key action *after* the election creates the true conflict at the heart of the performance, when the victor's vision for governing is pitted against a multitude of characters and forces, seen and unseen. Who will prevail, what will result, how will life change—all these unknowns produce dramatic tension far beyond who beats whom at the polls.

The more discerning audience, an involved citizenry, sticks around for the next acts and actively engages in the unfolding drama that will affect lives and community long after the election in the first act. They suspect where the real drama lies—in the day-to-day struggles to select a new police chief, guide community growth and development, spark economic vitality, sustain neighborhoods, squeeze budgets, protect equal rights, secure energy resources—and this committed audience of citizens would never miss the second and third acts.

SHORTAGES: GAS, POWER, WATER

After her election and dramatic first test in choosing a new police chief, my mother faced a new series of conflicts. Out of the wings came clashes over energy conservation, the city's electric power system, and alternative sources of energy—spurred by threatened energy shortages and spiraling costs of fuel. Before the 1973 OPEC oil embargo, Lincolnites, like other Americans, took for granted their use of cheap and plentiful petroleum. With expanded automobile use and suburban sprawl, oil consumption in the United States had more than doubled between 1950 and 1974. That picture changed drastically with the embargo, which doubled the price of crude oil at the refinery, caused widespread shortages at the pump, and exacerbated the recession.

At one point, drivers in some parts of the country were restricted to purchasing gas on even- or odd-numbered days, depending on their license plate numbers. A national advertising campaign urged citizens

21. The mayor takes the bus to work

to hang tags from light switches saying, "Last out, Lights out: Don't Be Fuelish." The crisis prompted studies of energy conservation measures and the search for alternative and renewable energy sources.

Lincoln's mayor urged that city government be a model for others to conserve energy. She asked her department heads to encourage employees to ride the bus or organize carpools. Later, with federal funds, the city initiated a carpooling program for city employees and for business firms located near city hall as the nucleus of a citywide program. She ordered thermostats in all city buildings to be set at sixty-five degrees during the winter, and over time the city met its overall goal of reducing city energy consumption across the board (including fleet operations) by 10 percent.

The mayor herself set an example for using the Lincoln Transportation System (LTS) by riding the bus to city hall, even though other mayors had been typically provided the use of official city cars. LTS ran ads with pictures of my mother on a bus with the slogan, "The 'Easy Ridin' bus takes her Honor to work."

Soon after Mom began commuting by bus to promote energy conservation, her administrative aide, Mike Merwick, received a call from one of the bus drivers. "Hey Mike, did somebody file a complaint on me? The mayor was on my bus this morning!" Merwick assured him no, she was just riding the bus. The driver argued, "Don't lie to me. If somebody's going to fire me, I want to know!" Merwick told the driver to expect the mayor tomorrow and the day after—she was just trying to encourage the public to ride the bus.

A roast of Lincoln's first woman mayor by the all-male Gridiron Club featured a song by Chauncey Barney on Mom's use of public transportation:

Boosalis, the Queen of the City
Big sister to you and to me
Serene, enlightened and witty
Protector of each little tree.
Our traffic will never flow better
No matter how much drivers cuss
Traffic jams just don't upset her
Queen Helen rides home on the bus.

After several months of the mayor's bus riding, newly appointed Police Chief Hansen urged my mother to curtail her public transit use for safety reasons, as she kept a schedule that required waiting at deserted bus stops in the dark, morning and evening. "She's on the job before most of her employees show up at work and she's among the last to leave," noted one reporter.

Believing that local government should take the lead in finding ways to conserve energy, the mayor appointed an Energy Action Committee to develop programs to encourage citizens and businesses to reduce energy consumption. The eighteen-member committee reflected her commitment to involve all segments of Lincoln's population—cochaired by a homemaker and an electric utility executive, with members as diverse as an Amtrak ticket agent, a department store manager, a physics professor, and a high school junior. One example of the Energy Action Committee's encouragement of energy conservation measures was its award/recognition of a realty firm's use of chartered city buses to transport realtors on open-house tours; rather than each agent driving a car, realtors would present listings information on the bus between homes on the tour.

But generally consumers remained largely apathetic to energy conservation measures. They were unwilling to cut back on automobile use, and they realized little direct financial benefit for conserving power as their electric bills continued to rise astronomically. High electric rates commanded the attention of city government and citizens alike.

Lincoln Electric System, the city-owned public power utility, raised its own revenues for operations and did not rely on taxes. In two years the city's electricity rates had increased more than 80 percent, yet LES said it had secured enough power to meet demand only until 1978. To help meet electricity demand after 1978, the LES board considered building its own steam-generating plant, perhaps using solid waste (garbage) as a source of fuel.

With prospects of near-term electricity shortages and the knowledge that the city's landfill would be full in less than ten years, the city-county "Common" (the city council, the county board, and the mayor) studied garbage-fueled generation of electricity in other cities. But a consultant's report concluded that power generated by burning garbage would not be economical for LES until *1990. The mayor vowed to monitor changes in technology and pricing that could someday make garbage-fired power generation economically feasible, and she involved citizens like Curt Donaldson in the effort. "Helen brought people into their government. I was a carpenter at the time with no special expertise in government," Donaldson recalled, "but she was interested in my views. When I became informed on energy, I would watch energy issues for her and discuss them with her."

Another alternative energy source studied was solar-powered energy. The federal government and Honeywell tested a mobile solar energy lab in Lincoln because of the favorable conditions for solar energy—heating season length, cost of fuel, and high number of Nebraska sunny days. But the economics of solar energy proved as unfavorable as power generated by solid waste.

Neither solar energy nor the use of solid waste to generate power came to fruition as solutions to the 1970s energy crisis, but the oil embargo of late 1973 underscored the susceptibility of power plants to fuel shortages and focused attention on the expansion of nuclear power. LES administrator Walter Canney predicted future power shortages that even the most optimistic energy conservation plans could not prevent. Canney and the LES board urged the mayor and city council to consider adding nuclear power to its future power supply program—specifically, Lincoln's participation in constructing Omaha Public Power District's (OPPD's) second nuclear plant at Fort Calhoun. (Lincoln's share would be 13 percent of the estimated $1 billion cost.)

Citizens split on the controversial nuclear power issue. Because of skyrocketing electric rates, many Lincolnites supported the nuclear option in hopes of future rate relief. Others opposed nuclear power on economic and safety grounds and cited the experience of other large utilities nationally in canceling the construction of nuclear plants due to cost overruns, inflationary pressures, and safety shutdowns.

On a close 4–3 vote (Bailey, Robinson, Jeambey, Denney), the city council rejected Lincoln Electric System's participation in the nuclear power plant, even though the LES board had already signed a contract with OPPD to buy into the plant without first consulting the city council.

The council's rejection completely upended LES's ten-year power supply plan.

The mayor agreed with the council's action. "I'm very skeptical of the economies of going nuclear," she said, anticipating that Lincoln's share would greatly exceed the $129 million estimate and that the city would get "very little control for our money." Regardless of Lincoln's opting out, the state approved OPPD's building its second nuclear power plant.

After that state approval, Councilman Jeambey (one of the four votes against Lincoln's participation in the nuclear plant) proposed a compromise to set a maximum ceiling of $129 million for Lincoln's share (rather than an open-ended 13 percent share). Jeambey's compromise proposal passed 4–3 because he switched his earlier vote. Even though OPPD subsequently rejected Lincoln's compromise terms, the proposal legally constituted a continued offer by Lincoln to participate in the project and, therefore, OPPD would be entitled to accept the offer in the future.

Whenever the council approved an ordinance or resolution, the mayor had eight days to approve or veto it. Overriding a mayoral veto required five council votes. With only minutes to spare on the eighth day, Mom vetoed the city council's approval of Lincoln's participation in OPPD's nuclear power plant, once again dashing LES's hopes for nuclear power.

The nuclear power plant issue came to an ironic end. Less than two years after the mayor's veto, OPPD itself canceled the nuclear plant because of skyrocketing final cost estimates and projected rate increases of up to 60 percent if the plant were built. OPPD had to swallow $40 million in contract cancellation costs rather than proceed with escalating costs of well over $1 billion; plus OPPD was sued for another $30 million that the Nebraska Public Power District had paid toward construction of the defunct plant. OPPD's cancellation vindicated the mayor's veto and votes of the council minority. The City of Lincoln continued to attack the energy crisis without taking the nuclear power route.

Lincoln's water supply also presented issues of future scarcity. Those who have not lived in parts of the West or Midwest may not fully appreciate the magnitude and complexity of water resource issues. City and state governments in water-scarce areas face tough decisions about financing and securing adequate future water supplies. Early in Mom's mayoral term, Nebraska Planning and Programming director Don Nelson gave legislative testimony that "the great crisis of the 1980s and 1990s will be water" and that it would "make the current energy crisis look like a school picnic."

Using her strong-mayor authority, my mother set an aggressive agenda for acquiring more water lands. Because much of its groundwater is salty, Lincoln was forced in 1930 to acquire land for water wells along the Platte River at Ashland, Nebraska, but the combined Ashland and Lincoln wells were not an adequate future water supply for a growing city. The mayor and her administrators met with Sarpy County officials to initiate the acquisition of nearly a thousand additional acres of land just across the Platte River that would ensure the city's water supply for the next twenty-five years. Although the water land acquisition had a hefty price tag, one can only guess how much higher the costs would have been in later *years. "Lincoln is paying a price it deserves to pay" due to the "neglect of past administrations," an editorial claimed. "The city should have had the foresight years ago to make adequate provision for its future water needs."

The mayor wasn't interested in being a mere caretaker during her time in office, passing off the tough problems to the next mayor. By securing a dependable water supply and supporting energy conservation and alternative energy measures, she helped ensure a healthy future for her growing community long after her job as mayor would end. As Richard Herman, former *Lincoln Journal* editorial pages editor, suggests, "LES is in far better financial shape now than it would have been had Helen and the city council approved the building of the nuclear power plant. She also looked way ahead in planning for Lincoln's future access to water, which Omaha now wishes it had."

THE COMPREHENSIVE PLAN AND STEVENS CREEK

After Mom's election and throughout 1976, new flashpoints erupted within the city council and between mayor and council over proposed policies to update the city's Comprehensive Plan, originally adopted in

1961 to guide the city's future growth and land use. When Mom was elected mayor, the Comprehensive Plan (Comp Plan) was being updated through an extensive, multi-year process of citizen involvement (Goals and Policies Committee). The most vehement Comp Plan arguments concerned proposed provisions that favored concentric city growth to the north, south, and west surrounding a strong downtown central business district core, and that also opposed the city's eastern expansion into the Stevens Creek watershed.

My mother's vocal opposition to the city's expansion into Stevens Creek began in her city council days, continued through the mayoral campaign against Sam Schwarzkopf, and would become a hallmark of her leadership as mayor. Council members Bailey, Jeambey, and Robinson shared my mother's philosophy that extending city utility services eastward into a different watershed (Stevens Creek)—before fully developing land to the north, south, and west that had existing streets and utility services—would be inefficient and exorbitantly costly to the city. Allowing development in Stevens Creek would only discourage concentric development in the existing watershed and weaken the central business district. But developers—particularly those with landholdings in Stevens Creek—and other business interests favored sooner development of Stevens Creek rather than postponement to allow for concentric development, and they found some sympathetic council ears.

As debate continued over the Comp Plan, a particular development proposal underscored the planning issues of eastward expansion into Stevens Creek. In 1976 Southeast Community College proposed locating a new campus for vocational classes on a 115-acre site in the Stevens Creek watershed and wanted city annexation of the site with extension of city sewer and water services. My mother expressed concern that allowing the college to build on the site would lead to more premature encroachment in Stevens Creek. The mayor and city planners offered to help the college locate a site closer to downtown that would avoid urbanization of a new watershed and conform to the concentric growth plan for the city intended to avoid "urban sprawl."

After negotiating with the college, my mother recommended the council approve a development agreement allowing the college to construct its desired facilities on the site's west end, which was not in the forbidden watershed, and to use the remainder for horticulture and recreational uses. The city, in turn, would annex only the building portion (not in Stevens Creek), extend city utilities and services (water, sewer, police), and retain approval powers over location of future buildings and parking.

The mayor's conditional annexation contract for the building portion of the Southeast Community College site—unprecedented but somewhat similar to the city's special-use permits—illustrated her creative approach to municipal problem solving. Mom found a way to support land development of positive value to the city while still protecting her consistent commitment to long-term land-use planning for a healthy city.

However, the Southeast Community College issue and the larger question of development in Stevens Creek only reinforced the perception in some quarters of the mayor as anti-business and anti-growth. The chamber of commerce and those business interests long anxious to "lift the Stevens Creek veil" supported the college's original plan and criticized the city, particularly Planning Director Doug Brogden, for having its head in the sand on Stevens Creek. On the other hand, city officials received editorial praise from the *Evening Journal* for their cost-sensitive planning:

> Expansion of residential subdivisions and business enterprises into the [Stevens Creek] watershed carries citywide economic and tax implications. In a private-enterprise sense, a developer can ignore associated community costs—such as extension of public services, fire and police protection, utilities, etc. Taxpayers can't. They help finance the growth.
>
> By saying "no, not yet," to further eastward spread until southern, northern and some western regions are built up around the Lincoln Center [downtown], elected officials are bravely trying to limit public costs almost always triggered by physical growth. Getting the greatest mileage out of lower public cost growth possibilities before moving on to more expensive ones is at the heart of the Stevens Creek-later policy. That kind of dollar squeezing is what most business people usually think government ought constantly to do. Not all, apparently.

Former *Lincoln Journal* editorial pages editor Richard Herman still agrees with the wisdom of the mayor's planning policy: "Helen waged tough battles on city planning. She managed to control the direction of growth pretty well by not extending streets and water and sewer lines until it made economic sense. The Stevens Creek line was held for thirty years against pressure from developer interests."

In January 1977, after several years of study and debate, the city council and the county board finally adopted the long-awaited updated Comprehensive Plan. The Comp Plan would serve until 2000 (with five-year updates) as a guideline for city growth and a blueprint for decisions on critical land-use issues: residential development; downtown redevelopment; limited eastward growth into Stevens Creek until more growth was achieved to the south, west, and north; hospital expansion; shopping centers; and public projects such as parks, schools, libraries, and streets. The Comp Plan guidelines were premised on future population growth projections (e.g., a projected doubling of the city's population to 325,000 by the year *2000).

With the mayor's help, the final 1977 Comp Plan also included a last-minute addition urged by the Citizen Task Force for Community Development: neighborhood improvement plans for the Malone, Near South, South Salt Creek, Havelock, and University Place neighborhoods. A Comprehensive Plan without specific focus on preservation and development of neighborhoods would have been sorely lacking in the mayor's *eyes.

THE 1977 CITY COUNCIL ELECTION: "BICKERING" AND A 5–2 SPLIT

Although the 1977 Comp Plan had gained city council approval, the plan's policies for guiding the city's growth and development would continue to engender heated debate for years, especially during political campaigns. The next city election, just a few months after the Comp Plan's adoption in January 1977, could shift the balance on the city council and greatly affect the implementation of the plan.

In the spring of 1977, two years after Mom's election as mayor, three council members' terms were expiring: Sue Bailey, John Robinson, and Council Chairman Max Denney. Denney announced that he would not seek reelection, but many speculated that he would later run for another political office, perhaps mayor. Without Denney in the race, the spring election could tip the balance on the city council toward those who generally supported the mayor (Bailey, Robinson, and Jeambey) or toward those who generally opposed her (Baker, Cook, and Sikyta). One political reporter forecast that if the mayor's opponents were to gain at least one ally, which appeared likely, "they could move into the Council driver's seat"; and if they were to capture two council seats, "they could become a real powerhouse" with added clout and the ability to override mayoral vetoes.

The 1977 city council primary election produced few surprises in the top six finishers who would vie in the general election for three open seats. Incumbent Sue Bailey led the pack, and incumbent John Robinson came in a strong third. Joe Hampton, president of a construction company and a developer with strong connections to the business community, finished second. Many recognized that Hampton, as a real estate developer with major landholdings, would have to declare more conflicts of interest on land-use decisions than other council candidates. A *Journal* endorsement of Hampton expressed reservations but took "Hampton at his word that he would do nothing in the next four years to cause or encourage any breaking of the Stevens Creek line."

Coming in fourth was Leo Scherer, tavern owner and likely spokesman for small-business interests, who had "no particular affection for Mayor Helen Boosalis." He had been the former director of Community Development and aide to Sam Schwarzkopf, Mom's predecessor. When she was elected mayor in 1975, Scherer said that "under no circumstances would he have remained at City Hall as a member of the Boosalis administration."

None of the city council candidates in 1977 injected the mayor into the campaign fray or publicly criticized her administration—surprising, since "any mayor, especially one as visible as Mrs. Boosalis, seems to be a sitting duck for political potshots." But the council newcomer campaigns did raise the matter of "bickering" between the council and the mayor as an impediment to resolving the city's problems. Hampton's well-financed campaign emphasized his pledge that he would help end the "bickering" in city hall. A *Star* editorial called "bickering" the phoniest issue in the council campaign, since bickering (aka disagreeing) is an entirely natural political phenomenon; it said that "the real issue, if we can probe through the smokescreen, is in electing one faction or another of councilmen who can *win* the bickering."

A major upset in the 1977 city council general election seated a formidable faction that would soon make Mom's first two years of "bickering" with the council seem like the good old days. Sue Bailey, my mom's greatest political ally on the council and longtime League of Women Voters colleague, went from finishing first in the primary election to fourth in the general election a month later, thus losing her seat. Bailey's defeat was an "unhappy stunner" in the light of most predictions of her shoo-in victory. Even Joe Hampton, who placed first in the general election, admitted that her loss "shocked the heck out of me."

The mayor was losing not only her greatest political ally on the city council but also the close relationship she and Bailey had developed through twenty years of working together on city problems. No one knew better than Mom how well suited Sue Bailey was to public service. A *Journal* editorial called her a "particularly fine council member, one who truly comprehends the sifting, reflective, open nature of the ideal legislator," while the *Star* posed, "Why such a good, decent, competent public servant should be turned out is a question difficult to answer and a fact hard to accept."

Some attributed Bailey's loss to overconfidence of her supporters because of her apparent shoo-in status after the primary, others to her spending the least of all the candidates, and others to a backlash from dissatisfaction with Mayor Boosalis or a general anti-female backlash. Council newcomer Leo Scherer, who moved up to second place after his fourth-place primary finish, interpreted Bailey's defeat as dissatisfaction with the Boosalis administration and an indication "that the University influence and the League of Women Voters have to be balanced with the total community." UNL political science professor and election expert Robert Sittig offered that Bailey did not fit the composite model of the "preferred candidate" that had been drawn from nationwide nonpartisan elections over the previous twenty years: "youngish white male with a business or professional background." That, he said, went a long way toward explaining why the winning newcomer candidates—

Joe Hampton and Leo Scherer—won and Sue Bailey lost in a very close race.

One reporter characterized the election's outcome as "homogenizing" the city council by electing two businessmen and ousting the council's only woman. In fact, this would be the first time in eighteen years (including Mom's sixteen-year city council tenure) that no woman would be serving on the council. A Paul Fell political cartoon in the *Lincoln Journal* depicted the anticipated five-man council majority crooning outside Mayor Helen Boosalis's office door, "A Woman's Place Is in the Home!"

With the election results, my mother and the media knew that she was in for "rough times." Much analysis and speculation ensued about the new 5–2 council split and its impact on my mother's mayoral leadership and potential future control of the mayor's office. A *Star* editorial examined the political alignments of the formidable new five-man majority: Bob Sikyta ("never been a fan of the mayor's, he says"); Dick Baker ("not as unreconstructed as Sikyta, but tends to make life miserable for the Mayor nevertheless"); Steve Cook ("long a political intimate of former Mayor Sam Schwarzkopf"); Joe Hampton ("instrumental . . . in bringing to Lincoln political malcontents from Boulder, Colorado and Madison, Wisconsin . . . to tell our voters that the city would go to hell if Mrs. Boosalis were elected"); and Leo Scherer ("Schwartzkopf's administrative assistant, . . . a department head for the former mayor, and one of his chief political lieutenants").

Just a few months after the 1977 election, *Star* reporter Gordon Winters noted that council members disagreed on the reasons for the 5–2 council split that the election produced, although all agreed that the traditional political labels "conservative" and "liberal" were misleading and could not explain the split. Neither were party labels illuminating, as only one council member was a Democrat (Robinson). Councilman Baker characterized the 5–2 split as business versus anti-business, while Councilman Robinson thought the split represented the divide between those who think government should help businessmen make a profit and those who consider what is best for the entire community.

Councilman Hampton claimed that those in the five-man majority "are men of action who arrive at decisions and implement them, while

Jeambey and Robinson [the two-man minority] are men of words who put off decisions." In turn, Councilman Jeambey took a simple view of the split: "There are five who are committed to making the mayor look bad." Both Jeambey and Robinson felt that the other five members of the council "try to manipulate events . . . to downgrade the public's perception of the mayor's performance."

Whether or not the 5–2 council split reflected "lingering resentment by those who backed incumbent Sam Schwartzkopf in the 1975 mayoral campaign," it gave all indications of being intractable. A super-majority of five had the power to override mayoral vetoes and appeared unstoppable.

Squaring off on the minority side of the 5–2 equation was my mother, who had not hesitated to flex her strong-mayor muscles over the previous two years. As a *Journal* editorial put it, "While the City Council majority has the clout to run over everybody else, it doesn't own the mayor." She would prove able to stand up to this powerful majority, again and again. Jan Gauger, then Lancaster County commissioner, could identify with the forces at play: "When I was elected to the County Board [in 1972] I, too, was up against the good old boys club that Helen was up against. They oppose you when you're weak—and when you're strong, they *really* oppose you."

Councilman Baker was voted chairman of the newly constituted council on a 5–2 vote, prompting one front-row observer to comment, "That's the way the votes are going to go for the next two years [until the next council election]." Chairman Baker called for a meeting with the council, mayor, and city legal department to define the duties of the council and the mayor's office. The move was on to pull in the reins of the feisty mayor by devising a formal procedure to restrict Mayor Boosalis in addressing the council because council members complained that "Mrs. Boosalis pops up and addresses the Council without first being recognized."

From afar I was concerned about the extraordinary stress that I imagined my mother was enduring. Not only had she lost Sue Bailey, her close colleague and confidante on the council, but now she faced an impenetrable wall of resistance to her vision for the city. From my vantage point in Chicago, I cringed to hear her talk of the new five-man council majority that generally opposed her, and how much time and effort she spent anticipating their next moves, trying to stay a step or two ahead of the five-man offense.

Whether as a preemptive move or a genuine effort to promote more harmonious relations, the mayor sent a peace offering to the new council—a new transportation department, which Councilman Sikyta had been urging for two years. My mother had resisted increasing the number of city departments and preferred a transportation division within an existing department. Nonetheless, she pulled this surprise turnaround, saying she "guessed she had been hung up in her opposition."

The move was considered politically adept. "Mayor Boosalis demonstrates she has practical political moxie," read a *Journal* editorial. "By recommending a new consolidated transportation department," it continued, "the mayor did a couple of things. She made a significant public showing of willingness to cooperate with the new City Council majority on matters of great substance to leaders of that majority. This goes beyond tokenism. Second, she beat the majority to the punch, since it is capable of and maybe even anxious to demonstrate its macho."

Unfortunately, the mayor's olive branch gesture did not turn out to signal a new and improved era in council-mayor relations. "The heralded end of bickering will not come, it appears, before the next city elections," lamented one editorial. The next city election was two years away, and indeed the bickering persisted and frequently escalated to all-out council-mayor wars. No important issue remained unscathed by the warfare.

Issues of energy production and rates stayed in the spotlight. Given the enormous public investment in the electric system and citizens' concerns about skyrocketing rates and capital outlays, in 1978 the mayor proposed that city officials and citizens be allowed increased participation in LES's planning process for meeting future power needs. In response to her proposal, Councilman Hampton fired back, "I think we ought to keep our cotton-picking hands out of the day-to-day administration of LES." Mom agreed that city government should not involve itself in day-to-day LES operations, but she warned against allowing LES to operate in isolation. A *Star* editorial criticized the council majority's rejection of the mayor's LES planning proposal: "It was a vindictive

slap at the mayor—and a shortsighted action. . . . The council majority
. . . seemed to be more interested in saying 'no' to the mayor than in
recognizing citizen interest in the enormous investment in the electric
system."

The adopted 1977 Comprehensive Plan became another target of
the new council majority. The battle over Stevens Creek development
waged on despite the Comp Plan's "resolution" of that issue. The five-
man majority began "making mincemeat of the Comprehensive Plan
to the ultimate detriment of the city," said a *Star* editorial in late 1977.
The number of council approvals of land-use changes that were clearly
prohibited by the Comp Plan continued to mount—for example, approval of industrial zoning for a thirty-acre tract along Salt Creek
(owned by the former mayor's brother) that had been designated for
park development in the Comp Plan, as well as approval of a forty-
one-acre rural housing development in the Stevens Creek watershed.
The mayor's veto power was largely ineffective as the five consistent
council votes were sufficient to stomp her vetoes. "Real estate developers and speculators would have to be blind not to see the holes advan-
tageously blasted through the Comprehensive Plan for them by Councilmen Baker, Cook, Hampton, Scherer and Sikyta," warned a *Journal*
editorial.

Amid the ongoing friction over land use designated in the Comp
Plan, a working committee was named to begin the task of preparing a
revised zoning code to implement the Comp Plan. City and county officials and one citizen made up the committee, staffed by the city Planning Director Doug Brogden. But the council majority wanted to retain
more control over zoning, observed a *Journal* editorial: "Reflecting its
animus of Brogden and the Boosalis administration, the Council majority decided to hire its own experts on the subject. The bland explanation
which went with the Council's independent action was that the city
dads—women having been banished from the City Council by the electorate—wanted to know what kind of innovative things are being done
in other places dealing with city planning and zoning."

The council's outside consultant report must have been a joy to read
for the five-man council majority. The consultants did not favor the use
of zoning or restricting extension of public utilities in order to slow city

growth to the east (including Stevens Creek) until concentric development to the north, south, and west could balance it. They found that
incentives for eastward city growth were too strong to control because
of existing "prestige" factors in east Lincoln, such as golf courses, parks,
hospitals, shopping facilities, and scenic views. The report touched off
new rounds of council fire and opened up the scarcely healing wounds
from years of fighting over the Comprehensive Plan.

No sooner was the consultant report released, however, than Councilman Jeambey (of the anemic two-vote minority bloc) charged that
some council members had privately lobbied the consultants to ensure
that the report would support their viewpoint. Hampton, Sikyta, and
Cook conceded that they had lunch with the consultants and took them
on a tour of east Lincoln before the report was written, but they denied
trying to influence the *report.

So rather than settling Comp Plan issues, the consultant report—
and its suspect objectivity—guaranteed that the fight over city land use,
development, and growth would continue throughout my mother's
term in office, gobbling enormous amounts of her time and attention.
The ongoing dispute boiled down to a basic difference in philosophies:
whether community growth—where and when—should be controlled
more by developers and landowners than by the public, or whether cities should try to direct and influence community growth.

DOWNTOWN REVITALIZATION AND BEAUTIFICATION

The mayor found more support than usual from her city council adversaries for her vision to revitalize downtown Lincoln. She knew from
the experience of other cities how easily a city's downtown retail center
could lose its prominence and viability. One way to prevent that scenario was to make the protection of Lincoln Center (the downtown)
an "iron condition" of the Comprehensive Plan, with zoning restrictions on location and phasing of future outlying shopping center development. Existing outlying shopping centers (such as Gateway) had
already diluted somewhat the strength of the downtown retail core,
but zoning restrictions could help stem the retail drain. Zoning could
be used to encourage theaters, restaurants, and other entertainment
venues to bring people and vitality to downtown.

Mom introduced downtown street festivals, including the first Lincolnfest where she cajoled pork producers to supply the BBQ, drawing thousands of people downtown. She hoped to purchase and redevelop the old federal building as a downtown performing arts complex, but the idea was later defeated in a bond issue referendum. As part of efforts to attract a mix of people, the mayor experimented with providing temporary senior center sites downtown. Involving her old neighborhood friends Sue Shelley, Sue Blomgren, and Betty Pfeifer in the project, a permanent site for the city's senior center was located on O Street in the heart of downtown.

To strengthen the downtown core, my mother's administration completed a beautification project along downtown O Street a little more than two years after her election as mayor—street and sidewalk improvements, trees, bricks, benches, and other amenities. The redevelopment plan was originated in the early 1970s by leaders of downtown property owners, but it had stalled over a cost-sharing arrangement between the owners and the city. Although some downtown merchants complained during two summers of construction and blocked traffic from the beautification project, most were pleased with the results, and so was the mayor. "We didn't let our downtown area get as shabby as other cities did before we began our planning," she said. "There's been a lot of hard work and cooperation between elected officials and the business community."

Many in Lincoln still positively associate my mother's era as mayor with transformative downtown beautification and tree planting, but there were those in the 1970s who belittled the beautification efforts as predictable concerns of a woman mayor. According to political reporter Don Walton, "Part of Helen's anti-business label was gender-based and reinforced by her concern for neighborhoods and for the beauty of the city, such as planting trees on O Street."

Lack of adequate parking remained a significant downtown problem. With boundless enthusiasm for downtown revitalization, the mayor embarked on an ambitious project called the Centrum—the redevelopment of an entire downtown block, with a large parking garage financed by the city on half the block and a retail complex financed by private enterprise on the other half. The project utilized one of my mother's favorite development tools: public-private partnership. She proposed raising parking fines and meter fees (then only five cents) to help pay for the city's parking garage portion of the Centrum.

Once the city council lined up behind the project, Mom's administration began negotiations to acquire the property and negotiate with all forty-four property interests on the Centrum block. The mayor grew impatient with the process, saying, "I wish we could move faster on it. There's a critical need for more parking downtown. With each month's delay, the costs go up." After purchasing 80 percent of the block, the city was forced to file eminent domain proceedings against holdout landowners and filed the first condemnation lawsuit to obtain the building that housed the Adult Book and Cinema Store.

The summer of 1976 the mayor took special delight in throwing bricks through several downtown windows, rather than a typical ribbon cutting, to launch the demolition of buildings for the Centrum project one year after she took office as mayor. The chairman of her Downtown Advisory Committee, Dick White, described the Centrum project as "the most important key to the maintenance of a strong central business district in downtown Lincoln." Her administration solicited developer proposals to construct the retail portion of the Centrum, and the council approved Minneapolis developer Watson Centers. My mother had always been fond of the downtown skywalks in her hometown of Minneapolis, so an option for skywalks connecting the Centrum with other downtown buildings was included in the plans.

Two years later the Centrum's retail segment had to be scaled back because of spiraling construction costs due to double-digit inflation after the original financial projections. Meeting with the developers to assure herself and the city council that everything possible had been tried to avoid scaling down the project, the mayor recognized her responsibility for its success: "If the Centrum doesn't fly, I know very well where the blame will be aimed . . . and I accept that." For once the mayor and city council put up a united front, approving project modifications and expressing confidence in the completion of the Centrum. The city-financed parking garage went forward as planned to provide over one thousand precious downtown parking spaces.

NEIGHBORHOOD REDEVELOPMENT

Mom's focus on downtown redevelopment in no way diminished her concern with redevelopment needs of commercial areas in older neighborhoods. She found less cooperation from the council for these lower-profile areas than for the downtown business and commercial center. But downtown revitalization composed only part of her strong urban development program, which included redevelopment of the older Havelock and University Place commercial areas and the Malone and Clinton neighborhoods.

These neighborhood redevelopment efforts formed a perfect fit with my mother's commitment to citizen involvement. Giving citizens a voice and means to help renew their own neighborhoods was an ideal way to share government responsibilities with community residents. The mayor's restructured Urban Development Department became the organizing force behind neighborhood redevelopment, and its new director, George Chick, brought as much energy and commitment to the task as his boss.

Federal funds for neighborhood redevelopment flowed through the Community Development Block Grant (CDBG) program. The federal strings attached required citizen participation programs in neighborhoods receiving grant funds—not at all onerous for a city administration already committed to citizen input. Lincoln's Urban Development Department added a neighborhood assistance office for coordinating resident involvement in the redevelopment of targeted communities.

As a result, strong and vocal neighborhood organizations multiplied and grew. The federal Department of Housing and Urban Development recognized Lincoln for having one of the best neighborhood assistance programs in the country. The city had never heard so much from its neighborhood citizens as they became effective and empowered communicators of community need. The mayor welcomed citizens taking responsibility for improving their neighborhoods, not only through matching dollars but also through matching commitment, input, and hard work.

The growing power of neighborhoods in Lincoln, with strong encouragement from the mayor, mirrored a self-government movement gaining traction nationally. According to a presidential commission on neighborhoods, neighborhood power could decrease government by returning to residents the ability to influence policy making. "The neighborhood movement represents demand for self-government," said the commission report, "and for de-bureaucratizing America." Neighborhood residents began feeling less alienated from city hall, which had previously seemed "as distant as Capitol Hill." In Lincoln, many neighborhood organizations that formed in the early 1970s in reaction to perceived threats to neighborhoods (zoning changes, street building, air pollution) were now inspired to be proactive in helping shape city decisions affecting their areas, such as parks, swimming pools, and district elections.

While encouraging active resident participation in neighborhood redevelopment, the mayor viewed neighborhood and business development as complementary. "Helen made sure that staff represented the *city* in working with neighborhoods, that they represented a city-wide perspective and not just neighborhoods," recalls former administrative director Mike Merwick. "She did not favor the neighborhoods over business, but wanted the neighborhoods to be on a par with business interests and have an equal voice, a level playing field."

Some council members, however, were far less enamored with actively involved neighborhood organizations and complained that the city's Urban Development Department (particularly its neighborhood assistance office) played too much of an "activist" role by empowering neighborhoods to work against positions favored by the city council. Councilman Hampton argued that the Urban Development Department should represent city hall in the neighborhoods and "not advocate the change or overthrow of city policy . . . and we find that happening." Councilman Sikyta wanted to eliminate the Urban Development Department to avoid duplication of planning and save taxpayers money. The mayor railed against the "activist" charges directed at the new department, arguing that neighborhood assistance staff "can't effectively assist neighborhoods by being passive. . . . There are people who will be threatened by neighborhood involvement. I am not one of those people."

The new five-man council majority initiated an independent performance audit of the Urban Development Department, hoping to curtail the city's active role with neighborhood organizations. But a *Journal* editorial surmised that the audit findings must have disappointed the complaining council members: "There's been a suspicion some of the community's movers and shakers had hoped the audit would turn the largely federally-financed agency into something of a public relations rock around the Boosalis administration's neck." Instead, the nationally recognized firm of Peat, Marwick and Mitchell reported that the city's new Urban Development Department had discharged its responsibilities in an effective manner. The editorial recognized the positive role of neighborhoods in the city's urban development effort: "It certainly was easier for municipal government to have its say years ago. Neighborhoods were less cohesive and active. But restoration of the Daddy Knows Best condition is not likely soon."

ALL-AMERICA CITY

The high level of citizen involvement in neighborhood development and so many other areas of city governance propelled Lincoln's designation as an All-America City in 1978, my mother's third year as mayor. Out of 470 nominations and 100 finalist cities, Lincoln was one of ten cities to win the distinguished All-America City award from the National Municipal League in its competition titled "Responsible Citizens and Responsive Government."

Representing the range of Lincoln's citizen involvement in downtown revitalization, neighborhood redevelopment, and the Comprehensive Plan, three *citizens accompanied Mom to Denver to make a presentation before the All-America City jury of public and private leaders headed by Dr. George Gallup, public opinion analyst and foreman of the jury for twenty-five years. Nationally syndicated columnist Neal Peirce wrote about Lincoln's winning the coveted award based on its citizen participation: "Like other cities, Lincoln has faced obstacles: getting downtown merchants to believe in downtown revitalization in the face of outlying shopping center growth and maintaining citizens' interest once immediate crisis situations have been resolved. But with some justification, Mayor Helen Boosalis says her city has become a 'stronghold of citizen participation.'"

Lincoln celebrated winning the All-America City award with an all-city picnic, band concert, and ceremony in Antelope Park on June 13, 1978. But even such a positive event honoring Lincoln's recognition could not erase the deep political division between my mother and the council's five-man majority. As the mayor accepted the All-America City award from George Gallup, only Councilmen Jeambey and Robinson joined her on the bandstand stage. The absence of the other city council members prompted one official to quip from the stage, "Will you look under things out there and see if you can find any more of them?" Later, in response to criticism of his absence from the celebration, Councilman Baker said, "I didn't think it was a big thing not to be there . . . there's something for us (councilmen) to do every night if we want to." The more likely reason for the absence of the council majority was that the celebration "was Lincoln's party and the Mayor's show."

Despite the conspicuous absence of so many city fathers, the spirit of the occasion could not be dampened. "The Mayor was everywhere," said one reporter. "One of her own countrymen said she reminded him of 'a Greek mother' keeping all the guests happy." And from the bandstand, George Gallup, generous in his praise for Lincoln, said its citizen mobilization set an example for the nation. "Informed competent citizens . . . are the key to good local, national and state government," he said. "I don't know of another city where citizen participation has been handled so intelligently and the results so well used and implemented." Although the five absent councilmen did not hear his words, Gallup's praise was not lost on the broader community, as an editorial in the *Star* noted the following day:

> Gallup's comments are greatly appreciated by those people in Lincoln who have worked with Mayor Helen Boosalis in cultivating citizen interest and participation in local affairs. It was fitting that Mrs. Boosalis accepted the plaque on behalf of the city. . . . It was somewhat fitting, too, that those city council members who have most strongly opposed the idea of citizen participation were among the five councilmen who failed to attend the ceremony.
>
> It is easy to be cynical about citizen involvement in local government. It is, like the broader democratic concept, cumber-

some, time-consuming, at times inefficient. . . . In Lincoln, citizens speak and have spoken their will through the neighborhood organizations, through the Goals and Policies Committee and on the city's boards and commissions as a result of a policy seeking broad representation in appointive offices.

My mother, who has never liked receiving awards as an individual, was unmistakenly proud of this special All-America City award to the city of Lincoln and its citizen volunteers.

MORE BUDGETING, MORE BICKERING

Lincoln's receipt of the prestigious All-America City award did not suggest that the mayor and the city could rest on past laurels. The award gave a well-deserved boost of recognition to the hard work that so many citizens were contributing to their community's well-being, and to the role of my mother and her staff in encouraging those contributions. But no award could measure the total effort it took—mostly behind the scenes—to keep city operations running smoothly.

From her city hall office, the mayor directed the nuts-and-bolts work for the relentless annual budget process: crunching numbers, trimming expenses, forecasting revenues. In 1976, in the face of increasing costs, high inflation, and a cutback in federal revenue *sharing, my mother had issued strict budgeting guidelines for department heads: to maintain and work toward consolidation of existing levels of service with no new programs, to reassign personnel to improve productivity, and to hold the line on personnel expenditures (from an already-reduced level).

With the new 5–2 majority, council review of the mayor's proposed budget in 1977 was more intense than ever. Frustrated by their inability to find places to cut in her lean budgets—similar to Governor Jim Exon's "perennial success in straight jacketing the Legislature at budget time"—some councilmen looked for areas to add spending. According to the *Star*, "The old budget-cutter, Councilman Bob Sikyta, commented that 'I feel as frustrated as much not knowing what to add in as not knowing what to cut.'"

By her fourth annual proposed budget, in 1978, my mother had wrestled the twin monsters of decreasing revenues and rising costs due to "galloping inflation"; she had come out at least even, if not on top. Those who had questioned the business competence of the woman mayor, with her pie-in-the-sky belief in citizen involvement, had to notice how tightly she was running the fiscal ship of state—even those on the council dedicated to exposing any fiscal weakness they could find in the mayor. The *Journal* reflected on Mom's fiscal performance during these challenging economic times:

> After several weeks of intensive checking under the rocks and prodding suspicious-looking figures with pointed sticks, the City Council has completed its preliminary scrutiny of Mayor Boosalis' proposed new budget. Does it seem to you remarkable that after such tough auditing the council made an aggregate cut of only $2,291 in the Mayor's recommended tax-supported budget? . . . What that says, at least superficially, is that Mayor Boosalis submitted a budget with almost no fat. . . .
>
> When Helen Boosalis was voted Lincoln's chief executive, our judgment was that her most difficult continuing challenge would be on the fiscal front. She seems to have met that challenge. Successive city councils have found it anything but easy to pare Boosalis budgets.

Despite the mayor's success in proposing lean, mean budgets that stood up under intense council scrutiny, council-mayor relations continued to deteriorate. Mom had been a thorn in the side of Councilman Sikyta ("the mayor's most vocal critic") since their days as council colleagues, and her attending council meetings nearly drove him wild when he became council chairman in 1978, as *Journal* reporter Warren Weber had predicted: "Friction and power clashes between chairman Sikyta and Mayor Helen Boosalis are also automatically assumed." Councilman Cook agreed that the mayor should be ruled out of order when making remarks to the council unless asked a direct question. "Cook pointedly says that he thinks the mayor ought to stay in her office during council meetings," confirmed Weber, and that "if she wants to keep up with council proceedings she could listen to the council squawk box the way former Mayor Sam Schwartzkopf did."

After one year on the council, Councilman Hampton proposed a referendum for amending the City Charter to ensure the legislative branch open access to information from city departments. When the city attorney confirmed that the City Charter already guaranteed council access to such information, Councilman Hampton withdrew his proposed charter amendment. Editorials examined Hampton's motivation for introducing the amendment and concluded that "the real thrust of the Hampton amendment is to erode Lincoln's strong mayor form of municipal government" and "to harass and embarrass the present mayor—for no good reason."

The bickering among council members took a particularly ugly turn in November 1977 during a four-hour public hearing in packed city council chambers on a proposed ordinance to strengthen the power of the Human Rights Commission. Councilman Hampton opposed granting the commission the power to subpoena, initiate complaints, and assess damages; he proposed that only businesses employing fifteen or more persons be subject to discrimination charges. In response to Hampton's statement "I don't see any point in us being the trailblazer," Human Rights Commission chairman Dr. Richard Powell argued, "We're not a bunch of flaming liberals. Some of our Commission members are as conservative or more than the people on the council."

After the vehement debate on the proposed ordinance and his proposed amendments to water it down, Councilman Hampton used the most disparaging racial *slur to attack his fellow councilman John Robinson. The council bickering had reached new heights—or depths. An editorial in the *Star* captured reaction not only to Hampton's remark but also to the heightened discord at city hall:

> We never did believe that Councilman Joe Hampton's campaign pledge to "end the bickering" at City Hall was in reality one of his top priorities. He did not "end the bickering"; indeed, he has thoroughly poisoned the air with his attack on Council colleague John Robinson last week. . . .
>
> This is a sad time for Lincoln. Something is happening here

that hasn't happened in our memory. Goodwill and cooperation seem to have vanished from the City Council chambers. . . . People who would gladly serve the city are being rejected right and left by a majority of council members. . . . Polarization is more apparent now than it ever was before the politically fraudulent "end the bickering" campaign.

Despite the dissension, my mother's administration kept hurtling forward to accomplish her long list of ambitious plans in what Mom knew would be a short four-year time frame. But the second half of her term—after the 1977 election produced the 5–2 council split—must have been excruciatingly painful at times, even with her optimistic nature.

To some, the political turmoil at city hall was inevitable. The five-man council majority shared a commitment to recapturing the mayor's office for one of their own, and the *Star* predicted a protracted battle: "Add the fact that the mayor is a woman to a burning desire to return the mayor's office to forces which felt much more welcome there prior to May 1975, and you have the makings of a marathon political grudge match which might culminate only after the city election of 1979, depending on the outcome of that election."

The coming city election in 1979 to choose the mayor and four city council members would prove to be more than the culmination of a political grudge match. It would turn out to give new meaning to the admonition of the Greek philosopher Heraclitus: "Expect the unexpected."

Roots—All Greek to Me
1909–1951

"Your mother's values and my values—an obligation to give back to society—were very much rooted in the sacrifice and trailblazing of our immigrant families. A lot of what we've been able to accomplish had to do with who they were."—GEORGE V. VOINOVICH, U.S. senator (Ohio), governor of Ohio, 1990–98, mayor of Cleveland, 1979–88

"Your mother's working in the family restaurant business confirms what a Greek American friend once told me: 'The restaurant business is the perfect preparation for politics—you have to deal with everyone who walks in the door.'"—PAUL SARBANES, U.S. senator (Maryland), 1977–2007

My mother is a great storyteller. In gatherings of most any size and purpose—family, social, political—folks love to hear Mom's stories. That doesn't mean she is a poor listener or monopolizes conversations; to the contrary, she draws out the quiet person in a group with her interested questions and inclusive comments. But when she tells stories, she can enliven a group of actuaries on a slow day.

I grew up listening to my mom's stories about her childhood and asked to hear them over and over. Her world as a first-generation child of immigrant parents growing up during the Great Depression was completely alien to me, and exotic. Having requested and heard the tales so many times, I can recite my mother's family lore almost in her own voice. If I get a few facts wrong, then she probably got them wrong, too, when she related them to my five-year-old, eight-year-old,

fourteen-year-old, fifty-year-old self. I'm sure she wouldn't mind if I tell
the stories in as close to her words as my memory allows.

So imagine climbing into her lap as I did, or being tucked into bed,
or sitting late at the kitchen table . . . listening to stories about her childhood in my mom's own voice, not mine.

Long before I was Helen Boosalis, I was Helen (Eleni) Geankoplis. My
maternal grandparents, Yionna and George Flogeras, were like my
second set of parents, only older. They lived close to our family for
most of my growing-up years in Minneapolis and only spoke Greek
to us kids, which is why I speak Greek fluently. I couldn't remember a
time without them, but long before I was born they married and had
four children in Greece—Bertha (my mother), Gus, Anna, and Betty.
When Gus was fifteen, he and my grandfather journeyed by boat to the
United States to find a better life, leaving my grandmother with three
young daughters in Greece. My grandfather and Gus settled in Brooklyn, where Gus hoisted beer on delivery trucks to support both of them
and the family back in Greece.

This arrangement lasted for a few years until my grandmother picked
up a transoceanic rumor that her husband had a "lady friend" in Brooklyn, and she made up her mind to get to America. In 1909 she packed up
the three girls and finagled space in steerage on an immigrant-crammed
boat. My mother (Bertha), who was only nine and a sickly child, almost
did not survive the grueling trip, but she would never forget the sight of
the Statue of Liberty coming into New York harbor.

Overwhelmed by foreign sights and sounds and language they
couldn't understand, my grandmother and her three young daughters
made their way through the snaking, endless lines of immigrants at Ellis Island for admission to their new *country. My grandfather and Gus,
somewhat Americanized after three years, led my grandmother and the
girls through the frightening city to their tenement home.

Over the next several years, my mother and her struggling family
lived in Brooklyn, and my grandparents sold fish-and-chips from a de-

crepit lean-to on Sheepshead Bay. The three girls went to public elementary school. My mother, Bertha, was very smart and loved school, even though she would sometimes come home crying when the kids made fun of her for being Greek. Her father would say, "Next time, take a knife and when they tease you, use it." While her younger sisters stayed in school, my mother was allowed only to finish fifth grade before being sent to work at a Spalding factory in Brooklyn, where she sewed baseball covers. I can hardly believe that my bright and "with it" mother, who so loved to talk about current affairs and politics, completed only the fifth grade. Her curiosity and intelligence must have propelled her remarkable self-education.

While the factory work was difficult and she continued to have health problems that left her virtually blind in one eye, my mother and her sister Anna managed to have some fun as teenagers. They loved going to the amusement park on Coney Island, not far from their parents' fish-and-chips stand. One summer evening when the sisters went to Coney Island, my mother met a "nice young man," Louie Greene, and fell in love. Anna kept the secret of her sister's feelings for Louie.

My mother's youthful Coney Island romance with Louie Greene was thwarted when her entire family moved from New York to Minneapolis. No one in the family would ever confirm or discuss the reason for the move, although one story was that Gus was in some kind of trouble in New York and had to leave, so the whole family moved with him.

After moving to Minneapolis my grandparents worked out an arranged marriage for my mother, as was the Greek custom then, to a Greek restaurateur in Minneapolis, George Geankoplis. When Anna learned of the arrangement, she told their mother about Bertha's Louie Greene in New York. My grandmother took Bertha aside. "You don't love this Louie Greene, do you?" Bertha, an obedient Greek daughter who would never consider crossing her parents' wishes, assured her mother that she did *not.

My mother's arranged marriage to George Geankoplis, my father, went forward as planned on September 2, 1918, in Minneapolis. When they married, my mother was eighteen years old and my father was forty. He had left his parents in Greece at the age of fifteen. On arriving in this country he worked for a relative in Indiana, then went to Chi-

22. Helen's parents, Bertha and George Geankoplis

cago where he survived by buying fruit at the Maxwell Street market and reselling it for a few pennies more. He eventually made his way to Minneapolis to join his older brother Jim.

George Geankoplis was not only more than twice my mother's age, but the supposedly well-off restaurant owner and attractive catch for the arranged marriage turned out to be co-owner (with his brother Jim) of the Minnehaha Café—a floundering restaurant and homemade candy store on Lake Street near Minnehaha Avenue in Minneapolis. Later a family member figured out that my grandparents believed they had arranged the marriage of their daughter Bertha to the rich Geankoplis in Minneapolis—my dad's cousin Nick, owner of the Sixth and Hennepin Café. Instead, they had mistakenly arranged my mother's marriage to an anything-but-rich Geankoplis—my father, George. My mother, the young bride, immediately faced what would be years of scrimping, saving, scraping by, economizing to make ends meet through a progression of my father's failing businesses.

I was born on August 28, 1919, a year after they were married, and my sisters, Tina and Ione, and my brother, Andy, were born within the next five years. I was the only one of the four born in a hospital, probably because my dad went into the Fairview Hospital delivery room about an

23. Helen Geankoplis at age three

hour after I was born and found me in a delivery basket that had fallen to the floor. (I've sustained numerous falls without injury throughout my life, apparently beginning with my entry into the world.)

As the first child and grandchild, I rarely occupied my crib nor was allowed to cry; someone always picked me up and held me. Because my mother was only nineteen and in somewhat fragile health when I was born, her twelve-year-old sister, Betty, came to live with us for two years to help care for me. Close enough in age to be my older sister, my spirited Aunt Betty became one of my all-time favorite people. After she moved back with my grandparents, Betty's visits were my best-loved childhood events. When I was three or four, I once got so excited hearing Betty's voice after the doorbell rang that I jumped off the toilet to go see her without pulling my pants up and tumbled head over heels all the way down the stairs.

24. Helen (*far left*) and her siblings (*from left*) Ione, Andy, and Tina

We lived then at 3115 Forty-first Avenue South in Minneapolis, a two-story house with two bedrooms upstairs. As my three siblings came along after me within five years, my sister Tina and I were pushed out of the upstairs bedroom and slept together on the pull-out couch in the living room. When Tina got pneumonia and nearly died, my mother was convinced that it was from her sleeping on the couch in the stairway draft.

I went with my folks to visit Tina in the hospital, where steam kettles surrounded her bed and ice packs were used to lower her temperature. Penicillin had not yet been discovered, and pneumonia was a common killer. As sick as Tina was, I remember thinking how lucky she was to get so many dolls and presents from our relatives and friends.

Although I didn't get to be hospitalized, I did receive lots of attention as a five-year-old when my smallpox vaccination became severely infected, probably from an unsterile needle. My arm swelled like a watermelon and oozed ugly fluid from the infection. The doctor came to the house and poked under my arm with wooden sticks burned at one end—at the sight, my mother passed out cold. Without the benefit of antibiotics, the doctor told my folks that if the arm were not better by morning, it would have to be amputated. All night in the upstairs bedroom my parents and grandparents prayed before Greek Orthodox icons and *kandili* (a wick in water and oil, always lit). By morning, the infection had receded, my arm was saved, and I was left with an unsightly scar to remind me of the painful, prayerful night.

It is amazing that the four of us lived through all the illnesses that dominated our childhood. As the oldest, I started school and brought home every possible contagious illness—measles, mumps, scarlet fever, diphtheria—and the other three would succumb one by one, sometimes even my mother. We were quarantined for most of one entire year and rarely in school. Even my dad had to live away; I would catch glimpses of him as he passed essentials to my mother through the side door.

During one long bout of sickness, my grandparents arrived with a live chicken to entertain us kids. We laughed ourselves silly watching our mother trying to chase down the flying bird to put a little diaper on it so it would not leave droppings all over the furniture. We had a grand time with the chicken that day until my grandmother took it out back, chopped off its head, and cleaned and cooked it for supper, just as she had done in Greece. That night we kids used our illness as excuse for our lack of hunger and sadly crawled back to our sickbeds.

My mother stayed home with us when we were very little. Besides caring for sick children, she tended a beautiful vegetable and flower garden. She loved everything about nature and often spoke wistfully of the lovely vegetation in her tiny hometown of Ayianni in Sparta (the Peloponnese) where she freely roamed as a young child. I regret she was never able to return to visit her hometown in Greece, but perhaps savoring her child's memories was as pleasurable as reality.

Mother was a magnificent seamstress. She sewed all our clothes and often dressed Tina and me in matching outfits, which was fine until we got older and I felt like a big baby wearing twin clothes. Even in our strapped financial state my mother had fine taste in fabric and style, and I was proud of how modern she dressed compared to my friends' mothers. She not only sewed for our family but often made pajamas and robes for the sick and took the streetcar long distances (on a single transfer) to deliver them along with home-cooked meals. Years later I understood how remarkably compassionate she had been while struggling to keep her own family afloat in dire times.

Because everyone we knew in the neighborhood lived much like we did, I didn't feel poor. For amusement, we siblings had each other and loads of neighbor playmates. We built elaborate forts for snowball fights during the long Minnesota winters, flooded the yard for an ice rink, and constructed a pond where our goldfish died when its water seeped through the stones into the ground. In one of our entrepreneurial efforts we made colored water by soaking different shades of crepe paper, then used the water to dye sand that we gathered from the Mississippi River and layered the sand in rainbow designs in glass jars to sell for a penny at our front-yard stand.

My mother was the family disciplinarian. Whenever one of us had a major punishment coming, we were sent to the yard to cut a thin branch from the bushes for Mother to use on our backsides. I didn't always succumb to punishment meekly; in fact, I devised a good system for escaping Mother's control by running three times around the dining-room table and then out the front door. Once, on my third lap, I glanced over my shoulder to see how far back I had left the old girl (in her twenties). The shock of seeing her right behind me made me faint, which terrified my mother so she let me off the hook.

Leaving child rearing and discipline to my mother, my dad encouraged me from a young age to stand up and fight for myself. I came home crying from second grade because some kids were teasing me. "You cannot cry for that, Elenitsa ['little Helen']," he said. "You must be strong. Remember, you are a Spartan!" My dad would smile if he knew how many times I have thought of his words during my political life.

With that encouragement, I began to think of myself as a tough kid and defender of the underdog. Whenever my younger brother, Andy, was chased home from school by older boys, I would stand in the doorway with my arms crossed over my chest and glare at the would-be attackers until they ran away. I liked my reputation as a force to be reckoned with, and it built my confidence.

A big freckled, red-haired bully in my fourth grade class, Edmund, mercilessly teased our classmate Eleanor, who was even poorer than most of us at Cooper Elementary. Edmund taunted her for living above a butcher shop, for wearing funny clothes, for being scrawny. I, too, was a scrawny ten-year-old, but Edmund didn't intimidate me. One day I told him to stop teasing Eleanor, and when he continued I knocked him down and hit him with my fists. Like all bullies, he was not nearly as tough as he acted, and that put an end to his domination. Afraid to go home with clothes torn from my Edmund attack, I sneaked in our back door. But when they heard the saga, Mother and Dad were proud that I stood up for Eleanor. That stuck with me.

My dad could rarely leave his Minnehaha Café, but when he did our biggest treat was to pile into his Model T Ford and take a drive over the Mendota Bridge, which we thought was the longest bridge in the *world. The closest we came to taking a family vacation was our fifty-mile drive once to Taylor Park for a picnic.

I'm ashamed to say I felt compelled to embellish my vacation history in answer to the inevitable autumn classroom question, "How was your summer vacation?" Most of the kids had at least gone to a Minnesota lake and some even out of state, so when the teacher asked if anybody had ever been out of the country, I found myself raising my hand. "Greece," I lied. "Oh, Helen, tell the class about Greece." "I can't remember. I was just a baby." Still, the kids in my class were impressed with my infant travels, especially my friend Dorothy, who always introduced me as her friend who had been to Europe.

My dad was rarely home, not only because he was in the restaurant business but also because his restaurant was failing. He and his brother Jim lost the Minnehaha Café and bought a small grocery store at Thirty-sixth and Lake where they also sold homemade chocolates. But the grocery store business soon failed, too. My parents had to give up the house when I was ten, and we moved to a rented duplex at 417 Second Avenue Southeast. The six of us lived on the first floor, and above us lived my grandparents and their as-yet-unmarried offspring,

Gus and Betty. (Anna had by then married Christ Legeros, who owned the Rainbow Café, a Minneapolis landmark that the Legeros family operated from 1919 to 1979.)

Our lives changed dramatically when we moved. Mother went to work to help in my dad's next solo try at the restaurant business—the Fairmont Café on East Hennepin between Fourth and Fifth. I worked at the Fairmont, too; every morning before school, I typed the day's menus and made copies using a messy duplicating contraption. I would run the extra eight blocks to elementary school but was late nearly every day. My principal called my mother in to complain that I was the worst student because I was never on time. Mother's explanation of my menu-typing duties did not fall on sympathetic ears. My ten-year-old's typing skills improved over time but not my tardiness.

Although Mother was working long hours at my dad's restaurant, my grandparents and Betty lived upstairs and could fill in watching over us kids, ranging then from ages five to ten. My grandparents, who spent hours every day playing the Greek card game Kolitsina, simply moved their game downstairs to watch us while Mother was at work.

My grandmother (in Greek, "Yiayia"), short and shapeless, wore her hair pinned in a knot at the top back of her head; when she let it down each evening, her hair fell almost to the ground. She was illiterate in both Greek and English. To use Minneapolis streetcars, she recognized letters in the route name as symbols—the Johnson Avenue streetcar was the one with the upside-down cane (J), the Como and Lake streetcar had two circles (Como). Yiayia told us stories from the old country, always in Greek since she spoke no English; my favorite was the Greek version of Thumbelina. Her greatest sorrow, she told us, was in being an *orphano*, her mother having died giving birth to her. All of us, especially our young mother, followed Yiayia's advice, particularly her medical remedies.

My grandfather (in Greek, "Papouli"), tall and stately, considered himself educated because he could read and write in Greek. Every day he walked to Sibley Park in his black suit, his watch on a gold chain stretched across his vest, wearing a starched shirt and tie and a black derby. He carried a cane—for effect, I now think—and cut quite a dashing figure. In the park he read his entire Greek newspaper, akin to his

earlier days in Greece when he spent hours at the coffeehouse, finger-
ing his *komboloi* (worry beads) and arguing politics with other men at
the *cafenia*. Papouli prided himself on refusing to learn one "scrap" of
English. I was fascinated by his white handlebar mustache and by his
slender feet when he stomped on grapes to make *wine. Papouli insisted that we children kiss his hand whenever we saw him, which only
added to his authority and aristocratic air.

Undoubtedly from smoking two or three packs of cigarettes a day,
my grandfather was hospitalized periodically for ulcer problems. My
grandmother greatly envied the attention he received during his hospital stays. Not until Yiayia was eighty did she have her big chance. She
slipped on the ice and dislocated her collarbone. Unfortunately, her son,
Gus, contacted a doctor friend who came to the emergency room, fixed
the collarbone, and sent her home. Yiayia was so disappointed.

My grandparents were the centerpiece of our family. After my
grandfather died at eighty-five (from an infected cut on his heel after
stumbling on a footstool), my dear little grandmother, who rarely
drank alcohol in her life, needed a shot of Metaxa (brandy and wine) in
the morning—doctor's orders—just to get her out of bed.

Because my father left Greece (Theologos, in Sparta, the Peloponn-
nese) at age fifteen and never went back, we never knew his parents.
My dad was typical of most Greek immigrants of the time who came
to America to make their fortune and intended to return to Greece.
Most did neither. They worked long hours for a relative in the restaurant business or tried to make a go of it themselves, struggling to support their families and give their children opportunities for a better life.
If they couldn't realize the dream that pulled them across the ocean,
then by God their children would. When I was twelve or thirteen I
found my dad reading a letter from Greece with tears streaming down
his cheeks—his mother, whom he had not seen for more than forty
years, had died.

After my dad lost both the Minnehaha Café and the grocery store
and we moved to the duplex, his Fairmont Café soon went from bad
to worse—even with Mother's working long hours to help him—and
he lost yet another business. My mother could have then gone to work

at her brother-in-law Christ Legeros's Rainbow Café, but she was too proud to be the "poor relation" working for her sister's husband.

Instead my mother went to work for my dad's cousin Christie Geankoplis at the Bridge Café. Christie admired my vivacious mother and treated her with dignity as she worked as hard as any man to help support the family. She walked to the Bridge every morning to open before 7 a.m. as she had done at my dad's Fairmont Café. She was blessed with boundless energy and charisma, making her popular with customers. I so admire the strength, courage, and stamina it took for her to work long hours in the restaurant, raise four children, and care for my dad when he developed heart problems.

Since my sister Tina was now old enough to type the daily menus, I moved up to greater responsibilities of making sundaes behind the soda fountain, waiting tables, and sometimes taking cash. Christie went to Greece the next summer and left my mother in charge of the Bridge. At twelve I was paid seven dollars a week; Christie said if I did a good job, my mother should give me a dollar raise. I never collected on the promised raise because Mother thought that would be "taking advantage."

That summer we four kids had more chores than usual since my mother was always at the Bridge, even on Saturdays. We played poker to determine who would do which chores. We would play cards for most of the morning, then rush to do our work before Mother got home. More often than not she would walk in, find dusting and other tasks unfinished, turn around, slam the door, and leave. We felt terrible then because we knew how hard she was working. Most people saw only my charming, lively mother; at home we also knew her highstrung, often depressed side.

About the time Mother went to work at the Bridge, she walked all over southeast Minneapolis searching for a bigger house, since the four of us kids were getting too old to share a bedroom in the duplex. She found one at *428 Fourth Street se, just a few blocks away from my grandparents. Christie moved in with us to make it financially feasible. We regarded him as our family's salvation during those toughest of times.

My father, meanwhile, went into yet another business with a younger partner, Tony DeMuse—the Sports *Center, at East Hennepin and Central. They served sandwiches and beer and had pool tables. With my mother working at the Bridge and my dad's Sports Center business and our move to the new house, my parents felt a small degree of financial stability that had eluded them for many years.

Family closeness was paramount to the immigrant groups who came to America in droves in the early 1900s, and our family was no exception. When my mother's immediate family migrated to Minneapolis from their first home in Brooklyn, they found a substantial Greek population in the Twin Cities that included more branches of the family—more second and third cousins, aunts, uncles, shirt-tale relatives, and those who might have been related if anyone could untangle the variations on family names assigned by Ellis Island officials. (Our family name, Geankoplis, derived from the Greek name Giannakopoulos, spelled phonetically in English.)

Our biggest family celebrations were not for family members' birthdays but for their name days—the feast days of the Greek Orthodox saints for whom they were named. My dad's name day was April 23, the feast day of St. George, so my folks always had an open house that day with a feast laid out for family and friends who came to call. We looked forward to Christmas most of all, not only for all the usual childhood reasons but because it was also our uncle Christ Legeros's name day. It seemed every Greek in Minneapolis came to celebrate Uncle Christ's name day, singing and Greek dancing late into the night on Christmas. We kids circled the table in awe at the roasted whole suckling pig with an apple in its mouth that Aunt Anna always served along with traditional lamb.

Whether on name days, holidays, or Sunday dinners after church, passionate political argument—not polite conversation—dominated our dinner table. The depression, New Deal, the labor movement, unemployment lines, whatever President Roosevelt said that day—all were debated, argued, never settled.

Most liberal at the table were my parents, fervent Roosevelt Democrats. My mother claimed that her Greek relatives began as liberal Democrats when they first came to this country and were hungry, but as soon as they had "two nickels to rub together in their pockets" they turned conservative and some even became Republicans. Mother and

Dad were always talking about America, our government, our community. Voting was a big deal at our house, never to be taken for granted.

Sharing my parents' liberal views in weekly dinner-table arguments was my mother's brother, Gus *Florest. Gus and Ted Phillips owned the East Hennepin Café, a popular restaurant and bar for Democratic politicians and later a favorite gathering spot of Hubert *Humphrey and his *DFLers. Uncle Gus often took me with him to see his friends at work in the state legislature, where I remember the clock was once covered to extend the close of the legislative session. I became hooked on politics.

Not only U.S. but Greek politics, too, was fodder for the extended family clan. Even my immediate family was split on the issue of the Greek monarchy. My grandfather was a monarchist and went to St. George's Greek Orthodox Church in southeast Minneapolis because it had a monarchist congregation, while my dad favored the overthrow of the monarchy in Greece and took our family to St. Mary's, with its like-minded anti-monarchist congregants. My mother would get a little nervous when the family bunch of hotheaded Greeks at Sunday dinner started shouting and carrying on. I loved it.

As captivating as I found the family political free-for-alls, the best part of every Sunday was when dinner was over and the grown-ups settled down for hours of poker playing—men at one table and women at the other. (The genders mixed at the poker table only many years later when aging husbands and wives began to die, and the men had to tolerate playing poker with the women.) During poker games we kids had a ball with our four Legeros cousins (Aunt Anna's children)—Elaine, George, John, and Con—who were just a little younger than the four of us.

Being the oldest of the cousins (and the bossiest), I was generally the ringleader of our wonderfully unsupervised Sunday adventures. I used to corral the little kids into a closet and tell the scariest stories I could think up, but once I had to beg to be let out when I scared myself silly. When our Legeros cousins moved to their "mansion" by Lake Calhoun (thanks to the Rainbow Café's success), we were treated to swimming in the lake. In our part of town, we had no lake and seldom went to the indoor city pool (Ryan) because it cost twenty cents for the four of us to swim there, a rare extravagance for our family.

We always spent Greek Easter at my grandparents' house. The Good Friday service, almost never the same date as my American friends' Good Friday, was my most beloved church service. The music in minor key was hauntingly melancholy as the huge wooden cross was carried through the church by the oldest in the community (usually my grandfather). Then came the *epitaphio* (golden tomb of Christ), covered with hundreds of fresh carnations and carried by a procession of church elders all dressed in black. On Saturday of Easter weekend we all took naps, then attended the midnight church service of the Resurrection.

After the church service, at about 2 a.m. we went to my grandparents' for the traditional Easter feast: *patsa* (a soup made with lamb intestines), *magiritsa* (another soup made of lamb livers and kidneys and who knows what else), roast leg of lamb, and Greek pastries—*baklava, diples, koulourakia,* and *kourabiethes*—which my grandmother spent weeks preparing. I tried to avoid the soups. Deep red hard-boiled eggs were passed and each of us would smack the end of our egg against someone else's until the winner—the one left with an uncracked egg—was declared. We went home about 5 a.m. and were crabby all the next day.

We didn't live in the Greek immigrant enclave in south Minneapolis but rather in southeast Minneapolis, where the dominant immigrants were Swedes. We observed all the Greek traditions in our family, but I didn't suffocate from the old-world culture and rules as did many of my Greek American peers. We first-generation children felt a mixture of pride and shame in our heritage. We had a foot in each world—Greek and American. Among Greeks I was proud of my family—especially my mother, who was so up-to-date compared to other Greek mothers—yet outside the world of Greek immigrants we just wanted to be Americans. We were embarrassed if my mother spoke Greek on the streetcar, and my brother, Andy, felt a burning shame whenever he was called a "dirty Greek."

One inescapable torture of being first generation was the painful exercise that none of my non-Greek friends had to suffer—Greek school. From age ten, three days a week after regular school I took one streetcar, then transferred to a second and walked several blocks to Greek school at our church on Lake Street across from Sears Roebuck. Our taskmaster teacher, Mr. Lambrinides, used a wooden ruler to slap the hands of boys who did not perform well. Once he made one misbehaving boy take off his pants and walk around the classroom in his long winter underwear, and we all had to swear to secrecy.

Even though I spoke Greek at home with my grandparents at all times and with my parents sometimes, I still had to attend the dreaded Greek school for several years. I felt sorry for myself—I thought my childhood was being ruined. I must have been a tired kid, since my school days started so early typing menus and ended most days with forty-five-minute streetcar rides to and from Greek school. I resented not being able to go to after-school activities with my friends, and I was ashamed to tell them I had to do something so weird and different.

The whole point of Greek school seemed to be showing off Mr. Lambrinides's pupils every year at the March 25 Greek Independence Day celebration at church. All year we worked to learn Greek poetry, plays, and songs that we recited with much fanfare. We dressed in Greek costumes, the boys wearing skirted *fustanellas*, the uniforms of the elite Greek soldiers (Evzones). If only their American friends could see them now, I secretly thought. At the end of the lengthy productions, swords in hand, we stood on chairs and shouted "Zito I Hellas!" ("Long live Greece!"). My parents were proud, my grandparents wept. Maybe Greek school was worth a little, if just for that.

My mother usurped what little time was left after Greek school obligations. She dreamed that she could nurture her children's hidden (very hidden) musical talents. She somehow negotiated a cut-rate deal on an old baby grand piano. Although depressing the keys required real finger strength, Tina and I took piano lessons together for fifty cents an hour. Soon even the bargain piano installment purchase plan of five dollars a month proved too expensive, and more than once we hid from the man who came to our door to collect. After two years I stopped piano lessons. (That's why I jumped at the chance to resume my early music career and restart piano lessons at the age of eighty-three.)

My dad brought home a violin left as a deposit by a losing pool player at the Sports Center, so I also took violin lessons. Ione and Andy played instruments from school—saxophone and trumpet—and my folks loved to listen to us play together, oblivious to the horrible sounds we produced. From his school trumpet Andy contracted trench mouth, which spread throughout the family, thus ending our family band.

When I was thirteen my mother paid three dollars to have a used tennis racket restrung, and I became quite a good tennis player. A year later she found a secondhand set of golf clubs, which Christie taught me how to use. No matter that Mother had ulterior motives for encouraging my interest in sports rather than accept my developing interest in boys. I played both tennis and golf for most of my life, thanks to my mother.

Perhaps it was no coincidence that Mother's enthusiasm for my participation in sports came on the heels of a stupid stunt I pulled. Across our driveway on Fourth Street lived two high school brothers. One day after school my friend Franny Boyle and I noticed that several good-looking football players had congregated next door. We girlish twelve-year-olds craved the attention of these manly heartthrobs, so we devised a plan.

We sat at our kitchen table by a window so the boys could see us from across the driveway. We brought out my dad's Metaxa, kept the top on the bottle, faked pouring brandy into cordial glasses, and pretended to drink—glass after glass. Within a short time the front doorbell rang. The rowdy group of boys barged in and immediately broke into my dad's liquor cabinet.

From brandy-drinking pseudo-sophisticates, Franny and I dissolved into frightened little girls. We had no idea how to stop the boys' mischief. They made a mess. My folks were furious and I thought they would never trust me again. But I was a pretty good kid, hid better my future indiscretions, and eventually earned back their confidence.

In high school I devoted much time to sports—tennis, golf, captain of the girls' basketball team. Most of my women friends now tell me that they had no opportunity to be in sports as girls, so I was fortunate. I was on the student council and news editor of the school newspaper. Math and English were favorite subjects but I detested home economics, especially sewing (contrary to my enjoyment of homemaking, particularly sewing, as an adult). I enrolled in college-prep courses but also took typing and shorthand—essential preparation for women's jobs then. I rarely studied until tests were given but usually did well and pleased my folks.

25. Helen's 1937 graduation photo, Marshall High School, Minneapolis

My parents were strict about dating and boyfriends, so my social life revolved around a group of girlfriends—we called ourselves "Just Us Girls." We had countless sleepovers and typical teenage crushes. We waited in subzero weather outside Northrop Hall to catch a glimpse of Nelson Eddy, and when he didn't show we lurked for hours in the lobby of the Radisson Hotel where we had heard he was staying. We gathered after school at Svoboda Drug Store, about two blocks from Marshall High, to smoke. At my house we would hang our heads out the bathroom window to smoke, then burn bacon and carry the smoky pan through the rooms to cover any cigarette smell before my mother got home from work. We even made my little sister Ione smoke one cigarette so she wouldn't tell on us.

Thank goodness my folks had no problem with my having American girlfriends. We were luckier than most of the other first-generation

Greek American kids we knew from church, even our cousins, whose parents didn't allow them to have American friends. Although my parents frowned on steady boyfriends and dating, especially non-Greek boys, they still gave me far more rope than most of the Greek girls had. I actually went to the prom with a non-Greek boy, Don Dowden, who sadly became one of the first casualties of World War II.

After my high school graduation in 1937, I had few aspirations for attending college; my folks, like most Greek immigrants then, saw little need for a daughter's higher education. My mother harbored high hopes for her only son, Andy, to become a dentist, but after high school he enlisted in the marines, and that was that. If the University of Minnesota hadn't been located so close to our house and tuition hadn't been so inexpensive, I wouldn't have enrolled.

As the oldest child I felt my first obligation was to help support the family, so I worked alongside my mother at the Bridge Café when I wasn't attending classes. Through Uncle Gus and his political friends at his East Hennepin Café, I worked a few summers at the streetcar company answering phones and fabricating route charts and schedules. By the end of my second year in college I'd grown impatient with classes and studying. I left college for a real job with a real salary.

I got a full-time job, through Uncle Gus, at the unemployment compensation division of the Minnesota Department of Employment Security. Once World War II began, jobs were plentiful and fewer people applied for unemployment compensation, so I moved to the employment division and eventually became a supervisor. I was still living with my parents, happily giving my paychecks to my father and helping Mother at the Bridge Café. Now that all the kids were old enough to drive the old Ford, our sibling squabbles centered on who would get the car. We devised a cutthroat game of buying a dime's worth of gas to see how little we could leave in the tank for the next person.

While waiting tables at the Bridge Café, I noticed a good-looking, short fellow who came in often for dinner, always wearing the strangest long, black coat . . .

Stories of Mom growing up in the 1920s and 1930s filled my own childhood with wonder and curiosity about such a different time; but it is my father's accounts of his meeting, falling in love, and marrying my mother that I remember about that era of her life. World War II was for me as dramatic and exotic a backdrop for my dad's courtship stories as Greek immigrant family life in America was in Mom's childhood stories.

My dad, Mike Boosalis—far more reserved and reticent than my mother (despite his "bring the house down" sense of humor)—didn't tell me his stories over and over as Mom did, and so I cannot recite them by heart. I asked him years ago if he would write down for me and for his grandsons the stories of his childhood, schooling, World War II service, career, and life with Mom. And so he did, sitting at his living-room desk, writing on yellow pads just as I recall him doing to prepare for his university classes when I was a little girl.

I'd love to relate all the yellow-pad chronicles of my dad's growing up as one of eight children of Greek immigrant parents (Mary and Gus Boosalis) who owned the Olympia Café in Faribault, Minnesota; his being sent at the age of six to live in Greece for five years with his maternal grandparents; his flying fifty air force combat missions with his b-24 crew; his university teaching and research on fungal diseases of wheat, soybeans, and corn. Instead, I include only the portions of Dad's written accounts that describe his meeting, courting, and marrying my mother so that the story can continue where we left her as a young woman working at the Bridge Café—these stories now in my dad's voice.

MIKE'S STORY

My brother Nick and I roomed at the College Inn Hotel in Dinky Town at the University of Minnesota in Minneapolis. Nick was a pre-med student and I was majoring in Technical Science (botany and plant pathology) at the College of Agriculture on the St. Paul campus. Our room was about a half mile from the Bridge Café, where I first saw Helen and fell in love with her.

When I wasn't taking dinner at a nearby boardinghouse, I frequently had dinner at the Bridge Café, not because of the good food but because Helen was there. I didn't have the nerve and confidence to introduce myself. I got to know her sister Tina first. I lacked the courage to tell Tina I wanted to meet her sister. Helen now says she noticed my presence at the Bridge Café and thought I was a strange-looking fellow because I was wearing a long, outdated black winter coat. Apparently, she paid more attention to my coat than to me.

I finally mustered enough nerve to ask her for a date, in a round-about way. I asked my good friend Harry Karlos to call Helen and inform her of my intention to ask her for a date. I wanted her to have enough time to think about me and not about my coat! My clever plan was to have her join me in a double date to Excelsior Park with Harry and his girlfriend, Georgia Branditsas.

Harry called Helen while we were at my Aunt Kiriaka's house. I don't know what he said to her, but unexpectedly he handed me the phone to continue the conversation. I said a few meaningless words before I asked Helen for a date. I didn't expect her to accept my invitation, and when she said yes I was so surprised I was speechless for a long time. For a moment Helen thought I had hung up the phone, but I gathered my senses and continued the most delightful phone conversation with her. We went to Excelsior Park and had a marvelous time, and this was the beginning of my courtship with the lovely Helen.

After breaking the ice with Helen and after that first date, I increased my dining at the Bridge Café. I purchased meal tickets, which saved me money eating there regularly. I timed my dinner to coincide with the time Helen finished working so I could walk her home.

I took Helen to Faribault to meet my parents and my younger siblings still at home—Georgia, Ted, and Elaine. My parents liked Helen the first day they met her. My brothers John, George, and Bill had been working at my dad's Olympia Café but had all joined the navy air corps by then; my brother and former roommate, Nick, had graduated from medical school and volunteered for military service, to serve as a medical officer in the paratroops. (Even eight-year-old Teddy went to the post office to try to enlist.) So my four brothers in the service did not meet Helen until much later.

My mother was soon to have five stars in her window, signifying five sons in active service during World War II. When I graduated from the University of Minnesota in 1941 I was drafted into the army, taking me away from Helen. Inductees were to serve one year, but that changed during my first week in the service. I was on KP duty peeling a bushel

26. Helen Geankoplis dates Mike Boosalis, 1942

of potatoes when I heard a frenzied radio announcement that Pearl Harbor had been bombed. With America's entry into World War II, my anticipated one year in the service turned into almost four years.

During my stint in the service Helen wrote to me nearly every day. Her letters bolstered my spirits and made it easier to tolerate my transition into army regimentation. I was assigned to Fort Riley, Kansas, for basic training and to serve in the horse cavalry, based on the classification officer's assumption that my college plant pathology major had

27. Helen Geankoplis, engaged, 1944

something to do with animals. Thank goodness Helen never saw me in my cavalry uniform—much too big due to my short stature and, instead of tapering at the knees, the flared part of my trousers tapered at my calves. I looked much like a flying squirrel. After four months of basic infantry training and working with horses at Fort Riley, my cavalry days ended with my failed attempts to keep my horse in line.

Posted on the Fort Riley camp bulletin board was my next assignment to the infantry at, of all places, Fort Snelling, Minnesota. What glorious news! I couldn't believe my good fortune (nor could my buddies) with an assignment returning me to my home state and to Helen. If the army had known, it wouldn't have bestowed such a welcome transfer.

28. Mike Boosalis, U.S. Army Air Forces

During my one-year stay at Fort Snelling I spent all my spare time with my dear Helen. Since I had no car, Helen would pick me up at Fort Snelling, and we sometimes went to her home or to Faribault to visit my family. I thoroughly enjoyed being with Helen, playing tennis and golf and going to movies, restaurants, amusement parks, and occasionally to bars for a few beers, although Helen didn't like beer.

Time flew too fast while stationed at Fort Snelling because I fell more deeply in love with Helen. I knew she was the one, the only one, for me. I was captivated by her intelligence, beauty, compassion, worldliness, and dazzling personality. Besides all of that she was a Democrat and a Spartan! During this time we decided to get married as soon as I was discharged.

But all good things must end. It was a dismal day for me when soldiers qualified for combat were notified that we were to be replaced by incoming limited-service draftees (those not qualified for combat). I had a choice to make—either stay in the army infantry or apply for another branch of the service.

I decided to apply for the army air corps to become a fighter pilot. I had fears about passing the physical for the army air corps because I wore glasses. To improve this defect I started drinking gallons of carrot juice in the weeks before my physical. Whether or not the carrot juice improved my eyesight, I qualified for the army air corps but not for pilot training as I had hoped. Instead, I reluctantly left Helen and Minnesota to train as a navigator at Selman Field in Monroe, Louisiana.

But I didn't complete my navigation training. We trained in AT-7 airplanes manned by a pilot, a navigator-officer-instructor, and three navigator cadets. I was one of three cadets who were "washed out" from navigation school because of what happened on our last training flight before graduation. We ran into bad weather at night; we got completely lost when our radio and compass malfunctioned; the plane ran out of gasoline; and we had to parachute into what we thought was the Gulf of Mexico but turned out to be a flooded Louisiana rice paddy. We three cadets were immediately reassigned to bombardier school, perhaps due to a shortage of bombardiers. I didn't tell Helen about my parachuting close call for quite awhile.

After my miserable cavalry experience and aborted navigation training, I did complete my third training in bombardier school in San Angelo, Texas, and was finally commissioned second lieutenant. I joined pilot Ken Volk's B-24 heavy bomber crew and started combat training in Wichita, Kansas.

Before departing for Italy as part of the Fifteenth Air Force (376th Heavy Bomb Group, 515th Squadron), we were allowed to invite wives and girlfriends to join us for a few days. Of course I invited Helen, and our crew had a marvelous time with our loved ones—nightclubs, dancing, dining.

While I was stationed in Lecci, Italy, Helen wrote frequent morale-booster letters, which I read over and over. She told me of working as a Red Cross nurse's aide at Minneapolis General Hospital, where she

29. Mike Boosalis (*back row, left*) with B-24 flight crew

volunteered twenty to thirty hours a week on top of her full-time job for the state. She wrote funny stories about her trips to the train station to pick up my four brothers when they were home on leave—so often that the station parking lot attendant started calling her "Buttercup," probably thinking she was a prostitute because she picked up so many different men.

Helen seemed so far away, but her letters gave me hope for a future beyond the war. Our squadron was flying combat missions over fortified bombing targets in Munich and Wiener Neustadt and over the heavily defended oil refineries in Ploesti, Romania, which supplied much of the fuel for Germany's war machine. As bombardier I had control of our plane during the final, ten-minute approach to the target, which seemed an eternity through the dense smoke screen covering the target and black barrage of flak (anti-aircraft artillery) that was "so thick you could walk on it." The longer we flew in combat, the more we dwelled on the probability of being killed.

Many planes were lost on those missions, and it was a miracle that only one member of our flight crew was injured. As the first aid officer (with minimal training), I applied a tourniquet when our flight engineer was hit. I then nervously grabbed a small packet I thought was sulfa powder to pour into the gaping shrapnel wound. The packet turned out to be coffee grounds. I was relieved to learn later that my novel treatment was harmless, but the crew teased me mercilessly that my patient had developed a huge craving for coffee. I wrote to Helen about this humorous incident, not about the dangers of our missions.

The night before the last of my fifty combat missions I kept praying, "This is my last mission in Europe. Please, Lord, make it a safe one, and not Ploesti." It wasn't Ploesti, and we did survive our last mission. Some of us returned to the States via ships, wanting to play it safe after months of flying combat missions. Before starting "retooling" training to prepare for assignment to the Pacific theater, I received a long furlough and immediately headed for Minneapolis to my gal, Helen.

The entire Geankoplis clan and friends welcomed me at Helen's house. The male relatives kissed me on the cheek, a custom unfamiliar to me that took me by surprise. After all, I was a World War II combat veteran! I was smitten with Helen's entire family, especially her mother, Bertha, a lovely, energetic, intelligent woman who was direct and "told it like it was." Helen's father, George, a tall, handsome man with an engaging personality and calm disposition, treated me with kindness and advised me to invest in real estate, which I was willing to do but lacked the resources! It was clear to me that Helen had her father's easy disposition and her mother's energy, intelligence, sense of humor, compassion, and generosity.

During this long furlough we got married on February 15, 1945, in the Greek Orthodox Church in Minneapolis. Just two weeks earlier we attended my brother John's marriage to Kay Christopoulos in Sioux Falls. Kay and Helen had been friends for years—each blessed with a marvelous sense of humor—and we appreciated our nearly simultaneous wartime weddings. Men our age were absent from both weddings. The only serviceman attending our wedding was my cousin Jim "Chop" Boosalis; my four brothers and Helen's brother, Andy, were all on active duty in the service. (Thankfully, all five brothers would survive the war, but John's plane went down in the South Pacific on the same day that George's training plane crashed stateside; Nick was in the Los Baños raid to liberate American POWs; Bill was subjected to kamikaze air at-

30. "Just Married"—Mike and Helen Boosalis, 1945

tacks at Okinawa; and Andy took part in marine amphibious assaults on Tarawa.) We greatly missed our brothers at our wedding. Soon I would rejoin them, but first the joy of marrying Helen.

Helen wore a beautiful satin wedding dress that her mother had sewn, and I wore my air force uniform. The Greek wedding ceremony itself was so long (almost two hours) that Helen got a little queasy from the candle smoke. We made it to the end of the service, wearing wreaths around our heads connected by ribbon and walking around the altar three times to symbolize our new life together.

We went to Miami Beach for our honeymoon, thanks to Uncle Sam's generosity in sponsoring rest leaves for returning air combat crews. As soon as we returned to Minneapolis I was assigned to the army air base in Midland, Texas, for training to fly bombing missions in the Pacific theater. I didn't care for the training and missed my old B-24 crew, but Helen would be joining me as soon as I found a suitable place to live. In the meantime she stayed with my brother John and his new bride, living in Corpus Christi where John was retooling to fly navy airplanes.

After days of intensive searching in an area jammed with service personnel all needing housing, I finally found somewhere to live on a small farm about three miles outside Midland. It was far from a luxurious place, really a marginal place—actually, a barely livable place: a converted chicken coop with no bathroom, an outdoor faucet (no sink), a lightbulb on a hanging cord—nothing was too good for the little woman. The landlady of our chicken coop told Helen with considerable pride that the bed had belonged to her grandmother. That wasn't hard to believe in view of its deplorable condition. In such a seller's market, the chicken coop's rent was unconscionable.

But Helen took the coop in stride and did her best to improve it. She never complained and frequently complimented me for finding a place when rentals were so scarce. Helen purchased a warming electric plate that she used to heat pastry and coffee for our breakfast every morning before I reported to the base at 6 a.m. I didn't want to spoil her newlywed domesticity by telling her that the officers club at the base served a bountiful breakfast of eggs, bacon, sausage, pancakes, oatmeal, fruit, yogurt, and toast. What the heck, Helen's rolls and coffee were good— and love endures all.

I know she didn't relish having to walk three miles to the air base to use a bathroom (rather than the outhouse near the chicken coop), especially since she was afraid of dogs and had to pass by several vicious ones. This wretched situation inspired Helen's miles of walking in search of better living quarters, and she found the perfect place on a ranch near town.

The ranchers, Mr. and Mrs. Brunson, rented us a spacious, clean room with kitchen privileges. Pa Brunson managed the ranch, and Ma Brunson worked in town at a women's clothing store. This couple, bless them, were generous, friendly people and treated us like family. On my days off I helped Pa Brunson round up cattle, and Helen helped Ma Brunson with house chores.

We had a wonderful time living on the ranch, and Helen learned a little about rural life. I'll never forget the day Ma Brunson informed Helen that one of the cows was having a difficult time aborting a calf so Pa Brunson had to administer medication to save her. Helen said, "Mike, let's go out there and see the poor mother cow." As we were walking through the corral searching for the mother cow, we came across a doleful looking creature and Helen said, "Look, Mike, that must be the mother cow. Look how sad her eyes look." At the sight of the cow I started laughing and said to my dear city wife, "That dejected-looking cow with the sad eyes is a bull."

After one of my combat training flights, Helen met my plane with the shocking news that President Roosevelt had died. She was crying and felt deep sorrow for a long time, as did I. Most servicemen and civilians held the president in the highest esteem for his leadership of the country through time of war.

Our newlywed life on the ranch ended a few months later when Japan surrendered, and I was honorably discharged as first lieutenant from the air force. We headed home to Minnesota. Housing was difficult to find, so Helen's parents generously invited us to live in a room in their attic. We pondered our future—whether I should seek employment or continue my education. I knew for certain I wasn't interested in or suited for the restaurant business so prevalent in both our families. I received a job offer from a hybrid seed company in Faribault where I had worked before being drafted. I turned down the stingy offer, as the salary was much less than my pay from the air force. Besides, there was no opportunity for advancement.

While in Faribault visiting my family, I ran into one of my former college professors and asked him if I was qualified to pursue graduate studies in plant pathology. He recalled that I had a good scholastic record and said he would send me an application for graduate school. A few months later the University of Minnesota Department of Plant Pathology accepted me and offered me an assistantship. My career in the exciting, dynamic field of plant pathology commenced.

Helen supplemented my meager assistant's pay by returning to her old job at the Department of Employment Security. We benefited from the GI Bill, which paid for my tuition and books. Helen typed and edited all my graduate school papers and could impeccably recite the scientific name for the pathogen inciting a fungal root disease on soybeans that was the subject of my master's thesis: *Rhizoctonia solani*.

After living in my in-laws' attic for a year, we rented an apartment in the same St. Paul building where Helen's sister Tina and her husband, Andy Vavoulis, lived. We then moved to an apartment in Minneapolis close to Helen's beloved Aunt Betty until I got my degree. I carpooled to work with three other plant pathology graduate students, not only saving money but also enjoying stimulating plant disease discussions to and from work.

On June 7, 1948, Mary Beth "Sunshine" (as Helen's mother, Bertha, called her) was born. What a marvelous event. Next to the happy day I married Helen, this was the happiest day of my life—of our lives. We had fun squeezing M.B. into our tiny bedroom—so small, the joke went, that you couldn't change your mind, let alone your clothes.

The Geankoplis clan with its innumerable cousins, uncles, aunts, sisters, and brothers frequently visited our small apartment and showered endless attention and love on the new addition to the family. Bertha (whom M.B. would later call Gram) insisted that the baby be bundled in warm clothing, even in the hot summer, so M.B. developed a terrible heat rash. Helen's sister Ione and her Aunt Betty (Nellas) and children, JoAnne and Tom, spent countless hours at our apartment entertaining little Mary Beth.

We often visited my family, who lived only fifty miles away in Faribault. My mother adored M.B. and loved to sing Greek songs to her. My mother was thirteen when she immigrated to this country from the same hometown as my father—Niata (in Sparta, the Peloponnese)—and she sang the old-country songs to my daughter that she had sung to her eight children when we were small. She still had the care of my younger siblings at home, Elaine and Ted, but they were growing up. By this time my brother Nick had returned from the paratroopers to resume his medical practice, and my brothers George, Bill, and John had returned from their navy service to become co-partners in the Olympia Café, taking over from my dad, who was in poor health. My sister Georgia had worked hard to help Dad keep the Olympia going in her brothers' absence.

Dad was a diehard Republican, and his political views were dramatically opposite Helen's and mine; in fact, I believe I was the only Democrat among all my siblings and my parents. Helen and Dad often engaged in friendly political debate, and he looked forward to our visits and these political polemics with Helen. I think Helen was the only Democrat whose political views Dad respected and tolerated.

I completed my PhD in 1951 and accepted a research and teaching position at the University of Nebraska–Lincoln. Although she cherished our close family and friends in Minneapolis, Helen had no qualms about moving to Nebraska. We found a house on South Forty-eighth Street for seventeen thousand dollars, and with less than a thousand dollars in savings we left Minnesota and drove with three-year-old Mary Beth in a deluge of rain to start our new life in the great state of Nebraska.

I hoped after we were settled in Lincoln that Helen would finish her undergraduate studies and perhaps go to law school. But she would have none of that—she wanted to stay home and devote her time to raising Mary Beth. Helen quickly developed a wide circle of friends and became very active in the League of Women Voters. Not in our wildest dreams could we have contemplated the adventures that lay ahead of us in Lincoln.

Chapter Five

Expect the Unexpected

Spring 1979

"Although Helen had her detractors because she was principled, most were delighted that this bright, handsome woman would stand up to the powers that be."—ROBERT E. KNOLL, Professor Emeritus of English, University of Nebraska–Lincoln

"The qualities that made Helen a good mayor were her perseverance and stubbornness, her loyalty, and the fact that she didn't suffer fools—she knows who's sincere and honest. Helen was the first strong woman in local politics. It was really hard for some of the guys to swallow. To this day, they blame her for anything that's gone wrong in Lincoln."—ROSS E. HECHT, retired president, Lincoln State Bank

A DOUBLE-BARRELED ANNOUNCEMENT

The mayor's ongoing battles with the city council 5–2 majority elected in 1977 could not obscure another looming battleground. The 1979 municipal election of mayor and four council members was just around the corner. Following her earlier pattern, my mother would not lay to rest early speculation about her running for a second term as mayor.

Mom's typical reluctance to think about reelection or to tip her hand, even if she was considering running again, did not discourage challengers from emerging. Stan Matzke, who had a "Boosalis for Mayor" sign in his front yard in the 1975 mayoral campaign, stepped forward to oppose the mayor in late 1978. Matzke knew he must start early to plan a campaign against an incumbent who had been on the city's political scene for twenty years.

Speculation soon surfaced that Matzke—former Nebraska Department of Administrative Services director, son of a former state senator, former candidate for secretary of state, registered Democrat—wanted to be mayor in order to launch a run for governor in four years and to carry on the Matzke name in local and state politics. Even though she hadn't declared her reelection candidacy, an editorial considered the mayor the stronger candidate, "lingering anti-woman sentiment among the electorate notwithstanding," yet it also judged Matzke a "formidable candidate."

When Matzke paid a courtesy visit in November 1978 to tell the mayor of his plans to run against her, she gave him no clue whether she would seek a second term. Given my mother's typically late decisions to run for office, she probably wasn't ready to declare her intentions six months before the spring election, even though conjecture about her potential challengers had begun soon after she was elected mayor in 1975.

For example, when Council Chairman Max Denney announced he would not seek reelection when his term ended in 1977, he was barraged with questions about his potential plans to run against Helen Boosalis for mayor in 1979, which he did not rule out. Even former mayor Sam Schwartzkopf began attending city council meetings in the spring of 1977, fueling predictions that he had his eye on running again in the 1979 mayoral election. But as the 1979 election approached, neither of these flash-from-the-past candidacies emerged; instead, it was the municipal political newcomer, Stan Matzke.

Amid speculation about the mayor's challengers and her reelection plans, the issue that had threatened to engulf my mother in her first few months as mayor now surfaced again in the final months of her term: her police chief appointment. After his incendiary appointment, Police Chief Hansen had performed an exemplary job and won over even his harshest initial critics. He overhauled the police department, changing from a traditional military model to a "team policing" model that diffused authority to lower-ranking officers—a power-sharing concept in sync with the mayor's philosophy.

Editorials lauded the mayor's tough decision to appoint Hansen, which had initially divided the community, and in a rare display of unanimity the city council agreed that Chief Hansen had been innovative, competent, and in tune with changing times. The three council members (Cook, Sikyta, and Baker) who had voted against Hansen's confirmation in 1975 and pushed for the appointment of Dale Adams (later elected Lancaster County sheriff) "are probably the chief's biggest supporters today [1978]," said Councilman Baker. "Maybe in retrospect it was a good decision to go outside because we got to see a different philosophy and now have a department that's better off because of it." Even Councilmen Scherer and Hampton, who were not on the city council when Hansen was confirmed, were uncharacteristically complimentary of the mayor's choice. Scherer called Mayor Boosalis's decision to select Hansen "one of the most positive things I've seen from the administration," and Hampton labeled Hansen a good cop and a good manager.

By the time the pot began to boil in anticipation of the 1979 spring mayoral election, Hansen's three years on the job as chief paralleled my mother's three years as mayor. Like the mayor, he had brought great change. They made a great team. But on December 19, 1978, Chief Hansen submitted his resignation letter to the mayor to accept the position of police chief of Fresno, California. In his letter, he told my mother that working for and with her "has been a truly rewarding experience. Your deep compassion for people, the support you have given the Police Department, your sense of fiscal responsibility and your continuing concern for the community as a whole, represent the attributes of an outstanding mayor and manager."

In an odd twist of fate, December 19 was the day the mayor had planned to declare her decision to run for a second term. Mom went forward with a "double-barreled announcement" at a city hall press conference: announcing her candidacy for mayor and the chief's resignation. A *Star* editorial viewed the coincidental timing as appropriate since the new mayor's appointment of Hansen had demonstrated "her capacity for tough decision-making and for moving in new directions for the betterment of the city," and her early decision had been vindicated by Hansen's stellar performance.

Now, under far different circumstances, the seasoned mayor instantly moved to replace her police chief with a veteran on the force with quality credentials—Assistant Chief Dean Leitner. Even Council Chairman Sikyta complimented the mayor on her choice. Only Councilman Scherer voiced his mistrust of the mayor's appointment, even questioning whether Leitner had made promises to the mayor to secure the chief's job.

Although her decision to seek a second term was not a great surprise, the mayor managed to surprise many folks by adding to her announcement that she would not run for mayor again if reelected for a second term. Councilman Sikyta promptly announced his intent to run for another city council term and to postpone his run for mayor rather than run against my mother in 1979, as he had been considering (he had even had a medical exam to determine if he could handle the pressure of being mayor). "It is no secret that Sikyta had no appetite for challenging Mrs. Boosalis head-to-head in a race for mayor," wrote the *Star*. "To Sikyta, losing to Mrs. Boosalis would doubtless be a fate worse than death." In a rather obvious move, Councilman Sikyta proposed a City Charter amendment to allow the city's mayor to serve part-time. He proposed removing charter language that required the mayor "to devote full time to the duties of office," which in his view "prevented people in the business community [like himself] from running for mayor by forcing them to give up their business interests while in office." The amendment, proposed by the likely future mayoral candidate, failed.

The same *Star* editorial considered Mayor Boosalis an early favorite to win reelection (despite "reports of her being in political trouble") because of her political acumen, name recognition, appetite for campaigning, and record of achievement:

- Containing property taxes and spending despite inflation
- Redeveloping the downtown core and older neighborhoods
- Improving Lincoln's bond rating to AAA and managing fiscal control in a time when urban areas nationally were facing dire financial problems
- Reorganizing city departments for greater efficiency and maintaining city services with fewer employees despite the city's growth in area and population

- Practicing her belief that citizens should participate in decision making and policy formation, spotlighted by Lincoln's recognition as an All-America City

Although deemed the early favorite, the mayor still faced a "tough re-election battle." Her critics pointed to parking and traffic problems associated with downtown beautification efforts and to "downzoning" provisions in the proposed zoning code implementing the Comprehensive Plan. Her thorny relationship with the council majority, posited the editorial, could also make her vulnerable in a reelection bid because of "the criticism and obstruction on the part of several members of the City Council who try to undermine her position whenever they get a chance and who oppose her both because she sometimes stands in the way of certain economic interests which compete with the overall community interest, and because in 1975 she had the audacity to challenge an incumbent and win."

THE 1979 MAYORAL PRIMARY ELECTION OPPONENTS

Like a siren call, my mother's December 1978 declaration of her reelection bid soon brought forth a flood of suitors for the mayor's job. By February 1979, almost a month before the filing deadline, ten candidates had announced or filed to run for mayor—a "colorful lot" that included a former police officer who had sued the mayor after his dismissal from the force, a twenty-three-year-old juvenile group home counselor proposing to replace what he termed "regressive" city sales and wheel taxes with an income tax, and a medical supply company president who stressed the city's need for a mayor with "constructive business experience."

Perhaps the most colorful of the lot was Bob Scanlon, a body shop owner, who acknowledged that although the mayor was doing the best job she could, there were times when a mayor needs to get tough and women cannot do that. He lamented how difficult it is for a group of guys like the city department heads to take orders from a woman. On women in politics, Scanlon said, "It's a man's world. Women shouldn't be involved in positions like mayor. A woman's place is in the *home."

Perhaps Scanlon was voicing the silent views of many others with misgivings about a woman as mayor.

Susan Welch, then chair of the UNL Political Science Department, cited a survey of 264 cities with populations greater than twenty-five thousand showing that only 6 percent had women mayors. (Few of those would have been "strong mayors.") While nationally women held 13 percent of city council seats, 40 percent of the survey cities had not a single female council member. The crowded field of male candidates seeking my mother's mayoral seat in the spring of 1979 would give voters the chance to undo their apparently aberrant choice for mayor four years earlier.

Why so much interest in the mayor's race? Did those coming forward smell blood based on a perception that the incumbent was in trouble? If so, how did that jibe with the absence from the race of the mayor's most vocal political rivals from the city council? Did Councilmen Sikyta's and Cook's decisions not to run for mayor "say more about Mrs. Boosalis' political strength than the large field of candidates says about her perceived weakness"?

Hard to imagine that members of the council 5–2 majority, who had spent the last two years fighting the mayor at almost every turn, would sit back and watch the weighty advantage of incumbency carry her to a second term. If they wouldn't run against her, what role would her councilmen critics play in the campaign?

In this crowded mayoral primary field, Stan Matzke was viewed as by far the strongest challenger. So why then didn't my mother's city council foes quickly jump on Matzke's bandwagon? Matzke's being a Democrat may have given them pause, as perhaps did his support of Helen Boosalis in her first mayoral campaign. Perhaps they didn't view him as truly one of them. "[Matzke's] work in the public sector and political background may not prove to be sufficiently worthy credentials for some of Mrs. Boosalis' most rabid political opponents," surmised a *Star* editorial. "They are said to be still recruiting a true blue business community candidate since Councilmen Bob Sikyta and Steve Cook have decided against a head-to-head confrontation with Mrs. Boosalis."

Matzke's lack of business credentials may have made him a lukewarm alternative for the anti-Boosalis council majority, but the mayor's anti-business reputation provided their rallying cry urging her defeat. In deferring his own candidacy for mayor until 1983 (when my mother said she would not run again), Councilman Sikyta claimed that Lincoln needed a mayor with more business experience than Mayor Boosalis. A *Journal* editorial deciphered the code: what ignited her opponents was not really the mayor's lack of business experience but rather her failure to give preferential treatment to business interests.

Reflecting back, *Lincoln Journal Star* editor Kathleen Rutledge recalled, "My sense is that her no-growth, anti-business label came from the fact that you couldn't 'play' Helen. That was irritating to those who were able to 'play' people in office to serve their own interests." Similarly, Mom's communications consultant for the mayoral campaign, Rich Bailey, believes that "Helen received a bum rap in being labeled as 'anti-business.' Her genuine interest in people and their concerns scared some people of the establishment—if she was willing to pay attention to everybody and anybody, that meant there were no longer just a few who could get access. So that translated into their view of her being anti-business."

The mayor held a positive view of her evolving relationship with the business community, as did many others. John Rosenow, Arbor Day Foundation president, recalls that the mayor's "approach was inclusive. She reached out to involve citizens, yet she also continued to engage the traditional leadership in business. Everyone had a voice—it felt balanced." The chamber of commerce may not have been thrilled with Mom's encouragement of the newly energized neighborhood organizations in the city's comprehensive planning process, but many business interests applauded her commitment to redevelopment and beautification of the downtown business district. And other measures, such as her sixty visits to Lincoln businesses to keep in touch with their concerns, also earned more business support for the mayor than she had when she took office four years earlier. She had convinced some in business, though far from all, that she was "not the wild radical I was feared to be."

In his formal announcement of candidacy on February 14, 1979, Stan Matzke admitted that Helen Boosalis had been a good mayor but said that he believed he would be a better one. Matzke said he had had difficulty deciding to run because he had been a Boosalis supporter four years earlier and had "a great deal of respect for her as a person and a public servant." The campaign was just beginning, but so far the civility level seemed quite high.

Matzke emphasized his desire to bring a different leadership style to the mayor's office. "There are many similarities between Helen and I," Matzke continued, but "the major campaign issue will be the difference in leadership styles. If I were mayor, you'd certainly know who is in charge." Matzke claimed the mayor had been indecisive, letting decisions linger on controversial issues like the Northeast Radial and downzoning provisions in the proposed zoning code. He claimed that "no one seems to be in charge" of the proposed zoning code and that Planning Director Doug Brogden was a political liability for the mayor. And implying the mayor's anti-business reputation, Matzke promised to work to establish a climate supportive of business progress.

The mayor's first-term record posed both problem and opportunity for Matzke and the long list of other challengers. It was against her record that "what all the other candidates have to offer" would be judged, warned a *Star* editorial, "and what the candidates have to offer should consist of more than vague charges and wish lists that cannot realistically be granted. It is not enough to *want* to be mayor." Apparently, more initial candidates "wanted" to be mayor than were prepared to take on my mother and her record—the final number of challengers fell from ten to six by the filing deadline in mid-March 1979.

Having failed to produce a "true blue business community candidate" of their own, Councilmen Sikyta, Hampton, and Scherer eventually declared their support for Matzke. From their council seats the three were presumed by a *Journal* editorial to be "in tactical position to ambush and hammer the chief executive"—nothing new, except now they had the added incentive of beating her at the polls—and "thus Mrs. Boosalis necessarily must be engaged in a multiple-front campaign," both inside and outside city hall.

The support of Councilmen Sikyta, Hampton, and Scherer for Matzke's candidacy raised the question of whether an affinity actually existed among the three councilmen (Republicans all) and Democrat Matzke or whether their support for Matzke was based primarily on "dislike for Mrs. Boosalis." An editorial in the *Lincoln Star* offered its view of the real reasons behind the councilmen's decisions to back Matzke for mayor: "It's not surprising that Lincoln City Councilmen Joe Hampton, Leo Scherer and Bob Sikyta would admit to joining the Stan Matzke mayoral campaign. They've spent the better part of two years trying to undermine the administration of Mayor Helen Boosalis with baseless criticism, unwarranted obstruction, constant bickering, and petty politicking. With those long months of meticulous, orchestrated preparation invested, it figures they would ultimately throw in with the candidate who might give Mrs. Boosalis the most potent challenge. Matzke just happened along. It easily could have been another candidate," the editorial observed of the three councilmen's support of Matzke. It then examined what role the mayor's performance may have played in their decision:

> We're not arguing against legitimate challenges to elected leadership. No incumbent owns a job. What is of concern is the quality of criticism aimed weekly at the mayor by her opponents on the council—the ceaseless, senseless attempts to bait her, to trap her, to embarrass her; the distortion of the record and of the issues.
>
> What are the complaints? High taxes? No, the mayor's budgets have held the line on taxes. Is it Government grown fat? No, during the past four years the administration has kept it lean and worked to increase its efficiency. Has the city administration ignored its responsibility to work with the private sector in maintaining a strong, attractive center city? The comparative health and physical attractiveness of Lincoln's downtown speaks for itself. Is the issue closed doors at City Hall? No, the mayor has opened them wider than ever before.

The *Star* concluded with its assessment of what was really at stake in this election: "One senses that the real issue is the unrealized goal of the council majority and its supporters of allowing interests to run rampant which up to this point have prospered but nevertheless chafe under the necessary controls which have helped shape this remarkable city and its excellent quality of life. Mrs. Boosalis' presence in City Hall threatens the realization of their goal. That is why, along with the grudge against her because she won four years ago, the council members in question so willingly climb aboard another's campaign train."

In such an impassioned editorial I hear the voice of one who closely observed the two-year reign of the five-person council majority and had simply had enough of the unreasonable behavior and extreme antagonism directed at the mayor. The strong editorial conclusions reached by the *Lincoln Star*'s longtime (1969–82) editorial page editor, Bob Schrepf, further illuminate for me my mother's plight. From my distant life in Illinois, I didn't fully understand at the time that my mother had been forced to engage in constant warfare in such an adversarial environment. I cannot imagine how she not only survived but also continued to fight for the good of her city, to inspire and engage others in the fight, and to succeed on many fronts against all odds.

When I asked Mom how she had continued to get out of bed in the morning for yet another day of battle, she was matter-of-fact in her response: "I could feel that the people were behind me. Whenever and wherever I went out into the community—to neighborhoods, to businesses, to speaking engagements—people would make an effort to come up and tell me they were behind me and not to give up. If I didn't feel all that support coming from regular folks—not just from those with vested interests—I wouldn't have had the strength to keep going like I did. The people were what saved me." Likewise, years after writing editorials for the *Star*, Bob Schrepf reflected, "I think the source of her optimism was her faith in people," he said. "Her experience with people allowed her to be optimistic."

My mother's other saving grace during the onslaught of attacks and obstructionism by the council majority was my dad's support. He was the cut man in her corner, ensuring that she was ready to go another round. He was her sounding board and confidante.

The importance of my parents' unique partnership to my mother's political life was apparent to those around them. Mike Merwick, administrative aide in the mayor's office, said that "Helen's biggest support was from Mike. It was hard enough at that time to be accepted as a woman leader by society at large, but it was even more important to have support at home," Merwick observed. "What a remarkable relationship they had—it didn't matter who was doing what, they were both in there supporting each other. He was key to what she was able to do. That was not at all common then." Likewise, Nancy McClelland, who worked with the mayor on city disability issues, offered, "I think we need a word for someone like Mike Boosalis because it's the men behind women like Helen who make all the difference. I loved when Mike would say, 'Go get 'em, Helen.' They are an amazing couple," she said. "What was really special was how clear it was that your parents were a team," said Keven Donnellan, AARP's chief communications officer. "You don't see that in a lot of political couples. Your father was so supportive of your mother and she always talked proudly of your dad's latest research. It's what kept them both so grounded in reality."

As a small child I sometimes heard my parents talking at bedtime, sharing the day's ups and downs. Not only did my mother share her skirmishes inside city hall and on the campaign trail, but listening to my father talk about his work from a different world than politics was undoubtedly a refreshing respite. At the end of her politically jagged days as mayor, soothing music could not have been more calming than hearing about Dad's fight against corn, wheat, and soybean diseases as she drifted off to rest up for the next day on the front.

THE 1979 MAYORAL PRIMARY ELECTION ISSUES

Once the March 1979 deadline for municipal candidacy filings passed, there were only twenty days until the primary election, followed a month later by the general election. The campaign was mercifully short, especially by today's standards, which meant that only a few issues could make their way to the top.

One of those issues spotlighted by Mom's chief opponent was "downzoning" under the proposed new zoning code to implement the Comprehensive Plan. Matzke charged that the proposed downzoning—when a piece of property receives a more restrictive zoning classification, often lowering its value—was "totally unfair to property owners" and "almost like robbery engineered by city hall administrators." Downzoning was a perfectly timed campaign issue, since public hearings on the zoning code had just ended, and Council Chairman Sikyta estimated a two-month review of the code by the council before taking final action—coincidentally, the same period of time before the primary election. That timing would allow, forecast an editorial, "Mayor Boosalis' opponents on the council to wring as much political advantage out of the [zoning code] controversy as possible."

The mayor would not be drawn into defending the proposed zoning code. In a news conference, she reminded the council and her opponent that she played no role in developing the proposed zoning code, which came from the citizen Planning Commission staffed by the city's Planning Department. The mayor had responsibility only to approve or disapprove the council's final action on the code as a whole; the City Charter and state law prohibited her from directing the Planning Department to include or delete proposed code provisions. She, too, was concerned about some of the code's controversial downzoning provisions and said that if the council approved the zoning code ordinance as proposed, she would veto it. That somewhat deflated the issue for the Matzke campaign.

While the zoning code wars continued on the council floor, Matzke chose an additional vehicle for criticizing the mayor. During the lengthy process to overhaul the zoning code, the city's longtime planning director, Doug Brogden, had come under fire from land speculators, developers, affected property owners—and from their city council champions—for his role in preparing the proposed zoning code, especially the controversial downzoning provisions. Matzke crafted a campaign issue criticizing Brogden, who reported to the mayor. With significant developer and business support, Matzke pressed the mayor to take a stand on Brogden's job performance and suggested that his days as director could be numbered.

A Matzke campaign ad in his series "Who's In Charge at City Hall?" questioned, "Who Is Doug Brogden Working For?" In the ad, Matzke promised to "control and if need be oversee the day to day activities of every department. . . . There will be no place in the Matzke administration for internal bureaucracies or fiefdoms who are not responsible to the mayor and the people of Lincoln."

At first ignoring Matzke's charges, the mayor later refused to "be bullied into promising Brogden's scalp as a price to pay for political support," as characterized by an editorial. In fact, she came out with both barrels blasting: "My integrity and my sense of fairness do not permit me to be pressured into firing or promising to fire the planning director because his proposals, prepared in the line of his duties . . . have met with disapproval from certain citizens affected by them." She pointed out that the planning director's job was to make zoning code proposals based on the Comprehensive Plan, not to make policy. "The City Council makes policy," she said. "It is up to the City Council to decide, based upon input from citizens at the public hearings already held, whether they are in agreement with those proposals."

My mother was not insensitive to legitimate grievances about the performance of one of her key administrators; she had her own issues with parts of the proposed zoning code and even perhaps with her planning director's perceived concentration of power over land use. But her sense of justice and fair play prevented her from publicly evaluating a subordinate's performance or promising his termination in response to heated campaign pressure. Matzke's blaming the mayor's planning director for downzoning proposals that Matzke claimed unjustly robbed "citizens of Lincoln who have worked hard for the property they now own" would probably strike a chord with voters. But this was the kind of issue to which my mother would have responded, "To heck with the campaign. I'm going to do the right thing."

Matzke conducted a typical challenger-incumbent primary campaign. "As the challenger," he said, "I have to point out the weaknesses of the current administration. That gives me a sort of negative point of view." His charges leveled at the mayor included her lack of a clear set of priorities, bad snow-removal policy, lack of interest in street safety, and "lacking in the ability to make the necessary tough decisions demanded of the city's chief executive officer." With little time in the primary campaign to address many issues, Matzke's central campaign theme was to criticize the mayor's leadership and management style. He echoed the majority council members' objections to her attending council meetings. "It's like the governor sitting in the back of the legislative chamber," he said. "Our mayor doesn't understand the concept of separation of powers."

While fielding campaign jabs from her strongest challenger and also reminding voters of her administration's accomplishments, Mom was simultaneously handling daily challenges as the city's chief executive—far different circumstances than her first mayoral campaign. She had to compromise her natural door-to-door, person-to-person campaign style. "During the 1975 campaign," a reporter observed, "Mrs. Boosalis campaigned 18 hours a day, relying more on personal contact than advertisements. Ironically, she says, the job she's trying to keep is preventing her from campaigning the way she knows and likes best—door to door."

THE UNEXPECTED

Although time was short between the filing deadline and the primary and general elections, there was enough time for the emergence of a lightning-rod campaign issue that no one had anticipated—a phenomenon that occurs in the course of many campaigns. Campaign strategists strive mightily to identify and focus on issues showcasing their candidate's strengths, but often an event external to campaign strategies will emerge to swamp all best-laid plans. Such was the case in the campaigns for mayor and city council in the spring of 1979.

Enter onstage an unlikely campaign lightning-rod issue: the proposed leasing of the city-owned Lincoln General Hospital.

Lincoln General, a public hospital, was planning in 1979 a major construction project requiring city-issued revenue bonds to finance project costs. In the mid-1960s, ownership and budget control of the hospital had passed to the city (and the public) in a deal where the city government issued revenue bonds to finance construction of the modern hospital plant. Since then the hospital administration had managed the facility's day-to-day operations, but the city owned the hospital and was responsible for board appointments, budget review, and other oversight functions. The split-control arrangement between the hospital and city had not always worked smoothly, but the hospital provided high-quality services while retaining its "public" character by providing health services to underserved populations.

In the spring of 1979—square in the middle of the municipal campaigns for mayor and city council—Lincoln General's request for a new city bond issue to fund additional construction took an unexpected turn. Lehman Bros., New York underwriter for the bonds, advised the city council that the split control between the city and hospital could adversely affect the bond interest rates. Without changes to the hospital-city arrangement, the bond rate penalty could be about .5 percent—about $50,000 a year more in city bond interest payments, or $1.5 million over the course of the thirty-year repayment period.

Lincoln General was only too happy to receive this Wall Street advice and quickly proposed a new arrangement with the city under a dramatically revised lease and operating agreement: administration of Lincoln General would reside solely in the private Lincoln General Hospital Association, extinguishing the city's budgetary and oversight authority and greatly limiting the city's power to appoint hospital board members. Under the hospital's lease proposal, the city would retain legal ownership, but that was about all—city control would effectively end. "Only in the legal and technical sense," an editorial asserted, "would Lincoln General remain a 'public' hospital. The proposed lease authorizes the private Lincoln Hospital Association to run the entity with almost complete autonomy."

Those who had long opposed city oversight of the hospital—especially the mayor's power to appoint hospital board members (with council confirmation)—applauded the hospital's proposed leasing arrangement. In essence, the proposed lease/operating agreement would convert city-owned Lincoln General Hospital into a privately operated health care institution akin to other private hospitals in the city; the hospital, not its city owner, would enjoy almost total autonomy while still enjoying the benefits of access to the city's credit card.

What offspring wouldn't love such an arrangement, and what parent would allow it? In retaining ownership but no budgetary and financial control over the hospital, the city would play no part in the hospital's operation other than as the hospital's sugar daddy when it needed the city's credit for issuing millions in revenue bonds to finance hospital construction, equipment purchase, and related legal fees.

At the March 26, 1979, city council public hearing on the proposed lease, Lincoln General's chief of staff urged the city to "relinquish control of Lincoln General Hospital for the good of the hospital and the city of Lincoln." He described the stigma attached to being a city-owned hospital that derived from the public perception that its facilities were not as good as those of private hospitals in Lincoln.

Council members also heard from another impassioned player—the mayor. Why, she asked, should the city, as owner, give up its review of hospital budgets and rates as well as its selection of hospital board members in return for a rubber-stamping function? If the council's real concern were to save money in lower bond interest costs, the mayor said, then it should consider a general obligation bond issue (voted on by the public) to fund the hospital project, since that would be cheaper than revenue bond financing. The mayor also expressed her fear that under the hospital's proposed lease arrangement Lincoln General would lose "some of its mandate for public access, or public service, if control becomes private." On the other hand, the mayor was not necessarily opposed to all forms of private administration of the hospital. Even if turning over total hospital control to a private organization were an appropriate option, she argued, the city council should solicit offers from other private entities in addition to the Lincoln General Hospital Association.

In fact, just such an alternative private organization did enter the scene: the health services group of the Mid-America Conference of the Seventh Day *Adventists. The Adventists group asked the council to delay action on the hospital-proposed lease in order to allow time to prepare its own proposal to operate the city-owned hospital. The mayor was not necessarily supportive of the Adventists' potential offer, but she believed their entry onto the field would ensure that all options would be considered.

The Adventists' renewed interest in operating the hospital presented a possible foil to what appeared to be a cut-and-dried arrangement—favored by the council majority—to wrest control of the hospital from the city into the all-too-eager hands of the Lincoln General Hospital Association. The Adventists' request to bid on assuming hospital operations would perhaps broaden discussion before the council could make what seemed to be a preordained decision in favor of the current hospital administration.

After the public hearing and entry of the new player, an editorial in the *Lincoln Journal* summarized arguments against approving the hospital-proposed lease but also acknowledged the inevitability that the lease would be adopted by the city council. First, the editorial maintained, even if the hospital's Wall Street consultant was correct, it would still be worth $25,000 to $75,000 more a year in increased city bond interest costs for "the public's elected representatives to continue having the opportunity to scrutinize, question and even influence Lincoln General's purse string decisions." Second, nothing in the hospital-proposed fifty-seven-page lease required the private hospital association's management to "give special attention to public services, the kind which public hospitals are initially chartered to provide." And finally, even if it were the appropriate time for the city to get out of the hospital business altogether, all the more reason, urged the *Journal*, to check out all potential parties interested in taking over the hospital.

The council delayed action on the lease for one week at the request of Councilman Hampton, supposedly to assure the council of its power to rescind the lease in the event of hospital mismanagement. He emphasized that his request for delay was not related to the Adventists' new proposal, which he viewed as "not germane to the issue." Hampton believed that consideration of a second proposal by the council would represent bad faith after the council's working with the Lincoln General Hospital Association on hospital expansion plans.

The council decided to delay action on the hospital lease just one day before the city's April 3 primary to elect the top two contenders for mayor as well as the field of council candidates for the general election a month later. Perhaps my mother went to bed the night before the primary thinking about what further leadership she could exert to protect the public interest in the city-owned hospital—but she awoke to a primary election day that would threaten to annihilate her mayoral leadership altogether.

THE 1979 CITY COUNCIL PRIMARY ELECTION: NEW DISTRICTS

During the mayor's primary campaign against her chief opponent, Stan Matzke, the city council had its own full plate: grappling with the massive zoning code overhaul to implement the Comprehensive Plan and also negotiating the proposed Lincoln General Hospital lease. The council majority hoped these two issues would join to defeat the mayor's reelection bid. Three of the five-person council majority were up for reelection themselves, though not as "at-large" candidates, as they had originally been elected.

This was the first city council election to use a partial district system, which had been vehemently opposed by the current council majority but decisively approved by voters. District elections were hailed by the *Star* as the "biggest change on the local political scene since implementation of the strong mayor form of government in the early 1960s," and the council district system proved to encourage more neighborhood activist candidates than the more costly, at-large elections.

Of the seven city council seats, four were up for election in 1979 and designated under the new system as district seats assigned to the four geographic quadrants of the city: northeast, northwest, southeast, and southwest. Council members Bob Sikyta, Steve Cook, and Arlyss Brown (appointed to fill Baker's term when he resigned) all filed to run for re-election in their newly designated districts; thus three of the five-member council majority who had consistently opposed the mayor were up for reelection. The fourth district was an open seat vacated by "burned out" Councilman Jeambey, who decided not to run for *reelection. The other three seats, occupied by Hampton, Scherer, and Robinson, would remain seats to be elected at large, not by district; candidates for those three seats would run citywide at the next city election in 1981, two years away.

How the new district system would affect the makeup of the next council was anyone's guess. Would all three incumbents win their new district seats and possibly add the winner of the open fourth district seat to their ranks, thereby creating a formidable *six*-member majority opposed to the mayor? Or would one or more of the incumbents lose their district races and weaken their majority hold of the legislative body? And how would the district council elections affect the heated citywide campaign for mayor?

Were the three incumbent council members who had conducted a vendetta against the mayor now running scared in their reelection bids? Would they suffer consequences at the polls from their self-created negative image? Was the power of incumbency enough to ensure their reelection, or did the March 31 editorial in the *Star* reflect public opinion? "The election may serve as a referendum on a council majority which consists sometimes of four but mainly of five members. Three of them, Arlyss Brown, Steve Cook, and Bob Sikyta, will be the ones to collect the roses or brickbats, since their terms have expired," the editorial warned. "The council majority is most responsible for the image received publicly of a city law and policy-making body grown surly, uncooperative and insensitive except to development needs; a council fearful of political expression except from establishment sources; a council which cannot get along with itself, let alone the executive branch; a council comprised of some members whose economic self-interest gets bound up too often with council business."

This was anything but a ho-hum local election. Much was at stake. My mother's election as mayor four years earlier had shaken the political tree, but whether that was just an aberration would be revealed not only in her bid for reelection but in the new district council races as well.

From their safe, not-up-for-election seats, Councilmen Hampton and Scherer labeled the prime challengers for the district seats—Eric Youngberg, Donna Frohardt, Mike Steinman, and Margrethe Ahlschwede—a "liberal slate" who had supported the advent of district elections in order to capture control of the council. Steinman and Ahlschwede were linked to the Lincoln Alliance, "perceived by some as an anti-establishment pressure group that uses roughshod tactics such as packing the city council chambers as a show of force to accomplish its goals." Councilman Hampton contended that the Alliance, in concert with liberal political leaders, was behind the "liberal slate" of council candidates. Alliance members, on the other hand, viewed the Alliance coalition of church, neighborhood, and civic organizations as a vehicle for citizen involvement in such projects as school safety and study of redlining charges against lending institutions.

Ads targeted Steinman's and Ahlschwede's membership in the Alliance and accused it of making "a possible power play for control of your city's government . . . patterned after the ideas of radical sociologist Saul Alinsky"—tactics reminiscent of my mother's first campaign for mayor when the university connection was used to taint her and other candidates in similar fear-evoking ads. Once again, the old guard apparently hoped through scare tactics to crush grassroots efforts outside its control.

The district council races intensified after the April primary election produced stronger-than-expected challenges to the incumbents for the general election. No doubt the three incumbent councilmen were feeling pressure from the threatening vote totals garnered by their primary opponents and from editorial criticism of their performance in office: "The council majority—[including] incumbent candidates Arlyss Brown, Steve Cook and Bob Sikyta—while figuratively declaring war against Mayor Boosalis, neighborhoods, the city's environment and the average citizen, has formed a hospitality committee for almost every special interest in the city," a *Star* editorial read. "Philosophically, the council majority seems continually at odds with the proposition that the average citizen ought to have much of a voice in governmental affairs. Those council members feel more comfortable when government is a closed shop." The primary vote tally put the three council incumbents on notice—they would face tougher general election campaigns against their district challengers than they had expected.

THE 1979 MAYORAL GENERAL
ELECTION CAMPAIGN: BOOSALIS V. MATZKE

Against this backdrop of district council candidates posing viable challenges to the anti-Boosalis incumbent candidates, Mayor Boosalis and Stan Matzke surprised no one by winning the top two spots in the primary election for mayor.

But to almost everyone's surprise and shock, Boosalis placed second behind Matzke. Matzke picked up a lead of 7 percentage points over the mayor—his 49 percent to her 42 percent—while the other five mayoral candidates combined accounted for 9 percent of the vote. Matzke expressed his surprise that the outcome put him further ahead than he had expected, and he predicted that the votes for the other five primary candidates would also go to him in the general election.

While recognizing the difficult come-from-behind campaign that lay ahead of her, my mother predicted that Matzke's primary lead would not translate into a victory in the general election. She surmised that the 29 percent primary voter turnout might have meant that pro-Boosalis supporters did not come out to vote. "People kept telling me I was a shoo-in, but I said, 'No, an incumbent is never a shoo-in.'" Perhaps the complacency of Boosalis supporters was responsible for the mayor's second-place showing, just as in the defeat of her close colleague Sue Bailey for a return trip to the council two years earlier.

The Boosalis primary "victory" party was a sobering affair, but my mother voiced an optimistic yet urgent battle cry encouraging her troops for the general election. The many well-wishers and volunteers who gathered again on primary election night at my Uncle John's restaurant accepted their candidate's charge, repeating again and again, "We'll have to work harder!" Indeed, it was time for the hundreds of Boosalis volunteers to turn up the heat. Mom's mayoral campaign volunteer coordinator, Betty Peterson, explained, "My job was not asking for money but asking for people's time. People rarely turned me down. Would you believe that we had eleven hundred volunteers? I know because I kept a card file on each volunteer."

While Mom's second-place primary showing didn't deter her optimism, editorials in both Lincoln newspapers painted a pessimistic picture of her chances of winning the general election. "Challenger Stan Matzke now must be reckoned as the clear favorite for the May 1 mayoral general election," read the *Journal* editorial. "This is not to say Helen Boosalis can't win a second show-down popularity contest. Her political task is formidable, however. Matzke's capture of 49 percent of all votes in a seven-person race suggests he should be now more able to attract the resources and commitment of the commercial and real estate development interests who have been big-dollar backers."

Equally discouraging was the editorial in the *Star*, which said that "Mayor Helen Boosalis is hardly out of the running, but faces an uphill struggle to retain her job," though it also offered constructive advice: "If Mrs. Boosalis is to win, she cannot take it for granted that people know she has done a good job as mayor—which she has. She must take her case to the people, attempt to back Matzke into a corner where he can't weasel on the issues and she must draw the line for voters between what she stands for and what the people who want to drive her from office stand for."

Were these editorial opinions accurate predictions of how tough the campaign would be for my mother to win another term? And did they draw instructive blueprints for changes in her general election campaign strategy? The answer appeared to be yes on both accounts, as Mom charged out of primary election night with her trademark take-it-to-the-people campaign style and a revamping of her entire campaign strategy.

First to be addressed was one stream of Mom's pre-primary advertising. The mayor had pegged her reelection campaign in part on her leadership in developing Lincoln's high quality of life and in keeping at bay urban fiscal problems that were plaguing other cities. Some campaign committee volunteers had pushed a concept for a series of print ads to contrast just how good things were in Lincoln compared to how bad they were in other cities.

One pre-primary Boosalis ad in the series—headlined "Some Cities Are Dying. But Not Lincoln"—showed a large picture of a run-down, decaying commercial area with a seedy tavern and boarded-up windows. The text of the ad was positive, highlighting Lincoln's vitality in its downtown and neighborhood development; but the accompanying photo, which occupied half the ad space, was so dismal that the impression on voters must have been overwhelmingly negative—some might even have thought that the seedy site was in Lincoln. The readers' association between the dreary picture and the ad's slogan, "Helen Boosalis On the Job," was likely a negative one.

Other Boosalis ads in the same series included one headlined "Some Cities Are Bankrupt. But Not Lincoln," with a close-up photo of a padlocked security gate displaying a small hand-printed sign—"Library Closed." Again, the ad's written text, which positively portrayed the city's fiscal condition, did not overcome the overall negativity created by the photo.

The worst of the lot was a photo accompanying the ad headlined "Some Cities Are Dangerous. But Not Lincoln." When I turned the page in my dad's clippings book and unfolded this ad, the picture literally took my breath away. The photo was nearly all door—opened just a crack to reveal a sliver of an elderly woman's face—one wrinkled, baggy, and frightened eye peering through the crack, one hand clutching the door's chain lock.

The disquieting, gloomy effect of the photos in the ad series was antithetical to my mother's positive, upbeat nature. How could she have thought this approach reflected who she was, and why did she approve this line of advertising? When I asked, she said that some volunteer advisers on her campaign committee who had more experience in higher-level political campaigns had urged her to try this different approach to capture voter attention; they insisted the theme of the ads would, by showing how bad things were in other places, bring into focus how good life was in Lincoln, thanks to her leadership. "I deferred to those who knew more than I about such things even though I wasn't keen on the ads," she told me. "I've always encouraged others' input in decision making, but in this case I neglected the fact that in the end the decisions are mine."

These weren't the only ads in my mother's pre-primary media campaign, but they dropped from sight after her second-place primary finish in favor of ads much more in keeping with Mom's character and image. For example, one ad series carried the theme, "She works with people . . . TO GET THINGS DONE! Helen Boosalis On the Job." This series used photos, too, but this time positive ones—a photo of the newly built Centrum (text: "The Centrum. It didn't cost a penny in property tax money!") and another of kids playing in a renovated park (text: "Our Neighborhoods. A place to raise kids and put down roots").

Another ad series headlined the mayor's personal qualities and experience and used quotes from news stories to substantiate the claims: "Honest & Decisive!" . . . "Proven Leadership" . . . "Lowered Taxes" . . . "Your Special Interests!" One even addressed her detractors' claim that she was anti-business, but this time in a post-primary positive style— "Helen Boosalis Means Business!"—quoting a business magazine article extolling Lincoln's "strong city administration that doesn't look at business and industry as ogres."

The mayor's advertising message had recovered from its primary election stumble and was back on track for the general election.

Meanwhile, the challenger's ads honed in on the discord at city hall, laying the blame at the mayor's feet. Matzke even picked up on terminology used by the city council majority in their promise to end the "bickering" at city hall. An ad showing Matzke, tie loosened, suit jacket slung over one shoulder, read: "I'll take the hassle out of city government. Lincoln doesn't need a mayor who argues all the time. My philosophy has always been that you can disagree without being disagreeable. There's no time for bickering when there is so much that can be done for the good of Lincoln." Matzke stressed his theme of "disagreeing without being disagreeable" in ads and on the stump throughout his campaign for mayor.

Other Matzke ads purported that Lincoln was rife with problems resulting from the mayor's poor leadership and indecision; other ads diminished the mayor's positive achievements, such as minimizing her role in Lincoln's recognition as an All-America City. "We didn't become an All-America City because of any one person. We all pitched in"; and "You and I and a whole lot of other people helped make Lincoln an All America City."

A series of Matzke ads titled "Who's In Charge at City Hall?" attacked the mayor's management of her administration, from lack of control over her planning director to lack of adequate snow removal. Lest anyone think that only in a smaller city could snow removal be a serious campaign issue, one need only look to the mayoral campaign in Chicago that same winter of 1979, when Mayor Michael Bilandic became the victim of his failure to remove the city's record ninety inches of snow and lost his job to Chicago's first woman mayor, Jane Byrne.

Matzke also played the anti-business card in ads using code words to his anybody-but-Boosalis business base: "I love Lincoln. . . . But the fact of the matter is our 'All America City' has problems. Big problems. . . . If you're a businessman, you know the problems I'm talking about . . . the restrictions that frustrate you every day. . . . If you're a property owner, you've felt the squeeze play from City Hall." Matzke's advertising slogan—"The best man for the job"—was "an integral part of Matzke's campaign effort." Would "businessmen," "property owners," and perhaps "men" in general respond to this call to reassert their power over who would run city hall after Lincoln's first woman mayor?

Campaign advertising alone rarely wins elections, at least not in local campaigns twenty-five years ago. Mom's dismal pre-primary ad series did not cause her second-place finish, but perhaps those ads had a greater impact because they were not counterbalanced by her typical door-to-door, grassroots campaigning. The day-to-day demands of the mayor's office put more distance between her and the voters. Support of the people had taken Mom through four tough years. Now she needed to find ways both to do her job as mayor and personally take her campaign to the people; she needed all her supporters to vote in the general election.

While she could not abandon city hall to knock on every door in Lincoln, Mom knew she needed to take on her opponent directly—to be "far more aggressive"—so that voters could see the differences between them and remember her work on their behalf. Her strategy included challenging Matzke three days after the primary to debate "so we can find out what his positions are. I think the public would like to know what programs are proposed to deal with what my opponent says are the 'big problems of Lincoln,' how they will be implemented and how we will pay for them."

Matzke's far-from-eager response to the mayor's proposed debates: "It's a question of whether they can be scheduled. My calendar is pretty filled already." He speculated that the mayor wanted debates to show that he was not informed about city hall matters. He predicted that her plan would "backfire" and that debates would show that the mayor was more a technician, and he a leader and manager dealing in "the larger concepts."

A "warm-up" debate on April 20 between the mayoral hopefuls produced no startling results. Matzke focused on the mayor's poor relationship with the council and reasserted his ability to "disagree without being disagreeable." The mayor responded that she had tried to maintain a good relationship with the council, but ultimately the voters should decide who was to blame for the friction. (Although she supported cooperation between the mayor and council, Mom clarified in a later debate that "cooperation does not mean capitulation.")

Matzke reiterated his claim that Planning Director Brogden wielded too much power in the Boosalis administration. The mayor responded that Brogden had only the power granted by the city council; if he got his way all the time, she said, "he must have four council members in his hip pocket. Would you believe that?" So went the initial debate—the two sparred, but no knockout.

In a second mayoral debate just a few days later, on April 22, one debate topic "on which there were fresh statements concerned the fast-developing issue of the Lincoln General Hospital lease." Fast-developing issue—yes. An important city council vote on the hospital lease was scheduled for April 23, the next day.

MAYOR'S VETO: LINCOLN GENERAL HOSPITAL LEASE

Flash back to the day before the April 3, 1979, primary election when the city council, on Councilman Hampton's motion, delayed a vote on the proposed lease of Lincoln General that would essentially change the character of the hospital from public to private. Just one day later came the primary election with its surprising results: Mayor Boosalis placed second behind challenger Stan Matzke. This chronology drove the hospital lease question squarely into the mix of the all-out battle between the two mayoral candidates, now pitted head-to-head for the few weeks before the voters would go to the general election polls.

Boosalis and Matzke did not really disagree on the substance of the hospital lease issue, but how the lease controversy unfolded in the month before the general election would prove to have a radically different impact on each candidacy.

On April 9, six days after the primary election, the city council approved the proposed hospital lease by a veto-proof vote of 5–2, dismissing the Adventists' offer to submit an alternative lease proposal under which the city stood to receive payment of $50,000 per year. In contrast, the city would receive no payment under the hospital-proposed lease but might save up to $50,000 a year in bond interest costs by severing city control over the hospital, according to the bond issue underwriters. The financial difference between the two proposals was essentially a wash, but city control would be lost under the hospital's proposed lease.

The mayor wasted no time. The day after the vote, Mom pledged to veto the council's lease approval, calling it a *"giveaway"* and calling the council's action "the most arrogant abuse of the responsibility of elected officials I have seen since I've been involved in city government. To give away the public control of a hospital in which the citizens of this community have invested . . . abrogates the first principle of re-sponsible government." If the hospital were to be turned over to private control, "it should only be through a vote of the people."

As I read these words I can hear my mother's tone of voice, the tone that I rarely heard growing up but when I did, I snapped to attention—it meant she was unmistakably riled up. An editorial in the *Star* on April 11 also recognized her vehemence: "For a person normally given to re-straint, her choice of words underlines the gravity of the situation." An editorial in the *Journal* that same day cheered my mother's impassioned position:

> If the Big Five on the Lincoln City Council wanted the city to get out of the public hospital business, why in the name of all that's rea-sonable didn't they simply put Lincoln General Hospital up for sale to the highest bidder? At least that way the people of Lincoln argu-ably might have picked up some cash. City government could have received something back from the multi-million-dollar investment it has made in the hospital over the past several years.
>
> But the deal approved by the City Council majority Monday unites the worst of two worlds: it transfers operational control of Lincoln General from the public to a private organization while simultane-ously granting that private group an exclusive pipeline to use the city's public credit for its private hospital expansion purposes.
>
> Mayor Boosalis, who intends to veto the lease, calls the council action a "giveaway." There's no big quarrel here with the mayor's description and none at all with her decision to veto, even in the face of certain failure.

As promised, the mayor vetoed the lease on April 17, "using the oc-casion to deliver a stinging indictment of the city council decision. In what is probably the strongest-worded veto message she has issued dur-ing her four years in office, the mayor said, 'the public deserves more than to have public control of this operation (Lincoln General) abruptly and highhandedly thrown away.'" Mom's veto message denounced the council decision as "hastily conceived, ill considered, based on errone-ous and speculative assumptions and clearly not in the best interest of the citizens and hospital ratepayers of the city of Lincoln." The lease agreement was proposed "under the guise of being a prudent financial step calculated to save money" on hospital bonds, but such savings were the "sheerest speculation," she argued, since bond consultants could not guarantee that severing the ties between the hospital and city would result in better interest rates. Instead, the mayor said, city control of the Lincoln General budget and rates had been "cavalierly thrown away by the City Council."

The mayor's blazing four-page veto message said that city control had not been a yoke around the hospital's neck but, instead, had been mutually satisfying. Mom went on to praise the historic city-hospital link: "I perceive the present city control of the hospital as a relationship which has allowed Lincoln General to expand, to remain financially solvent, and to provide outstanding health services. Lincoln General stands as an example of a truly functional citizen-owned operation from which the public has reaped benefits and in which the public has a continuing concern."

The hospital administration was not about to take this barrage, especially from the mayor, sitting down. The same day Mom issued her veto message, Lincoln General Hospital administrator Robert Brungard distributed a lengthy report to hospital employees that outlined reasons to support the lease agreement. The report "pointed out how individual council members voted on the lease, explicitly noted Mayor Boosalis' hostility, and urged hospital people to 'get out and vote' May 1"—leaving little guesswork for whom his hospital employees should vote. In turn, my mother charged that Brungard's report to his employees violated the city's code of ethics: "He has forgotten the public nature of his employment in what is still a city hospital."

LINCOLN GENERAL PETITION DRIVE

The hospital lease question not only inflamed the sentiments of those in positions of power at both city hall and Lincoln General but soon became a wildfire at the grassroots level. Three days after the mayor's veto of the council's 5–2 approval of the lease, Lincoln citizen Charles Brown announced that he and more than a hundred volunteers would launch a petition drive if the council were to override the mayor's veto as anticipated. People were angered by the "lousy deal" represented by the lease, Brown said, as well as by the council's arbitrary refusal to hear any proposals from others interested in operating the hospital.

Brown recognized that overturning legislation is no easy task. To suspend the enacted lease ordinance and submit the issue to voters, petition gatherers would have to collect almost five thousand signatures within fifteen days of the lease's final approval. If enough petition signatures were collected, the lease would be suspended; if the council then failed to repeal the lease, it would be submitted to voters in a referendum. Brown's interpretation of the date from which to calculate the fifteen-day petition deadline was April 23 (the date of the council's expected veto override), since the lease approval would truly be "final" on that date. Fifteen days from April 23 would put the petitions' due date after the looming city elections on May 1.

City Attorney Bill Austin, however, had bad news for Brown and his fellow petitioners. Austin gave the mayor his legal opinion that the fifteen-day petition time frame had begun on the date the council voted to approve the lease, April 9, regardless of the date of the mayor's veto or potential veto override. Brown and his volunteers did not have the luxury of waiting to see if the council would override the mayor's veto on April 23 before beginning their fifteen-day mission to collect enough signatures to overturn the lease. No, Brown and his petition troops were shocked to learn on Friday, April 20, that they had less than *four days*—until April 24—to collect thousands of signatures. Brown and his petition volunteers frantically hit the streets over the weekend. It seemed truly a mission impossible.

Austin, newly appointed as city attorney, remembers his trepidation in giving the mayor his legal opinion on the petition drive timing: "It was at this point that I thought I was going to have the shortest career as a City Attorney in the history of Lincoln," he said. "Despite a jaw clenched tighter than her own fiscal policies, she accepted my opinion . . . what I learned, however, was that my new boss had a tremendous respect for the law and that she would follow it even when it was difficult."

On Monday, April 23, just eight days before the general election, the city council voted to override the mayor's veto by the same 5–2 vote that had originally approved the hospital lease. The prevailing council members came to the meeting prepared not only to vote to override the mayor's veto but also to voice their anger. Four of them read from prepared statements rather than speak extemporaneously on the council floor as was the norm. Chairman Sikyta claimed that Lincolnites were "grossly misled" if they relied on the mayor for their information on the hospital lease proposal. The most vitriolic remarks came from Councilman Hampton: "The mayor has finally come out with how vindictive she can be when anyone has the conviction to disagree with her."

Meanwhile, as the combative Monday council meeting concluded with the council majority overriding the mayor's veto, Charles Brown's petition volunteers scattered across the city, still madly collecting signatures in hopes of meeting their April 24 deadline set to expire in twenty-four hours. Over the weekend, the number of volunteers circulating petitions had swelled to three hundred. Even former mayor Dean Peterson came to city hall to pick up petitions.

Brown brought petitions that weekend to the mayoral debate, surmising that the venue would be fertile ground for gathering signatures. Apparently, his request for a petition signature took one person quite off guard—mayoral debater Stan Matzke.

The second debate was more "low-key than spirited" except for the Lincoln General lease issue. A debate question to the mayor asked about her immediate and unequivocal opposition to the lease when it was originally proposed to the council. She told the debate audience that some of her supporters had urged her to hold back on the controversial issue because it could go either way and could mean big trouble for her campaign. She had countered those advisers, believing the hospital "giveaway" was one of the most important city issues she had faced. "If it cost 10,000 votes and the election, I had no choice but to veto it."

The obvious debate question for Matzke, then, was where he stood on the lease. Matzke, "who previously hedged on questions relating to his stance on the lease," said that he, like the mayor, also would have vetoed the lease approval. He told the debate audience that he probably would sign a petition in order to force a vote of the public on the matter. The debate over, up stepped Charles Brown to give Matzke the golden opportunity to sign a petition as he had declared only moments earlier that he "probably" would do. And sign the petition Matzke did.

But in a strange maneuver, he immediately scratched out his name. Defending his flip-flop, Matzke said that he removed his name from the petition "because he had not read it and because he became skeptical when the person who put the petition before him was Charles Brown"; Matzke claimed that Brown had recently come to Matzke's workplace looking for information detrimental to his campaign. After crossing out his name, Matzke said, "If I'm going to sign one, I'll sign somebody else's. It's a personal thing."

The day after the debate, Matzke did sign a petition at a League of Women Voters meeting—presumably one circulated by someone more acceptable to him. But in contrast to his campaign advertising themes, which stressed bold and resolute leadership, his post-debate moment of indecision in the last week of the mayoral campaign may have reinforced a public perception, or at least created doubt, about Matzke's decisiveness as the city's next chief executive. "That Matzke reportedly signed someone else's petition later does not completely sponge away an impression of indecisiveness," stated a *Journal* editorial.

In contrast, the results of the petition drive showed little citizen indecision on the hospital lease question. The final signature count was not even a close call. On the day the petition deadline expired, which was also the day after the council override of the mayor's veto, Charles Brown and his burgeoning band of volunteers gleefully submitted 6,293 signatures, far more than the required 4,914.

An editorial in the *Journal* echoed seemingly universal amazement: "Has there ever been any popular political response quite like it in these parts? The securing of 6,293 petition signatures in only four days, asking a reversal or referendum vote of the City Council's decision to lease away public control over taxpayer-owned Lincoln General Hospital, is just what Mayor Helen Boosalis said it is: "Phenomenal!" The editorial continued by condemning the council majority's miscalculation and disregard of the depth of public feeling about the hospital lease: "The council majority can try to split public responsibility and public accountability, as the hospital lease does, and safely slap around Mayor Boosalis in the process by overriding her veto, but the reaction of an outraged citizenry is something else. . . . Lincolnites have demonstrated they care, and care very deeply, about meaningful continuing public control over the hospital, so long as it remains a public institution. If the hospital's status is to change, the public wants lots more discussion of the option."

Called "spontaneous and unorchestrated" in a *Star* editorial, the petition drive was "one of the most remarkable political phenomena seen in this city in memory . . . [and] clearly vindicates and reinforces Mayor Boosalis' veto." Besides broad-based opposition to the terms of the lease, other factors might have contributed to the petition drive's success. The editorial surmised that some signers might have felt that the council proceeded too quickly without exploring alternatives; others might have wanted the city to sell, not lease, the hospital; others perhaps wanted to put the issue up to public vote. "Most, we think, regard the hospital as a public asset which should be subject to public control as long as it remains such."

The success of the petition drive pleased the mayor enormously. "The proponents of the lease agreement appear to have underestimated public concern about the accountability of the hospital," she said. "Those people who feel that the public is unconcerned about how public property should be managed may have their eyes opened by the success of this petition drive." When asked whether the petitions would have repercussions in the mayoral election only a week away, the mayor said she did not know; nor did she believe that the petition drive necessarily "vindicated" her veto of the lease. "When I vetoed the lease, I had no way of knowing what the citizens thought. I did it because I thought it was a bad lease. At the time, it appeared it [my veto] might be an unpopular decision politically."

With the general election just a few days away, my mother's words might seem to have been strategically spoken, but they made me reflect on the conviction of her position when the lease issue first surfaced, not weeks later when the water had been tested and hindsight perfected. Just days after the primary election, my mom—still reeling from her poor showing in the primary—did not shrink from taking the strongest of stands on an issue that came out of left field and carried unknown repercussions on public opinion.

Whatever the political fallout from the mayor's taking such an out-front position, its potential threat to her come-from-behind bid for re-election was real. With only a few weeks until the general election, any negative public opinion of her stand on Lincoln General would be all too fresh on election day. Her advisers had good reason to caution her to tread lightly on the hospital lease issue, but Mom's decision to pursue it full throttle had little to do with trying to calculate the issue's impact on her election—and everything to do with her gut sense of doing the right thing.

Even if campaigning (and governing) "by poll numbers" were as om-nipresent in 1979 as it is now, I'm sure Mom would have had principled disdain for deciding issues based on poll numbers and for advice per-suading candidates and officeholders to change course with whichever way the popular winds blow. I call it courage. She may simply call it freedom from fear of failure. Whichever it was, it set her apart from many other politicians, then or now.

THE 1979 MAYORAL GENERAL ELECTION: OUTCOME

With the timing of the council majority's override of the mayor's veto and, concurrently, the stunning success of the petition drive, the hospi-tal lease issue dominated media and public attention all during that final week of the 1979 mayoral and city council campaigns. The pro-lease positions of the council majority—three of whom were up for reelec-tion (Sikyta, Cook, and Brown)—were unequivocal; the mayor's voice was equally clear through her veto and condemnation of the council's "giveaway." The triumph of the last-minute petition drive indicated the high level of public awareness of the issue. Only the mayoral challenger, Stan Matzke, seemed out of the fray and lacking an audible voice on the issue, since he had no official role to play in the commanding drama playing out in city hall.

So the hospital lease issue that had been on no one's radar screen just a few weeks earlier injected an unpredictable element in the final week's campaign stretch. This can happen in campaigns—and the tim-ing of the peak and denouement of such unpredictable forces can pro-duce election winners and losers. A stirred-up frenzy filled Lincoln's electoral air.

Both mayoral and council campaigns were surely doing all the usual end-of-campaign stuff—phone and mail vote reminders, advertising blitzes, door-to-door pamphlet drops—but all within a context of uncertainty over the fate of Lincoln General. Boosalis supporters, energized by their candidate's leadership, were committed to reversing their candidate's second-place primary finish. The city council campaigns had also swung into high gear, propelled by the momentum of the hospital lease struggle in the eleventh hour before balloting would begin.

Boosalis endorsements by both newspapers further revved up my mother's supporters. The *Lincoln Journal* cited its earlier prediction that "Mrs. Boosalis' toughest test would be to live within stiff revenue restraints. She's passed that business world challenge in a fashion that should please some of the starchiest of fiscal conservative collars." (The Boosalis endorsement concluded, however, by refuting—based on the integrity of the Matzke family name—any implications that Matzke was "a cardboard front man for real estate development and business interests who are providing so much of his campaign financing.") The *Lincoln Star* reminded voters of Helen Boosalis's four-year record as their mayor:

- From her reorganization of the Lincoln Police Department upon taking office in 1975 to the veto of the Lincoln General Hospital lease agreement last week, the Mayor has exercised that kind of strong leadership the city needs.
- During her first term the budgets have held the line. . . . Few city governments have Lincoln's fiscal health and stability. . . .
- The Boosalis administration has been committed to the city maintaining a partnership with the private sector. . . .
- The administration has advocated transportation planning which recognizes future energy limits. . . .
- During the years she has served the city the Boosalis name has been synonymous with honesty, integrity and openness. The hallmark of her political career has been the encouragement of citizen involvement in government. . . .
- Lastly, Mrs. Boosalis has been fiercely independent and not beholden to any special interests.

Charged with excitement and new confidence in the campaign's final week, the Boosalis camp hit a brick wall on Sunday, April 29, 1979, two days before the election. A poll released by the *Sunday Journal and Star* showed Matzke with a substantial lead—45 percent for Matzke, 37 percent for Boosalis, and 18 percent undecided. The poll results echoed the earlier primary election outcome when Matzke led Boosalis by 7 percentage points—49 to 42. The margin of error in the citywide poll was 5 percentage points, but the pollster said that undecided Lincoln voters typically vote against the incumbent. News of the poll could not have been worse for Mom, nor come at a worse time with only two days to go before the May 1 general election.

After the final week's surge of what felt like positive momentum, Boosalis campaign workers read the poll results with disbelief. My mother's indomitable can-do spirit kicked into high gear as she exhorted her supporters to corral every Boosalis vote for Tuesday's election, but even she must have had doubts during the campaign's last forty-eight hours.

If the poll was correct, and if undecided votes were to fall in Matzke's favor, as the pollster predicted, the mayor would lose by a significant margin and her second-act vision for the city would go unrealized. But even if the poll was wrong and had missed the mark, beyond the margin of error, would the poll's outcome negatively affect a close election by influencing voters just two days before the election?

The headlines on May 2 told the story: "Mayor Jubilant Over Reelection" and "Win Amazes Mayor" (accompanied by a photo capturing Mom's exuberant expression at the moment she learned of her victory). My mother's come-from-behind win over Matzke was decisive: Boosalis, 54 percent; Matzke, 46 percent.

Uncle John's restaurant was a far different election-night scene than the evening of the primary election a month earlier. Throngs of well-wishers continued to jam into the Knolls for hours, all wanting to congratulate and hug their victorious mayor. Mom repeated in a voice hoarse from nonstop campaigning, "Isn't it great? Fantastic! This is even better than the last time!"

My mother told the crowd she had expected a tight race but felt the momentum change the last ten days of the campaign. She credited old-

31. "Win Amazes Mayor" reads the headline

fashioned grassroots campaigning by her supporters: "I have never seen anything like the effort that the hundreds of people in this room put together." Max and I, giddy and relieved, viewed from our corner of the packed room the same scene that a reporter described: "It was Helen Boosalis' night. She was the heroine."

And what about those erroneous poll results released two days earlier, predicting a substantial Matzke victory? The pollsters tried to explain that Tuesday's election was the one example out of twenty when

32. Mike and Helen Boosalis, Bertha Geankoplis, and Max and Beth Davis celebrate Helen's 1979 mayoral reelection

election results did not substantiate scientific polling. Much of the 18 percent undecided vote in the poll must have gone to the mayor, even though earlier Lincoln voting patterns typically gave non-incumbents the clear advantage on election day. Both the pollster and the newspaper editor who published the poll speculated that the dynamics of the final days of the mayor's race, particularly the Lincoln General issue, could explain the difference between the poll and the contrary election results.

At 10:55 p.m. on election night, Stan Matzke "traveled across town at the hour of his greatest disappointment" to congratulate his opponent. He made his way through the boisterous throng and stepped up on the small platform with the mayor. "You're a heck of a campaigner," he told my mother as the crowd erupted with applause. "And he's a definite class act," I shouted in Max's ear.

In response to reporters' questions, both my mother and Matzke identified the hospital lease as a critical factor in the erosion of Matzke's lead in the primary. Before leaving his subdued election-night party to congratulate my mother, he had candidly told his supporters, "Something happened and it probably had something to do with Lincoln General." Although the lease issue clearly played a role in the outcome of the mayoral race, a *Star* editorial cautioned against its overemphasis in post-election analysis: "While the mayor was given credit for her decisiveness in vetoing the lease, she most likely won because of her overall good first-term record and the fact that her friends got out the vote in the general election."

THE 1979 CITY COUNCIL GENERAL ELECTION: OUTCOME

The hospital lease issue did not merely explain my mother's victory and Matzke's defeat, however; it also highlighted the strife between the mayor and council and reminded voters of the majority's obstructionism. Matzke himself acknowledged in defeat that "he had become identified with the City Council majority opposed to Mrs. Boosalis" and that "the anti-council incumbent sentiment expressed by the voters may have carried over to his candidacy." He speculated that the lease issue coupled with "what he said may have been an anti-council, antibusiness vote" may have cost him the election.

And what an anti-council vote there was! In Lincoln's first council election by districts, the three incumbents—Bob Sikyta, Steve Cook, and Arlyss Brown—were defeated by Donna Frohardt, Eric Youngberg, and Mike Steinman, respectively, while the fourth seat, vacated by Bob Jeambey, went to Margrethe Ahlschwede. The formidable five-person majority that had continually clashed with the mayor was now decimated, and only two members of its formerly powerful ranks remained on the council: at-large council members Joe Hampton and Leo Scherer, who were not up for reelection until 1981.

Suddenly the veto-proof 5–2 majority of the prior council completely switched to an opposite 2–5 split, as the elected novices were generally "presumed to be supportive of the policies Mrs. Boosalis has formulated in her first four years as mayor." The predicted new and improved five-person majority was composed of the four newly elected district members and at-large member John Robinson, although the newcomers were quick to emphasize that they were individual, independent thinkers and would not be part of any "bloc voting."

Mom looked forward to more harmonious relations with the new council group and joked with her election-night supporters about losing her voice, "Maybe I won't need my voice with the new council that was elected!" One thing seemed certain: the endless bickering and antagonism between the old city council majority and the mayor had come to an end. "The electorate took surprising steps to resolve the problem of 'bickering' in City Hall by ending the service of three incumbent members of the Council and re-electing the mayor—rather than vice versa as had been forecast by many," a *Star* editorial observed. "There was a statement in those election results against the imperious treatment of people."

Members of the former council majority expressed anger and bitterness at the election results. Council Chairman Sikyta was astounded at his defeat; after all, he had already voiced his intent to serve only one more council term before running for mayor. "I thought with eight years on the council and what I've been trying to accomplish that people were behind me." With the new council lineup, Sikyta continued, "No longer can I be picked on as the one causing trouble for the Mayor. She ought to be able to wheel and deal as much as she wants."

Councilman Hampton expressed his dismay at losing his majority colleagues and said he would now be "a voice in the wilderness." With four inexperienced council members, Hampton predicted "the sheer reality of the situation is that it places almost total control of city government in the hands of the Mayor for the time being." Councilman Scherer, Hampton's only compatriot from the disbanded former majority, expressed wait-and-see skepticism: "I see myself as a watchdog. I want the new council members to prove that they can be responsive to the needs of the total city first and then to their districts."

Yes, a critical factor cited for the electoral wipeout of council incumbent candidates was the modified district election plan, which "radically changed Lincoln's municipal politics," claimed a *Star* editorial. Those who futilely fought against the district election plan six months earlier (led by the council majority) had undoubtedly recognized that representation by districts "would be a political threat to the status quo. District election would be the great equalizer; it would diminish much of the advantage of incumbency and name recognition."

The three incumbents' losses could be viewed as a collective defeat based on their group performance on the council. "The council majority's decision to ram through the lease and override a Boosalis veto was a thunderous political error by the very people who probably had the election won two weeks ago," said a *Journal* editorial on the day after the election. "It allowed the council majority to be perceived as a bloc—homogeneous, rigid and high handed. The astonishing success in only four days of a referendum petition drive stopping the lease dead was the tip-off." *Journal* reporter Karen Maguire observed that voters must have responded to the council majority's shared negative behavior: "Arrogance may have been the deciding factor in the City Council election, according to voters and victors. There was some talk of a liberal-conservative split between incumbents and challengers, but winners and losers mostly agreed that the vote was influenced more by negative reaction to the so-called council majority."

Others characterized the election results in traditional political terms as a victory of liberals over conservatives, although Mom took exception to that broad-brush view. "I'm a liberal where human rights and constitutional safeguards are concerned," she said, "and a conservative where fiscal matters are involved." The *Star* saw a broader confluence of factors at work: "Describing Tuesday night as the victory of local lefties does not accurately describe what happened, nor who and what made it happen. . . . There has been, moreover, no adequate definition of the terms liberal and conservative as they relate to municipal issues. It was, rather, the 'ins' against 'outs'; entrenched arrogance as opposed to the promise of decent treatment and open minds, and an anti-incumbent trend bucked only by Mrs. Boosalis." The editorial found in the election results an alternative to the traditional labeling of liberals: "it was the victory not of liberals and refugees from the campus riots of the 1960s, as Joe Hampton would have it, but of what [Mike] Steinman likes to call the 'good government types'; those who place high value on openness, accountability and other civic and political virtues and who are inclined to view special interests skeptically. The good government types doubtless were aided by large numbers of voters both Democrat and Republican who consider themselves good government types."

NEW DAY

Between the election on May 1 and the swearing in of the new council and reelected mayor on May 14, a bit of old business commanded the attention of the old council. After a two-year marathon of meetings to draft a new zoning code implementing the Comprehensive Plan adopted in 1977, the lame-duck council rushed to reach agreement on the controversial zoning code before the new council, with its strong neighborhood representation by district, would take office. The lame-duck council—about to lose four of its members—was determined to enact the zoning code based on its years of work and negotiations.

Because Councilman Cook could not vote on the zoning code due to conflict of interest, the lame-duck majority did not have the five votes needed to override a mayoral veto. Since the mayor had the old council somewhat "over the barrel," she offered for council reconsideration her list of suggested changes to zoning code provisions already approved. The old council and the mayor agreed on a compromise version of the zoning code, which contained far less downzoning than the original drafted by the Planning Department but also recognized major neighborhood *concerns.

As one of their last acts, the previously powerful majority members of the old council were forced to join in a unanimous vote to repeal their earlier approval of the Lincoln General lease. It must have been a bitter pill to swallow for the three council members who had just been defeated at the polls at least in part because they had approved the very lease they were now forced to repeal. The five council members who had originally approved the lease and cavalierly overridden the mayor's veto before being redressed by citizens through petition and ballot could not resist taking a few parting shots. Even as they voted to repeal the lease that had been their nemesis, they maintained that "they were correct in their original votes."

After adjournment of the lame-duck council meeting, my mother was sworn in for her second term as mayor, and I wager she did not have one word to say about the old council's repeal of the ill-fated hospital lease. The election said it all. The four new district council members were sworn in, and as if to signal the electoral sea change that had

just occurred, the new council voted 5–2 in favor of authorizing application for federal funds to boost the city's ride-sharing car-pool/van-pool
program—an application the old council had rejected the week before
on an opposite 5–2 vote.

That spring of 1979 Mom had once again been the victor on the political electoral battleground, but political strategy had driven neither
her decisions as mayor nor her leadership in governing. Her touchstone
through four years as mayor had been and would continue to be, not
special interests, but the best interests of the people she represented; she
would go on using the powers of her office to open city government to
their voices and provide effective leadership to serve their needs. "This
being Mrs. Boosalis' final term in office, she is beyond any personal
political ambition," the *Journal* stated, "although her commitment to
the well-being of Lincoln always has been paramount." The people carried her into another term as mayor, and they would feed her energy to
work on their behalf for another four years.

Whatever combination of factors produced her stunning victory and
the upset of her city council foes, Mom anticipated her second term
with delight at the prospect of working with a cooperative legislative
body but also with sobering knowledge of the difficult issues facing her
city. She recognized that "the next four years will be tougher than the
last four. The problems facing the city will be harder to handle."

Just as the euphoria of her underdog victory four years earlier did
not obscure my mother's realistic view of the challenges she would
face in her first term, neither did the elation at this come-from-behind
victory four years later cloud her vision of the work ahead. Mom's four
years as mayor had further developed her leadership and administrative skills, especially her fiscal toughness, but the economically turbu-
lent and inflationary times would continue to hurl great obstacles at all
those who took on the job of steering their cities through the late 1970s
and early 1980s.

Getting to Know You
Summer 1986

With both boys in Lincoln for the summer of their Grami's campaign for governor, I grew accustomed to dropping them off at day care and going to work in the makeshift campaign offices downtown. The Boosalis state campaign headquarters occupied the second floor of an old building on Eleventh Street between O and P, the Lancaster County campaign office occupied a portion of the first floor below, and Sandy's Bar occupied the remainder. Getting from the Boosalis county office on the first floor to the state headquarters upstairs required going outside, through another door, and up the steps where a dozen or so offices housed the fifteen paid staff of the Boosalis for Governor campaign, the occupants identified by elegant magic marker scrawls on their office doors.

To get to my cozy cubicle, I crossed the threadbare carpet of the cavernous reception/workroom with its donated metal desks, assortment of chairs, worktables, and filing cabinets. A paper scroll covered one length of wall—"Helen Boosalis" in huge red letters. The offices opened at 7:00 a.m., and on most days folks were still there at midnight.

My mother spent little time at her campaign offices. On the rare days she was not on the road campaigning, the fund-raising staff chained her to the desk in her office to make solicitation calls—her least-favorite campaign activity. Kay Orr didn't have an office in her campaign headquarters. Since she had chosen not to resign her position as state treasurer when she decided to run for governor—as Mom had resigned her state cabinet position as director of the Department on Aging—Orr still occupied her office in the state capitol when she was not out campaigning.

For the primary campaign, Mom had hired as her campaign manager Marg Badura, former executive director of the Nebraska Democratic Party, who had worked on Democrat Jane Eskind's nomination bid for Tennessee governor before returning to Nebraska to work on the Boosalis campaign. Mom added Omaha attorney Tom Litjen as co-manager of her campaign after the primary. Litjen, an important guide to the tricky political landscape in Omaha, had been an aide to former Democratic congressman John Cavanaugh of Omaha and to Republican congressman Doug Bereuter. The campaign organizational plan was for Badura to oversee issues and political strategy, while Litjen was in charge of fund-raising and overseeing staff and volunteers.

The division of labor between the co-managers seemed logical, but as the race progressed some questioned whether the Boosalis campaign was being run by committee, and some insiders groused that no one person was calling the shots. One political analyst suggested the campaign needed a Steve Smith—"the mean member of the Kennedy clan [who] won elections for his in-laws by being decisive, if almost always acerbic." I can't judge if the criticism was on the mark; from my vantage point Mom seemed to call most of the important shots of the campaign. Perhaps at the level of day-to-day operations it was challenging for two captains to run a tight ship.

I do know that Mom's paid staff, as well as her thousands of volunteers throughout the state, were totally committed to her successful candidacy. Working for a campaign is no way to make a living. For example, Brian Rockey, who was then Governor Kerrey's press aide, took a five-month leave of absence to join the Boosalis campaign as scheduler. His salary was $24,000 a year on Kerrey's staff, but he took a 50 percent pay cut to work for Mom's campaign. Why take such a step? "Because it's Helen," Rockey said. "It's a good cause and a very winnable race. Besides, nobody goes to a campaign to make money."

My mother's relationship with her campaign staff reminded me of her rapport with previous staffs as mayor and state director—she was tough and demanding but also fair and understanding. As with her former staffs, she insisted that her campaign aides not limit information they gave her to what they thought she wanted to hear. "You're not doing me a favor by saying 'yes' to me," she told them. Yet I know everyone in the governor's campaign wanted to please her, including me.

With her organization in place, my mother hit the summer campaign trail for points west. With fall elections distant, voters typically do not pay close attention to candidates' messages in the summer months, but they do welcome opportunities to rub elbows with them, especially at outdoor events. Soon after her victory in the primary, Mom had her first "debate"—under a tent with Thomas Jefferson in Minden as part of Nebraska Chatauqua festivities. Jefferson (played by a law professor commissioned by the National Endowment for the Humanities for the Constitution's bicentennial) told the Chatauqua crowd that he never campaigned, made speeches, or debated opponents during his lifetime and that he found "pressing the flesh to be a vulgar practice." Mom enjoyed hamming it up in the playful sparring with Jefferson and reminded her audience that Nebraska agricultural and economic development issues were similar to those in Jefferson's time.

My favorite summer campaign events were Fourth of July parades, which stretched over a period of days so that each small town could have its own celebration without competing with neighboring towns. The little town of Dodge, Nebraska, population 820, swelled to about fifteen thousand spectators to watch the three hundred entries in the Dodge Centennial parade. On the Fourth of July itself, Mom managed to attend events in all three Nebraska congressional districts—the dedication of the Calamus Dam in Burwell, parades in Ralston and Seward, and finally the fireworks in Holmes Park in Lincoln.

My boys never had such an exciting Fourth of July. They rode in a parade in an antique car with their Grami—waving and waving to the sidewalk crowds as if they had been little celebrities all their lives—and stayed up late watching fireworks and chasing fireflies. Spending the day with the boys temporarily lessened my guilt for the long hours I spent away from them at the Boosalis campaign fund-raising factory and for dragging them to Nebraska and leaving them in the care of strangers. Yet I felt no guilt over my shameless exploitation in putting sandwich boards on the little guys that read, "Please Vote for My Grammy!" as we passed out Boosalis for Governor brochures.

33. Grandsons, Michael and Christopher Davis, and daughter, Beth, campaign for Helen Boosalis for governor

I know my friends in Chicago, New York, and Los Angeles would snicker if they heard me talk about growing up in "urban" Lincoln, Nebraska, but positively urban is how I felt when we campaigned in some of the tiny towns in the state's vast prairie west of Lincoln and Omaha. I found each town charming and friendly and sad—sad because of the struggle to survive in the devastating agricultural economy. Nebraska farm families for generations had chosen and cherished, despite the hardships, a way of life that could no longer be sustained without drastic change. Grown children of farm families were leaving not only their farms and rural communities in droves but also leaving Nebraska for better opportunities. Visiting those small, struggling towns during the summer campaign reminded me of one more reason why Mom was running for governor.

The boys' summer ended with another spectacular event—the Ringling Bros. and Barnum and Bailey Circus came to town. At their ages (almost six and three), the circus was a big deal for them no matter what. But what if you got to see your grandmother actually riding a circus elephant? That spectacle commanded some higher level of excitement—for my mother, too, I'm sure.

Ever the willing sport, Mom swung her almost-sixty-seven-year-old self up on her assigned elephant as her twenty-year-younger opponent did the same, and down the street they came to the shrieking delight of both my boys and all the other children (and some adults) watching the lumbering procession. My mother joked that she was not uncomfortable riding the symbol of the Republican Party. Her campaign communications director, Roger Aden, called it symbolic of Helen's support for all Nebraskans. For her grandsons, however, it was just the coolest thing they had seen their Grami do yet.

With little more than parades and elephant rides and small-town visits to distinguish the candidates before Labor Day—the traditional start of campaigns in earnest—the media continued to blur the differences between Boosalis and Orr by highlighting the generic two-woman aspect of the race and blending their strengths as candidates. "The candidates are battle-hardened professionals who worked their way to leadership," wrote a Minneapolis commentator. "Mrs. Boosalis and Mrs. Orr are personable, smart, tough as boot leather, good organizers, quick thinkers, terrific campaigners. Each unleashed a finish in the primary that left opponents gasping."

Debate on issues would later divide and differentiate them, but distinctions in philosophy and personal style began emerging earlier. A New York–based feature writer for *US* magazine observed differences between the two candidates during her three days of interviews: "Boosalis is always relaxed and at ease with people in public and at home. But Orr needs to soften her public image. There is a split between Orr's public and private persona that Boosalis doesn't have." Many who worked with Mom throughout her public service emphasize her wholeness—the lack of difference between her public persona and her private persona. They variously describe Helen as genuine, authentic, the real deal, a straight shooter, without a phony bone in her body.

According to former governor and U.S. senator Bob Kerrey, "Helen is authentic. Her authenticity makes her the same in public and in private. When you see that, you know you're seeing something special." And another former Nebraska governor, Mike Johanns, told me, "In high-visibility positions, it's awfully easy to develop a public persona. Helen was Helen. What she stood for privately, she stood for publicly." Former St. Paul mayor George Latimer observed, "People trusted her because she was 'unvarnished.' I can't remember Helen saying anything that rang hollow or false. There was no phoniness—she was unpretentious. What she said she believed." Likewise, the mother/wife/grandmother whom we know within our own family is no different from the councilwoman/mayor/candidate-for-governor we've seen in the public spotlight.

In the summer of 1986, reporters made comparisons between the two candidates' personal styles on the campaign trail. "Each has an easy approach to campaigning," wrote a *Lincoln Journal* reporter. "Orr seems warm but reserved. Boosalis displays a jaunty enthusiasm." In a post-primary *Omaha World-Herald* profile, the two words used most by those interviewed to describe Boosalis were "energy" and "warmth." Even Joe Hampton, Mom's perennial city council opponent when she was mayor, called Boosalis "energetic, bright and hardworking" (but in the same breath he also called her "a true believer—wherever there's a problem, there is a government solution"). UNL political scientist and

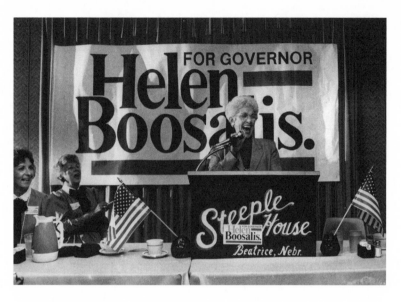

34. Helen takes her campaign for governor across the state

Republican Robert Sittig said, "Helen's got an unbelievable ability to relate to anyone in the public arena, from the lowest to the highest."

When the press wanted to know the sixty-seven-year-old Boosalis's secret for sustaining her high level of energy from the start of her campaign day at 5:30 a.m. until midnight, Mom responded, "I don't have a secret formula. I'm fortunate to have a lot of energy. And I like what I'm doing—meeting and listening to people." When asked what part of campaigning for governor she liked best, Mom said it was being with people—"knowing you can make a difference and convincing people they can make a difference." My dad shared with reporters his own theories about Mom's stamina: "She doesn't get real uptight. She has a positive attitude. She doesn't use her energy uselessly. She's well organized. She's having a lot of fun (running for governor)."

The Lincoln press was more likely to know that the former mayor "leaves men and women half her age panting for breath as they try to catch up with her," but reporters from *U.S. News and World Report* asked Bill Giovanni, former Lincoln finance director, how city staff had kept up with the energetic former mayor. Giovanni recalled a fellow administrator who tried to impress Mayor Boosalis: "First, he showed up at quarter to 8:00 but Helen was already there. Then, he showed up at 7:30. He kept coming in earlier and earlier, but she was always there first. Finally, he gave up."

Even with her high energy, one would think that my mother must have abandoned the home front altogether during the governor's race, but not so. On Sundays she cooked meals for the rest of the week— stews or soups in big quantities that could be frozen and easily reheated by Dad. Throughout her political life Mom kept as top priority her husband, family, and home. She did have to relinquish some homemaking tasks during the hectic years as mayor and even hired cleaning help, but she didn't abandon her role as homemaker. Mom's mayoral campaign manager, Beatty Brasch, recalls, "During one campaign, I remember someone asking Helen how she could remain so human and down to earth, doing what she was doing. Helen replied, 'I have to wash the toilets every Sunday night and that reminds me who I am.'"

During the governor's campaign I saw firsthand how Mom did it all—by sleeping very little, being efficient and highly organized, motivating people around her to do more than they thought they could, and functioning at warp speed. As Chris Beutler, one of her young (age forty-one) Democratic gubernatorial primary opponents, said after losing the primary to Mom, "This woman is high energy. When I got out of the primary, I felt like I had been scorched by a comet."

In addition to observing the energy she would bring to the job as governor, voters outside Lincoln were also getting to know the Democratic candidate's philosophy of government. At the launch of the general election campaign, Governor Kerrey emphasized my mother's mayoral record of citizen involvement in government: "Helen listened to the neighborhoods, to individuals, to children, to older people. She stood fast for the people every single time. It was the people first and foremost. And the city of Lincoln kept getting better."

When asked during the campaign for governor to describe her philosophy of government, my mother said she viewed government as a tool to allow people to accomplish their goals. "If you have a stake in something, you have part ownership of it, you are going to have more pride in maintaining it. I think that's the trouble with many of the [government] programs around the country—too much pouring money into the problems and not enough reaching out to the people and having them be part of it," Mom said, sounding just like her former mayoral self. "Government is there to serve people. It's not there to serve ourselves or the bureaucrats or the narrow interests."

For those who were quick to slap the conservative-liberal labels on the candidates, my mother's twenty-four-year stint in nonpartisan elected office supported her own view that she was a moderate. "My greatest strength is solving problems—pulling people and parties together to solve problems," she said. "Is that conservative or is that liberal? Those are political labels used to discredit individuals. The liberal Democrats didn't think I was liberal enough. I've been a moderate all my life." U.S. senator Jim Exon agreed: "Never in my memory have the Republicans nominated such a right-winger [as Orr]. Boosalis may appear liberal next to Mrs. Orr, but by her actions and attitudes and long history in office, Helen is a moderate."

As the electorate acquired a deeper knowledge of the two nominees they had elected in the primary, voters developed interest in the candidates' families, particularly in the husbands of the two women vying for the governor's job. Both spouses shared a common start in traditional marriages—the husbands worked and their wives stayed home and assumed volunteer jobs that evolved into full-time political careers.

After the primary, reporters descended on my dad's office at UNL's Department of Plant Pathology, where he divided his time among teaching, research, extension work with farmers, and administration. Never one to seek the limelight, he was patient with their questions about his wife's historic race for governor. Whether my mother was running for city council, mayor, or governor, my dad's reaction to her pursuit of a nontraditional political career has always been straightforward, unforced, and *genuine. "I knew she had the potential to do or be whatever she wanted," Dad told a *Lincoln Star* reporter. "I didn't know where this would lead. I think people should do whatever they want and the spouse should encourage them, whether it's staying home or going out to work." When asked about men who are threatened by women who succeed, Dad responded, "I'm delighted I don't have that hangup. She has her thing to do and I have mine. I think I'm a pretty good plant pathologist," he added.

As far as being a role model for men in two-career households, my dad simply said, "I'm not a role model. I'm just Mike Boosalis." He stated that he wouldn't have made it through grad school without Mom's help, and said that they discuss their work and learn from each other. And what about being "First Man" if his wife were elected governor? "First Man? I don't know. I just want to continue to be the first man in Helen's life."

When asked during the campaign if he had to do more household chores now that his wife was running for governor, Dad got that twinkle in his eye that he gets when he sees an opening for one of his funny stories. Yes, he told the reporter, he was spending more time on household chores and had recently mentioned that to his secretary. She, in turn, went home and asked her husband if he, too, would help her more with house chores, like Mike Boosalis. Her husband replied, "I will when you run for governor!"

Because I had virtually relocated to Nebraska for the campaign, I was also interviewed for a few newspaper articles featuring the elected mother/elected daughter angle. "My mother is a unique and very special kind of leader," I told a reporter. "I've been around politics myself now and I think that when times are tough, you need tougher and more talented people. She's strong and decisive and she's never become removed from the people." My entering politics had added a new dimension, I said, to our already close relationship, and I could seek her advice on my Evanston City Council issues. When asked if my mother would campaign for me next spring when I would be up for city council reelection, I responded, "As governor of Nebraska, I don't think she'll have much time." A later *Chicago Sun-Times* article titled "Politics in 1986: Women on the Move" noted that although Kay Orr and Helen Boosalis might not have had political role models, Boosalis had provided just that for her daughter. "More women at the top will bring more women to the top," Mom told the Chicago *reporter.

And so the summer passed—parades, fund-raising, elephants, organizing, Nebraskans getting acquainted with their gubernatorial candidates. By August the two campaigns appeared to have adopted different strategies. Orr's campaign co-chair Art Knox said that Orr had spent the summer "listening," and as in the primary, the early stages of her campaign seemed geared to building organization rather than visibility. As a reporter for the *Star* noted, "Boosalis may project more down-home warmth. Orr may be more skilled in terms of campaign mechanics and strategy." In contrast, my mother began discussing issues with voters early in the summer and released several detailed issue papers—not waiting until Labor Day to talk with voters across the state about problems, plans, and priorities. "She wants to be sure people understand her positions," said Boosalis campaign co-chair Ben Nelson.

But the best-laid plans . . .

Chapter Six

Everything Old Is New Again
1979–1983

"Helen could have a heated debate on an issue, get over it, and go on to the next issue, even with the same people. She had no carryover of animus. Why? Because she worked for the people—it was not personal with her."
—BEN NELSON, U.S. senator (Nebraska), governor of Nebraska, 1991–99

"In all my years in government, I've never met anyone like Helen. She was totally committed to the city. Many start out with good political rhetoric, but once they get in office it's a different story. Not Helen—she was the real deal."
—MICHAEL MERWICK, administrative aide, administrative director, fire chief, City of Lincoln, 1975–83

I get breathless when reading or writing about my mother's elections, like her 1979 come-from-behind reelection win—caught up in the drama and suspense even when I know the endings. I somewhat understand the psyche of "campaign junkies," those nomads who wander the political desert between campaigns and are inevitably drawn to the next oasis of hope, the next campaign promising a winner or at least the good fight. As the candidate's daughter (and as a candidate myself) I could never get past the jitters and state of high anxiety, so I never experienced the high sought by campaign junkies. Yet I can understand the appeal of campaigns—living moment to moment, creating and reacting to the unexpected, enduring the agony and thrill of polls and election nights, dancing on the edge between victory and defeat.

But my mother was no campaign junkie. As energized and energizing as she was in full campaign mode, she got her kicks not before but *after* elections—her highs came from governing. I am captivated by the courage and fortitude of political candidates who put it all on the line, subjecting themselves to a thumbs-up or thumbs-down vote by folks they've never met. My mother, on the other hand, would say her courage was tested most while *in* office, not by running *for* it.

If Mom were telling her own political life story, would she minimize accounts of her campaigns as simply being the means to an end? Would she instead focus on her days in office, much as a mother's attention to childbirth gives way to engagement with the being who has been born? Never the victim of post-campaign letdown or even plain old exhaustion, my mother welcomed the campaign finish line because then she could charge full tilt toward her goals for improving life in Lincoln for, and with the help of, its citizens.

NEW POLS

In May 1979, as my mother began her second term as mayor in a worsening national economy, at least she wasn't also facing constant battles with the city council, as she did during much of her first term. The new council, with four new district members, quickly went to work to resolve and in some cases undo several controversial issues from the old council's agenda.

The new council revisited some previous council decisions of limited scope, such as appointment to the Lincoln Electric System board of Joyce Durand, whose confirmation had been blocked earlier by the council's "petty politics"; some decisions on timely opportunities with long-range benefits, such as the city's purchase of the old federal building and post office (deemed a "white elephant" by dissenting Councilmen Hampton and Scherer); and a few larger issues of such complexity and controversy that they had remained unresolved for years, such as construction of a proposed cross-town roadway, the Northeast Radial. The new city council jumped in to exercise constructive legislative leadership that complemented, rather than battled, the mayor's executive leadership.

The 1979 city council didn't just flip, however, from the previous council's predictable 5–2 votes opposing the mayor to equally predictable 5–2 votes supporting her. While a predictably supportive council vote pattern would have made Mom's job a little easier, she didn't want the kind of bloc voting—even in her favor—that had characterized the preceding council. She wanted healthy debate leading to rational decisions for the good of the whole city—not automatic acquiescence to preconceived judgments. While the mayor supported spirited debate, she also welcomed the more congenial style that the new district-elected majority brought to the council. She didn't miss the strain of ongoing preparation for combat with the former majority, and she appreciated her ability—with new blood on the council—to move ahead on projects that had been stalled or defeated by the previous council.

In the aftermath of the first district elections, business interests that had lost council majority representation began to squirm. A series of articles by a team of *Sunday Journal and Star* reporters analyzed the historical emergence of political forces challenging traditional community leadership in Lincoln. Reporter Karen Maguire called the change a loosening of "the knot that once bound Lincoln's business community to civic leadership. Traditional business-oriented community leaders now are sharing power with neighborhood leaders."

Examining the changing forces at play after the 1979 city election, the analysis found that "among the neighborhood-allied leaders—the New Pols—are Mayor Helen Boosalis and City Council members Mike Steinman, Eric Youngberg and Margrethe Ahlschwede. . . . The New Pols want a strong downtown, development in established neighborhoods and housing in the downtown core. They look to other cities for innovations. . . . Development west and north of Lincoln is a priority and continued eastern and southeastern expansion is seen as a threat to a strong downtown. In their view, Lincoln must be more progressive. Mass transit and other alternatives to the automobile and large roads, and aggressive energy conservation are major items" on the agenda of the New Pols, the series noted.

"The Old Pols see too much government interference," said one series article, which identified Joe Hampton—whose support came from groups like the chamber of commerce, builders, and developers—as an acknowledged leader of the business-allied faction, the Old Pols. "They say private enterprise can do a better job of meeting people's needs. . . . In their view, economic growth is a predominant concern for the community, and they contend that overly restrictive zoning and inadequate planning for street needs would be dangerous to Lincoln's economic growth. . . . [I]t isn't realistic to use zoning regulations to force balanced residential growth in all directions from the downtown business district," according to the Old Pols, because "the city can't force people to live where they don't want to live."

The series analysis looked back to a 1977 interview with Joe Hampton about Lincoln's power structure, when Hampton said most community leaders would continue to come from the world of business and asked, "Where else would you get your leadership?" The analysis concluded that "the answer came in 1979. The leadership is coming from Lincoln's neighborhoods and other non-traditional sources. The 1979 city election brought four political neophytes into Lincoln's political arena and removed persons who were considered allies of the business community. During that same election, Mayor Boosalis was returned for a second term, in spite of loud opposition from portions of the business community that actively supported her opponent, Stan Matzke. . . . Mayor Boosalis' commitment to the neighborhoods helped put her in office."

As the neophyte council members learned how to flex their political muscles, the "Old Pol" Councilman Scherer strongly criticized the mayor and his new council colleagues. He charged that none of the four district council members could have been elected at large, that the new council was anti-business and anti-growth, and that a new council philosophy was developing: "Whatever Helen (Boosalis) wants, Helen's going to get." Scherer reiterated his long-standing suspicion that a "power play plan" had been coordinated to "run city government" by some combination of churches, neighborhood organizations, university, state senators, and newspaper people. Scherer sometimes vented his frustration in letters to the editor. "I still don't support the results of the Boosalis re-election or the election of some of the new council members," he wrote in November 1979. "I wasn't elected to the City

Council as an at-large member to be a 'yes-man' for the Boosalis administration."

Revealing the depth of his irritation with his new minority position on the council by the spring of 1980, an enraged Scherer contended that the mayor did not invite him to be an early guest on her hosted local cablevision program, *Lincoln in View*, because he disagreed with her politically. Although she planned to rotate appearances of council members on the biweekly half-hour program, Scherer filed a complaint with cablevision officials and was offered equal time. "I'm tired of being pushed, tired of being kicked and I'm going to fight back," Scherer lashed out at his perceived rebuff by Mayor Boosalis, whom, a reporter noted, "he considers one of his political enemies."

I find surprising my mom's ability to go toe-to-toe on an issue with those who considered her a "political enemy" and then work together with those same folks on other issues for the good of the city—surprising because I have observed that male politicians are often better at such practical switching of gears. Men seem agile in forming and re-forming political alliances that will help achieve their ultimate goals, while women (and I include myself) more often seem guided by judgments about the character and worthiness of those with whom they choose to ally on issues. As an alderman myself, I could have used more of Mom's pragmatism that made her willing to work with just about anyone in order to accomplish her goals for the city.

Although Councilman Scherer viewed her as a political enemy, the mayor worked with him to create an Economic Development Commission. "Scherer authored the idea and has worked with Mrs. Boosalis in developing the proposal," noted an editorial. "That partnership is a somewhat remarkable and welcome development." At its first meeting, the mayor warned the new Economic Development Commission not to be complacent about the economy. Although Lincoln had enjoyed low unemployment, she warned that the university and state government would contribute far less to the city's economy in the future, that the "depression-like" state of the building industry required attention, and that the hard-hit downtown needed help to continue as Lincoln's prime retail center.

DOWNTOWN: NEW AGAIN

The makeup of Lincoln's city council changed—sometimes dramatically—every two years, but regardless of who held the council reins,
Mom used the executive power of the mayor's office and her own leadership abilities to keep the city moving in a positive direction. She had
to be nimble in shifting strategies and rerouting around roadblocks
that some council members erected along the way, but the start of her
second term brought smoother sailing with a council majority whose
goals were more in sync with hers.

I find it laudable that during difficult economic times, no matter
how smooth or difficult the mayor's relations with each succeeding city
council, Lincoln's health and vitality remained strong during my mother's tenure as mayor. A good example was the city's redevelopment of a
viable downtown core in an era when many cities witnessed the demise
of their downtown centers.

Centrum Plaza, the ambitious public-private redevelopment in central downtown that was fast-tracked in my mother's first term, officially
opened six months after her reelection in the spring of 1979. Minneapolis developer Steve Watson noted that Centrum Plaza had the distinction of being "one of the all-time fast" downtown shopping center developments. Comparable projects averaged five years from the time of
a developer's involvement—the Centrum took less than half that time.

Centrum Plaza was editorially praised as the outcome of both "leadership of public and private interests" and "cooperative public and private investment." The skywalk system, unusual for a city of Lincoln's
size, was deemed a delight. Although economists at the time were predicting the 1979 holidays to be tough for retailers, the Centrum brought
shoppers downtown. In spite of the dismal economy throughout the
country, retail business boomed in downtown Lincoln that year, with
sales far exceeding those of recent years. Much of the increase in sales
was attributed to attracting more out-of-town shoppers who had previously gone to Omaha shopping centers—not to a shift of Lincoln shoppers from outlying malls to the downtown.

The Centrum attracted an initial twenty retail tenants because of
its location adjacent to existing anchor retailers (Brandeis; Miller and

Paine) and its planned skywalk linkage to other downtown businesses to form a regional shopping complex. By the following holiday season, Centrum Plaza was near full occupancy with thirty-three tenants and continued strong sales; and by the summer of 1982 it had a waiting list of tenants for space.

But the path to sustained vitality and viability in downtown Lincoln was not without significant challenges and setbacks. In July 1980, less than a year after the exciting opening of Centrum Plaza, the management of the fifteen-store Brandeis chain announced the closing of its stores in downtown Lincoln and Omaha. Operated under a long-term lease in the block-long former Gold's department store (site of Mom's infamous bargain hunting), Lincoln's Brandeis was one of two key anchors linked by skywalk to the new Centrum. The closing announcement came as a shock to the Gold family, employees, businesses, and city government. Brandeis management explained that although the rejuvenated retail environment in downtown Lincoln had reduced losses at its Lincoln store, they were unable to reverse its long-standing unprofitable history. The general manager expressed confidence in downtown Lincoln and blamed the chain's closings in Lincoln and Omaha on "today's economic *conditions."

What a blow the Brandeis closing was to the city's long-range hopes for the Centrum, which was doing well but just getting off the ground. "I think it's pretty short-sighted of Brandeis to make this move," the mayor lamented. "Lincoln is strong and it's viable and if Brandeis had been able to hang on, it probably would have seen acceptable profits. But rather than view it as a disaster," she continued, choosing to look on the positive side, "it should be viewed optimistically as an opportunity to entice and draw in another large department store."

The mayor's political opponents seized a different kind of opportunity—to blame the Brandeis store closing on business disruption from the city's concurrent downtown beautification project and construction of the Centrum. Yet revenues of Miller and Paine, the other anchor linked by skywalk to the Centrum, had increased substantially since the opening of the Centrum parking garage and skywalk system, according to President John Campbell.

The mayor moved quickly to address the void in the city's downtown plan created by the Brandeis closing. Within days of the closing announcement, she asked the Downtown Advisory Committee to form a task force to study development strategies for the landmark Brandeis store. Mom asked the task force to make recommendations on potential tax incentives; on the building's relationship to revitalizing the Haymarket area and old city hall; on alternative uses for the site, such as a grocery store to support downtown housing; and on the Brandeis building's role in the total plan for downtown.

In requesting task force recommendations and also encouraging the chamber of commerce to help take the lead, the mayor said that "the announcement of the Brandeis closing shocked the entire community. While many people have indicated that this is a sign of the times and is a fact we must accept, I am convinced that we can find a new tenant for that beautiful building which is located in the most vibrant and exciting central business district in the United States." But she also cautioned, "I'm not so naive to think that we will have department stores knocking on our doors, fighting one another about who gets to have it—times are tough and very few large businesses are relocating downtown, even in shopping malls." Mom reached out to citizens and business to help, because "the Brandeis closing is more than just a downtown problem— it's a total community problem."

While the closing of Brandeis was a blow to the city's plans for Lincoln's downtown, my mother's resolve to move the downtown, forward never wavered. By reaching out to citizen advisers and the larger business community, she enlisted their expertise and vested interests in working on the problem. "The Downtown Advisory Committee's task force study of the Brandeis store vacancy, suggested by Mayor Boosalis, is an action with hope for the future," noted a *Star* editorial. "It is the only approach to the matter that really makes any sense. . . . With justification, Lincoln is proud of its downtown area. It is an attractive, vibrant and largely successful place of business, especially compared to the near disasters that have befallen many downtowns throughout the country."

Within a year of the Brandeis store closing, a developer (Cherry Hill Company) negotiated and signed purchase contracts with the Gold family for the Brandeis property. A feasibility study of the site recom-

35. The mayor's door is always open

mended that the vacated department store become a retail "galleria" linked to the Centrum, the Atrium, and Miller and Paine and that it also include office space, since a 3 percent downtown office vacancy rate showed a critical need. The mayor was delighted with the news of the building purchase, having earlier met with Cherry Hill developers and offered the city's assistance. Other downtown merchants were equally delighted, although they had not yet suffered loss of business following the closing of Brandeis and, in fact, sales in Centrum Plaza shops were up 20 percent over the previous year.

Within six months at a press conference in the mayor's office, the developer revealed architectural plans for an $8–$10 million renovation of the building. The office and retail complex was named Gold's Galleria, in honor of the Nathan Gold family's operation of Gold's department store from 1902 to 1964, when the business was sold and property leased to the Omaha-based Brandeis chain. The renovation would include a six-story, half-block-long atrium capped by a barrel-vaulted skylight, with walkways on each floor bridging the atrium to create an indoor streetscape atmosphere. Forty percent of the space was pre-leased within four months of the building purchase. The new Galleria complex was off and running.

With all indications that downtown Lincoln was weathering both the national economic downturn and the closure of a major downtown department store, the mayor might have breathed a little easier, but the closing of Brandeis and its redevelopment as Gold's Galleria was not the only significant downtown challenge during this period. Another entire block adjacent to downtown retailers was also in jeopardy when the Cornhusker Hotel closed just prior to the beginning of Mom's second term in 1979. The large, antiquated hotel building sat empty for three years while the city searched for ways to encourage redevelopment by providing partial public funding. A Wisconsin developer (Carley Capital Group) proposed a new $34 million hotel and convention center complex and asked the city to contribute $10 million in financing.

To assemble such a large public funding package, in early 1980 the city and the chamber of commerce sought state legislative approval for the city's use of tax increment *financing to fund the public elements in the proposed Cornhusker redevelopment—convention center, skywalks, and public parking. The city then applied for a federal Urban Development Action Grant (UDAG) intended to leverage private investment for projects in "distressed areas" or in "pockets of *poverty," for which the city hoped the area surrounding the old Cornhusker Hotel would qualify.

The mayor contended that the low-income area around the vacant hotel would greatly benefit from jobs provided by the project, but Lincoln's relatively sound economy within the faltering national economic climate worked against its favorable consideration for UDAG "pockets of poverty" federal financing of the Cornhusker project. Lincoln's UDAG application was not selected for funding in early 1980 by HUD, which had received 270 applications from cities requesting $1 billion in UDAG funding when only $160 million of funding was available.

Undaunted, the mayor said the city would go forward with plans to redevelop the Cornhusker block through private financing sources, since Lincoln had a good track record of completing major projects without federal funding. But soaring interest rates on a First National Bank loan that had been secured to finance the private portion of the project prevented the developer from moving forward and threatened to postpone the project indefinitely (the prime rate at the time was 20 percent). Attempts by the city to redevelop the Cornhusker with the Wisconsin developer had come to an end by June 1981.

Out of the ashes just two months later came reports of interest in developing the Cornhusker site for a new hotel-convention center from David Murdock, a Los Angeles developer-investor. Burnham Yates, retired board chair of First National Bank, which acquired the hotel in 1978, had suggested to Murdock that he consider the Cornhusker opportunity. Murdock had already made investments in Lincoln, including the First National Bank building, the regional distribution center for Ace Hardware Corporation, and Yankee Hill Brick Manufacturing Company; he was also constructing two large office buildings in downtown Omaha.

Murdock's early concept involved razing the vacant hotel to build an entirely new $40 million complex, with possible city tax increment financing for land acquisition, site improvement, and the convention center, depending on whether the hotel area could be considered "blighted" under Nebraska law. The mayor sent her young administrative team, headed by Administrative Director Elaine Carpenter, to California to negotiate with the developer giant. They returned to Nebraska with a deal, but one that would test the city's capabilities and agility.

In the subsequent whirlwind, the Murdock hotel project ("Cornhusker Square") advanced at great speed. My mother described the project as one of the most exciting public-private partnerships and invigorating relationships she experienced during her mayoral years. "Even Superman couldn't have gone through the city's red tape faster than the Cornhusker Square project, one of the largest developments in Lincoln's history," a reporter declared. "It went through faster than a speeding bullet," said Planning Commission chairman Bob Hans.

Murdock's Cornhusker Square project was announced on December 19, 1981 (the old Cornhusker Hotel had closed in 1978), and Murdock told the mayor that the project would be scrapped if ground could not be broken by April 1, 1982. Her department heads said that the three-month time frame could not possibly be met, but the mayor and Council Chairman Hampton worked together to put the project on an ultra-fast track. By the April 1 deadline, the old Cornhusker Hotel building was demolished (by implosion), the site was prepared for construction, a redevelopment plan and design were approved, an architect was chosen, utilities were relocated, and $5.4 million in city *bonds were authorized for building the project's public portions (the convention center and parking garage).

The redevelopment of both the vacated Brandeis store and the Cornhusker Hotel—each representing an entire downtown city block—averted the threats that their closings had posed to the viability of downtown Lincoln. A responsive and supportive city hall played a major role in the success of both projects.

During this period the city also targeted for redevelopment a large area known as Haymarket. This historic area bordering downtown and the Burlington Northern Railroad yards contained more than forty commercial properties dating from the 1870s to the 1920s. For years the city had hoped to rehab and convert the deteriorating district into a historic area of shops and restaurants, but efforts to gain the area's listing on the National Register of Historic Places had been blocked by a

Burlington Northern lawsuit objecting to inclusion of its train depot in the national historic listing and to accompanying property restrictions.

However, after federal tax laws changed in 1981 to provide incentives to rehabilitate historic buildings registered either nationally or locally, the city's preservation planner initiated the process for local historic designation of the Haymarket Landmark District, despite Burlington's continued objections that could threaten federal tax credit approval. In an attempt to resolve the impasse, the mayor contacted Burlington Northern in August 1982 to negotiate city concessions in return for the railroad's withdrawing objections to inclusion of its property in the historic district. She received Burlington's response a week later agreeing to withdraw its objections and crediting its change of heart to concessions made by the city: the deletion of part of the track from the district, the allowance of a high communications tower, and the assurance of no city control of railroad operations or long-range plans for the depot. The path was clear for approval of the Haymarket district's local historic designation and for several developers who were interested in the historic district's tax *incentives.

During my mother's second mayoral term, construction was well under way on multiple multimillion-dollar projects in downtown Lincoln, even in the midst of a national recession. Tenants had moved into lower floors of the Gold's Galleria office-retail complex connected to the skywalk system. The new construction of Cornhusker Square's hotel-convention center was ahead of schedule for its planned 1984 *opening. In the Haymarket district, "lamplighted cobblestone and brick walks, turn-of-the-century storefronts with canopied windows and arched entrances" were no longer architectural drawings but reality; new tenants inhabited The Candy Factory (a former seventy-four-year-old candy plant) and Haymarket Square (a former collar factory converted to uses like restaurants, offices, shops).

Even with so much commercial development downtown, an expansion of high-density housing downtown—long the mayor's dream and recommended by her appointed Downtown Advisory Committee—had not yet become reality. But a strong and growing downtown commercial base made prospects brighter for future downtown housing in Lincoln.

The city recognized that areas surrounding the downtown also con-tribute to its character and vitality. Adjacent to downtown Lincoln rises the magnificent Nebraska state capitol, the "tower on the plains." Ber-tram Goodhue, architect of this first statehouse design to depart from the U.S. Capitol prototype, proposed that a mall extend from each side of the towering building into the surrounding community. Centennial Mall, the first, was completed in 1972 between the capitol and the Uni-versity of Nebraska, adjacent to downtown.

The architect of Centennial Mall was Larry *Enersen, whose land-scape architectural designs were showcased throughout Lincoln: Fol-som Children's Zoo, Wilderness Park, Lincoln Foundation Garden, Lincoln Community Playhouse Theatre, Pioneers Park Pinewood Bowl stage, Crescent Green park system along the banks of Salt Creek, resto-ration of the old city hall, and the Rock Island depot. Seeking to honor Enersen's many contributions, the Nebraska Statewide Arboretum ap-proached the mayor for ideas. Mom was eager for development of the second mall—Lincoln Mall—joining the capitol and the County-City Building, also in the downtown area. She suggested that Enersen design it and that, without his prior knowledge, he should be honored at the mall's dedication for his lasting influence on the city and "improving life through architectural quality, design excellence and environmental order."

Lincoln Mall, funded by private contributions, became another last-ing beautification effort benefiting downtown, surrounding neighbor-hoods, and Lincoln citizens for generations to come. At its dedication in 1983, Enersen spoke of his satisfaction in directing tree planting down-town, which he said took twenty years to convince skeptical politicians and business owners to do. To share a love for trees with a tree-plant-ing champion like Mayor Boosalis, Enersen said, helped him achieve an important goal. In turn, the mayor said, "It would be difficult to travel around Lincoln without seeing Enersen's work. He has communicated the values of a community, the joy of living. He understands the need for trees to soften the harsh prairie landscape." Mom's deep respect for this unassuming architect who had left such a mark on the city ex-plained their simpatico vision for Lincoln's enduring beauty.

ENERGY: GAS, GARBAGE, GENERATING POWER

Issues of energy production, consumption, and conservation continued as high priorities in my mother's second term as cities and the country struggled to find new solutions to rising costs of energy. Securing funding and getting the public to carpool and use public transportation was one energy-related focus for the mayor in her second term. Soon after her reelection, the U.S. Department of Transportation awarded a grant for a ride-sharing demonstration project in three Lincoln residential areas, one of seventeen national awards focused on altering suburban transportation habits in cities with existing ride-sharing programs.

Less than two years later, the city received a much larger federal grant to encourage carpooling, use of public transit, and flexible work hours to relieve traffic congestion. "The [federal transportation grant] award was notable not only because of the budget massacre going on in Washington, but because of Lincoln's excellent record in energy conservation," noted a *Star* editorial in May 1981. "Lincoln has taken significant steps to hold down fuel consumption in the past few years under Mrs. Boosalis' leadership and generally with city council cooperation."

The success of the city's mayor-championed carpooling program fluctuated annually with changes in gas prices. In its first years of operation, 1978 and 1979, the program showed 50 percent enrollment increases when gas prices soared, but enrollment slowed when gas prices decreased. Compared to other cities (e.g., Denver, Los Angeles, St. Louis, San Francisco), Lincoln had a relatively high percentage of its labor force carpooling (22 percent) and a low percentage driving to and from work alone (64 percent). While the city's program made respectable progress during her tenure as mayor, my mother wanted more Lincoln residents to carpool or use public transportation. But she was battling Americans' love affair with their automobiles that is still in full bloom today, no matter how high gas prices climb.

Carpooling wasn't the only city-promoted alternative to single-passenger automobile use. "Soaring" gas prices ($1.45 in 1980) also increased Lincoln bus ridership by almost 30 percent. But even with increased ridership, Lincoln Transportation System faced increasing fuel costs simultaneously with massive cuts in federal transportation subsidies to cities. Municipal transit systems nationally were caught in the bind of having to raise fares because of federal subsidy cuts, which in turn lowered ridership—a vicious cycle that undermined most of the country's mass *transportation.

Shortly after her reelection, the mayor charged her Energy Action Committee to study and make recommendations on a waste-burning plant for converting garbage into steam. The plant could drive electric generators or heat buildings and also help address the city's shortage of landfill space for the 560 tons of garbage produced in the city every day. Lincoln Electric System (LES) administrator Walt Canney agreed that the technology for burning solid waste to make steam had improved in the previous two years: utilizing the steam in combination with a coal-fired plant to produce power had become much more economical. A Nebraska Energy Office study of solid waste plants throughout the United States and Canada showed that Lincoln would be an ideal city for such a plant, with the university as an ideal customer.

Despite the mayor's strong support for a waste-burning, steam-generating plant, the council was not as enthusiastic. Councilman Hampton opposed having taxpayers subsidize the plant, and Councilman Youngberg favored composting garbage for fertilizer rather than burning it for power. After a lengthy public hearing in September 1980 on the city's applying for a $25 million federal grant to offset the plant's projected $65–$85 million price tag, the council voted not to apply for federal funds but, instead, to study the feasibility of composting solid waste for *fertilizer.

The mayor, disappointed at the council's rejection of the solid waste plant, said that "time will tell whether that was a good decision or not." She viewed the council's action as "just an honest difference of opinion" but thought that the "loss is to the community." Going on to fight another day was easier for Mom because when she lost on an issue she did not regard it as a personal loss—not loss of power, or respect, or personal stature. After pursuing what she considered good for the city, trying to "convince and cajole" the council, and being thwarted in that pursuit, she attributed the loss to an honest difference of opinion—her proposal had simply not gained enough support to carry the day. Often she sought and found another way to achieve her goal; sometimes she accepted the defeat and let it rest; and at other times she was convinced by her opponents and changed her mind. Rarely, if ever, did she personally agonize over a defeat.

In late 1980 consumers angrily protested proposed Lincoln Electric System rate hikes of 20 percent. But the electricity rate controversy did not resurrect nuclear power as an option, primarily because LES had greatly overestimated future demand for power and the need for system growth back when it urged Lincoln's participation in Omaha's nuclear power plant during Mom's first term. Since then, a Nebraska Power Association study had recommended against utilities building nuclear power plants because of nuclear power's high capital costs, environmental objections, and problems of waste disposal and fuel availability.

LES had become more cooperative in its dealings with the mayor and city council since my mother's first term. Given the public's anger over electricity rate hikes, an editorial in March 1981 urged citizens to "support continuing efforts by Mayor Boosalis and some members of the City Council to make the LES board a more consumer-oriented body, sympathetic and responsive to ratepayer frustrations." By the mayor's second term, LES had become more "sensitive to customers faced with inflated utility costs, proud of its efforts in conservation and of programs to diversify energy sources and is seeking to shed some of that excess capacity."

For example, to help support consumer conservation, LES became the first public utility company in the industry to implement a residential conservation service plan called "The Home Energy (T.H.E.) Audit." For a fifteen-dollar fee, the groundbreaking program sent a trained energy auditor into a home to provide the homeowner with written recommendations for reducing energy consumption, along with cost estimates and projected savings. The positive consumer response encouraged LES to expand the program to small businesses, offices, schools, restaurants, churches, and medical clinics.

By 1981 city government, too, had surpassed the mayor's goal of reducing energy consumption by 10 percent through such measures as turning down thermostats, cutting gas consumption, switching to diesel-powered equipment, and using weatherizing techniques.

COMPREHENSIVE PLAN, ZONING CODE: PRESSURE TO REVISE

Since adoption of the Comprehensive Plan in 1977, the city had received kudos for its exemplary planning process and its model Comp Plan— Lincoln's blueprint for growth until 2000. In late 1979, the Canadian government asked an American consulting firm to identify the best U.S. community models for planning and implementing efficient uses of land. After finding the best 150 U.S. community planning models, the consultants reduced the number to just two: Portland and Lincoln. These two cities, the consultant concluded, "are absolute leaders in comprehensive planning and related energy policies. They are far away ahead of the rest." Although just about everything in Lincoln's Comp Plan impressed the consultants, they cited the "rare" kind of citizen involvement in setting community planning goals and policies, the on-going dialogue between strong neighborhoods and a strong business community, and the process for monitoring the plan that would be viable even after the departure of "an exceptional mayor."

Even the more urbane Omaha, which rarely looked to Lincoln as a model for anything, was urged by a state legislative study committee to follow Lincoln's lead by developing its own comprehensive plan for urban growth and a process for citizen input. "The plan should resemble the Comprehensive Plan of the city of Lincoln," the committee recommended, "which has been cited as one of the best comprehensive plans in the entire country by a recent Canadian study." The legislative study criticized Omaha's allowing outlying large suburban shopping centers to drain business from downtown and contribute to its decay; but it commended Lincoln for limiting the growth of commercial areas outside of downtown and for paying "particular attention to maintaining and improving the downtown area before it had a chance to deteriorate."

While the external accolades were gratifying, they did not diminish the increasing pressure from Lincoln developers and the business community to alter the Comp Plan and ease zoning restrictions as the economy continued to slow and new development declined. For example, developers of a proposed large-scale office building and residential apartment complex applied for a zoning change that would be in total noncompliance with the Comp Plan. The complex was to be located near Southeast Community College, itself the center of a zoning dispute years earlier. The developer argued that the Comp Plan unfairly prohibited most non-residential development outside the downtown, thus joining the chorus of developers who were requesting zoning changes based on the depressed state of the building economy.

In June 1982 the mayor vetoed the council's approval of the zoning change for the office-residential complex, using her veto message to reiterate her philosophy about zoning in the context of prevailing economic conditions. "While many would suggest that present economic conditions mandate acceptance and approval of nearly any proposed project that involves immediate construction," she said, "I simply cannot subscribe wholeheartedly to a theory of planning by expediency. While I certainly am not oblivious to the current difficult economic conditions, the future orderly growth of Lincoln cannot be mortgaged to haphazard and erratic planning decisions responding solely to what we hope are temporary economic problems."

Persuaded by the veto message, enough council members refused to override the mayor's veto, thereby denying the requested zoning change. A *Journal* editorial characterized the veto as "evidence of the kind of steely resolution wanted in leadership positions—usually wanted more by political conservatives than liberals."

With such zoning restrictions on land use and development, Councilman Hampton criticized as "anti-business" the final zoning code enacted to implement the Comp Plan, even though the code was "fashioned after unprecedented public input and passed by a council dominated at the time by a so-called pro-business majority, of which he was one." He also criticized the anti-business predilection of the Comp Plan's champion, Mayor Boosalis. Since his election to the council in 1977, Hampton's ongoing beef with the mayor was her commitment to balanced growth and comprehensive planning through zoning and land-use controls.

Councilman Hampton often raised his favorite example of the mayor's anti-business bias in land-use and development issues: his opinion that the city had let a potential IBM development slip through its fingers because it would have violated Comp Plan land-use goals. He told a chamber of commerce forum in July 1979, shortly after Mom's reelection, "In our complacency, we do not welcome a new industry like IBM. I can't think of a more positive, blue chip industry than IBM." City officials, he said, should have been wooing the technology giant rather than restricting conditions under which it could build a plant on its large site in Stevens Creek.

IBM had acquired eight hundred acres in the Stevens Creek watershed in 1970 as part of IBM's national land banking program. Before the adoption of the 1977 Comprehensive Plan, the city asked IBM about its plans for the Stevens Creek property because of its impact on the land-use goals of the Comp Plan. IBM replied that it had no development plans for the property; that the land was acquired because of its location in Lincoln, not because of its specific location in Stevens Creek; and that the acquisition was one of eight added to IBM's land bank as possible future sites for plants and laboratories, but it had a low likelihood of development by IBM.

It didn't matter to Councilman Hampton that "the city, rather than closing the door to IBM, encouraged it to build a plant here and offered it incentives to do so." His accusation that the city and the mayor discouraged IBM from developing its land in Lincoln provided the refrain for a chorus of opponents who claimed the mayor was "anti-business," a claim that dogged her through her entire political *career.

Developer and Council Chairman Joe Hampton himself incited another zoning showdown in April 1982 by requesting rezoning of property he owned. The city Planning Department opposed Councilman Hampton's request to rezone thirteen acres of residentially zoned land to permit a ten-building office park because there was too much vacant office space in the city, because other office sites were available elsewhere, and because the rezoning would be "completely out of sync with the Comprehensive Plan." Although the city's Economic Development Commission supported Hampton's development project, the City-County Planning Commission nixed the office park zoning change. "Bad economic conditions don't to me provide a reason for a change of zone," said Planning Commissioner Bob Hans.

When the council split 3–3 after Hampton declared his conflict of interest and did not vote, Councilman Hampton "lashed out" at the no-growth policy at city hall for areas other than downtown. He argued that his proposed office park would create jobs and broaden the tax base and that the Comp Plan should serve only as a general guideline. Hampton charged that Lincoln's planning process "presents more of a problem to the economic well-being of this city than it does a solution." But some viewed Hampton's justification for his project as equating the city's economic well-being with his own. Most people are aware, the *Star* said, of the "big difference between an individual's economic well-being and the community's economic well-being."

Councilman Hampton's stated zoning philosophy reflected that of many of his developer colleagues: unless a zoning change "is clearly detrimental to the city," the decision should be left to the marketplace. Many developers held views on zoning in direct opposition to the mayor's philosophy: hers in favor of planned, balanced, steady, concentric growth of the city, and theirs in favor of unlimited growth in any direction depending on market forces.

But which view did the public share? Had economic hard times changed the community's desire for planned growth as embodied in the Comprehensive Plan? That question was explored during the thorough process established to review and update the Comprehensive Plan every five years: the 1977 Comp Plan was scheduled for an update in 1982. At the first hearing, in September 1982, of the Lincoln-Lancaster Goals and Policies *Committee, the citizen body charged with making recommendations for updating the Comp Plan, four hundred citizens showed up to hear proposed changes to the plan and register to vote on the recommendations at the next *meeting.

During this 1982 Comp Plan update process, the issue of development in the Stevens Creek watershed reared its head once again. Former councilman Sikyta, then a member of the Goals and Policies monitoring board, proposed that the Comp Plan be amended to allow planning for development in Stevens Creek. But views had changed since he fought the Stevens Creek battle as a council member during my mother's first term as mayor. His latest proposal to allow planning for Stevens Creek development was killed by a virtually unanimous vote of the large citizen Goals and Policies Committee, with no debate.

Both neighborhoods and business interests were able to claim some victories in the final 1982 update to the Comp Plan, and the expected fireworks never materialized—"a tribute to the desire of the [several hundred] committee members to do what they believe is good for the city, even if they don't agree." By leaving the 1977 Comp Plan mostly intact, the Goals and Policies Committee did not buy the argument that land-use and zoning restrictions on development and growth were undermining the community's economic health. Their actions indicated that sweeping changes to the 1977 Comp Plan were not needed—it was standing up well to tests of time and economic change.

The mayor applauded the concerted effort by citizens who took part in the highly democratic, nationally lauded Goals and Policies Committee process in 1982 to update the Comp Plan, just as she had applauded the long-awaited approval of the 1977 Comp Plan during her first term. Her faith in the wisdom of the people was once again confirmed. And every time she vetoed a rezoning request and stood up to those who called her "anti-business" and a "no growth-er," she demonstrated the depth of her commitment to the ideals of balanced growth and planned development for the good of the entire community.

For my mother, prudent land-use planning and zoning did not represent a municipal power game; rather, it was intrinsic to her vision for Lincoln's long-term health and viability. "Helen was forward-looking, a visionary," said Coleen Seng, Lincoln's second woman mayor. "She looked at issues well into the future. That's not easy because the day-to-day issues in local government can swallow you alive."

BUDGET PAIN: CUT, CUT, CUT

Against the sobering backdrop of a faltering national economy and its effect on the economic well-being of cities nationwide, budgeting for even a relatively healthy city like Lincoln continued to command my mother's focused attention in her second term. Although Mom was experienced by then in constructing tight budgets, her budgets reflected the fiscal constraints imposed by relentlessly increasing inflation and decreasing revenues.

The mayor's proposed 1979–80 budget contained a 7 percent increase over the previous budget and stayed within the state-imposed 7 percent lid on spending from property tax *revenue. Although the budget increase sounds generous by today's standards, the state lid imposed a significant financial restraint on Lincoln and other Nebraska cities, both because inflation was increasing far beyond the lid and because the city was growing, creating increased demand and costs for city services. Through her first term, the mayor had managed to propose, and the council had managed to adopt, budgets that stayed within the 7 percent state spending lid without large cuts in city services. But in her second term, inflationary pressures were too great to avoid hefty budget short-falls without major reductions in services.

My mother proposed for council consideration five alternatives for closing the 1980–81 projected budget shortfall. Two alternatives called for substantial reductions in city staff and major spending cuts in de-partmental budgets and in city services; the other three contemplated increased revenues through raising taxes to help keep pace with infla-tion. Mom favored the spending reduction alternatives over those re-quiring increased taxes. A *Journal* editorial criticized the mayor's prefer-ence for cuts in employees and services over generating new revenue but also recognized that budgeting during such economic hard times was a "melancholy process of retrenchment."

The city council—after studying her "glum-sounding alternatives"— preliminarily approved the mayor's preferred alternative to cut employ-ees and services and awaited her revised budget proposal. Once Mom's proposed 1980–81 budget reached the council for debate, it had elimi-nated sixty-five full-time city employees. The mayor's budget message explained the necessity for cuts ranging across all city departments, even in the face of additional demands for city services due to popula-tion growth. Because of the combined effect of high inflation rates (14.7 percent for the twelve months ending in April 1980, during the mayor's budget preparation) and the state's 7 percent lid on local government spending, she said, "We're just going to have to learn to live with lower levels of service."

Not content with arguing the merits of the mayor's austere budget proposal, Councilman Hampton quarreled with the accuracy of em-ployee figures submitted by the mayor and claimed that the number of city employees had increased during my mother's tenure. A *Star* editorial countered that the mayor had held the line on city expenditures, including employees, throughout her term in office in severely inflationary times and that she "has been as conservative as any self-admitted conservative, such as Hampton, would probably be if in the same position. That is almost too much for 'conservatives' to take. It galls them when someone they try to paint as a liberal, big spender turns out to be prudent with tax funds."

Labor negotiations on salary increases for city employees were a tricky component in every budget cycle, but they were even trickier for the 1980–81 proposed budget. The mayor relied on her personnel director to negotiate equitable compensation contracts with city employee unions. Before the council vote on the 1980–81 budget, three unions (firefighters, transit, and city employees) had accepted an 8.5 percent wage and benefit package. The fourth bargaining unit, the police union, rejected the city's contract offer, even after federal mediation, and asked the state Commission of Industrial Relations to determine a wage rate.

The police union's gamble to improve on the city's offer of an enhanced 8.5 percent package ultimately cost union members dearly. The state Commission of Industrial Relations, in an unprecedented ruling, determined that the police union did not prove that they were entitled to *any* compensation increase, based on a comparison of Lincoln police wages with those in similar cities. Many officers had believed that if the union lost before the commission they would at least receive the pay increase last offered by the city—"a total wipeout was unthinkable."

Following the commission's unexpected decision, the mayor and council did not re-offer the 8.5 percent increase to the police union, since the commission's ruling was binding. If the city were to renegotiate a wage increase, a taxpayer could sue the city for paying more than the commission ordered. In the wake of the commission's "stunning and bitter blow to the police union," the union's legal counsel resigned. The union president summarized the grim outcome: "We were aware of what we were getting into, we took a chance. We got in a street fight and got beat this time." The mayor's only comment: "I think we bargained in good faith with the police union. It was their idea to go to the Commission of Industrial Relations."

In the end the council approved most of the mayor's proposed 1980–81 budget and even added back several items not included in the mayor's budget. Mom complimented the council on its working over her budget. While she did not agree with them on adding expenditure items that she had not recommended, she recognized that "they're the policy-making body and should make those kinds of decisions."

As my mother's second term progressed, the city fiscal picture grew worse. Double-digit inflation persisted, with a 1980 average inflation rate of 13.48 percent. The recession of the early 1980s was even deeper than the 1973–75 recession sparked by the Arab oil embargo and was considered a "double dip" recession—actually two separate recessions interrupted by a short, two-quarter economic expansion. The second "dip," in 1982, was the worst recession to date, and the unemployment rate reached double digits for the first time since the depression. Business bankruptcies increased 50 percent over the previous year, with the farm economy especially hard hit.

In her usual "Sound Off to City Hall" sessions in the neighborhoods in February 1981, the mayor noticed a higher level of citizen knowledge about local government budgeting. Mom rarely heard people asking for new services and programs, as in the past, and many citizens attending seemed to be aware of the confluence of economic restrictions the city was facing.

NORTHEAST RADIAL: ROAD TO NOWHERE

At the start of Mom's second mayor term in 1979, the long-standing controversy over building a proposed Northeast Radial roadway appeared to be settled and buried once and for all. The short version of the very long history of the Northeast Radial began way back in 1952 when a radial roadway to connect northeast Lincoln with the downtown via a diagonal expressway was proposed in the Comprehensive Plan. The Northeast Radial's design was revised many times before the city began acquiring property along the Radial corridor in the late 1960s and early 1970s, eventually acquiring 297 parcels of property totaling eighty-three acres.

Shortly before my mother became mayor, the council stopped acquiring property because the Radial had become so contentious. Residents of neighborhoods bordering the Radial corridor expressed increasing anger that twenty years of city indecision about constructing the expressway had led to deterioration of homes and streets in the area, with homeowners unable to secure loans because of the unsettling possibility of the road's construction.

The Radial was one neighborhood issue that had sparked the district election plan, so it was no surprise that most of the new district council members elected in 1979 opposed the Radial, as did the mayor. In September 1979 the new council appointed a Northeast Radial Reuse Task Force of neighborhood and business representatives to recommend alternative uses for the land acquired by the city in the Radial corridor. Councilman Hampton and other Radial supporters wanted the task force to have the option of keeping some of the acquired land—a potential end-run effort to retain the possibility of building the Radial. In December the council approved Hampton's motion to clarify the task force's charge and to direct the task force to consider, among the reuse options, retaining a 120-foot-wide strip of city-owned Radial corridor land. The mayor warned that the word "corridor" spells "Radial" to many persons in the community and could keep alive the prospect of building a Radial in the future.

After ten months of input from residents, business representatives, city staff, and a visiting design team from the American Institute of Architects, the task force issued its report in August 1980. The group proposed that most of the city-owned Radial land (from Twenty-seventh to Forty-eighth streets) be returned to the tax rolls for residential and industrial development, with a twenty-five-foot-wide strip of land retained as a "linear park" buffer (recreational or bikeway use) between residential and industrial uses. My mother said she "wanted to stand up and applaud" when the task force completed its presentation. The council approved the task force plan, with only Councilmen Hampton and Scherer voting no.

That left the issue whether to build a shortened Radial between downtown and Twenty-seventh Street. Over two hundred citizens (most wearing "No Radial" buttons) appeared at a public hearing on the shortened Radial options. When the mayor concluded that "a strong public consensus in favor of the Radial did not exist," a *Journal* editorial criticized her. "She knows better than almost anybody in office that the broad public mass does not turn out at such events," it said. "Those present have particular or personal interests. Drawing a sweeping generality from an isolated event is treacherous business."

Before the council vote on a shortened Radial, the mayor declared her intent to veto it, if passed. The *Journal* criticized her for announcing her veto early, when "heretofore, the mayor has made it a virtual ironclad practice not to tip her decisions in advance of City Council voting." On the other hand, the *Star* called the mayor's veto announcement "an exercise of commendable political leadership, as well as being correct on the issue." In any case, the council voted 5–2 *not* to build the shortened Radial, finally "culminating more than 20 years of indecision about the issue." But that decisive vote in November 1980 was the gauntlet thrown down for Radial proponents (including the chamber of commerce), who began circulating petitions for a Radial referendum in the 1981 city election.

Although the *Star* said that in voting down the Radial the council had acted "as a take-charge legislative body intent upon disposing of chronic city problems and controversies," Councilman Hampton vehemently disagreed. "I'm glad the Mayor came out of the closet [by announcing her intended veto]," he said. "It appears that she and some members of this council must believe that they can make it so disagreeable for people to operate their cars that they can literally legislate them out of them."

The petition drive gained enough signatures to put the Radial question on the ballot. Voters would approve or reject the shortened Radial plan (downtown to Twenty-seventh Street) and the city's retention of a corridor (Twenty-seventh Street to Forty-eighth Street) for possible future Radial extension. The referendum's outcome was difficult to predict, and so was its potential effect on those running for city council who would share the ballot with the referendum in the upcoming 1981 election.

The mayor's visible leadership in opposing the Radial could influence the referendum, as the petition organizers recognized. Mom's opposition had many grounds—the energy situation, damage to neighborhoods that needed revitalizing, lack of evidence for relief from traffic congestion, shrinking federal assistance dollars ("no 'Uncle Sugar' in Washington who is going to fund this project"), and the city's own limited resources. "I do not believe that we can encourage this elaborate expansion of our street system," she said, one that "simply does not provide enough citywide benefits for its enormous costs."

Councilman Hampton, whose own reelection bid would share the same ballot with the Radial referendum, retorted: "Helen Boosalis is probably the most serious obstacle to the development of a safe and orderly traffic system in the city." City council candidates on both sides of the issue could agree with one primary candidate, Curt Donaldson, who wanted to end the Radial war once and for all, either way: "This thing has dragged on for as long as it took to build the whole U.S. highway system."

THE 1981 CITY ELECTION: ANOTHER RACE, ANOTHER COUNCIL

The Radial referendum was not the only question to be settled by the municipal election in the spring of 1981. Also to be decided was who would fill the three at-large city council seats currently held by Councilmen Scherer, Hampton, and Robinson.

In August 1980, almost a year before the end of his first term, Councilman Scherer announced that he would not seek reelection. "I don't see where my point of view is having much effect in City Hall," he said. "It isn't worth the hassle." He acknowledged that since the election of the new district council members, he and Joe Hampton were often in the minority on major issues. He considered "the Big Three" leaders of the majority—Eric Youngberg, Margrethe Ahlschwede, and Mike Steinman—an arrogant "clique at City Hall" who were controlled by the Lincoln *Alliance. Scherer predicted that the council he was leaving "may go down as the worst council in history." (Councilman Hampton later concurred, saying that his first four years in office were like "split terms—the first two years with a realistic oriented council, and the last two with an idealistic oriented council.") Scherer also announced that he had been appointed by the Republican National Committee to coordinate a program to get Democrats and Independents to vote for

Republican candidates. Knowing that Mom was a state coordinator for Jimmy Carter's reelection campaign, Scherer couldn't resist taunting, "I love to challenge the Mayor. This will just be at a different level."

The second at-large council member to declare his intention not to seek reelection in 1981 was John Robinson—the only minority council member and the one considered to be a moderating force between the "Old Pols" and "New Pols." With Robinson out of the race, Councilman Hampton was left as the only potential incumbent council candidate in 1981. Whether Hampton was a member of the 5–2 majority in the first half of his term or of the 2–5 minority in the last half, his consistent refrain in opposing the mayor had been that she was "anti-business," although on rare occasions he had praise, albeit mixed, for her fiscal acumen. "She is fiscally oriented and good with a dollar," he had said soon after my mother's reelection, "although I don't always agree with where she's allocated it."

As Hampton approached his 1981 reelection bid, his rhetoric against the mayor became stronger. When Councilman Mike Steinman presented a resolution in February to protect citizens who participated in local government decision making from being harassed by public officials, Hampton tried to turn the issue around to protect members of the council from harassment by Mayor Boosalis. "She was elected mayor, she was not elected eighth member of this council. I want to make it crystal clear, no one intimidates me." He referred to letters from the public that asked him "to speak out against the social science that now prevails in city hall."

When Councilman Hampton announced his decision to run for city council reelection in March 1981, he declared his intent to focus on the need for more private-sector jobs and for balanced representation on the council. He did not consider himself "the business community's candidate," he said, "but I think I can also say that Joe Hampton understands how business functions, what it takes to make it function, and what is necessary to provide a tax base for the city." If he didn't run for reelection, he reasoned, "there would not be any depth or background" on the council.

With Hampton the only incumbent in the 1981 council election, speculation about other candidates for the two open at-large seats yielded several names, the most interesting to me being Christie Schwartzkopf, my old junior high friend and daughter of the previous mayor; and Bob Kerrey, a local businessman who did not end up running for council but became governor a year later in his first elected office, and later U.S. senator and presidential candidate.

The 1981 city council general election produced three Republican, business-oriented victors to fill the at-large city council seats: Bill Danley, real estate broker; incumbent Joe Hampton, who admitted to being "less than pleased at his second place finish"; and Louis Shackelford, retired manager of downtown's Hovland Swanson clothing store. In contrast to the result of the 1979 election, the neighborhood-oriented candidates in 1981 were all defeated. First-place winner Danley viewed this result as a change in voter philosophy. Others analyzed the shift from neighborhood to business representation in 1981 as the natural result of the greater financial resources needed to run at-large council campaigns compared to district campaigns.

The ability of at-large candidates to mount a citywide campaign through incumbency (Hampton) or greater campaign spending (Danley, Shackelford) seemed to trump the candidates' identification with issues, even an issue as controversial as the Radial. Voters rejected the Northeast Radial in the election, 60 to 40 percent, even though all three council winners supported it, suggesting that voters "did not tie issues and personalities together." The *Star* called the resounding margin of the Radial's defeat "an impressive political *victory for Mayor Helen Boosalis, those district council members who opposed the road . . . and neighborhood groups who worked hard without much money compared to their opponents."

The mayor greeted the outcome of the city council election with equanimity, calling the three men elected "competent people who will do well for the city of Lincoln." She expected to get along with the new council and believed that any pressure to create factions would come from external forces, not from within the council. She objected to predictions of a council split between business-oriented and neighborhood-oriented legislators, calling such labeling "preposterous" and the result of "false perceptions"—just as attempts by some to label her as anti-business had been.

Some argued that the 1981 election of three businessmen for the at-large council seats, and its contrast to the 1979 election of four neighborhood newcomers for the district council seats, demonstrated that growing concern over the economy in 1981 had topped voters' scorecards. The mayor, on the other hand, assumed that the new council would recognize the importance of the economic base that business provided as well as the necessity for maintaining healthy neighborhoods. "We need all of it to make the city work," she said. "During my 22 years in city government, I've always found that people in this community come together for the total good." My mother avoided reinforcing the neighborhood-business dichotomy that her political foes and the political analysts so often emphasized. "We all should have an interest in the total community."

The mayor called "nonsense" the perception that the business community and neighborhoods did not have the same interests and said that maintaining the community would take a total community effort. "If we have big depressed areas, it erodes the tax base, leads to crime and vandalism, creates a climate that is not attractive to new industry, resulting in fewer jobs, investments and revenues." Mom argued that, in the face of federal cutbacks, neighborhoods and the private sector should work together, not as adversaries, on revitalization efforts. With fewer federal dollars, neighborhoods would have to become more self-sufficient and rely more on local businesses, volunteers, and foundations to achieve their goals.

Regardless of the 1981 shift in representation of business and neighborhood interests on the city council, my mother strived to elicit a community-wide perspective from all members of the council because the city's issues were big, the economy was poor, and federal aid was shrinking. No matter what voting split might develop on the new council, the national economy made it certain that all council members—conservative or liberal, business or neighborhood—together with the mayor would "be locked into a tight fiscal situation from which there is no escape."

One False Move and ...
August–October 1986

Have words ever popped out of your mouth and you later wished you could hit a verbal delete button? Most of us, I suspect, have had that experience. Most of the time, we suffer no terrible consequences and can leave the words behind us. Next time that happens, be glad you aren't running for governor.

Given my limited local campaign experience, I thought I'd learned quite a bit during my mother's gubernatorial primary campaign about the critical influence of television advertising—its timing and content—on the outcome of statewide campaigns. Mom's ads before the primary built on her already strong name recognition and voters' familiarity with her experience as mayor, conveying positive messages on why Boosalis was the best candidate for governor. The ads aired at the peak campaign moment, elevated Mom well above her six primary opponents, and helped propel her to a primary win. But if I thought after the May 1986 primary election that I knew something about the role of advertising in winning and losing statewide campaigns, well then someone should have told me, "You ain't seen nothin' yet."

Many campaigns geared to November general elections keep a relatively low profile during the summer months before kicking into a higher gear at the traditional Labor Day starting line. Voters don't pay much attention to candidates during the summer, which makes it a good opportunity for campaign staffs to organize fieldwork, plan strategy, and raise money.

Mom altered this traditional pattern by traveling the state and giving speeches outlining her policy proposals during the summer of 1986. Because she genuinely wanted to know what issues people cared about and also wanted them to understand her positions, she had always engaged in extensive dialogue with voters when both seeking and serving in elected office. Her statewide campaign for governor required much more effort to reach voters scattered across so much geography, so that was how she wanted to spend her summer campaign time when not on the phone raising money or walking in parades or riding elephants.

In early August—dog days of summer, swimming holes, and campaigns—Mom went on a stump swing through Hastings, Wayne, and Omaha to speak on state public education issues. "If Nebraskans are to share the benefits of education, we must share the burden of furnishing that education." She continued her education speech:

> That's why as governor, I will work with the unicameral to fulfill the *promise made to Nebraskans in the 1960s to have: one-third of our taxes from the property tax, one-third from sales tax and one-third from the income tax. We can fulfill these promises without a tax increase.

David Kotok, a reporter for the *Omaha World-Herald*, picked up a phrase from Mom's speech ("one-third . . . one-third . . . one-third") and did his own calculation of the effect on sales and income taxes of the Boosalis "proposal," according to his interpretation. His August 9 article began:

> A property tax reduction plan outlined Friday by Helen Boosalis, Democratic candidate for governor, would require more than a *60 percent increase in the state sales tax rate and a 40 percent boost in the income tax rates*. The plan, which she said would be "a goal" of a Boosalis administration, would reduce property taxes by *42 percent. (emphasis added)

In the article Kotok admitted that the percentage increases in sales and income taxes were derived by the reporter himself and not specifically proposed by my mother. "Specifically, Mrs. Boosalis proposed that Nebraskans' sales taxes, income taxes and property taxes raise equal amounts of revenue. She did not mention the specific percentages by which the three taxes would increase or decrease. *The percentages were arrived at by a reporter's application of her proposed formula* to State Department of Revenue figures for tax receipts" (emphasis added).

The article gave more credence to the reporter's independently designed calculation of Boosalis's "proposed tax rate increases" than it did to the candidate's own words from her speech: my mother had specifically said the goal of eventually equalizing the three taxes could be accomplished "without a tax increase." Besides pointing to the words from her speech, Mom further explained her position to the reporter:

> When told what the formula [of thirds] would do to Nebraska tax rates if it were in place now, Mrs. Boosalis said she meant the plan to be only a goal. . . . Later Friday Mrs. Boosalis said she does not want any tax rates raised, with the exception of the 1-cent sales tax in *LB662. . . .
>
> Setting goals, such as equal receipts from the three types of taxation, is necessary, Mrs. Boosalis said in an interview. "All I have said is I will work with the Legislature to fulfill that promise [made in the 1960s]." . . .
>
> In her speech, Mrs. Boosalis spoke out against tax increases. . . . [She said] "Nebraskans' per capita income earned in 1985 was less than it was in 1973. That means that most of our citizens are in no position for a tax increase."

Not only did my mother oppose any rate increases in sales and income taxes in order to achieve an equalization of revenues from the three taxes, but she argued that the reporter's calculations made it appear that she envisioned a shift to one-third sales taxes, one-third income taxes, and one-third property taxes occurring all at once. "I'm not saying it would be done in a year or two. No one can say exactly when it will be done. But if you don't start, it will never be done." How long such a shift would take would depend on such factors as the state's rate of economic growth, changes in the federal income tax law, and future actions of the legislature.

So how could a gradual equalization of the three taxes occur without Kotok's predicted tax rate increases? More revenue from sales and income taxes could occur over time by applying current tax rates to an expanding tax base, rather than applying Kotok's concocted increased tax rates of 60 percent and 40 percent to a static tax base. Some of the shift to more revenue from sales and income taxes would occur naturally, since revenue from property taxes would not increase as rapidly as revenue from sales and income taxes (assuming constant tax rates). With both a faster growth in sales and income tax *revenues* plus greater cost savings from government efficiencies, my mother said that a gradual shift to equalizing the amounts raised by sales, income, and property taxes could occur—without increasing the *rates* of sales or income taxes.

The often confusing distinction between increased tax rates and tax revenues made Kay Orr's own tax position inscrutable. On September 1, an editorial in the *Lincoln Journal* examined inconsistencies in Orr's assertions about tax increases: "Unless one anticipates an absolutely stagnant economy, there are constantly changing relationships between tax revenue and tax rates. Is Orr's campaign flag nailed to holding the line on tax dollars or tax rates? She seems to be going in both directions." In a debate at the state fairgrounds Orr said, "I will not take any more money from the taxpayers' pocket than is already being sent to the state," so the editorial queried: "Isn't that reasonably clear? She's talking about tax dollars—revenue—and on that basis, someone would be entitled to think Orr means to have state budgets rigidly controlled for four years by the net general fund receipts for the current year."

In contrast, the *Journal* found in other remarks that Orr had gone in a completely different direction: "Staying with tax rates in existence when Bob Kerrey leaves office . . . appears Orr's declared tax policy. Just Tuesday Orr speculated before the Lincoln Independent Business Association that improved private economic conditions could provide additional revenue to the state with existing state tax rates." The editorial again queried: "Could such additional revenue be called 'higher taxes,' which seem prohibited [by Orr] in another context?"

A *Lincoln Star* editorial criticized, from a different perspective, the claim that Boosalis's "tax proposal" translated into gigantic tax increases. "True enough if you raised all three [taxes] to the income producing level of the highest of the group. On the other hand, if you reduced them all to the level of the lowest of the group, you would have a drastic tax *decrease*"—a calculation just as cavalier as Kotok's. The editorial went on to identify the fallacy of the claim that my mother's proposal would require tax increases: "Boosalis did not say and does not intend that she would, if elected, immediately move to a point of equal income from all three taxes. It is a goal toward which she would work over a period of time."

But the genie could not be cajoled, coerced, or crammed back into the bottle. My mother and scores of others kept pointing to the explicit language in her speech, and she unequivocally refuted the *World-Herald* reporter's interpretation of the single sentence. During a rare moment in the campaign when Mom and I were home (and awake) at the same time, I overheard her side of a heated phone exchange with David Kotok as she tried to set him straight on what he had reported was her "tax proposal."

Too late. The Orr campaign seized on the opening that the article created. In a telephone interview with the *World-Herald* the day after the Kotok article appeared, Orr claimed that she read Boosalis's tax proposal "with alarm." Referring to the reporter's calculations of a 60 percent increase in sales tax and a 40 percent increase in income tax as though they had actually been proposed by my mother, Orr said, "There is no question we need property tax relief, but this (plan) appears to be ill-considered. . . . That kind of huge increase in the sales tax would have a devastating impact on the elderly" and on business.

The Orr campaign must have been dancing in the streets. Their candidate's Democratic opponent had initiated a tax increase issue via the helpful reporting of the state's major newspaper. Just four days earlier a *poll reportedly conducted for the Orr campaign had shown Orr trailing Boosalis. The contrived tax issue was the perfect instrument to reverse Orr's own purportedly negative polling results.

It was a typically sweltering Nebraska August, but the tax issue snowballed, gathering daily speed and momentum thanks to new Orr television ads hammering home the Boosalis "proposed tax increases." After seeing the ads once or twice, I couldn't bear to witness the relentless bashing. I had the exaggerated sense that the ads were playing twenty-four hours a day. Whenever an Orr tax ad came on the air, my dad would pace and shake his head and periodically appear to be on the verge of exploding.

I can close my eyes today and see the despicable ads, almost frame by frame. One opened with a chart purporting to be Mom's tax plan for Nebraska. As a male voice announces the numbers produced by the "Boosalis tax plan," a red column representing the sales tax and a gold column representing the income tax enlarge to engulf the entire screen.

My dad and I found little comfort in other commentary that recognized what had actually transpired. An August 31 column by *Journal* statehouse reporter Kathleen Rutledge warned that "what could loom very large" in the election "is one line in an August 8 speech." Mom's insistence that the *World-Herald* reporter's interpretation of that line was wrong would not negate the potential effect of Orr's relentless ads to create their own truth. "There's nothing like being able to accuse your opponent of favoring higher taxes," wrote Rutledge, "and the Orr campaign has taken full advantage of the opportunity. Orr reminded a group of Lincoln businessmen last week that *she* doesn't advocate raising the sales tax by 60% and the income tax by 40%. The message is being drummed into television viewers' heads in an Orr campaign commercial. . . . Whether voters perceive this as fair warning or as exaggeration of Boosalis' intent could shift the balance in this dead-even race" (emphasis added).

Similarly, *Lincoln Star* political reporter Don Walton observed that "Orr's commercials tying her opponent to a plan that would hike state tax rates continue to tick away on TV screens like a time bomb. That's the wild card right now in a tight gubernatorial race." And on September 1 the *Lincoln Journal* issued a strong editorial response to the tax issue frenzy:

> Strictly as a tactical move in a tough race for Governor, Helen Boosalis made a campaign error last month saying her long-distance goal was movement toward a state and local revenue system based approximately equally on the legs of the property tax, the sales tax, and the income tax. That opening allowed an *Omaha World-Herald* reporter to include in his coverage of the Democratic nominee's remarks the reporter's own rough calculation of how much state sales and income taxes (in dollars) theoretically would have to increase immediately so as to bring the local prop-

erty tax burden immediately down to an arithmetic semblance of parity. . . .

By now the Boosalis statement, as conditioned by the *Omaha World-Herald*'s reportage, has taken on a life of its own. It has furnished the raw meat for a Kay Orr television advertisement, as anyone with political moxie knew it would. The hammered intended message, playing to Nebraska demonology, is that Boosalis is a taxer and spender. . . .

All of Boosalis' assertions that the ad distorts and misrepresents her position are not likely to quiet the hardball Republican opposition.

By putting Boosalis on the campaign defensive, Republican Orr generally escapes being probed about her own tax policy assertions. That's a great campaign spot to be in.

Mom had immediately denied that the *World-Herald* story represented her tax plan and restated her opposition to raising taxes. She had reiterated that her long-term goal of equalizing revenue from sales, income, and property taxes could be achieved through economic growth and increased government efficiency. What more could she do?

Orr's campaign representative, Barry Kennedy, admitted that he didn't recall seeing any account of Boosalis's advocating the tax increases as calculated in the *World-Herald* story, but he argued that increasing the rates of sales tax and income tax was the only way to achieve her equalization goal. Orr herself had not made any detailed tax proposals but said she "hopes to have recommendations before the election from a group studying taxes for her." No such recommendation from Orr or her tax study group materialized before the *election.

Time and again Mom had to explain herself on the tax issue, to the exclusion of other campaign issues she preferred to discuss. To a roomful of newspaper editors in late September, she reiterated ("with irritation in her voice"), "I have been adamant. I have been firm. I have never deviated and my record shows I do not support tax increases. Period. Anything beyond that is a complete distortion." Among the newspapers represented in that room, the *Des Moines Register* analyzed how Kay Orr was able to whipsaw the Democratic nominee on the tax issue:

For decades relief from high property taxes, which provide 57 percent of government revenues in the state, has been near the top of
the political agenda. Deep into her [August] speech on education,
Boosalis embraced the goal of shifting taxes until the property, sales
and income taxes each supported about one-third the total cost of
government.

Her position—hardly a new concept among Cornhusker politicians—might have gone unnoticed but an Omaha newspaper reporter put pencil to paper and figured out that Boosalis' proposal to
reduce reliance on property taxes would cause increases of 60% in
the sales tax rate and 40% in the income tax rate.

Within days, the Orr campaign was on television with commercials warning Nebraskans about the whopping tax increases in store
for them if they elect Boosalis.

How would voters in Lincoln, western Nebraska, and Omaha—the
real campaign "battleground"—perceive Orr's attack ads on taxes?
Richard Shugrue, Creighton University law professor and political analyst, said it was a major advantage for Boosalis to be running even or
slightly ahead of Orr at the end of August. He couldn't remember a
non-incumbent Democrat running neck and neck with the Republican
at the beginning of the fall campaign. No wonder, he said, Orr had to
"take some risks by throwing the first real punch of the campaign with
a commercial critical of Mrs. Boosalis on taxes."

Bill Lee, who produced ads for Democratic primary candidate Chris
Beutler, characterized Orr's ads as striking Boosalis hard: "It's going to
get a lot bloodier before it gets over. These two women are going to
make a lot of the men's campaigns look like kid stuff. Beginning with
Orr's tax commercial they're starting probably the first television attack campaign in Nebraska. It's going to be interesting how Nebraskans
view that kind of attack."

Neil Oxman quickly produced Mom's advertising response to Orr's
damning tax ads. One Boosalis ad replayed part of an Orr ad while an
announcer intoned, "Kay Orr is misleading the public. Her false TV ads
want you to believe Helen Boosalis is for raising taxes. That's not true."
Mom's ad continued, "Helen Boosalis is against raising taxes and her re-

cord proves it again and again. Helen Boosalis, not Kay Orr, is the only candidate to have managed a major government budget. And she did it by controlling spending and without raising taxes."

To further complicate the unanticipated tax issue, the November ballot for electing Nebraska's governor also included a referendum on whether to retain legislation on school consolidation and state funding of public schools (LB662), which the legislature had already enacted in 1985. The original purpose of the bill was twofold: first, to reduce the number of school districts through mandatory consolidation; and second, to provide an adequate financing system for public education that would reduce the overall property tax burden. The consolidation part of the legislation was highly controversial in itself, but a last-minute amendment to the bill to provide a 1 percent increase in state sales tax (from 3.5 percent to 4.5 percent) to finance public education and thereby reduce the burden on property taxes only heightened the controversy. A citizens group organized a petition effort to repeal LB662 by referendum vote on the November 1986 general election ballot—the same ballot as the vote for governor.

My mother, most Democrats, and the Nebraska State Education Association (nineteen thousand teachers) opposed the referendum to repeal LB662—in other words, favored retaining the already enacted bill to reduce the number of school districts (955) by consolidation and to impose a 1 percent increase in state sales tax to relieve the local property tax burden for funding education. Orr, most Republicans, and business interests opposed LB662 and wanted it repealed.

Orr had already launched a barrage of thirty-second ads that capitalized on the Kotok article; now she could use additional ads to suggest that Boosalis's support for retaining LB662 was further evidence of the Democrat's larger sinister scheme to raise taxes. "No doubt about it," said an Orr ad voice-over. "Helen Boosalis wants to raise your taxes and Kay Orr does not."

So, misinterpret the recipe for a one-third/one-third/one-third tax stew, sprinkle with the LB662 referendum, step back, and watch the pot boil.

And boil it did—boiled over. The tax issue—as construed by the *World-Herald* reporter and used to advantage in Orr's TV ads—engulfed

Mom's campaign. On September 4, in the first Boosalis-Orr public debate, my mother tried to put the issue to rest by flatly opposing any new tax increases. Orr was asked about her shift to negative campaigning after telling reporters earlier that she planned to run a positive campaign and avoid talking about her opponent. Orr responded that she abandoned that strategy because of "public confusion about their differences. I had to make it clear what I stand for and let them know about my opponent." State GOP vice-chair Bee Whitmore agreed with her candidate, saying that when the tax issue arose in August, "Kay had to decide to move on it and seize it."

The new Boosalis ads directly responding to Orr's tax assault began airing September 6 to try to fend off the attack, but Orr's ads, which began on August 24, were taking hold, her attack strategy paying off. A *Sunday Journal and Star* poll taken in mid-August showed the race even, 37.8 percent to 37.4 percent, but only a month later the *World-Herald* published the results of its poll taken between September 9 and 11—after Kotok's article and after Orr's pounding TV ads—showing Orr leading by a sobering 11 points: 44 percent to 33 percent.

The timing of the *World-Herald* poll could not have been better for Orr. Her negative spots attacking Boosalis on taxes had played incessantly for more than two weeks immediately before the poll, while Mom's response ads had just begun to air as the poll got under way. Both campaigns agreed that Orr's advertising influenced the September *World-Herald* poll.

My mother continued to assert that the purported tax plan featured in the Orr ads was "not mine. It originated in the pages of the *World-Herald*." In response to her plummeting mid-September poll results, Mom said, "Given the turn the campaign has taken, I am not surprised about the poll results. Orr has been on TV for weeks with an ad that distorts and misrepresents my tax record. When people learn of the deliberate distortion and dishonesty involved in that ad campaign, the polls will turn around." Voters would make up their minds based on "substance and integrity," she said, and when asked whether she was questioning Orr's integrity, my mother replied that she would let the voters make that judgment.

After Mom's 11-point drop in the September poll, Boosalis headquarters was like a funeral parlor—Doris's receptionist voice several decibels lower and the typically bustling hallway empty of staffers squirreled away in their cubicles, moping. Even the persistent phone ringing sounded subdued. Had my mom been in her campaign office right after the disheartening *World-Herald* poll, she undoubtedly would have greeted her demoralized troops with encouraging words and an upbeat story, perhaps recounting the discouraging poll published just a few days before her second mayoral victory in 1979.

Instead, Helen Boosalis was visiting livestock sales barns in the Platte Valley, where she told reporters that the unfavorable poll would only make her work harder. Although I wasn't with Mom on that trip, political reporter Don Walton's description of the candidate after such a disappointing setback was vintage Mom. I could visualize the set of her jaw, her redoubled energy, and her unflagging optimism, greeting farmers one by one as she climbed "up and down the steep rows of seats, her red suit the only splash of color in the [livestock sales] barn dominated by overalls and grunting hogs." Walton mused that "if she had been staggered by a weekend newspaper poll that suddenly showed her 11 points behind Kay Orr in a gubernatorial race that had been rated dead-even, it didn't show. Or it had been short-lived. Her mood was upbeat as she marched armed with her legendary store of energy through an overcast day."

This was the upbeat, energetic Helen Boosalis that her campaign continued to project to voters, with positive advertising emphasizing her experience and leadership. Neil Oxman said at the time that the task for his media consulting firm was "to capture the essence of Helen and communicate it to Nebraskans. Our crew fell in love with her. This is a lady who is a true professional. She is extraordinarily secure."

Orr's campaign added fresh versions of their tax ads and other assaults about the number of new manufacturing jobs created under my mother's terms as mayor. My mother's campaign continued on its positive advertising track but also responded to correct Orr's distortion of the Boosalis record on taxes and jobs. One Boosalis ad countered, "It's time Kay Orr stopped the negative campaign," and quoted a newspaper claim that "Kay Orr is no more than mudslinging. That's not leadership."

Mom not only used advertising to defend her position against the Orr tax attack ads but also took her case directly to the people, as in her spirited North Platte speech on September 20:

> The stakes are too high to sit back and let our opponents spout half-truths, distortions and outright fabrications and not challenge them. The stakes are too high to sit back and let our farmers and ranchers hear how great the ag economy is from people who wouldn't know a corn stalk from a palm tree. The stakes are too high to let a few wealthy big shots from outside our state tell us in Nebraska what's good for us. It's time to turn the fire up in this campaign and send these Orr Republican elephants back to the circus where they belong.

In a Boosalis ad late in the campaign, Governor Kerrey spoke directly to the voters about my mother, with no mention of Orr. "A governor's job is to fight for all Nebraskans," he said. "It takes independence and experience, and only Helen Boosalis has it. Helen Boosalis is an extraordinary woman who can lead Nebraska. She cares about people. As a voter, that's what I'm looking for in our next governor. We've come a long way in the last four years. Now is not the time to turn back." The Orr campaign kept "on the shelf" an unbroadcast ad of President Reagan speaking in Omaha on Orr's behalf. Apparently, Orr's campaign believed her tax ads were doing the job, without help from the Gipper.

In the unlikely event that a voter somehow missed Orr's omnipresent television tax ads, a lower-tech rendition was delivered by mail in the last few days of the campaign in a brown envelope marked: "Open Immediately. Tax Information Enclosed." The letter, signed by Orr's campaign treasurer, began, "Do you want to pay higher taxes? Of course not—but you will if Helen Boosalis has her way." At least one voter (not my father) resented this approach and wrote a letter to the editor of the *Journal*:

> I am a registered Republican, a party contributor and a person who voted for Kay Orr in the primary. . . . The recent mailing of "Open Immediately (Tax Information Enclosed)" in the plain brown envelope hinted something more than campaign material. . . . I have no

302 | *Flash Forward*

idea what the *Omaha World-Herald* piece actually reported, but I do
know both these ladies want to be governor too badly to ever make
such a tax proposal. The campaign advice that resulted in this mail-
ing suggests that the Nebraska voters are stupid and deserve no respect. . . . Pollsters should move my voter support over to the other
lady.

The staggering damage inflicted by the Orr tax ads was apparent in
the September poll results, but would the damage be lasting? In Chicago in late October, Max gagged on his morning coffee as he read a
Chicago Sun-Times article recounting how "Boosalis got in trouble" by
suggesting property tax relief through greater reliance on sales and income *taxes, which a newspaper story portrayed as an immediate tax
increase. The *Sun-Times* described what happened in the aftermath of
that story: "Orr, who has offered no tax plan, then unleashed a TV ad
accusing Boosalis of wanting to raise taxes, and shot ahead for a time
in a mid-September *Omaha World-Herald* poll." Indeed, Orr's accusation
that her opponent wanted to raise taxes, though vehemently denied by
my mother, was "clearly an echo of Reagan's stinging 'tax and spend'
label for Democrats [that] hit a nerve with voters," the *Denver Post* reported.

Like a recurring nightmare, those ads played in my head on continu-
ous reel as the campaign churned forward. In a confusion of nightmare
and reality, a scathing Orr tax ad gained a prominent airing at a particularly crucial moment.

On October 6, the third and final hour-long televised debate between
the two candidates covered campaign issues such as economic development, agriculture, groundwater, liability insurance, telephone deregu-
lation, and, of course, taxes. My mother was well prepared, with her
tabbed organized debate book thoroughly researched by Greg Hayden,
campaign head of policy research, with help from Sue Bailey and other
campaign advisers. Both candidates did well, and, most important in
debates, neither made a misstep. Both supporter camps in the debate
audience were pleased and inspired by their candidate as the debate
ended.

After each candidate had her last word and the studio lights dimmed at the debate's conclusion, those watching the studio monitors and those at home watching the televised debate were surprised to hear from one of the candidates yet one more time. Orr managed to have truly the last word as her blistering ad attacking my mother on taxes flashed on the TV screen. There was a collective gasp in the television studio, perhaps even from some in the Orr camp. The inequity and favoritism of airing one candidate's political ad at the very moment of the debate's conclusion was apparent to all.

Omaha station KETV's policy prohibited the airing of campaign ads immediately before or after a debate broadcast. The station's general sales manager, Howard Shrier, said that airing Orr's ad after the debate was a result of "human error." He said that Orr's ad had been submitted late for a spot to be aired during the *Monday Night Football* broadcast; all those spots were filled, so it was manually scheduled for 8:00 p.m.—"coincidentally" right after the debate—by station staff unfamiliar with the debate schedule. "It just kind of backfired," Shrier said. In an impotent, too-late-now gesture the station sales manager promised that a letter would be drafted by KETV to apologize to Helen Boosalis.

The tax issue had truly acquired its own life—a recurring specter through the rest of the campaign—confirming my childhood certainty that you really cannot kill the bogeyman.

The tax issue is permanently embedded in my memory and the subject of one of my most vivid recollections of my mother's race for governor—the autumn day in 1986 when Orr's tax attack against my mother provoked the Boosalis campaign to examine its true character and determine its ultimate course to election day. This powerful image, which is still with me, taught me less about political missteps and winning campaign strategies than it instructed me on principles versus expediency and the meaning of integrity.

The strained drive from Lincoln to Omaha seemed longer than sixty miles. The normal campaign chatter of Mom and her campaign co-manager was reduced to half-phrased, halfhearted comments on innocuous subjects. I sat in the backseat. Traveling separately to the Omaha campaign meeting were Neil Oxman and Mom's Washington DC pollster, Harrison Hickman.

Childhood impressions of Omaha skittered among my gloomy thoughts. I

304 | Flash Forward

had traveled to Omaha less than half a dozen times in my childhood. Although Lincoln's sibling in proximity, Omaha seemed to me when I was growing up to have a bit of an attitude. Perhaps it was a member of Nebraska's down-to-earth family of little pretense, but Omaha was the big-city cousin, putting on airs and just tolerating the rest of us folks at reunions.

Pushing aside my childhood thoughts of familial rivalry, I thought about Omaha's importance to any Democratic campaign for statewide office. Its sheer voting numbers could neutralize the votes of the conservative and sprawling but sparsely populated western part of the state. Omaha is a must-win for statewide Democratic candidates, yet because of the more conservative views of its significant population of blue-collar Democrats, it is far from a slam dunk for most Democratic campaigns. In the preceding gubernatorial election, Democrat Bob Kerrey narrowly won because of his slim but decisive win in Omaha.

My thoughts halted as the car pulled into the parking lot of a nondescript Omaha office building. The tension of the last few days showed on the faces of our weary band as we made our way to the office conference room of Boosalis campaign co-chairman Ben Nelson. Each of us wore the strain of months of sleep deprivation, junk food, and bad coffee.

Even my mother had lost the usual spring in her step, and the corners of her mouth curled slightly down in disgust, as though she had just flipped on a TV and caught one of Orr's scorching ads against her. How many times I had seen her, dog-tired from nonstop speeches and merciless campaign wear and tear, but the moment she entered a populated room she seemed to inhale the energy and life force from every body there, like a transfusion restoring her vibrant, charismatic self. But not on this day—not on this mission.

Ben Nelson, looking acutely worried, was waiting for us. "Helen," he nodded. "Everyone's here. Come this way." He pushed open the oversize doors to the inner sanctum. There they were—the Omaha Big Boys, as I had secretly dubbed them—seated stone-like at the far end of the long conference table. These were Omaha Democratic Party bigwigs, and they weren't happy; in fact, they looked irritated, angry, almost menacing. The boardroom table seemed to elongate as I took visual attendance. In my mind's eye, my mother seemed to shrink, and I could feel myself disappearing altogether.

There were no social niceties or how are you's. As we took our seats a voice from the end of the table erupted, "Helen, you've got to blast back at Orr.

36. "Take Off the Gloves" editorial cartoon of race between Kay Orr and Helen Boosalis

They've created a tax issue and they're running with it. It doesn't matter that it's distorted, it doesn't matter that it's not factual. There's no time to clarify the issue or explain it. You can't let these attack ads play over and over again unchallenged." He turned to the media consultant. "Neil, what kind of ads can we do quickly to blast back hard—to hit below the belt? Now's the time."

"Several ways we could go. The camera could . . ."

"Just a minute, Neil," my mother cut in. "Listen, I'm as frustrated as all of you. The World-Herald story's given Orr a huge opening. But I've said from the beginning, I will win this on the high road or no road. I will not stoop to doing negative attack ads."

Another of the Omaha Big Boys slammed his fist on the table. My stomach began to churn. "You've got to take the gloves off, Helen! Hit 'em back hard with an even stronger negative message than theirs. Get in the ring and start slugging. And out of the ring, you gotta get down in the mud, if that's what it takes. We've got so little time. The election's at stake, for God's sake!"

"Look, I'm the one on the line here. I know the election's at stake—my candidacy's at stake. But so are my integrity and the reputation I've built through *twenty-four years in office. You know I'm tough. You know I'm no shrinking violet. I'll fight to the end to win this thing. But I won't fight dirty."*

"Dirty, hell! We have to do what it takes. Do you . . ."

"Excuse me, excuse me for interrupting." Harrison Hickman's soft-spoken drawl could barely be heard over the boom-box voices in the room. "Gentlemen, the truth is that no one knows what works best in a situation like this, where two women are running against each other and one has gone negative, more negative than the normal comparative stuff. No pollster, no media guy, no campaign manager knows the right response. There's been so little experience. And just what does 'taking the gloves off' look like with two women in the ring? No one knows. So now we have to work through this dilemma—calmly and rationally."

At last there was silence in the room.

Chapter Seven

Mayors' Mayor
1975–1983

"Helen had a national reputation as a great administrator of a well-governed city and was a model for other mayors. She believed in running things right. Helen's concerns for cities cut across partisanship and reflected her deep, passionate beliefs about government serving people."—GEORGE LATIMER, mayor of St. Paul, 1976–90

"Although Mayor Boosalis was U.S. Conference of Mayors president when the Reagan administration was trying to dismantle the federal government, her leadership made a difference. We succeeded in stabilizing the cuts in federal urban aid. Without her leadership, we could have lost it all."—TOM COCHRAN, executive director, U.S. Conference of Mayors

No doubt about it, I mused from the back row: if you want to be a powerful mayor, your name must begin with "B". The other mayors of middling to larger U.S. cities had quietly taken their places at the imposing half-moon table. The four seats behind the placards with "B" mayor names were still empty when the doors swung open, heads craned, and the cavernous conference room's undercurrent of low voices transformed to a loud buzz.

Each with his own entourage of briefcased advisers, assistants, assistants to the assistants, and thick-necked bodyguards, the big three city mayors slowly ascended to their seats: Beame of New York, Bilandic of Chicago, and Bradley of Los Angeles. The remaining empty "B" seat at the grand table had been filled without notice during the regal male procession by the petite, white-haired woman who now pounded her gavel.

"The meeting of the 1977 Resolutions Committee of the U.S. Conference of Mayors will now come to order." I smiled at the familiar authoritative voice ("Pick up your room this instant, Mary Beth!") of Mayor Boosalis of Lincoln, Nebraska—Helen Boosalis, my mother.

U.S CONFERENCE OF MAYORS: TRACK TO LEADERSHIP

My mother's appointment in 1977 as chair of the Resolutions Committee of the U.S. Conference of Mayors showcased the first woman ever so appointed in the forty-five-year history of the national *organization. The Resolutions Committee, like the floor of the stock exchange after the opening bell, held the heated core of fiery policy debate among mayors at U.S. Conference of Mayors meetings. It forged comprehensive municipal policy positions for the organization's leadership to recommend to Congress and the White House.

Meetings of the Resolutions Committee often devolved into clashes between big city–small city, sun belt–frost belt, urban-suburban-rural, liberal-conservative forces, each with a differing perspective on desired federal urban policy. The typical combat at the Resolutions Committee eventually produced policy recommendations for adoption by the U.S. Conference of Mayors general membership (mayors of cities larger than thirty thousand). Floor debate sometimes ensued in the full body of mayors on the most controversial items, but without the level of heated discourse common at the Resolutions Committee.

I joined my folks in Tucson for the 1977 U.S. Conference of Mayors meetings, primarily so I could witness how Mom would handle her chairmanship of the Resolutions Committee with its agenda that included incendiary issues such as gun control and national health insurance. Thinking about her presiding over this powerful group of opinionated, outspoken city bosses tied knots in my stomach. Would these macho politicos take direction from a woman chair, even a strong and competent woman like my mother?

Mayor Boosalis ran the contentious Resolutions Committee meeting with calm decisiveness, even when tempers flared among the mayoral heavyweights. As I watched, I understood why she needed a crash review of Robert's Rules of Order. She had to prepare herself for the inevitable parliamentary maneuvering of these savvy politicians, even with the U.S. Conference of Mayors parliamentarian at her elbow. At one point, a vociferous mayor seemed bent on challenging her rulings as chair and derailing the meeting based on some obscure parliamentary point. When my mother hesitated a moment, Mayor George Moscone jumped in and "saved" her, as Mom later gratefully acknowledged to the charismatic San Francisco mayor, who was assassinated just a year later in his city hall office.

Several such moments of argument arose among the mayors of vastly different political stripes. In the end my nail biting was for nothing. My mother's job as Resolutions Committee chair earned the respect of her peers by the time she gaveled the meeting to a close several hours later. Her committee approved an impressive list of urban policy resolutions ready for recommendation to the full body of mayors, where Mayor Boosalis would defend the work of her spirited Resolutions Committee members.

Chairing the Resolutions Committee was not my mother's first leadership role at the U.S. Conference of Mayors. From her initial meeting in Boston just two months after her first election as mayor, in 1975, she was targeted as a rising star among the ranks of her fellow mayors (who were, indeed, mostly "fellows"). She and a powerhouse group of mayors traveled straight from the Boston meeting of the U.S. Conference of Mayors to the White House to urge President Ford to continue federal revenue sharing.

After the 1976 presidential election, Mom and several big-city mayors were appointed by the U.S. Conference of Mayors president to meet with the new Carter administration on its proposed urban policy. While in Washington the mayors of Lincoln, Chicago, Syracuse, New Orleans, Denver, Milwaukee, Portland, and San Juan also testified before the Senate Intergovernmental Relations Committee.

During Carter's first year, the mayors pressed for a well-financed federal urban policy and sought response to questions about Carter's plan for cities:

- Will Carter target federal aid to distressed big cities or to small towns and rural areas as well?
- Should states be given the primary role to administer and distribute urban aid? How will the mayors react to a greater state role "after decades of antagonism"?
- Who will be in charge of the new federal urban policy? "HUD? The Commerce Department? A new cabinet agency? A White House urban czar? Fifty governors in fifty states?"
- Will Carter's urban program rely on business incentives, or earmark funds for urban neighborhoods and social services?
- Should federal dollars be used to relocate the unemployed, or to bring jobs back to places where unemployment is high?

Shortly after President Carter's State of the Union message in January 1978, the U.S. Conference of Mayors mid-winter meeting in Washington DC criticized the lack of federal commitment to urban aid as reflected in Carter's budget. "We are not knocking on the federal door asking for handouts," my mother told her fellow mayors. "We just want the assistance we need so we can help ourselves. In Lincoln, we consider the federal government to be catalysts—the institution which gets our local initiatives and resources underway. . . . Unfortunately, this budget is not a catalyst even hot enough to boil water."

After several meetings with Carter's cabinet members, a meeting with President Carter and Vice-President Mondale, and a lengthy roll-up-the-sleeves session with Stuart Eizenstat, the White House adviser on domestic affairs (whom my mother greatly respected for his attention to cities' needs), the mayors found encouragement that their recommendations would be incorporated into the administration's urban policy. The mayors continued to work closely with the White House on implementing the president's urban policy throughout the Carter years.

"Listen Up, Jimmy, Helen Boosalis Has Something to Tell You" was the funny headline for an article outlining the mayors' efforts to influence Carter's urban policy in the February 7, 1978, *Lincoln Journal*. The president must have listened, because the following month, Helen Boosalis joined a group of mayors invited to the White House for the

37. President Carter meets at White House with U.S. Conference of Mayors executive committee

unveiling of Carter's urban program, which she characterized not so much as a "panacea" for cities' ills as "a positive beginning."

Overall, Lincoln's mayor was "pleased that the President and his staff have been listening to the cities" and that Carter kept his pre-nomination promise to be "a friend, an ally and a partner" to the nation's mayors. She called Carter's comprehensive urban policy a "tremendous effort," noting that this was the first time such an attempt had been made at the federal level. On a more parochial note, she was pleased that the policy reflected "an interest in healthy cities that still have pockets of problems, as we do in our city."

My mom continued her visits to the White House with other mayors from the U.S. Conference of Mayors to hammer out revisions to Carter's urban policy and plans for its implementation. Differences among cities' needs surfaced between mayors of growing cities (mostly sun belt) and mayors of older cities (mostly frost belt) over appropriate distribution of federal urban aid. Mayors of newer, growing cities argued that they lost out in federal funding formulas even though they contained "pockets of poverty" as severe as more widespread poverty in the older cities of the Northeast and Midwest.

The mayors worked out a compromise strategy so that they could speak with one voice in Washington. Mom and others urged officials in the Carter administration to address the *prevention* of urban decay. She argued that cities like Lincoln, which are neither "distressed" nor growing rapidly, should be considered eligible for federal funds to help prevent urban decline and not be ignored in favor of declining, older cities. "I really think it makes good business to invest before a problem becomes so great it can't be corrected," she said. "You don't wait to repaint the house until the wood is rotten." (Her words recall my dad, up on the ladder every spring, scraping and painting the woodwork of the older houses where I grew up—no rotten wood under his watchful eye.)

In addition to bringing the message of the nation's mayors to Carter's urban policy, Lincoln's mayor spoke at national forums on a host of issues facing cities across the country. "Part of Mayor Boosalis' leadership was her practical, common sense way of talking about issues," recalled U.S. Conference of Mayors executive director Tom Cochran. "She had a Hubert Humphrey way about her. She could get people to listen. She could cut through to the heart of issues." At a Kansas City conference on urban growth and economic development sponsored by HUD, Mom touted the revitalization efforts in Lincoln's older neighborhoods and central business district and stressed the need for partnerships between city government and private enterprise to stabilize and revitalize cities' central cores. "The forum could not have had a better authority on the subject," noted a *Star* editorial.

As chair of the Human Development Standing Committee of the U.S. Conference of Mayors (the first woman to chair a policy standing committee), my mother called a conference in Washington DC of city human services directors to identify municipal human services *needs. Many cities were reluctant to take on major responsibility for human services, which was viewed then as going beyond traditional municipal responsibilities for public safety (police and fire), sanitation, sewers, and streets. Providing a range of human services necessary to meet the needs of citizens was not considered a primary role for city government but was seen instead as the responsibility of the county, state, or federal governments—in short, somebody *else. Lincoln's mayor related that her city had spent nearly a third of its funds from federal revenue sharing on human services in areas of health, human rights, aging, addiction treatment, employment, and job training.

Mom's work on urban policy at the national level helped her understand other cities' struggles to budget for the rising costs of public services and infrastructure needs in a worsening economy—a time when the ability of cities to band together to ensure continued federal assistance was particularly crucial. Nearly fifty years earlier, during times of record unemployment in the Depression economy, the U.S. Conference of Mayors was founded to strengthen the capacity of mayors to manage serious economic problems in their cities and to seek assistance from the federal government.

In the context of cities nationally, Lincoln was fortunate in one respect—its rate of unemployment lagged far behind the national *average. In fact, during my mother's increasingly active leadership in the U.S. Conference of Mayors, Lincoln's positive employment picture made national news in the fall of 1980. Lincoln's 3.2 percent unemployment rate was the lowest among metropolitan cities in the country at a time when the national rate was 7.5 percent and the economy was in a *recession. Lincoln did not share the desperate unemployment conditions of some of its fellow cities, but like them, Lincoln's ability to finance municipal services and operations was further and further tested by the worsening national economy and rising inflation. All faced an economic plight.

Lincoln's mayor began her second term in 1979 not only with the confidence Lincoln voters had shown that she could steer them through serious economic times but also with the confidence of her mayor colleagues nationwide. Two months after her mayoral reelection she was elected chair of the Advisory Board of the U.S. Conference of Mayors, the third-ranking post in the organization's hierarchy. That position put her on track for election as president of the U.S. Conference of Mayors in 1981.

To be slated for president of the U.S. Conference of Mayors was a big deal. Moreover, the mayor of Lincoln (eightieth-largest U.S. city in the 1980 census) would be the national organization's first woman president. "For the first time in its 47-year history, the U.S. Conference of Mayors has placed a woman in line to become its president and leading advocate on urban policy," reported the *Pittsburgh Press*. "That would give the 59-year-old Democrat regular access to the President of the United States, as well as an opportunity to wield considerable influence in the mayors' organization."

A *U.S. News and World Report* story on big-city women mayors (including Chicago's Jane Byrne and San Francisco's Diane Feinstein) featured a picture of the U.S. Conference of Mayors' president-in-waiting and described her as "peppery." At her biweekly news conference, Lincoln's mayor "shrugged off her new fame." She said, "I haven't been besieged to be on talk shows." When asked about the reported 750 women mayors in 18,800 municipalities of all sizes, Mom said she hoped the number of women mayors would increase faster and that more women would view running for office as an extension of their civic duty.

With my mother's rising leadership role in the U.S. Conference of Mayors, her trips to Washington DC grew more frequent. Mom continued to meet with Carter's urban policy team and others in the administration of importance to cities. President Carter had tapped two of Mom's mayor colleagues for cabinet positions—Moon Landrieu (New Orleans mayor and father of current U.S. senator Mary Landrieu) as HUD secretary, and Neil Goldschmidt (mayor of Portland) as transportation *secretary. Mom valued and utilized these administration connections in transportation and urban development. For example, she led a delegation of city, county, and state officials to urge Congress to pass the Federal Public Transportation Act of 1980, including reform of transit funding to cities to take into account a city's level of transit services and not just its population; Mom also explored HUD funding programs to assist Lincoln's downtown redevelopment efforts. (My mom's frequent Washington appearances had one downside. After one trip when she walked nonstop over the marble floors of the Capitol in high heels, she could barely walk when she got home and had to undergo foot surgery.)

U.S. CONFERENCE OF MAYORS: PRESIDENT-ELECT

At the June 7 opening press conference of the 1980 U.S. Conference of Mayors meeting in Seattle, Lincoln's mayor shared the podium with mayors Charles Royer of Seattle, Edward Koch of New York City, and Richard Hatcher of Gary, Indiana. "You might well wonder what in the world the mayor of New York City and the mayor of Lincoln, Nebraska, have in common," my mother told reporters. With its relatively low rate of unemployment, Lincoln was "insulated somewhat" from the effects of the recession, she explained, but it "is having a devastating effect on all of us." She said that Mayor Koch agreed with her contention that federal fiscal support for cities like Lincoln, which had not been as severely damaged by the weak economy, was important "preventative medicine."

As anticipated, at the Seattle meeting my mother moved up in the leadership lineup to be elected U.S. Conference of Mayors vice-president. Traditionally, the sitting U.S. president would come to address the mayors, and this presidential election year was no exception. President Carter, who had listened to the problems of cities and fashioned an urban policy to address them, received a warm welcome from the assembled mayors. A photo of Carter addressing the mayors appeared on the June 11 front page of the *Washington Post*; standing next to him, applauding, was the smiling, white-haired mayor of Lincoln, Nebraska.

My mother downplayed her quick rise to leadership in the national organization composed of many powerful leaders in their own right. "The only reason I'm up for the presidency is that they were overdue to have a woman president," she said. "Let's face it; that's the way it is." But Barbara Goldman, Lincoln's former Washington lobbyist, said she had watched "Helen go from being one of the most well-liked mayors, to being one of the most respected. And that's not an easy task with these people as your peers." Carolyn Chaney, Lincoln's Washington lobbyist since 1979, told reporters at the Seattle meeting that once Helen Boosalis became affiliated with the U.S. Conference of Mayors, you no longer heard: "Lincoln? Where? I don't think the people back home know it, but they have an ambassador in Helen." As an example, Chaney credited my mother for her role in getting the "pockets of poverty" provision added to the Urban Development Action Grant program.

38. Mayor Helen Boosalis applauds President Jimmy Carter at 1980 U.S. Conference of Mayors meeting

When she returned from the 1980 U.S. Conference of Mayors meeting, Mayor Boosalis was "bubbling with enthusiasm . . . [her] head filled with ideas she will share with Lincolnites for weeks to come." By then the 1980 presidential campaigns were in full swing. During her twenty years in nonpartisan elected office, Mom had not played an active role in party politics, though she considered herself, and was considered, a good Democrat. ("Mrs. Boosalis acknowledged she is not closely involved in party politics, either at the local or national level.") But with her visible national leadership of the U.S. Conference of Mayors and her growing influence in Washington and with mayors across the country, she had been "wooed" by the presidential primary campaigns of both President Carter and Senator Ted Kennedy.

Consequently, Mom's endorsement of President Carter in early April 1980 was "especially important," wrote a *Journal* reporter, "because the Mayor was courted late last year by Kennedy supporters and her work with the U.S. Conference of Mayors makes her endorsement useful in Nebraska as well as nationally." She also announced that she had agreed to be one of three Nebraska co-chairs for the Carter-Mondale campaign, including current U.S. senator Ben Nelson. President Carter, she said, "is the only one in my recollection to understand cities as the valuable resources that they are."

The week after her appointment as co-chair, my mother met with President Carter in the Oval Office to discuss Midwest concerns (perhaps including farmers' disappointment in the recent U.S. grain embargo to Russia). She had attended other meetings in the White House, but this was her first one-on-one with the president. She didn't even try to mask her excitement when reporters asked what she remembered about the Oval Office—like a ten-year-old she said the rug, the flag, and the desk. She missed sharing details of her White House visit with my dad, who at the time was in Australia for five weeks of consulting with Australian farmers on conservation tillage and ecofallow cropping practices.

Before the May 1980 presidential primary, my mother was concerned that Carter would lose votes to Kennedy because of the ten-cents-a-gallon surcharge on gasoline that the president had ordered to reduce oil imports. However, Carter easily won the Nebraska Democratic primary, and at 9:30 p.m. on primary election night he called my mother to thank her for her help.

President Carter made another phone call to my mother four months later—a call unrelated to the close race he was running against his formidable opponent, Ronald Reagan. In mid-September 1980, shortly after the birth of our older son, Michael, the phone rang in the Lincoln mayor's kitchen. Mom was ready for bed, with pajamas on and rollers in her hair, when she picked up the phone and sat down at the glass-topped breakfast table. A voice said, "Please hold for the president of the United States." A moment later my mother heard, "Hello, Helen? Jimmy here. I'm just calling to congratulate you on the birth of your first grandchild."

My mom, flabbergasted, later said it was lucky she did not respond to what she thought was surely a joke—but was not. It was, indeed, the president taking a moment from the fight of his political life to celebrate a new life in one distant midwestern family. President Carter's call made a big impression on me, the mother of that baby, if not the baby himself, who now rolls his eyes at the telling of the story of the president's call to his grandmother on the occasion of his birth.

Despite her role in the presidential campaign and her many U.S. Conference of Mayors responsibilities, my mother's "first and foremost" job was as mayor. True to her word, she withdrew her name as a delegate to the National Democratic Convention because the convention in New York would be held before completion of Lincoln's 1980–81 budget deliberations in August.

REPRESENTING MAYORS INTERNATIONALLY

Keeping up the pace of running the city at home while playing a national and even international role in representing cities must have taxed even my mother's enormous energy reserves. Prior to the November 1980 presidential election, she and Dad traveled to Taiwan as part of a ten-mayor delegation from the U.S. Conference of Mayors. It was an intriguing time in U.S.-Taiwan diplomatic and trade relations, as President Carter had announced his decision the year before to extend diplomatic recognition to mainland China and thus withdraw recognition from Taiwan. In their five-day visit, the mayors met with many public officials, including the governor of Taiwan Province and the mayor of Taipei, Lee Teng-hui, who later returned the visit and lectured at the University of Nebraska–Lincoln.

Unexpectedly added to the mayors' schedule was a meeting with Sun Yun-suan, premier of the Republic of China, a chief architect of Taiwan's "economic *miracle." The U.S. mayors also traveled from Taipei to visit a marble factory in Hualien, steel and shipbuilding plants in Kaohsiung, and Taichung Harbor. They met with private-sector members of the Chinese National Association of Industry and Commerce. Just reading Mom's five-day Taiwan schedule left me breathless, but she and my dad loved every minute.

My mom was glad to have Dad with her in Taiwan, as he had been unable to go with her to the USSR in 1976. At that time, Lincoln's new mayor and three other mayors from the U.S. Conference of Mayors represented American cities through a U.S. State Department exchange program established in the 1973 summit conference between President Nixon and Soviet general secretary Leonid Brezhnev.

My mother's visit to the USSR with the mayors of Denver, Dayton, and Spokane was her first venture out of the country (notwithstanding her childhood fib about going to Greece as a baby). In 1976 not many Americans had visited Russia, given the cold war history. The mayors delegation visited Moscow, Leningrad (now St. Petersburg), Minsk, and Sochi. My mother still speaks glowingly of her visit to the Hermitage with its vast collection of art treasures in more than a thousand rooms. In Moscow the mayors were shown modern city public improvements, such as the impressive subway system, but were not taken to visit common shopping areas where consumer goods were in short supply.

During her Russian sojourn, my mother learned to dispose of Russian vodka in potted palms. The Russian host officials were fond of toasting their guests on every conceivable occasion, perhaps testing whether the American mayors could hold their liquor. After many vodka toasts one night, one of her colleagues got so sick as the delegation wound its way down from a mountain reception that Mom swore he looked green for the rest of the Russian trip.

Lincoln's mayor had a bit of a scare while staying in a St. Petersburg hotel. The only woman in the U.S. mayors delegation, she stayed in a small room with a single twin bed, signaling the presence of a woman traveling alone. In the middle of the night someone knocked, then tried to break in. She could not reach the front desk for help (since instructions were in Russian) or escape through the window, which was several floors above the Neva River. Eyeing the flimsy chain, my mother moved nearly every piece of furniture against the door. When the other mayors retrieved her the next morning, they found a pile of cigarette ashes outside her doorway—leavings from her would-be intruder.

After her 1976 Russia and 1980 Taiwan trips, my mother, as president-elect of the U.S. Conference of Mayors, led a delegation in 1981 of eight American mayors to the international Jerusalem Conference of Mayors, joining mayors from Canada, Brazil, Germany, Switzerland, Australia, and Denmark. The conference, hosted by Jerusalem mayor Teddy Kolleck, addressed city strategies when declining revenues force the cutting of traditional municipal services. My mother spoke to the group on the importance of neighborhood and citizen participation.

When the U.S. delegation stepped off the plane in Jerusalem, they were invited to go immediately to the home of Prime Minister Menachem Begin. The prime minister opened his home weekly and held prayer services, often inviting foreign visitors. Although exhausted from the grueling plane ride, neither my mother nor the mayor of Sydney could pass up the opportunity, as the other U.S. mayors did, to meet the prime minister in his own home. My parents were moved by Begin's warm hospitality and struck by his unassuming, modest home. Mom found it difficult to reconcile Begin's reputation as a fierce military warrior with their mild-mannered, soft-spoken host. The *Jerusalem Post* later featured a photo of my mother with Prime Minister Begin.

After their astonishing first evening with the prime minister my folks toured Jerusalem, including a visit to the Western Wall. When the five-day conference concluded, they spent two days on a whirlwind tour of Israel, including Masada, the Dead Sea, Jericho, Tiberias, a northern kibbutz, Yad Vashem, and the Golan Heights. My mother thought about her mother, as Gram had often talked about her dream of visiting Israel. Gram wanted to go to Israel even more than she wanted to return to her native Greece, which she had left at the age of nine. Unfortunately, she never had the opportunity to do either. By the time international travel became more accessible to middle-class Americans, Gram was too frail and afraid to risk such an adventure. But she loved hearing every detail of her mayor daughter's visit to Israel.

NEW FEDERALISM: MADAME PRESIDENT VS. MR. PRESIDENT

During my mother's year as president-elect of the U.S. Conference of Mayors (1980–81), an enormous change transpired in Washington that would largely define her course for the next year as president of the organization: the mayors lost their sympathetic ear in the White House— Ronald Reagan defeated Jimmy Carter.

Anxious to set a positive tone, twenty-five mayors of the U.S. Conference of Mayors Legislative Committee met in Chicago the week after Reagan's election and pledged cooperation with the new administration. Although the mayors would take a wait-and-see attitude toward the president-elect's yet-unknown urban policies, the U.S. Conference of Mayors' own president-elect, Mayor Helen Boosalis, declared that the mayors wanted to "cooperate with the administration to try to resolve the problems of the cities."

During their Chicago legislative meeting, the mayors received the good news that the lame-duck Congress had approved the continuation of federal revenue sharing to cities for three more years. Cities had been fighting hard to prevent cuts in general revenue sharing—a popular urban funding source because few federal strings were attached. "The federal government is pretty good at collecting moneys, but they should be returned to local governments with as few strings as necessary," Lincoln's mayor urged at the meeting.

After his inauguration, President Reagan invited my mother and a group of twelve mayors from the nation's largest cities to meet with him. When they heard Reagan outline his contemplated across-the-board cuts in Community Development Block Grant (CDBG), Urban Mass Transit Administration (UMTA), and Comprehensive Employment and Training Act (CETA) programs, as well as total elimination of the Urban Development Action Grant (UDAG) program, one mayor said he "felt as though he'd been invited to participate in his own execution."

As Mom prepared to take the reins as president of the U.S. Conference of Mayors midway through Reagan's first year in office in 1981, President Reagan summoned five governors and five mayors to Washington to attempt to build support for his controversial block grants proposal—the consolidation of about ninety federal categorical grant programs into seven block grant programs. Most categorical grants had been made directly to cities; the Reagan administration was proposing that consolidated block grants be funneled through state governments.

Among the group of governors and mayors meeting with President Reagan was Lincoln's mayor and Nebraska's Republican governor, Charles Thone. Mayor Boosalis conveyed general support from mayors for consolidation of federal programs into the proposed block grants as long as the grants would go straight to cities rather than to states. The cities did not want to substitute state-level bureaucracy for federal bureaucracy. "I tried to make the point at the White House, with all due respect to the states, that I felt state block grants may ignore the workhorse of the federal system—the cities," said Mayor Boosalis.

If the cities were the workhorse of the federal system, then the horse would soon be put out to pasture. As the country's mayors assembled in Louisville in June 1981 for their first annual U.S. Conference of Mayors meeting since Reagan's election, they came ready to focus on Reagan's "new federalism"—a term coined to describe the new administration's plans to give states the authority to distribute federal funding in non-specific block grants through the states and to cut urban funding.

Democratic mayors came to Louisville ready to attack Reagan's new federalism plan, charging that "the nation's financially strapped cities will bear the brunt of the federal cuts and be cast upon the mercy of unsympathetic states." The mayors suspected that "Reagan's true goal is to eliminate most federal funding and return taxing powers to the states." Republican mayors at the Democrat-dominated U.S. Conference of Mayors meeting raised only a weak defense of President Reagan, as their cities also stood to suffer at the hands of his new federalism.

Lincoln's mayor was elected president of the U.S. Conference of Mayors at the end of the impassioned Louisville meeting in June 1981. My mother's biggest challenge lay not in being the organization's first woman leader in its forty-nine-year history but in uniting into a single strong voice the disparate and angry outcries of mayors who felt abandoned by their federal government at a time of economic crisis when they most needed help. She would have to be a conciliator among her fellow mayors and also a strong advocate and tough negotiator when she took their message to Washington. That was an enormous dual role to fill while at the same time facing equally challenging economic stress in her own city. U.S. senator Paul Sarbanes recalled Mom's leadership of the nation's mayors: "Helen's commitment, drive and high energy were obvious from the moment she walked in the door. She had an incredible reputation as mayor and was picked by her peers to head the U.S. Conference of Mayors because she was a 'fighter.'"

The 1981 U.S. Conference of Mayors meeting in Louisville was "acrimonious" but ended on a hopeful and conciliatory note. In her inaugural address as president, my mom pledged to bring to the conference "greater unity" and renewed influence in Washington through "constructive dialog" with the Reagan administration, the New York Times reported. "We must respect the people who must be moved," she told her fellow mayors. "We must recognize the possibility that at times we may be wrong."

Max and I went to Louisville to witness and celebrate Mom's election as U.S. Conference of Mayors president, but I worried on two fronts—as a new parent I worried about leaving nine-month-old Michael for the first time, and as a daughter I worried about how much was on my mother's plate. I did see my first horse race at Louisville's Churchill Downs and placed a ten-dollar bet on a horse with the right name: Greek Boss. When my horse won, I took it as a sign that another Greek Boss would do just fine. I knew my mother had enormous staying power and would call on her bottomless energy reserves for the home stretch.

Folks back in Lincoln were mighty proud of their mayor taking the helm of the U.S. Conference of Mayors. A *Journal* editorial headline on June 10, 1981, said it all: "That's Our Helen Up There." The editorial began, "One week from today, Helen Boosalis of Lincoln, Nebraska, will make national history. She's to be inaugurated president of the U.S. Conference of Mayors, the first woman executive ever so honored. That leadership recognition reflects great personal credit to Mrs. Boosalis, and redounds to the credit as well of the citizens of this All-America city," the *Journal* puffed with hometown pride. "In most recent years, the conference's flag role has been entrusted only to mayors of great urban or metropolitan areas, or to figures of significant national political stature. Helen Boosalis fits in neither of those two particular classifications. In terms of competence, intelligence and strength of character, however, she rates at the very top of any listing."

On my mother's return from Louisville, the *Lincoln Star* was not the only one to say, "Welcome home, mayor, we're proud of you." A committee of well-wishers hosted several surprise festivities on the day the mayor returned home to honor her installation as U.S. Conference of Mayors president. The public was invited to greet her along with the lieutenant governor and other dignitaries when her plane arrived, followed by a motorcade to the County-City Building with "her honor" and my dad riding in a sign-decorated open antique car, owned and driven by Lincoln architect Bill Schlaebitz. That evening, supporters gathered at our family's usual spot for celebrating election nights, weddings and now national leadership—where else but my Uncle John's Knolls restaurant.

As the one-year term of my mother's U.S. Conference of Mayors

39. U.S. Conference of Mayors president Helen Boosalis meets with President Ronald Reagan

presidency began in June 1981, the mayors focused on a single push: influencing the Reagan administration and Congress to rework Reagan's new federalism and his proposed cuts in federal urban aid. A month after her installation as president, Mom met briefly with President Reagan in the Oval Office, but she was able to do little more than express the cities' concerns about his proposed federal block grant program.

She left the Oval Office for extended meetings with other White House officials, including Chief of Staff James Baker and Rich Williamson, the president's assistant on intergovernmental affairs. In get-acquainted sessions they discussed the new federalism, the return of general revenues to cities, and the administration's enterprise zone proposal. The staffers said that Reagan intended to continue to redefine the roles of states and cities and their relationship to the federal government through the block grant program. My mother expressed mayors' concerns about states' control over administration of block grants. She pointed out, for example, that Nebraska governor Thone had failed to include any city representation on a task force he had recently formed to study the block grant *program.

The following month President Reagan continued to push his proposals for a massive economic overhaul and achieved some overwhelming victories in Congress. The Reagan administration planned to reduce federal subsidies to local mass transit by 30 percent per year until entirely eliminated. Lincoln City Council chairman Joe Hampton viewed the transit cuts as "impending disaster" as the council struggled with the substantial impact of the cuts in annual city budget deliberations. Large public transit systems in Chicago and New York City, already in financial trouble, stood to lose the most. Bailout by the states was considered unlikely; cities' options for increasing fares would drive passengers away, making transit systems even more dependent on subsidies and encouraging folks who had learned to take transit back into their cars.

The new federal block grant program through the states and the proposed cutbacks in federal aid to cities for mass transit, street construction, and water-treatment plants were only a part of larger Reagan administration economic plans. The tax bill approved by Congress in 1981—mainly authored by the Reagan administration—created a huge shift to supply-side economics, allowing business and individuals to retain more income in order to prompt more investments to spur the economy.

The Reagan administration's economic package continued to steamroll through Congress; the effects on funding urban programs rocked cities nationwide during Mom's presidency of their mayors. When Congress enacted Reagan's new federalism by combining federal funding programs into nine block grants to states, the state of Nebraska prepared to lose more than 10 percent of its federal funding in the first year (beginning October 1, 1981), with the largest cut occurring in the social services block grant—more than 20 percent. Nebraska's governor warned local bodies not to expect help from the state and promised to veto any state legislative attempt to replace lost federal funds with state funds. The governor did not have to act on that promise, as Nebraska's legislature supported his position. That scenario was repeated in many states nationwide.

In a speech at the Nebraska League of Municipalities, Lincoln's mayor articulated the frustration of mayors across the country. "In the past," she said, "mayors have had a 'tin-cup image' in approaching the federal government for money. The growth of federal aid programs brought progress to cities and moved them from providing basic fire and police protection into many other areas." Mom cautioned that large-scale cuts in federal aid to cities during an economic crisis meant that mayors would face an enormous challenge similar to the one they faced during the Depression when the U.S. Conference of Mayors was founded.

The discouraging picture for cities only grew worse. A second round of Reagan proposed budget cuts in September 1981 followed closely on the heels of the first round with additional 12 percent across-the-board cuts in federal aid to local governments in such areas as community development, job training, economic development, and, again, public transit. The additional proposed reductions on top of budget cuts already made in July threw a grenade into most cities' planning and budgeting efforts, leaving them little choice but to slash programs and services. Cities in most states were caught in a bind between federal cuts and unresponsive state governments.

In Washington a crowd of 240,000 people protested the federal budget cuts. On Saturday, September 19, members of the AFL-CIO, NAACP, and NOW joined others like Coretta Scott King in the mass march from the Washington Monument to the Capitol. The Reagan administration dismissed the massive demonstration as "partisan" and the president vowed to continue slashing the federal budget, labeling critics of his program "Chicken Littles."

Like the marchers, the nation's mayors were up in arms. When they got wind that Reagan's second round of cuts included revenue sharing and that Budget Director David Stockman had urged the president to phase out revenue sharing altogether within two years, mayors and thousands of local officials nationwide barraged the president with telegrams of protest. The outpouring persuaded Reagan to postpone his decision on the ultimate fate of revenue sharing, but the cuts in revenue-sharing funds went forward with other cuts in urban aid.

Reagan's decision to include revenue sharing in his meat-ax cutting of aid to cities flew in the face of his assurances to the mayors at their U.S. Conference of Mayors meeting in Louisville shortly after his election. Explaining why "America's governors, mayors and county officials are perturbed about President Reagan's latest round of proposed budget cuts and ought to be boiling mad," *Washington Post* columnist Neal Peirce wrote: "What annoys many state and local government leaders is that the full weight of the budget ax is falling on them even while some of the most dangerously expansive elements of the federal budget remain almost inviolate. The President rejects anything but the most token cuts in the snowballing Pentagon budget with its massive cost overruns . . . [and] has yet to bite the bullet on the single most inflationary element of Social Security."

Peirce continued recounting the mayors' grievances and summarized remarks of U.S. Conference of Mayors president Helen Boosalis: "By first considering extinguishing revenue sharing, and then including it under his 12 percent across-the-board cuts, President Reagan is reneging on an oft-repeated 1980 campaign promise to decentralize power and resources by revenue sharing. The only result will be increased local property taxes, or more likely, cuts in police, fire and social services."

With Reagan's cuts breezing through Congress at record speed to take effect at the start of the federal fiscal year on October 1, the nation's mayors needed to channel their concerns into an effective action plan. My mother called for a special Chicago convening of mayors on urban federalism in mid-November 1981 to give mayors an opportunity to question President Reagan's budget and economic strategies and to formulate their own strategy in response. "The new chief of the U.S. Conference of Mayors is planning to pin the Reagan Administration down on what it is planning for the future," reported the *Boston Herald American*.

In the *Herald American* interview about her call for a mayors' "summit" on urban federalism, my mother said, "I'm not sure we know what Reagan's view of federalism really is—who is responsible for what. This is a big dramatic change. We need to have a national debate on these issues." The article noted that the absence of just such a national debate was credited by many as "the key to Reagan's stunning budget and tax successes" in his first year in office—"a riverboat gamble," as Senate Majority Leader Howard Baker called it. "But no one succeeded in slowing Reagan's momentum or penetrating his simplistic, back-to-basics and small-is-beautiful concepts about the nature of government. Whether the mayors can do so now is questionable—but Boosalis is determined to try."

In early November, just a few days before convening her urban federalism summit of mayors in Chicago, Mom had two visitors to Lincoln with opposing views on Reagan's new federalism. My mother's close colleague Moon Landrieu, a potential presidential candidate (and formerly HUD secretary, mayor of New Orleans, and U.S. Conference of Mayors president), came to Lincoln for a Democratic fund-raiser. Landrieu called Reagan's domestic policies "devastating" for American cities, shifting responsibility for the poor, mass transit, housing, and community development to cities "without giving them the wherewithal" to perform. "Giveaways in the President's tax package were disgraceful," he said. "Across-the-board tax cuts and the size of domestic budget cuts were unwarranted."

The morning after Landrieu's visit, Lincoln's mayor greeted Vice-President George H. W. Bush at the Nebraska Air National Guard airfield when he arrived for a speaking engagement with the state Republican Party. At a Lincoln news conference, the vice-president confirmed that President Reagan was not going to back off his economic recovery plans, including social program cuts, just because of poor economic news like the recent 8 percent national unemployment figure. "We're prepared to take some political flak," he said. Bush was no longer using the term he had coined in his 1980 GOP primary campaign against Reagan—"voodoo economics"—which he had predicted would result in increasing inflation and enormous federal deficits.

News accounts spoke of a necessary "alteration" to Vice-President Bush's Lincoln speaking schedule. His Saturday speech at the state Republican Party fund-raiser at Lincoln's Pershing Auditorium coincided with a Nebraska football "away" game. But when ABC announced it had decided to televise the Nebraska–Oklahoma State game, large television screens were quickly installed in the civic auditorium so that attendees of the Republican event wouldn't have to miss the game. Bush's speech had to be choreographed to squeeze into the game halftime slot if he expected to have an audience. As I know only too well, neither a vice-presidential speech to party loyalists nor a wedding can trump a football game for Go Big Red Nebraska fans.

On November 12, 1981, after the back-to-back Lincoln visits of Landrieu and Bush, president Helen Boosalis of the U.S. Conference of Mayors welcomed 125 mayors to the two-day National Urban Conference on Federalism that she had called in Chicago. "Not since the formation of the Conference of Mayors 50 years ago has there been such a dramatic shift as is occurring now. There's nothing more important on the agenda right now," Mom told reporters as she left Lincoln.

My mother tried to set a positive tone in opening the summit meeting of angry and dispirited mayors, saying, "I'm sure that all of the Mayors here today . . . would like the name of President Ronald Reagan to be added to that list of Presidents with whom we worked to build and to improve America's cities. . . . We want this to be a time for reaffirmation of the shared responsibility for the welfare of our citizens, and reaffirmation of the unity of our goals." She was firm about the embattled cities' expectations of their federal government: "It is essential that federal tax dollars continue to be invested in our cities, in the development of our urban economies, our urban communities, our urban residents. It is essential that the direct links between the cities and Washington be preserved to the extent possible."

At the urban federalism summit in Chicago, the mayors avoided the kind of inflammatory political rhetoric that had dominated their Louisville meeting some months earlier; yet they made it clear they had suffered all they could at the hands of the Reagan budget cutters and could withstand no further cuts unless the administration could find alternative funding sources for cities. Speaking for her mayor colleagues, my mother said, "When you talk about further cuts, you're talking about cuts in basic services—firemen, police—not frills."

U.S. Conference of Mayors executive director Tom Cochran recalls that "as U.S. Conference of Mayors president, Mayor Boosalis had the total support of the giants [big cities]. She spoke powerfully for cities of all sizes in saying, 'With all due respect, Mr. President, you're wrong. We *do* need the federal government to help us with these problems. These are not local problems, they are national problems.'" At the summit, Mom expressed hope for a reopening of dialogue with the White House that had not occurred in the earlier rounds of cuts, and hope that Reagan's agreement to delay a decision on the termination of federal revenue sharing might signal the coming end to the withering cuts. Yet the fact that Vice-President Bush and presidential aides James Baker and Ed Meese had declined an invitation to attend the Chicago mayors' summit was a signal of another sort.

Summit keynoter and Harvard economist John Kenneth Galbraith told the assembled mayors that their cities had been singled out as "special victims" of the Reagan economic programs. In contrast, the administration and Congress had increased aid to sugar, peanut, tobacco, and dairy farmers. "As mayors you are the economic and social targets of President Reagan's economic policies," Galbraith said. "You have been singled out for attention, nearly all of it negative. Not previously in our history have we seen a fiscal revolution so comprehensively crafted against our urban centers and our city populations."

In the Windy City, the mayors discussed the changing roles of local and federal government and the meaning of federalism. All opposed further cuts in federal funding to cities, and many supported a pending proposal by Vermont's Republican governor Richard Snelling for a two-year moratorium on further federal cuts. Recommendations at the summit from the six policy standing committees of the U.S. Conference of Mayors—urban economic policy, arts and recreation, housing and community development, energy and environment, transportation, and human development—reflected the mayors' acceptance of the need for a reasonable realignment of responsibilities among federal, state, and city governments.

The mayors did more than voice their opposition to the massive federal cuts in aid to cities—they worked to contribute to the changing definition of federalism and a workable division of responsibilities among federal, state, and local governments. But when they left Chicago they were not optimistic about their influence on President Reagan, who was "rather firm on his program" according to his assistant on intergovernmental affairs.

Results of a U.S. Conference of Mayors national survey of cities, released shortly after the Chicago summit in November 1981, showed that federal cuts had already deeply affected city recreation and parks programs and also health and human services for the poor. Many cities, in efforts to absorb federal cutbacks, had reduced services substantially (e.g., garbage collection, library operations, police and fire protection) and had deferred capital spending such as road and bridge maintenance. Testifying before a House banking subcommittee, Lincoln's mayor said, "The picture that emerges is stark."

The survey also showed that 75 percent of responding cities had laid off employees and almost half planned to raise taxes to meet rising costs, although many cities were restricted by state law from doing so. The mayor of one western city noted on his survey, "We are paring our essential services to the bone. Where do we go from here?" My mother's response to the survey was reported in the *Washington Post*: "Mayors are wrestling with federal cuts at the same time they are wrestling with the effects of a recession, tight money and rising unemployment." President Reagan's response: "There must be some pain" until the economy revives and inflation eases.

A key component in Reagan's new federalism was his belief in private sector responsibility: "The push for expanded private sector roles in public sector service delivery is part of the President's design for reducing federal responsibility for community services," explained an article in *The Mayor*. President Reagan formed a Private Sector Initiatives Task Force to engage the business sector in providing services that local governments could not afford. He appointed Mayor Boosalis, as U.S. Conference of Mayors president, to his task force with forty-three other members representing private corporations, nonprofit organizations, government, civic, religious, and education groups. The board chairman of Armco chaired the task force; other elected officials included Delaware governor Pierre du Pont and U.S. senator David Durenberger of Minnesota. Commenting on her appointment to the task force, Mom said she recognized how much the private sector could contribute to meeting needs of cities but that "private organizations cannot replace the contributions that have been made by the federal government. We cannot expect the private sector to make up for the dramatic cuts in federal spending that we are *seeing."

About the time of her appointment to Reagan's task force, my mom played a key role in advancing an innovative private-sector initiative in Lincoln. During her visits to local businesses to learn how city government could support them, she had developed a friendly relationship with the management of the Kawasaki plant, which had manufactured four hundred thousand motorcycles, recreational watercraft, utility cycles, and snowmobiles since opening in Lincoln in 1975.

When Kawasaki experienced a slowdown in the faltering economy of late 1981, the company proposed an innovative idea to the mayor: to lend its excess employees to Lincoln's municipal government as temporary workers instead of laying them off. Employees would continue to be paid by Kawasaki while they worked for the city, and they would return to the plant assembly line when sales rebounded. Kawasaki admitted that the plan was not entirely altruistic on its part, reported the *New York Times*; it would be cheaper to keep paying experienced workers than to break in new employees later.

The mayor's enthusiasm for the plan was immediate. The Kawasaki employees did not replace city employees but were assigned special projects such as painting a public works maintenance center and stripping woodwork in the old city hall. My mother said the initiative "reaffirmed the public-private partnership that has existed in this community for *years." President Reagan, in telegrams to the president of Lincoln's Kawasaki plant, Kichiro Ando, and to Mayor Boosalis praised the partnership for reflecting "an admirable spirit of cooperation between the public and private sectors. This is precisely the kind of effort which I am attempting to encourage throughout the country. I am pleased to know that you as President of the U.S. Conference of Mayors have taken the initiative in this area," Reagan wrote to Mom.

Whatever role the private sector might eventually come to play in supporting local public services, cities' pain in the wake of the federal cuts was immediate and sustained. Whatever hopes the mayors had for influencing the Reagan administration's philosophy concerning federal aid to cities were dashed by continuing assaults on federal urban programs. Just a few weeks after the mayors' summit in Chicago, Reagan's budget director proposed *ending* federal subsidies for low-income housing construction within a year and phasing out two of the federal government's chief urban aid programs—the CDBG and UDAG programs. But by February 1982 the administration "sought to buy peace with the mayors this time around by sparing three aid and economic development programs—general revenue sharing, the Community Development Block Grant program, and the Urban Development Action Grant program—from budget director David Stockman's axe. The mayors indicated strong support for these programs."

While those federal urban aid programs were saved for the time being, Reagan's yet additional 10.7 percent cuts in federal funding to cities and states in his fiscal year 1983 proposed budget would mean more layoffs and service reductions in cities around the nation and also increased local taxes. "The damage that the FY 1983 budget proposal would inflict on our cities and the suffering it would inflict on so many of our citizens cannot be overstated," Lincoln's mayor told the *Washington Post* on behalf of the nation's cities. "Mayors know that the most basic needs of city residents will not be met in the months ahead unless the cuts in federal urban programs are stopped and stopped now."

This latest blitz of proposed federal spending cuts left city and housing officials in shock, even those among President Reagan's own cabinet. "HUD Secretary Samuel Pierce, described as angry, plans to appeal the reductions to President Reagan," the *Star* reported. Also included in Reagan's package of deep spending cuts (in non-defense programs) were reductions in environmental protection, job-training and employment programs for the poor, and a host of other individual assistance programs. My mother expressed her frustration in my favorite quote of her U.S. Conference of Mayors presidency: "I wonder if we are moving toward a time when the only imperatives of our national government are the manufacture of money, stamps and *missiles."

On the heels of Reagan's latest round of cuts in his fiscal year 1983 proposed budget came news that the nation's unemployment figures had taken another jump, to *8.8 percent, representing a post-Depression record of nearly 10 million unemployed Americans. The president was not shaken by this news, although he termed the high number of unemployed "a very great tragedy." He insisted he would make no change in plans for an economic recovery, even as his press secretary defended his sensitivity to the plight of the unemployed: "He often has said that if there is one person who wants to work and cannot do so, that's one too many."

Lincoln's mayor said the unemployment increase "provides a grim backdrop for the deep cuts in human service and economic development programs which the Reagan Administration is seeking." Mom argued that the unemployment rate is "a statistic that reflects human suffering among Americans" and called on Congress for "a moratorium on further federal budget cuts and for a re-examination of the cuts that have already been made."

Congressional Democrats agreed. House Speaker Tip O'Neill called the Reagan economic plan "a cruel hoax" that had brought about "the worst economic slump since the Great Depression," and he predicted that unemployment would reach 9.5 percent and remain at high levels for at least nine more *months. Senator Daniel Moynihan said, "Reaganomics has brought on the sharpest and soonest recession we've had since 1919—the last time there were only 12 months between recessions. This is a man-made recession, a devastating one and an unnecessary one."

In March 1982 Mom testified before the House Budget Committee, urging Congress to adopt a budget that "invests in the human and physical capital necessary for this country to become productive and internationally competitive once again." Lincoln's mayor testified that whatever support existed for Reagan's new federalism had been undermined by his budget cuts and reduced funding turned back to the states: "These proposed cuts in urban programs would be difficult to accept in a more favorable economic climate, but when we consider the many, many urban families who cannot find affordable housing, the millions of Americans who are unemployed and need job training; when we pause for only a moment to think about the condition of our nation's transportation system and the finiteness of our natural resources; when we all know that the ability of our country to remain strong depends to a large extent on an educated citizenry—these proposed cuts become simply intolerable."

With the change in presidents, the nation's mayors faced a precipi-tous slam of the federal door at the same time they were coping with a deep economic recession. The Reagan administration would not be deterred from its chosen path, and even the collectively loud and in-creasingly plaintive voices of the country's mayors fell on deaf ears in Washington.

When I consider Mom's year as president of the U.S. Conference of Mayors, I am alternately sad that she had the misfortune to rise to that prominent position at the outset of the Reagan administration and its frontal assault on federal aid to cities, but also proud that she took on the responsibility of representing cities nationwide with such commit-ment and fire. The struggle was not the first but surely the most lop-sided for the diminutive mayor of a medium-sized city in the Midwest.

As Lincoln's mayor headed into the final days of her U.S. Conference of Mayors presidency, how did folks in Lincoln view her year in the national spotlight? *Star* reporter George Hendrix recounted her presi-dency year in terms of travel, power, and publicity: "Helen Boosalis has had the sort of year politicians dream of. Jetting around the nation in near constant motion, Lincoln's mayor has rubbed elbows with the men and women who strum the strings of political and corporate America." Hendrix concluded, tongue in cheek, his description of Mom's whirl-wind year: "She's gained power—she talks, and the movers and shakers listen, well, most of them. She's been showered with publicity: columns by Washington pundits on her views on the nation's cities, interviews on the 'Today Show,' pictures and headlines in *The New York Times*, ap-pointments to national committees, appearances before Congress, and official White House photos of Helen Boosalis and the Gipper smiling over a shared anecdote."

Mom even received publicity for her involvement in the baseball strike, sending a telegram as U.S. Conference of Mayors president to baseball commissioner Bowie Kuhn urging the parties to settle the strike—the cities having suffered by mid-season the loss of at least $10 million in tax revenues and a total economic loss in the hundreds of *millions.

"Aware of the worth of all that publicity," Mom's political opponents in Lincoln remained skeptical that she would not seek a third mayoral term in May 1983. Some pooh-poohed the value to Lincoln of the mayor's national role. Councilman Hampton did not view the mayor's out-of-state visits as doing Lincoln any good, since she was only talking with fellow politicians and not making calls on industrial prospects for the city. She had, however, repeatedly solicited business contacts from the Lincoln Chamber of Commerce to make calls on prospective industries during her U.S. Conference of Mayors travels throughout the country, but the chamber "never used me or asked me to visit prospects."

When asked to assess her year as chief spokesperson for American cities, my mother viewed her biggest accomplishment as helping focus attention on President Reagan's new federalism and its impact on cities and on mayors' concerns about transferring federal purse strings to the states, which had never shown much sympathy toward cities. Although Reagan remained unswayed on his economic policy and related budget cuts, he had shifted some of his positions on federalism, largely because the mayors had effectively exerted pressure on Congress, which had in turn balked at some of Reagan's proposals.

U.S. CONFERENCE OF MAYORS PRESIDENT: END OF TERM

Mayor Boosalis's high-profile but frustrating year as president of the U.S. Conference of Mayors drew to a close with its 1982 annual meeting—its *fiftieth anniversary—in Minneapolis. In addition to all her official duties in presiding over the meeting, Mom looked forward to one of those rare full-circle life moments: to return to her hometown of Minneapolis—not only as a mayor but as a sort of "mayor of mayors"—and to be joined by her eighty-two-year-old mother (Gram), sisters Tina and Ione, Dad, Max, and me for the festivities honoring her year's service as president.

The annual June meeting opened in Minneapolis with a Saturday press conference; its tone contrasted with the 1981 mayors' press conference in Louisville, which had "degenerated into an oratorical battle between Republican and Democratic mayors." In fact, at the Minneapolis press conference, only Minneapolis mayor Don Fraser and St. Paul mayor George Latimer joined my mother on the podium, creating the impression that "much of the bitterness toward Reagan that surfaced at the meeting last year seemed to have abated and been replaced by resignation."

The more moderate tone must have been a relief to my mom, as she had made it her goal over the previous year both to curb Reagan's assault on cities and to improve relations between the White House and the U.S. Conference of Mayors. If so, she had only one night to enjoy the calm.

The next day, "moderation gave way to shock" when the *New York Times* exposed a draft of the Reagan administration's first comprehensive urban policy. The White House document charged that twenty years of federal aid had transformed city officials "from bold leaders of self-reliant cities to wily stalkers of federal funds." The leaked administration document called for even further cuts in urban grants and more reliance by cities on states and on themselves. Rich Williamson, Reagan's assistant for intergovernmental affairs, acknowledged that the report reflected the views of many in the administration, but he defended the president, who had just seen the report and sent it back as unacceptable. "The President does not feel the federal government should turn its back on the cities of this country," Williamson said.

The administration's leaked urban policy had already done its damage, however, and most mayors were outraged; those who had been supporters of the administration were put on the defensive. Some mayors charged that the report "almost seems to draw a battle line between the White House and the mayors of these cities." My mother lamented that after all the time spent working with the Reagan administration, she wondered if anyone at the White House had been listening.

That night Max and I read Mom's welcoming address for the next day's opening U.S. Conference of Mayors plenary session. Perfectionistic young lawyers as we were back then, we thought her speech needed revising and tightening up. We took it back to our hotel room, worked on it for several hours, and slipped it under my parents' door in the wee hours. Later, in retrospect, Max remarked how arrogant we had been to revise her speech. I disagreed with him at the time and argued we were only trying to be helpful; but after reading the clippings of the incredibly challenging year my mom had just finished as U.S. Conference of Mayors president and particularly the difficult day she had just faced with the leak of Reagan's inflammatory urban policy, I now agree with Max. The last thing my mother probably had on her mind was a perfectly crafted speech that would read like a logically tight legal brief.

Even with such a dramatically frustrating ending to her tenure as president, my mother's leadership of her fellow mayors was strongly praised. She "wowed city leaders throughout the nation with her performance," and mayors from cities of all sizes and geography gave her an "A+." Republican mayors praised her ability to present a balanced view while representing the majority opinion. Peoria mayor Richard Carver, a Reagan ally, said, "Boosalis has done an absolutely superb job balancing the partisan concerns with those of the overall Conference."

Reflecting on his colleague's leadership of the U.S. Conference of Mayors, former St. Paul mayor George Latimer said, "Helen possessed true statesmanship. She did not view holding a position of leadership as her opportunity to push her own priorities or particular set of issues. She thought about the mission of the whole organization and, just as she brought to her community, she represented all constituents."

Democratic mayors applauded her success in holding the U.S. Conference of Mayors together during tough economic times and the partisan struggle for control of the organization. Gary mayor Richard Hatcher, Mom's immediate predecessor as president and an outspoken Reagan critic, commended her skills as compromiser and leader in bringing the mayors together: "Helen's a bridge builder. She attempts to see all sides of the question. She tries to find a common basis to work together. She's a fighter. She really stands up for what she believes. Beneath her kind, genteel exterior, she is a very strong and firm woman."

Mayors lauded Mayor Helen Boosalis for calling national attention to their problems, acknowledging she could control neither the national economy nor the Reagan administration. They recognized it was not easy to inherit the split between the U.S. Conference of Mayors and the Reagan administration and to preside over mayors with widely divergent interests, especially during a time of recession, federal cutbacks, deteriorating infrastructure, and skyrocketing unemployment.

And so the country's mayors thanked their colleague Helen Boosalis for forcefully advocating for the role of cities in setting national priorities and the urban agenda. They applauded her focus on public-private cooperation and her calling together the nation's mayors in Chicago for the National Urban Conference on Federalism. On June 23, 1982, Lincoln's mayor relinquished the gavel to her successor, Detroit mayor Coleman Young, knowing that she had given it her best.

My mother continued in a national leadership role as immediate past president of the U.S. Conference of Mayors. She was featured speaker at national forums on cities' roles in the old and new federalism. She helped draft an economic recovery plan to submit to President Reagan and the new Congress elected in the fall of 1982, joining other mayors on the front lines of battle to save their cities: Ed Koch of New York City, Coleman Young of Detroit, Jane Byrne of Chicago, George Voinovich of Cleveland, Henry Cisneros of San Antonio, Richard Fulton of Nashville, Henry Maier of Milwaukee, "Dutch" Morial of New Orleans, William Hudnut of Indianapolis, Kathy Whitmire of Houston, Joe Riley of Charleston, and Ted Wilson of Salt Lake City. Just as on her home turf in Lincoln, my mother continued the fight to equip the nation's cities to meet the needs of their people in the toughest of economic times.

Issues, Debates, Polls, and Other Irrelevancies
Summer and Fall 1986

Before the tax issue swamped my mother's campaign for governor, she
had outlined the three major issues she expected to be her campaign focus. During August Czech Days the week before the provocative *Omaha
World-Herald* tax article, Mom told folks in Wilbur ("Czech Capital of
the U.S.A.") that her campaign for governor would address the worsening farm economy, economic development to increase jobs and industry, and improvement of the educational system.

"Every farm closing is a tragedy to a farm family and is felt by every
town in Nebraska," she said of the state's agricultural problems when
she announced her candidacy. But as an urban mayor and former president of the U.S. Conference of Mayors, she was asked at the Douglas
County Democratic Forum whether she could relate to farmers and rural residents of her state. "I wasn't born on a farm," she responded, "but
then I wasn't born in a family of politicians either." While Mom had
learned about some agricultural issues during my father's thirty-five
years' work on crop diseases at the University of Nebraska–Lincoln,
she would do more homework on agriculture, consult with experts,
and listen to the people most affected—the farmers—just as she had
done on other issues all through her political career.

Before the primary election my mother had proposed an Agricultural Revitalization Plan to restructure agricultural debt, expand the
role of the state's Department of Agriculture to include agricultural
advocacy in addition to regulation and inspection, and establish a family

farm technology research center at the university. Her immediate goal was to organize with other farm states a regional coalition of governors and congressional representatives with other farm states as a viable lobbying force for a decent federal farm bill and policies more supportive of family farming. "We are not looking for handouts," she said in announcing her candidacy, "but we should demand fair treatment. Washington is not providing answers. Washington, in fact, is part of the problem."

After Orr and Boosalis emerged from the primary as party nominees, my mother added more specifics to her plan to revitalize the state's agricultural economy and embarked on a summer statewide agricultural issues tour. Governor Ed Herschler of neighboring Wyoming came to Nebraska in early August to support Mom's regional lobbying plan to change federal trade and farm debt policies. He agreed that a regional coalition could "put the heat on Washington," as successfully done during the Ford and Carter administrations. After President Reagan's fall visit raised $200,000 for Kay Orr, an impressive Farm Policy Reform Rally in Omaha protesting Reagan's federal farm policy attracted hundreds of farmers in tractors and pickup trucks, labor leaders, and midwestern politicians (including U.S. senator Tom Harkin).

The most controversial farm-related issue of the gubernatorial campaign was the proposed repeal of Initiative 300, an amendment to the state constitution that would restrict corporate ownership of farmland in Nebraska. Orr and the Republican Party supported repealing the amendment and allowing unrestricted corporate farm ownership, while Boosalis opposed repealing the amendment in favor of making moderate revisions to fix it. My mother admitted that the measure only treated the symptoms of the state's farming ills, not their causes, but said that continued restriction on corporate farm ownership was critical in such an unstable farm economy. Supporters of Orr's position in favor of unrestricted corporate farming launched a petition drive for a referendum to appeal the amendment. When the drive failed, the emotional decibel level of the corporate farming issue diminished and both candidates' positions became more flexible.

My mother, the Democratic nominee, stressed that farming and economic development were not unrelated campaign issues but rather the double keys to Nebraska's success: "The two are tied so closely together—agriculture is our biggest and most basic industry." Therefore, the Boosalis twelve-point economic plan included such proposals as creating new markets for Nebraska farm products; promoting development of agriculture-related industries, such as food processing; and increasing research on alternative crops and new uses of Nebraska agricultural products.

My mother launched another summer statewide issues tour when she introduced her economic development plan at Isco, the scientific instruments manufacturing firm where she had announced her candidacy for governor six months earlier. Founded in a garage and growing in thirty years to four hundred employees and exporting worldwide, Isco was a shining example of homegrown economic development. My mom explained her plans as governor to support and encourage similar business growth and attract new industry: "We can't sit with our arms folded in a corner hoping new business comes and asks us to dance. We've got to get on our feet and move!"

My mother's talk of business and economic development during the campaign often sparked the old "anti-business" and "anti-growth" labels she had acquired from disgruntled business interests and political foes during her mayoral years. It was inevitable that this old grudge would be rehashed in the bigger, brighter arena of the governor's race. Mom flicked off the charges as she would a pesky gnat, but I knew she was irritated every time they reappeared. "Nonsense," she responded to a reporter's query about her anti-business reputation. "Look at the record. That anti-business stuff comes from the few people who wanted to make big bucks on land development through a change in zoning that was not in the best interest of the city."

On the campaign stump in October for my mother, Governor Bob Kerrey said that Boosalis's reputation for "being anti-business is a 'mythical notion'!" What she did as mayor, Kerrey said, was to protect the integrity of the city's Comprehensive Plan from erosion by special business interests. He described his unsuccessful attempts to get Mayor Boosalis's support for a zoning change that would have benefited his own property development but was contrary to Lincoln's Comprehensive Plan. "She said no to me a helluva lot more times than I would have liked. 'I have the people of the city of Lincoln to be concerned about,'

40. Governor Bob Kerrey and former governor Frank Morrison join Helen Boosalis on the campaign trail

she said." UNL political scientist Robert Sittig speculated in a *World-Herald* interview that Mrs. Boosalis "drew the antipathy of some business groups, particularly developers, because she came to politics as a university housewife involved in the League of Women Voters and other civic organizations. Unlike most in city government, Mrs. Boosalis had no economic interest to advocate." Sittig told reporters, "She had no apparent economic reason to be involved."

Eager to land a one-two punch after launching her venomous Boosalis tax increase ads, Orr joined the ancient chorus still singing chants of Boosalis as anti-business and anti-growth. She claimed that Boosalis had a no-growth philosophy when she was mayor and would not be a state leader for economic development and job creation. On this issue, however, Orr could not land a credible blow. Mom's economic development record as mayor was too solid, and she fired back at Orr with ease and confidence.

The third Boosalis priority campaign issue—education—was dominated by LB662, the bill passed by the legislature in 1985 mandating all elementary-only school districts to consolidate or affiliate with K–12

school districts. The bill resulted from years of legislative efforts to reduce the number of Nebraska school districts (955). LB662 also imposed
an additional one-cent sales tax to finance an increase in state aid for
public education and to reduce local property taxes. The legislature had
passed the bill in 1985 after a bitter fight; Governor Kerrey had agonized
before deciding to sign the bill and hoped that its flaws would later be
*fixed.

A petition drive succeeded in placing a referendum to repeal LB662
on the November ballot along with the election of a new governor.
Those opposing repeal of LB662 (Boosalis, Kerrey, Democrats) supported the bill's improvement of the quality of education and promotion of tax equity; those who wanted LB662 repealed (Orr, Republicans)
were concerned about loss of local control over schools and lack of
specific guarantee of local property tax relief.

The crux of the dispute between the two gubernatorial candidates
on LB662 was the one-cent sales tax increase for education. Orr claimed
that a tax increase is a tax increase is a tax increase—she opposed all tax
increases. My mother argued that the one-cent sales tax increase was
a substitute for local property taxes and not an additional tax burden.
She vowed that as governor she would ensure that every dollar raised
by the one-cent sales tax increase would go to property tax relief and
would not be a windfall for local governments; if not, she would push
for its repeal.

Mom's position on repealing LB662 gave more traction to Orr's accusation that Helen Boosalis favored tax increases; it helped Orr create for
voters a cumulative impression that her Democratic opponent would
raise their taxes through the roof. Orr used Mom's support of LB662 to
augment and reinforce her tax ads charging that Boosalis favored massive sales tax and income tax increases (60 percent and 40 percent) based
on David Kotok's interpretation in the *World-Herald*. Unlike Initiative
300 (restricting corporate farm ownership), which fizzled out as a campaign issue after its referendum petition drive failed, Orr and Boosalis's
opposing positions on repealing LB662 grew to be a major differentiat-
ing issue in the general election campaign for governor.

No matter what priority issues my mother envisioned for her campaign, Orr's "gotcha" tax issue threatened to drown out all the rest. The

three televised hour-long debates were barometers of how prominent the issue of taxes had become. The first debate, on September 4, was held in an open-air auditorium at the state fairgrounds in Lincoln. Mom in her hot-pink suit and Orr in her lavender dress were primarily objects of political curiosity: How would two women debate? What would they wear? How would they sound? Would they be mean to each other?

The first debate was "tame stuff" and a "ho hum affair" covering familiar themes of agricultural policy, school consolidation and financing, corporate farming restrictions, women's issues, taxes. Orr had just launched her first offensive tax ads, but the first debate was before the September poll that would reveal the devastating effect of the Orr ads on Boosalis's polling numbers. Kathleen Rutledge, then *Journal* statehouse reporter, described the meeting of women combatants at that first debate: "Boosalis isn't known for being an attack politician, although she earned a reputation for toughness as mayor of Lincoln and was adept at baiting Council Chairman Joe Hampton. And Orr has been working to soften the 'Dragon Lady' image she acquired at the Statehouse when she was an aide to Governor Charles Thone. Hence, an essentially polite exchange between two candidates, each of whom emphasized she had a vision for Nebraska and the experience to implement it."

In the three weeks between the first debate and the second, on September 21 in North Platte, the 11-percentage-point drop in my mother's polling numbers after Orr's tax ads engendered disagreement within the Boosalis campaign and among political analysts as to how my mother should respond to the ads and try to recapture the momentum. Strategists on both sides of the race agreed that "the tax issue dominated the first twenty days of September." Orr contended that by continuously pressing the tax issue, she was being "informational," not "negative." Democratic analyst and Creighton law professor Richard Shugrue urged Boosalis to show she was "a tough street fighter. She has to turn it around, capture the initiative." Robert Sittig disagreed, however, and said that she should "do the same thing she's been doing—stress her broader experience, be natural, and don't do anything unusual." Campaign co-chair Ben Nelson urged Mom to emphasize more strongly the differences between the candidates.

My stomach was in knots as I caught wind of so many competing views in the wake of the tax debacle, but my mother seemed to keep a clear head. She knew who she was and what she stood for. She was not about to "take off the gloves" by suddenly morphing into an attack politician, but neither would she lie down for unfair attacks against her. Her years as mayor in frequent hand-to-hand combat with city council opponents equipped her with the toughness she needed to fight back. As Kathleen Rutledge observed years later, "Even if she was urged to 'take off the gloves,' I know that Helen is very principled. Her energy and drive comes from her sense of what's right."

"Tame" and "ho hum" certainly did not characterize the second televised debate. Among sharp exchanges on a host of issues, my mother reminded the audience of Orr's ties to Governor Thone and questioned her fiscal record as chief of staff of his administration, citing state budget increases under Thone of more than 13 percent per year. Orr responded: "I don't know how Mrs. Boosalis thinks a chief of staff operates in the governor's office, but my governor, Charley Thone, did not let the chief of staff set policy. I certainly didn't." My mother shot back that based on her record as mayor, "I don't preach fiscal conservatism. I've done it. While others talk about tax relief, we did it." Greg Hayden, UNL economics professor and head of policy research in the Boosalis for Governor campaign, recalls that "in the debates with Orr, your mother would put a picture of her grandsons on the podium to remind her not to get testy or defensive in the debate."

After the second debate, Orr had to defend her own fiscal record. Governor Kerrey and his chief of staff, Don Nelson, criticized Orr for trying to disassociate herself from former governor Thone. State Democratic Party chairman Tom Monaghan accused Orr of "wanting it both ways"—touting her administrative experience as chief of staff under Governor Thone, but denying any responsibility for that administration's budget problems, such as the 38 percent increase in state spending when Orr was Thone's chief of staff and the drop from the state's surplus of $116 million in 1979–80 to a $15 million deficit in 1981–82.

At the third and final debate, on October 6, Orr and Boosalis "traded blows on taxes once again. . . . Only this time it was Helen who took the offensive." Mom told the debate audience that voters had a choice between her record of holding the line on tax rates as mayor and Orr's record of voting for tax rate hikes as state treasurer and member of the state Board of Equalization—two hikes in income tax rates and one increase in the sales tax rate in 1982 brought about by the "crisis management" of the Thone administration. Although the third debate covered some new ground, the candidates returned again and again to taxes but Mom had recovered her balance from Orr's devastating tax ads in early September.

The progression of polling numbers through the campaign appeared to bear out a Boosalis recovery and, indeed, her recapturing momentum. If campaigns put too much emphasis on polls, they find themselves chasing voter sentiment at an elusive moment in time that is already past; yet campaign workers thrive on the latest poll numbers, especially if the numbers are positive. Early in a race, the candidates must rely almost exclusively on their own polling before enough voter interest in the campaign compels independent polling.

Back in June, more than a month after the May primary election, the Boosalis campaign had commissioned a poll by Hickman-Maslin Research of Washington DC, which showed the race dead even: 43 percent for each candidate, with 14 percent undecided. At that time both primary nominees had 83 percent name recognition and both had favorable ratings of 56 percent. This early private poll showed that Boosalis drew more support from Republicans than Orr did from Democrats—a good sign for any Democrat who hopes to win in Nebraska. Late in August another private poll, this time conducted by the Orr campaign, reportedly showed Boosalis in the lead. Although Orr's campaign would not comment on the poll, they did say they agreed with Boosalis's June poll results showing the candidates tied at 43 percent.

A *Sunday Journal-Star* poll in mid-August showed a dead heat: Boosalis at 37.8 percent, Orr at 37.4 percent, and 24.8 percent undecided. Both campaigns confirmed that the results were generally consistent with their private polls. The newspaper poll also reported that Boosalis's support was stronger among younger voters, while Orr attracted more senior voters. Mom's campaign co-chair Marg Badura speculated that Helen "electrified" younger voters, while older voters were more reluctant about her candidacy because they knew that the last thing they themselves would want to do was run for governor.

348 | Flash Forward

Then came the shocking early September poll in the *World-Herald* reporting Mom's precipitous 11-percentage-point drop after Orr's relentless television tax ads. Richard Shugrue, in an opinion piece, noted about this poll: "Whether by design, the poll just happened to be conducted right smack in the first Orr media blitz, when her negative campaign heightened her own recognition and left unanswered questions about Boosalis' program. It also was conducted before Boosalis had begun her own advertising."

After the plummeting September poll results, the Boosalis campaign commissioned another poll by Mom's Washington pollster Harrison Hickman. These mid-September results showed Boosalis trailing Orr by 4 percent: Orr 46 percent, Boosalis 42 percent, 12 percent undecided, and a 4-point margin of error. This poll was taken after my mother's response ads to Orr's tax attack ads had been running for five or six days. There is no question that the *World-Herald* poll "caught us at a low point," Hickman said, but his new poll taken in mid-September "shows that the Boosalis campaign got the ship turned around in the water and moving in the right direction."

A "toss up" was what the governor's race was called after the results of an ABC–*Washington Post* poll taken a month later in mid-October, after all three televised debates: Orr at 50.5 percent, Boosalis 49.5 percent, with an 8 percent margin of error. The next *World-Herald* poll, on October 26, confirmed that Boosalis had reversed the steep drop shown in its September poll: instead of trailing Orr by 11 percentage points, Boosalis was now down by only 3 percent. The *World-Herald* pollster said the poll results were so close that "there is no statistically significant difference." And the election was just a little more than a week away.

My mother could feel the momentum shifting to her in the final days of the campaign. More than the candidate's wishful thinking, there was a growing perception that the race was extremely close. "Whereas September clearly belonged to Orr, October hasn't," wrote Don Walton in the *Lincoln Star* on October 22. "She [Boosalis] has stopped the momentum that seemed to be clearly Orr's in September. And that means either candidate is in a position to win it in these last two weeks."

Both candidates were optimistic and stepped up the pace of their campaigns—hard to imagine possible in Mom's case. In fund-raising, each had cracked the $1 million mark, breaking campaign fund-raising records in Nebraska. With a week still to go, Orr had raised $1.26 million, Boosalis $1.03 *million (compared to the 1982 record of $1.1 million for Thone and $900,000 for Kerrey). The Boosalis campaign staff continued to work away raising funds, as I had done for months from the desk where I had thrown all those pencils at Neil.

By this point I was no longer spending my days raising money. I spent the last days of the campaign with my mom on the campaign trail, amazed at her stamina and good humor. I wanted to be a supportive, upbeat companion and I tried mightily, but mostly I was exhausted.

With a week to go, my mother was scheduled for a full day of campaigning in Omaha, still the key election battleground, and I went along. Don Walton from the *Star* was riding with the candidate to do an end-of-campaign story. The campaign driver, David Wiese, and I managed to get my mother in and out of three luncheon events where she was featured speaker. We stopped at a senior housing center where Mom walked up to a man in a wheelchair who looked up blankly, then broke into a big grin and said, "Oh, you're the lady!"

We made endless stops at Omaha drugstores and supermarkets where Mom cruised the aisles and checkout lines with the same cosmic level of energy she had when she began the campaign a year earlier. As she passed the meat counter in one grocery store she paused to lament, "I should be shopping. Look at the cheap prices!" I remember virtually all the shoppers reaching toward her, wanting to shake her hand and wish her good luck. Don Walton observed the same phenomenon: "The recognition was extraordinary, the tone of the reception friendly," Walton wrote. "Just the signs that Helen Boosalis might hope to see in Omaha, the center of Democratic voter strength in Nebraska, during the crucial final days before election day. It's the city she has to win. Television had worked its magic, turning the Democratic gubernatorial nominee from Lincoln with the crown of snow-white hair into a recognizable celebrity in the one city in the state that is virtually impossible for a candidate to penetrate on foot."

After a big rally at the National Guard Armory that night, we drove the fifty miles back to Lincoln, still wired from the day and sensing the surging momentum but wary of expressing it out loud. Mom tried to ignore a cough that she had been fighting for weeks. We hoped her raspy voice would last for another week, but that didn't stop her from chatting with me in the backseat. We exchanged old family stories and reminisced about the crazy stunts she had done as mayor.

My mother had us in stitches as she recounted her adventure as the mayor contestant in an ostrich race. She climbed onto the little surrey seat, just big enough to sit on and sturdy enough to be dragged along the ground as the ostrich ran forward. As she eased herself down and was handed a broom, the cowboy (maybe ostrichboy) shouted all kinds of instructions over the cheering crowd—how to sit, how to hold on, how to steer ("hold the broom on one side or the other of the ostrich's head, depending on which direction you want to go"). Amidst our laughter at the picture of my rather refined-looking, white-haired mother trying to steer a galloping ostrich with a broom, I asked whether she worried about remembering all those instructions during the race? "Oh no! Once we got started, I just wanted to win!" Yes, that explained the last year, I thought, as our car pulled into the driveway of our house where my dad was upstairs sleeping.

The momentum shift that we had been afraid to acknowledge seemed to pop out of the cake by the next weekend, two days before the November 4 election, when the *Sunday Journal-Star* published the results of its final poll. "I think a person would be a fool to say who's going to win," said pollster Doug Evans, whose firm conducted the poll. He told the *World-Herald* that "this poll and others show that the momentum in the race is on Mrs. Boosalis's side. He said her strength during the course of the latest poll seemed to build from day to day." Indeed, the poll showed:

- Boosalis: 44 percent
- Orr: 43 percent
- Undecided: 13 percent

Essentially, the numbers were right back where they were in June at the outset of the general election campaign—after all the work, all the money, all the travel, all the ads, all the bad coffee, all the angst.

But there we were—elated, excited, nervous, scared, charged—only two days before the only real poll that counted: the election.

Chapter Eight

Another Time Around
1979–1983

"What makes Helen different from other politicians is her lack of ego. By that, I don't mean a lack of personhood or strength. I mean the personal ego that seems inevitably to come into play when people run for office. To a remarkable degree, Helen was immune to the glories of 'living in the mansion'—she was focused on what she could do with the power rather than on having it."
—KATHLEEN RUTLEDGE, editor, *Lincoln Journal Star*, 2001–2007

"Unlike most politicians, Helen never thought she should be treated differently than anyone else. Most politicians start to think they are better than others or their motivations change, but Helen never did change. And most surround themselves with people who tell them they're perfect—she didn't."
—BEATTY BRASCH, campaign coordinator and campaign manager, Boosalis mayoral campaigns

BUDGETING: CLOSING THE GAP

As president of the U.S. Conference of Mayors in 1981–82, my mother led the nation's cities in their fight against the Reagan administration's dismantling of most of the federal support system for cities. Like many other mayors who joined in that national effort, Lincoln's mayor was fighting for her city also at the state level to replace, at least in part, lost federal revenues when city budgets could be cut no further.

The plight of cities that were caught in the middle was described in the *Wall Street Journal* in March 1982: "The federal money spigot is dry-ing up, and most states can't or won't replace the aid cities have been counting on. At the same time, cities often can't get state permission to try to make up the lost funds through new taxes on their own. Many [cities] have already reduced street cleaning, library hours, recreation programs and programs for the elderly and children. And they are borrowing from the future by the perilous expedient of delaying maintenance on structures like bridges and sewers." The article identified Lincoln as one of many cities that "must beg the state legislature for permission to levy taxes" and quoted its mayor: "We don't have the wherewithal to raise revenue. We're creatures of the state."

In February 1982, during her U.S. Conference of Mayors presidency, Lincoln's mayor lobbied the Nebraska legislature to permit an increase in Lincoln's sales tax from 1 percent to 1.5 percent to replace shrinking federal transit funding and to finance needed public works *projects. Federal transit funding covered nearly 50 percent of Lincoln Transportation System's deficits but was slated by the Reagan administration for total phaseout by 1985. Lincoln's transit system was in jeopardy, but loss of federal transit funding alone would not win state legislative support for a sales tax increase. Transit wasn't a major issue in most small Nebraska towns, and only nine municipalities statewide even levied a sales tax. As one mayor put it, "I have trouble imagining a rural legislator will give a tinker's damn about mass transit."

My mother took Lincoln's quest for the sales tax increase to the legislature "wrapped in a call for courage in dealing with President Reagan's New Federalism." With the reduction in federal aid and a shift of programs back to the local level, she argued, comes the burden on local officials to raise the money to keep programs going; although supporting increased taxes is always a political risk, local officials must either "take up that challenge or accept responsibility for deteriorating cities and loss of vital services."

Joining her in presenting Lincoln's case were the city's finance director, its transportation director, and the sponsor of the bill to boost Lincoln's sales tax—state senator Dave Landis, my high school classmate. My mother and Landis stressed that the bill would not impose the additional sales tax without first getting voter approval, giving residents the "opportunity" to raise additional tax revenues for desired and critical services. The additional sales tax would help Lincoln retain its AAA bond rating, the envy of many other cities during those difficult economic times. Their arguments did not prevail, and the bill to increase the sales tax fell two votes short of passage by the Nebraska unicameral. Some legislators opposed it based strictly on their belief that a sales tax should be a revenue source reserved exclusively for state government.

The defeat came as a relief to the Lincoln Chamber of Commerce, which had written a letter to state legislators opposing the increased sales tax bill. My mother was "surprised, confused and, of course, disappointed" by the letter, since the chamber had not communicated its views to her or met with city officials on budget or sales tax issues. My mother's support of a Lincoln sales tax increase to compensate for loss of federal revenue was undoubtedly seen, to those already convinced, as yet more evidence of her "anti-business" attitude.

I wonder if Mom's lobbying for a sales tax increase satisfied Councilman Hampton. During an earlier council debate on whether to retain a legislative lobbyist in the mayor's proposed budget, Hampton had said, "Maybe it's time for the mayor and council to get off their duffs and quit fooling around with some of the penny-ante issues, and get over (to the Statehouse) and lobby." My mother coolly countered, "If I got off my duff any more, I don't think I'd get into bed at *night."

The mayor presented her 1981–82 budget to another new council, elected in 1981, and called for restraint by proposing an increase of less than 3.5 percent over the previous year. Her proposed budget included extensive service cuts and elimination of thirty-two more full-time staff positions (but adding eight new police officer positions). She made substantial cuts in the city's six-year capital improvement program, cutting capital expenditures to less than half of what they were in her 1979–80 budget.

Of the full-time positions eliminated, 23 came from the Parks and Recreation Department, which had lost a total 130 positions since 1977—a devastating blow to all aspects of the parks and recreation system. The department bore more than half the service and job cuts in the mayor's budget in yet another year of cutting services and jobs. (Services deemed essential, such as police and fire protection, could not easily be cut and, in fact, often required staffing increases because of the city's growth, further exacerbating the need to cut from other areas.) There seemed an understanding of the necessity for such extreme measures. Chairman of the Parks and Recreation Advisory Board, Clancy Woolman, expressed surprising support for the mayor's budget plan: "I commend the Mayor. In a tough situation, she did a hell of a job." He said the city would have to rely more on volunteers. "If residents realize they do not have the services, I think they will provide them by helping us out."

Having long promoted citizens' stewardship of their city, the mayor encouraged city departments to use volunteers to help sustain existing programs facing budget cuts. She asked her department heads to make lists of jobs that could be done by volunteers and asked community groups to expand their existing volunteer efforts. Over time, numerous volunteer opportunities had emerged, such as tree planting and care; painting benches, fire hydrants, and fences; delivering books; cutting weeds on median strips; cleaning bus shelters; assisting in programs for seniors, children, and those with special needs; and maintaining playground equipment—the possibilities seemed endless. "The whole spirit of citizens volunteering to take care of their city started with Helen," recalled Betty Peterson, Boosalis campaign volunteer coordinator. "The city would have come to a standstill during bad economic times if it weren't for volunteers at the libraries, parks, schools, programs all over."

Parks board chairman Woolman was right about his fellow residents' willingness to assist the city, but he could not have imagined one particular person who would be among the first citizens to step forward to help with city park maintenance—the mayor's husband, Mike Boosalis. With her stepped-up call for public volunteerism to help counterbalance budget cuts in city departments, Mom had apparently found a receptive ear in her own home. My dad called the Parks and Recreation Department and offered to use two of his vacation days to work full-time on city park maintenance, knowing that the department was in dire straits due to (his wife's) budget cuts.

My mother loved the notion. "It was his idea," she told the *Star*. "He's heard me talking so much about volunteerism, he took it upon himself to do it. He just wanted to help where he was needed." When asked if her husband, chairman of the university's Plant Pathology Department, might be overqualified for his status as "city lawn mower extraordinaire," the mayor said that my dad loved to do yard work and that they used to pull weeds together before she became mayor and had less time.

What began as a rather "cute-sy" human-interest story about the mayor's husband became a visible example of volunteerism used to spawn a citywide campaign for getting volunteer help in park maintenance. When the sales manager of the Journal-Star Printing Company saw the news story about my dad's civic spirit, he contacted his boss and together they approached the city with a scheme for publicizing the need for park volunteers. Both daily newspapers, the *Journal* and the *Star*, ran free full-page ads inviting Lincolnites to "Be a V.I.P."—Volunteer in the Parks. The ads urged the public—rather than complain about the lack of mowing and weed control due to budget cuts—to volunteer as individuals or groups from their neighborhoods, businesses, churches, civic groups, sports teams to help maintain the beauty of their parks by cutting grass, collecting litter, painting benches, and planting flowers.

The day after the first ad appeared, dozens of people showed up at the V.I.P. campaign kickoff and saw the mayor buzzing around on a lawnmower. Among them were a mother and daughter who volunteered to take care of a mini-park near their home for the rest of the summer. One individual who came to volunteer said, "I don't consider myself 'civic-minded.' But if you're interested in the city, you should give them a hand. It came as a shock to me how short-handed they were." Others came in groups—employee groups from Minnegasco and Goodyear volunteered to mow and trim two parks all summer, postal workers took on maintenance of median plantings near post offices, a church mowed and collected litter from a nearby park, school groups took on several parks. After more ads, so many residents volunteered that the Parks and Recreation Department ran short of industrial-type lawnmowers and put out a call for the donated use of those as well.

The V.I.P. program, spontaneously "spurred by a news story about Mike Boosalis" with minimal but enthusiastic planning, took on a life of its own and continued for years, reaffirming "Lincoln's long tradition of outstanding community service by volunteers . . . a characteristic that many other places envy and are going to have to develop in a period of pinched governmental capacity."

The popular V.I.P. program, a small example of the mayor's commitment to citizen involvement, received significant media attention along with another city volunteer effort that year during the holiday season. The mayor issued the city's holiday wish list in a forty-page "Catalog of Gifts" to give citizens other opportunities to contribute to the needs of their city. The catalog, tested in a few other cities, was also an effective way to educate the public about the costs of their government. It displayed gifts in a broad price range that any citizen, company, or organization could buy for the city: fluorescent lights ($150), jaws of life ($6,700), fire truck ($75,000), jogging path ($800), four lighted ball fields ($460,000), eight swat team caps ($25), a device to help police search for buried bodies ($8,995), license tags for cats and dogs ($.05 per tag). Something for everyone.

The gift catalog also included requests for priceless volunteer help and even prompted some unsolicited monetary and in-kind donations, including typewriters, office chairs, a stepladder, and a three-year-old buffalo (valued at $600 and placed in the Pioneers Park zoo). A Wyoming man offered his 1934 fire truck if the city would come get it—one of the few offers the city turned down. In its first year the catalog produced $231,383 in cash and gifts. During a trip to testify before a congressional Banking Subcommittee on growing city problems due to federal budget cuts, my mother was asked for an interview about the catalog on nbc's *Today* show.

While Lincoln's creative use of volunteers and gift catalogs reinforced citizens' sense of community ownership and increased understanding of city finances, severe budget strains continued to plague the city for the duration of my mother's second term.

EQUAL RIGHTS

Not all city issues during the national economic crisis in Mom's second mayoral term were budgetary. In late 1981 the city council considered an amendment to Lincoln's anti-discrimination law to protect against discrimination on the basis of sexual orientation.

Dubbed the "gay rights amendment," the proposal drew more than two hundred people at a November 1981 public hearing of the city's Human Rights Commission and prompted almost five hours of testimony. At the standing-room-only hearing, impassioned speakers took the microphone on both sides of the issue. Many of those opposed to the amendment referred to what they termed the immorality and perversion of the homosexual lifestyle, as one who declared, "If this amendment is allowed, I and my family will have no choice but to leave the city." The city attorney gave his legal opinion that by enacting the amendment, the city would be exceeding its authority under the state human rights law. The Nebraska Civil Liberties Union and others challenged his opinion, and the mayor said she would have "no qualms" about ratifying a potential city council vote approving the amendment.

More than three months later, a second hearing, this time before the city council, drew more than three hundred citizens. Six hours of testimony commenced after police and firemen searched the council chambers for a bomb after receiving a phoned threat. Just after midnight, the council unanimously voted to put the issue on the ballot at a special May election. In May 1982 voters resoundingly defeated the measure by a 4–1 margin. The active endorsement of the amendment by the mayor and Councilmen Steinman and Youngberg did not make a dent in the passionate opposition. Other elected officials "maintained a carefully neutral public stance."

The mayor was puzzled by the overwhelming defeat of the amendment. She normally could predict the outcomes on local referenda with some degree of confidence based on activity in the months leading up to an election, but this one took her by surprise. She speculated that the mix of issues on the special election ballot—gay rights, a jail bond issue, Sunday liquor sales—drew an unusual mixture of voters with widely divergent interests and made the outcome unpredictable. "I think maybe the margin of defeat was the surprise," she said. "What a personal and emotional issue it is."

Although gay rights remains a "personal and emotional issue" more than twenty-five years later, it was still startling to read an account of the Lincoln performance of the San Francisco Gay Men's Chorus a month after the amendment's defeat. The mayor was asked to welcome the chorus at their performance at First Plymouth Church. Because of the recent gay rights amendment controversy, media coverage was high and some members of the mayor's staff thought she might want to back out of her scheduled welcoming of the chorus. It was rumored that she would not show up for the event because it would be politically unpopular, as had happened with elected officials in other cities. But Mom had no intention of canceling and was enthusiastic about having the group perform. When she walked down the church aisle to welcome the chorus, the exuberant audience gave out "whoops" and cheers, none of which was reported by the media.

However, while the mayor's welcome and the San Francisco Gay Men's Chorus event proceeded without incident or protest, KOLN-KGIN TV, the local CBS affiliate, canceled a scheduled performance by the chorus on its *Morning Show*. Station president A. James Ebel stated: "Our public affairs committee decided that 82 percent of our viewers outside Lincoln would not appreciate the lifestyle represented by the chorus. We saw no reason to irritate viewers watching the 'Morning Show,' which is not designed to carry any torches for causes."

My mother's commitment to civil rights was apparent throughout her years in elected office, beginning with her first city council term in 1959. Throughout her tenure she worked closely with residents of the Malone neighborhood, the area with the city's largest minority population, on efforts to strengthen the neighborhood, including the Malone Community Center, and to secure federal and city funding for neighborhood redevelopment. She also worked for years with minority residents to address troubling law enforcement issues, a critical consideration in her police chief search and in establishing a citizens police review board.

So, too, her work for the rights of citizens with disabilities was of long standing. During her first campaign for mayor, my mother disagreed with the incumbent by supporting direct city funding of the Mayor's Committee on Opportunities for the Disabled to address citywide needs of those with disabilities. She used her national platform with the U.S. Conference of Mayors to testify in U.S. Department of Education hearings on Section 504 of the Rehabilitation Act and the Education of Handicapped Children Act, including the right of children to be educated in the "least restrictive environment." Long before the 1990 Americans with Disabilities Act guaranteed accessibility of public facilities to those with disabilities, my mother worked on access issues with Lincoln's League of Human Dignity and other advocacy groups. The mayor and her department heads spent hours in wheelchairs to assess firsthand the many County-City Building accessibility barriers—elevators, steep ramps, drinking fountains.

In March 1975 a letter to the editor from the mother of an adult son with disabilities described my mother's responsiveness as city council member to issues affecting people with disabilities. "Several years ago I visited with Mrs. Boosalis in regard to my problem in lifting my son in his wheel chair up and down the curbs," she wrote. "Mrs. Boosalis presented my problem to the entire body of the City Council and today there are curb ramps! It is with deep respect, admiration and appreciation for this lady that I write this letter to relate to the people of Lincoln that she listened to me and did something about it."

Nancy McClelland, who chaired the Mayor's Committee on Employment of the Handicapped in the late 1970s, credits Mom's work with the committee to champion handicapped parking and curb cuts long before other communities had them. McClelland underscores my mother's lasting influence on her: "Today whenever I have a really tough task that intimidates me, I say to myself, 'Act like Helen Boosalis. Get the ball rolling, get it done, then get on to the next task. You can do it.'"

My mother's work for women's rights represents another arena where she spent considerable energy throughout her elected life. One of her early acts as mayor had been to create the Lincoln-Lancaster Commission on the Status of Women. With the threatened elimination of commission funding under the federal Comprehensive Employment Training Act during her second term, my mother and County Commissioner Jan Gauger worked to merge staffing for the women's commission and the city's Human Rights Commission. Even with smaller staffing than it had as an independent quasi-government body, the move to the city saved the fledgling Commission on the Status of Women. Thirty years later the Lincoln-Lancaster Women's Commission continues to inform the mayor, city council, and county board on issues that affect women in the *community.

A popular speaker for women's groups, the mayor spoke about the "superwoman myth" to adolescent girls at the YWCA Teen Center in March 1980. "The myth about superwoman," she said, "is that all you need to do is to work hard, be a perfect wife and mother, and in addition, successfully develop a professional career. The reality is that the woman who tries to balance these roles needs a very clear sense of priorities and realistic expectations of her own personal limits." With more women working outside the home, Mom cautioned, "Most women continue to do most of the cooking, cleaning, child care, run the kids to dancing lessons, piano lessons, Scouting and Campfire duties." Even when husbands and children assume more responsibilities, she said, it is often viewed as "helping out the women."

When she first became mayor, Mom, too, still subscribed to the superwoman myth and tried to continue all her housekeeping duties on top of her demanding job as Lincoln's chief executive. She soon recognized that she had to set priorities and that something had to give. To find a balance between home and work, she had to get real about which homemaking tasks were essential (and could be shared with outside cleaning help), which ones she wanted to keep doing herself for personal satisfaction, and which ones were nonessential but demonstrated (even to herself) that she was still a great homemaker while working outside the home—that is, a superwoman. An example of the nonessential was her annual baking of hundreds of holiday cookies in numerous varieties and bringing them on large platters to city hall to the "oohs and aahs" of city staff and her city council colleagues. As mayor, those nonessential tasks simply had to go. Superwoman had to go.

Reading about Mom discussing the superwoman myth, I realized I had also bought into the myth, just as my mother—also raised by a superwoman—had done. If I had been in her audience of teenage girls in 1980, the year my first child was born, I might have better understood my own feelings of inadequacy as a young mother both at home and on the job, and why I felt constantly overwhelmed. But who ever listens to advice coming from one's parents? And my generation really did believe that we could have it all and, moreover, that we were entitled to have it all. We should have asked and we should have listened to our mothers.

As Mom confronted her own superwoman expectations while traversing uncharted territory as a woman elected chief executive, her commitment to feminism deepened. She spoke frequently on the subject and actively encouraged other women to run for elected office. She prodded women, cajoled them, pushed them to take the next step by becoming active participants in local government. She would urge women's groups as well as individuals: "Start observing government at all levels, read about it, take an interest in it, don't be afraid to become involved. Once you have decided that you are knowledgeable enough and have something to offer, bite the bullet and run for office."

The mayor acknowledged both the advantages and the hurdles that women candidates faced. "Many women who are political candidates lack the egotism of their male counterparts and are reluctant to toot their own horns, but they are also helped by the perception that they are less tainted in politics," she told a UNL psychology class in 1981. "Raising money is a major obstacle for potential women candidates. Since women are considered improbable winners, who wants to put money on a loser? Women lack access to certain groups such as the Chamber of Commerce, and women themselves are not big contributors to campaigns." She noted that increases in the number of elected women had been disappointingly small—women were not the "better half" but the "missing half" among elected representatives.

In 1980, the sixtieth anniversary of women's suffrage, Colorado congresswoman Pat Schroeder spoke to Nebraska women at an Equality Day celebration on August 23. Urging the passage of the Equal Rights Amendment, she accused ERA opponent Phyllis Schlafly of taking the rights won by her "foremothers" for granted: "We don't want to walk in front of men. We don't want to walk in back of men. We want our historical position beside men." My mother also spoke at the Equality Day event, where a *World-Herald* reporter observed: "As a nationally known mayor, Helen Boosalis could easily put her feet up on her city hall desk and feel as if she had done her part for the women's movement. Instead, she speaks in measured tones of the anger she feels toward those who benefit from strides some women have made in gaining equality, yet have no interest in the cause."

I am struck by how much of what Mom said on Equality Day in 1980 still applies today: "Unlike the suffragists, we have no single issue to devote our lives to. Instead, we face a multitude of issues that we care about: the ERA, quality child care, displaced homemakers, family violence, sexual assault and sexual harassment, upward mobility, equal pay for work of equal value, reproductive freedom, educational equity, single parenting, and many more." Mom continued, "We often must divide our energies among several of these issues. To make matters even more complicated, we all face and care about other issues of a more general concern: the economic health of our nation, the need to conserve our country's resources, the defense budget, the continuing needs of the disadvantaged, to name but a few. So we must learn to care for ourselves and each other during the long process of involvement in these issues."

My mother concluded by reminding the Equality Day celebrants that people cannot be complacent about achieving equal rights for women and minorities. It is the same, she said, as working for good government: "I tell citizens continually you've got to keep working at it. It's the same thing with the women's movement."

Not long after that celebration, the ERA had its rendezvous with death. At midnight on June 30, 1982, the ratification of the proposed Twenty-seventh Amendment fell three states short of the thirty-eight needed to ratify a constitutional amendment. The next day, Lincoln's mayor held a noon rally on the steps of the state capitol to proclaim "A New Day: Beyond ERA" and to rededicate support for the expired amendment. "Tell those who oppose us that they will not stop our struggle for full and equal rights," Mom urged the crowd. "If you are unhappy with the current lawmakers' view of women, then you have the power to change it. Public policy must be made more sensitive to the needs of women, at the local and state levels. I urge you not to wait until the 'right politician' comes along. I urge you, instead, to *become* those policymakers."

At her biweekly press conference, the mayor asserted that the ERA's defeat would not hold women back: "We'll just have to fight a little longer, a little harder to get the rights women should have had from the beginning." When a reporter pointed out that the mayor had become a highly successful woman without the ERA, she appeared to straighten taller than her five-foot, four-inch frame and countered that she had found success only "because of the work for equality by a large number of women over many years. Too many people forget that—that none of us do it alone." Her words echo those of a more recent trailblazing woman, U.S. Supreme Court justice Ruth Bader Ginsburg: "I think about how much we owe to the women who went before us—legions of women, some known but many more unknown. I applaud the bravery and resilience of those who helped all of us—you and me—to be here today."

No doubt the unsuccessful struggle to gain passage of the ERA helped mold and sharpen my mother's feminism, but Mom didn't identify with the more militant wing of the women's rights movement, nor did she consider herself a model for other women to emulate. She supported and encouraged other women to run for office or to push ahead in their fields not because they should follow her example but because they should use and develop their own talents to the maximum. "She winces when you ask if she's a role model," observed a *Star* reporter, "but ask young professional women in Lincoln, and they will tell you: 'She meant a lot to me just being there.'"

Her "just being there" influenced far more "women" of all ages than my mother could possibly know. She loved speaking to classrooms of children in Lincoln and small rural *towns. During Mom's last month as mayor, a six-year-old girl who was born during the early Boosalis mayoral years was surprised when she heard that Joe Hampton and Roland Luedtke were running for mayor. "Oh!" she said. "You mean a man can be mayor?"

POMP, CEREMONY, AND DARING

Not all the mayor's duties involved matters of great consequence. Although her role as Lincoln's chief executive did not leave much room for frivolity, Mom executed the ceremonial duties of the job with great panache. She accepted every request for the mayor's presence that her schedule allowed. Not only did she get a kick out of mingling at events with the people whom she was in office to serve, but she also wanted citizens to feel a personal connection to their mayor. One day they would read in the paper about her congressional testimony in Wash-

41. Helen prepares to fly in 1926 Swallow biplane

ington or her latest showdown with a city councilman; the next day they might shake hands at a city recreation event with their fun-loving mayor who expressed warm interest in every person she met. Mom felt these appearances were one way to dispel the image of a dignified, white-haired, remote mayor out of touch with her constituency. She especially loved frequent encounters on the street "when young kids would yell, 'Hi, Helen!'"

Ceremonial requests for the mayor's presence ran the gamut from the typical welcoming of groups, cutting of ribbons, and throwing of the first pitch at baseball games to more outlandish events such as goat-milking contests and ostrich races. Organizations were eager to schedule the energetic mayor. Mom's adventurous nature even compelled her to agree to a few daring airborne feats: a ride in a hot-air balloon and a flight in a two-seat open-cockpit Swallow biplane, which had made the first air-mail flight in 1926 at a cruising altitude of a thousand feet. Earlier in the day of the biplane flight, the plucky mayor told a United Way meeting, "This might be the next to my last public appearance."

42. Helen prepares for an ostrich race

Her most audacious venture came from an invitation to celebrate the Nebraska Air National Guard's thirty-fifth anniversary in July 1981. To honor that event, the mayor joined the ranks of only two other women who had copiloted an F-4 fighter reconnaissance jet (RCF-4 Phantom II) capable of flying at sixteen hundred miles per hour (more than twice the speed of sound). It was not all smooth sailing (or flying), since a low

43. Helen "copilots" an F-4 fighter reconnaissance jet

cloud ceiling delayed the start of the air show and then a fuel leak was discovered in my mother's lead plane as it taxied down the runway. The forty thousand shivering observers watched in the windy cold as my mother transferred to a spare F-4 fighter plane.

Mom had prepared for the flight by going through "egress" training. She was fitted with a too-tight helmet, a flight suit, and a harness attached to her parachute; she then practiced getting out of the Phantom in the event of an emergency. I wondered if she was thinking about her father teaching her not to be afraid of anything—she was a Spartan.

The ground crew was placing bets that "her ladyship will become ill and probably black and blue as she pulls Gs (reverses gravity pull)," but they underestimated the mayor. Not only had her adolescent hero been Amelia Earhardt, but I know Mom would have willed herself to come through any flying experience unscathed. And of course that's exactly what happened.

"Her plane had just executed two screaming, thunderous pass-throughs, smoke billowing behind all four jets, flying in diamond formation," observed a *Star* reporter at the scene. "They whooshed in before the audience, two camouflage painted planes at a time, parachutes billowing behind. General's stars taped to her shoulders, helmet on head, Mrs. Boosalis jumped out of the back seat, waving to the crowd." Describing her thrilling ride, Mom said, "Of course I felt great. I loved every minute of it." As the mayor-pilot signed autographs in the brisk twelve-mile-an-hour wind, "a shivering, blue-lipped six-year-old" asked his mother, "Why is the mayor doing this airplane trip anyway?" The mayor turned to him. "Because I was asked," she said. "I couldn't pass it up."

For her performance as copilot (and just for being game, I suppose) she was presented with a pilot's silk scarf with patches for the 173rd and 155th Tactical Reconnaissance Groups and an RF4-C insignia. The flight seemed to capture the public's attention, and for months afterward people would stop her on the street and say, "Oh, I always wanted to do that!"

THE 1983 MAYORAL ELECTION: JUST SAY NO

It took some convincing on the mayor's part to assure "an army of doubters" that she was not being coy, as politicians sometimes are, about her decision not to run for a third term. Many could not believe that the mayor would not change her mind, capitalizing on her outstanding record and all the fresh publicity from her year as president of the U.S. Conference of Mayors. At a speech to the county Democratic Party six months before the 1983 spring election, she was asked whether she would reconsider. She responded with exasperation. "No, I have been saying that for 3½ years, and I haven't been saying it to play little games. I've been saying it because I mean it."

A growing group of those considering a run at the mayor's office might have harbored lingering doubt about the finality of her decision, but most finally accepted that the portrait of Helen Boosalis as Lincoln's forty-fourth mayor would, indeed, be hung the following spring next to the forty-three men who had preceded her.

The mayor's on-the-record plan to leave office at the end of her second term provoked what the *Journal* had predicted would be "a crafty positioning of opposing political forces—even political parties—on se-

44. Lincoln's first woman mayor stands before portraits of her forty-three male predecessors

lective issues in advance of the 1983 elections." Both sides of the council divide—the three at-large council members (all businessmen) and the four district council members—tried to label each other as the mouthpiece for either business interests or neighborhood interests. Many believed the two constituencies represented on the council had finally achieved parity: neighborhoods had established themselves as an equal power, and the business community no longer held a one-dimensional view but was a diverse mix of business interests. With business and neighborhood interests having traded power in council elections several times during my mother's eight years as mayor, and given their fairly equal power in her last two years, the capturing of the mayor's office had now become the prized symbol of political dominance in the upcoming 1983 election.

Many agreed with a *Star* editorial that said "there is no one in sight who could beat the mayor if she had chosen to run again." But who would run for mayor now that folks finally believed that her decision not to run was real? My mother's opponent who had placed first, ahead of her, in the 1979 mayoral primary—Stan Matzke—seemed to have designs on making another run, this time without the powerful incumbent woman mayor in his path. Two years before the 1983 mayoral election, he fueled speculation by leaving the Democratic Party to become a Republican, and when asked if he had plans to run for the nonpartisan mayor's post he said, "I'm very open on it. It depends on the situation at the time." But Matzke's second mayoral candidacy never materialized.

Of little surprise was Councilman Hampton's announcement of his candidacy for mayor in the fall of 1982. Hampton assured voters that he would not represent only business interests and stressed his positive relationship with most of the city's neighborhoods; many, however, considered the neighborhoods to be strongholds for an anti-Hampton vote. He also said that if elected mayor he would not open up the Stevens Creek watershed for development, which he regarded as "sheer folly"; nor would he "pave the whole town." His campaign promises, as compared to his actual record on both issues, would be judged by the voters.

Also judged by voters would be Hampton's ongoing criticism of the popular outgoing mayor, which he downplayed at the press conference announcing his candidacy for mayor. At the press conference, "Hampton took a white gloves approach to Mayor Helen Boosalis, a powerful political opponent whom he often has been at grips with," a *Star* reporter observed. "No overt jabs were directed at the two-term incumbent who has announced she will not seek re-election. Hampton instead noted that he and the Mayor 'agree on about 85 per cent of the issues.'" During his mayoral campaign that followed, he put forward some sound plans for the city's future, such as his economic program to strengthen local industry and provide jobs.

Hampton also continued to raise his long-standing favorite issue— his claim that IBM bypassed development of its land in Lincoln in favor of developing elsewhere because eight years earlier (1975) city officials asked the company to consider a northwest rather than northeast site to avoid encouraging eastward city growth. As mayoral candidate, Hampton continued to blame city officials for IBM's failure to develop the site, despite IBM's repeated assurances that it was "not unusual" for the company to "hold land for more than 10 years without developing it" and that IBM was banking the land for "possible future company use as a plant-lab site." When specifically asked during the 1983 mayoral campaign about Hampton's charge, a New York IBM spokesman said that "there is no truth to the allegation" that negative city administration comments cost Lincoln an IBM development. Even Hampton admitted that when he talked with company officials in 1982 they "never did say they skipped over Lincoln because of a negative attitude, but they told me that Lincoln did not fit into their overall planning at this point."

His six years on the city council and his visible role as council chairman made Hampton a frontrunner, but it was a crowded race for mayor with twelve candidates seeking to replace Mayor Boosalis in the 1983 spring primary. At her regular press conferences, the mayor was repeatedly asked whether she would endorse a candidate to succeed her before the primary, and who that candidate might be. "When Boosalis steps down in May after a quarter century in city government she will leave behind a healthy share of enemies and a fortune of amassed loyalties," wrote George Hendrix in the *Star* on March 31, 1983. "Boosalis is the champion of the old and most active neighborhood associations. She has gained national recognition in recent years. Her local status has reached that of elder stateswoman. That her status and her followers might come into play for election purposes is a savory prospect to some. Overt backing by Boosalis will throw weight."

The mayor did not consider endorsing Councilman Hampton. Of others in the primary field, Roland Luedtke and Roger Lott were Hampton's strongest challengers, and both would have much to gain from the mayor's endorsement—Luedtke, a moderate Republican, attorney, and former legislator and lieutenant *governor, and Lott, a moderate Democrat and attorney. Many considered Luedtke's advantage for winning the mayor's endorsement to be his campaign manager, Lloyd Hinkley, a former city council colleague of my mother's and rumored to be her first choice for *mayor. On the other hand, Lott was perceived as the candidate whose positions most closely matched the mayor's.

The two winners of the mayoral primary who would face off in the general election—Hampton and Luedtke—surprised few. But with late polls showing Hampton in the lead, the surprise came in his second-place primary finish, trailing Luedtke by almost 6 percent. The week after the primary the mayor weighed in on her "preference" for mayor, without using the word "endorsement" and without criticizing or even referring to Hampton. She praised Luedtke's leadership skills and said he "is committed to open government and citizen participation, two necessary ingredients for allowing our citizens to feel a part of their community."

Hampton attacked the Boosalis "endorsement" of Luedtke and charged that the mayor had allowed her feelings against him to affect her decision. "It's unfortunate that after a long and successful career in city hall, she's having difficulty laying down the reins and is allowing a personal vendetta to affect her judgment," he told reporters. Those interview comments were toned down when Hampton issued a press release about the Boosalis endorsement in which he seemed to take pains not to criticize the mayor; instead, he positively compared the mayor to himself: "I think it's unfortunate that our differences have been exaggerated. I have many of the same qualifications Helen did before she became mayor. I believe my business background adds a further positive dimension to my qualifications."

A pragmatist, Hampton was not about to distance himself from the mayor or her legions of supporters in this nonpartisan mayoral race between two Republicans. "Helen Boosalis has been a good mayor," he said, "perhaps one of the best Lincoln has had in many ways. She and I have shared the goal of making Lincoln a thriving, prosperous community with a high quality of life. . . . Only time will tell if I can lead the city as effectively as Helen Boosalis has, but I am not running against her."

As the 1983 mayoral campaign lurched toward the general election and the end of my mother's days as mayor, Councilman Hampton became more strident. He believed that Luedtke was benefiting from an anti-Hampton campaign based on Hampton's reputation for divisiveness and generating political foes, including the mayor. "I can't believe that the Mayor is supporting Roland [Luedtke] because of his administrative abilities," he said. "To my mind, she is simply opposing me." With just one week to go, Hampton had already set a new spending *record for a mayoral campaign: $41,000. The Lincoln newspapers were split—one endorsed Hampton, the other endorsed Luedtke.

FOLLOWING FOOTSTEPS

My mother was watching closely the race to elect her successor, but she was also watching another race of great personal interest five hundred miles away: my campaign for city council in Evanston, Illinois. Certain that I would never be a candidate myself after witnessing my mother's harrowing campaigns, I found myself running for city council the same spring of 1983 that Mom was finishing her final term as mayor.

I hadn't meant to go that route. Sure, I had inherited the belief that community involvement was both a cherished value and an obligation. In moving from Chicago to Evanston after finishing law school, I hoped to find a greater connection to community, and I did. After volunteering in a few local campaigns, I welcomed opportunities to serve on Evanston's business district redevelopment commission and its economic development committee—familiar territory for someone who grew up hearing talk of zoning and downtown development around the dinner table. A comfortable niche, I thought—to be involved and contribute to my community behind the scenes, without the angst of campaigns and headaches of elected office.

But my interest and involvement led a politically active group in my ward to urge me to run for the Third Ward city council seat being vacated by Ned Lauterbach, a popular, progressive Evanston alderman. I was honored by the group's confidence, but being an alderman was not a role I sought—that was Mom's arena. Even if I were to consider running for city council in the future, I told the group, the timing at that moment was not good—with my law practice and a two-year-old, I was barely keeping afloat. Thanks, but no thanks.

I met with the candidate-seeking group on Thanksgiving weekend in 1982 while my folks were visiting. I thought my mom would get a kick out of hearing about my meeting with local politicos. Instead, she related the story of the young man's advice when she was considering running for mayor in 1975: the brass ring often comes round only once—opportunities rarely present themselves at the perfect time. She asked me how I felt about my work on city committees and about my community. By the time we went to bed that night, I knew I would run.

It wasn't that Mom talked me into running *for* elected office—she helped me see that I need not run *from* the opportunity because I feared trying to "follow in her footsteps." And that "brass ring" advice? It proved valuable in making that decision, as it has in many life decisions since then. With more than a little uncertainty, I threw my own hat in the ring—not one of Mom's uniquely dashing hat creations but a practical, low-key version for serving my own community.

Knocking on doors in my own campaign that spring of 1983, I often sensed my ten-year-old self who campaigned for Mom in 1959, walking alongside me—astonished at being part of something so important and grownup.

My campaign seemed a familiar repeat of Mom's early grassroots city council campaigns, only slightly more sophisticated with its (+) (-) (0) identification of *voters. But there was an even bigger difference between my mother's first city council campaign and mine. Two weeks after filing my official candidacy I discovered I was pregnant, so unborn Christopher accompanied me on my after-dinner door knocking and was born three months after my swearing in as alderman. Greeting me at the city council meeting nine days after his birth was a resolution declaring Christopher as Evanston's official "alderbaby"—it passed unanimously.

Mom came from Lincoln to celebrate my victory on election night, April 12, 1983. Inevitably, Lincoln newspapers featured angles on "passing the torch" and "following in the *footsteps of her mother," one noting that my political career started out five years ahead of my mother's, which began with her first city council election at age thirty-nine. I told one reporter that both my parents had instilled in me from childhood the importance of giving "as much to the community as you can. They've always been models for my personal and professional life, and now for my political life. I hope I can do as good as job as she [Mom] has. She really lives the whole idea of what representative government is about. She always said that you have to remember that in public office, it's the people you represent. That's my *goal."

LEGACIES

As I was preparing for a new chapter of my life in local elected office, my mother was closing multiple chapters in hers. She had poured herself into each and every day of her eight years as mayor, holding nothing back, building no reserves. Every day she somehow started with a full tank, gave it her all, and almost ran on empty by day's end—then got up the next day and started again. After she returned from her trip to Evanston for my election, I am certain she spent every day of her last month as mayor in the same manner.

Assessment of Mom's performance as mayor as well as sentimental looks back at her mayoral tenure dominated the local news as much as the 1983 mayoral campaign to replace her. One month before her last day as mayor, Tom White of the *Lincoln Star* wrote a comprehensive retrospective of her lasting contributions to Lincoln—her "vision to push Lincoln from just a neat and clean Midwestern city to one of vitality, energy and greater equality. And to do that, she opened up government, promoted more responsible involvement and shared the power." Noted was Mom's simply stated philosophy of social responsibility: "Everyone can make the world a better place. You occupy some space so do something worthwhile with it—for other people."

Even in editorial endorsements of the mayoral candidates hoping to succeed her, comments about my mother's own performance nearly overshadowed the endorsements. For example, before the 1983 mayoral primary, the *Lincoln Journal*'s endorsement of Hampton and Luedtke as primary winners outlined the skills needed to be mayor—all in terms of skills my mother possessed: "The business of serving as mayor of Lincoln involves more than being a decisive, crackerjack executive and manager (as Helen Boosalis has been). It also requires a skill of cooperatively working with many groups, bringing people together, touching private sector bases, understanding enormously complex governmental programs and relationships, reacting compassionately and always showing informed, sensitive leadership. (Come to think of it, that, too, also pretty much describes Helen Boosalis' tenure.)"

So, too, a *Journal* editorial endorsing Luedtke for mayor in the general election began with a lengthy salute to my mother that seemed to be more an endorsement of *her* candidacy:

> Helen Boosalis has been a superb mayor of Lincoln. Not perfect, because no one can be. But very, very good. The record of quality achievements in Lincoln in which Mayor Boosalis has had a direct

hand thoroughly discredits her scare-tactic campaign foes of eight years ago. They paraded visions of grass covering the streets of a stunted, no-growth, overtaxed, anti-business town . . . should Boosalis be elected.

Instead, during the Boosalis years, Lincoln won All-America City recognition, once had the lowest unemployment of any metropolitan area in the nation, can point to balanced private growth with public partnership and enjoys a downtown so unlike the shabby national model as to constantly provoke visitor wonder and admiration. Helen Boosalis thus leaves a benchmark combining high activism, humanitarianism and fiscal conservatism. Which is a tough act to follow.

And how did such editorial assessment jibe with citizen approval ratings? In 1980, after five years as mayor, Mom's approval rating was 61 percent, disapproval 27 percent. Midway through her second term, her approval rating was even higher at 70 percent, disapproval 21 percent— to which she responded, "I guess I'm pleased but I'm always working to improve. We're here for one reason, to serve the people, and if people have a good perception of that, I'm pleased obviously. But it's not enough and I'm going to work harder to make it better."

What does make a good mayor? In a syndicated column at the time, humorist Andy Rooney compared mayors and governors: "Mayors almost never grow up to be president, the way a lot of governors have in the past, but mayors are often more interesting people. Governors, even when they're faking it, are more likely to act like statesmen. Mayors have to get right in there and wrestle with the bears." My mother certainly wrestled with more than her share of bears and often pinned more than her share. To do that day after day and to take it on with more confidence than fear required a clear sense of purpose and mission. Her purpose, in a word, was the people—to represent them, involve them, serve them.

What did my mother identify as the qualities of a good mayor? In her second term she told a reporter that the ideal mayor cares and is interested in the entire community, has the ability to work with diverse groups, and encourages participation from all types of people. What she said about political power appears self-evident and yet sets a standard that only some in public office seem to meet: "Elected officials should use the power vested in them only for the public good." When asked at the time to describe her own best and worst qualities, the mayor answered in rare personal terms: "Sometimes I'm very blunt but I am very honest. I listen and I'm fair in examining issues thoroughly. And I'm a pretty good organizer because I always want to get things done."

My mother seemed more comfortable with questions about her accomplishments than about personal qualities that made her a good mayor. A year into her second term, she said she was most proud of opening up city government to the people and of helping to revitalize neighborhoods and *downtown. I suspect those achievements still led her list at the end of her tenure.

"Politician" is not a word Mom would have used to describe herself; she seemed to find the concept rather distasteful. Yet, politician she was in the best sense of the word: "Helen may not regard herself as primarily a politician, but reporters and observers who have watched her for the last eight years tell you she has mastered the art form," wrote reporter Tom White. "She's coy without being dishonest, open but never spills the beans, shrewd but not shrill. She knows when to stand tough and when to duck. Most of all, she's everywhere, shaking hands, talking to people, celebrating moments of success, pointing out the positive. She has an uncanny knack of getting people to give what they can and to feel good about it."

A range of those with whom my mother shared political battles—not all on the same side—gave opinions of her public office service in an *Omaha World-Herald* retrospective on March 16, 1997, fourteen years after she left the mayor's office. Sue Bailey, her old League of Women Voters and city council compatriot, called her "the most dedicated public servant I've ever seen. She just enjoys herself. I guess that's her secret. I think she sees decision-making and problem solving as fun." Stan Matzke, whom Mom defeated in the 1979 mayor's race, described her as "a marvelously committed, intelligent woman. She's honest, hardworking and sincere." And according to Bob Sikyta, council chairman during her first term and one of her most frequent adversaries, "She is a lady you'd like to have next door as your neighbor. If you were in trouble, you'd want Helen on your side. She's not a talker. She's a doer."

Almost twenty-five years after Mom left city hall, her local and national colleagues paint for me a still-vibrant picture of her leadership as mayor. In Lincoln, John Rosenow of the Arbor Day Foundation told me, "During Helen's years as mayor, I witnessed the widespread good feeling that came from having a mayor who was emotionally and intellectually engaged and committed to doing the right thing for the city. That was a fabulous thing—for citizens to feel so good about their city. Whether or not a given issue had broad support to start with, citizens knew Helen would take it on if she thought it was the right thing to do."

And in Washington DC, U.S. senator George Voinovich of Ohio said, "In the mayor's office, there's not a Republican way or a Democratic way to do it—there's a right way and a wrong way. . . . Helen's sincerity about what she was doing was inspiring. She didn't go through the motions—when she got involved with something she was genuine and serious and everyone knew it—no game playing, no hidden motive. She was straight out and open, and that gave people a sense of comfort and confidence."

On a long drive from Lincoln to Chicago in 2001, I asked my mother what she thought were the most important attributes for serving in public office, now that she had been out of the mayor's office for almost twenty years. Her answer, which I jotted down at the next rest stop, sounded to me like a description of the attributes she had demonstrated as mayor. But I doubt Mom would have answered the same way had I asked her to describe herself—then her list would have been much shorter, more modest and matter-of-fact.

- Courage, willingness to take risks
- Knowledge and preparation
- Commitment to hard work
- Creativity
- Integrity
- Ability to bring people together
- Appointing bright people who are not afraid to challenge
- Letting others help and sharing credit
- Showing enthusiasm—it's infectious

- Building a strong base of support through an enlightened, informed, and involved citizenry

When we got back in the car, I wanted to know more about her notion of risk taking, since that has always seemed to me an intimidating
part of serving in public office, where risks are public and so are failures
that sometimes occur after taking risks. Mom thought for a moment
and said, "What's always made risk taking fairly simple for me was that
the risks I took were in and for the public interest only—not for my own
personal or political gain. Besides, actions that appear to be risky often
are not—when you step back and think about it, there is really only one
right course of action." I have reflected often on Mom's words about
risk taking—not just in the political context but also in life. Part of her
comfort with taking risks was her attitude toward failure. She once told
a journalist that she was not afraid of failing: "I don't have a big ego. If
I've done my best and I fail, I can let it go. It doesn't bother me."

In one of Mom's last newspaper interviews before leaving the may-
or's office, *Journal* reporter David Swartzlander noted her 72 percent
approval *rating in Lincoln public opinion polls and suggested that she
had become one of the most popular mayors in Lincoln's history and
a role model for other women. "Legacies and role models—all that
stuff is embarrassing to me," my mother responded. "I'm a people's
rights activist. I strongly believe people should have an opportunity to
do what they're most capable of doing." Swartzlander then asked how
she wanted to be remembered. "As someone who really cares about
people," she said. "As someone who really listens to people, anyone and
everyone. And that I've had a little hand in continuing to build the kind
of city the people really want it to be."

A few days before handing over the mayor's office to her successor,
Roland Luedtke, my mother wrote a condolence letter to Mrs. George
Hansen, wife of the man she had chosen as police chief in her first test
of office eight years earlier. Upon learning of George Hansen's death
in her final days as mayor, Mom reflected on her earliest days in the
letter to his widow: "I learned so much from George, I can't begin to
enumerate the lessons. He was a top-notch administrator and, as an
inexperienced and brand new one, I soaked up all I could of his con-

siderable talent and expertise. Even though I was sorry to see you and George leave Lincoln, I was grateful that you were here during a very critical time for me."

On Friday, May 13, 1983—a "truly unlucky day" for supporters of Lincoln mayor Helen Boosalis—a Mayor's Appreciation Committee held a celebration of Mom's twenty-four years of elected service. Co-chairing the event were Gates Minnick, CEO of DuTeau Chevrolet, and Coleen *Seng, neighborhood activist in the University Place Community Organization—appropriately representing both business and neighborhood appreciation of the mayor. The committee had no trouble getting donations for the reception, which was expected to host "more than 2,000 people."

But far more than the expected number showed up to thank their mayor. My mother stood—her shoes eventually abandoned—greeting and hugging more than five thousand "school children, politicians, firefighters, friends and just plain citizens who stood in line for hours to say 'thanks' for her twenty-four years of service to the city." She was moved to see even Larry Enersen, architect of so much of the city's beauty, slowly make his way up the steps to thank her in the last days of his terminal illness. The thanks were mutual.

It was Mom's kind of party—guests from all generations, all walks of life. The lobby of the County-City Building was filled with more than three thousand helium balloons saying "Thanks, Helen!" Restaurants donated tons of food, and Greek pastries were made by friends from the Greek Orthodox church. The mayor joined in Greek line dancing as well as with other neighborhood ethnic dancers and singers. Brightly colored banners hung from the second-floor balcony bearing the names of the city's sixteen neighborhood organizations, all of which had thrived with the mayor's encouragement. Donated flowers everywhere and displays of pictures "showing the humorous and reflective moments in her long career" vied for space with the people who continued to flow through the doors. In short, it was "a tribute to the type of administration Boosalis said she wanted to be remembered as striving for—responsive, open, people-oriented."

An eight-page newspaper publication titled "Thanks, Helen!" (produced compliments of Journal-Star Printing Company) provided an

45. The mayor greets five thousand well-wishers as she leaves office

affectionate retrospective of the mayor's contributions to her city and captured the vibrancy, energy, and humor of "the people's *mayor" in a collage of photographs—Helen boarding a city bus, exiting the Phantom jet, dedicating the Cornhusker Hotel, staking a campaign yard sign, meeting with President Carter, riding a fire truck, reading to schoolchildren, using her sewing machine, and on and on. *Lincoln Journal* manag-

46. Mike, Beth, and Helen at the mayor's farewell appreciation party

ing editor Gil Savery's introduction to the retrospective piece captured some of the rich and lasting legacy Mom left her fellow citizens:

> Mayor Helen switched from local legislator and framer of ordinances to an administrator who gave meaning to "strong" in the mayor's office. So her administration was marked by strengthened roles for her directors, but even stronger accountability to the mayor's office. Neighborhood voices grew and citizen advisory groups helped shape city policy, downtown beautification became a reality, the Centrum was built and Cornhusker Square started. City purse strings became a bit tattered from her tugs implementing tight fiscal policy. So effective was Helen's administration of this All-America City that she became known nationwide and was elected president of the U.S. Conference of Mayors. The luster of her tenure places a heavy burden on successors.

I can't imagine the mix of emotions as Mom wrote her last letter from the mayor's office on May 16, 1983, to thank her citizen "Friends" for the mayor's appreciation celebration two days earlier and for their larger commitment to the community. "In a few hours I will leave the Mayors' office. I leave with confidence knowing that this city is composed of citizens like you who will give your all to the betterment of our community. I am sure you will provide the same level of support to our new Mayor and City Council. Together, we can demonstrate that we are equal to the challenges that lie ahead for our city."

Together, with citizens. That's what my mother's era as mayor had been all about.

Eight years after she took her solemn oath of office as mayor of Lincoln, I know my mother, Helen Boosalis, had lived up to her mayor's oath and fulfilled as well the Athenian Oath of ancient Greece:

> *We will never bring disgrace on this our City by an act of dishonesty or cowardice. We will fight for the ideals and Sacred Things of the City both alone and with many. We will revere and obey the City's laws, and will do our best to incite a like reverence and respect in those above us who are prone to annul them or set them at naught. We will strive increasingly to quicken the public's sense of civic duty. Thus in all these ways we will transmit this City, not only not less, but greater and more beautiful than it was transmitted to us.*

Trail's End
November 1986

How do you calm yourself in anticipation of a yes-or-no verdict, all-or-nothing jackpot, win-or-lose election, after wanting and working for and thinking of little else for months?

The last few days of the governor's campaign in 1986 were mostly a blur. We took Michael out of his first grade class and Christopher out of preschool so that the four of us could be together in Nebraska for election night. Max's nerves were out of control, so I tried to steer clear of him and let him manage the boys, who were inhaling the air's excitement and behaving as if on a massive sugar high.

My own nervousness typically translates into a quest for control, driving me to overprepare for whatever situation is causing the nervousness or to steep myself in useless information so it feels more familiar and less scary. To drown out anxiety about what could go wrong before the election, or what else the campaign (especially I) should or shouldn't have done, or what to do or say or feel if my mom actually lost, I tried controlling my racing mind by going over election statistics I had picked up in the campaign.

Here's a sampling: Nebraska's population in 1986 was 1.6 million, with about 850,000 registered voters. Therefore, if the voter turnout on Tuesday were a record 71 percent, or 600,000, as predicted by Nebraska's secretary of state, then we only had to get a measly 300,001 votes for Mom. Surely I had personally seen 300,001 friendly, supportive faces in the last seven months. Then, let's see, 51 percent of the registered voters were Republican and 42 percent were Democrats. (That's why, as Neil

Oxman said, the object of our campaign plan was "to hold onto Democrats, get a reasonable share of Independents, and not get completely shut out by Republicans because the state has such an overwhelming number of Republicans.") How many of those 51 percent registered Republicans and 42 percent registered Democrats would come out to vote? No, I thought, these percentages were not consoling statistics on election day. Move on.

Eighty percent of the population lived in the eastern third of the state, primarily in Omaha, Lincoln, Bellevue (site of the Strategic Air Command and Offutt Air Force Base), and Grand Island (which lost its ranking every Nebraska football Saturday when the 76,000 fans in Lincoln's Memorial Stadium made the stadium the third-most-populated site in the state). Now I was off track, but how soothing it was to think about non-election trivia.

I still couldn't get the 51–42 split between Republican and Democratic registered voters out of my head. I tried to focus on the positive history of Democratic candidates for governor who had beaten the party odds. The Nebraska governorship had rotated frequently between the two major parties since 1900—there had been fifteen Republican governors and ten Democratic governors (of varying lengths in office). That sounded more encouraging.

I moved on to think about the Democrats who had won five out of the last six statewide races for the U.S. Senate and the governorship, even with all those registered Republican voters. And Democrats had won a miraculous seven out of the last nine governor's races, which had produced three Democratic and two Republican governors; moreover, both Republican governors were defeated as incumbents when they sought a second term. Sounding better all the time, Mom's race seeming more and more winnable.

Then I focused on the very last governor's election. Democrat Bob Kerrey won the 1982 election by 7,233 votes—only 50.6 percent—and he had won in less than a third of the state's counties (twenty-nine of ninety-three). But the point was, he won! Voter turnout had been the key. If Republican incumbent Charles Thone had gotten four more votes per precinct, he would have been reelected. And that made me think about the Boosalis campaign's field operations—surely they were prepared to squeeze four more votes out of every precinct. Surely, but what if—and off I would go again.

So that was the state of my whirling mind as the hours ticked by toward election day—November 4, 1986. I don't know what my mother did to stay calm, but she was busy darting here and there for one more appearance, one more handshake, one more vote, so I guess she had no time to fret. Besides, fretting is not her thing. I tried not to pay attention to prognosticators, who had kicked into high gear, but it was like trying to ignore a box of chocolates that may or may not have any caramels left.

Voter turnout was predicted to be at a record level based on the notorious two-woman feature of the race, but some thought the controversial referendum on school consolidation and financing (LB662) would also draw more voters out. I went into worry overdrive when I learned that Fred Lockwood, member of the Republican State Central Committee, found encouraging the prospect of more voters turning out for the LB662 referendum. "Quite frankly, that's the biggest plus at this stage for Kay Orr." I found a fellow fretter in Gary Goldberg, Democratic chair of the Third Congressional District, where LB662's mandatory school consolidation was especially disliked; he was concerned that voters might not distinguish between their opposition to LB662 and their choice for governor.

I preferred reading more encouraging predictions, such as former Democratic congressman John Cavanaugh's prognosis that Orr had campaigned negatively against Boosalis for too long. That gave Orr, he said, an initial lead but did not in the end give voters positive reasons to vote for her. That's right, that's right—I silently screamed to all the undecided voters.

To calm my nerves I taped above the bathroom mirror the Lincoln papers' positive endorsements of my mother. The *Star*, after praising her many accomplishments as mayor, based its endorsement of Boosalis for governor on "her philosophy of government as both an economic catalyst and the protector of the people's interests. . . . Helen's vigor, toughness and personal warmth are rare in one individual and are well tailored to the demands of the state's top job." The *Journal*, too, reminded readers of my mother's impressive record and tough fiscal choices as mayor, her national leadership, and a host of other reasons for endorsing her as governor: "Boosalis' demonstrated leadership style consistently seems to cast a wider constituency net. . . . [A]n effective Governor must work persuasively with diverse constituencies, forming coalitions and gaining consensus. . . . Behind Helen's upbeat chemistry and vitality is a proven, tested substance and an extraordinary talent for providing service."

I couldn't keep from sneaking a few peeks at some of the Orr endorsements as well, such as the *Grand Island Independent*: "We don't think that Helen Boosalis would be a spendthrift governor, any more than is the incumbent Democrat Bob Kerrey. But we do think that Boosalis' constituency—unions, teachers, educators, urbanites—are a lot more demanding of services than those backing Orr. We also think that Orr has better rapport with business and professional people, and therefore the greater potential to help reverse the present difficulties." But I couldn't bring myself to read the *Omaha World-Herald*'s endorsement of Orr.

On the last full day of the campaign, November 3, Mom and Dad boarded a small, private plane for a thousand-mile swing through the state with stops in Scottsbluff, North Platte, Grand Island, South Sioux City, Omaha, Beatrice, and back to Lincoln. Joining the fourteen-hour final campaign swing were Frank Morrison (governor, 1961–67), U.S. senator Jim Exon (governor, 1971–79), Lieutenant Governor Don McGinley (Mom's running mate), and state senator Chris *Beutler (one of Mom's opponents in the gubernatorial primary). Accompanying this "wealth of Democratic statehouse experience" in a second plane were members of the press, including Kathleen Rutledge of the *Lincoln Journal* and David Kotok of the *Omaha World-Herald*.

Between campaign stops, former governor Morrison, with his droll humor and Walter Matthau–like deadpan delivery, regaled the politicos with stories of past campaigns. My mother chimed in with a story of once sharing a platform with Governor Morrison in the early 1960s when she was on the city council. She was seated next to the governor at the head table, which was on risers. Waiting to speak, my mother sat, canary-like in a stovepipe yellow straw hat and matching silk dress, with the imposing (six-foot three) governor towering next to her. Suddenly, out of the corner of her eye, she glimpsed the governor's hulking torso falling toward her, as if in slow motion, and simultaneously felt the risers collapsing beneath them. On the floor in a tangle of chairs, Morrison on top of Mom, her yellow hat askew, they couldn't stop laughing at the ridiculous scene they presented. Now in the small plane flying around the state to help elect as governor the woman he nearly crushed twenty-five years earlier, Morrison added to Mom's story: "Big as I am, I was afraid I'd hurt the lady. You can tell how far I'd advanced in life because there I was, caught in this position with a lovely young woman, and what did I say? 'I'm sorry!'"

The traveling band of political heavyweights spoke on my mother's behalf at stop after stop, gaining momentum fueled by the large, enthusiastic crowds who turned out to cheer their next governor. In Omaha, the election's key battleground, the powerhouse group added Governor Kerrey to their ranks. Kerrey rallied the crowd to turn out to vote for Helen Boosalis the next day, his message reinforced by the "Nebraska-Gram" that the Boosalis campaign delivered to voters across the state:

NEBRASKA-GRAM NEBRASKA-GRAM NEBRASKA-GRAM

TUESDAY IS ELECTION DAY AND IT IS CRITICAL THAT YOU TAKE
THE TIME TO VOTE FOR HELEN BOOSALIS.

REMEMBER, IN 1982—I WAS ELECTED BY AN AVERAGE OF ONLY
FOUR VOTES PER PRECINCT.

IF YOU ARE CONCERNED ABOUT THE FUTURE OF NEBRASKA,
PLEASE JOIN WITH ME IN VOTING FOR HELEN BOOSALIS.

GOVERNOR BOB KERREY

Having squeezed every moment from this final, grueling effort, Mom seemed calm going into election day, elated by the positive feel of the last day of campaigning. As the small plane landed in Lincoln she told the others she had found the jam-packed trip "relaxing." Frank Morrison turned to her and said, "Helen, you have a strange way of relaxing."

On election day, Mom and Dad and I crept out of the house at 6:00 a.m., the boys and Max still asleep, to meet campaign volunteers for the 6:30 shift change at the Burlington Northern shops. The three of us had done the same daybreak campaigning at Burlington on election day in my mother's first campaign for mayor. That was such a simpler time, I mused. We had only to reach Lincoln voters then, the same voters who had come to know my mother through her four terms on the city council, who would call her to complain about an issue or stop her in the grocery store to thank her. There was such a personal quality to campaigning then—a one-on-one relationship with voters, supporters and critics alike.

Armed with Boosalis for Governor brochures, we waited for the hordes of departing Burlington employees just as we had waited eleven years earlier, in 1975, wearing our Boosalis for Mayor buttons. But I was older and, if not wiser, then somewhat jaded in my view of statewide electoral politics—where exorbitant media advertising trumps personal grassroots campaigning, consultant-sculpted message overshadows candidate discourse on issues, and raising money eclipses all other campaign efforts.

A few more cynical thoughts breezed by me before the worker throngs emerged from the railroad shops, and then the familiar election-day rituals began. I glanced over at Mom, who looked as fresh and upbeat as on the day she announced her candidacy for governor nine months earlier, even though she had been fighting a respiratory illness for weeks. I, on the other hand, longed for sleep and hoped that adrenaline would carry me through the day.

Mom and Dad went to vote, surrounded by cameras and reporters. I can't remember how I spent the rest of the day—whether I made any more campaign stops with my folks, whether I went to Boosalis headquarters as I had for the last seven months to help with last-minute details, or whether I was just too nervous for any of that and went back to the house to prepare the boys for the long day and evening ahead. Part of preparing the boys involved significant bribes for good behavior during their Grami's election night. I hoped to avoid any major meltdowns—theirs or mine—in front of television cameras.

The six of us—Mom, Dad, Max, Michael, Christopher, and I—went for an early dinner before driving to Omaha for the first returns. I missed Gram, who had been there for Mom's mayoral election nights; she had

47. Mike and Helen Boosalis cast their votes for governor in the November 4, 1986, general election

died the year before. I doubt that any of us ate much, and certainly not my mother, who spent the entire dinner greeting well-wishers who came to the table. Our collective mood was positive, even high spirited—early exit polls showed my mother in good position. We drove off to Omaha, our expectations high—or in the case of my father and Max, as high as their anxious selves would allow.

We went to Omaha first because the returns from densely populated Douglas and Sarpy counties historically had come in first, closely followed by results from Lancaster County, where Lincoln is located. Conventional wisdom said that if my mother were to have a comfortable early lead in Douglas and Sarpy counties, she might win; on the other hand, if Orr were ahead in Omaha or close at that point, she would likely win.

Shortly after the polls closed, we walked into Omaha's Old Mill Holiday Inn for the post-election party. It was early and the crowd had not yet grown, but anticipatory excitement had already arrived in the form of streamers and balloons and huge signs and camera platforms and television lights and scurrying campaign staff and volunteers readying the large hall for the night's festivities. The boys' eyes grew wide at what looked like the makings for a gigantic birthday party, and I caught my breath as it sunk in that by the end of the evening, Mom could very well be governor.

Then I saw the mayor of Omaha, Mike Boyle, down the foyer walking toward us. His eyes didn't look right to me, even as he smiled and hugged my mother. We bunched close to him, not to miss a word. He said it was very early with returns just coming in, and that Mom was ahead, but not by as much as they hoped to see in Omaha. We would have to wait it out for later returns, which he hoped would widen her lead. My mother reacted to Boyle's news optimistically, "It's a great way to start the night ahead, Mike. We're going to do fine." My stomach hurt.

People began to pour into the hall, and Mom was swept into the teeming congratulatory mass. Assembled on the podium platform was a who's who of state Democratic officials, and each delivered a rousing on-to-victory speech. U.S. senator Ed Zorinsky bounded to the microphone: "Helen is coming along like a steamroller! The scent of victory is in the air!" Her running mate, Don McGinley, reminded the crowd of the election night four years earlier, which ended in the "Kerrey-Mc-Ginley landslide of six-tenths of 1%."

Campaign co-chair Ben Nelson introduced "the next governor of Nebraska," and my mother took the stage to unbridled ovations. The crowd sensed a win, and Boosalis supporters basked in their own participation in it. My mother's remarks were brief. I only remember her comparing the culmination of the nine-month campaign, which began on February 5, 1986, to her experience thirty-eight years earlier when her "daughter, Mary Beth, was born." This was not yet a victory speech, but she "exuded confidence that she would win." When she finished she stepped back where my dad and I were standing, and the three of us joined hands overhead while the crowd roared.

On to Lincoln to the election-night party at the Cornhusker Hotel, which had played such a significant role in revitalizing downtown during my mother's second term as mayor. With the polls now closed a good while, the Cornhusker ballroom was already overflowing with celebrating supporters when we walked in. But "the complexion of the returns, favorable when she left Omaha, changed by the time she reached Lincoln." Undaunted, my mother circulated through the ballroom for at least ninety minutes, shaking hands, accepting hugs and kisses, thanking nearly each and every one of her supporters for their help. It became less and less likely that late returns from the Third Congressional District out west would turn the numbers around. About midnight, Mom and I slipped out of the ballroom to confer with state Democratic chairman Tom Monaghan.

It was over. With most poll returns in, Helen Boosalis was losing 52 percent to *48 percent. She took a deep breath and went back to the ballroom where she and my dad stepped up to the podium platform. I found Max and the boys, grabbed Christopher in my arms while Max carried Michael, and the four of us joined my folks at the podium. Christopher sucked his thumb, Michael covered his eyes from the glare of television lights and flashbulbs, Max bit his lip, and I tried harder than I ever have in my life not to cry as my mother began her concession speech at 12:20 a.m. on November 5: "We have conducted an open, honest, forthright campaign. But my dear, good friends, it has become increasingly apparent as the returns come in that the people of Nebraska have made their choice for governor. . . . I hope each of you will pledge to help the governor these next four years. During this campaign we ran as representatives of two parties, but we're all Nebraskans. And we're going to do as Nebraskans have always done—we're going to work together—Republicans and Democrats—to make life in our state the best it can possibly be."

"Smiling and dry-eyed," she thanked her supporters and said they were a "class act" throughout her campaign. But on this seventh and last of her election nights, the truly class act was my mother. I cannot imagine to this day how she was able to concede as she did—with genuineness, acceptance, grace. Even the *Omaha World-Herald*, which had far from supported her candidacy, praised Mom's poise on election night:

48. Helen Boosalis delivers concession speech

"Helen Boosalis ended her campaign for governor of Nebraska with class and dignity. . . . To swallow the hurt of defeat and proceed without displaying bitterness is the mark of a leader. . . . Mrs. Boosalis has earned her spot in the history books, and her gracious election night performance enhances her reputation."

I tried to fall in with Mom's example, but all I wanted was to leave the Cornhusker, run away, escape from everyone's woebegone expressions and well-meaning sympathy. Surely it was a bad dream and I would soon wake to the euphoria and promise of just a few hours ago. But my misery felt too real even for a nightmare. My mother's sister Tina gave me a comforting hug, and I burst into tears and had to flee the room.

I hated Kay Orr and her stupid campaign and all campaigns and politics in general. None of it was worthy of my mother, and the people who voted for Orr would get just what they deserved. So went my election-night gnashing and moaning, which diminished only slightly over the next several days and eventually healed over, but with a stubborn scar.

I couldn't bear to read the postmortems, the endless analysis of what Orr's campaign did right and what my mother's did wrong. The newspapers carried nothing but that for weeks, whether I cared to read them or not. The voting breakdown showed that Orr won by running nearly even in traditionally Democratic Douglas County (Omaha) and by carrying most of the typically Republican small towns and rural western counties.

Orr knew she couldn't carry Lincoln, a Boosalis stronghold, and she said she had concentrated more attention on typically Democratic Omaha, especially in south Omaha. After the election, Orr felt that two positions helped her run nearly even in Omaha: her pro-life position and her fiscal conservatism. She claimed that her opposition to LB662 helped further define the difference between the candidates on taxes.

Early in the campaign, when the two candidates first took their positions on LB662, public opinion polls showed that more people supported than opposed it. By the time of the election, however, two voters wanted the 1985 legislation repealed for every voter who still supported it. There was disagreement whether it was the mandatory school consolidation part of the bill or the one-cent sales tax increase for public education that caused the measure's defeat by referendum. But in either case, most agreed that LB662 brought its opponents to the polls in great numbers—both those who wanted to keep local control of small school districts and those who opposed increased sales taxes to finance public education—causing the high voter turnout (68 percent) in Nebraska's *1986 election.

Did the overwhelming number of voters who opposed LB662 (66 percent) also provide the narrow winning margin for fellow LB662 opponent and gubernatorial candidate Kay Orr? It's impossible to know for sure, but much post-election analysis concluded that what sank my mother's candidacy was the overall issue of taxes: the *perception* of her support for increased sales and income taxes touted by Orr's television tax ads, compounded by her support of LB662. Some pundits agreed that Orr's attack ads distorting Mom's position on taxes had precipitated the drop in Boosalis support in September, but that the Boosalis campaign had come roaring back to even the race and commandeered the momentum going into the election—but ultimately fell just short on time.

"Taxes was it. We were not able to get the tax increase label off," lamented Tom Monaghan. "The tax issue hurt us all over, and especially in Omaha. It's going to be interesting. We will be watching to see how Kay manages the state these next four years without a tax increase." (Ironically, Orr would lose the governorship four years later to my mother's campaign co-chairman Ben Nelson, whose challenge to Orr's first-term record as governor included two key issues: her support of a proposed low-level nuclear waste dump and—her tax restructuring plan, which resulted in tax *increases.)

The day after the election, Lincoln editorial writers further analyzed Omaha's critical role in the fate of Democratic candidates. "The election of 1986 once more demonstrated the shallowness of the Democratic base in Douglas County, despite its overwhelming Democratic registration," the *Journal* emphasized. "Time after time since World War II, majoritarian Douglas County Democrats have failed their party's nominee for President, the national legislature, and governor, either with weak support or plain rejection, as was the case again Tuesday."

Governor Kerrey, who had come from behind just four years earlier to narrowly defeat Orr's mentor, Governor Thone, said that my mother "ran a spectacular campaign and almost won. In my judgment, Helen Boosalis was an exceptional candidate who ran an exceptional campaign. She was able to come from behind to make the race close on her personal strengths." Kerrey pointed out that Democrats are at a disadvantage when running for an open governor's seat in Nebraska because Republican registered voters so outnumber Democrats—both Kerrey's and Exon's gubernatorial wins came against Republican incumbents. In races against incumbents, Democrats "can run on the issues."

Don Walton's post-election analysis in the *Star* focused on the unique tone and new records set by the historic campaign: "The gubernatorial race that Boosalis and Orr waged this year was the most vigorous in my memory. Both candidates left campaign workers panting. Orr always set a brisk pace. But Boosalis is world class—a dynamo overflowing with self-renewing energy that somehow seems to build on itself, ever expanding and growing. In a way, I guess, Helen Boosalis functions sorta like a nuclear explosion—with much better results. But if you're a campaign aide, especially one assigned to keep up with her, it must be awfully frightening." Walton continued with a focus on Mom's fund-raising success: "Besides smashing the gender barrier and establishing a new energy standard, Nebraska's two gubernatorial candidates broke some other new ground. . . . The most surprising aspect of the campaign to me was Boosalis' ability to raise big money. A million bucks. Democrats can't do that. Especially if they're not incumbents. But Helen Boosalis did."

Had I been willing to read the *newspapers the day after the excruciating election result, I would have found some solace in the *Journal's* editorial: "In defeat, Democrat Helen Boosalis rates cheers for her terrific campaign. That she is an extraordinary person unselfishly devoted to the public welfare is a fact established long ago. If the literary description of the 'perfect knight' can be brushed up, Boosalis is one of the rare ones on whom it fits." And the hometown paper itself took comfort, as I did, in the level of Mom's support from Lincoln voters: "Beloved is not a bad word to use either. A telling measure of Boosalis' status in her home community was the . . . 60%–40% margin she gained in Lancaster County, also Kay Orr's home for nearly a quarter century. . . . One can't imagine Helen Boosalis going into retirement. . . . Leadership such as hers is a rare commodity, and of those to whom much is given, much is usually asked."

We all survived the crushing disappointment of the 1986 gubernatorial election night, my mother faring the best of all of us. I crawled back to Evanston with Max and the boys, where we put our normal lives back together and got used to living in one household again, though I fought a daily desire to pull the covers over my *head.

Their house quiet except for the phone ringing every few minutes with either consoling words or requests for interviews, my mom and dad hit the road for a change of scene and much-needed rest. They stopped overnight at a small motel in Nebraska City where, my dad told me later, "the lady clerk changed from a friendly to an unfriendly disposition when she saw the name Boosalis on the registration pad— evidently she was a strong supporter of the other political party."

The next day they played golf at a municipal course, but they weren't in the mood to enjoy the game and quit playing long before the eighteenth hole. My father told me years later that on that afternoon he saw my mother shed her only tears over losing the governor's race, breaking down as he had never seen her do. Her deep sorrow, he said, came not from losing the election but from letting down all her supporters, campaign workers, and friends.

That made perfect sense to me. I knew that my mother's pursuit of elected office was not a grab for personal power but an outgrowth of her faith in people and her desire to involve them in their own governance. It wasn't personal ambition but a desire to give people their voice that finally prevailed in each of her last-minute decisions to run for office. It didn't at all surprise me that letting people down was sadder for her than her sense of personal *loss.

After leaving Nebraska City, my folks drove on to Independence, Missouri, to visit Harry Truman's Presidential Museum and Library. Relieved at Mom's lift in spirits after spending the afternoon reading Truman's life history, my dad surmised that she could identify with the trials that inevitably come with choosing a political life. After leaving Independence to return home to Lincoln, he said, my mother has not since dwelled on her electoral loss.

Mom must have also found comfort knowing that while she may have narrowly lost the gubernatorial election, she did so with her gloves on and her integrity intact. For my dad and me, the closeness of the race just made it harder to take, and the two of us continued for years to pick at the scab of defeat with disillusionment and anger. In contrast, my mother did not wallow in what might have been but rather threw herself into a score of non-elected volunteer efforts, back where she had begun her long, successful path in public *office.

The only indication that my mother was feeling worse about the governor's race than she let on was her avoidance of post-election interviews. She must have needed time to digest her loss and recuperate from the demanding campaign. Six months after the election she agreed to sit down with the *Star*'s Don Walton over a 7:30 a.m. breakfast at a neighborhood restaurant. ("Helen's a morning person. But then she's an afternoon person and a night person, too.") Walton reported that while Helen had not won the previous November, she was going strong with her service on national and local boards and her frequent speaking engagements in and out of state. On the subject of the election she responded only briefly, he noted, preferring to talk about the

49. Helen and Mike at home, post–governor's race

future and ending that phase of the interview with "a conclusive nod of the head." She characterized her gubernatorial bid as "a positive experience—only the ending wasn't."

"Helen's energy level . . . remains in overdrive," Walton observed, "and at 67, she continues to grow." Six months after her disappointing defeat my mother's optimism was intact, her resilience apparent. "Personal growth and service—those are the important things," she told Walton. "I want to help encourage people to go beyond what they think they're capable of doing. That's what they did with me. You can accomplish what you didn't dream was possible. Take a little risk. Be prepared. Set your goals high."

The interview concluded, Walton observed my mother as she stopped at several tables to respond to greetings and thanks for her public service. And then, on that day more than twenty years ago, as every day since, "Helen Boosalis walks out into another bright morning in her life."

Chapter Nine

Life ~~After~~ Is Politics

1983–2007

"If Helen has a political philosophy it could be described in one word: community. She is the embodiment of community. Helen believes everyone should participate in community building, and she made sure every person was welcome in that effort."—F. GREGORY HAYDEN, professor of economics, University of Nebraska–Lincoln

"Helen brought a level of enthusiasm to office that most public officials don't have—a curiosity and an enthusiasm for the challenge. She genuinely wanted to make a difference and approached her whole career that way. You know it's real because since then, she continues to bring that enthusiasm to so many good causes."—RICH BAILEY, retired chairman, Bailey Lauerman Marketing/ Communications

When my mother announced her bid for reelection as mayor in 1979, she surprised many by simultaneously declaring that if elected she would not seek a third mayoral term. Why in 1983 did she feel compelled to stick with that four-year-old promise? It isn't unusual for politicians to reconsider their earlier statements of intent to step down based on changed circumstances, unfinished business, or a reluctance (unstated) to give up power. Others willingly leave office for the proverbial opportunity to "spend more time with family"—a few because they mean it, some because they have read the tea leaves of a losing campaign ahead.

None of the typical motivations or excuses for voluntarily leaving elected office seemed to apply to Mom. After two terms, her popularity and effectiveness as mayor were not waning, nor did she feel stuck with a stale promise to step down. Despite the urging of supporters—my father chief among them—to run for a third term, when Mom left the mayor's office on May 16, 1983, she had "no regrets about my decision not to run for re-election. Eight years is long enough for anyone to serve as mayor." Not only did she feel that eight years was enough time to accomplish her goals, but she feared that a longer term could lead to satisfaction with the status quo. Perhaps the self-imposed finite term as Lincoln's chief executive had spurred her boundless energy and drive to get things done, which had in turn inspired those around her to step up the pace. Add to that the momentum from the increased involvement of citizens, and Mom's eight years as mayor proved enough to "make a good city better."

NEBRASKA DEPARTMENT ON AGING: DIRECTOR

In any event, Mom had no time for second thoughts as she began her new job as director of the Nebraska Department on Aging on June 1, 1983, just two weeks after leaving the mayor's office. Appointed by Governor Bob Kerrey in the first year of his new administration, my mother became the first permanent director since the state legislature had granted department status to the agency on aging in 1982. In announcing his appointment of Helen Boosalis to his cabinet, Governor Kerrey said, "I know she will bring a special sensitivity to the problems of local government. Moreover, her national reputation will be a special benefit to all the people of Nebraska, and especially to its older citizens."

Governor Kerrey's appointment of the barely retired mayor presented "the perfect marriage—an unqualified asset for the Kerrey administration, a most appropriate service for the mayor, and a 10-strike for the Department on Aging." It was reported that when Mom learned an acquaintance had asked my dad if his wife was being "put out to pasture," my mother said, "When you see him again, you tell him that's exactly why I'm going to take this job—so that people won't be put out to pasture who don't want to be put out to pasture."

While her new responsibilities were far narrower than those she had as mayor, Mom brought to her state executive position the valuable administrative and fiscal management skills she had honed in the mayor's office. Years later, Bob Kerrey reflected on his appointment of my mother as director of the Nebraska Department on Aging: "Helen was such an exceptional executive and administrator, she could have filled any cabinet position. Given her undeserved anti-business reputation, poetic justice would have been to put her in charge of economic development."

The state's Department on Aging did not operate direct services for seniors but rather administered funding and monitored programs through eight area agencies. My mother viewed her major role as that of advocating on behalf of older Nebraskans. She relied on her capable department administrator, Patty Kuehl, to oversee department administrative operations so that Mom could speak to groups across the state about senior issues such as in-home services to prevent unnecessary and costly institutionalization, rising costs of health care, volunteer and paying jobs, housing options, increasing utility costs, nutrition, and transportation.

Mom's approach as director of the Department on Aging was inclusive, just as when she was mayor. In two years she visited more than 150 senior groups across the state, because "bringing people into the process is my method of governance. People should be part of the decisions that affect their lives." Everywhere she spoke, my mother encouraged seniors to participate in their communities however they could—through government, organizations, neighborhoods. She no longer held elected office, but her focus continued on citizen involvement in community, including senior citizen involvement. My mother utilized her experience and contacts from her mayoral years in her role as statewide advocate for seniors. In 1984, after a year in her new position, the *Star* reported the former mayor was "as effervescent about aging programs today as she was about streets and comprehensive plans in years past."

When asked if she was thinking of retirement after four or possibly eight years as director of the Department on Aging, my mother responded, "I just hope I have the choice. You don't retire just because you reach a certain age. There are people far more productive who are past 80 than others are at 45." Mom didn't retire, but she did resign her position after two and a half years to run for governor. Nor did she retire when she didn't win the governor's race in 1986. Nor is she yet fully retired at age eighty-eight.

AFTER THE GOVERNOR'S RACE: CONTINUING SERVICE

Retirement from public life did not follow my mother's losing the governor's race. Mom kept almost a full-time schedule through a broad array of volunteer leadership positions. The intensity of her eight years as Lincoln's chief executive, her subsequent tenure as director of a state agency, and her year's nonstop gubernatorial campaign all combined with her natural energy to keep her engine running on high idle. She welcomed new paths after the governor's campaign in 1986.

After twenty-four years in elected municipal office and a few more in appointed state office, my mother seemed to have no difficulty switching gears or adjusting to life after politics. Why? For Mom, politics is not separate from normal, everyday life. For her, different rules do not apply to the world of politics, nor does she think politicians should get to create their own special rules. She didn't believe that public office conferred power to elevate her wishes above others', but rather that it gave her the means to represent fairly the people's interests and involve them in their own governance.

Mom had learned over her quarter century of public service how best to wield the tools of public office to effect change and get things done, but she always knew that the real power resided in the people and not in her. That's why after the governor's race she was able to use or find or create other tools to advance the public good. It was only the setting that changed when she left public office—her public purpose did not.

Throughout her years in office my mother had done a lot of speaking to groups. Now she could accept even more invitations for speaking engagements, many about the critical importance of citizen participation in government. Averaging a few speeches a week in Lincoln and greater Nebraska, she also kept a busy travel schedule for out-of-state talks. Her visibility as former president of the U.S. Conference of Mayors and as a high-profile candidate in the country's first two-woman gubernatorial race made her a sought-after speaker for national meetings.

Mom was also in great demand to serve on local, state, and national boards, and she said yes to those causes in which she most believed. She brought new perspectives to her board service. By their nature, governing boards can become captive over time to narrower interests than those envisioned by an organization's mission; as in city government, having Helen Boosalis as a board member virtually guaranteed a board's opening up to new voices and outside perspectives.

Her style of asking probing questions of an organization's staff, soliciting input from those affected by its policies or service, and requesting current reasons to justify "the way things have always been done" opened boardroom doors to winds of change and new energy once she entered. Not a gadfly or disruptive force, my mother frequently stirs the pot. Her elected experience has often been unique on a board, and her commitment to openness and inclusion—giving others a voice—frequently changes board dynamics. While not always in agreement with my mother's positions, several board colleagues told me they appreciated livelier, meatier board meetings once Helen joined their boards.

AARP: CHAIRMAN OF THE BOARD

While still director of the Nebraska Department on Aging, my mother was appointed in 1985 to AARP's National Legislative Council, where she served for the next six years. The twenty-two-member council developed AARP's state and federal legislative public policy agenda for recommendation to the board of directors. It met regularly in Washington DC for briefings from congressional leaders, business, leading institutions, and government staff; the council also sought the input of AARP members through hearings held throughout the country.

Developing legislative policy must have been a refreshing change for Mom after traveling the combative campaign trail for governor. A forceful advocate for seniors during her tenure as state aging director, she brought a depth of knowledge to AARP's federal policy agenda focused on the health care system, retiree pension and health care benefits, long-term care, and Social Security and Medicare.

While she no longer held elected office, my mother did not leave her special brand of political leadership at the AARP doorstep. According to AARP's chief communications officer, Kevin Donnellan, "Helen brought to AARP a passion for broader issues beyond those directly affecting seniors. At AARP she continued to carry the same sense of responsibility for representing the interests of all people that she had when she was in elected office."

Wherever possible, Mom helped move the organization from a focus on traditional senior issues such as Social Security and Medicare to a broader range of issues also of concern to older people, including education, children in poverty, literacy, workforce issues, consumer protection, and campaign finance reform. She believed that AARP should use its tremendous power of over thirty-three million members to influence not only policy decisions affecting the lives of seniors today but also policies that would affect the legacy left to their children and grandchildren and reflect the desire of seniors to make the world a better place for future generations.

Donnellan described his respect for my mother's ability to champion advocacy issues—such as campaign finance reform—and to move them decisively to AARP's legislative policy agenda. He said that Mom would put an issue on the table in such a persuasive way that few could disagree without looking silly, and consensus on moving the issue forward would nearly always follow. Donnellan called this maneuver the "Boosalis approach" and said that twenty years later, AARP staff from my mother's era still utilize and refer to the "Boosalis approach."

My mother encouraged efforts to expand AARP's advocacy work and helped launch the organization's Public Policy Institute and its nonpartisan voter education project, AARP/VOTE. She served on the board of trustees for AARP/VOTE, originally established as a separate trust funded by contributions from interested AARP members. Some feared that the organization's first foray into national electoral politics, even on a nonpartisan basis, would prove objectionable to the broader membership. On the contrary, the voter education effort turned into one of AARP's most popular, broad-based, and visible programs.

To encourage the broadening of AARP's public policy and advocacy work, my mother supported the organization's decentralization through a network of statewide offices to encourage grassroots efforts. Even within the context of a behemoth national organization, this effort was reminiscent of Mom's outreach as mayor to neighborhoods and grassroots organizations to give people a voice in decisions made on their behalf.

After she served six years on AARP's National Legislative Council, the membership elected my mother in 1992 to AARP's fifteen-member board of directors, responsible not only for the legislative public policy agenda but also for oversight of AARP's $500 million budget, administration, and broad array of programs for seniors.

My mother brought to AARP's board the same fiscal watchdog attributes that she had applied so tenaciously to city finances as mayor. In addition to raising more than the usual number of questions about the organization's expenditures and fiscal management, she also asked about the business practices of contractors providing services or products to AARP. She recognized the power of an organization to drive the marketplace by pressing potential contractors on their business practices such as employee benefits and hiring policies. Some of the issues she raised did not reflect the thinking of the board majority or management, but they often provoked lively meeting discussion.

During her second year on the AARP Board of Directors, Mom was appointed chair of the National Commission on Manufactured Housing, a congressional commission charged by Congress with improving quality standards for mobile homes—the only type of housing built to federal standards. The commission was composed of representatives of the manufactured housing industry, consumers, and public officials. AARP's representation derived from the significant number of seniors living in mobile homes. My mother refereed heated debate among the commissioners, who represented widely disparate constituencies—still somewhat tame compared to her former city council–mayor battles.

Also during her first term on the AARP board, Mom was appointed as one of fifteen members of the Consumer Advisory Council to the Securities and Exchange Commission (SEC). She met over lunch with SEC chairman Arthur Levitt (with whom she had served on President

50. Senator Jim Exon (NE) meets with AARP National Legislative Council member Helen Boosalis, 1989

Reagan's Private Sector Initiatives Task Force) about his plans for a campaign to protect small investors from fraud as part of the SEC's role in consumer protection. Levitt hoped the new advisory council would help the SEC determine investor concerns and resolve their complaints. Protecting consumers was right up Mom's alley; she threw herself into learning about uninsured bank products and investments marketed to older people whose life savings could be at risk.

My mother was elected chairman of the AARP Board of Directors for a two-year term at AARP's biennial meeting in Denver in May 1996. "Helen's leadership kept the board united," AARP director of policy and strategy John Rother said. "She had a midwestern, populist style; she cared about people and was clear thinking, direct and always upbeat. She was a pleasure to work with because of her constructive attitude—'we're going to get this done.'"

51. Vice President Al Gore meets with chair of the AARP Board of Directors, Helen Boosalis, 1998

During her time as AARP board chair Mom spent an average of ten days a month in Washington DC working with AARP staff, testifying before congressional committees, and meeting with advocacy groups and public officials. She traveled to AARP regional offices throughout the country and was a frequent speaker at national forums on AARP's legislative policy agenda. Mom's frequent flights took her through Chicago and we were fortunate to see her often, just as when she traveled extensively as president of the U.S. Conference of Mayors fifteen years earlier. When home in Lincoln between trips, she devoted almost full-time to AARP work, expedited by learning—in her seventies—how to use a computer.

AARP's board chairmanship was an inside leadership role responsible for the board's oversight and direction of the organization. The board chair did not typically serve as the external face of the organization, a role normally reserved for the president. But because of my mother's background in elected office, her comfort with the press and understanding of messaging and framing of issues, and her nonpartisan approach, she served as an articulate public spokesperson for AARP during her tenure as board chair. "Because Helen was such a good speaker and great on the issues, we tried to use her as much as we could at public events," Rother said.

For example, Mom was frequently tapped as spokesperson for AARP's national campaign to educate consumers about fraudulent telemarketing businesses, a campaign developed by AARP during Clinton's second term when Congress was preoccupied with nonlegislative matters. Her message to a large senior event in Shreveport, Louisiana: "Older people are vulnerable to telemarketing fraud. AARP has interviewed hundreds of victims who were often too trusting and too blasted nice to hang the phone up on a caller who was trying to cheat them out of their money."

Mom's approach to issues facing seniors nationwide was nonpartisan. "Helen was able to apply her great public experience without wearing the party hat," Donnellan reflected. "She didn't have to stand on the Democratic Party platform to talk about issues." However, she did manage to raise the partisan ire of at least one U.S. senator. When Republican senator Alan Simpson of Wyoming became a one-man crusade taking on the "monstrous" AARP and its finances and policies, and seeking congressional investigation of the group's nonprofit status, he was invited to address the AARP board about his concerns. Upon entering the boardroom he said, "I know who of you are Democrats," looking straight at my mother. Throughout his remarks Simpson continued to pick on her, which only further united the board against him, but "Helen was neither taken aback nor ruffled," Rother remembers. Simpson undoubtedly was equally unfazed by the board's response to him; he said in a later interview that leaving the Senate in 1997 gave him "the freedom to just beat the brains out of the AARP and I do that all over America."

As AARP board chair, my mom used countless national public forums to advocate for AARP's legislative policy, but she also connected to groups of seniors on their home turf with her message urging individual involvement, like her plainspoken urging of seniors in North Platte, Nebraska, to help erase the "greedy geezer" image people have about seniors and social security: "Stay active in your community. There are so many needs out there: children, literacy, poverty, health. Be involved. There's no excuse for anyone to say there's nothing to do. . . . Visit a nursing home. Be a friend to someone who has no family. Giving one's own time brings many rewards. Get involved with children. Isolation can be destructive."

My mother's national leadership role in AARP exemplified what she urged all seniors to do—stay active, get involved, contribute to community. As profiled in the *Omaha World-Herald*, "Helen Boosalis proved two decades ago that a strong, popular Lincoln mayor need not be a man. Now she's demonstrating that a leader of the world's largest retirement organization need not possess the slightest interest in retiring."

NATIONAL TRUST FOR HISTORIC PRESERVATION: TRUSTEE

The year following the governor's race in 1986, the National Trust for Historic Preservation sought to bring my mother's "deep experience as a dynamic mayor" and her expertise in municipal issues to its board of trustees, since the "first line of preservation . . . occurs at the local, municipal level." The organization's early reputation for saving magnificent old houses of the wealthy was then giving way to its emphasis on preserving sites and buildings that embrace American history, culture, and architecture. Trust president, Richard Moe, described the preservation movement's evolution "from a reactive, don't-tear-it-down movement to more proactive strategies for using assets for the benefit of the whole community. Helen's understanding of communities was vital in making the shift in emphasis and in helping the Trust focus more on cities and what it takes to make cities work."

My mother, Moe said, "commanded people's attention with the power of her ideas and ability to express them" during her nine years as trustee; she brought insights from her experience in the city trenches, where she had balanced efforts to encourage new development with preserving neighborhood assets and community viability as a whole.

Mom's practical experience using preservation as a tool for community development and using comprehensive planning and zoning to control sprawl and encourage "smart growth" demonstrated the kind of positive outcomes the National Trust hoped to foster in cities nationwide.

In her speech at a 1990 National Trust for Historic Preservation conference on the "Widening Influence of Growth Management Strategies on Historic Preservation," the former Lincoln mayor cautioned that city growth management policies were often criticized as anti-business by the growth-at-any-cost advocates. She emphasized the need for preservation advocates and elected leaders to build consensus and a broader base of support for city growth and development goals, including preservation. Her experience as mayor, Mom told the audience, had taught her that "political leadership, particularly at the local level, can play an enormously significant role in shaping our cities and in determining whether preservation will be a major player. It's pretty tough in times of economic insecurity and dwindling resources to make the case for preservation before city councils and county boards when the buzz-words in politics are jobs and economic development."

My mother admitted that she had not been a strong advocate of historic preservation until a preservationist in Lincoln, Phyllis Narveson, came to the mayor's office asking, "Isn't it time Lincoln got into preservation?" That comment awakened my mom's latent interest and sparked a curiosity to learn more. During a time of major recession and budget restraints, Mom spearheaded the appointment of Lincoln's Preservation Commission, the adoption of a preservation ordinance, and the hiring of a preservation planner—all the result of one citizen getting the ball rolling and enlisting my mother's leadership, eventually creating broader community awareness and support where little had earlier existed.

During her service on the board of trustees of the National Trust for Historic Preservation, my mother experienced an event neither historic nor preservationist but just plain terrifying. She was attending a National Trust meeting in New Orleans when she and two fellow trustees were held up at gunpoint as they passed through an underpass on the way to a restaurant. The nervous assailants did not notice Mom's maneuver to hide her purse under the large paisley scarf draped over her shoulder, but they ordered the two women to remove their rings and the man, his watch, before they ran off.

My mother thought she would never see her ring again but preferred its loss to the three of them being shot. Sentimental but not valuable, the ring was a gift from my dad; a colleague in Australia, where Dad spent five weeks consulting on wheat diseases, gave him the uncut sapphire later used to make the ring. What a surprise when she received a letter from the office of New Orleans district attorney Harry Connick informing her of the armed robber's arrest and, even more surprising, the ring's recovery. I now wear the ring and sometimes think of its checkered past, my mother's knuckles too swollen now from arthritis for her to wear it.

ARBOR DAY FOUNDATION: CHAIRMAN OF THE BOARD

Closer to home but still at the national level is Mom's service on the board of trustees of the Arbor Day Foundation, devoted to volunteer tree planting and promoting healthy communities through urban and community forestry programs nationwide. The Arbor Day Foundation board service was a natural for the former mayor committed to Lincoln's quality forestry program, care of its extensive park system, and acquisition of new city park land even during times of fiscal austerity. My mother's love for trees (inherited from her mother) was reflected in the city's major downtown beautification project when she was mayor. The Bradford pear trees lining downtown O Street and other parts of the city gave citizens a lovely welcome to spring after long Nebraska winters. "Helen understood the extraordinary importance of quality of life measures, such as tree planting, to the vitality of a city—how they both enrich citizens' lives and support success of businesses," said the national foundation's president, John Rosenow.

It is little wonder that my mother still serves with pleasure on the board of the Arbor Day Foundation (she served as board chair from 1996 to 1998) to help support the foundation's expanding programs on trees, conservation, and environmental stewardship and the development of its historic Arbor Day Farm and the Lied Lodge and Conference Center in Nebraska City. Rosenow, the foundation's visionary founder,

52. Helen, Mike, and Beth at 2005 dedication of the Helen Boosalis Trail in Lincoln

values Mom's practical community experience as mayor, her national perspective on cities across the country, and her energetic enthusiasm for inspiring people to plant, nurture, and celebrate trees. "She helps us keep our eye on the ball and remember the people we're here to serve," he says.

Since she left office, the former mayor's love of trees and parks has been tangibly honored. Mom has always disliked and discouraged personal awards and public namings in her honor, because she knows that public achievements are the result of collective efforts—not those of one person. Yet she took great pleasure in two such namings because of their attachment to the beauty and recreational opportunities afforded by the city's parks and trees. First, Helen Boosalis Park, an eight-hundred-acre area (former landfill), was dedicated on her last day in office in 1983 for future development as a regional park to anchor the city's planned eight-mile linear Crescent Green along Salt Creek. Second, the Helen Boosalis Trail, part of the city's extensive park trail system that she helped initiate as mayor, was dedicated in 2005 with a plaque honoring Mom's lasting contributions to Lincoln:

> *Vision and energetic leadership*
> in developing a healthy, vibrant and livable city
> *Commitment to fairness*
> and representing constituencies in all walks of life
> *Belief in open government*
> and citizen participation in building community

COMMUNITY INVOLVEMENT: NEVER-ENDING

Given the critical role that the Lincoln General Hospital lease issue played in my mother's reelection as mayor in 1979, how fitting was her appointment twenty years later by Lincoln mayor Don Wesely to the Community Health Endowment Board of Trustees. The Community Health Endowment was established from the net proceeds ($37 million) of the eventual sale of Lincoln General Hospital by the City of Lincoln to Bryan Memorial Hospital in 1997. From the endowment's growing assets, its board of trustees allocates over $1 million a year to meet community needs in health and human services.

Who knows if the city's lucrative sale of Lincoln General Hospital in 1997 and the resulting endowment would have occurred if the 1979 petition drive to stop the lease of Lincoln General had failed. But the petition drive did succeed, the hospital remained under city control, Mom was reelected mayor in 1979, Lincoln General was sold almost twenty years later with an endowment created from sale proceeds, and eventually my mom helped allocate endowment funds from that sale for community health needs. The circles of history.

Mom also served on a bipartisan task force of the state chapter of Common Cause to promote campaign finance reform, a cause she has long supported, to address the excessive amount of money poured into political campaigns. One of her colleagues in that effort, former state senator Jim McFarland, summed up why so many organizations and causes continue to seek my mother's involvement long after her days in public office have ended: "She has vision and she can dedicate herself to a goal without alienating people who don't share it. I really think she's a woman of principle. She has a real social conscience."

Describing Mom's participation after the governor's race on many local boards would fill pages; what I find most remarkable is that organizations today still ask her to serve even though she is in her late eighties. Few people of any age have her breadth of local and national experience to bring to her wide spectrum of community board service, including the Nebraska Community Foundation, Nebraska Commission on the Status of Women, Lincoln/Lancaster Public Health Foundation, University of Nebraska–Lincoln Osher Lifelong Learning Institute, Greek Orthodox Church of the Annunciation, Mayor's Committee for International Friendship, Nebraska Appleseed Center for Law in the Public Interest, Community Health Charities, Southeast Nebraska Cancer Foundation, and Health Partners Initiatives.

On the political front, my mother remains eager to support good candidates for public office and is often asked to help campaign for local candidates or to do radio spots for referenda such as public bond issues. She regularly chews the political fat at monthly breakfast sessions with her old bipartisan reelection strategy group that worked so hard to reverse her second-place primary finish in her 1979 run for mayor: Beatty Brasch, Lloyd Hinkley, Curt Donaldson, Jan Gauger, Ross Hecht, Glenda Peterson, and Dick Herman (who joined the group after retiring from the *Lincoln Journal*). The only ones missing from the original 1979 strategy group are Sue Bailey, Mom's close city council colleague, and Sue Shelley, Mom's dear friend from the old Forty-eighth Street neighborhood, both of whom have died.

I've joined a few of the strategy group's lively breakfasts—with

53. Jan Gauger and Helen are honored in 2007 as founders of the Lincoln–Lancaster Commission on the Status of Women

four Democrats and four Republicans, good-humored political digs are rampant. After more than twenty-five years, they rarely miss their monthly sessions—"Helen won't let you," Lloyd Hinkley, Mom's 1960s council colleague, told a reporter. This diverse, close-knit group represents Mom's favorite combination of good folks, politics, and plenty of laughter.

My mother has more time now than during her days in elected office to keep up with her extensive network of friends from all quarters—the old neighborhood, the Greek Orthodox Church, the large number of organizations where she has volunteered—all ages, all walks of life. She keeps in touch with those who live away by writing notes, sometimes several a day. And, like Gram, she is the kind of loyal friend you want if you're sick or in need—she'll show up at the door with a big bowl of homemade *rizogolo* (Greek rice pudding).

It is only recently that my folks have given up their poker game, after playing for more than thirty years with UNL math professors Lloyd Jackson and Bill Leavitt, psychology professor Frank Dudek, and spouses. According to Mom's administrative director, Mike Merwick, even during her hectic years as mayor, the secretaries in the mayor's office knew "never to schedule anything that conflicted with 'POK' in her calendar." The love of the game must have passed down from Gram, whose Greek immigrant family and friends played poker every Sunday night in Minneapolis when Mom was growing up.

For more than twenty-five years Mom and Dad have co-hosted "mystery guest" dinners (with retired federal judge Warren Urbom and his wife, Joyce; Ann and Dick Johnson; and, recently, Mike Seacrest and Tom Davies); the host couple invites guests unknown to the other two couples to be the evening's "mystery guests." At their advanced age, I marvel that my folks continue to enlarge their already large circle of friends and interests.

I describe some of Mom's continuing community contributions (and fun) not in an effort to cram more activities on her résumé already packed with a lifetime of accomplishment. Rather, her ongoing civic engagement and community involvement tell me that losing the governorship was neither the climax of her story nor the ending of a typical political career defined by climbing to the next position of power. My mother was an effective city council member and a superb mayor, and I believe she would have made an excellent governor—but those positions were her tools, not ends in themselves. She used elected office to further her goals of representing and involving people in ways to best serve community need, not to advance her personal political game plan. When she didn't win the governor's seat, she simply found other means to carry on her service.

In fact, if you were to ask my mother today about losing the governor's race, she would tell you it was for the best, that it was meant to be. Part of that response springs from her acceptance of what is and from her instinct to look forward with optimism—not backward with regret. But a more concrete reason for Mom's sanguine response about the outcome of the governor's race springs from her regard for the roles that she values and honors more than any other—daughter, wife, mother, grandmother, mother-in-law. And, she says, had she been elected governor, she might have had to compromise her cherished roles as mother and grandmother at the very time when her family needed her most.

MOTHERING: GRANDMOTHER, MOTHER, MOTHER-IN-LAW

November 14, 1990. I walked off the elevator in my New York hotel, delighted to see my old friends Ruth Messinger and Andrew Lachman sitting in hallway chairs opposite the elevator. I had met Ruth at my first National League of Cities meeting after my city council election in 1983. She was then on the New York City Council and a generous mentor for women who were, like me, new to municipal elected office. We became fast friends and formed our own little cell of cohorts within the National League of Cities that included Mayor Jim Scheibel of St. Paul, Mayor Alice Wolf of Cambridge, and Councilwoman Margaret Barrett of Jackson, Mississippi. We traveled together to League of Cities meetings across the country and became close enough friends to eat from each other's plates when trying new restaurants in strange cities.

So I was thrilled to see my old friends, and in my pleasure at their unexpected visit I didn't register the strangeness of their sitting in my hotel hallway. We exchanged hugs, then Ruth dropped the bombshell: "Max has had a stroke. He's alive. They've sent a plane for you. We need to get you packed."

My brain shut down. All I remember from the next hour is the image of Andrew taking underwear from the hotel bureau to pack in my suitcase, my fleeting thought how bizarre that was. Ruth and Andrew drove me to a New Jersey airfield where one of Max's Centel Corporation colleagues, Al Kurtze, and the company plane were waiting for me. Al told me that Max, then forty-two, was in a meeting when he began to slur his words and then collapsed. He was rushed to a nearby hospital and later transferred to Evanston.

The lurch through darkness back to Chicago is a blur. I walked into the blue-white lights of Evanston Hospital's intensive care unit about 3:00 a.m. Max, awake, raised his head, his eyes darting like a cornered animal's. He tried to talk but made only guttural sounds. His right arm limp, his left hand squeezed mine for help. I was helpless.

Over the next several hours I learned that Max's stroke was massive, blocking blood to the left side of his brain, causing loss of speech and paralysis to the right side of his body. Prognosis: unknown. "Go home, arrange for your children, get some rest."

Rest was out of the question, but I did arrange for my children. I called my mother. Whatever she was doing at that moment—and for months to come—she dropped. She immediately came to Evanston.

My memory is a blur of time so frightening and painful it swallowed us whole. Max slept more and more, growing less alert and slipping further toward unconsciousness.

Just months earlier we had attended his twenty-fifth Hammond High School reunion, Max's first reunion ever, and sat next to Joan Vatz, whom he had not seen since high school, and her husband, Ken. We discovered in conversation the coincidence that Joan had been a lab partner of my cousin George Vavoulis at the University of Minnesota Medical School many years earlier. We told Joan that George had suffered a stroke during his neurosurgery residency at Duke. Ken was most interested in the story—he was a neurologist.

As Max's condition grew worse the first week after the stroke, I recalled our evening with Joan and Ken and called Ken from the waiting room outside of intensive care. I hoped he could give me reassurance that everything would be fine—he could not—but he recommended an Evanston neurologist, Dan Homer. Dr. Homer put Max in a drug-induced coma, where machines would do the work of his heart and lungs to give his swelling brain a chance to rest. A surgeon implanted a monitor inside Max's skull to track the swelling of his brain.

I stayed at the hospital with Max eighteen hours a day, watching every change in numbers on the intracranial monitor screen. During the week of the coma (and for several weeks after) I was not a mother. My mom was mother and grandmother to the boys. Although they must have been frightened, at ages ten and seven, by all the changes in our household, she kept their lives as normal as possible.

Mom took the boys to the pet store to pick out tropical fish for an old aquarium she found in our basement. She took Michael to Little League practice and one evening took him to store after store searching for erasable pens that he just had to have for school. She made up elaborate bedtime stories as she always had when she visited (like "Willie and the Clouds"), but this time she took special pleasure in making the little guys squeal with laughter at her story about the dirtiest man in the world. The boys were in good—no, the most loving and tender—hands.

Mom cooked meals and washed and rearranged my cupboards (as always) and fielded millions of calls and food bequests from concerned friends and family. She kept a careful notebook of all these contacts so I could someday read with appreciation the outpouring of good wishes for Max and our family.

My whole world was the hospital. In the few minutes a day Mom and I might see or talk to each other, she didn't press me for details or thoughts or anything else. She knew I was barely keeping it together and didn't want to burden me with the tiniest demand, even where the boys' mittens were kept. She managed a city; she could manage our household just fine.

My mother did insist that I do one thing during that terrible post-stroke coma week—she thought I should come home from the hospital for Thanksgiving dinner for the sake of some normalcy for the boys. I agreed. After only a half day riveted to Max's brain monitor, I left the hospital to come home. I realized on the way home that I had neither talked to Max that day—which I did every day he was in the coma, whether he could hear me or not—nor said good-bye when I left. I nearly turned the car around to go back to the hospital but knew I would be even later for Thanksgiving dinner, so did not.

I realized as I drove home that Max had seemed different that day. Outwardly he looked the same—hooked up to every kind of medical machine imaginable—but something was different about his presence, or lack of it—like he was not there, only his body. I thought maybe that was why I had not spoken to him that day, had not said good-bye—he was not there to say good-bye *to*. My thoughts scattered as I pulled into the drive and the boys came screaming out the door into my arms. I don't think they noticed, but we had a pretend real Thanksgiving.

I fell into bed early that night but was awakened by the oddest sensation that something was slowly covering my body. A strange dream, I thought. An hour or so later I awoke again, calling out "Mom" and sitting straight up in bed. I felt the same sensation, like a light mist creeping over my body. This time I made sure I was awake and not in a semiconscious dream state. I wasn't afraid, just confounded. The same thing happened two or three more times during the night. Once I closed my eyes tight and tried to "see" what it was—I saw nothing. I'm overtired and overwrought, I thought.

I got up from my restless night, kissed the boys and Mom good-bye, and headed back to the hospital. When I walked into Max's room and said good morning, I realized everything had changed from the day before. Max was back, his presence was back, he was there in the bed—not just his body. I gave thanks, my real thanksgiving.

Two days later the doctors brought Max out of the coma. The brain swelling was reduced. It was now safe for his heart and lungs to do their own work. No one could say what was going to happen in terms of recovery, but all rejoiced that he had made it through the week. Dr. Homer's induced coma saved Max's life.

Later his surgeon told me that Max had been close to death and that few of the doctors on his case thought he would live through the coma. He explained that the brain of a young man like Max is larger than an older person's; therefore, he had less room inside the skull for the brain to swell before shutting down organs like heart and lungs. It is not by way of science that I knew my Thanksgiving-night awakenings came from Max, hovering between life and death.

Max survived the life-threatening stage of his stroke. The next four months in the hospital were survival of a different order—of spirit, of will, of stamina. After a month in critical care at Evanston Hospital, Max transferred by ambulance to the Rehabilitation Institute of Chicago, where he spent three more months in grueling six-hour days of speech, physical, and occupational therapy. Our sister-in-law Annie took leave from her job and picked me up every morning at 7:30 a.m., spent the whole day with us in therapy, and drove me home late at night.

I saw the boys a little more than I had those first weeks after the stroke, but I was still totally focused on Max and his recovery. With Mom's boundless care and attention the boys were thriving, even when they would go to the hospital to visit and find their dad unable to speak their names. Max came home from the Rehabilitation Institute on March 16, 1991, almost four months to the day after his stroke. We had a twin celebration with streamers and balloons—for Max's homecoming and for the birthday of Roman Marczewski, the lovely new Polish

54. Helen Boosalis in Lincoln, 1999

man in our lives who would help with physical lifting of Max, with his physical therapy exercises, and even with his speech, as Roman was also learning to speak English at the same time.

The story of Max's courageous battle to recover partially and adjust to the permanent effects of his stroke is another story entirely, but part of that story belongs here. Just as the doctors saved Max's life after his stroke, so did my mother save the life of our family during that most terrible of times.

She was selfless, she was sympathetic, she was strong, she was funny—in short, she was Grami and she was Mom. From the day she hurriedly packed her suitcase and left my dad and her life in Lincoln, it had been four months. Time to go home. I can hear her voice, "So you see how things work out. If I had been elected governor . . ."

55. Helen and Beth, mother and daughter

Losing the governor's race didn't keep my mother from finding new ways to contribute, to making her community and world a better place and to supporting with love her family and friends. It is what she does—without thinking, without sacrifice, without ego, but with great purpose. I know her greatest wish at age eighty-eight is to have both opportunity and ability to keep on doing her life's work, which to her is not work but reason to be. She has, indeed, used her very special talents to the fullest, as my dad always hoped she would and always encouraged her to do.

Yet I now view Mom's talents not as those of one perched on some pedestal high above the rest of us but as those of an ordinary woman with an extraordinary belief in people and in the value of each person's ability to contribute to community, to family, and to the world. Her faith in people is the wellspring for her optimism, her resilience, and all those leadership traits I used to think she had from birth. True, Mom has given much as an exceptional leader, but she would say her leadership comes from "the people"—all the people in her life—through their belief in her, in one another, and in community.

Afterword

People have long memories of leaders trusted and admired. In Gram's house right up to 1985 when she died, one would think that Franklin Roosevelt had just left office, that Eleanor was still out fighting for another good cause. The passion and respect for these long-past leaders always felt palpably alive in the inevitable political conversations at Gram's dinner table.

When visiting my parents in Lincoln, I have often witnessed similar expressions of feelings about my mother. Now in her late eighties, Mom has long been out of public office, yet often wherever we go—restaurants, plays, shopping malls, street corners—strangers come up to shake hands or pat her on the back.

"Hey, Mayor. When're you running again? We need you."

"Helen, you're the best damn mayor this city's ever had."

"Thanks, Mayor, for doing so much for Lincoln."

I've seen parents and grandparents drag shy children over to meet the mayor, who always finds a way to engage with them. I'm awed by the genuine warmth and gratitude these folks feel for my mother even if they've never before met her, especially since she left the mayor's office twenty-five years ago. At times I'm puzzled by the age of some of her fans—surely they were only children when my mother was mayor.

I sense that most of them, regardless of age, do not hold in their heads a list of the mayor's historical accomplishments for which they are grateful. Instead, they deeply appreciate how seriously my mother held in trust her service to the public, how much respect she held for citizens, how persistent she was in seeking their participation in governing, and how dedicated she was to representing all interests fairly. Yes, she left behind scores of tangible improvements to the city, but mostly she left a legacy of leadership in its purest form, leadership used not for purposes of personal power but for empowerment of others.

This legacy was reflected once again during my visit to Lincoln a few years ago. Mom and I went to breakfast at the Green Gateau, where I ordered the crunchy whole grain blueberry pancakes. We were deep in conversation about her grandchildren's lives when two women in their twenties or early thirties, one holding a newborn, sat down at the table next to ours. When we got up to leave after our third cup of coffee, the young mother stood and introduced herself to Mom as a member of the Divas. When we got outside, I asked my mom who the Divas are.

"They're a group of young Democratic women. It's so encouraging to see women their age committed to taking an active role in politics."

"What does 'Divas' stand for?" I asked.

"I don't think it's an acronym—just an expression of the group's strength and independence."

"How do you know about them?"

"They've invited me to several of their meetings, even though I'm more than fifty years older than many of them."

I unlocked the car door for Mom and told her I'd be right back. Returning to the restaurant, I stopped at the young women's table. I explained I'd like to hear more about the Divas—Democratic Divas of Nebraska, I learned—and asked if I could get in touch with them on a future trip to Lincoln. Holding her newborn while writing her e-mail address on a bank deposit slip, Leirion Baird looked up, "I'd love to talk to you. Your mother is our absolute hero."

I was moved by her sincerity—this woman who likely was not yet born the year Helen Boosalis was first elected mayor and perhaps was in grade school when Mom ran for governor.

I knew then with greater clarity why I feel compelled to tell my mother's story. I'm not just writing her political history. I'm writing of the lasting influence of one woman's life and character on the political arena where she served, on the community she governed, and, most important, on the people she continues to inspire.

That's why winning or losing the governor's race is not the ending of Mom's story but just one tributary flowing into the rushing currents of her life, a life reflecting her optimism and faith in people. By calling forth the best in citizens to build community for the good of all, she stirs all of us to embrace our highest aspirations . . . for our leaders and ourselves.

Photo Acknowledgments

1. Helen, the seamstress: Courtesy of and reprinted with permission from the *Lincoln Journal Star*.
2. Helen, the homemaker: Courtesy of and reprinted with permission from the *Lincoln Journal Star*.
3. 1959 Boosalis for City Council campaign card: Courtesy of Richard H. Blomgren.
4. Boosalis family campaigns in Helen's 1959 city council race: Courtesy of and reprinted with permission from the *Lincoln Journal Star*.
5. Helen Boosalis, city council chair, 1974: Courtesy of and reprinted with permission from the *Lincoln Journal Star*.
6. Mike Boosalis in his university lab, 1975: Courtesy of and reprinted with permission from the *Lincoln Journal Star*.
7. 1986 Boosalis for Governor campaign sticker.
8. Flanked by her grandsons, Helen shares Mother's Day with her family during governor's race: Reprinted with permission from the *Omaha World-Herald*.
9. Helen Boosalis accepts Democratic primary election nomination for Nebraska governor: Courtesy of and reprinted with permission from the *Lincoln Journal Star*.
10. Helen Boosalis supporters celebrate her gubernatorial primary win, May 13, 1986: Courtesy of and reprinted with permission from the *Lincoln Journal Star*.
11. Democratic unity event after the gubernatorial primary: Courtesy of and reprinted with permission from the *Lincoln Journal Star*.
12. 1975 Boosalis for Mayor campaign brochure: Courtesy of Richard H. Blomgren.
13. 1975 mayor's race: Schwartzkopf v. Boosalis: Courtesy of and reprinted with permission from the *Lincoln Journal Star*.
14. Helen stakes her own yard signs in 1975 mayoral campaign: Courtesy of and reprinted with permission from the *Lincoln Journal Star*.
15. Democrat Helen Boosalis and Republican Kay Orr in front of the state capitol: Reprinted with permission from the *Omaha World-Herald*.
16. Helen takes oath of office as mayor, 1975: Courtesy of and reprinted with permission from the *Lincoln Journal Star*.
17. Mayor Boosalis appoints of Police Chief George Hansen: Courtesy of and reprinted with permission from the *Lincoln Journal Star*.

426 | Photo Acknowledgments

18. Senator Bill Bradley (NJ) (*center*) comes to Nebraska for Boosalis for Governor campaign: Reprinted with permission from the *Omaha World-Herald*.

19. Former Atlanta mayor Maynard Jackson touts Helen's national reputation as mayor during governor's campaign: Courtesy of and reprinted with permission from the *Lincoln Journal Star*.

20. Senator Gary Hart (CO) (*right*) rallies Boosalis voters at press conference: Reprinted with permission from the *Omaha World-Herald*.

21. The mayor takes the bus to work: Courtesy of and reprinted with permission from the *Lincoln Journal Star*.

22. Helen's parents, Bertha and George Geankoplis: From the author's collection.

23. Helen Geankoplis at age three: By S. Kierski Studio, Minneapolis, Minnesota. From the author's collection.

24. Helen and siblings: Ione, Andy, and Tina: From the author's collection.

25. Helen's 1937 graduation photo, Marshall High School, Minneapolis: From the author's collection.

26. Helen Geankoplis dates Mike Boosalis, 1942: From the author's collection.

27. Helen Geankoplis, engaged, 1944: By Barry Studio, Minneapolis, Minnesota. From the author's collection.

28. Mike Boosalis, U.S. Army Air Forces: By Fritsch Studio, Faribault, Minnesota. From the author's collection.

29. Mike Boosalis (*back row, left*) with B-24 flight crew: From the author's collection.

30. "Just Married"—Mike and Helen Boosalis, 1945: From the author's collection.

31. "Win Amazes Mayor," reads the headline: Courtesy of and reprinted with permission from the *Lincoln Journal Star*.

32. Mike and Helen Boosalis, Bertha Geankoplis, and Max and Beth Davis celebrate Helen's 1979 mayoral reelection: Courtesy of Richard H. Blomgren.

33. Grandsons, Michael and Christopher Davis, and daughter, Beth, campaign for Helen Boosalis for governor: From the author's collection.

34. Helen takes her campaign for governor across the state: Reprinted with permission from the *Omaha World-Herald*.

35. The mayor's door is always open: Courtesy of and reprinted with permission from the *Lincoln Journal Star*.

36. "Take Off the Gloves" editorial cartoon of race between Kay Orr and Helen Boosalis: Courtesy of and reprinted with permission from the *Lincoln Journal Star*.

37. President Carter meets at White House with U.S. Conference of Mayors executive committee: Reprinted with permission of AP Laserphoto.

38. Mayor Helen Boosalis applauds President Jimmy Carter at 1980 U.S. Confer-

ence of Mayors meeting: Wide World Photos, with permission of AP Laserphoto.

39. U.S. Conference of Mayors president Helen Boosalis meets with President Ronald Reagan: Public domain.

40. Governor Bob Kerrey and former governor Frank Morrison join Helen Boo-salis on the campaign trail: Courtesy of and reprinted with permission from the *Lincoln Journal Star*.

41. Helen prepares to fly in 1926 Swallow biplane: Courtesy of and reprinted with permission from the *Lincoln Journal Star*.

42. Helen prepares for an ostrich race: Courtesy of and reprinted with permission from the *Lincoln Journal Star*.

43. Helen "copilots" an F-4 fighter reconnaissance jet: Courtesy of and reprinted with permission from the *Lincoln Journal Star*.

44. Lincoln's first woman mayor stands before portraits of her forty-three male predecessors: Courtesy of and reprinted with permission from the *Lincoln Journal Star*.

45. The mayor greets five thousand well-wishers as she leaves office: Courtesy of and reprinted with permission from the *Lincoln Journal Star*.

46. Mike, Beth, and Helen at the mayor's farewell appreciation party: From the author's collection.

47. Mike and Helen Boosalis cast their votes for governor in the November 4, 1986, general election: Courtesy of and reprinted with permission from the *Lincoln Journal Star*.

48. Helen Boosalis delivers concession speech: Courtesy of and reprinted with permission from the *Lincoln Journal Star*.

49. Helen and Mike at home, post–governor's race: Courtesy of Richard H. Blomgren.

50. Senator Jim Exon (NE) meets with AARP National Legislative Council member Helen Boosalis, 1989: Courtesy of AARP.

51. Vice President Al Gore meets with chair of the AARP Board of Directors, Helen Boosalis, 1998: Public domain.

52. Helen, Mike, and Beth at 2005 dedication of the Helen Boosalis Trail in Lincoln: Courtesy of Elaine Hammer.

53. Jan Gauger and Helen are honored in 2007 as founders of the Lincoln–Lancaster Commission on the Status of Women: Used with the permission of Dennis Buckley.

54. Helen Boosalis in Lincoln, 1999: Courtesy of Richard S. Hay.

55. Helen and Beth, mother and daughter: From the author's collection.

Appendix 1

1919	Born in Minneapolis, Minnesota
1945	Married Mike Boosalis
1948	Birth of daughter, Mary Beth
1951	Moved to Lincoln, Nebraska
1957–59	President, Lincoln League of Women Voters
1959–75	Lincoln City Councilmember (elected to 4 terms)
1975–83	Mayor, City of Lincoln (elected to 2 terms)
1981–82	President, U.S. Conference of Mayors
1981–82	Member, President's Private Sector Initiatives Task Force
1983–86	Director, Nebraska Department on Aging
1986	Democratic nominee for governor of Nebraska
1988–97	Trustee, National Trust for Historic Preservation
1993–95	Chair, National Commission on Manufactured Housing
1994–96	Member, SEC Consumer Advisory Council
1996–98	Chair, Arbor Day Foundation Board of Trustees
1996–98	Chair, AARP Board of Directors

LINCOLN CITY COUNCILS, 1975–1983

1975–77 CITY COUNCIL

Sue Bailey
John Robinson
Bob Jeambey
Max Denney

Bob Sikyta
Steve Cook
Dick Baker

1977–79 CITY COUNCIL

John Robinson
Bob Jeambey

Bob Sikyta
Steve Cook
Dick Baker / Arlyss Brown
Joe Hampton
Leo Scherer

1979–81 CITY COUNCIL

John Robinson
Mike Steinman*
Eric Youngberg*
Margrethe Ahlschwede*
Donna Frohardt*

Joe Hampton
Leo Scherer

1981–83 CITY COUNCIL

Mike Steinman*
Eric Youngberg*
Margrethe Ahlschwede*
Donna Frohardt*

Joe Hampton
Bill Danley
Lou Shackelford

*District representative

Notes

FLASH FORWARD: CALLING ME HOME

2 Governor Kerrey made his surprise: "Gubernatorial Primaries May Make
   History," *Scottsbluff (NE) Star-Herald*, May 11, 1986.

2 One reporter speculated that Kerrey's absence: Thomas A. Fogarty, "Kerrey
   Decision Sends Surge of Ambition through State," *Sunday Journal-Star*, October 20, 1985.

2 "charismatic and sometimes controversial": C. David Kotok, "Kearney Politicians Say '86 Campaign Lacks Excitement," *Omaha World-Herald*, May 11,
   1986.
   On the Democratic side: Fogarty, "Kerrey Decision."

3 My mother responded to: Kathleen Rutledge, "Boosalis '98% Sure' of Candidacy," *Lincoln Journal*, October 29, 1985.

3 Several other Democrats: Fred Knapp, "Boosalis Bids to Be Governor," *Lincoln Journal*, February 3, 1986.

3 "did all the motherly": C. David Kotok, "Mrs. Boosalis Shuns Liberal Label,"
   Omaha World-Herald, April 15, 1986.

3 She had planned to launch: "Boosalis Formally Opens Race for Gubernatorial Nod," *Holdrege (NE) Citizen*, February 3, 1986.

4 Unadilla, population 291: www.neded.org/files/research/stathand/bsect5b
   .htm.

4 breakfast at Horstman's: Francis D. Moul, "Ramblins," *Syracuse (NE) Journal-
   Democrat*, February 6, 1986.

4 On home turf in Lincoln: Don Walton, "Boosalis Enters Governor Race,"
   Lincoln Star, February 3, 1986.

4 "You are going to give": C. David Kotok, "Mrs. Boosalis Tells Crowd of 450:
   I'm a People Person," *Omaha World-Herald*, February 6, 1986.

4 With the primary only: C. David Kotok, "Observers Say 2 Women Hold the
   Early Lead," *Omaha World-Herald*, February 24, 1986.

5 A month after her announcement: "Co-Chairmen Named in Boosalis Campaign," *Omaha World-Herald*, March 11, 1986; "Shickley Woman Works for
   Boosalis," *Hastings (NE) Tribune*, March 18, 1986.

5 record of fourteen in 1934: AP, "Record 15 Candidates Vie for Governor of
   Nebraska," *Des Moines Register*, May 14, 1986.

5 In most non-presidential primaries: C. David Kotok, "Poll: Close, 3-Way
   Races for Governor Indicated," *Sunday World-Herald*, March 30, 1986; Larry

Batson (*Minneapolis Star and Tribune*), "Economy Overshadows Gender in Nebraska's Prairie Classic," *Sunday World-Herald*, August 17, 1986.

5   "performance overflowing with actors": Don Walton, "From the Crowded Pack, Two Will Emerge," *Lincoln Star*, May 12, 1986.

5   An *Omaha World-Herald* poll: Kotok, "Poll: Close, 3-Way Races."

5   some questioned whether her campaign: Don Walton, "Political Perceptions, Realities Differ," *Lincoln Star*, March 28, 1986; Kotok, "Poll: Close, 3-Way Races."

6   "The Democratic Party has": "Boosalis Wins Frank Morrison Endorsement," *Lincoln Star*, May 9, 1986.

6   "voters take the opportunity": Don Walton, "Tiemann's Words Hint of GOP Division," *Lincoln Star*, April 7, 1986.

6   "earned . . . permanent foes": Editorial, "Helen Boosalis Has Credentials to Be an Effective Governor," *Lincoln Journal*, April 7, 1986.

6   "I know people who are old": AP, "Democrats Woo Voters with Ideas," *York (NE) News-Times*, May 2, 1986.

6   "This may be more of a contest": Walton, "Political Perceptions, Realities Differ."

CHAPTER I. CALL TO ACTION

12   "Your mother thinks democracy": Sue Bailey Jackson, interview.

12   "The important traits Helen had": Lloyd D. Hinkley, interview.

21   "Charter Bombshell Dropped": Leo Scherer, "Charter Bombshell Dropped, Women Voters Unit Threatens Fight," *Lincoln Evening Journal*, January 26, 1959.

21   "quite surprised with the action": Scherer, "Charter Bombshell Dropped."

21   "You are uninformed": Scherer, "Charter Bombshell Dropped."

21   "The plan still strengthens": Virgil Falloon, "Women Voters Hit Charter Changes, League to Oppose All Proposals Because Mayor Power Weakened," *Lincoln Star*, January 27, 1959.

31   "new look in city government": Virgil Falloon, "Pat Boyles Elected Mayor, Smashing Vote Ousts Martin," *Lincoln Star*, May 6, 1959.

32   "It was a surprise": Falloon, "Pat Boyles Elected Mayor."

32   "Pat Boyles Elected Mayor": Headline, *Lincoln Star*, May 6, 1959.

32   "Council Seat to Mrs. Boosalis": Headline, *Lincoln Star*, May 6, 1959.

35   "Operation Understanding": Sandi Risser, "Countdown on Nebraska 'Missilewomen' Is 28," *Nebraska Education News*, March 21, 1963.

36   "Under Mayor Boyles": Editorial, "Council Developing City by Sensible Budget," *Lincoln Evening Journal*, July 27, 1960.

36   "The newest member": "Mrs. Councilwoman," *Lincoln Star*, May 18, 1959.

38 "Of the many candidates": Editorial, "Boosalis Service Needed," *Lincoln Evening Journal*, May 1, 1967.

38 "One great thing about working": Lloyd D. Hinkley, interview.

39 "an exceptionally intelligent": Editorial, "Crowded Council Race," *Lincoln Evening Journal*, April 2, 1971.

40 "He's my husband": "Boosalis Reportedly to Quit NU for Position at Michigan State," *Lincoln Star*, October 4, 1973.

40 Even without the move: "Helen Boosalis Will Resign from Council," *Lincoln Evening Journal*, October 5, 1973.

41 "It is a rarity": William O. Dobler, "In Perspective," *Lincoln Star*, October 16, 1973.

42 "Helen Boosalis has been": Editorial, "Statesmanship in City Affairs," *Lincoln Star*, October 8, 1973.

42 "an institution unto herself": Scott Hoober and Roger Hirsch, "Primary Vote Results Reveal a 'Mixed Bag,'" *Lincoln Evening Journal*, April 7, 1971.

FLASH FORWARD: DOWN TO TWO

43 the *Sunday World-Herald* published: C. David Kotok, "Poll: Close 3-Way Races for Governor Indicated," *Sunday World-Herald*, March 30, 1986.

43 The next *World-Herald* poll: AP, "Beutler Invites Boosalis to Series of Debates," *Lincoln Journal*, April 24, 1986.

43 Then, just a few days: AP, "Gubernatorial Primaries May Make History," *Scottsbluff (NE) Star-Herald*, May 11, 1986.

45 "I could not be happier": Fred Knapp and Kathleen Rutledge, "Boosalis, Orr Write National History," *Lincoln Journal*, May 14, 1986.

46 Nebraska ("of all places"): Claude Lewis, "Women Gaining in Politics," *Philadelphia Inquirer*, May 28, 1986.

46 "While this contest": Don Walton, "More Than a Contest between Women," *Lincoln Star*, May 16, 1986.

47 As a businessman, Kerrey: C. David Kotok, "Mrs. Boosalis, Defeated Democrats Move Swiftly to Show Party Unity," *Omaha World-Herald*, May 15, 1986.

48 "has proven experience, she has a (political base)": Evan Roth and Tom Allan, "Both Camps Say Wins Grew from Grass Roots," *Omaha World-Herald*, May 14, 1986.

48 "Every Democrat is comfortable": C. David Kotok, "Mrs. Boosalis Toasted in Omaha," *Omaha World-Herald*, June 6, 1986.

49 "I've never seen another candidate": Evan Roth and C. David Kotok, "Candidates for Governor Try to Rally the Party Faithful," *Omaha World-Herald*, June 8, 1986.

49 "Mrs. Boosalis had a much easier": C. David Kotok, "1st Woman-vs.-Woman

Governor's Race: Nebraskans Write History on Ballots," *Omaha World-Herald*, May 14, 1986.

49   Until Governor Kerrey made: C. David Kotok, "Kay Orr's Victory Scores Firsts for Nebraska, GOP," *Omaha World-Herald*, November 5, 1986.

49   "GOP loyalists as": Don Walton, "Orr Wins GOP Nomination with Strong Outstate Vote," *Lincoln Star*, May 14, 1986.

49   Orr applied her skills: Walton, "More Than a Contest Between Women."

50   Her strength among Democrats: Don Walton, "Boosalis Coasts to Win: Nebraska Has First Two-Woman Race for Governor," *Lincoln Star*, May 14, 1986.

50   "Helen's gubernatorial primary win": Robert F. Sittig Sr., interview.

50   "Helen had never been": George Latimer, interview.

50   Some post-primary news analysis: Walton, "More Than a Contest between Women."

50   "saving money for a late": C. David Kotok, "Kearney Politicians Say '86 Campaign Lacks Excitement," *Omaha World-Herald*, May 11, 1986.

51   Brashear and Domina AP, "Big Losses Faced by Losers in Gubernatorial Primaries," *Scottsbluff (NE) Star-Herald*, June 26, 1986.

51   *Lincoln Journal* post-primary editorial: Editorial, "Especially on THIS Morning After: There Is No Place Like . . . ," *Lincoln Journal*, May 14, 1986.

51   "played most of his cards": Walton, "Boosalis Coasts to Win."

52   "It's an opportunity": Don Walton, "Nominees Pause to Assess Race," *Lincoln Star*, May 15, 1986.

52   "Well, it sounds like": Ed Howard, "The Candidates: Helen Boosalis: Happy with Opportunities," *Grand Island (NE) Independent*, May 15, 1986.

52   Orr, also besieged by: Walton, "Nominees Pause to Assess Race."

52   The day after the primary: C. David Kotok, "'Getting to Know You' 1st-Day Theme," *Omaha World-Herald*, May 15, 1986.

52   To launch her campaign for: "Boosalis Delays Her 'Thank You' Trip," *Lincoln Journal*, May 16, 1986.

CHAPTER 2. MADAME MAYOR

54   "Helen knew who she was": Chuck Hagel, interview.

54   "Women are good at coalition": Barbara A. Mikulski, interview.

55   "tacit admission that": Evans, *Personal Politics*, 16.

55   The commission's 1963 report: Evans, *Personal Politics*, 17.

56   "to transform how women view themselves": Denise L. Baer, "The Political Interests of Women: Movement Politics, Political Reform, and Women's Organizations," in Whitaker, *Women in Politics*, 99.

56   *time: David Broder observed that the formation of the National Organiza-

tion for Women (NOW) in 1966 was not even covered by the *Washington Post* and was reported by the *New York Times* on the "Food, Fashion, Family and Furnishings" page, below the recipes for a Thanksgiving menu. Broder explained that the women's movement did not make news on the front pages of the *Post* or *Times* until August 1970, when Betty Friedan, NOW's founder, organized a strike of women workers (housewives, office and factory workers) and protest marches in Washington DC, New York City, and other cities to debate issues of pay and employment discrimination, passage of ERA, childcare, and abortion. Lois Duke Whitaker, "Women and Sex Stereotypes: Cultural Reflections in the Mass Media," in Whitaker, *Women in Politics*, 90.

56 "the *Equal Rights Movement*": Baer, "Political Interests of Women," 102.

56 Women's community activism: Ann Bookman and Sandra Morgan, ed., *Women and the Politics of Empowerment*, cited in Carroll, *Women and American Politics*, 13.

56 *slow: "Women grassroots community activists have been the subjects of study, but the relationship of their community involvement to their recruitment to electoral politics has not been fully explored." Marianne Githins, "Accounting for Women's Political Involvement: The Perennial Problem of Recruitment," in Carroll, *Women and American Politics*, 42.

56 *Representatives: As of January 2007, of the 11,811 people who have served in Congress, only 238 (2 percent) have been women. "Facts and Findings: Women Office Holders: Historical," Center for American Women and Politics, Eagleton Institute of Politics, Rutgers University, www.cawp.rutgers .edu.

56 records of women mayors in 1989: Sue Tolleson-Rinehart, "Do Women Leaders Make a Difference?" in Carroll, *The Impact of Women in Public Office*, 150.

56 percentage remained unchanged in 2006: Fact Sheet: "Women in Elective Office 2007," www.cawp.rutgers.edu.

56 Data on numbers of women state: www.cawp.rutgers.edu.

59 "flood of mail and calls": "Mrs. Boosalis to Run for Mayor," *Lincoln Star*, March 4, 1975.

59 "home from work when": Robert F. Sittig Sr., interview.

59 "anoint themselves for positions of power": Wilson, *Closing the Leadership Gap*, 53.

59 "soft-sell their ambition": Wilson, *Closing the Leadership Gap*, 55.

60 Nancy Pelosi described: Wilson, *Closing the Leadership Gap*, 54.

60 In a 2001 political science study: Moncrief, Squire, and Jewell, *Who Runs for Legislature?* table 5.5, 102, cited in Wilson, *Closing the Leadership Gap*, 61.

60 *Nebraska: Schwartzkopf's daughter Christie was one of my best friends in junior high. We had grown apart while attending different high schools, but it was still awkward with our parents as mayoral election opponents.

60   Schwartzkopf easily won his: Lynn Zerschling, "Schwartzkopf Doing 'Lot of Work' in Struggle to Retain Mayor's Seat," *Lincoln Star*, April 30, 1975.

60   "I told your mother": Sue Bailey Jackson, interview.

61   "surprise . . . that the 16-year council": Editorial, "Toward a Spring Showdown," *Lincoln Star*, March 5, 1975.

61   "Is Lincoln ready for a woman": Editorial, "Toward a Spring Showdown."

62   *ratification: The proposed Equal Rights Amendment read: "Equality of rights under the law shall not be denied or abridged by the United States or by any state on account of sex."

62   After Bella Abzug: Rowbotham, *A Century of Women*, 437.

62   *1928: Bertha Knight Landes professed surprise and reluctance at being urged to run in 1922 for an open seat on Seattle's city council and filed her last-minute candidacy when the primary election was only a month away. Four years later she filed her candidacy for mayor two hours before the deadline and only after a deluge of public encouragement. Landes dismissed gender as an issue in the race for mayor, believing that her candidacy could bring Seattle "an executive familiar with city business, one who could work in harmony with the Council, and one committed to the purpose of selecting capable heads of departments, regardless of personal or political entanglements." Haarsager, *Bertha Knight Landes*, 126.

62   "the issue of her gender": Haarsager, *Bertha Knight Landes*, 126.

62   *Midwest: Lincoln's population in 1975 was 166,000 (or estimated 183,400 Metropolitan Statistical Area [MSA]). http://recenter.tamu.edu/data/popm/pm4360.htm. In a listing of "major American cities," Lincoln ranked seventy-seventh in 2000, with a population of 226,000 (or 250,000 MSA). Wright, *New York Times 2007 Almanac*, 240.

62   People often make distinctions: Leonie Huddy and Nayda Terkildsen, "Gender Stereotypes and the Perception of Male and Female Candidates," *American Journal of Political Science* 37, no. 1 (1993): 119–47, cited in Carroll, *The Impact of Women in Public Office*, 151.

63   *candidate: Pat Schroeder, former Democratic Colorado congresswoman and 1988 presidential candidate, said that many people told her she didn't look "presidential" and asked, "Why are you running as a woman?" She responded, "What choice do I have?" Caitlin Johnson, "When It Comes to Politics, Where Are the Women?" *ABC News*, February 8, 2006, http://abc news.go.com/politics/print?id=1533331.

63   Mom predicted that being female: "'Realist' Boosalis Runs for Mayor," *The Oracle*, March 20, 1975.

63   "dynamic, positive leadership": "Mrs. Boosalis to Run for Mayor," *Lincoln Star*, March 4, 1975.

63   "The leader needs to": Wills, *Certain Trumpets*, 16.

63 "I strongly feel that government is there": "'Realist' Boosalis Runs for Mayor."

63 overemphasis on "brick and mortar": "Boosalis Pushes Human Services," *Lincoln Star*, March 4, 1975.

64 "because of the times, she stood": Rich Bailey, interview.

64 "facing an acknowledged uphill battle": Editorial, "Toward a Spring Show-down."

64 Schwartzkopf led the field with 42 percent: Editorial, "Mayor's Race Warming, *Lincoln Evening Journal*, March 5, 1975."

64 "If not wildly popular": Editorial, "Mayor's Race Warming."

64 "as of now, it's doubtful": Editorial, "Mayor's Race Warming."

65 *voters: In 1975 registered Republicans and registered Democrats in Lincoln were evenly split. "One of 4 Voters Expected Out for Primary," *Lincoln Star*, April 2, 1975.

65 "a small faction representing": Editorial, "Ultra-Ridiculous," *Lincoln Star*, March 27, 1975.

65 "few people have worked": Editorial, "Ultra-Ridiculous."

65 42 percent Schwartzkopf, 41 percent Boosalis: Warren Weber, "Poll: Sam, Helen Neck and Neck in Mayor's Race Home Stretch," *Sunday Journal and Star*, March 30, 1975.

66 "I just don't believe": "Contributions Over $100 Out for Boosalis," *Lincoln Evening Journal*, March 7, 1975.

66 Schwartzkopf hadn't yet raised: "Schwartzkopf Leads Spending Race," *Lincoln Star*, April 3, 1975.

66 "She is popular": Lynn Zerschling, "Boosalis Giving Schwartzkopf Run for Money," *Lincoln Star*, April 4, 1975.

66 "the most spirited race": Editorial, "Premier Election for Council," *Lincoln Evening Journal*, April 4, 1975.

66 "energy freak": Lynn Zerschling, "Mrs. Boosalis' Garden Waits, But She's Doing Lots of Walking," *Lincoln Star*, April 29, 1975.

68 *13 percent: The top two vote-getters in Lincoln's mayoral primary would face each other in the general election a month later, even if one received more than 50 percent of the votes cast in the primary.

68 "The council president's commanding": Lynn Zerschling, "Boosalis Runs Strong . . . Schwartzkopf Trails in Primary," *Lincoln Star*, April 9, 1975.

68 "Mrs. Boosalis' grassroots campaign": Zerschling, "Boosalis Runs Strong."

68 "Mrs. Boosalis has grabbed": Editorial, "Leadership the Issue," *Lincoln Star*, April 10, 1975.

68 "Boosalis' strong showing reinforces": Warren Weber, "Leadership Campaign Theme for Boosalis, Schwartzkopf," *Lincoln Evening Journal*, April 9, 1975.

68 "I was assigned a precinct": Robert F. Sittig Sr., interview.

69 Schwartzkopf "can be expected": Editorial, "Leadership the Issue."

69 "dismayed at having lost": Warren Weber, "Schwartzkopf Left Hard Road after Big Boosalis Victory," *Lincoln Evening Journal*, April 11, 1975.

69 credited my mother's 13 percent lead: Zerschling, "Boosalis Runs Strong."

73 "rather snappy with": Weber, "Schwartzkopf Left Hard Road."

73 "This is just the first half": Weber, "Leadership Campaign Theme."

73 maintained a low public profile: Warren Weber, "Sam and Helen Offer Voters Little in Common," *Sunday Journal and Star*, May 4, 1975.

74 "Stevens Creek is the hidden": "Mayoral Candidates Appear Together for 1st Time in Race," *Lincoln Evening Journal*, April 3, 1975.

75 "There's a real struggle": Editorial, "Ahhh, Those Ads," *Lincoln Evening Journal*, May 3, 1975.

75 "Is this the majority you want": Paid advertisement, *Lincoln Star*, April 30, May 2, 3, 4, 5, 1975.

75 "an advertising blitz": Warren Weber, "Sam's Advertising Is New Campaign Issue," *Lincoln Evening Journal*, May 1, 1975.

76 "took a more personal approach": Lynn Zerschling, "Style More Than Issues Separates Candidates," *Lincoln Star*, May 3, 1975.

76 "Dear Mrs. Boosalis: As a council": Paid advertisement, *Lincoln Star*, May 1, 1975.

76 "felt this was the only way": Zerschling, "Style More Than Issues."

76 "Never, it seems, have the politics": Editorial, "Below-the-Belt Campaigning," *Lincoln Star*, May 1, 1975.

77 mostly held private her view: Weber, "Sam and Helen."

77 "Citizens for Balanced Representation": Richard Haws, "Christenson Goes to Nebraska to Rap 'Liberal-Radical' Soglin," *Wisconsin State Journal*, May 6, 1975.

77 working with a partner in the advertising firm: Bart Becker, "Imbalance Decried," *Lincoln Evening Journal*, May 1, 1975.

77 ("a group closely associated with"): Haws, "Christenson Goes to Nebraska."

77 "liberal/radical regime": Haws, "Christenson Goes to Nebraska."

77 Stressing Madison's comparability to Lincoln: Becker, "Imbalance Decried."

77 "new breed of police chief": Haws, "Christenson Goes to Nebraska."

77 Mom's communications consultant: Weber, "Sam's Advertising."

78 "Helen's business opponents": Coleen J. Seng, interview.

78 "because they fear his opponent": Weber, "Sam and Helen."

79 *election: One reporter, after examining the candidates' required financial campaign reports ten days before the election, queried, "Where do people with the last name of Amen get all that money? The name Amen showed up 18 times in Schwartzkopf's report." Gordon Winters, "Campaign Reports Show Individuality," *Lincoln Star*, April 25, 1975.

79   "will not only promise": Advertisement, *Lincoln Star*, May 2, 1975.

79   poll showed Boosalis with 56 percent: Warren Weber, "Helen Boosalis Will Become Mayor If She Keeps 56%–34% Poll Lead," *Sunday Journal and Star*, April 27, 1975.

79   *newspapers: "When he was first elected mayor eight years ago Sam Schwartz-kopf was . . . a listener, eager to learn the ropes, welcoming good advice and interested in hearing what Lincolnites all across the spectrum had to say. With his smashing re-election triumph four years ago, Mayor Sam stopped listening, in our opinion, and that is one of the major problems facing the city today. . . . Although Sam Schwartzkopf has been 'not a bad mayor,' that is not enough for Lincoln. This city deserves the best mayor it can elect.

"Lincoln voters on May 6 have the opportunity to vote for a candidate, Helen Boosalis, who in our opinion would be an excellent mayor of the City of Lincoln.

"Mrs. Boosalis has been president of the City Council during these past few years when the council was forced, by default, to take on executive as well as legislative functions. . . . [F]ew Lincolnites have as deep and thorough an understanding of Lincoln municipal affairs as does Helen Boosalis. And few public servants have been as open and as sensitive to the needs of differing elements of the community as she.

"And one of those elements with needs she has been sensitive to is the business community. . . . The fact that she is willing to listen to any and all interests, however, and the fact that she speaks her own mind and is fiercely independent may stick in the throats of some, but we think a vast majority of Lincolnites respect those qualities.

"Something exciting is happening in this town. Increasingly, by greater numbers, average citizens who never were a part of it before are beginning to realize that they can affect the decisions which affect them. They can have input in government; they can be a part of building the future of their city. Helen Boosalis has asked for that input and interest and welcomes it. It is a cliché but it applies in this instance: Helen Boosalis is a public official who listens. Through her, the people will have a voice." Editorial, "Making a Good City Better," *Lincoln Star*, April 28, 1975.

"Contrasting Schwartzkopf's eight years as mayor with the 16 years invested in public service by Mrs. Boosalis on the city council, this newspaper believes Mrs. Boosalis' style would promote a greater general sense of citizen participation and confidence in municipal government, at no cost to substance.

"The marvelous character of the free access by any person to the Lincoln City Council is due in part to Mrs. Boosalis. She has operated in the same way—willing always to respectfully listen—in personal relationships. . . . As mayor, Mrs. Boosalis is likely to be more of a visible, take-charge individual in the administrative front, and will be held directly accountable for the actions of subordinates.

"A number of thoughtful students of the Lincoln municipal scene suspect the community never has really given its 'strong mayor' governmental form a fair trial. Schwartzkopf permitted considerable decision-making to come from the ferment of council-department director interchanges. With Mrs. Boosalis as mayor, the 'strong mayor' structure is apt to receive a test.

"The salad days of municipal revenue growth and ever-expanding resources are over. . . . In her 16 years on the council, Mrs. Boosalis gained an unparalleled background of this city's problems, priorities, attitudes and governmental machinery. She is the kind of experienced, tested, disciplined and responsible person the community would want at the administrative helm in matching restricted resources with problems." Editorial, "Mrs. Boosalis for Mayor," *Lincoln Evening Journal*, April 28, 1975.

82   "This is the guy who started": Deborah Fairley, "Husband Gets Share of Boosalis Cheers," *Omaha World-Herald*, May 8, 1975.

82   *empowerment: The only other election night where I've seen a similar response was in a Chicago hotel ballroom the night that Barack Obama won the Illinois Democratic primary for the U.S. Senate.

83   my mother "is not the kind": Fairley, "Husband Gets Share."

83   "What I'll bring is my belief": Jana Miller, "Boosalis First Woman to Grip Helm of City Government," *Lincoln Evening Journal*, May 7, 1975.

83   "I've always felt that if any community": Deborah Fairley, "Lincoln's Boosalis to Take City Reins," *Omaha World-Herald*, May 7, 1975.

83   "labels are preposterous": Fairley, "Husband Gets Share."

83   "If the citizens of Lincoln": Editorial, "The Day After," *Lincoln Evening Journal*, May 7, 1975.

84   "It is safe to say": Editorial, "Lincoln's New Mayor," *Lincoln Star*, May 8, 1975.

84   "The next time a study": Editorial, "A Madison-Lincoln Link," *Lincoln Star*, May 10, 1975.

84   "If he had been left alone": Editorial, "Lincoln's New Mayor."

85   In assessing his loss: "Mayor Sam: Sorry He's Out," *Lincoln Sun*, May 21, 1975.

85   "signal[ed] a demise": Lynn Zerschling, "Boosalis Expected to Be Vocal, Visible Mayor," *Lincoln Star*, May 8, 1975.

85   "what apparently has been taking place": Warren Weber, "Business Community Loses Political Clout," *Lincoln Evening Journal*, May 7, 1975.

85   *gang: O Street is the major arterial through the center of downtown Lincoln. The term "O Street gang" was originally coined to describe, literally, Lincoln's business civic caretakers, led by large retailers on O Street (e.g.,

Gold's, Miller and Paine). A group of downtown property owners "who thought and acted business," the O Street gang once dominated Lincoln city government, as was common in many cities (George Hendrix, "There's More to It Than Labels Imply," *Lincoln Star*, March 21, 1983). As the influence of the earlier O Street Gang gave way to broader business interests and also to neighborhood interests, the use of the term "O Street gang" took on a negative connotation, describing not the traditional business civic caretakers but rather the segment of the business community motivated by self-interest and the desire to exert influence and control over city hall, especially over the regulation of land use and development.

85 "pressure group in Lincoln is dead": Weber, "Business Community Loses Political Clout."

85 The power struggle between business: Hendrix, "There's More to It."

85 "the rift took on definition": Hendrix, "There's More to It."

86 *shake: Bob Schrepf, who wrote *Lincoln Star* editorials as editorial page editor from 1969 to 1982, told me recently that "Helen's unfair anti-business label stuck because she was not a businessman" (Robert K. Schrepf, interview). Former city councilman (and humorist) Curt Donaldson put it this way: "Her anti-business label came from the fact that she didn't smoke cigars and hang out at the Nebraska Club. She just wasn't from the business world in their eyes" (Curt Donaldson, interview).

86 "Her record during 16 years": Editorial, "Making a Good City Better."

86 "waking up to the fact": Weber, "Business Community Loses Political Clout."

FLASH FORWARD: MAY THE BEST WOMAN . . .

87 "Gals Vie for Gov.": *Dodge (NE) Criterion*, May 15, 1986.

87 On the heels of Geraldine: Robert Wagman, "Woman vs. woman," *Scottsbluff (NE) Star-Herald*, October 29, 1986.

88 *age: The Nineteenth Amendment was signed into law on August 26, 1920, two days before my mother's first birthday.

88 On the congressional front: Fred Knapp and Kathleen Rutledge, "Boosalis, Orr Write National History," *Lincoln Journal*, May 14, 1986.

88 "At that rate": John Dillin, "In Nebraska, a Double Win for Women in Politics," *Christian Science Monitor*, May 15, 1986.

89 Women state legislators fared: Dillin, "In Nebraska, a Double Win."

89 "Many federal races have": Dillin, "In Nebraska, a Double Win."

89 the power of incumbency: Dillin, "In Nebraska, a Double Win."

89 *men: "There is enormous advantage to incumbency in the U.S. electoral system, and you have a system with minimal [numbers of] women participat-

ing," said former Massachusetts governor Jane Switt. "Incumbents win 90% of the time. Unless we come up with something dramatic, progress will continue to be slow." Caitlin Johnson, "When It Comes to Politics, Where Are the Women?" *ABC News*, February 8, 2006, http://abcnews.go.com/politics/print?id=1533331.

89 He had observed common perceptions: Robin Toner, "Facing Preconceptions of Women as Candidates," *New York Times*, October 3, 1986.

90 *1986: "Three major contests on Election Day will be all-female affairs. Mikulski and Chavez are only the second pair of women in U.S. history to win the nominations of both major parties in a Senate campaign. [The first pair: incumbent Senator Margaret Chase Smith vs. Lucy Cormier in Maine.] In Nebraska, State Treasurer Kay Orr, a Republican, is running against former Lincoln Mayor Helen Boosalis, a Democrat, in the country's first all-woman gubernatorial race. In Maryland's 2nd Congressional District, Democrat Kathleen Kennedy Townsend, Robert Kennedy's daughter, will oppose incumbent Helen Delich Bentley." Amy Wilentz, "No More Petticoat Politics: Women Are Running Tough Campaigns for Major Offices," *Time*, September 22, 1986.

90 "It's the absolute natural progression": Marla Paul, "Politics in 1986: Women on the Move," *Chicago Sun-Times*, October 9, 1986.

90 "The interesting thing about women": "Women of '86 Are 'Proven Vote Getters,'" *Omaha World-Herald*, September 11, 1986.

90 "the fruits of the third wave": David Broder (*Washington Post*), "Nebraska Candidates Part of 'Breakthrough': Women Pay Their Dues, Earn Success at Polls," *Omaha World-Herald*, September 14, 1986.

91 "During the 1986 gubernatorial race": Sara J. Weir, "The Feminist Face of State Executive Leadership: Women as Governors." www.ac.wwu.edu/~sweir/womengovs98.htm.

92 "The two-woman aspect of my 1986": Barbara A. Mikulski, interview.

92 "My state is making history": Helen Boosalis, "Equality Is Not Being Newsworthy," *USA Today*, May 20, 1986.

92 "Why did their [Boosalis's and Orr's] victories": Editorial, "The Best Candidate," *New York Times*, May 22, 1986.

93 "Who would have thought": Raad Cawthon, "In Nebraska Election, May Best Woman Win," *Atlanta Journal and Constitution*, May 25, 1986.

93 "hard hit Nebraska": AP, William M. Welch, "Nebraska Race Is Headliner," *McCook (NE) Gazette*, September 29, 1986.

93 "Why such a first": Michael Doan and Michael Bosc, "Kay Orr and Helen Boosalis: Woman Power on the Prairie," *U.S. News and World Report*, May 26, 1986.

93 "Nebraska, of all places": Claude Lewis, "Women Gaining in Politics," *Philadelphia Inquirer*, May 28, 1986.

93   "Let's face it": Lynn Cutler, "Perspectives," *Newsweek*, May 26, 1986; AP, "State Gubernatorial Race Attracts National Interest," *Lincoln Journal*, May 19, 1986.

93   "Everybody says New York": Thomas Oliphant, "Ferraro's Legacy," *Boston Globe*, May 27, 1986.

93   "outsiders seemed more struck": "Women Win Both Primaries in Nebraska," *New York Times*, May 18, 1986.

94   "Nebraska is not all": William Robbins, "2 Women Leading in Nebraska Race," *New York Times*, March 30, 1986.

94   "Nebraska will defy the historians": Francis D. Moul, "Stage Set," *Johnson County Courier*, May 15, 1986.

94   "It is not surprising that": Robert E. Knoll, interview.

94   "myth of Nebraska conservatism": Robbins, "2 Women Leading."

94   "Nebraskans are independent": Richard Benedetto, "19 Vie for Governorship in 12 States," *USA Today*, May 13, 1986.

94   Nebraska needed a mother—"someone": C. David Kotok (*Omaha World Herald*), "Nebraska: A Singular State for Genderless Politics," *Los Angeles Times*, May 25, 1986.

94   With so much attention: Doan and Bosc, "Kay Orr and Helen Boosalis."

94   "Only Boosalis brings women's": Benedetto, "19 Vie for Governorship."

95   "on two key women's issues": Oliphant, "Ferraro's Legacy."

95   that she was *personally* opposed: C. David Kotok, "Mrs. Boosalis Tells Forum She Is against Abortion," *Omaha World-Herald*, February 22, 1986.

95   *Nebraska: A recent *Boston Globe* article highlighted the continuing complexity of abortion as a political issue in Nebraska today: "This state [Nebraska] is more conservative than most, but polls indicate that Nebraskans view abortion rights much as the rest of the country does: A 2000 survey conducted by the *Omaha World-Herald* found that 72 percent of residents favor keeping abortion legal at least in limited circumstances. Yet Nebraska has some of the most restrictive abortion laws in the country. . . . The apparent disconnect between public opinion and public policy speaks to the way the abortion-rights debate is perceived in Nebraska, according to longtime political observers. . . .

". . . [A]fter the Alito nomination, [former Nebraska governor and U.S. senator Bob Kerrey] said it is clear that abortion-rights supporters need to reframe the debate. Kerrey said Democrats need to work to reduce the number of abortions, and accept some limits to abortion access, such as spousal and parental notification requirements.

"Many Nebraskans who support abortion rights clearly abhor the practice. The 2000 statewide poll showed that 38%—more than half of those who support legalized abortion—said it should be legal in only 'a few circumstances.' . . . [T]he majority of the state's residents probably support an absolute right to terminate pregnancies only in narrowly defined circumstances, such as rape or incest, or where the life of the mother is in jeopardy, Kerrey said." Rick Klein, "Push in Nebraska Highlights New Abortion Dynamic," *Boston Globe*, January 23, 2006.

95   *Omaha: Before losing the gubernatorial primary election to Helen Boosalis, David Domina was "the chosen favorite of key Omaha Democrats and the single issue anti-abortion movement." Editorial, "Helen Boosalis Has Credentials to Be an Effective Governor," *Lincoln Journal*, April 4, 1986.

95   "force me to simply stay out": Evan Roth and C. David Kotok, "Candidates for Governor Try to Rally the Party Faithful," *Sunday World-Herald*, June 8, 1986.

95   Other Democrats felt the abortion: Roth and Kotok, "Candidates for Governor."

96   "I do not believe in whole scale": Kathleen Rutledge, "Taxes More Likely to Spark Debate: Women's Issues Not Seen in Race," *Sunday Journal-Star*, August 31, 1986.

96   national effort to engage evangelical: "Evangelical Role in GOP Rises," *Lincoln Star*, June 16, 1986.

96   *future: "The lack of a gubernatorial endorsement 'does not take away from the fact that I'm excited there will be a woman governor of Nebraska,' said Irene Natividad [head of the National Women's Political Caucus in Washington DC]." Fred Knapp, "Candidates' Abortion Positions Cited; Caucus Probably Won't Back Boosalis or Orr," *Lincoln Journal*, July 15, 1986.

96   Their enthusiasm was tempered: AP, "Feminist Leaders Hail Race Results," *Grand Island (NE) Independent*, May 16, 1986.

96   *no-(wo)man's-land: Don Walton, longtime political reporter for the *Lincoln Journal Star*, told me recently, "I talked with [former governor and U.S. senator] Jim Exon ten days before he died. His opinion was that the abortion issue had severely damaged the Democratic Party in Nebraska because the national party had become deaf to people on the other side" (Walton, interview).

96   "This will be a historic": Robert McMorris, "History-Minded Stalwarts Cautiously Swap Party Fliers," *Omaha World-Herald*, May 15, 1986.

97   "There are probably some cowboy": T. R. Reid, "Women Likely to Lead Both Tickets in Nebraska," *Washington Post*, May 12, 1986.

97   "Nebraska is running a state prom": "Petition Candidacy Possible: DeCamp Says Race for Governor Has Become a Prom Queen Contest," *Lincoln Journal*, June 16, 1986.

97   "The nominations of [Orr and Boosalis]": C. David Kotok, "Sileven Says Nomination of Women 'God's Curse,'" *Omaha World-Herald*, July 24, 1986.

97   "Most people took the nomination": Mike Royko (*Chicago Tribune*), "Rev. Sileven Gives God a Bum Rap," *Lincoln Star*, July 31, 1986.

CHAPTER 3. THIS IS NOT YOUR FATHER'S CITY HALL

99   "Helen always understood": Bob Kerrey, interview.

99   "Helen truly was the prime": Mike Johanns, interview.

101   *members: The seven Lincoln City Council members and the mayor each held four-year terms. Council members were elected on a staggered basis: a city election to select four city council members was followed two years later by an election to select the other three city council members; then the cycle repeated. Although the mayor held office for four years, every two years the composition of the city council could change quite dramatically, as my mother experienced as mayor. Such swings often made for dynamic changes in mayor-council relationships, depending on the numbers of council members who were generally supportive or generally opposed to the mayor's leadership and goals.

101   "fly either blind or unprotected": Editorial, "Score One for Mayor," *Lincoln Evening Journal*, May 31, 1975.

101   "all the facts on why": Lynn Zerschling, "She Keeps a Black Book," *Lincoln Star*, July 3, 1975.

101   "That's accountability": Editorial, "Score One for Mayor."

102   "during those long and often boring": Warren Weber, "Mayor's Hair, Office Operation Alike: Everything Smooth, in Place," *Sunday Journal and Star*, December 21, 1975.

102   "there is only one administrative policy": Gordon Winters, "Boosalis Questioned on Authority Bounds," *Lincoln Star*, June 1, 1977.

102   "Before Helen was mayor": Michael Merwick, interview.

102   Humble's opinion clarified: Winters, "Boosalis Questioned on Authority Bounds."

102   "restiveness by a council majority": Editorial, "City Hall Tensions," *Lincoln Journal*, April 14, 1977.

103   *chief: The mayor's authority to appoint the police chief with confirmation by the city council was part of the City Charter amendment conversion to the "strong mayor" form of government.

105   mayor appointed the finalist selection: Lynn Zerschling, "Police Chief Panel Named by Mayor," *Lincoln Star*, August 1, 1975.

106   "good, sound background": Lynn Zerschling, "Police Chief Field Narrowed to 22 Men," *Lincoln Star*, July 19, 1975.

107   "help Mayor Boosalis make an appointment": "Petition Supports Adams for Police Chief," *Lincoln Star*, August 6, 1975.

107   "would take a dim view": "Petition Supports Adams for Police Chief."

107   The six finalists: "Adams and Wessel among Contenders," *Lincoln Evening Journal*, August 23, 1975.

107   One candidate stood out: "If Hansen Not Confirmed, Mayor Says Search Process Will Resume," *Lincoln Star*, September 4, 1975.

108   Emerging from the breakfast meeting: Warren Weber, "Split City Council Vote Seen on Police Chief Confirmation," *Lincoln Evening Journal*, September 4, 1975.

108   Meanwhile, the acting chief: "2nd Place Frustrates Adams; Acting Chief's Plans Indefinite," *Lincoln Evening Journal*, September 3, 1975.

108   The leader of the newly formed: Nancy Hicks and Gordon Winters, "Council Opinion Split on New Police Chief," *Lincoln Star*, September 4, 1975.

108   She would not put forward: Hicks and Winters, "Council Opinion Split."

108   Councilman Cook contended: Weber, "Split City Council Vote."

108   "I think it's quite a blow": Hicks and Winters, "Council Opinion Split."

108   Agreeing with the mayor: Editorial, "New Chief Proposed," *Lincoln Evening Journal*, September 4, 1975.

109   "A fair guess is that": Editorial, "New Chief Proposed."

109   Included in the group were: John Gleason and John Roberts, "Lincolnites Mounting Opposition to Police Chief Nominee Hansen," *Sunday Journal and Star*, September 7, 1975.

109   Rumors were aired: Gleason and Roberts, "Lincolnites Mounting Opposition."

109   *chief: The rumor of the comment by Hansen's son was later squashed when my mother confirmed that she met Hansen for the first time when he came to Lincoln to interview for the police chief position, and that she did not ask him or anyone else to apply for the job. Gleason and Roberts, "Lincolnites Mounting Opposition."

109   The possibility of even seeking a recall: Gleason and Roberts, "Lincolnites Mounting Opposition."

110   "I have great respect": Hicks and Winters, "Council Opinion Split."

110   He received more calls urging: Gleason and Roberts, "Lincolnites Mounting Opposition."

111   "If the [citizen] committee hadn't been": Gordon Winters and Nancy Hicks, "Council Votes 4–3 to Confirm Hansen as Police Chief," *Lincoln Star*, September 9, 1975.

111   "speaking emotionally, his hands": Warren Weber, "Council Okays Hansen under Heavy Fire," *Lincoln Evening Journal*, September 9, 1975.

111   "Don't screw up what good": Winters and Hicks, "Council Votes 4–3."

111   The vice-president of a large: Winters and Hicks, "Council Votes 4–3."

111   "I think this is the hardest": Winters and Hicks, "Council Votes 4–3."

III "the end of a very difficult": Gordon Winters, "Hansen Looks Forward to Taking Chief's Post," *Lincoln Star*, September 9, 1975.

112 "some citizens still are not convinced": Editorial, "New Police Chief," *Lincoln Evening Journal*, September 9, 1975.

112 "—Mayor Helen Boosalis' courage": Editorial, "A Time of Trial," *Lincoln Star*, September 10, 1975.

112 *neighbors: In a poll conducted for the *Sunday Journal and Star* the week following the city council police chief vote, 46 percent of Lincolnites polled approved of Hansen's selection, 31 percent disapproved, and 23 percent were undecided. Richard Paxson, "George Hansen Given 46% Support in Poll," *Sunday Journal and Star*, September 14, 1975.

112 "tradition, loyalty, friendship": Editorial, "A Time of Trial."

112 "I think the hardest thing Helen": Jan Gauger, interview.

113 several serious law enforcement: Editorial, "Hansen's New Beginning," *Lincoln Star*, October 1, 1975.

113 "a substantial racial credibility gap": Editorial, "Hansen's New Beginning."

114 "Police or Killers?": Liane Guenther, "'Screaming' Signs Draw Only Glances from Most," *Lincoln Star*, September 26, 1975.

114 The explosion gave rise: H. L. Hoffmaster and Jim Camden, "Elevator Explodes . . . Four Critical, One Missing," *Lincoln Star*, September 26, 1975.

114 cache of twenty handguns: "Guns Stolen from Pawn Shop," *Lincoln Star*, September 26, 1975.

114 City and county officials committed: Bart Becker, "Law Enforcement Policies to Be Reviewed," *Lincoln Evening Journal*, September 30, 1975.

114 Civil Rights Division of the U.S. Justice: Warren Weber and Steve Kadel, "Federal Agents Probe Shooting," *Lincoln Journal*, September 26, 1975.

114 The mayor also called for mediators: Nancy Hicks and Lynn Zerschling, "Mayor Wants Assistance of Justice Department," *Lincoln Star*, October 9, 1975; Wes Albers, "Lewis Panel Seeks Grand Jury," *Lincoln Star*, October 11, 1975.

115 Also, she wanted to revamp: Warren Weber, "Boosalis Remains Undecided on Administrative Shake-ups," *Lincoln Evening Journal*, July 2, 1975.

116 Taking office in late May: Bart Becker, "City Council Cuts Salary Requests: Sikyta Heats Budget Sessions," *Lincoln Evening Journal*, August 7, 1975.

116 *budget: The total city budget included operations of Lincoln General Hospital and Lincoln Electric System, which were supported by fee revenue, not local taxes. The city budget also included operations for the city water system and public bus system, sometimes operated in other cities (e.g., Omaha) by separate independent districts. Mayor Helen Boosalis, Point of View, "Boosalis Points to City's Uniqueness," *Lincoln Star*, August 31, 1982.

116 My mother's election as mayor: Warren Weber, "Economic Storm Clouds

Gather as Mrs. Boosalis Begins Mayoralty," *Lincoln Evening Journal*, May 22, 1975.

116 During the previous administration: Editorial, "Mrs. Boosalis for Mayor," *Lincoln Evening Journal*, April 28, 1975.

116 "what amounted to extra money": Weber, "Economic Storm Clouds Gather."

116 "Lincoln's governmental progress": Editorial, "Mrs. Boosalis for Mayor."

117 *inflation: Inflation figures in my mother's 1975–79 term as mayor began at 8.98 percent (1975) and ended at 11.28 percent (1979). John J. McCusker, "What Was the Inflation Rate Then?" Economic History Services, 2001, http://www.eh.net/hmit/inflation.

117 With high inflation, the increased costs: Weber, "Economic Storm Clouds Gather."

117 "If I don't have the right": Lynn Zerschling, "City Council Cuts Money for Salaries," *Lincoln Star*, August 7, 1975.

117 "You are the policy making body": Zerschling, "City Council Cuts."

117 "Mrs. Boosalis had the stamina": Lynn Zerschling, "Mayor Wins Battle for Aide," *Lincoln Star*, August 12, 1975.

118 "Helen made the city staff into": Michael Merwick, interview.

118 "Helen was able to handle": Beatty Brasch, interview.

118 "The mayor's budget represents": Editorial, "Boosalis Holds Line," *Lincoln Star*, July 19, 1976.

119 the only layoff of municipal employees: "City Trying to Aid 48 to Be Laid Off," *Lincoln Journal*, August 18, 1976.

119 recession of 1973–75 "is remembered primarily": Marc Labonte and Gail Makinen, "The Current Economic Recession: How Long, How Deep, and How Different from the Past?" Congressional Research Service, Library of Congress, CRS Report RL31237, CRS-15, January 10, 2002.

119 "the darkest period in modern financial market history": Editorial, "The Return of Stagflation," Blanchard Economic Research, December 30, 2000, http://www.gold-eagle.com/editorials_00/blanchard123oopv.html.

119 "The explosion in oil prices": "Oil and the Coming Global Economic Slowdown," www.stratford.com, in Editorial, "The Return of Stagflation."

120 *jobs: At my mother's first U.S. Conference of Mayors meeting in Boston in 1975, Mayor Richard J. Daley of Chicago was asked by a reporter, "You get re-elected over and over again and Chicago still seems to work—what's the secret?" Chicago's seventy-two-year-old boss replied, "You gotta have a lot of friends. And you can't spend more than you take in." As the elevator doors closed he added, "And you gotta have courage. You have to go to the people when you need more revenue." Jeremiah V. Murphy, "Mayor Daley's

Secret for Keeping Chicago Out of Financial Mess," *Boston Globe*, July 8, 1975.

120 *bankruptcy: New York City was poised to default on billions in municipal bonds and notes (over $12 billion, or 21 percent of all those in the market place). Gene Kelly, "Mallon Unruffled Over Bond Market," *Lincoln Evening Journal*, October 11, 1975. Mayor Beame's plea to President Ford for underwriting New York City loans had been rejected the month before the 1975 U.S. Conference of Mayors meeting in Boston. Martin F. Nolan, "Mayors Lobby Ford for Funds Tomorrow," *Boston Globe*, July 9, 1975.

120 the mayors called for $2 billion: "Big City Mayors Issue Aid Alarm," *Lincoln Evening Journal* (reprinted from *New York Times*), July 6, 1975.

120 "the recession hits the cities": "Big City Mayors Issue Aid Alarm."

120 My mother was a sponge: Martin F. Nolan, "US Mayors Meet in Boston to Air Mutual Woes," *Boston Globe*, July 5, 1975.

120 "Our cities have borne": Martin F. Nolan, "Ford Neglects Cities, Kennedy Charges," *Boston Globe*, July 8, 1975.

120 Councilwoman Louise Day Hicks: Nolan, "Mayors Lobby Ford."

120 Boston had just gone through: Editorial, "Mayors Converge on Boston," *Boston Globe*, July 5, 1975.

121 "what they think doesn't count": Ian Menzies, "Nation Is Demoralized, Says Harris," *Boston Globe*, July 9, 1975.

121 "The public wants men of hope": Menzies, "Nation Is Demoralized."

121 *mayors: Other mayors included in the mayors' 1975 White House visit with President Ford were Chicago's Richard J. Daley, New York's Abe Beame, Atlanta's Maynard Jackson, Newark's Kenneth Gibson, Gary's Richard Hatcher, San Francisco's Joseph Alioto, Milwaukee's Henry Maier, Detroit's Coleman Young, and Boston's Kevin White.

121 White House to meet with President Ford: Lynn Zerschling, "Boosalis, Other Mayors to Meet with President," *Lincoln Star*, July 10, 1975.

121 revenue sharing set to expire: "Big City Mayors Issue Aid Alarm."

121 "As long as the major decisions": Rich Tillson, "What Does the Federal Government Do Here?" *Third Dimension/Daily Nebraskan*, November 11, 1976.

122 "an open administration was 'not idle'": Editorial, "Her Honor Takes Command," *Lincoln Star*, May 21, 1975.

122 "Helen was a master in": F. Gregory Hayden, interview.

122 "Helen never forgot who": Mike Johanns, interview.

122 The mayor ordered simple logistical: "City to Install Recorder to Tape After-Hours Calls," *Lincoln Star*, July 29, 1975.

123 She scheduled city-neighborhood: J. L. Schmidt, "Neighborhood Forums to Make Government More 'Accessible,'" *Lincoln Star*, April 5, 1978.

123 ("Sound Off to City Hall"): Karen Maguire, "Budget to Be Topic at Four City Forums," *Sunday Journal and Star,* February 17, 1980.

123 Some citizens suggested spending reductions: "Road Priorities Change," *Lincoln Star,* March 13, 1980.

123 but many more suggested: Editorial, "Budget Limitations: Easier to Talk Than Cut," *Lincoln Star,* February 23, 1980.

123 "Helen had a lasting influence": Jacquelyn R. Herman, interview.

124 "Frankenstein monster": Editorial, "Neighborhoods Too Interested?" *Lincoln Star,* November 22, 1976.

124 used the neighborhood forums to solicit: Jerry Loos, "Helen Boosalis Wins in Lincoln," *Nebraska Democrat,* June 1975.

124 Citizens Resource Bank: "Boosalis Would Set Up Citizen Resource Bank," *Lincoln Evening Journal,* April 22, 1975.

124 A disgruntled letter to the editor: Letter to the editor, "Saying and Doing," *Lincoln Star,* April 24, 1975.

125 During a dozen straw-vote stalemates: Nancy Hicks, "Mayor, Council Agree on LES Nominations," *Lincoln Star,* December 30, 1975.

125 "I'll probably be committing political suicide": Steve Kadel, "Four Nominees Chosen for LES Board," *Lincoln Evening Journal,* December 30, 1975.

125 "Look at the record": Kadel, "Four Nominees Chosen."

125 if the council chose to limit: Tom Lansworth, "Council, Mayor Still Disagree on Appointments," *Lincoln Journal,* August 4, 1977.

125 she had appointed 86 women: Gordon Winters, "Not a Matter of Numbers," *Lincoln Star,* February 21, 1977.

126 the mayor refused to reappoint: Lansworth, "Council, Mayor Still Disagree."

126 Twelve-year-old bike rider: Patty Beutler, "She Peddles Ideas to Improve Cycling," *Lincoln Star,* April 2, 1977.

126 "True, Shanks, educated as a lawyer": Editorial, "Council Majority Wants Dutiful, Lock-Step City," *Lincoln Star,* September 21, 1977.

127 When interviewed after his humiliating: Editorial, "An Example of Class," *Lincoln Journal,* September 22, 1977.

127 "Mrs. Boosalis asked me": Warren Weber, "Shanks Rejection Seen as Conservative Ploy," *Lincoln Journal,* September 20, 1977.

127 approved the mayor's appointment of Shanks: "Council Approves Shanks Appointment," *Lincoln Star,* May 23, 1978.

127 "Now Kauffman joins": Editorial, "Vendetta against Mayor: Sikyta Stars in Latest Act," *Lincoln Star,* October 27, 1977.

128 Councilman Sikyta later apologized: "Sikyta Apologizes to Kauffman," *Lincoln Star,* October 28, 1977.

128 "[Mayor Boosalis] has encouraged participation": Editorial, "Council Ob-

stinate Beyond Reason; Hang in There, Mayor," *Lincoln Star*, August 8, 1977.

128 "What in the world": Editorial, "Power Sharing Comes Hard," *Lincoln Journal*, August 5, 1977.

129 "What are the councilmen trying": Editorial, "Two Faces of City Council: Executive Self in Command," *Lincoln Star*, August 16, 1978.

129 My mother received mixed reviews: Warren Weber, "Some Rate Her Hot, Some Rate Her Cold," *Sunday Journal and Star*, June 13, 1976.

129 "I think it's healthy": Weber, "Some Rate Her Hot."

129 "I'll be the first to admit": "Centrum Razing Begins in Summer," *Lincoln Evening Journal*, March 31, 1976.

130 "rather candid for a politician": Weber, "Mayor's Hair, Office Operation Alike."

130 Councilman Sikyta even called: Gordon Winters, "Sikyta Says City Bogged by Personality Conflicts," *Lincoln Star*, April 21, 1977.

130 "The genesis of the problem": Editorial, "Personality Problem Besets Council," *Lincoln Star*, April 25, 1977.

130 was headlined, "Mayor's Hair": Weber, "Mayor's Hair, Office Operation Alike."

130 "Mayor Boosalis, not a hair": Warren Weber, "To Comprehend Work on Comprehensive Plan Requires Comprehension," *Lincoln Evening Journal*, December 8, 1976.

131 "bathing cap snapped over": "Mayor Dunked," *Sunday Journal and Star*, June 13, 1976.

131 "Under Mayor Boosalis' Immaculate": Warren Weber, "Under Mayor Boosalis' Immaculate Coiffure Is Person Ranked First in Lincoln Power Poll," *Lincoln Journal*, June 17, 1977.

131 "My hairstyles and fashion choices": Chrystal Patterson, "Hillary at Rutgers," April 20, 2007, http://www.hillaryclinton.com/blog/view/?id=4465.

131 Mayor's Commission on the Status of Women: "Boosalis to Appoint Women's Status Board," *Lincoln Evening Journal*, October 29, 1975.

132 executed on the last day of 1975: Ron Ruggles, "Sex Differences Receive Commission's Undivided Attention," *Lincoln Sun*, July 28, 1976.

132 After the national elections: Joy Stilley, "Women's Impact Felt in Bicentennial Year," *Grand Island (NE) Independent*, January 4, 1977.

FLASH FORWARD: MONEY TALKS . . .

134 "Compared to other candidates": Neil Oxman, interview.

135 total costs of the Orr and Boosalis campaigns: "State Gubernatorial Race Attracts National Interest," *Lincoln Journal*, May 19, 1986.

135 "We have to keep": C. David Kotok, "Governor's Race Pulls Attention in Washington," *Sunday World-Herald*, May 18, 1986.

135 Governor Mario Cuomo was honorary: "Ex-Nebraskans Plan NYC Boosalis Rally," *Lincoln Star*, September 12, 1986.

136 "The trouble is, you will see": "State Gubernatorial Race Attracts National Interest."

136 Reagan's September 1986 appearance: C. David Kotok, "Nominees: Reagan Visit Will Not Have a Major Effect," *Omaha World-Herald*, September 11, 1986.

136 highlighting the importance: C. David Kotok, "Lobbyist: Nebraska Race Hot Topic in Washington," *Omaha World-Herald*, September 17, 1986.

136 "Times have begun to get better": Gabriella Stern, "Kerrey Says Reagan Is Wrong in Saying Farmers' Plight Improving," *Omaha World-Herald*, September 26, 1986.

136 "I've felt for some time": AP, "Exon Criticizes Reagan's Speech," *Norfolk (NE) News*, September 26, 1986.

136 "Money's always a problem": Don Walton, "Boosalis Backers Say the Worst Is Past," *Lincoln Star*, October 9, 1986.

136 "if the natural ability": Melvin Paul, "Campaigners Seek $$ Now, Votes in Fall," *Nebraska Newspaper*, July/August 1986.

137 Following the lead of Reagan: C. David Kotok, "Stars Come Out in Race for Governor," *Sunday World-Herald*, September 28, 1986.

137 "I like Helen because she's a no-nonsense": "Bradley: Boosalis' Connections Nationally Can Help Nebraska," *Lincoln Journal*, October 21, 1986.

139 Although hardly matching the fund-raising: "Governor's Race a Gallery of Stars," *Grand Island (NE) Independent*, September 28, 1986; "Senators Say Mrs. Boosalis Can Cooperate," *Omaha World-Herald*, October 29, 1986.

139 Mayor Coleman Young hosted: jdt, *David City (NE) Banner Press*, September 25, 1986.

139 "displayed a blend of toughness": "St. Paul Mayor Backs Mrs. Boosalis," *Omaha World-Herald*, April 28, 1986.

140 "The truth is that being mayor": James Joyce, "Jackson Speaks Out for Boosalis," *Lincoln Star*, October 17, 1986.

141 "If I have anything to say": "Boosalis Seeking Funds from Greek-Americans," *North Platte (NE) Telegraph*, October 2, 1986.

CHAPTER 4. ROLL UP HER SLEEVES

146 "Key to Helen's effectiveness": Jan Gauger, interview.

146 "Helen was energetic, empathetic": Jerry L. Petr, interview.

147 With expanded automobile use: "1973 Oil Crisis," http://en.wikipedia.org/w/index.php?title=1973_oil_crisis.

149   model for others to conserve energy: Lynn Zerschling, "How to Curtail Cars Discussed," *Lincoln Star*, September 19, 1975.

149   She ordered thermostats: "Boosalis Orders Thermostats Lowered," *Lincoln Star*, February 2, 1977.

149   city met its overall goal: "Mayor Boosalis Says City Is Nearing Energy Goal," *Lincoln Journal*, January 26, 1978.

149   "Hey Mike, did somebody file": Michael Merwick, interview.

149   "Boosalis, the Queen of the City": "Lincolnites Are Roasted in 'Concord to Discord,'" *Lincoln Evening Journal*, April 6, 1976.

150   "She's on the job": Lynn Zerschling, "She Keeps a Black Book," *Lincoln Star*, July 3, 1975.

150   One example of the Energy Action: "Woods Realty Wins Energy Award," *Lincoln Star*, March 3, 1977.

150   In two years the city's electricity rates: Bart Becker, "Lincoln Utilities: Up 81.7%, Up 24.8%, Up $1, Up 45%," *Sunday Journal and Star*, May 9, 1976.

150   With prospects of near-term electricity shortages: Gordon Winters, "NPPD Interested in Lincoln's Garbage," *Lincoln Star*, June 8, 1976.

150   But a consultant's report concluded: Harold Simmons, "Garbage Power Feasible, but Costly, Study Reports," *Lincoln Journal*, April 15, 1977; Gordon Winters, "Burning Garbage for Power Appears Uneconomical," *Lincoln Star*, April 16, 1977.

151   *1990: Costs of generating power by burning solid waste were projected as high as $27 per ton of garbage in the first year and $13 a ton after ten years, compared to $1.75 a ton to bury garbage in a landfill. Winters, "Burning Garbage."

151   "Helen brought people": Curt Donaldson, interview.

151   favorable conditions for solar energy: Bob Guenther, "'Solar Energy Potential High,'" *Lincoln Star*, December 5, 1975.

151   Canney predicted future power shortages: Harold Simmons, "LES Chief: Power Shortage, Mandatory Cutoffs Approaching Fast," *Sunday Journal and Star*, January 18, 1976.

151   many Lincolnites supported the nuclear: Harold Simmons, "Poll Shows Backing for More N-Plants," *Sunday Journal and Star*, May 23, 1976.

151   Others opposed nuclear power: Roy Scheele, "LES Statistics 'Wishful Thinking,'" *Lincoln Evening Journal*, October 14, 1975.

151   On a close 4–3 vote: Lynn Zerschling, "City Council Rejects Nuclear Power Deal," *Lincoln Star*, September 30, 1975.

152   The council's rejection: Lynn Zerschling, "Council Reaffirms N-Plant Vote," *Lincoln Star*, October 21, 1975.

152   "I'm very skeptical": Lynn Zerschling, "Mayor Supports Council Veto of LES Nuclear Power Deal," *Lincoln Star*, October 1, 1975.

152   Regardless of Lincoln's opting out: Bob Guenther, "OPPD Can Build Ft. Cal-
       houn Plant," *Lincoln Star*, October 24, 1975.

152   OPPD had to swallow $40 million: Editorial, "OPPD Follows Lincoln Council in
       Rejecting Power Plant," *Lincoln Star*, February 3, 1977.

152   OPPD was sued for another $30 million: Harold Simmons, "NPPD Plans to Sue
       over Nuclear Plant," *Lincoln Star*, April 29, 1977.

153   "the great crisis of the 1980s": Editorial, "The Future Rests on Water," *Lincoln
       Star*, November 12, 1976.

153   Lincoln was forced in 1930: "Boosalis Hits Plan to Divert Platte Water into
       Little Blue River Basin," *Lincoln Journal*, July 22, 1978.

153   The mayor and her administrators met: Richard Passon, "Trickle of Protest
       Voiced: Lincoln-Sarpy Well Rights Recognized," *Lincoln Evening Journal*, May
       11, 1976; "City to Acquire Sarpy Wellfield," *Lincoln Star*, May 12, 1976.

153   ensure the city's water: Bob Guenther, "Lincoln's Land Hunt Draws Neigh-
       bors' Ire," *Lincoln Star*, February 26, 1976.

153   Although the water land acquisition had a hefty: "City Land Appetite Is Ex-
       pensive," *Lincoln Evening Journal*, January 4, 1977.

153   *years: Elected officials often face dilemmas of financing the huge costs of
       deferred infrastructure maintenance or construction inherited from their
       predecessors. When I was on the Evanston City Council in the 1980s we had
       to bite the bullet to finance a long-overdue overhaul of the city sewer system,
       which a study had deemed seriously inadequate—in 1939. No previous coun-
       cil had been willing to weather the political fallout from the increased sewer
       fees or taxes necessary to finance the huge sewer project.

153   "Lincoln is paying a price": Editorial, "Sarpy County Rip-off," *Lincoln Star*,
       December 27, 1977.

153   "LES is in far better financial shape": Richard D. Herman, interview.

154   In 1976, Southeast Community College: Jack Kennedy, "Chamber Looks to-
       ward Suburban SeTech Site," *Lincoln Evening Journal*, June 9, 1976. Richard
       Paxson, "Poll: 58% Favor 84th-O Site for College," *Lincoln Evening Journal*,
       July 28, 1976.

154   My mother expressed concern: "SeTech Board, City Not Tiffing—Mayor,"
       Lincoln Evening Journal, June 10, 1976.

154   The mayor and city planners offered: J. L. Schmidt, "Mayor Says City Not
       Necessarily against Campus," *Lincoln Star*, June 10, 1976.

154   After negotiating with the college: "SCC Officials Still Want Campus at 86th
       and O," *Lincoln Evening Journal*, July 6, 1976; "Mayor Wants Part of Campus
       Annexed," *Lincoln Star*, July 30, 1976.

155   The chamber of commerce and those business: Editorial, "Tech College Site,"
       Lincoln Star, August 27, 1976.

155   "Expansion of residential subdivisions": Editorial, "Breaking Stevens Creek
       Line; Start with a College Campus," *Lincoln Evening Journal*, August 27, 1976.

156 "Helen waged tough battles": Richard D. Herman, interview.

156 long-awaited updated Comprehensive Plan: Gordon Winters, "Comprehensive Plan Gets OK after Final Skirmish," *Lincoln Star*, January 26, 1977.

156 The Comp Plan would serve: Winters, "Comprehensive Plan Gets OK."

156 *2000: Lincoln's actual population by 2000—the time frame for the 1977 Comprehensive Plan—grew to 226,000 (or 250,000 Metropolitan Statistical Area), not to 325,000 as projected in 1977. However, a last-minute Comp Plan revision in 1977 linked future building projects to *actual* population growth in the event the projected population figures did not materialize.

156 mayor's help, the final 1977 Comp Plan: Vince Boucher, "Final Views Heard on Comprehensive Plan," *Lincoln Star*, January 25, 1977.

156 A Comprehensive Plan without specific focus: Editorial, "Citizens Have Final Shot Tonight at 'Comp Plan'; Changes Necessary," *Lincoln Evening Journal*, January 24, 1977.

156 *eyes: Although the comprehensive planning process required a study of all land uses within the city, my mother discovered that the city had not kept records of all public property. She directed her staff to do a firsttime inventory of city-owned land after a visit from Marty Pritchard, director of the Indian Center, seeking help in locating and acquiring a site for construction of a new Indian Center to provide day care, senior services, a halfway house, alcohol rehabilitation, and education. The inventory turned up a parcel near Salt Creek, which the city agreed to lease for $1 since federal funding would not cover the center's land costs. The center to this day is an important focal point in Lincoln for American Indians. "$1 Million Federal Grant Okayed for New Lincoln Indian Center," *Lincoln Journal*, September 28, 1977.

156 The next city election: Editorial, "Another Election Upcoming," *Lincoln Star*, November 8, 1976.

156 Denney announced that he would not: Warren Weber, "Denney Won't Seek Council Reelection, May Run for Future Political Office," *Lincoln Evening Journal*, November 5, 1976.

157 "they could move into": Warren Weber, "Council Race Is Conservatives' Key to Power," *Lincoln Journal*, April 28, 1977.

157 Many recognized that Hampton: Editorial, "Conflict Issue Raised in City Council Race," *Lincoln Star*, April 23, 1977.

157 took "Hampton at his word": Editorial, "Incumbency and Diversity; Factors in Council Choices," *Lincoln Journal*, April 24, 1977.

157 "no particular affection for Mayor": Editorial, "Preliminaries Are Over," *Lincoln Evening Journal*, April 6, 1977.

157 Scherer said that "under no circumstances": Warren Weber, "Scherer Goal to Reduce Citizen–City Hall Friction," *Lincoln Evening Journal*, April 1, 1977.

157 "any mayor, especially one as visible": Warren Weber, "Campaign Spotlight Flickers, Dims," *Lincoln Journal*, April 29, 1977.

157 Hampton's well-financed campaign: Gordon Winters, "Bailey Defeated in Turnaround Election," *Lincoln Star*, May 4, 1977.

158 "the real issue, if we": Editorial, "There's Trouble Ahead If the 'Bickering' Stops," *Lincoln Star*, April 30, 1977.

158 Bailey's defeat was an "unhappy stunner": Editorial, "Once Again, Voters Speak," *Lincoln Journal*, May 4, 1977.

158 "shocked the heck out of me": Winters, "Bailey Defeated in Turnaround Election."

158 "particularly fine council member": Editorial, "Incumbency and Diversity."

158 "Why such a good, decent": Editorial, "Election Results Forecast Changes in Council Policy," *Lincoln Star*, May 5, 1977.

158 Some attributed Bailey's loss: Warren Weber, "Shoo-In Shooed Out Because . . . ?" *Sunday Journal and Star*, May 8, 1977.

158 others to her spending the least: "Money Equals Votes Formula Is Accurate Except for Bailey," *Lincoln Star*, May 24, 1977.

158 others to a backlash: Weber, "Shoo-In Shooed Out."

158 "that the University influence": Warren Weber, "Incumbent Bailey Big Loser in Council Race," *Lincoln Journal*, May 4, 1977.

158 "youngish white male with a business": Warren Weber, "UNL Prof: Preferred-Candidate Model Helps Explain Council Race," *Sunday Journal and Star*, May 29, 1977.

159 election's outcome as "homogenizing": Gordon Winters, "Male, Business Image Reflected in Council Winners," *Lincoln Star*, May 4, 1977.

159 A Paul Fell political cartoon: Paul Fell, cartoon, "A Woman's Place Is in the Home," *Lincoln Journal*, May 9, 1977.

159 she was in for "rough times": Editorial, "Election Results Forecast Changes."

159 A *Star* editorial examined the political: Editorial, "Past Political Alignments Shape Current City Hall Battle," *Lincoln Star*, October 11, 1977.

159 *Star* reporter Gordon Winters: Gordon Winters, "Political Labels Garbled in Council Split Shuffle," *Lincoln Star*, October 11, 1977.

159 "are men of action": Winters, "Political Labels Garbled."

160 "try to manipulate events": Gordon Winters, "Issue of Control of Mayoralty Is Simmering," *Lincoln Star*, October 10, 1977.

160 "lingering resentment by those": Winters, "Issue of Control."

160 "While the City Council majority": Editorial, "Macho at City Hall," *Lincoln Journal*, October 5, 1977.

160 "When I was elected": Jan Gauger, interview.

160 "That's the way the votes": Gordon Winters, "Amidst Ritual, Council Shifts Character," *Lincoln Star*, May 17, 1977.

160 "Mrs. Boosalis pops up": "City Council to Be More Formal?" *Lincoln Journal*, May 24, 1977.

161 "guessed she had been hung up": Warren Weber, "Mayor Sends Council Olive Branch Shaped Like Transportation Agency," *Lincoln Journal*, May 17, 1977.

161 "Mayor Boosalis demonstrates": Editorial, "Moxie and Flexibility," *Lincoln Journal*, May 18, 1977.

161 "The heralded end of bickering": Editorial, "The 'Bickering' Goes On," *Lincoln Star*, June 22, 1977.

161 "I think we ought to keep our cotton-picking": Gordon Winters, "Council Vetoes Mayor's LES Ideas," *Lincoln Star*, June 6, 1978.

161 Mom agreed that city government: Editorial, "Citizen Participation Issue Sparks Council-Mayor Rift," *Lincoln Star*, June 7, 1978.

161 "It was a vindictive slap": Editorial, "Outside Involvement Knocked: A Pattern Clearly Emerges," *Lincoln Star*, June 19, 1978.

162 "making mincemeat of the Comprehensive": Editorial, "Another Attack on the Plan," *Lincoln Star*, November 24, 1977.

162 The number of council approvals of land-use: Editorial, "For Council Majority, Developers' Desires Take Priority over City's Plan," *Lincoln Journal*, November 23, 1977.

162 "Reflecting its animus": Dick Herman, "Implicit Questions in Report of City Council's Consultants: Does, Should Public 'Shape' Growth?" *Lincoln Journal*, March 22, 1978.

162 The consultants did not favor the use of zoning: Tom Cook, "Consultant Apparently Urging Stevens Creek Development," *Lincoln Journal*, March 10, 1978.

163 Hampton, Sikyta, and Cook conceded: Gordon Winters, "Consultants' Report Felt Unduly Influenced," *Lincoln Star*, March 21, 1978.

163 *report: Responding to Councilman Jeambey's lobbying charges, Councilman Cook said he actually disagreed with the planning consultants on Stevens Creek and believed the city should continue to restrict growth to the east and southeast, perhaps allowing development only in Stevens Creek's north end. "City's Eastward Growth Gets Consultants' Nod," *Lincoln Star*, March 11, 1978. Councilman Hampton denied favoring immediate expansion into Stevens Creek but said the city should consider it in the future. Winters, "Consultants' Report Felt Unduly Influenced."

163 The ongoing dispute boiled down: Herman, "Implicit Questions."

164 The redevelopment plan was originated: Gordon Winters, "Beautified O St. to Reopen Today," *Lincoln Star*, August 5, 1977.

164 "We didn't let our downtown": "Mayor Boosalis Encourages Citizen Involvement," *Lincoln Living*, August 1977.

164 "Part of Helen's anti-business": Don Walton, interview.

165 "I wish we could move faster": Lynn Zerschling, "Centrum Project Making Progress," *Lincoln Star*, December 4, 1975.

165   After purchasing 80 percent: Lynn Zerschling, "City Files Lawsuit to Obtain Building," *Lincoln Star*, January 31, 1976.

165   The chairman of her Downtown: Frank Partsch, "Downtown Demolition: Lincoln Mayor Leads 'Vandals,'" *Omaha World-Herald*, August 12, 1976.

165   Two years later the Centrum's retail segment: Editorial, "Centrum Needs a Boost," *Lincoln Journal*, July 29, 1978.

165   "If the Centrum doesn't fly": Tom Cook, "Downtown Businesses Concerned about Any Centrum Complex Delay," *Lincoln Journal*, August 1, 1978.

165   The city-financed parking garage: "Centrum Garage Can Now Handle 1,038 Vehicles," *Lincoln Journal*, December 14, 1978.

166   The federal Department of Housing: Karen Maguire, "Neighborhood Assistance Office Stirs Controversy on City Council, HUD Praise," *Sunday Journal and Star*, December 17, 1978.

167   "The neighborhood movement represents a demand": Dave Goldberg, "Power to the Neighborhoods: Little City Halls Link People to Government," *Sunday Journal and Star*, April 29, 1979.

167   "as distant as Capitol Hill": Goldberg, "Power to the Neighborhoods."

167   In Lincoln, many neighborhood: "Lincoln Neighborhood Groups Come of Age," *Sunday Journal and Star*, April 29, 1979.

167   "Helen made sure that staff": Michael Merwick, interview.

167   Councilman Hampton argued that the Urban: Maguire, "Neighborhood Assistance Office Stirs Controversy."

167   Sikyta wanted to eliminate: Tom Cook, "Urban Development Discussed: Neighborhood Planning Might Be Overhauled Because of Audit," *Lincoln Journal*, June 12, 1978.

167   "can't effectively assist neighborhoods": Maguire, "Neighborhood Assistance Office Stirs Controversy."

168   "There's been a suspicion": Editorial, "Plus for Urban Development," *Sunday Journal and Star*, July 16, 1978.

168   Lincoln was one of ten cities: Dick Piersol, "Traveling Road Show Trying to Sell Lincoln," *Lincoln Journal*, November 13, 1977.

168   Representing the range of Lincoln's: Piersol, "Traveling Road Show."

168   *citizens: In addition to the mayor, three citizens joined Lincoln's presentation to the All-America City award jury in Denver. Dick White, past chairman of the Downtown Advisory Committee, described how businesses worked with city government to develop a downtown redevelopment plan. Jacqueline Herman, past chair of the Community Development Task Force and Near South Neighborhood Association member, related how city government and neighborhood organizations worked together on housing and neighborhood redevelopment, arts festivals, clean-up campaigns, etc. Bob Hans, past chairman of the Goals and Policies Committee, explained efforts

to elicit citizen views on updating the Comprehensive Plan for guiding Lincoln's growth and land use through the year 2000. Piersol, "Traveling Road Show."

168 "Like other cities, Lincoln": Neal R. Peirce (*Washington Post*), "Grass-Roots Citizen Activism Thriving in U.S. Cities Large and Small," *Sunday Journal and Star*, May 14, 1978.

169 "Will you look": Dick Piersol, "All-America Forest Missing Some Trees," *Lincoln Journal*, June 14, 1978.

169 "I didn't think": "Absent Council Members Respond," *Lincoln Journal*, June 14, 1978.

169 "was Lincoln's party": Piersol, "All-America Forest."

169 "The Mayor was everywhere": Piersol, "All-America Forest."

169 "I don't know of another city": Gordon Winters, "Gallup Praises Lincoln for Citizen Involvement," *Lincoln Star*, June 14, 1978.

169 "Gallup's comments are greatly": Editorial, "Citizen Involvement Big Plus in Lincoln's Winning Award," *Lincoln Star*, June 15, 1978.

170 *sharing: Lincoln's federal revenue-sharing funds were used to support the Lincoln Transportation System, fire and police, parks and recreation, finance (e.g., budget accounting system), storm sewers, public works (e.g., traffic signals), and human services. "Revenue Plan Wins First Round," *Lincoln Star*, June 10, 1977.

170 my mother had issued strict budgeting: Lynn Zerschling, "Mayor Does Not Believe Tax Cut Likely Next Year," *Lincoln Star*, February 19, 1976.

170 "perennial success in straight jacketing": Editorial, "New City Council Majority Sits on Consolidation Issue," *Lincoln Star*, July 20, 1977.

171 due to "galloping inflation": "Mayor's Report Confirms Crunch," *Lincoln Journal*, February 7, 1978.

171 "After several weeks of": Editorial, "Hard-to-Slash Budget," *Lincoln Journal*, August 3, 1978.

171 "the mayor's most vocal critic": Warren Weber, "Conservatives Set Their Goals," *Sunday Journal and Star*, May 21, 1978.

171 "Friction and power clashes": Warren Weber, "Sikyta to Head Council," *Sunday Journal and Star*, May 14, 1978.

171 "Cook pointedly says that he thinks": Weber, "Conservatives Set Their Goals."

172 "the real thrust of the Hampton amendment": Editorial, "Council Should Hire Own Staff," *Lincoln Journal*, September 12, 1978.

172 "to harass and embarrass": Editorial, "A Groundless Proposal," *Lincoln Star*, September 9, 1978.

172 Councilman Hampton opposed granting: Sandy Mohr, "Hampton against Rights Unit?" *Lincoln Journal*, October 27, 1977.

172   In response to Hampton's statement: Gordon Winters, "Hampton, Rights
       Agency at Odds," *Lincoln Star*, October 28, 1977.

172   *slur: "City Councilman Joe Hampton used a racially derogatory term to
       describe fellow Councilman John Robinson after a sometimes fiery public
       hearing Monday night. Though the two men disagree on the exact wording,
       Hampton admitted that he did use the word 'nigger' to describe Robinson's
       actions throughout the council debates on changing the city's anti-discrimi-
       nation laws" (Nancy Hicks, "Hampton Admits Using Word 'Nigger,'" *Lincoln
       Star*, November 5, 1977). After Hampton apologized to Robinson privately,
       Robinson declared in a council meeting that he would not settle for anything
       short of a public apology and said, "The statement was an affront to all black
       citizens, consequently I won't accept any private apology" (J. L. Schmidt,
       "Hampton Apology Rejected," *Lincoln Star*, November 8, 1977; see also War-
       ren Weber, "Robinson Doesn't Accept Apology," *Lincoln Journal*, November
       8, 1977).

172   "We never did believe": Editorial, "Hampton's Low-Level Attack Poisons the
       Atmosphere," *Lincoln Star*, November 9, 1977.

173   "Add the fact that": Editorial, "Past Political Alignments."

FLASH BACKWARD: ROOTS—ALL GREEK TO ME

174   "Your mother's values and my values": George V. Voinovich, interview.

174   "Your mother's working in the family restaurant": Paul Sarbanes, interview.

175   *country: In 2003 Mary Beth took me to New York and we visited the re-
       stored Ellis Island. We stood at the upper-level railing above the large room
       where bedraggled immigrants had waited in lines for entry to new lives in
       America. We could almost hear their ghostly whispers in scores of languages.
       I imagined my mother, Bertha, at age nine and her sisters, grabbing tightly to
       their frightened but determined mother. I was moved at the view from Ellis
       Island of the Statue of Liberty, remembering how my mother described the
       thrill of seeing the great lady at the end of her miserable voyage from
       Greece in 1909.

176   *not: My mother, Bertha, did not tell me the story of her romance with
       Louie Greene until the 1960s. Her sister Anna and Anna's husband, Christ
       Legeros, were vacationing in Florida when a handsome older man came to
       their restaurant table and asked, "Are you Anna Flogeras?" When Anna re-
       plied yes, the man said, "You probably don't remember me. I'm Louie
       Greene. I knew you in New York. How is your sister Bertha?" After return-
       ing to Minneapolis, Anna told Bertha, widowed by then for many years, that
       she had seen Louie Greene and that he was a wealthy businessman who had
       never married. When Mary Beth heard the story she urged her Gram to

contact Louie Greene, but my mother, Bertha, answered simply, "I've lived my life, honey. All of that is past."

182   *world: Mendota Bridge, the final bridge over the Minnesota River before it flows into the Mississippi, was the longest concrete arch bridge in the world when it was built in 1926 and was called the "mile-long bridge."

184   *wine: I realized as an adult that my grandfather made his own wine, not because he liked doing it, but because of Prohibition.

185   *428 Fourth Street SE: Mike and I were visiting Mary Beth, Max, and our grandsons in Evanston for Christmas 2006. I couldn't sleep one night and pulled a thin book from the bookshelf in Michael's old bedroom. It was an old, beat-up book of poetry, and as I thumbed through it I recognized many of the Eugene Field poems, such as "Jest 'Fore Christmas" and "Little Boy Blue." Remembering from my childhood, I could recite them by heart.

The next morning I took the little book downstairs to ask Mary Beth where she had gotten it. She said she had picked it up from a street vendor's sidewalk table of used books in New York City a few years earlier, along with a Greek history book she had sent to her Uncle Nick and a book on Yeats that she sent to a former Carleton professor. "Why did you buy this one?" I asked. She said she likes poetry and also thought the book looked really old, perhaps like an old treasure that turns up on *Antiques Road Show*, but she had forgotten it until I pulled it off the shelf.

I recited some of the poems from my childhood as we poured through the pages together. What I hadn't noticed the night before were some faint pencil markings on the front pages—"Minneapolis Minnesota" and "Elaine Geankop"—the latter went to the edge of the page, as if the writer had run out of room. The next page was scrawled in the same handwriting "Halan." Impossible—but could this be my book from my childhood? We both had goose bumps. But why *"Elaine* Geankop"? Mary Beth came up with a theory that one of my Greek relatives wrote "Elaine," the American version of my Greek name, Eleni, and then was corrected by another Greek who might have said, "No, her name is Halan" (which is how Helen sounds with a Greek accent).

By this time, our husbands, Max and Mike, joined in our unsolved mystery/twilight zone conversation, and Max cautioned that we were getting carried away. After all, what were the odds that my actual childhood book would make its way to a street vendor in New York and that my daughter would unknowingly purchase it some seventy years later? Mike, the careful scientist, perused the book, page by page. He found the answer.

On a back page in even fainter pencil, written so close to the spine of the book that you would miss it if the page were not opened completely flat, was an address: "428 4th Street SE, Minneapolis Minn." Unbelievable—the poetry book was mine.

185   *Center: During the summer of 2006, Mary Beth and I drove to Minneapolis to visit my sisters. We stopped to eat at Cuzzy's, a restaurant near our hotel. In after-dinner conversation about southeast Minneapolis with the cook, I was astonished to discover his family relationship to Tony DeMuse, my dad's Sports Center partner of seventy years ago.

187   *Florest: Florest is a more Americanized version of my grandparents' name, Flogeras.

187   *Humphrey: Because of Uncle Gus Florest's close friendship with Hubert Humphrey, my folks bought Humphrey's house when he moved to Washington DC after being elected U.S. senator.

187   *DFLers: DFL is the Minnesota Democratic-Farmer-Labor Party, a merger of the Minnesota Democratic Party and Farmer-Labor Party that Humphrey was instrumental in forging.

CHAPTER 5. EXPECT THE UNEXPECTED

206   "Although Helen had her": Robert E. Knoll, interview.

206   "The qualities that made Helen": Ross E. Hecht, interview.

206   "Boosalis for Mayor" sign: Gordon Winters, "Matzke Plans Race for Mayor," *Lincoln Star*, December 2, 1978.

207   Speculation soon surfaced: "Matzke on the Go," *Sunday Journal and Star*, December 17, 1978.

207   "lingering anti-woman sentiment": Editorial, "Matzke First to Announce Mayor's Race Is On," *Lincoln Star*, December 4, 1978.

207   When Matzke paid a courtesy visit: Winters, "Matzke Plans Race for Mayor."

207   Max Denney announced: Warren Weber, "Denney Will Run, Maybe, for Mayor," *Lincoln Journal*, April 1, 1977.

207   Even former mayor Sam: "Schwartzkopf May Seek Mayor Post," *Lincoln Journal*, May 24, 1977.

207   He overhauled the police department: Paula Dittrick, "Lincoln Team Policing Approach Said a First," *Lincoln Star*, June 19, 1978.

208   Editorials lauded the mayor's tough: Editorial, "Burglary Rate Is Falling," *Sunday Journal and Star*, June 13, 1976.

208   council agreed that Chief: Warren Weber, "Council Applauds Hansen's Work," *Sunday Journal and Star*, January 29, 1978.

208   "has been a truly rewarding": George Hansen, Chief of Police, to Mayor Helen Boosalis, December 19, 1978.

208   "her capacity for tough": Editorial, "City Hall Announcements Bring Record into Focus," *Lincoln Star*, December 20, 1978.

209   Even Council Chairman Sikyta: Editorial, "Thank You George Hansen," *Lincoln Journal*, December 20, 1978.

209 Only Councilman Scherer: Gary Seacrest, "Council oκ of Leitner Is Expected," *Sunday Journal and Star*, January 7, 1979.

209 even had a medical exam: Gordon Winters, "Sikyta Council Candidate This Time," *Lincoln Star*, January 19, 1979.

209 "It is no secret": Editorial, "In Eight Years, the World," *Lincoln Star*, January 19, 1979.

209 "prevented people in the business": Bob Reeves, "Part-Time Mayor Plan Advocated by Sikyta," *Lincoln Star*, February 15, 1979.

209 The same *Star* editorial considered: Editorial, "City Hall Announcements Bring Record into Focus."

210 "tough re-election battle": Editorial, "City Hall Announcements Bring Record into Focus."

210 ten candidates had announced: Editorial, "A Crucial Election Yields Few Candidates," *Lincoln Star*, February 19, 1979.

210 "colorful lot": Editorial, "Large, and Growing, Field," *Lincoln Star*, February 8, 1979.

210 a former police officer: Joe Hudson, "Two More Seek Boosalis Post," *Lincoln Star*, December 23, 1978.

210 juvenile group home counselor: "Mayoral Candidate Kushner Favors Income Tax for Lincoln," *Lincoln Star*, February 6, 1979.

210 medical supply company president: Hudson, "Two More Seek Boosalis Post."

210 "It's a man's world": Warren Weber, "Bob Scanlon in Race for Mayor," *Lincoln Journal*, February 7, 1979.

210 *home: Apparently, Scanlon changed his mind about electing women mayors. I discovered a half-inch newspaper ad (perhaps from the personals) that ran before the 1979 general election: "Vote Helen Boosalis for Mayor. Paid for by Bob Scanlon."

211 Susan Welch, then chair of the uNL Political Science: Gordon Winters, "Sex Not Considered City Election Issue," *Lincoln Star*, April 12, 1979.

211 "say more about Mrs. Boosalis' political": Editorial, "Large, and Growing, Field."

211 "[Matzke's] work in the public": Editorial, "Large, and Growing, Field."

212 A *Journal* editorial deciphered the code: Editorial, "Sikyta Sets Election Agenda," *Lincoln Journal*, January 22, 1979.

212 "My sense is that her": Kathleen Rutledge, interview.

212 "Helen received a bum rap": Rich Bailey, interview.

212 "approach was inclusive": John Rosenow, interview.

212 sixty visits to Lincoln businesses: Gordon Winters, "Both Boosalis, Matzke Want to Do Well in Primary," *Lincoln Star*, March 30, 1979.

212 earned more business support: Warren Weber, "Ho-hum Boosalis-Matzke

(etc.) Mayoral Race Probably Will Speed Up," *Sunday Journal and Star*, March 25, 1979.

212   "not the wild radical": Warren Weber, "Under Mayor Boosalis' Immaculate Coiffure Is Person Ranked First in Lincoln Power Poll," *Lincoln Journal*, June 17, 1977.

213   "a great deal of respect": Bob Reeves, "Matzke Perceives Major Issue as Different 'Leadership Styles,'" *Lincoln Star*, February 15, 1979.

213   "no one seems to be": Warren Weber, "Matzke Opens Campaign with Kind Words," *Lincoln Journal*, February 14, 1979.

213   "what all the other candidates": Editorial, "A Good Record Is Tough to Challenge," *Lincoln Star*, February 16, 1979.

213   "in tactical position to ambush": Editorial, "They're Off and Running!" *Lincoln Journal*, March 15, 1979.

213   "dislike for Mrs. Boosalis": Winters, "Both Boosalis, Matzke Want to Do Well."

214   "It's not surprising": Editorial, "Beware of Councilmen Promising Support," *Lincoln Star*, March 17, 1979.

215   "I think the source of": Robert K. Schrepf, interview.

215   "Helen's biggest support was": Michael Merwick, interview.

216   "I think we need a word": Nancy McClelland, interview.

216   "What was really special": Kevin J. Donnellan, interview.

216   downzoning—when a piece of property: Gordon Winters, "Citizens' Planning Group Which Published Ad Has 2 Members," *Lincoln Star*, January 26, 1979.

216   "totally unfair to property owners": "Downzoning Downgraded by Matzke," *Lincoln Journal*, January 26, 1979.

217   "Mayor Boosalis' opponents": Editorial, "Council to Take Time on Proposed Zoning Code," *Lincoln Star*, February 5, 1979.

217   In a news conference, she reminded: "Without Study, Mayor Would Veto Zoning," *Lincoln Star*, January 27, 1979.

217   Matzke pressed the mayor: "Boosalis Is Mum on Brogden," *Lincoln Star*, February 22, 1979.

217   "control and if need be oversee": Political advertisement, *Lincoln Journal*, March 5, 1979.

217   "be bullied into promising": Editorial, "Mayor Won't Succumb to Political Pressure," *Lincoln Star*, March 1, 1979.

218   "My integrity and my sense": Editorial, "Mayor Won't Succumb to Political Pressure."

218   "citizens of Lincoln who have worked": Letter to editor from Stan Matzke, "Zoning Code," *Lincoln Star*, February 7, 1979.

218   "As the challenger": Karen Maguire, "Family Tradition Part of Why Matzke Cares," *Lincoln Journal*, March 28, 1979.

218 "It's like the governor": Letter to the editor from Russell Dodworth, "Mayor Is There," *Lincoln Star*, March 19, 1979.

218 "During the 1975 campaign": "Boosalis Doesn't See Easy Win," *Lincoln Journal*, March 28, 1979.

220 the bond rate penalty: Gordon Winters, "Lincoln General's Ties to City Questioned Anew," *Lincoln Star*, March 3, 1979.

220 extinguishing the city's budgetary: Gordon Winters, "City Urged to Loosen LGH Ties," *Lincoln Star*, March 28, 1979.

220 "Only in the legal": Editorial, "New Route to Old Goal," *Lincoln Star*, March 5, 1979.

220 needed the city's credit: Editorial, "Proposed Lincoln General Lease Raises Many Public Policy Issues," *Lincoln Journal*, March 24, 1979.

220 "relinquish control of Lincoln General": "Council Hears Pros, Cons to Change City-Hospital Pact," *Lincoln Journal*, March 27, 1979.

220 He described the stigma: Winters, "City Urged to Loosen LGH Ties."

221 If the council's real concern: Gordon Winters, "Action on Hospital Lease Postponed for One Week," *Lincoln Star*, April 3, 1979.

221 "some of its mandate": "Council Hears Pros, Cons."

221 *Adventists: In 1979 the Adventists' health services group operated more than four hundred hospitals worldwide and sixty hospitals nationwide, with ability to purchase hospital supplies at a 25 percent reduction. Winters, "City Urged to Loosen LGH Ties." In 1976 Union College, operated by the Seventh-day Adventist church, had expressed interest in buying the hospital if it was for sale.

221 The Adventists group asked: "Lincoln General: Adventists Want to Run Hospital," *Lincoln Journal*, April 2, 1979.

221 *Lincoln Journal* summarized: Editorial, "City Must Pull Bond Issue Oars, Whether Hospital Lease Goes or Not," *Lincoln Journal*, March 30, 1979.

222 "not germane": Winters, "Action on Hospital Lease Postponed."

223 "biggest change on the local political scene": Editorial, "One Incumbent Says 'No,'" *Lincoln Star*, January 6, 1979.

223 "burned out" Councilman Jeambey: Karen Maguire, "Jeambey Won't Run for Re-election to City Council," *Lincoln Journal*, January 5, 1979.

223 *reelection: Jeambey, a Presbyterian minister, said his last two years on the council—when he was in the two-man minority—were marked by back-room caucuses, economic self-interests, and political posturing, which he defined overall as "trying to make the Mayor look bad." Warren Weber, "Jeambey Reflects as Council Term Ends," *Lincoln Journal*, April 27, 1979.

224 "The election may serve": Editorial, "Negative Council Image to Be an Election Factor?" *Lincoln Star*, March 31, 1979.

224 a "liberal slate": Warren Weber, "Conservatives Claim Liberal Slate Push," *Lincoln Journal*, March 28, 1979.

224 "perceived by some as an anti-establishment": Warren Weber, "Lincoln Alliance Back in Picture," *Lincoln Journal*, April 26, 1979.

224 Hampton contended that the Alliance: Weber, "Lincoln Alliance Back in Picture."

224 "a possible power play": Political advertisement, *Lincoln Star*, April 26, 1979.

225 "The council majority": Editorial, "City Council Record Demands a Change," *Lincoln Star*, April 25, 1979.

225 Matzke expressed his surprise: Bob Reeves, "Mayor Admits Campaign Will Be Hard," *Lincoln Star*, April 4, 1979.

225 my mother predicted that Matzke's primary lead: Warren Weber, "Matzke Surprised by Mayoral Lead; Boosalis Didn't See Shoo-in Election," *Lincoln Journal*, April 4, 1979.

226 "People kept telling me": Reeves, "Mayor Admits Campaign Will Be Hard."

226 "We'll have to work": Weber, "Matzke Surprised by Mayoral Lead."

226 "My job was not asking": Elizabeth A. Peterson, interview.

226 "Challenger Stan Matzke now must be reckoned": Editorial, "Sorting Election Results," *Lincoln Journal*, April 4, 1979.

227 "Mayor Helen Boosalis is hardly": Editorial, "Incumbency Not Helpful in Some Primary Races," *Lincoln Star*, April 5, 1979.

227 "Some Cities Are Dying": Political advertisement, *Lincoln Journal*, March 18, 1979.

228 "Some Cities Are Dangerous": Political advertisement, *Sunday Journal and Star*, April 1, 1979.

229 Lincoln's "strong city administration": Quoting article in *Advertising Age*, December 1977.

229 "I'll take the hassle": Political advertisement, *Sunday Journal and Star*, April 1, 1979.

229 "We didn't become an All America City": Political advertisement, *Sunday Journal and Star*, April 1, 1979.

229 series of Matzke ads: Political advertisements, *Lincoln Star*, March 3, 5, 1979.

229 mayoral campaign in Chicago: Editorial, "Gee, Look What the Voters Did," *Lincoln Journal*, February 28, 1979.

229 "I love Lincoln": Political advertisement, *Lincoln Star*, March 31, 1979.

229 "an integral part of Matzke's": Weber, "Matzke Surprised by Mayoral Lead."

230 "far more agressive": "Boosalis, Matzke Scheduled to Debate," *Daily Nebraskan*, April 11, 1979.

230 "so we can find out": Gordon Winters, "Matzke Will Debate, If He Can Fit It into His Schedule," *Lincoln Star*, April 7, 1979.

230 "It's a question": Winters, "Matzke Will Debate."

230 "the larger concepts": Winters, "Matzke Will Debate."

230 A "warm-up" debate: Gordon Winters, "Mayoral Hopefuls Spar at Warm-up Debate," *Lincoln Star*, April 20, 1979.

230 "cooperation does not mean": Tom Prentiss, "Matzke, Boosalis and Candidates Debate City Issues," *Daily Nebraskan*, April 30, 1977.

230 "he must have four": Winters, "Mayoral Hopefuls Spar."

231 "on which there were fresh statements": Gordon Winters, "Debate Brings Few Ripples," *Lincoln Star*, April 23, 1979.

231 council approved the proposed hospital: Gordon Winters, "Lincoln General Lease Is ok'd," *Lincoln Star*, April 10, 1979.

231 "the most arrogant abuse": Gordon Winters, "Mayor to Veto Hospital 'Giveaway,'" *Lincoln Star*, April 11, 1979.

232 "For a person normally": Editorial, "lgh Lease Provides No Relief from Politics, *Lincoln Star*, April 11, 1979.

232 "If the Big Five": Editorial, "Of Hospital Leases and 'Giveaways,'" *Lincoln Journal*, April 11, 1979.

232 "using the occasion to deliver": Warren Weber, "Mayor Condemns Council in Vetoing Hospital Lease," *Lincoln Journal*, April 19, 1979.

233 "I perceive the present city": Gordon Winters, "Boosalis Vetoes Lease for Lincoln General," *Lincoln Star*, April 18, 1979.

233 The report "pointed out how": Editorial, "Issue in Hospital Lease Remains Control, Not Trust or Economics," *Lincoln Journal*, April 20, 1979.

233 "He has forgotten the public": "Boosalis: Brungard Actions Unethical," *Lincoln Journal*, April 23, 1979.

233 Charles Brown announced: Warren Weber, "Petitioners Ready If Hospital Lease Veto Fails," *Lincoln Journal*, April 20, 1979.

234 If enough petition signatures: Jim Camden, "Petition Drive Seems Success," *Lincoln Star*, April 25, 1979.

234 "It was at this point": William F. Austin, remarks at Community Builder Award luncheon honoring Helen Boosalis, May 7, 2002, Lincoln.

235 "grossly misled": Karen Maguire, "Hospital Lease Is Center of Council, Petition Duel," *Lincoln Journal*, April 24, 1979.

235 "The mayor has finally come out": Maguire, "Hospital Lease."

235 "low-key than spirited": Winters, "Debate Brings Few Ripples."

235 "If it cost 10,000 votes": Winters, "Debate Brings Few Ripples."

235 "who previously hedged": Warren Weber, "Matzke Would Have Vetoed Hospital Lease," *Lincoln Journal*, April 23, 1979.

235 He told the debate audience: Winters, "Debate Brings Few Ripples."

236 "because he had not read it": Winters, "Debate Brings Few Ripples."

236 Matzke claimed that Brown: Weber, "Matzke Would Have Vetoed."

236 "If I'm going to sign one": Tom Prentiss, "Matzke Supports Mayor's Hospital Veto, Criticized Zoning," *Daily Nebraskan*, April 23, 1979.

236 Matzke did sign a petition: Tom Prentiss, "Matzke, Boosalis and Candidates Debate City Issues."

236 "That Matzke reportedly signed": Editorial, "Boosalis Deserves Second Term," *Lincoln Journal*, April 26, 1979.

236 "Has there ever been": Editorial, "People Care about Hospital!" *Lincoln Journal*, April 25, 1979.

237 Called "spontaneous and unorchestrated": Editorial, "They Sent 'Em a Message," *Lincoln Star*, April 25, 1979.

237 "Most, we think, regard": Editorial, "They Sent 'Em a Message."

237 "The proponents of": "Mayor Hails Hospital Lease Petition Drive," *Lincoln Journal*, April 25, 1979.

237 "When I vetoed the lease": Camden, "Petition Drive Seems Success."

239 "Mrs. Boosalis' toughest test would be": Editorial, "Boosalis Deserves Second Term."

239 "From her reorganization": Editorial, "The Boosalis Record: A Promise Kept," *Lincoln Star*, April 24, 1979.

240 45 percent for Matzke: Karen Maguire, "Mayor Poll Shows Matzke Ahead," *Sunday Journal and Star*, April 29, 1979.

240 "Isn't it great?": Warren Weber, "Mayor Jubilant over Re-election," *Lincoln Journal*, May 2, 1979.

240 My mother told the crowd: Weber, "Mayor Jubilant over Re-election."

241 "I have never seen": "Boosalis Wins with Unexpected Ease," *Daily Nebraskan*, May 2, 1979.

241 "It was Helen Boosalis' night": Weber, "Mayor Jubilant over Re-election."

241 The pollsters tried to explain: C. David Kotok, "sri Pollsters Say Election Was the One Example in 20," *Lincoln Journal*, May 2, 1979.

242 Both the pollster and the newspaper editor: Kotok, "sri Pollsters."

242 "traveled across town at the hour": Editorial, "The Good Stretch Run," *Lincoln Star*, May 3, 1979.

242 "You're a heck": Weber, "Mayor Jubilant over Re-election."

242 "Something happened": Gordon Winters, "Win Amazes Mayor," *Lincoln Star*, May 2, 1979.

243 "While the mayor was given credit": Editorial, "Politics Overemphasized in Hospital Controversy," *Lincoln Star*, July 4, 1979.

243 "he had become identified": Winters, "Win Amazes Mayor."

243 "what he said may have been": Weber, "Mayor Jubilant over Re-election."

243 "presumed to be supportive": Winters, "Win Amazes Mayor."

244 "Maybe I won't need": "Boosalis Wins with Unexpected Ease."

244 "The electorate took surprising": Editorial, "Beyond Change in Style, No Point to Predictions," *Lincoln Star*, May 14, 1979.

244 "I thought with eight": "Sikyta 'Surprised' by Frohardt Win," *Lincoln Star*, May 2, 1979.

244 "a voice in the wilderness": Karen Maguire, "Arrogance Said Council Race Role," *Lincoln Journal*, May 2, 1979.

244   "the sheer reality": Bill Kreifel, "No Earthshaking Events Foreseen When New City Council Takes Office," *Sunday Journal and Star*, May 13, 1979.

244   "radically changed Lincoln's": Editorial, "A Time to Remember: The 'Liberals' Waltz In," *Lincoln Star*, May 3, 1979.

244   "would be a political threat": Editorial, "History Backs Guess That City Can Adapt," *Lincoln Star*, May 7, 1979.

245   "The council majority's decision": Editorial, "OK Corral, Revisited; or Looking at Election Results," *Lincoln Journal*, May 2, 1979.

245   "Arrogance may have been": Maguire, "Arrogance Said Council Race Role."

245   "I'm a liberal": Kreifel, "No Earthshaking Events Foreseen."

245   "Describing Tuesday night": Editorial, "A Time to Remember."

246   lame-duck council rushed to reach: Gordon Winters, "Council Sprinting to Pass Zoning Code," *Lincoln Star*, May 8, 1979.

246   "over the barrel": Editorial, "New Zoning Ordinance Ends Lengthy Process," *Lincoln Star*, May 11, 1979.

246   The old council and the mayor: Karen Maguire, "Neighborhood Leaders Say New Zoning Code Workable," *Lincoln Journal*, May 9, 1979; Gordon Winters, "Mayor Wins Compromise," *Lincoln Star*, May 9, 1979.

246   *concerns: The new zoning code respected most land-use designations made in the 1977 Comp Plan by (1) encouraging residential and commercial growth to the north, west, and south of Lincoln Center and discouraging it to the east (Stevens Creed watershed); (2) reserving sizable blocks of land for future industrial development; (3) discouraging urban sprawl; and (4) helping preserve existing housing in older neighborhoods. Editorial, "At Last, New Zoning Code," *Lincoln Journal*, May 11, 1979.

246   "they were correct": "Lincoln General's Lease to Association Repealed," *Lincoln Star*, May 15, 1979.

247   the new council voted 5–2: Gordon Winters, "New Blood Takes Over in Council Transfusion," *Lincoln Star*, May 15, 1979.

247   "This being Mrs. Boosalis' final term": Editorial, "OK Corral, Revisited."

247   "the next four years": Editorial, "The Good Stretch Run."

FLASH FORWARD: GETTING TO KNOW YOU

248   The offices opened at: Nancy Hicks, "Pace Grows Faster at Two Campaign Headquarters," *Lincoln Star*, October 16, 1986.

248   Kay Orr didn't have an office: Hicks, "Pace Grows Faster."

249   campaign manager Marg Badura: "State Gubernatorial Race Attracts National Interest," *Lincoln Journal*, May 19, 1986.

249   added Omaha attorney Tom Litjen: C. David Kotok, "Mrs. Boosalis Toasted in Omaha," *Omaha World-Herald*, June 6, 1986.

249   The campaign organizational plan: Kathleen Rutledge, "Duo Splits Boosalis Campaign Work," *Sunday Journal-Star*, August 10, 1986.

249   "mean member of the Kennedy": Richard Shugrue, editorial, *Omaha Daily Record*, September 22, 1986.

249   "Because it's Helen": "Kerrey Aide to Help Boosalis Campaign," *Omaha World-Herald*, June 25, 1986.

250   "You're not doing me a favor": "Helen Boosalis: The Campaign Has Been Fun," *Grand Island (NE) Independent*, October 30, 1986.

250   "pressing the flesh to be": Dorraine Harris, "Boosalis, Jefferson Swap Views," *Hastings (NE) Tribune*, June 30, 1986.

250   The little town of Dodge: "Dodge Crowded as Parade Passes," *Fremont (NE) Tribune*, July 7, 1986.

250   On the Fourth of July itself: C. David Kotok, "Candidates Shaking Hands across Nebraska," *Omaha World-Herald*, July 4, 1986.

252   not uncomfortable riding the symbol: Henry J. Cordes, "2 Governor Hopefuls Ride Elephants," *Omaha World-Herald*, August 26, 1986.

252   "The candidates are battle-hardened": Larry Batson (*Minneapolis Star and Tribune*), "'Economy Overshadows Gender in Nebraska's Prairie Classic,'" *Sunday World-Herald*, August 17, 1986.

253   "Boosalis is always relaxed": Quoted in Melvin Paul, "Campaigners Seek $$ Now, Votes in Fall," *Nebraska Newspaper*, July / August 1986.

253   "Helen is authentic": Bob Kerrey, interview.

253   "In high-visibility positions": Mike Johanns, interview.

253   "People trusted her": George Latimer, interview.

253   "Each has an easy approach": Kathleen Rutledge, "Gubernatorial Candidates Boosalis, Orr Return to the Basics on Campaign Trail," *Lincoln Journal*, September 19, 1986.

253   were "energy" and "warmth": "Mrs. Boosalis: Ex-Mayor Relishes Making It Happen," *Omaha World-Herald*, October 9, 1986.

254   "I don't have a secret formula": "Boosalis Leaves Age Critics Panting for Breath," *Sunday Journal-Star*, September 7, 1986.

254   "knowing you can make a difference": "Mrs. Boosalis: Ex-Mayor Relishes Making It Happen."

254   "She doesn't get real uptight": "Boosalis Leaves Age Critics Panting."

254   "leaves men and women half her age": "Boosalis Leaves Age Critics Panting."

254   "First, he showed up at": Michael Doan and Michel Bosc, "Women Power on the Prairie," *U.S. News and World Report*, May 26, 1986.

255   "During one campaign, I remember": Beatty Brasch, interview.

255   "This woman is high energy": Kathleen Rutledge and Fred Knapp, "Orr and Boosalis Make Final Pitches," *Lincoln Journal*, November 3, 1986.

255   "Helen listened to the neighborhoods": Don Walton, "Boosalis Launches Election Campaign," *Lincoln Star*, July 29, 1986.

255 "If you have a stake": "Mrs. Boosalis: Ex-Mayor Relishes Making It Happen."

256 "My greatest strength is": C. David Kotok, "Mrs. Boosalis Shuns Liberal Label," *Omaha World-Herald*, April 15, 1986.

256 "Never in my memory": C. David Kotok, "Governor's Race Pulls Attention in Washington," *Sunday World-Herald*, May 18, 1986.

256 *genuine: My dad's encouragement of and respect for my mother's political life remained unchanged from that reported in 1978 when his wife was mayor: "You don't have to visit with Mike Boosalis very long to discover that he is not intimidated, threatened or resentful of his wife's position as head of city government; instead, he is an articulate enthusiast, eager to tell you about her 'many attributes,' such as her 'marvelous disposition.'" Jim Raglin, "Close to Home," *Lincoln Journal*, January 6, 1978.

256 "I knew she had the potential": Nancy Hicks, "Candidates' Husbands Are Supportive," *Lincoln Star*, June 9, 1986.

257 "I will when you run": Evan Roth, "Helen, Mike Boosalis at Ease in Spotlight," *Sunday World-Herald*, May 18, 1986.

257 "My mother is a unique": "Mary Boosalis-Davis Still Campaigns for Her Mom," *Sunday Journal-Star*, August 17, 1986.

257 "More women at the top": Maria Paul, "Politics in 1986: Women on the Move," *Chicago Sun-Times*, October 9, 1986.

257 *reporter: Expressing similar sentiments twenty years later, Justice Ruth Bader Ginsburg said in a speech to the Chicago Foundation for Women (December 10, 2005): "In her [Justice Sandra Day O'Connor's] own words, 'For both men and women, the first step in getting power is to become visible to others—and then to put on an impressive show.' As women achieve power, the barriers will fall. As society sees what women can do, *as women see what women can do*, there will be more women out there doing things, and we'll all be better off for it" (emphasis added). Transcript, "Honoring a Pioneer in Women's Rights: A Conversation with Supreme Court Justice Ruth Bader Ginsberg," hosted by Chicago Foundation for Women, December 10, 2005.

257 Orr's campaign co-chair Art Knox: C. David Kotok, "Orr, Boosalis Strategies Contrast Early in Race," *Omaha World-Herald*, August 17, 1986.

258 "Boosalis may project more": Don Walton, "The Governor's Race Is Off and Running," *Lincoln Star*, August 1, 1986.

258 "She wants to be sure people understand": Kotok, "Orr, Boosalis Strategies Contrast."

CHAPTER 6. EVERYTHING OLD IS NEW AGAIN

259 "Helen could have a heated debate": E. Benjamin Nelson, interview.
259 "In all my years in government": Michael Merwick, interview.

260   "petty politics": Editorial, "LES Slate Promising," *Lincoln Star*, July 4, 1979.

260   deemed a "white elephant": "Council Majority Votes to Buy Old Federal Building, Post Office," *Lincoln Journal*, July 3, 1979.

261   "the knot that once bound": Karen Maguire, "Lincoln: Struggle for Power," *Sunday Journal and Star*, September 21, 1980.

261   "among the neighborhood-allied leaders": Maguire, "Lincoln: Struggle for Power."

261   "The Old Pols see too much": Maguire, "Lincoln: Struggle for Power."

262   "the answer came in 1979": Maguire, "Lincoln: Struggle for Power."

262   "Whatever Helen (Boosalis) wants": Karen Maguire, "City Councilman Scherer: City Hall in Power Play," *Lincoln Star*, August 8, 1979.

262   "power play plan": Editorial, "Still Fighting the Last War," *Lincoln Star*, August 11, 1979.

262   "I still don't support": Letter to editor from Leo Scherer, "No Yes Man," *Lincoln Star*, November 10, 1979.

263   he disagreed with her politically: "Leo Scherer Incensed at Lack of TV Invite," *Lincoln Journal*, April 29, 1980.

263   "I'm tired of being pushed": "TV Show 'Snub' Angers Scherer," *Lincoln Star*, April 29, 1980.

263   "he considers one of his political enemies": "TV Show 'Snub' Angers Scherer."

263   create an Economic Development Commission: "City Staff Proposed for Promotion Unit," *Lincoln Star*, February 10, 1981.

263   "Scherer authored the idea": Editorial, "A New Commission?" *Lincoln Star*, February 13, 1981.

263   Although Lincoln had enjoyed: Matt Truell, "Boosalis Dampens Economic Session," *Lincoln Journal*, May 15, 1981.

264   "one of the all-time fast": Gene Kelly, "Centrum Plaza Is Deep in Heart of Watson Country," *Lincoln Journal*, October 2, 1979.

264   "leadership of public and private": Editorial, "Centrum, Another Lincoln Asset," *Lincoln Journal*, October 5, 1979.

264   retail business boomed: Gerry Switzer, "Centrum Given Much of Credit for Booming Downtown Business," *Lincoln Star*, November 23, 1979.

264   Much of the increase: Gerry Switzer, "Centrum Impact on Businesses Said Big Business," *Lincoln Star*, February 11, 1980.

265   form a regional shopping complex: Kelly, "Centrum Plaza Is Deep in Heart."

265   Centrum Plaza was near full occupancy: Gene Kelly, "Centrum Plaza Merchants Registering Good Sales Year," *Sunday Journal and Star*, October 5, 1980.

265   waiting list of tenants: "Centrum Now Has Waiting List," *Lincoln Star*, July 14, 1982.

265 Brandeis management explained: Gerry Switzer, "Brandeis Will Close 4 Stores," *Lincoln Star*, July 22, 1980; "Businessmen Echo Hope for Store to Replace Brandeis," *Lincoln Star*, July 22, 1980.

265 The general manager expressed confidence: Gene Kelly, "Downtown Brandeis Store 1 of 4 Closing," *Lincoln Journal*, July 21, 1980.

265 *conditions: The economic slump had brought mass layoffs in the construction industry and in other Lincoln businesses such as Outboard Marine, Goodyear plants, Square D, and Snyder Industries. Gerry Switzer, "Lincoln Layoffs Total More Than 1000 Employees," *Lincoln Star*, July 23, 1980.

265 "I think it's pretty short-sighted": "Officials, Merchants Lament Brandeis News," *Lincoln Journal*, July 21, 1980.

265 Yet revenues of Miller and Paine: Gerry Switzer, "Downtown Panel Urges Sale of Haymarket Lot," *Lincoln Star*, September 20, 1980.

265 The mayor moved quickly: Bob Reeves, "DAC Task Force to Study Future of Brandeis Store," *Lincoln Star*, August 15, 1980.

266 "the announcement of the Brandeis closing": Reeves, "DAC Task Force."

266 "The Downtown Advisory Committee's task force": Editorial, "Boosalis and DAC Off on Right Track," *Lincoln Star*, August 19, 1980.

266 A feasibility study of the site: Gerry Switzer, "Brandeis Contract Signed," *Lincoln Star*, September 3, 1981.

268 sales in Centrum Plaza shops: Gerry Switzer, "Downtown Survives Loss," *Lincoln Star*, September 3, 1981.

268 Within six months at a press: L. Kent Wolgamott, "Brandeis Building to Be Remodeled," *Lincoln Journal*, March 5, 1982.

268 The office and retail complex: Gerry Switzer, "Brandeis Store to Be Gold's Galleria," *Lincoln Star*, May 13, 1982.

268 Forty percent of the space: Gene Kelly, "Historic Building Fast Taking on a New Look: Galleria at 11th and O Worth Its Weight in Gold," *Sunday Journal and Star*, July 18, 1982.

268 A Wisconsin developer: Karen Maguire, "Tax Increment Financing Considered for Cornhusker Convention Complex," *Sunday Journal and Star*, April 20, 1980.

268 To assemble such a large: James Joyce, "Cornhusker Bill over First Hurdle," *Lincoln Star*, March 5, 1980; Thomas A. Fogarty, "Lawmakers OK Bill on Cornhusker Block," *Lincoln Journal*, March 27, 1980.

268 *financing: Tax increment financing allows cities to raise money to help finance private projects by selling bonds. The increased property tax revenues from the finished project are earmarked for a period of time to pay off the bonds, thus reducing the developer's financing costs. After the bonds are paid off, all property tax revenues from the project can then be used for normal government expenses. George Hendrix, "Cornhusker Hotel Plan May Hinge on Survey," *Lincoln Star*, November 12, 1981.

269 The city then applied: Maguire, "Tax Increment Financing Considered."

269 *poverty: "Pockets of poverty" were defined as neighborhoods or areas within cities where more than 85 percent of the residents had incomes below 80 percent of the median income of the city and more than 35 percent had incomes below the national poverty level. Projects like hotels and shopping centers were viewed favorably for federal Urban Development Action Grants because they offered jobs for unskilled and semiskilled laborers living within the pockets of poverty. Bob Reeves, "Council OKS $5.6 Million Grant Application," *Lincoln Star*, April 29, 1980.

269 but Lincoln's relatively sound economy: Bob Reeves, "Mayor Feels Future Bright," *Lincoln Star*, November 27, 1980.

269 Lincoln's UDAG application: Bob Reeves, "City Hasn't Given Up Hope for Cornhusker Block Aid," *Lincoln Star*, December 30, 1980.

269 Lincoln had a good track record: Jake Thompson, "Grant Request Belly-up for Cornhusker Block," *Lincoln Journal*, December 24, 1980.

269 But soaring interest rates: David Swartzlander, "Boosalis Withdraws Cornhusker Bid," *Lincoln Journal*, June 3, 1981.

269 Out of the ashes: David Swartzlander and Gene Kelly, "Murdock Pondering Cornhusker Project," *Lincoln Journal*, August 13, 1981.

269 Murdock's early concept involved: Gerry Switzer, "Plans to Raze Cornhusker Hotel Again in Works," *Lincoln Star*, August 19, 1981.

269 could be considered "blighted": Hendrix, "Cornhusker Hotel Plan."

270 "Even Superman couldn't": David Swartzlander, "Murdock Expertise Cuts City Red Tape," *Sunday Journal and Star*, March 14, 1982.

270 mayor and Council Chairman Hampton: Swartzlander, "Murdock Expertise."

270 *bonds: Two types of bonds were sold for the Cornhusker Square project: $3.8 in tax-allocation bonds for the civic center to be paid back over fifteen years using taxing increment financing, and $1.6 million in parking revenue bonds. "Cornhusker Interest Rates Are Approved," *Lincoln Journal*, March 23, 1982.

270 area's listing on the National Register: George Hendrix, "Landmark Designation Sought," *Lincoln Star*, August 26, 1981.

271 after federal tax laws changed: Hendrix, "Landmark Designation Sought."

271 She received Burlington's response: George Hendrix, "Haymarket OK with BN," *Lincoln Star*, August 9, 1982.

271 *incentives: Newly enacted federal investment tax credits offered incentives to property owners for rehabilitation of their income-producing buildings that were registered as historic structures either nationally *or* locally. Lincoln's Historic Preservation Commission promptly applied for a *local* historic designation of the Haymarket area under Lincoln's preservation ordinance.

"Much of the credit for Lincoln's interest in historic preservation goes to Dan Kidd, the city's first preservation planner hired by the Mayor in December 1980. Kidd took advantage of the Economic Recovery Tax Act of 1981 to help developers recoup some of the expenses of renovation [through tax credits]." Tom Ineck, "Planner: Look at Preservation Must Include Look to Future," *Lincoln Journal*, May 17, 1984.

271   *opening: Construction of Cornhusker Square moved rapidly to completion. The mayor and the hotel's general manager christened the last load of concrete in topping-off ceremonies one year from the day the old hotel was imploded. The Cornhusker opened its doors in December 1983, months ahead of schedule and just months after the end of my mother's second term as mayor. A letter thanking her for "bringing an ambitious and far-reaching concept into actual reality" was signed by Murdock Development Company's senior vice-president, H. R. Haldeman.

271   "lamplighted cobblestone and brick walks": Gerry Switzer, "Downtown's a' Bustle with Building Projects," *Lincoln Star*, January 31, 1983.

271   expansion of high-density housing: "Mayor Plans Downtown Housing Study Group," *Lincoln Star*, June 6, 1979.

272   The architect of Centennial Mall: "Architect's Impact Is All Around Lincoln," *Sunday Journal and Star*, April 17, 1983.

272   *Enersen: After graduating from Harvard's Graduate School of Design in 1945, Larry Enersen stopped in Lincoln to visit college friend Ken Clark. Clark enticed him to form a partnership in Lincoln, and the two began practicing "on a rickety drafting table" in Clark's basement. Out of that basement eventually grew the firm Clark Enersen Partners, which in 1983 had twenty-four architects, landscape architects, and planners ("Architect's Impact"). Enersen's wife, Eleanore, was an outspoken advocate of services for people with disabilities. One summer in high school I worked for her at a day camp for children with disabilities and learned some of the most important lessons of my life.

272   "improving life through architectural": Glenda Peterson, "New Lincoln Mall Debuts on Friday," *Sunday Journal and Star*, April 17, 1983.

272   "It would be difficult to travel around Lincoln without seeing": Matt Truell, "Mall Architect Enersen Praised during Dedication," *Lincoln Journal*, April 12, 1983.

273   awarded a grant for a ride-sharing: George Hendrix, "City to Battle Single-Rider Cars," *Lincoln Star*, August 17, 1981.

273   Less than two years later: Don Walton, "Lincoln Gets $817,500," *Lincoln Star*, May 1, 1981.

273   "[federal transportation grant] award": Editorial, "Transportation Grant Due to Lincoln Record," *Lincoln Star*, May 4, 1981.

273 In its first years of operation: Melanie Gray, "Carpool/Vanpool Nets 12% Gain," *Lincoln Journal*, January 1, 1983.

273 "Soaring" gas prices: Editorial, "Buses, Yes, and Pooling, too," *Lincoln Journal*, April 14, 1980.

273 But even with increased ridership: Reid Warren, "LTS Doing Well, but Trouble Is on Horizon," *Lincoln Star*, September 8, 1981.

274 Municipal transit systems nationally: L. Kent Wolgamott, "LTS Expects $120,000 in Federal Cuts," *Lincoln Journal*, October 13, 1981.

274 *transportation: Financing Lincoln's bus system became a major impetus for the mayor and other elected officials to seek approval from the state legislature for an increase in the city's sales tax. "Cities Feeling Pinch of 7 Percent Lid," *Lincoln Journal*, October 19, 1981.

274 charged her Energy Action Committee: "Conversion of Trash to Fuel Subject of $44,000 Study," *Lincoln Star*, March 17, 1980; Gary Seacrest, "Energy Group Plan Runs into Roadblock," *Lincoln Journal*, March 18, 1980.

274 A Nebraska Energy Office study: Mitchel Benson, "Solid Waste 'Could Be Used' for Fuel," *Lincoln Journal*, July 28, 1979.

274 *fertilizer: UNL economist Greg Hayden spoke against the city's federal grant proposal to fund a solid waste plant because of rising fertilizer shortages that made municipal waste a "valuable national resource" for composting. Fertilizer shortages could even lead to making it illegal for cities to burn their trash. Bob Reeves, "Council Votes Not to Apply for a Garbage Plant," *Lincoln Star*, September 3, 1980.

274 "time will tell": Jake Thompson, "Council Sets Match to Proposal for City Garbage-Burning Plant," *Lincoln Journal*, September 3, 1980.

274 "just an honest difference": Jake Thompson, "Mayor Says Council's Defeat of Garbage Plant Not Personal," *Lincoln Journal*, September 4, 1980.

274 "loss is to the community": Bob Reeves, "Garbage Plan Kaput—Mayor," *Lincoln Star*, September 4, 1980.

274 "convince and cajole": Thompson, "Mayor Says Council's Defeat."

275 In late 1980 consumers angrily: Bob Reeves, "LES Rate Hike Sparks Concern," *Lincoln Star*, November 20, 1980.

275 But the electricity rate controversy: Editorial, "N-waste Problem Grows," *Lincoln Journal*, January 2, 1981.

275 a Nebraska Power Association study: Jim Aucoin, "Rising Costs Tarnish Nuclear Power's Image," *Sunday Journal and Star*, May 31, 1981.

275 "support continuing efforts by Mayor": Editorial, "LES Rate Cap Proposal May Not Realize Goal," *Lincoln Star*, March 2, 1981.

275 "sensitive to customers faced": Editorial, "Progress at LES," *Lincoln Star*, July 12, 1982.

275 LES became the first: Editorial, "LES Energy Audit Program Is First in the Nation," *Lincoln Star*, November 3, 1980.

275 The positive consumer response: Mary Kay Roth, "Lincoln Electric to Expand Energy Audit Program," *Lincoln Star*, February 22, 1981.

275 By 1981 city government: "City Government Cuts Energy Use by 11%," *Lincoln Star*, February 4, 1982.

276 "are absolute leaders in comprehensive planning": Dick Herman, "Not Only an All-America City, but a 'Premier' One as Well," *Lincoln Journal*, November 1, 1979.

276 "The plan should resemble": UPI, "Omaha Advised to Follow Lincoln in Urban-Growth Plan," *Lincoln Journal*, January 5, 1980.

277 The developer argued that the Comp Plan: George Hendrix, "Mayor Vetoes Apartments, Offices at 84th and O Sts.," *Lincoln Star*, June 9, 1982.

277 "While many would suggest that": Hendrix, "Mayor Vetoes Apartments, Offices."

277 "evidence of the kind of steely": Editorial, "Wise Land-Use Decisions," *Lincoln Journal*, June 9, 1982.

277 "fashioned after unprecedented public input": Editorial, "'Fat, Dumb, Indifferent' and a Great Place to Live," *Lincoln Star*, July 14, 1979.

278 "In our complacency": Gordon Winters, "Hampton Labels City Indifferent," *Lincoln Star*, July 13, 1979.

278 IBM replied that: Nancy Hicks, "No IBM Plant Planned for Lincoln Site," *Lincoln Star*, April 17, 1975; editorial, "Lincoln Was the Attraction," *Lincoln Evening Journal*, April 17, 1975.

278 "the city, rather than closing": Editorial, "'Fat, Dumb, Indifferent.'"

278 *career: The mayor expressed at the end of her second term how frustrating she found the anti-business label. "I regret an element of the business community hasn't publicly accepted my leadership. We work together, and get along privately. I don't know whether it's sexism or political differences. I think it's more political. Sharing power is a very difficult thing. It comes down to that" (Tom White, "Helen Boosalis: Homemaker to City-Maker," *Lincoln Star*, April 16, 1983). While my mother may have regretted that a segment of the business community had not accepted her leadership, others knew the value of her contributions to business. "The truth is that Helen has been one of the best friends Lincoln business has ever had. Her policies and her leadership have been an outstanding asset to the Lincoln business community" (editorial, "No Hell Like Fury of Influence Lost," *Lincoln Star*, August 11, 1982).

278 "completely out of sync": David Swartzlander, "Mail Supports Hampton Plan for Office Park," *Lincoln Journal*, April 20, 1982.

278 Although the city's Economic Development: David Swartzlander, "Commission Favors Hampton's Project," *Lincoln Journal*, April 23, 1982.

278 "Bad economic conditions": George Hendrix, "Hampton Zone Change Opposed by Planners," *Lincoln Star*, April 29, 1982.

278 "lashed out": David Swartzlander, "Rezoning Denial Angers Hampton," *Lincoln Journal*, April 29, 1982.

279 He argued that his proposed office: David Swartzlander, "Hampton Promotes Office Complex," *Lincoln Journal*, April 22, 1982.

279 "presents more of a problem": Editorial, "Planning Has Helped, Not Hurt, Economy," *Lincoln Star*, June 9, 1982.

279 "big difference between an individual's": Editorial, "Planning Has Helped."

279 "is clearly detrimental to the city": George Hendrix, "Steinman Defection Sustains Mayor's Veto," *Lincoln Star*, June 15, 1982.

279 Many developers held views on zoning: "Boosalis Prefers Steady Growth to Spectacular, Unlimited Growth," *Lincoln Star*, June 22, 1979.

279 *Committee: The community's official "Goals and Policies" were the foundation of the Comprehensive Plan from which the city's growth and land-use strategies and zoning ordinances were drawn. Editorial, "Proposed Comprehensive Plan Redo Not Really Comprehensive," *Lincoln Journal*, September 20, 1982.

279 *meeting: By registering, citizens became voting members of the Goals and Policies Committee and were eligible to vote on recommended changes to the Comprehensive Plan as long as they did not miss two successive committee meetings. Characterized by some as an invitation to special-interest groups to pack the committee's voting membership, it was also "a most democratic process." After the Goals and Policies Committee voted on amendments to update the Comp Plan, the proposed amendments then went to the Planning Commission for review and recommendation and finally to the city council and county board for ultimate approval. Editorial, "No Perfect Answer to Planning Input," *Lincoln Star*, September 22, 1982.

279 Former councilman Sikyta: George Hendrix, "Planning in Stevens Creek Defeated," *Lincoln Star*, September 22, 1982.

280 "a tribute to the desire": L. Kent Wolgamott, "Neighborhood Forces Successful at Goals and Policies," *Lincoln Journal*, September 22, 1982.

280 Goals and Policies Committee did not buy: Editorial, "Proposed Comprehensive Plan Redo."

280 "Helen was forward-looking": Coleen J. Seng, interview.

280 *revenue: A simplified picture of the tax-supported portion of the mayor's 1979–80 proposed budget showed the breakdown of each dollar (excluding amounts for operation of the city's public "businesses"—LES and Lincoln General Hospital—and excluding revenue from state / federal aid):

Revenues:			*Spending:*	
Local property tax	$.40		Public Safety (police, fire)	$.35
Sales tax (1 cent)	.25		Libraries, parks, recreation	.17
Other taxes, fees	.12		Transportation	.11
			General government	.10
			Community plan/develop	.05
			Municipal court, jail	.05
			Environmental control	.03
			Health	.03

Bob Reeves, "Boosalis' City Budget Includes 7% Increase Over Current Year," *Lincoln Star,* July 7, 1979.

281 My mother proposed for council consideration: Karen Maguire, "Mayor Lists Ways to Close Budget Gap," *Lincoln Journal,* March 21, 1980.

281 "melancholy process of retrenchment": Editorial, "City Budget: Something Must Give," *Lincoln Journal,* March 25, 1980.

281 "glum-sounding alternatives": Bob Reeves, "Council to Stay within 7% Lid," *Lincoln Star,* March 25, 1980.

281 high inflation rates (14.7 percent for the twelve: "Mayor's Budget Proposal Said to Be Right on the Mark," *Lincoln Journal,* July 10, 1980.

281 "We're just going to have to learn": Bob Reeves, "Mayor Budgets Cuts in Most City Services," *Lincoln Star,* July 10, 1980.

281 Not content with arguing: Editorial, "'Massaging the Figures,'" *Lincoln Star,* July 2, 1980.

282 8.5 percent wage and benefit package: "Police Union Claims City Won't Negotiate," *Lincoln Star,* August 5, 1980.

282 The fourth bargaining unit: Karen Maguire, "Lincoln Police Nix Wage Offer; Industrial Relations Gets Case," *Lincoln Journal,* October 8, 1980.

282 The state Commission of Industrial Relations: Editorial, "Lessons, Bitter and Otherwise," *Lincoln Journal,* May 27, 1981; Dick Piersol, "Kibosh Put on Police Pay Raises," *Lincoln Journal,* May 20, 1981.

282 Many officers had believed: Barb Koenig, "Lincoln Police Union Counsel Resigns; Rosenberg and Yungblut Hired by Local," *Lincoln Journal,* August 13, 1981.

282 "a total wipeout": Editorial, "Lessons, Bitter and Otherwise."

282 If the city were to renegotiate: Dick Piersol, "Police to Start '81–'82 Pay Talks; May Appeal Commission Ruling," *Lincoln Journal,* May 22, 1981.

282 "stunning and bitter blow": Editorial, "Lessons, Bitter and Otherwise."

282 union's legal counsel resigned: Koenig, "Lincoln Police Union Counsel Resigns."

282 "We were aware of": Kathryn Haugstatter, "Police Officers Ready to 'Take Job, Shove It,'" *Lincoln Star,* May 22, 1981.

282 "I think we bargained": George Hendrix, "City Says Police Pay Settled," *Lincoln Star*, May 22, 1981.

283 "they're the policy-making body": Bob Reeves, "Mayor Says Council Did Good Job," *Lincoln Star*, August 9, 1980.

283 Double-digit inflation: John J. McCusker, "What Was the Inflation Rate Then?" Economic History Services, 2001, www.eh.net/hmit/inflation/.

283 The recession of the early 1980s: Marc Labonte and Gail Makinen, "The Current Economic Recession: How Long, How Deep, and How Different from the Past?" Congressional Research Service, Library of Congress, CRS Report RL31237, CRS-15, January 10, 2002.

283 Business bankruptcies increased 50 percent: "The Economy in the 1980s," http://economics.about.com/od/useconomichistory/a/economy-1980s.htm.

283 In her usual "Sound Off": Bill Kreifel, "Mayor: Sound Offs Show Citizens Knowledgeable," *Sunday Journal and Star*, March 1, 1981.

284 Radial had become so contentious: Chris Welsch, "Radial Corridor's History Reveals Changes, Changes and More Changes," *Daily Nebraskan*, January 28, 1983.

284 Residents of neighborhoods bordering: Karen Maguire, "Youngberg Paints Lines for the Radial's Demise," *Lincoln Journal*, June 14, 1979.

284 In September 1979 the new council: Karen Maguire, "Council Approves Radial Task Force," *Lincoln Journal*, September 5, 1979.

284 Councilman Hampton and other Radial supporters: Editorial, "A Lot of Empty Talk from Radial Boosters," *Lincoln Star*, September 4, 1979.

284 In December the council approved: "Council Instruction to Radial Panel Leaves Some in Dark."

284 warned that the word "corridor": "Council Instruction to Radial Panel Leaves Some in Dark," *Lincoln Journal*, December 16, 1979.

284 the task force issued its report: Bob Reeves, "Task Force Suggests Uses for Radial Land," *Lincoln Star*, August 13, 1980.

284 "wanted to stand up": Karen Maguire, "City Council Gives Rave Reviews, Boos to Radial-Corridor Proposal," *Lincoln Journal*, August 13, 1980.

285 "She knows better than": Editorial, "Representing Those Not Present," *Lincoln Journal*, November 1, 1980.

285 mayor declared her intent to veto: "Mayor Would Veto 22nd St.," *Lincoln Star*, November 13, 1980.

285 "heretofore, the mayor has made": Editorial, "A Touch of Hypocrisy, Perhaps?" *Lincoln Journal*, November 13, 1980.

285 "an exercise of commendable": Editorial, "Helen Clarifies the Issue," *Lincoln Star*, November 13, 1980.

285 "culminating more than": Bob Reeves, "Despite Council's 'No Build' Vote, Northeast Radial Isn't Dead," *Lincoln Star*, November 18, 1980.

285   "as a take-charge legislative body": Editorial, "Majority Decisiveness Is Typical of Council," *Lincoln Star*, November 18, 1980.

285   "I'm glad the Mayor": Karen Maguire, "Petition Drive Seeks City Vote on Radial," *Lincoln Journal*, November 18, 1980.

285   The petition drive gained enough: Karen Maguire, "Petitions Submitted on Northeast Radial," *Lincoln Journal*, January 15, 1981; "Northeast Radial Petitions Turned In," *Lincoln Star*, January 16, 1981.

285   The mayor's visible leadership: "Mayor Opposes Radial Spending," *Lincoln Journal*, March 19, 1981.

286   "no 'Uncle Sugar'": Editorial, "Northeast Radial Plan Hit Hard by Mayor," *Lincoln Star*, March 19, 1981.

286   "I do not believe": "Mayor Opposes Radial Spending."

286   "Helen Boosalis is probably": Bill Kreifel, "Hampton Reacts to Mayor," *Lincoln Journal*, March 20, 1981.

286   "This thing has dragged": Beth Headrick and Mary Louise Knapp, "City Council Candidates Discuss Issues at Forums," *Daily Nebraskan*, April 3, 1981.

286   "I don't see where": Bob Reeves, "Scherer Says Views Not Effective, Won't Seek Re-election," *Lincoln Star*, August 15, 1980.

286   *Alliance: Hampton shared Scherer's view of the Lincoln Alliance. Hampton said that in the previous eight years the city had started to fragment and polarize, beginning "when Saul Alinsky spoke in Lincoln and his presentation became a model for the Lincoln Alliance, a format of activism, and the deplorable tactic of inciting citizens against citizens in an attempt to destroy the orderly government. It makes me determined to do whatever I can to counter that because it could destroy the well-being of the community." Bill Kreifel, "Community Split Concerns Hampton," *Lincoln Journal*, March 26, 1981.

286   "may go down as the worst": Reeves, "Scherer Says Views Not Effective."

286   "split terms—the first two": Kreifel, "Community Split Concerns Hampton."

287   "I love to challenge": "Scherer to Be Five-State GOP Coordinator," *Lincoln Journal*, August 26, 1980.

287   between the "Old Pols" and "New Pols": Editorial, "The Man in the Middle Says 'No' to Third Term," *Lincoln Star*, February 14, 1981.

287   "She is fiscally oriented": Winters, "Hampton Labels City Indifferent."

287   "She was elected mayor": George Hendrix, "Council Tackles Harassment Issue," *Lincoln Star*, February 3, 1981.

287   "the business community's candidate": Kreifel, "Community Split Concerns Hampton."

287   "there would not be any depth": "Hampton Sees Economic Danger Signs," *Lincoln Star*, March 4, 1981.

287   speculation about other candidates: Editorial, "With 1983 Implications, Spring Election Nears," *Lincoln Star*, January 2, 1981.

288   "less than pleased": George Hendrix, "Danley Scores First-Place Finish," *Lincoln Star*, May 6, 1981.

288   First-place winner Danley viewed: Hendrix, "Danley Scores First-Place Finish."

288   Others analyzed the shift: Editorial, "Money Lends Edge in At-Large Contests?" *Lincoln Star*, May 1, 1981.

288   The ability of at-large candidates: Editorial, "Election Results: No Simple Analysis," *Lincoln Star*, April 10, 1981.

288   "did not tie issues": Editorial, "Dead, but Not Buried," *Lincoln Star*, April 9, 1981.

288   *victory: Eventually, the council put the Radial issue to bed just before the end of my mother's second mayoral term in 1983. After awaiting resolution of the Radial issue for twenty-four years, the mayor was "surprised and exuberant" when the council adopted the Radial redevelopment plan, with the unexpected vote of new Councilman Shackelford, for alternative use of the land originally acquired for the Radial. The plan included a blend of industrial and residential development, rehabilitation of existing housing, and a controversial and costly linear park running the length of the former Radial corridor to separate housing and industrial uses (George Hendrix, "City Council Adopts NE Radial Proposal," *Lincoln Star*, February 15, 1983). After winning the "sweet victory . . . a jubilant Boosalis hugged residents who had been living in the shadow of the Northeast Radial proposal for years" (David Swartzlander, "Council: Redevelop Radial Land," *Lincoln Journal*, February 15, 1983).

288   "competent people who will": Bill Kreifel, "Mayor Says New Council Members Are Competent and They'll Do Well," *Lincoln Journal*, May 12, 1981.

289   Some argued that the 1981 election: Editorial, "And the Winner Is . . . (Yawn) Apathy (Yawn)," *Lincoln Star*, May 7, 1981.

289   "We need all of it": Kreifel, "Mayor Says New Council Members Are Competent."

289   "We all should have": David Swartzlander, "Urban Renewers Hunt Elsewhere for Money," *Lincoln Journal*, March 25, 1982.

289   "be locked into a tight fiscal": Editorial, "No Real Surprises," *Lincoln Journal*, May 6, 1981.

FLASH FORWARD: ONE FALSE MOVE AND . . .

291   "If Nebraskans are to share": Robert Dorr, "Taxes Story Is Rebutted by Boosalis," *Omaha World-Herald*, August 11, 1986.

291 *promise: The referenced "promise" to equalize property, sales, and income taxes was advanced in the 1960s by legislative advocates for the state's adoption of sales and income taxes. C. David Kotok, "Leveling Off of 3 Taxes Is Proposed," *Omaha World-Herald*, August 9, 1986.

291 "A property tax reduction plan": Kotok, "Leveling Off of 3 Taxes Is Proposed."

291 *42 percent: In 1984, 57 percent of state revenue came from property taxes, 23 percent from income taxes, and 20 percent from sales taxes.

292 "When told what the formula": Kotok, "Leveling Off of 3 Taxes Is Proposed."

292 *LB662: As recognized in the *Omaha World-Herald* story, the only tax-rate increase Helen Boosalis supported in the 1986 governor's race was the one-cent increase in sales tax for education addressed in the finance portion of the school consolidation law (LB662). The state legislature had already passed LB662 in 1985, but voters would decide whether or not to retain it by referendum vote in the November 1986 election.

292 "I'm not saying it would be done": Dorr, "Taxes Story Is Rebutted."

293 Some of the shift to more revenue: Dorr, "Taxes Story Is Rebutted."

293 "Unless one anticipates an absolutely": Editorial, "'No Tax Increases' Means What? Dollars, or Tax Rates?" *Lincoln Journal*, September 1, 1986.

293 "True enough if you raised": Editorial, "Campaign for Governor Losing Part of Its Smile," *Lincoln Star*, September 16, 1986.

294 "There is no question we need": "Mrs. Orr Calls Boosalis Plan 'Ill-Considered,'" *Omaha World-Herald*, August 10, 1986.

294 *poll: The Orr campaign declined to comment in early August on Orr's purportedly poor showing in their own poll, claiming they had decided before the poll was taken that they would not release the numbers. Instead, Orr campaign coordinator Nancy Reckeway said, "We agree with Helen's numbers"—referring to "a Boosalis poll that showed the candidates dead even with 43 percent each." "Orr Backers Mum on Report Candidate Trailing Boosalis," *Lincoln Journal*, August 5, 1986.

295 "what could loom very large": Kathleen Rutledge, "Women's Issues Not Seen in Race," *Sunday Journal-Star*, August 31, 1986.

295 "Orr's commercials tying her": Don Walton, "Let's Take a Glance at Their First Debate," *Lincoln Star*, September 8, 1986.

295 "Strictly as a tactical move": Editorial, "'No Tax Increases' Means What?"

296 Orr's campaign representative: Fred Knapp, "Poll Showing Orr in Lead Is No Surprise to Boosalis," *Lincoln Journal*, September 15, 1986.

296 "hopes to have recommendations": Knapp, "Poll Showing Orr in Lead."

296 *election: Orr "has offered no tax plan" (Lynn Sweet, "Prediction: Woman Governor in Nebraska," *Chicago Sun-Times*, October 28, 1986). "A tax study

that she [Orr] talked about during the campaign should be completed and reviewed in about two weeks [mid-November]"—in other words, conveniently after the gubernatorial general election (AP, "Orr Wins Historic Governor's Race," *Grand Island (NE) Independent*, November 6, 1986).

296   "I have been adamant": Thomas A. Fogarty, "'Tax Deal' Won't Loosen Its Grip on Nebraska Race," *Des Moines Register*, September 29, 1986.

297   "For decades relief from": Fogarty, "'Tax Deal' Won't Loosen Its Grip."

297   the real campaign "battleground": C. David Kotok, "Omaha Could Be Key in Race for Governor," *Sunday World-Herald*, August 31, 1986.

297   Richard Shugrue, Creighton University law: Kotok, "Omaha Could Be Key."

297   "take some risks by throwing": Kotok, "Omaha Could Be Key."

297   "It's going to get a lot": Fred Knapp, "Orr, Boosalis TV Political Ads Watched, Evaluated, Debated," *Sunday Journal-Star*, September 14, 1986.

297   "Kay Orr is misleading": Fred Knapp, "Boosalis Says Orr Misleading Public on Tax-Raise Issue," *Lincoln Journal*, September 12, 1986.

298   Nebraska State Education Association: Fogarty, "'Tax Deal' Won't Loosen Its Grip."

298   "No doubt about it": C. David Kotok, "Orr Ads Hit Tax Issue; Boosalis Uses Kerrey," *Omaha World-Herald*, October 21, 1986.

299   "public confusion about their": C. David Kotok, "Mrs. Orr's Attacks Heat Up the Tempo of Governor's Race," *Sunday World-Herald*, September 14, 1986.

299   44 percent to 33 percent: Knapp, "Poll Showing Orr in Lead."

299   Her negative spots attacking: Don Walton, "Boosalis Backers Say the Worst Is Past," *Lincoln Star*, October 9, 1986.

299   Both campaigns agreed that Orr's: Kotok, "Orr Ads Hit Tax Issue."

299   "not mine. It originated": C. David Kotok, "Mrs. Boosalis Tries to Clarify Tax Position," *Omaha World-Herald*, September 16, 1986.

299   "Given the turn the campaign": Knapp, "Poll Showing Orr in Lead."

299   "substance and integrity": Kotok, "Boosalis Tries to Clarify Tax Position."

300   "up and down the steep": Don Walton, "Undaunted by Poll, Boosalis Steps up Pace," *Lincoln Star*, September 18, 1986.

300   "to capture the essence of Helen": C. David Kotok, "Advertising Is Covering Campaign Distances," *Sunday World-Herald*, October 12, 1986.

300   "It's time Kay Orr stopped": C. David Kotok, "Boosalis and Orr TV Ads Take Jabs at Each Other," *Omaha World-Herald*, October 29, 1986.

301   "The stakes are too high": Dan Moser, "Boosalis to Lead Demo 'Charge to Victory,'" *North Platte (NE) Telegraph*, September 21, 1986.

301   "A governor's job is": Kotok, "Orr Ads Hit Tax Issue."

301   The Orr campaign kept "on the shelf": Kotok, "Boosalis and Orr TV Ads."

301   "Do you want to pay": AP, "Orr, Boosalis Send Out Letters, Each Seeking Donations, Election-Day Vote," *Lincoln Star*, October 31, 1986.

301   "I am a registered Republican": Letter to editor from James E. Burch, "Change His Vote," *Lincoln Journal*, October 30, 1986.

302   "Boosalis got in trouble": Sweet, "Prediction."

302   *taxes: Former Illinois comptroller and state senator Dawn Clark Netsch ran for governor of Illinois eight years after she hosted the fund-raiser at her home in Chicago for my mother's campaign for governor. During her 1994 governor's race, Netsch proposed a fairer tax structure for funding education in Illinois: a "tax swap" plan that would raise state income taxes (from 3 percent to 4.25 percent) to increase education funding and to lower property taxes. Netsch believed that a mix of taxes ought to be more like one-third income tax, one-third sales/excise taxes, and one-third property taxes. (Sound familiar?)

     Her Republican opponent, Jim Edgar, spent millions in his advertising campaign to discredit Netsch's tax-swap plan and to "misrepresent" it, according to Netsch. (Perhaps Edgar took a lesson from Kay Orr's advertising playbook?) For example, Edgar's multimillion-dollar ad campaign claimed that the plan would result in a 41 percent tax increase. Netsch responded that many taxpayers would actually pay less tax when her proposed income tax increase and property tax reduction were combined. She said often on the gubernatorial campaign trail, "Gee, if it were really a 41% tax increase, I don't think I would vote for it myself."

     Edgar was elected Illinois governor in 1994, and many blame Netsch's tax-swap plan for dooming her candidacy (she received only 35 percent of the vote). Today, Netsch says that Edgar's misrepresentation of her tax plan is what she resents most (transcript, "Dawn Clark Netsch's Tax-Swap Proposal," *Chicago Matters*, Valuing Education series, "Chicago Tonight," WTTW, aired March 28, 2006). However, the tax-swap idea refused to die. Four years after Edgar became governor, he proposed a similar tax swap of higher state income taxes for lower property taxes, but he had inflicted so much damage to the concept during the campaign that his fellow Republicans blocked passage of his proposal.

     Since then Michigan has enacted a sweeping tax-swap plan to fund public education, but versions of Netsch's and Edgar's proposals have languished in the Illinois legislature. A *Chicago Sun-Times* reporter observed ten years after Netsch's gubernatorial defeat, "Now we are reaping what the state's lack of political will has sown over the last decade. Nearly 80 percent of the state's 891 school districts are running at a budget deficit even as rising property taxes threaten to drive some people from their homes" (Cindy Richards, "Netsch Plan May Catch on Yet," *Chicago Sun-Times*, February 18, 2004).

302   "Orr, who has offered no tax plan": Sweet, "Prediction."

302   "clearly an echo of Reagan's": Beth Frerking, "Governor Race a Women's Affair," *Denver Post*, October 5, 1986.

303   Omaha station KETV's policy prohibited: Jen Deselms, "Orr's Ad Scheduled by Mistake," *Daily Nebraskan*, October 8, 1986.

CHAPTER 7. MAYORS' MAYOR

307   "Helen had a national reputation": George Latimer, interview.

307   "Although Mayor Boosalis was": Tom Cochran, interview.

308   *organization: The U.S. Conference of Mayors is a national nonpartisan organization of member cities with populations of thirty thousand or more (about eight hundred cities in 1980 and more than eleven hundred today). The member cities strive to speak with one voice to the president and Congress on national urban policy. The organization began in 1932 in response to the desperate state of cities during the Great Depression and was successful in gaining passage of the country's first federal funding relief provided directly to cities.

309   Senate Intergovernmental Relations Committee: "Mayors Testify on Urban Policy, Meet with White House Officials," *The Mayor*, March 1, 1978 (*The Mayor* is the official publication of the U.S. Conference of Mayors).

309   questions about Carter's plan: "Urban Policy Stymies Carter; Mayors Will Lobby," *Sunday Journal and Star*, February 5, 1978.

310   "We are not knocking": "Mayor Wants Urban Commitment," *Lincoln Journal*, January 26, 1978.

310   After several meetings with Carter's: Newhouse News Service, "Mayors More Optimistic about Higher Federal Aid for Cities," *Lincoln Star*, January 28, 1978.

310   the funny headline: Tom Cook, "Listen Up, Jimmy, Helen Boosalis Has Something to Tell You," *Lincoln Journal*, February 7, 1978.

311   as "a positive beginning": Andy Montgomery, "Mayor Boosalis Encouraged by Urban Plan," *Lincoln Journal*, March 28, 1978.

311   "pleased that the President": Montgomery, "Mayor Boosalis Encouraged."

311   "an interest in healthy cities": "Healthy Cities Covered in Carter Urban Policy," *Lincoln Star*, March 28, 1978.

312   "pockets of poverty": "Prevention Called Key to Aid for City," *Omaha World-Herald*, September 30, 1978.

312   "I really think it makes good business": "Prevention Called Key to Aid for City."

312   "Part of Mayor Boosalis' leadership": Tom Cochran, interview.

312   At a Kansas City conference: "Boosalis Talks on Revitalization," *Lincoln Star*, June 8, 1977.

312   "The forum could not": Editorial, "Talk of Revitalization Puts Mayor in Spotlight," *Lincoln Star*, June 13, 1977.

312   *needs: "When Helen Boosalis chaired the U.S. Conference of Mayors Human Development Standing Committee, she brought together city human services directors to identify human needs in cities. She convened the first meeting of municipal human services professionals, and the group is still going today." Laura DeKoven Waxman, interview.

313   *else: Cities were slow to take on responsibility for human services long after my mother's early focus in the 1970s. When I was on the Evanston City Council and participated in the National League of Cities in the late 1980s and early 1990s, debate still continued about the appropriate role of cities in providing for such human services as child care, workforce training, addiction treatment, and homeless shelters. I remember Mayor Don Frasier of Minneapolis being a lone voice in urging cities to view the health and development of children as the most important municipal responsibility. By the end of my decade as alderman in 1993, I could see a shift in cities' recognition of their critical role as frontline coordinators of human services, even as funding for human services remained a staggering challenge.

313   Lincoln's mayor related: Journal Washington Bureau, "Mayor Hits Federal Policy-Setting," *Lincoln Journal*, October 31, 1977.

313   Nearly fifty years earlier: Holly Spence, "Nebraska's Metro Mayors Keep Strong Party Ties," *Nebraska Democrat*, November 1981, 1.

313   *average: The national unemployment rate reached as high as double digits during my mother's second term, while Lincoln's topped out at 6 percent (Nancy Hicks, "Lincoln Unemployment Hits New High," *Lincoln Star*, January 18, 1983). The depressed auto-industry town of Flint, Michigan, had the highest unemployment rate at 20.7 percent.

313   *3.2 percent: Several reasons for Lincoln's low unemployment were cited in a *New York Times* article (Iver Peterson, ". . . As Lincoln, Neb., Credits Diverse Economy for the Lowest, 3.2%," October 26, 1980):

- Diversity of commercial, industrial, and service employers (e.g., food-handling businesses, because "even in a recession, people keep eating").
- Low wages resulting from the relocation of farmers after World War II in the wake of farm consolidation and automation (migration from farms to Lincoln and Omaha produced a labor surplus, keeping wages low).
- Relatively undemanding attitude of workers from small towns who grew up "with an agrarian work ethic."
- Low percentage of workforce unionized (in 1980, 15 percent of

Nebraska's workforce was unionized, compared to 33 percent in Michigan and 37 percent in New York).

- Predominance of government employment, accounting for more than a quarter of the metropolitan area's workforce (government employment is typically more recession-proof).

314   "For the first time": Kathy Kiely, "Woman Mayor in Line as Group's President," *Pittsburgh Press*, June 11, 1979.

314   "peppery": "In More Big Cities, It's 'Her Honor the Mayor,'" *U.S. News and World Report*, July 16, 1979.

314   "shrugged off her new fame": Gordon Winters, "Magazine Reports Boosalis 'Peppery,'" *Lincoln Star*, July 12, 1979; Karen Maguire, "'Peppery' Boosalis Hits the Nation's Newsstands," *Lincoln Journal*, July 12, 1979.

314   *secretary: Before President Carter appointed Moon Landrieu and Neil Goldschmidt to his cabinet, the last two mayors to serve in federal cabinet positions were under Franklin Roosevelt and John Kennedy.

314   and not just its population: Journal Washington Bureau, "Boosalis Urges Public Transport," *Lincoln Journal*, November 20, 1980.

315   "You might well wonder": Karen Maguire, "Boosalis: Smaller Cities Not Immune," *Sunday Journal and Star*, June 8, 1980.

315   "The only reason I'm up": Karen Maguire, "She'll Lead Mayors Conference in 1981: Lincoln's Boosalis Is Steel in Velvet Glove," *Sunday Journal and Star*, June 15, 1980.

316   "bubbling with enthusiasm": Bob Reeves, "Boosalis 'Bubbling with Enthusiasm' after Mayors' Conference," *Lincoln Star*, June 13, 1980.

316   "Mrs. Boosalis acknowledged": "Boosalis against Open Demo Convention," *Lincoln Star*, August 7, 1980.

316   she had been "wooed": C. David Kotok, "Boosalis' Endorsement Courted by Carter, Kennedy Campaigns," *Sunday Journal and Star*, December 23, 1979.

316   "especially important," wrote a *Journal*: Thomas A. Fogarty, "Signs Indicate Nebraska Will Be Solid Carter Country," *Lincoln Journal*, March 25, 1980.

317   "is the only one": "Boosalis to Be Coordinator for Carter Nebraska Campaign," *Lincoln Star*, April 8, 1980.

317   mother met with President Carter: "Boosalis Gets Glimpse of Oval Office," *Lincoln Star*, April 17, 1980.

317   consulting with Australian farmers: "Boosalis among Scientists Traveling to Australia," *Lincoln Journal*, March 8, 1980.

317   ten-cents-a-gallon surcharge: Thomas A. Fogarty, "Reagan, Carter Find Good Life Very Good," *Lincoln Journal*, May 14, 1980.

318   "first and foremost" job: "Helen Boosalis to Be Carter Coordinator," *Lincoln Journal*, April 8, 1980.

318   she withdrew her name: "Mayor Decides to Withdraw as Delegate," *Lincoln Star*, June 19, 1980.

318   It was an intriguing time: Daniel Southerland, "Will China Keep Smiling at US, Taiwan?" *Christian Science Monitor*, October 29, 1979.

318   *miracle: Taiwan's "economic miracle" that was credited to Sun Yun-suan, premier of the Republic of China in 1980, included building the Chiang Kai-shek International Airport, nuclear power plant, and national expressway; establishing high-tech industries and semiconductor companies; and converting Taiwan's export industries, centered on textiles, toys, and agriculture, to petrochemicals and electronics. http://en.wikipedia.org/wiki/Sun_Yun-suan.

318   State Department exchange program: "Her Honor Boots Up for Big Red Journey," *Lincoln Journal*, October 22, 1976; Gordon Winters, "Mayor Buys Boots for Russia Trip," *Lincoln Star*, October 22, 1976.

319   hosted by Jerusalem mayor: "Lincoln Mayor to Attend Jerusalem Conference," *Lincoln Star*, April 22, 1981.

320   prime minister opened his home: Ellen Gordman, "Mayor Boosalis Reports on 'Remarkable' Israel," *Jewish Press*, June 5, 1981.

320   When the five-day conference: Gordman, "Mayor Boosalis Reports."

320   "cooperate with the administration": "Boosalis Sees Hope for Cities," *Lincoln Star*, November 15, 1980.

321   During their Chicago legislative meeting: Gordon Winters, "Mayor Praises City's Lobbyist for Doing Effective Job," *Lincoln Star*, April 24, 1980.

321   "The federal government is": "Boosalis Sees Hope for Cities."

321   "felt as though he'd been invited": George Hendrix, "Boosalis: City Is Hurting, Situation Is Deteriorating," *Lincoln Star*, February 5, 1981.

321   Most categorical grants had been: Darwin Olofson and Mary Kay Quinlan, "Two Nebraskans Meet with Reagan," *Omaha World-Herald*, June 2, 1981.

321   "I tried to make the point": Olofson and Quinlan, "Two Nebraskans Meet with Reagan."

322   "the nation's financially strapped cities: George Hendrix, "Nation's Mayors Debate Reagan's Intentions," *Lincoln Star*, June 15, 1981.

322   "Helen's commitment, drive": Paul Sarbanes, interview.

322   "We must respect the people": B. Drummond Ayres Jr., "Divided Mayors' Once-Steady Course Shifts in Reagan's Direction," *New York Times*, June 18, 1981.

323   "One week from today": Editorial, "That's Our Helen Up There," *Lincoln Journal*, June 10, 1981.

323   "Welcome home, mayor": Editorial, "Happy Homecoming, Madame President," *Lincoln Star*, June 18, 1981.

323   A committee of well-wishers: "'Surprises' Planned for Boosalis' Return," *Lincoln Journal*, June 15, 1981.

324   In get-acquainted sessions: George Hendrix, "Mayor Meets Reagan, Aides,"
      Lincoln Star, July 24, 1981.

325   *program: Although Governor Thone resisted pressure from my mother to
      include city participation in state block grant decision making, he finally ca-
      pitulated to her suggestion to form an advisory council of local and state of-
      ficials to recommend policies for the newly instituted federal block grant
      program. The resulting twenty-five-member Nebraska Advisory Commis-
      sion on Intergovernmental Affairs had five representatives each from city
      governments, county governments, the state legislature, the executive
      branch of state government, and the public at large. Thomas A. Fogarty,
      "New Advisory Council to Study Block Grants," *Lincoln Journal*, September
      15, 1981.

325   "impending disaster": Editorial, "Reagan Transit Policy Will Create Disas-
      ter," *Lincoln Star*, July 28, 1981.

325   When Congress enacted Reagan's: Thomas A. Fogarty, "State to Lose $6.9
      Million in Funding," *Lincoln Journal*, September 19, 1981.

325   Nebraska's governor warned: Nancy Hicks, "State Won't Plug Gaps in Loss
      of Federal Funds," *Lincoln Star*, September 19, 1981.

326   "mayors have had a 'tin cup image' in": "Mrs. Boosalis Tells Cities: Help Plan
      New Federalism," *Omaha World-Herald*, October 3, 1981.

326   A second round of Reagan: "President's Proposed Revenue Sharing Cuts Op-
      posed," *The Mayor*, October 1, 1981.

326   "Chicken Littles": AP, "Thousands Protest Cuts in Budgets," *Lincoln Journal*,
      September 19, 1981.

327   The outpouring persuaded Reagan: "President's Proposed Revenue Sharing
      Cuts Opposed."

327   "What annoys many state": Neal R. Peirce (*Washington Post*), "New Budget
      Cuts Irk Local Officials," *Lincoln Journal*, October 5, 1981.

327   "The new chief": Peggy Simpson, "Chief Mayor to Reagan: What Next?"
      Boston Herald American, August 31, 1981.

327   "I'm not sure we know": Simpson, "Chief Mayor to Reagan."

328   "But no one succeeded": Simpson, "Chief Mayor to Reagan."

328   "Giveaways in the President's": Don Walton, "Landrieu Criticizes Reagan
      Policy for Cities," *Lincoln Star*, November 7, 1981.

328   "We're prepared to take": Thomas A. Fogarty, "Bush Arrives in Lincoln,"
      Lincoln Journal, November 7, 1981.

329   "Not since the formation": "Mayors Open Talks on Federalism," *Lincoln Star*,
      November 11, 1981.

329   "I'm sure that all": "Mayors Announce Positions on Federalism at Close of
      Chicago Conference," *The Mayor*, December 1, 1981.

329   At the urban federalism summit: UPI, "Mayors Fearing Reduction in Police,
      Fire Protection," *Lincoln Journal*, November 13, 1981.

329 "When you talk about further cuts": UPI, "Mayors Fearing Reduction in Police, Fire Protection."

329 "as U.S. Conference of Mayors president": Tom Cochran, interview.

330 "As mayors you are the economic": "Mayors' Conference Opened by Boosalis," *Lincoln Star*, November 13, 1981.

331 "rather firm on his program": Bob Reeves, "Mayors Want Reagan to Hold the Line on Cuts," *Lincoln Star*, November 16, 1981.

331 "The picture that emerges": Andy Montgomery, "Mayor: Cuts Stall Cities," *Lincoln Journal*, December 15, 1981.

331 "We are paring our essential services": AP, "Budget Ax Falling on City Services," *Lincoln Star*, November 26, 1981.

331 "Mayors are wrestling with federal": AP, "Budget Ax Falling."

331 "The push for expanded": "Mayor Boosalis Appointed to President's Private Sector Task Force," *The Mayor*, December 15, 1981.

331 "private organizations cannot replace": "Mayor Boosalis Appointed."

332 *seeing: Given the Reagan administration's support for private-sector initiatives to replace government funding, my mother could not understand Reagan's push to eliminate the Urban Development Action Grant (UDAG) program, which required private investment in UDAG-funded public-private projects. Karen Maguire, "Mayor: Inflation, Lid May End Programs," *Lincoln Journal*, February 4, 1981.

332 Kawasaki plant, which had manufactured: Gene Kelly, "Confidence in Plant Underlined: Kawasaki Crews Note no. 400,000—Officials Laud Plant Adaptability," *Lincoln Journal*, May 20, 1982.

332 Kawasaki admitted that the plan: "Kawasaki Offers City Its Workers," *New York Times*, October 24, 1981.

332 The Kawasaki employees did not: Mike Butler, "Kawasaki Workers Shift Jobs," *Lincoln Star*, October 22, 1981.

332 "reaffirmed the public-private": "Kawasaki Layoffs Avoided by Arrangement with City," *Lincoln Journal*, October 21, 1981.

332 *years: Peter F. Drucker commended Lincoln for its use of public-private partnerships during my mother's years as mayor: "The city of Lincoln, Nebraska, has since 1975 pioneered in efforts to couple better service with lower costs" (Drucker, "Our Entrepreneurial Society," *Harvard Business Review*, January–February 1984, 60). John Rosenow, president of the Arbor Day Foundation, recently noted Drucker's references to Mayor Boosalis's leadership in contracting with the private sector for the benefit of the city. Rosenow said recently, "Helen created an early model for joining the efficiency of the private sector with the public purposes of the public sector" (Rosenow, interview).

332 "an admirable spirit of cooperation": "Kawasaki Layoffs Avoided."

333 "sought to buy peace": Herbert H. Denton, "Mayors Decry Proposed Cut in Federal Aid," *Washington Post*, February 12, 1982.

333 "The damage that the FY 1983 budget": Denton, "Mayors Decry Proposed Cut."

333 "Mayors know that the most": Caroline Atkinson and Herbert Denton, "Trust Fund Found Short by Billions," *Washington Post*, January 30, 1982.

333 "HUD Secretary Samuel Pierce": Owen Ullman, "Stockman's Plans Anger HUD, Mayors," *Lincoln Star*, December 2, 1981.

333 "I wonder if we are": George Hendrix, "Boosalis Has Spent Year Living Politician's Dream," *Lincoln Star*, June 14, 1982.

333 *missiles: My mother credits this quote to Mike Brown, partner, City Policy Associates, and former director of public affairs, U.S. Conference of Mayors.

333 *8.8 percent: The 8.8 percent national unemployment figure was for February 1982.

334 "a very great tragedy": "Jobless Blame Placed on Reagan," *Lincoln Star*, December 5, 1981.

334 "He often has said": UPI, "Jobs Dip; Reagan Unshaken," *Lincoln Star*, March 6, 1982.

334 "provides a grim backdrop": UPI, "Jobs Dip."

334 "a statistic that reflects": "Jobless Blame Placed on Reagan."

334 House Speaker Tip O'Neill: "Jobless Blame Placed on Reagan."

334 *months: The average national unemployment rate for calendar year 1982 was 9.7 percent. U.S. Department of Labor, Bureau of Labor Statistics, "Household Data Historical: A-1 Employment Status of the Civilian Noninstitutional Population 16 Years and Over, 1969 to Date," www.bls.gov.

334 "Reaganomics has brought on": "Jobless Blame Placed on Reagan."

334 "These proposed cuts in urban": "Boosalis Tells Congress Budget Cuts Intolerable," *Lincoln Journal*, March 10, 1982.

335 "Helen Boosalis has had": Hendrix, "Boosalis Has Spent Year."

335 baseball commissioner Bowie Kuhn: "Conference of Mayors Gets into the Strike Act," *Jamestown (NY) Post-Journal*, July 30, 1981.

335 *millions: Lincoln did not then have a professional baseball team. Now the Lincoln Saltdogs, whose name represents the importance of salt in the settlement of Lincoln and whose inaugural season was in 2002, is a professional team comparable to AA minor-league baseball.

335 "Aware of the worth": Hendrix, "Boosalis Has Spent Year."

336 Councilman Hampton did not view the mayor's: David Swartzlander, "Sharing of Lincoln's Mayor with Nation Is Liked, Disliked," *Sunday Journal and Star*, December 27, 1981.

336 "never used me or asked": David Swartzlander, "Retiring Mayor Says Lincoln Oasis Dream Fulfilled," *Lincoln Journal*, May 9, 1983.

336 When asked to assess her year: Hendrix, "Boosalis Has Spent Year."

336 *fiftieth: In June 2007 the U.S. Conference of Mayors celebrated its seventy-fifth anniversary and honored the organization's past presidents at its annual meeting in Los Angeles. I accompanied Mom to the mayors' meeting, where she was the most senior past president in attendance. (There have been three women presidents since her 1982 presidency—mayors of Houston, Salt Lake City, and Long Beach.) Moving more slowly than twenty-five years ago but with her lively humor intact, Mom regaled fellow mayors and veteran U.S. Conference of Mayors executive director Tom Cochran with stories from the past, such as how she rigged a watermelon-seed-spitting contest against Denver mayor Bill McNichols, her fellow Russia delegation colleague.

336 "degenerated into an oratorical": George Hendrix, "Urban Policy Statement Shocks Mayors," *Lincoln Star*, June 21, 1982.

337 "moderation gave way to shock": Hendrix, "Urban Policy Statement Shocks Mayors."

337 "from bold leaders of self-reliant cities": David Hoffman (*Washington Post*), "'It's War,' Mayor Says of Urban Policy Report," *Omaha World-Herald*, May 21, 1982.

337 "The President does not feel": Hendrix, "Urban Policy Statement Shocks Mayors."

337 "almost seems to draw a battle line": Hendrix, "Urban Policy Statement Shocks Mayors."

338 mother's leadership of her fellow mayors: David Swartzlander, "Mayors Give Boosalis A+ Grade as President," *Sunday Journal and Star*, June 20, 1982.

338 "Helen possessed true statesmanship": George Latimer, interview.

338 "Helen's a bridge builder": Swartzlander, "Mayors Give Boosalis A+ Grade."

339 She was featured speaker: "Boosalis Featured at NY Conference on Federalism," *Sunday Journal and Star*, April 3, 1982.

339 She helped draft an economic: UPI, "Boosalis, Other Mayors to Draft Recovery Plan," *Lincoln Journal*, November 10, 1982.

FLASH FORWARD: ISSUES, DEBATES, POLLS, AND OTHER IRRELEVANCIES

340 Mom told folks in Wilbur: Julian C. Jenson, "Meet Helen Boosalis," *Wilbur (NE) Republican*, August 6, 1986.

340 "Every farm closing is a tragedy": Fred Knapp, "Boosalis Bids to Be Governor," *Lincoln Journal*, February 3, 1986.

340 "I wasn't born on": C. David Kotok, "Mrs. Boosalis Tells Forum She Is against Abortion," *Omaha World-Herald*, February 22, 1986.

340   Agricultural Revitalization Plan: Mary Bargman, "Boosalis Outlines Ag, Rural Plan in NP," *North Platte (NE) Telegraph*, April 8, 1986.

341   "We are not looking": Don Walton, "Boosalis Enters Governor Race," *Lincoln Star*, February 3, 1986.

341   agricultural issues tour: "Boosalis to Make Ag Tour of State," *Alliance Times-Herald*, July 29, 1986.

341   "put the heat on": C. David Kotok, "Wyoming Governor Backs Mrs. Boosalis' Farm Plan," *Omaha World-Herald*, August 5, 1986.

341   Farm Policy Reform Rally: Kent Warneke, "Farm Rally No Place for Republicans," *Omaha World-Herald*, September 15, 1986.

341   The most controversial farm-related: C. David Kotok, "DeCamp Vow Aims to Boost Petition Drive," *Omaha World-Herald*, June 16, 1986.

341   My mother admitted that: "Boosalis Calls Initiative 'Wall of Protection,'" *Norfolk (NE) News*, April 9, 1986.

341   When the drive failed: C. David Kotok, "Candidates: Changes Worth Study in I-300," *Sunday World-Herald*, July 13, 1986.

341   the double keys to Nebraska's: Lynn Zerschling, "Boosalis Portrays Self as Tough Person Who Can Get Things Done," *Sioux City Journal*, April 25, 1986.

342   Boosalis twelve-point economic plan: James Joyce, "Boosalis, Orr Sing Economic Tune," *Lincoln Star*, October 7, 1986.

342   "We can't sit with our arms": Henry J. Cordes, "Mrs. Boosalis: Diversify Economy," *Omaha World-Herald*, August 19, 1986.

342   "Nonsense," she responded to a reporter's: C. David Kotok, "Boosalis Shuns Liberal Label," *Omaha World-Herald*, April 15, 1986.

342   "being anti-business is a 'mythical notion'": Don Walton, "Boosalis Stresses Her Budget Talents," *Lincoln Star*, October 10, 1986.

343   "drew the antipathy of some business": "Mrs. Boosalis: Ex-Mayor Relishes Making It Happen," *Omaha World-Herald*, October 9, 1986.

343   she claimed that: Don Walton, "Boosalis, Orr Each Leap to Offensive," *Lincoln Star*, September 22, 1986.

344   *fixed: In 1985 (the year before the governor's race) when the Nebraska legislature passed LB662 by a vote of 25–23, there were 24 Republicans, 24 Democrats, and 1 independent in Nebraska's nonpartisan unicameral legislature. Senator John DeCamp proposed an eleventh-hour amendment to LB662—adopted on a 29–6 vote—adding the one-cent sales tax increase to both increase education funding and reduce the state's reliance on "excessive or unfair property taxes" for financing public education. Although he proposed the one-cent sales tax increase amendment to the bill, DeCamp voted yes on LB662 until it received a majority of yes votes, then changed his vote to no. Democratic governor Bob Kerrey, who signed the bill into law in the last

minutes of his five-day veto consideration period, had concerns about the sales tax increase but favored LB662's incremental move toward tax uniformity and hoped the funding mechanism could be fixed later. "Story of TEEOSA (1985–1987): The Complete History of the Nebraska Tax Equity and Educational Opportunities Support Act (TEEOSA)," http://schoolfinance.ncsa.org/policy/fullhistory/1985–1987/a3.htm.

344 Those opposing repeal of LB662: "School Consolidation Bill Faces Fierce Fight," *McCook (NE) Gazette*, July 7, 1986.

344 not an additional tax burden: Editorial, "It Is Not a Tax Increase," *Cozad (NE) Tri-City Tribune*, October 21, 1986.

344 push for its repeal: C. David Kotok, "Mrs. Boosalis Tries to Clarify Tax Position," *Omaha World-Herald*, September 16, 1986.

345 first debate was "tame stuff": Kathleen Rutledge, "Boosalis, Orr Renew Familiar Themes," *Lincoln Journal*, September 4, 1986.

345 "Boosalis isn't known for": Kathleen Rutledge, "No Fireworks Set Off in State Fair Debate," *Sunday Journal-Star*, September 7, 1986.

345 "the tax issue dominated": C. David Kotok, "Boosalis, Orr Supporters Expect Aggressive Debate," *Omaha World-Herald*, September 21, 1986.

346 "Even if she was urged": Kathleen Rutledge, interview.

346 more than 13 percent per year: C. David Kotok, "Candidates Show 'Real Choice,'" *Omaha World-Herald*, September 22, 1986.

346 "I don't know how Mrs. Boosalis": Todd von Kampen, "Boosalis, Orr Square Off in Second Debate," *Daily Nebraskan*, September 22, 1986.

346 "I don't preach fiscal": Kotok, "Candidates Show 'Real Choice.'"

346 "in the debates with Orr": F. Gregory Hayden, interview.

346 Kerrey and his chief of staff: Gabriella Stern, "Kerrey Faults Kay Orr on Spending," *Omaha World-Herald*, September 19, 1986.

346 "wanting it both ways": "Democratic Leader Says Orr Trying to Have It Both Ways," *Lincoln Journal*, October 6, 1986.

346 "traded blows on taxes": Don Walton, "Candidates Spar on Taxes," *Lincoln Star*, October 7, 1986.

346 Mom told the debate audience: Walton, "Boosalis Stresses Her Budget Talents."

347 43 percent for each candidate: Kathleen Rutledge, "Poll Shows Boosalis, Orr Enjoy Equal Support," *Lincoln Journal*, June 28, 1986.

347 Although Orr's campaign would not: "Orr Backers Mum on Report Candidate Trailing Boosalis," *Lincoln Journal*, August 5, 1986.

347 A *Sunday Journal-Star* poll: Fred Knapp, "Race for Governor Said Neck and Neck," *Sunday Journal-Star*, August 17, 1986.

348 "Whether by design, the poll": Richard Shugrue, editorial, *Omaha Daily Record*, September 22, 1986.

348 "caught us at a low point": C. David Kotok, "Consultant Says Poll Indicates Boosalis Ship 'Turned Around,'" *Omaha World-Herald*, October 3, 1986.

348 A "toss up" was what: AP, "Boosalis-Orr Race Said Too Close to Call by Poll," *Lincoln Star*, October 18, 1986.

348 "there is no statistically significant": "Poll Indicated No Leader in '86 Race for Governor," *Omaha World-Herald*, October 26, 1986.

348 "Whereas September clearly": Don Walton, "Nebraska Governor's Race Coming Down to Perceptions," *Lincoln Star*, October 22, 1986.

349 In fund-raising, each had cracked: Don Walton, "Campaign Tops $2 Million," *Lincoln Star*, October 29, 1986.

349 *million: The final amounts raised in the 1986 governor's race were $1,506,000 by Orr and $1,266,000 by Boosalis. Nebraska Accountability and Disclosure Commission, "The 1986 State of Nebraska Primary and General Elections: A Summary of Political and Campaign Financing: The Candidates," vol. 1, pp. 5 (Orr), 36 (Boosalis).

349 "Oh, you're the lady!": Don Walton, "Boosalis Takes Aim at Big Omaha Vote," *Lincoln Star*, October 29, 1986.

350 the results of its final poll: Fred Knapp, "Both Sides Confident in Historic Race," *Sunday Journal-Star*, November 2, 1986.

350 "I think a person would be a fool": AP, "Pollster Passes on Prediction," *Omaha World-Herald,* November 3, 1986.

CHAPTER 8. ANOTHER TIME AROUND

351 "What makes Helen different": Kathleen Rutledge, interview.

351 "Unlike most politicians, Helen": Beatty Brasch, interview.

351 "The federal money spigot": William M. Bulkeley, "Cities Fear 'New Federalism' Will Further Pinch Budgets Already Hit by Tighter Government Aid," *Wall Street Journal*, March 2, 1982.

352 *projects: If the legislature were to grant Lincoln's requested sales tax increase, the state would have to exempt that amount from its 7 percent city spending lid on the grounds that it was local replacement of lost federal revenue.

352 only nine municipalities: George Hendrix, "Council to Lobby for Increase in City Sales Tax," *Lincoln Star*, November 3, 1981; David Swartzlander, "Lincoln Will Seek Hike in Sales Tax," *Lincoln Journal*, November 2, 1981.

352 "I have trouble imagining": Bulkeley, "Cities Fear 'New Federalism.'"

352 "wrapped in a call for courage": James Joyce, "Lincoln Officials Argue Sales Tax Case," *Lincoln Star*, February 4, 1982.

352 My mother and Landis stressed: Joyce, "Lincoln Officials Argue."

353 Their arguments did not prevail: Thomas A. Fogarty, "City Sales Tax Measure Falls Two Votes Short of Passage," *Lincoln Journal*, April 16, 1982.

353 Some legislators opposed it based: James Joyce and George Hendrix, "City Sales Tax Bill Falls on Slim Margin," *Lincoln Star*, April 17, 1982.

353 "surprised, confused and, of course": Mike Butler, "Mayor Surprised at Chamber's Letter," *Lincoln Star*, February 22, 1982.

353 "Maybe it's time for the mayor and council": Karen Maguire, "Council Trims Own Budget $25,000," *Lincoln Journal*, July 18, 1980.

353 *night: My father recently reminded me that the desk chair pillow in my old bedroom at home was given to my mother soon after this exchange with Councilman Hampton about lobbying was quoted in the newspaper. I had not known until then the meaning of a friend's hand-embroidered words on the pillow (other than the obvious): "My Duff."

353 The mayor presented her 1981–82: George Hendrix, "Boosalis Budget Up Only 3.46%," *Lincoln Star*, July 9, 1981.

353 She made substantial cuts: L. Kent Wolgamott, "Capital Budget Down 65%," *Lincoln Journal*, July 9, 1981.

353 23 came from the Parks: "Non-human Services to Feel Biggest Pinch," *Lincoln Star*, July 9, 1981.

353 130 positions since 1977: Editorial, "City Park Programs Taking Unwanted Turn," *Lincoln Star*, June 5, 1981.

354 "I commend the Mayor": "Budget Cut Plans May Slice 34 Jobs, including 24 with Parks Department," *Lincoln Journal*, July 9, 1981.

354 numerous volunteer opportunities: Karen Maguire, "Citizens Given Word: Penny-Pinching Time," *Lincoln Journal*, February 22, 1980; Bob Reeves, "City Officials Respond to Budget Restraints with Lists of Volunteer Jobs," *Lincoln Star*, February 25, 1980.

354 "The whole spirit of citizens": Elizabeth A. Peterson, interview.

354 My dad called the Parks: David Swartzlander, "'Cut the Grass,' Helen Said— and Mike Did," *Lincoln Journal*, May 18, 1982.

354 "It was his idea": "He's Out on Fairways, Mowing," *Lincoln Star*, May 18, 1982.

355 "Be a V.I.P.": Charles Flowerday, "Parks Need Mow Help, V.I.P.s Respond," *Sunday Journal and Star*, May 23, 1982.

355 "I don't consider myself": David Swartzlander, "City Has Volunteers; Now It Needs Lawnmowers," *Lincoln Journal*, May 27, 1982.

355 "spurred by a news story": Swartzlander, "City Has Volunteers."

355 "Lincoln's long tradition": Editorial, "Lot of Zip in vip," *Sunday Journal and Star*, May 30, 1982.

356 "Catalog of Gifts": George Hendrix, "Mayor Issues Catalog with Civic Gift Ideas," *Lincoln Star*, November 19, 1981.

356 It displayed gifts: David Swartzlander, "Fire Truck, New Bus among Top Items on City's Wish List," *Lincoln Journal*, November 19, 1981.

356   The gift catalog also included: "Boosalis Not Looking Gift Buffalo in Mouth," *Lincoln Journal*, December 9, 1981; "City's Wish List," *Tampa Tribune*, December 17, 1981; AP, "Well, So Much for Santa Claus," *Sacramento Union Paper*, December 17, 1981.

356   In its first: David Swartzlander, "Lincolnites, Others Respond Handsomely to Wish List Published by City," *Lincoln Journal*, December 25, 1982.

356   catalog on NBC's *Today* show: "Mayor Boosalis Interviewed on 'Today Show,'" *Lincoln Star*, December 16, 1982.

357   Dubbed the "gay rights amendment": "Boosalis Has 'No Qualms' about Ratifying Gay Rights," *Lincoln Star*, November 19, 1981.

357   "If this amendment is allowed": Joe Kreizinger, "Gay Ordinance Meeting Prompts Much Discussion," *Daily Nebraskan*, November 19, 1981.

357   "no qualms": "Boosalis Has 'No Qualms.'"

357   drew more than three hundred: Mike Butler and George Hendrix "Vote Set on Rights Measure," *Lincoln Star*, March 2, 1982.

357   Just after midnight: David Swartzlander, "Sexual Orientation Amendment on May Ballot," *Lincoln Journal*, March 2, 1982.

357   "maintained a carefully neutral": George Hendrix, "Voters Reject Gay Rights," *Lincoln Star*, May 12, 1982.

357   "I think maybe the margin": George Hendrix, "Mayor a Bit Puzzled by Election's Outcome," *Lincoln Star*, May 13, 1982.

358   "Our public affairs committee": Bart Becker, "Full Chorus Highlighted Men's Concert," *Lincoln Journal*, June 10, 1981.

358   Committee on Opportunities for the Disabled: Randal Blauvelt, "Candidates Disagree on Use of City Funds for Disabled Service," *Nebraska Reporter*, April 23, 1975.

358   She used her national platform: Jeff Goodwin, "Council Favors Keeping Current Disability Rules," *Daily Nebraskan*, September 1, 1982.

359   spent hours in wheelchairs: Lynn Zerschling, "Wheelchair Difficulties Noted," *Lincoln Star*, October 8, 1975.

359   "Several years ago I visited": Letter to editor from Mrs. Esther Arrison, "Curb Ramps Forthcoming," *Lincoln Evening Journal*, March 27, 1975.

359   "Today whenever I have a really tough": Nancy McClelland, interview.

359   With the threatened elimination: "Full-time Staff for 'Status of Women' Favored by Four," *Lincoln Star*, July 14, 1979.

359   Even with smaller staffing: Karen Maguire, "Council OKS City Incorporating Women's Commission," *Lincoln Journal*, July 18, 1979.

359   *community: "Helen Boosalis entered political life at a time when few women held elected positions. She helped lead the way for future women leaders," said Jan Potter of the Nebraska Commission on the Status of Women in 1997 (*Omaha World-Herald*, March 16, 1997). On International

Women's Day, March 7, 2007, Jan Gauger and my mother were honored as co-founders of the Lincoln-Lancaster Commission on the Status of Women in 1975.

360   "The myth about superwoman": Karen Maguire, "At Home, at Work, It's Mom—No, It's Superwoman," *Lincoln Journal*, March 11, 1980.

361   "Start observing government": "Women Mayors: Making a Difference," *The Best of America*, July 4, 1981.

361   "Many women who are political": Abby Maahs, "Mayor: Women Candidates Hindered," *Daily Nebraskan*, April 9, 1981.

361   "We don't want to walk": Justin Mitchell, "Congresswoman: Women Big Contributors to History," *Lincoln Journal*, August 23, 1980.

361   "As a nationally known mayor": A. J. McClanahan, "Lincoln Mayor Says Women Must Keep Momentum Going," *Omaha World-Herald*, September 1, 1980.

362   "Tell those who oppose": Melanie Gray, "250 Rededicate Themselves to Equal Rights for Women," *Lincoln Journal*, July 1, 1982.

362   "We'll just have to fight": David Swartzlander, "Boosalis: ERA Death Unfortunate," *Lincoln Journal*, June 30, 1982.

363   "because of the work for equality": George Hendrix, "Boosalis: Women Must Fight," *Lincoln Star*, July 1, 1982.

363   "I think about how much": "Living the Legacy: The Women's Rights Movement 1848–1998," www.Legacy98.org/move-hist.html.

363   "She winces when you ask": Tom White, "Helen Boosalis: Homemaker to City-maker," *Lincoln Star*, April 16, 1983.

363   *towns: A fourth grade girl from Seward, Nebraska, invited Helen Boosalis, candidate for governor and former mayor, to visit her school. Dressed in white patent-leather shoes and a new white dress her mother had sewn for the occasion, the little girl introduced Helen Boosalis to her class and later wrote a thank-you letter. "You inspired me a lot. Your stories were great. If I don't grow up to be a writer, I would like to follow in your footsteps." The letter was signed Danielle M. Nantkes—a lawyer elected to the Nebraska legislature in 2006, twenty years after that classroom visit.

I found in my mother's files scores of other letters from elementary school children whose classrooms Mom had visited as mayor or candidate for governor. In big block printing or newly learned cursive writing, the letters were both funny and touching. Some samples:

- "I've never really had anyone talk about the government that I really understood." Your friend, Kelly
- "I liked what you did to downtown Lincoln. I like you a lot even though I'm a Republican." Andrew

- "I would like to see all the homeless and the hungry get helped in some way because its sad to see them." Angie
- "I would like shorter school days because both my teacher and I think the extra 20 minutes are too long and boring. Both my grandma and I think you're the best." Annette
- "My Mom voted for you but my dad didn't." Melissa
- "You did everything just so perfect. We thought you were going to come in a limousine." Jenee
- "I'm glad I was born in time so I was alive when you were mayor." Your citizen, Elizabeth
- "I am excited there are two women canidates for govener. I watched you Wednesday on Good Morning America. If you become govener, please help the people who have problems on the farm." Gabe

363   "you mean a man": "Today's Corn," *Lincoln Star*, April 29, 1983.

364   "when young kids would yell": Don Walton, "Boosalis Building Statewide Familiarity," *Lincoln Star*, May 15, 1986.

364   "This might be the next": J. L. Schmidt, "Star's Flying Ace Takes Off," *Lincoln Star*, May 22, 1976.

365   Her most audacious venture: Melanie Gray, "Co-pilot Boosalis Soars over Capital," *Lincoln Journal*, July 27, 1981.

366   going through "egress" training: "Boosalis Will Fly with Air Guard," *Lincoln Journal*, July 20, 1981.

366   "her ladyship will become ill": Lynn Hawkins, "Mayor Flies with Great Ease," *Lincoln Star*, July 27, 1981.

366   "Her plane had just executed": Hawkins, "Mayor Flies with Great Ease."

367   "No, I have been saying": George Hendrix, "Possible Mayoral Candidates Now Testing Political Waters," *Lincoln Star*, November 15, 1982.

367   "a crafty positioning": Editorial, "No Real Surprises," *Lincoln Journal*, May 6, 1981.

368   finally achieved parity: George Hendrix, "There's More to It Than Labels Imply," *Lincoln Star*, March 21, 1983.

368   "there is no one in sight": Editorial, "Mayor's Contest Next," *Lincoln Star*, November 16, 1982.

369   "I'm very open on it": Thomas A. Fogarty, "Stan Matzke Unveils Plan to Become a Republican," *Lincoln Journal*, August 6, 1981.

369   not represent only business: David Swartzlander, "Hampton Announces Mayoral Bid," *Lincoln Journal*, November 24, 1982.

369   "Hampton took a white gloves": George Hendrix, "Hampton Is Positive as Mayoral Candidate," *Lincoln Star*, November 25, 1982.

369   During his mayoral campaign: "Hampton Unveils 5-Point Economic Development Plan," *Lincoln Star*, January 12, 1983.

369 his claim that IBM bypassed development: David Swartzlander, "IBM Confirms It Still Has Plans to Use Its Northeast Lincoln Site," *Sunday Journal and Star*, April 10, 1983.

369 "not unusual" for the company to "hold land": Swartzlander, "IBM Confirms."

370 "there is no truth": Swartzlander, "IBM Confirms."

370 His six years: Editorial, "Tuesday City Election Results Will Impact upon All Our Lives," *Lincoln Star*, March 31, 1983.

370 "When Boosalis steps down": George Hendrix, "Primary to 'Thin Out' Mayoral Field," *Lincoln Star*, March 31, 1983.

370 *governor: Roland Luedtke lost his position as lieutenant governor when Bob Kerrey defeated Governor Charles Thone by 7,233 votes (50.6 percent)— just months before Luedtke ran for mayor of Lincoln in 1983. C. David Kotok, "Governors' Camps Sound Battle Cry," *Sunday World-Herald*, November 2, 1986.

370 *mayor: Lloyd Hinkley, a realtor and former city councilman, argued during the 1983 mayoral campaign that Hampton would have too many real estate conflicts of interest if he were elected mayor, which is why Hinkley did not run for mayor himself. Hampton's response to the charge was that if Hinkley "has some concerns about his own integrity and his ability to maintain it, that's his concern." David Swartzlander, "Hinkley Says Interest Conflicts Could Snag Hampton as Mayor," *Sunday Journal and Star*, March 27, 1983.

370 Lott was perceived: Hendrix, "Primary to 'Thin Out' Mayoral Field."

370 his second-place primary finish: George Hendrix, "Hampton Plans 'Issues' Campaign," *Lincoln Star*, April 8, 1983.

370 her "preference" for mayor: George Hendrix, "Boosalis Would 'Prefer' Luedtke," *Lincoln Star*, April 15, 1983.

371 "is committed to open government": David Swartzlander, "Boosalis Endorses Luedtke," *Lincoln Journal*, April 14, 1983.

371 "It's unfortunate that after a long": George Hendrix, "Hampton Levels Charge at Luedtke," *Lincoln Star*, April 16, 1983.

371 "I think it's unfortunate that our differences": Hendrix, "Hampton Levels Charge."

371 "Helen Boosalis has been": David Swartzlander, "Lott Is Endorsing Luedtke for Mayor," *Lincoln Journal*, April 15, 1983.

371 He believed that Luedtke: David Swartzlander, "Hampton's Easy Going Image, Complex Personality Shown," *Lincoln Journal*, April 27, 1983.

371 "I can't believe that the Mayor": Swartzlander, "Hampton's Easy Going Image."

371 *record: My mother spent $37,500 in her reelection campaign for mayor in 1979.

371 The Lincoln newspapers were split: Editorial, "We're for Roland Luedtke,"

Lincoln Journal, April 22, 1983; Editorial, "Hampton Best Choice for This Point in Time," *Lincoln Star*, April 25, 1983.

373 *voters: Volunteer canvassers in my 1983 city council campaign went door-to-door and identified positive (pro-me) voters on the poll sheet with a (+) sign, negative voters with a (-) sign, and uncommitted voters with a (o) sign.

373 *footsteps: While footstep-following comparisons were media hype, I was startled to discover in my research a couple of real footsteps of my mother's that I did precisely follow. In her early leadership path at the U.S. Conference of Mayors in the late 1970s, Mom chaired the Human Development Standing Committee. More than ten years later, I, too, chaired the Human Development Policy Steering Committee as an Evanston alderman active in the National League of Cities—the national organization of cities and state municipal leagues that includes member cities and towns of all sizes (not just over 30,000 population) and includes city council participants as well as mayors.

Even so, Mom's footsteps were large. As Human Development chair, I was invited to a meeting at the White House, my first. After clearing the security post I walked up the White House drive, a little full of myself, thinking, "Here I am—not my mother—actually going to the White House for my own meeting." Just then, a long, black limousine pulled up and stopped, and U.S. senator Paul Simon from Illinois climbed out and waved. "How's your mother doing? Please say hello to her."

373 "as much to the community": David Swartzlander, "Davis Follows Footsteps of Mother, Boosalis," *Lincoln Journal*, April 13, 1983.

373 *goal: In 1986, three years after my mother stepped down as mayor and was running for governor, the *Chicago Sun-Times* did a similar mother-daughter story which quoted Mom saying that I never wanted to be a politician. "That was until three years ago, when she [Davis] became a second-generation pol by being elected alderman in Evanston." Ray Hanania, Mary Gillespie, and Alf Siewers, "In Nebraska, Best Woman *Will* Win," *Chicago Sun-Times*, May 27, 1986.

Also during the 1986 governor's race, Chicago cbs affiliate anchorwoman Susan Anderson came to our house in Evanston to interview me and do a video with Max, Michael, and Christopher for a news segment on family political dynasties—the Daleys, the Stevensons, and . . . (who?) mother-daughter politicians Helen Boosalis and Beth Boosalis Davis. We got a big laugh from the stretch comparison.

374 her "vision to push Lincoln": White, "Helen Boosalis."

374 "The business of serving": Editorial, "Mayor's Race Crowded," *Lincoln Journal*, March 31, 1983.

374 "Helen Boosalis has been": Editorial, "We're for Roland Luedtke."

375 approval rating was 61 percent: Karen Maguire, "Polled Lincolnites Rate Mayor, Council High," *Lincoln Journal*, April 5, 1980.

375 "I guess I'm pleased": Bill Kreifel, "Council's, Mayor's Performances Liked," *Sunday Journal and Star*, May 17, 1981.

375 "Mayors almost never grow": Andy Rooney (*Tribune* Company Syndicate), "It Wouldn't Be Much Fun, Being a Mayor," *Lincoln Star*, March 3, 1982.

375 In her second term she told: Holly Spence, "Nebraska's Metro Mayors Keep Strong Party Ties," *Nebraska Democrat*, November 1981, 1.

375 "Sometimes I'm very blunt": Diane Andersen, "Boosalis 'Does Her Thing' for the City as Mayor," *Daily Nebraskan*, August 26, 1980.

376 she was most proud of opening: Andersen, "Boosalis 'Does Her Thing.'"

376 *downtown: Years later my mother said that her greatest disappointment in her efforts as mayor was seeing the downtown fade as a retail shopping center after she left office. "One wonders whether there were other things we could have done." Doug Thomas, "Anything but Retiring," *Omaha World-Herald*, March 16, 1997.

376 "Helen may not regard herself": White, "Helen Boosalis."

376 A range of those with whom: Thomas, "Anything but Retiring."

377 "During Helen's years as mayor": John Rosenow, interview.

377 "In the mayor's office": George V. Voinovich, interview.

378 "I don't have a big ego": White, "Helen Boosalis."

378 *rating: At the end of Mom's second term as mayor in 1983, a *Lincoln Journal* poll of Lincoln residents reported 72 percent approval, 18 percent disapproval ratings for Mayor Helen Boosalis; 62 percent approval, 13 percent disapproval for Governor Bob Kerrey; and 48 percent approval, 39 percent disapproval for President Ronald Reagan. Kent L. Wolgamott, "Poll: 48% OK Reagan's Performance," *Lincoln Journal*, May 14, 1983.

378 "Legacies and role models": David Swartzlander, "Retiring Mayor Says Lincoln Oasis Dream Fulfilled," *Lincoln Journal*, May 9, 1983.

379 a "truly unlucky day": "Appreciation Party for Helen Friday," *Sunday Journal and Star*, May 8, 1983.

379 *Seng: Twenty years later, in 2003, Coleen Seng was elected Lincoln's second woman mayor. She did not run for a second term.

379 "more than 2,000 people": David Swartzlander, "72% Approve of Boosalis' Efforts as Mayor," *Sunday Journal and Star*, May 8, 1983.

379 "school children, politicians, firefighters": Michelle Carr, "5,000 Well-wishers Say 'Thanks' to Mayor for 24 Years of Service," *Lincoln Journal*, May 14, 1983.

379 The lobby of the County-City: Carr, "5,000 Well-wishers Say 'Thanks.'"

380 *mayor: Several of those I interviewed referred to Helen Boosalis as "the people's mayor."

381 "Mayor Helen switched from": Gil Savery, introduction, "Thanks, Helen!" Journal-Star Printing Co., May 13, 1983.

382 the Athenian Oath: "About Cities: Cities 101: Athenian Oath," National League of Cities, http://www.nlc.org/about_cities/cities_101/146.aspx.

FLASH FORWARD: TRAIL'S END

383 Nebraska's population in 1986: Larry Batson (*Minneapolis Star and Tribune*), "Economy Overshadows Gender in Nebraska's Prairie Classic," *Sunday World-Herald*, August 17, 1986; Fred Knapp, "Both Sides Confident in Historic Race," *Lincoln Journal*, November 2, 1986; "Today's Primaries," *USA Today*, May 13, 1986.

384 "to hold onto Democrats": Neil Oxman, interview.

384 Eighty percent of the population: Tim Sacco, "'Equality before the Law': In a Battle for the Nebraska Governorship, Two Women Bring the State's Motto a Modern Application," *America West* Airline Magazine, October 1986.

384 The Nebraska governorship had rotated: "Governor's Race a Historic Mark," *Falls City (NE) Journal*, May 22, 1986, citing Robert Miewald and Robert Sittig, "Nebraska Gubernatorial Elections 1866 to 1982," Nebraska Research Report No. 12. Department of Political Science, University of Nebraska–Lincoln.

384 there had been fifteen Republican: "Governors of Nebraska," www.lincoln-libraries.org/depts/ref/negovernors.htm, or http://en.wikipedia.org/wiki/List_of_Governors_of_Nebraska.

384 I moved on to think about the Democrats: Don Walton, "The Governor's Race Is Off and Running," *Lincoln Star*, August 1, 1986.

384 Democrat Bob Kerrey won: C. David Kotok, "Governors' Camps Sound Battle Cry," *Sunday World-Herald*, November 3, 1986.

385 "Quite frankly, that's the biggest": Knapp, "Both Sides Confident."

385 congressman John Cavanaugh's prognosis: Knapp, "Both Sides Confident."

385 "her philosophy of government": Editorial, "Boosalis Star's Choice," *Lincoln Star*, November 3, 1986.

386 "Boosalis' demonstrated leadership style": Editorial, "Preference for Boosalis," *Lincoln Journal*, October 27, 1986.

386 "We don't think that": AP, "Boosalis, Orr Gain Editorial Endorsements," *Beatrice (NE) Sun*, October 29, 1986.

386 *World-Herald's* endorsement: AP, "Two Newspapers Split on Top Endorsements," *Norfolk (NE) News*, October 30, 1986.

386 *Beutler: In 2007, twenty-one years after finishing second behind Helen Boosalis in the 1986 Democratic gubernatorial primary and then generously campaigning for her election as governor, Chris Beutler was elected mayor of Lincoln; Helen Boosalis campaigned for him.

386 "wealth of Democratic statehouse experience": C. David Kotok, "Mrs. Boo-salis Finds Pace 'Relaxing' on Election Eve," *Omaha World-Herald*, November 4, 1986.

387 "Helen, you have a strange way": Kotok, "Boosalis Finds Pace 'Relaxing.'"

389 Conventional wisdom said: Don Walton, "Omaha Voters May Hold Key to Victory," *Lincoln Star*, November 4, 1986.

390 "Helen is coming along like a steamroller": David Thompson, "Mrs. Boosalis Praises 'Class Act' of Backers during Her Campaign," *Omaha World-Herald*, November 5, 1986.

390 I only remember her comparing: Thompson, "Mrs. Boosalis Praises 'Class Act.'"

391 But "the complexion of the returns": Thompson, "Mrs. Boosalis Praises 'Class Act.'"

391 *48 percent: Final results of the 1986 Nebraska gubernatorial election were Kay Orr, 298,325 (53 percent); Helen Boosalis, 265,156 (47 percent). Secretary of State Allen J. Beerman, comp., *Official Report of the State Board of State Canvassers of the State of Nebraska, General Election, November 4, 1986* (Lincoln NE: Office of Secretary of State).

391 "We have conducted an open, honest": Thompson, "Mrs. Boosalis Praises 'Class Act'"; Helen Boosalis, concession speech, November 4, 1986, private files.

391 "Helen Boosalis ended her campaign": Editorial, "Class, Dignity in Boosalis Talk," *Omaha World-Herald*, November 9, 1986.

392 The voting breakdown showed: C. David Kotok, "Kay Orr's Victory Scores Firsts for Nebraska, GOP," *Omaha World-Herald*, November 5, 1986.

393 Orr felt that two positions: Kotok, "Kay Orr's Victory Scores Firsts."

393 Early in the campaign: C. David Kotok, "Boosalis Camp Says Sales Tax Issue Sank Her Effort," *Omaha World-Herald*, November 6, 1986.

393 disagreement whether it was the mandatory: Nebraska Council of School Administrators, "History of TEEOSA (1985–1987): The Complete History of the Nebraska Tax Equity and Educational Opportunities Support Act (TEEOSA)," http://schoolfinance.ncsa.org/policy/fullhistory/1985–1987/a3.htm.

393 *1986 election: The controversial combination and complexity of issues involved in LB662 gave rise to later speculation about the impetus and motives for enacting the legislation in 1985. "Given the partisan nature of the issue, one might ask whether LB662 was about school finance, school consolidation, a tax increase, or a means to shape the outcome of the 1986 gubernatorial election. Perhaps it was a little of each. . . . Some Republicans and party leaders may have felt that blaming the Democrats for the passage of LB662 [in 1985] would enhance the odds for a Republican victory in the [1986] gubernatorial race." Nebraska Council of School Administrators, "History of TEEOSA."

393 fell just short on time: Thompson, "Mrs. Boosalis Praises 'Class Act.'"

393 "Taxes was it": Kotok, "Kay Orr's Victory Scores Firsts."

394 *increases: "The Governor [Orr] has struggled for more than two years to lift a low approval rating that has dogged her since a revamping of the state's tax structure brought income tax increases in many categories. She has sponsored legislation to correct what she said was a mistake, but many people in this heavily Republican state still criticize her for it." William Robbins, "Politics Overtake Selecting Nuclear Waste Dump Sites," *New York Times*, September 30, 1990.

394 "The election of 1986": Editorial, "A Memorable Fight," *Lincoln Journal*, November 5, 1986.

394 "ran a spectacular campaign": Kotok, "Kay Orr's Victory Scores Firsts."

394 "The gubernatorial race": Don Walton, "Together, They Knocked Down the Barriers," *Lincoln Star*, November 7, 1986.

395 *newspapers: In addition to abundant post-election analysis of the 1986 governor's race in the press, individuals who closely observed the campaign had a variety of personal views. My mother's mayoral campaign communications consultant, Rich Bailey, recently reflected on the outcome of the governor's race. "Many voters in conservative, rock ribbed Republican country west of Seward probably said to themselves, 'OK, I'll have to vote for a woman because I have no other choice, but she better not be too damn liberal.'" Bailey also observed, "The issues and values that Helen stood for played so well in a community environment where she could express her warm personal interest in people. That doesn't work as well at the state level where the geography is huge" (Rich Bailey, interview). In a similar vein, former St. Paul mayor and unsuccessful candidate for governor of Minnesota, George Latimer, told me, "The relationship I had with the people of St. Paul was very intimate. Intimate doesn't translate into a statewide race" (George Latimer, interview).

395 "In defeat, Democrat Helen Boosalis": Editorial, "A Memorable Fight."

395 *head: Losing a hard-fought campaign is difficult not only for family, friends, and supporters of the candidate but also for the professionals who pour their hearts into the campaign. More than twenty years after my mother's race for governor, Neil Oxman—target of my early campaign pencil throwing—told me, "What do I do after a losing campaign? Get depressed—post-campaign depression. Our firm's won about three-quarters of the almost 600 races we've done, and the fact of the matter is, I rarely remember the winning campaigns. I remember the losing ones. It's somewhat better as I've gotten older and have other things to balance my life, but the losses stay with me way more than the wins." Neil Oxman, interview.

396 *loss: Betty Peterson, the volunteer coordinator for my mother's mayoral

and gubernatorial campaigns, told me, "Even though Helen handled the loss very well, I know she felt bad because she thought she had let everybody down. But she didn't let anybody down." Elizabeth A. Peterson, interview.

396 *office: Ten years after the 1986 election, my mother said to a reporter about the governor's race, "Things work out the way they're supposed to, I guess. I always put things behind me and go on to the next thing." Thomas, "Anything but Retiring."

396 "Helen's a morning person": Don Walton, "Boosalis Far from Retirement," *Lincoln Star*, May 18, 1987.

CHAPTER 9. LIFE ~~AFTER~~ IS POLITICS

398 "If Helen has a political philosophy": F. Gregory Hayden, interview.

398 "Helen brought a level": Rich Bailey, interview.

399 "no regrets about my": Gene Fadness, "Boosalis to Bring Youthful Vigor to State Department of Aging," *Lincoln Sun*, May 11, 1983.

399 "make a good city better": campaign slogan, Boosalis for Mayor campaign material, 1975.

399 "I know she will bring": Don Walton, "Boosalis Will Take Over Aging Dept.," *Lincoln Star*, January 5, 1983.

399 "the perfect marriage": Editorial, "More Appointments Are of Highest Merit," *Lincoln Star*, January 6, 1983.

399 "When you see him again": John Barrette, "Mayor Boosalis Out to Pasture? Not a Chance," *Omaha World-Herald*, January 18, 1983.

400 "Helen was such an exceptional executive": Bob Kerrey, interview.

400 "bringing people into the process": "Helen Boosalis: The Campaign Has Been Fun," *Grand Island (NE) Independent*, October 30, 1986.

400 "as effervescent about aging programs: Nancy Hicks, "Boosalis Spreading Word," *Lincoln Star*, May 21, 1984.

400 "I just hope I have the choice": Fadness, "Boosalis to Bring Youthful Vigor."

403 "Helen brought to AARP a passion": Kevin J. Donnellan, interview.

403 "Boosalis approach": Kevin J. Donnellan, interview.

405 "Helen's leadership kept the board": John Rother, interview.

407 "Because Helen was such a good speaker": John Rother, interview.

407 "Older people are vulnerable": Mary Sharon Thomas, "Senior Adults Celebrate Happy, Healthy Lives," *Shreveport (LA) Times*, September 29, 1996.

407 "Helen was able to apply": Kevin J. Donnellan, interview.

407 When Republican senator Alan Simpson: "Conversations with History: Institute of International Studies, UC Berkeley," interview of Alan Simpson by Harry Kreisler (September 17, 1997), http://globetrotter.berkeley.edu/conversations/Simpson/simpson6.html.

407 "Helen was neither taken aback": John Rother, interview.

407 "freedom to just beat the brains": "Conversations with History," interview of Alan Simpson by Harry Kreisler (September 17, 1997).

408 "Stay active in your community": Mary Pierce, "Seniors Rights Advocate Visits NP," *North Platte (NE) Telegraph*, October 16, 1998.

408 "Helen Boosalis proved two decades ago": Doug Thomas, "Anything but Retiring," *Omaha World-Herald*, March 16, 1997.

408 "deep experience as a dynamic mayor": Nomination by Royce Yeater of Helen Boosalis for trustee of the National Trust for Historic Preservation, July 13, 1987.

408 "from a reactive, don't-tear-it-down movement": Richard Moe, interview.

409 "political leadership, particularly": William R. Klein, "Widening Influence of Growth Management Strategies on Historic Preservation," *Preservation Forum* 4, no. 2 (1990): 12.

410 "Helen understood the extraordinary": John Rosenow, interview.

411 "She helps us keep our eye": John Rosenow, interview.

412 Helen Boosalis Park, an eight-hundred-acre: Al J. Laukaitis, "Boosalis Park Down in Dumps," *Lincoln Journal Star*, May 15, 1994.

413 Common Cause to promote campaign finance: Bill Avery, Local View, "Nebraskans' Feelings Clear about Excessive Campaign Spending," *Lincoln Journal Star*, May 24, 2005.

413 "She has vision": Thomas, "Anything but Retiring."

414 "Helen won't let you": Cindy Lange-Kubick, "Helen's People Still Offering Advice after All These Years," *Lincoln Journal Star*, December 8, 2002.

415 "never to schedule anything": Michael Merwick, interview.

Interviews

Rich Bailey, retired chairman, Bailey Lauerman Marketing/Communications; communications consultant in Boosalis mayoral campaigns. Interview by author, tape recording, Lincoln, October 12, 2001.

Sue Bailey Jackson, Lincoln City Council member, 1973–77; adviser in Boosalis city council, mayoral, and gubernatorial campaigns. Interview by author, tape recording, Lincoln, October 12, 2001.

Beatty Brasch, executive director, Center for People in Need; former executive director, Lincoln Action Program; former election commissioner; campaign coordinator and campaign manager in Boosalis mayoral campaigns. Interview by author, tape recording, Lincoln, October 12, 2001.

Tom Cochran, executive director, U.S. Conference of Mayors. Interview by author, tape recording, Washington DC, June 13, 2006.

Curt Donaldson, Lincoln City Council member, 1993–99; Boosalis mayoral campaign adviser. Interview by author, tape recording, Lincoln, May 2002.

Kevin J. Donnellan, chief communications officer, AARP. Interview by author, tape recording, Washington DC, June 13, 2006.

Jan Gauger, Lancaster County commissioner, 1972–88; co-founder, Lincoln-Lancaster Commission on the Status of Women; adviser in Boosalis mayoral and gubernatorial campaigns. Interview by author, tape recording, Lincoln, October 10, 2001.

Chuck Hagel, U.S. senator (NE). Interview by author, tape recording, Washington DC, June 12, 2006.

F. Gregory Hayden, professor of economics, University of Nebraska–Lincoln; head of policy research, campaign advisory committee member, and a manager in Boosalis gubernatorial campaign. Interview by author, tape recording, Lincoln, June 21, 2006.

Ross E. Hecht, retired president, Lincoln State Bank; adviser in Boosalis campaigns. Interview by author, tape recording, Lincoln, May 9, 2002.

Jacquelyn R. Herman, neighborhood activist. Interview by author, tape recording, Lincoln, October 10, 2001.

Richard D. Herman, *Lincoln Journal* editorial pages editor, 1973–93; political/legislative reporter, 1962–73. Interview by author, tape recording, Lincoln, October 10, 2001.

Lloyd D. Hinkley, realtor; Lincoln City Council member, 1961–69; adviser in the Boosalis campaigns. Interview by author, tape recording, Lincoln, October 12, 2001.

Mike Johanns, secretary of agriculture, U.S. Department of Agriculture, 2005–7; governor of Nebraska, 1999–2005; mayor of Lincoln, 1991–98. Interview by author, tape recording, Washington DC, June 14, 2006.

Bob Kerrey, president, The New School; U.S. senator (NE), 1989–2001; governor of Nebraska, 1983–87. Interview by author, tape recording, New York City, November 13, 2006.

Robert E. Knoll, professor emeritus of English, University of Nebraska–Lincoln. Interview by author, tape recording, Lincoln, October 12, 2001.

George Latimer, Distinguished Visiting Professor of Urban Studies, Macalester College; mayor of St. Paul, 1976–90. Interview by author, tape recording, St. Paul MN, February 6, 2002.

Nancy McClelland, former teacher, Lincoln Public Schools; former program specialist, League of Human Dignity; volunteer in Boosalis campaigns. Interview by author, tape recording, Lincoln, October 5, 2004.

Michael Merwick, director, Building and Safety Department, City of Lincoln; fire chief, City of Lincoln, 1980–83; administrative director and administrative aide, City of Lincoln, 1975–80. Interview by author, tape recording, Lincoln, October 12, 2001.

Barbara A. Mikulski, U.S. senator (MD). Interview by author, tape recording of phone conversation, Washington DC, June 15, 2006.

Richard Moe, president, National Trust for Historic Preservation. Interview by author, tape recording, Washington DC, June 12, 2006.

E. Benjamin Nelson, U.S. senator (NE); governor of Nebraska, 1991–99. Interview by author, tape recording, Washington DC, June 13, 2006.

Neil Oxman, president, Campaign Group; media consultant in Boosalis gubernatorial campaign. Interview by author, tape recording of phone conversation, Philadelphia, April 12, 2007.

Elizabeth A. (Betty) Peterson, volunteer coordinator in Boosalis mayoral reelection and gubernatorial campaigns; volunteer in Boosalis city council and mayoral campaigns. Interview by author, tape recording, Lincoln, May 2002.

Jerry L. Petr, retired professor of economics, University of Nebraska–Lincoln; supporter of Helen Boosalis in political campaigns. Interview by author, tape recording, Lincoln, October 5, 2004.

John Rosenow, president, Arbor Day Foundation. Interview by author, tape recording, Lincoln, June 21, 2006.

John Rother, director, policy and strategy, AARP. Interview by author, tape recording, Washington DC, June 13, 2006.

Kathleen Rutledge, editor, *Lincoln Journal Star*, 2001–7; former statehouse reporter. Interview by author, tape recording, Lincoln, June 22, 2006.

Paul Sarbanes, U.S. senator (MD), 1977–2007. Interview by author, tape recording, Washington DC, June 13, 2006.

Robert K. Schrepf, vice-president and editorial page editor, *Hartford Courant*; editorial page editor, *Lincoln Star*, 1969–82. Interview by author, tape recording, New York City, June 10, 2006.

Coleen J. Seng, mayor, City of Lincoln, 2003–7; Lincoln City Council member, 1987–2003; director of community ministries, First United Methodist Church, 1977–97. Interview by author, tape recording, Lincoln, October 10, 2001.

Robert F. Sittig Sr., professor of political science, University of Nebraska–Lincoln, 1962–2002; member, Lancaster County Republican Executive Committee, and delegate, Republican State Convention, 1970s–1980s; adviser/volunteer in Boosalis mayoral and gubernatorial campaigns. Interview by author, tape recording, Lincoln, October 12, 2001.

George V. Voinovich, U.S. senator (OH); governor of Ohio, 1990–98; mayor of Cleveland, 1979–88. Interview by author, tape recording of phone conversation, Washington DC, June 29, 2006.

Don Walton, political reporter, *Lincoln Journal Star*. Interview by author, tape recording, New York City, June 10, 2006.

Laura DeKoven Waxman, partner, City Policy Associates; former assistant executive director, U.S. Conference of Mayors. Interview by author, tape recording, Washington DC, June 13, 2006.

Bibliography

PERIODICALS

Boston Globe, January 1, 1975–January 31, 2006
Chicago Sun-Times, January 1–December 31, 1986
Chicago Tribune, January 1–December 31, 1986
Daily Nebraskan, January 1, 1975–December 31, 1986
Lincoln Evening Journal, January 1, 1959–April 9, 1977
Lincoln Journal, April 11, 1977–August 4, 1995
Lincoln Journal Star, August 7, 1995–December 31, 2002
Lincoln Star, January 1, 1959–August 4, 1995
New York Times, January 1, 1975–December 31, 1986
Omaha World-Herald, January 1, 1975–December 31, 1997
Time, January 1, 1975–December 31, 1986
USA Today, January 1, 1975–December 31, 1986
U.S. News and World Report, January 1, 1975–December 31, 1986
Washington Post, January 1, 1975–December 31, 1986

BOOKS

Carroll, Susan J., ed. *The Impact of Women in Public Office*. Bloomington: Indiana University Press, 2001.
———, ed. *Women and American Politics: New Questions, New Directions*. New York: Oxford University Press, 2003.
Evans, Sara. *Personal Politics: The Roots of Women's Liberation in the Civil Rights Movement and the New Left*. New York: Vintage Books, 1980.
Haarsager, Sandra. *Bertha Knight Landes of Seattle: Big City Mayor*. Norman: University of Oklahoma Press, 1994.
Rowbotham, Sheila. *A Century of Women: The History of Women in Britain and the United States*. New York: Viking Press, 1997.
Whitaker, Lois Duke. *Women in Politics: Outsiders or Insiders?* 3rd ed. Upper Saddle River NJ: Prentice-Hall, 1999.
Wills, Garry. *Certain Trumpets: The Call of Leaders*. New York: Simon and Schuster, 1994.
Wilson, Marie C. *Closing the Leadership Gap: Why Women Can and Must Help Run the World*. New York: Viking Press, 2004.
Wright, John W., ed. *The New York Times 2007 Almanac*. New York: Penguin Group, 2006.

Index

Page numbers in italic indicate photographs.

HB = *Helen Boosalis*; BD = *Beth Davis*

AARP, 402–8
abortion as issue, 94–96, 362, 443–44n
Abzug, Bella, 62, 88
Adams, Dale, 104, 107, 108–11, 208
Aden, Roger, 252
Adventists. *See* Seventh Day Adventists
age issue in gubernatorial campaign, 6
Agricultural Revitalization Plan, 340–41
agriculture as issue in governor's race, 94, 250, 252, 302, 340–42, 344–45
Ahlschwede, Margrethe, 224, 243, 261, 286
airplanes and ceremonial duties, *364, 364–67, 366*
Alesio, Mike, 10
Alinsky, Saul, 224, 481n
Alioto, Joseph, 120, 449n
All-America City recognition, 168–70, 210, 229, 375, 458n
Alliance. *See* Lincoln Alliance
Allington, Bob, 4, 10
alternative energy sources, 150–51, 274. *See also* energy use policy
Amen, Paul, 79, 438n
Anderson, R. D., 105, 111
Ando, Kichiro, 332
Angle, John and Catherine, 10
Angle, Margaret, 10
anti-business, accusations of, 441n, 477n; in 1975 mayoral election, 74, 78, 86; in 1975 mayoral term, 155, 164; in

1979 mayoral election, 212–13, 228, 229; in 1979 mayoral term, 277–78, 280, 287, 353, 441n, 477n; in governor's race, 342–43
approval ratings, 375, 378, 503
Arbor Day Foundation, 410–12
Ash, Pat, 30, 32
Athenian Oath and HB, 382
Athens, Andy, 141–42
Austin, Bill, 234

Badura, Marg, 8–9, 50–51, 136, 249, 347
Bailey, Rich, 64, 212, 398, 506n
Bailey, Sue: on 1975–77 city council, 101, 110, 124–25, 129, 151, 154; in 1977 city council election, 156–60; on city council with HB, 39–40; death of, 413; governor's race advisor, 302; on HB, 12, 376; and HB's first run for city council, 25; and mayoral campaign, 60, 75
Baird, Leirion, 424
Baker, Dick: on 1975–77 city council, 101, 108, 109, 124–25, 129; and 1977–79 city council, 160, 169, 208; and 1977 city council election, 159; on city council with HB, 39; resignation of, 223
Baker, Howard, 328
Baker, James, 324, 330
Barney, Chauncey, 149
Barrett, Margaret, 416
baseball strike (1981), 335
Beame, Abe, 307, 449n
beautification project, 146, 164, 265, 410

Begin, Menachem, 319–20
Bellamy, Carol, 93, 135
Bentley, Helen Delich, 442n
Bereuter, Doug, 249
Beutler, Chris, 2, 3, 5, 43, 47, 48, 50, 255, 386, 504
Bicycle Safety Committee, 126
Biegert, Maurine, 5
Bilandic, Michael, 229, 307
Blocker, Lee, 116
block grants, 321, 325, 490n
Blomgren, Sue, 164
Blomgren family, 26
"blue laws" controversy, 36
Boosalis, Bill (Mike's brother), 194, 200–201, 204
Boosalis, Elaine (Mike's sister), 194, 204
Boosalis, George (Mike's brother), 194, 200, 204
Boosalis, Georgia (Mike's sister), 194, 204
Boosalis, Helen: [personal data is cited here; events in her life are cited elsewhere in the index, by topic, e.g., mayoral campaign (1975)] courtship and marriage, 193–205, 215–16; education, 24; family history, 175–93; as grandmother, 3, 248, 250, 252, 317, 346, 415, 417–18, 420; as homemaker, 16–17, 190, 255, 360; as mother, 12–17, 26–27, 33, 257, 372–73, 415, 417–20; personal energy, 6, 66, 253–55, 300, 322, 380; relationship with staffs, 218, 249–50, 254–55; on risk taking, 24, 378; as role model, 132, 257, 363, 424n, 471n, 499–500n; service on boards, 402–13. See also Geankoplis, Helen
Boosalis, Helen, photos of: after governor's race, 397; with Al Gore, 406; with Beth, 421; with Bill Bradley, 137; with Bob Kerrey and Frank

Morrison, 343; city council chair, 40; in city council race, 28; editorial cartoon, 305; with family, 29, 45, 46, 242, 381; at farewell celebration, 380, 381; with Gary Hart, 139; with George Hansen, 115; in governor's race, 46, 47, 48, 254, 389, 392; and Helen Boosalis Trail, 411; as homemaker, 18, 19; with Jan Gauger, 414; with Jim Exon, 405; with Jimmy Carter, 311, 316; with Kay Orr, 91; with Maynard Jackson, 138; as mayor 100, 148, 267, 368, 380; in mayor's race (1975), 70, 72; in mayor's race (1979), 241, 242; with ostrich, 365; with planes, 364, 366; with Ronald Reagan, 324; with Sam Schwartz-kopf, 71; in Lincoln, 420; wedding, 201
Boosalis, Jim (Mike's cousin), 200
Boosalis, Kay Christopoulos (Mike's sister-in-law), 200
Boosalis, John (Mike's brother), 194, 200, 202, 204; and Knolls restaurant, 81–83, 226, 240, 323
Boosalis, Mary and Gus (Mike's mother and father), 193
Boosalis, Mike (HB's husband): in city council campaign, 26–27; consulting in Australia, 317, 410; courtship and marriage, 193–205; education, 203–5; as father, 7, 16, 17–18; in governor's race, 256–57, 294, 386–88; on HB, 254, 256; in mayoral campaign, 66–67, 76–77, 79–80, 82; military service, 194–200, 202–3; news clippings kept by, 67, 99, 146; offered job in Michigan, 40–42, 76; post-governor's race, 395–96; support for HB, 55, 66–67, 82, 215–16, 257, 399, 421, 471n; as UNL professor, 17–18, 27, 75–76, 193, 205, 256, 340; and U.S. Conference of

Mayors, 336; as volunteer in Parks and Recreation, 354–55

Boosalis, Mike (HB's husband), photos of: after governor's race, *397*; in Air Force uniform, *197*; with B-24 flight crew, *199*; celebrating 1979 election, *242*; city council campaign, *29*; with family, *45*; at farewell celebration, *381*; in governor's race, *389*; on Helen Boosalis Trail, *411*; with Helen Geankoplis, *195*; in university lab, *41*; wedding, *201*

Boosalis, Nick (Mike's brother), 193, 194, 200, 204

Boosalis, Ted (Mike's brother), 194, 204

"Boosalis approach," 403

Bornemeier, Nancy, 14

Boyle, Franny, 190

Boyle, Mike, 2, 3, 390

Boyles, E. Bartlett "Pat," 31–32, 34, 37

Bradley, Bill, *137*, 137–38

Bradley, Tom, 307

Brady, Teri, 14

Bragg, Jo, 65

Brandeis stores closing, 265–66, 268

Branditsas, Georgia, 194

Brasch, Beatty, 118, 255, 351, 413

Brashear, Kermit, 2, 5, 7, 43, 49

Brennan, Edward, 140

Brogden, Doug, 155, 162–63, 213, 217–18, 230. *See also* Planning Department

Brooks, Pierce, 105

Brown, Arlyss, 223, 224, 225, 238, 243

Brown, Charles, 233–36

Brown, Mike, 492n

Brungard, Robert, 233

Brunson, Mr. and Mrs., 202–3

budget process: in 1975 mayoral term, 116–19, 170–71, 447n; and citizen forums, 123; as issue facing mayor, 147;

mayoral term (1979), 280–83, 351–56, 447n, 478–79n

Burlington Northern Railroad, 270–71

Burlington rail yards, campaigning at, 80–81, 388

Bush, George H. W., 136, 328–29, 330

business community, 78, 85–86, 261–62, 276, 287, 289, 439n, 477n. *See also* anti-business, accusations of; "O Street gang"

Byrne, Jane, 229, 314, 339

campaign contributions: in mayoral campaign, 65–66, 50in. *See also* fundraising

campaign finance reform: and Common Cause, 413; and AARP, 403

campaign junkies, 259

Campbell, John, 265

Campbell, Robert E., 78

Candy Factory, 271

Canney, Walter, 151, 274

Carley Capital Group, 268–69

Carpenter, Elaine, 270

carpooling program, 149, 247, 273

Carroll, Joe, 103–4, 108, 109

Carter, Jimmy, *311*, *316*; HB's endorsement of, 287, 316–17; mayors in cabinet, 314; and U.S. Conference of Mayors, 309–12, 315–18

Carver, Richard, 338

"Catalog of Gifts" program, 356, 498n

Cavanaugh, John, 48, 94, 249, 385

CDBG (Community Development Block Grant) program, 166, 321, 333

Centennial Mall, 272

Centrum Plaza project, 164–65, 228, 264–65, 381

ceremonial duties of mayor, 363–67

CETA (Comprehensive Employment and Training Act) programs, 321, 359

Chamber of Commerce: board appointees from, 125; and HB's national role, 336; and Joe Hampton, 261; leadership by, 266; and mayoral races, 79, 212; and sales tax increase request, 353; and Stevens Creek development, 155; and support of Radial, 285; and tax increment financing proposal, 268

Chaney, Carolyn, 315

Charles, Reid, 117–18

Chavez, Linda, 88, 92

Cherry Hill developers, 266–68

Chicago IL: fundraising in, 140–45; mayoral campaign (1979), 229

Chick, George, 115, 166. *See also* Urban Development Department

Chisholm, Shirley, 62

choice, reproductive, as issue, 94–96, 362, 443–44n

Christenson, Doug, 77

Christy, Valerie, 126

Cisneros, Henry, 339

citizen involvement: and All-America City award, 168–70; and Comprehensive plan, 276, 458–59n; and district election system for city council, 223; in government, 106; and HB as mayor, 122–24, 126, 128, 210, 283; and HB's dialogues with voters, 291; as HB's philosophy of government, 255–56; as issue in mayoral campaign, 63; as legacy, 374–76, 381, 424; and neighborhood redevelopment, 123, 166–67; and police chief selection, 104; and seniors, 400, 408; speaking engagements on, 319, 401. *See also* volunteers

citizens advisory groups, 124

"Citizens for Balanced Representation," 77

"Citizens for Concerned Government," 75–76

Citizens Resource Bank, 124

Citizen Task Force for Community Development, 156, 458n

city and county government, consolidation of, 63

city council, HB's service on: first campaign for, 25–33; first term, 33–36; second term, 37–38; third and fourth terms, 38–39

city council (1975–77): and budget preparation, 117–18; conflicts with HB, 129; and HB's appointments, 124–25; staggered election of, 25, 445n

city council (1977–79): 1977 election, 156–59; and bickering, 156–63; and mayoral campaign (1979), 213–15;

city council (1979–81): 1979 election, 222–25, 238, 243–46; and budget, 280–82; and Radial project, 283–86; relationship with mayor, 261

city council (1981–83): 1981 election, 288–89; and budget, 353–54; and Radial referendum, 288, 482n

City-County Planning Commission. *See* Lincoln–Lancaster County Planning Commission

city-neighborhood forums, 123–24, 283

civil rights, 358. *See also* disabilities, citizens with; equal rights; gay rights amendment; human rights; women's rights

Clark, Ken, 475n

Clinton, Hillary, 131

Cochran, Tom, 307, 312, 329–30, 493n

Collins, Martha Layne, 88, 89, 139

Common Cause, 413

Community Development Block Grant program. *See* CDBG program

Community Health Charities, 413

Community Health Endowment, 412–13

composting, 274, 476n

Comprehensive Employment and Training Act (CETA) programs, 321, 359

Comprehensive Plan: in 1975 mayoral campaign, 63, 73–74; in 1975 mayoral term, 133, 153–56, 162–63, 455n, 458–59n, 469n; in 1979 mayoral campaign, 210, 216–18, 222; in 1979 mayoral term, 246, 276–80, 283, 478n; in governor's race, 342–43. *See also* zoning

Connick, Harry, 410

Consumer Advisory Council to the SEC, 404–5

consumer protection and AARP, 403, 407

Cook, Steve: on 1975–77 city council, 101, 108, 109, 115, 124, 129; and 1977–79 city council, 162–63, 171–72, 208, 246, 457n; and 1977 city council election, 159; in 1979 city council election, 223–25, 238, 243; on city council with HB, 39; decision not to run for mayor, 211

Cormier, Lucy, 442

Cornhusker Square development, 266–70, 271, 381, 391, 474n, 475n

corporate farming restrictions (Initiative 300), 341, 344. *See also* agriculture as issue in governor's race

Crosby, Robert, 109

Crounse, Jim, 48

Cuomo, Mario, 135

curb ramps, 359

Cutler, Lynn, 93, 135–36

Daley, Richard J., 121, 448n, 449n

Danley, Bill, 288

Daub, Hal, 3

Davies, Tom, 415

Davis, Beth Boosalis (HB's daughter): a.k.a. Mary Beth, 1; birth of, 204, 390; childhood of, 12–37; education of, 54–55; election to Evanston City Council, 372–73, 502n; fundraising in Chicago, 140–45; in governor's race, 7–11, 43–44, 95, 134, 140–45, 248–52, 257, 303–6, 349–50, 383–91, 395; and Gram's history, 460–61; and HB's childhood, 174–75, 461–62n; in HB's first city council run, 25–26, 27, 29–33; in HB's second city council run, 38; marriage, 55, 57; and mayoral campaigns, 67–68, 79–83, 86, 242; as mother, 1–2, 11, 53, 142, 248, 250, 252, 317, 323, 382; in National League of Cities, 487n, 507n; and superwoman, 360; at U.S. Conference of Mayors, 307–8, 322–23, 336–38, 493n; wedding of, 81

Davis, Beth Boosalis (HB's daughter), photos of: celebrating 1979 mayoral election, *242*; city council campaign, *29*; at farewell celebration, *381*; in governor's race, *45, 46, 251*; with HB, *421*; on Helen Boosalis Trail, *411*

Davis, Christopher (BD's son), *45, 46, 251*; during father's illness, 417–18; in gubernatorial campaign, 1, 7, 44, 142, 250–52, 383, 388, 391; as official alderbaby, 373

Davis, Max (BD's husband), *45, 46,* 242; in gubernatorial campaign, 2, 11, 383, 391; illness, 416–20; marriage, 55, 57; and mayoral general election, 79–81; siblings of, 81; at U.S. Conference of Mayors, 322–23, 336–38; at wedding, 81

Davis, Michael (BD's son), *45, 46, 251*; Carter's congratulations on birth

Davis, Michael (*continued*)
of, 317; during father's illness, 417; in
gubernatorial campaign, 2, 44, 142,
52, 250–52, 383, 388, 391
DeCamp, John, 97, 494n
Democratic Party: and gubernatorial
race, 2, 5, 51, 93, 136–38, 256, 385, 386,
394, 444n; HB's involvement with, 50,
316; in Nebraska, 383–84; unity session after 1986 primary, 47–48, 48. *See
also* Lancaster County Democratic
Party
DeMuse, Tony, 185, 462n
Denney, Max: on 1975–77 city council,
101, 108, 124, 129, 151; as council
chairman, 86; on police chief decision, 110–11, 112; as possible mayoral
opponent to HB, 207
Department on Aging, Nebraska, 48,
50, 399–401
disabilities, citizens with, 73, 358–59
district election system (partial) for city
council, 223, 244
Divas group, 424
dogs and rabies shots, 33
Dole, Bob, 137
Dole, Elizabeth, 137
Domina, David, 3, 5, 6, 7, 43, 47, 48, 48,
50, 51, 444
Donaldson, Curt, 151, 286, 413, 441n
Donnellan, Kevin, 216, 403, 407
Dow, Breta, 24
Dowden, Don, 192
Downtown Advisory Committee, 165,
266, 271, 458n
downtown revitalization: in 1975
mayoral term, 133, 163–65, 209; in
1979 mayoral term, 264–72; as issue
in mayoral campaign, 63; legacy, 375,
376, 381, 503n; and HUD grants, 314
downzoning issue. *See* zoning

Drucker, Peter F., 491
Dudek, Frank, 414
Dukakis, Mike, 141
du Pont, Pierre, 137, 331
Durand, Joyce, 260
Durenberger, David, 331

Ebel, A. James, 358
Ebeling, Bobby, 15
Ebeling, Dick, 26
Ebeling family, 14, 25, 26
economic conditions: in 1975 mayoral
term, 119–20, 123, 171; in 1979 mayoral
term, 247, 264, 268, 277–78, 280, 281,
283, 289, 313, 335, 338, 352, 356, 473n,
487n, 492n; and city services, 313; as
U.S. Conference of Mayors issue,
313–36
economic development: as issue in
governor's race, 94, 250, 302, 340,
341–43; and Urban Development
Department, 115, 123, 167
Economic Development Commission,
263, 278
Edgar, Jim, 485
education: as issue in governor's race,
94, 291, 297, 298, 340, 343–44, 385, 393,
494n; and AARP, 403. *See also* LB662
referendum
Eizenstat, Stuart, 310
Ellis Island, 460
Endicott, Don, 77–78
Energy Action Committee, 150, 274
energy use policy: in 1975 mayoral
term, 133, 147–53, 161; in 1979 mayoral
term, 261, 273–75, 276
Enerson, Eleanore, 475
Enerson, Larry, 272, 379, 475
Equal Employment Opportunity Act,
62
equal rights, 147, 356–63. *See also* civil

rights; disabilities, citizens with; women's rights

Equal Rights Amendment (ERA), 62, 94–95, 96, 361, 362–63, 436

Equal Rights Movement, 56

Eskind, Jane, 249

Evanston (Illinois) City Council, 257, 372–73, 454, 487n

Exon, J. James "Jim," 405; on abortion issue, 444n; campaigns for HB, 386; fundraising for governor's race, 135, 136; as governor, 170, 394; on HB, 256

fallout shelters, 35–36

family political dynasties, 502n

farm economy. *See* agriculture as issue in governor's race

federal building purchase by city, 260

federal cuts in aid to cities, 322, 325, 326–34, 336, 338; and low-income housing, 333; and transit funding, 352

federalism, new: HB on, 322, 324–36; National Urban Conference on Federalism, 327–31, 339; and Reagan budget cuts, 334, 491n; and sales tax proposal, 352

Federal Public Transportation Act (1980), 314

Feinstein, Diane, 314

Fell, Paul, 159

Ferguson, Miriam "Ma," 88

Ferraro, Geraldine, 87, 97

Flogeras, Yionna and George (HB's maternal grandparents), 175, 180, 183–84, 188–89

Florest (Flogeras), Gus (HB's uncle), 175, 176, 187, 192

football frenzy: and BD's wedding, 81; and Bush speech, 328–29; Memorial Stadium, 384

Ford, Gerald, 121, 309, 449n

Fraser, Don, 336, 487n

Friedan, Betty, 62, 435n

Frohardt, Donna, 224, 243

Fulton, Richard, 339

fundraising: in governor's race, 134–45, 248–49, 348–49, 394–95, 496n; in governor's primary race, 8–10, 50–51; and women political candidates, 361. *See also* campaign contributions

Galbraith, John Kenneth, 330

Gallup, George, 168–70

garbage-fueled generation of electricity, 150–51, 453, 476n. *See also* waste-burning plant

Gauger, Jan, 414; as county commissioner, 75, 160, 359, 499; on HB, 112–13, 146, 160; and Lincoln-Lancaster Commission on the Status of Women, 132; and reelection strategy group, 413

gay rights amendment, 356–57

Geankoplis, Andy (HB's brother), 177, 179, 201

Geankoplis, Bertha Flogeras (HB's mother), 175–76, 177, 180–81, 184–86, 189–92, 200, 204, 242, 460n. *See also* Gram (HB's mother)

Geankoplis, Christie (HB's father's cousin), 185

Geankoplis, George (HB's father), 176–77, 177, 180–86, 189, 191–92, 200, 462n

Geankoplis, Helen, 175–93; birth, 177–78; childhood, 178–90; courtship and marriage, 193–205; and high school/post–high school, 190–92. *See also* Boosalis, Helen

Geankoplis, Helen, photos of: at age three, 178; at engagement, 196; high

Geankoplis, Helen (*continued*)
  school graduation;, *191*; with Mike
  Boosalis, *195*; with siblings, *179*
Geankoplis, Jim (HB's uncle), 177
Geankoplis, Nick (HB's father's cousin),
  177
Gephardt, Richard, 139
Gibson, Kenneth, 449
Ginsburg, Ruth Bader, 363, 471
Giovanni, Bill, 254–55
Girl Scouts, 15, 16
Goals and Policies Committee, 74,
  279–80, 478n
Gold, Nate, 24, 78
Goldberg, Gary, 385
Gold family, 265, 266, 268
Goldman, Barbara, 315
Goldschmidt, Neil, 314
Gold's Galleria, 268, 271
Goodhue, Bertram, 272
Goodyear company, 473n; volunteers
  from, 355
Gore, Al, *406*
governors, women as, 88
governor's race. *See* gubernatorial
  campaign (1986)
Gram (HB's mother), *177*, *242*; death of,
  388–89; on HB's appearance, 131; and
  Israel, 320; as loyal friend, 80, 414;
  and mayoral campaign, 57–58, 80–82;
  on poker, 187, 415; political heroes of,
  423; at U.S. Conference of Mayors in
  Minneapolis, 336. *See also* Geankoplis,
  Bertha Flogeras (HB's mother)
Grasso, Ella, 88
Greek community: in BD's childhood,
  43; and fundraising, 141; in HB's
  childhood, 186, 188; at HB's farewell
  celebration, 379
Greek Orthodox Church, 43, 187, 188,
  414

Greek Orthodox Church of the Annunciation, 413
Greek school, 188–89
Greene, Louie, 176, 460n
groundwater as issue in governor's
  race, 302; as issue in 1975 mayoral
  term, 152–53
growth and land use policy: appointments related to, 126; and historic
  preservation, 409; as issue facing
  HB, 133, 277, 279; as issue in 1977 city
  council election, 156–63. *See also*
  Comprehensive Plan
gubernatorial campaign (1986). See
  "Flash Forward" chapters
gun control as issue at U.S. Conference
  of Mayors, 308

Hagel, Chuck, 54
hairstyles, media comments on, 130–31
Haldeman, H. R., 475n
Hamilton, Bruce, 85
Hampton, Joe: on 1977–79 city council,
  159, 161–62, 163, 167, 457n; in 1977 city
  council election, 157–59, 208, 222, 231;
  and 1979 city 223, 224, 244, 245; on
  1979–81 city council, 260, 261–62, 270,
  274, 277–79, 284–86; and 1980 budget
  shortfall, 281–82; in 1981 city council
  election, 286–88, 481n; on HB, 253,
  285–87, 336, 369, 371, 497n; run for
  mayor (1983), 363, 369–71, 374, 501n;
  and lobbying for sales tax increase,
  353, 487n; support for Matzke in
  1979 mayoral campaign, 213–15; and
  transit cuts, 325; and John Robinson,
  172–73, 460n
Hans, Bob, 278, 458
Hansen, George, *115*; condolence letter
  to wife of, 378–79; and curbing HB's
  bus riding, 150; in police chief con-

troversy, 107, 108, 111, 113, 114, 446n, 447n; resignation of, 207–8

Hanson, Richard, 42

Harris, Lous, 120–21

Hart, Gary, 139, *139*

Hatcher, Richard, 315, 338, 449

Hauder, Laurie, 131

Hawkins, Paula, 88

Hayden, Greg, 122, 302, 346, 398, 476

Haymarket Landmark District, 266, 270–71, 474n

health insurance, national, as issue at U.S. Conference of Mayors, 308

Health Partners Initiatives, 413

Hecht, Ross E., 206, 413

Hefner, Christie, 143–45

Helen Boosalis Park, 412

Helen Boosalis Trail, 412

Hendrix, George, 85, 335, 370

Herman, Jacquelyn, 123, 458

Herman, Richard "Dick," 153, 156, 413

Herschler, Ed, 341

Hickman, Harrison, 89, 303, 306, 347, 348

Higgins, Marge, 3

Hills, Carla, 120

Hinkley, Lloyd D., 12, 38–39, 370, 413–14, 501

historic preservation, 408–10, 474–75

Historic Preservation Commission, 409, 474–75

Hoch, Nancy, 2–3, 4, 5, 7, 43

Holbert, Fred, 105

Homer, Dan, 417, 419

housing, high-density downtown, 271–72

housing, manufactured (mobile homes), 404

Hudnut, William, 339

Human Rights Commission, 172, 356–57, 359

human services, city funding of, 459n; as issue in mayoral campaign, 63; and U.S. Conference of Mayors, 312–13, 487n

Humble, Charles, 102

Humphrey, Hubert, 120, 187, 312, 462n

IBM site in Lincoln, 277–78, 369–70. *See also* Stevens Creek development

Illinois gubernatorial campaign (1994), 485n

incumbency as electoral advantage, 89, 441–42n

Indian Center, 455

infrastructure maintenance, 331, 338, 454n

international representation of mayors, 318–20

Isco, 4, 10, 342

Israel, mayors' delegation to, 319–20

Jackson, Jacky, 14

Jackson, Lloyd, 414

Jackson, Maynard, *138*, 139–40, 449

Jackson, Sue Bailey. *See* Bailey, Sue

Jeambey, Bob: on 1975–77 city council, 101, 105, 110, 124, 129, 151–52, 154, 157, 163; on 1977–79 city council, 169, 457n; and 1977 city council election, 160; decision not to run for reelection (1979), 223, 465

Jerusalem Conference of Mayors, 319–20

Johanns, Mike, 99, 253

Johnson, Ann and Dick, 415

Johnson, Vard, 2

Karlos, Harry, 194

Kassebaum, Nancy, 88

Kauffman, Fred, 127–28

Kawasaki company, 332

Kelly, Jimmy, 14

Kemp, Jack, 137

Kennedy, Barry, 296

Kennedy, John F., 55

Kennedy, Ted, 120, 316

Kerrey, Bob, *46, 48, 137, 343*; in 1982 governor's race, 51, 135, 349, 384, 390, 394, 50m; and 1986 governor's race, 2, 3, 5, 6, 45, 47–48, 301, 342, 346, 386, 387, 394; and abortion issue, 95, 443–44n; on appointing HB to cabinet, 399–400; on HB, 99, 253, 255, 503n; and LB662, 344, 49m, 494–95n; and speculation on run for city council, 288

Kidd, Dan, 475

Knoll, Robert E., 94, 206

Knolls restaurant, 81–82, 226, 240, 323

Koch, Edward, 315, 339

Kolleck, Teddy, 319

Kotok, David, 291–94, , 298, 299, 344, 386

Kuehl, Patty, 400

Kuhn, Bowie, 335

Kunin, Madeleine, 88

Kurtze, Al, 416

Labedz, Bernice, 95

labor unions, municipal, 282. *See also* police union

Lachman, Andrew, 416

Lambrinides, Mr. (Greek teacher), 189

Lancaster County Democratic Party: endorsement in 1975 mayoral race, 65, 69. *See also* Democratic Party

Landes, Bertha Knight, 62, 436n

Landis, Dave, 352

Landrieu, Moon, 314, 328

Latimer, George, 50, 139, 253, 307, 336, 506n

Lauterbach, Ned, 372

LB662 referendum (school consolida-

tion and sales tax for education): as issue in governor's race, 298, 343–44, 345, 393, 483n, 494–95n, 505n; and voter turnout, 385, 393, 505

League of Human Dignity, 359

League of Women Voters: and the 1977 city council election, 158; and 1979 mayoral election, 236; in city charter battle, 20–23, 61; and governor's race, 343; HB in, 15, 18–19, 65; and HB's run for city council, 23–24, 27, 30; as source of HB appointments, 125

Leavitt, Bill, 414

Lee, Bill, 297

Lee Teng-hui, 318

Legeros, Anna Flogeras, 175, 176, 183, 460

Legeros, Christ, 183, 460n

Legeros, Elaine, George, John, and Con, 187

Leitner, Dean, 209

LES. *See* Lincoln Electric System (LES)

letters from school children, 499–500n

Levitt, Arthur, 404–5

Lewis, Kenneth, 30, 32

Lewis, Sherdell, shooting of, 113–14

Lincoln NE: city charter battle, 20–22; electoral system for mayor/city council, 437n, 445n; restructuring of city departments, 114–19, 161, 209; size of, 26, 436n, 455n; strong-mayor form of government, 20–22, 37, 61, 101–2, 172, 440n, 445n

Lincoln Alliance, 224–25, 286, 48m

Lincoln Comprehensive Plan. *See* Comprehensive Plan

Lincoln Electric System (LES): in 1975 mayoral term, 150–52, 161–62; in 1979 mayoral term, 274–75; and alternative energy sources, 150–52, 274–75; board appointments, 124–25, 127,

160; budget, 447; and nuclear power, 150–52, 275

Lincolnfest, 164

Lincoln General Hospital: board appointments, 127–28; budget, 447n; as issue in 1979 election, 219–22, 231–38, 242–43, 245; lease repeal, 246; lease veto, 231; petition drive, 233–38; proposed lease, 219–22, 231–33; sale of, 412–13

Lincoln in View (television program), 263

Lincoln-Lancaster Commission on the Status of Women, 131–32, 359

Lincoln–Lancaster County Planning Commission, 126, 278

Lincoln/Lancaster Public Health Foundation, 413

Lincoln Mall, 272

Lincoln Saltdogs, 492n

Lincoln Transportation System (LTS), 126, 149, 161, 273–74, 325, 476n

Litjen, Tom, 249

Lockwood, Fred, 385

Lott, Roger, 370

LTS. *See* Lincoln Transportation System (LTS)

Luedtke, Roland, 370–71, 374, 378, 501

Maguire, Karen, 245, 261

Mahoney, Gene, 2

Maier, Henry, 339, 449

Malone neighborhood, 113, 114, 156, 166, 358

Marczewski, Roman, 419–20

Marsh, Shirley, 49

Martin, Bennett "Abe," 21, 23, 31–32

mass transit: in 1979 mayoral term, 273–74, 476n; and 1979–81 city council, 261; budget, 447n, 459n, 479n; and Federal Public Transportation Act

(1980), 314; and Reagan administration cuts, 325–26, 330, 334, 352; sales tax increase request to state legislature, 352, 476n, 496n; and UMTA cuts, 321

Matzke, Stan: in 1979 mayoral general election campaign, 225–31, 235–36, 240, 242, 262; in 1979 mayoral primary campaign, 206–7, 211–14, 216–19; considers second run for mayor (1983), 368–69; support for HB, 206, 211, 376

mayoral campaign (1975), 57–86; analysis of, 68–69, 83–86; decision to run, 57–61, 372; endorsements, 439–40; general election campaign, 73–79; issues, 63; polls, 65, 79; primary campaign, 64–73; primary/general election system, 437n; victory, 79–86; as woman candidate, 61–64

mayoral campaign (1979), 206–47; advertising, 227–30; announcement for, 208–9; campaign spending in, 501n; debates in, 230–31, 235; general election, 225–31; issues, 209–14, 216–22, 228–38, 239; general election outcome, 238–43; primary, 210–19, 222–26; reunions with reelection strategy group, 413–14

mayoral election (1983), 367–71, 374, 378

mayoral term, 3rd, decision not to pursue, 209, 398–99

mayoral term (1975–79), 99–133, 146–73, 209–10, 239

mayoral term (1979–83), 260–89, 351–82

Mayor's Committee for International Friendship, 413

Mayor's Committee on Opportunities for the Disabled, 358–59

McClelland, Nancy, 216, 359

McFarland, Jim, 413

McGinley, Don, 386, 390
McGinn, Bobby, 132
McNichols, Bill, 318, 493n
Meese, Ed, 330
Merwick, Michael, 102, 106, 118, 149, 167, 215–16, 259, 414–15
Messinger, Ruth, 416
Mikulski, Barbara A., 54, 88, 89, 92
Minnegasco company, volunteers from, 355
Minnick, Gates, 379
Mitchell, Walt, 104
Moe, Richard, 408–9
Monaghan, Tom, 48, 346, 391, 393–94
Mondale, Walter, 310
Moore, Terry, 48–49
Morial, "Dutch," 339
Morrison, Frank, 5, 6, *343*, 386–87
Moscone, George, 309
Moul, Francis, 94
Moul, Maxine, 94
Moynihan, Daniel, 334
Murdock, David, 269–70, 475n
"mystery guest" dinners, 415

Nantkes, Danielle M., 499
Narveson, Phyllis, 409
National Commission on Manufactured Housing, 404
National League of Cities, 416, 487n, 502n
National Organization for Women, 56, 131, 434–35n
National Register of Historic Places, 270
National Trust for Historic Preservation, 408–10
National Urban Conference on Federalism, 327–31, 339
National Women's Political Caucus, 62, 88, 96, 444

Natividad, Irene, 444n
Nebraska: effect of Reagan administration cuts on, 325–26; sales tax increase request to legislature, 352–53, 496; as site of two-woman race/media coverage of, 93–94; voter statistics, 5, 383–85
Nebraska Advisory Commission on Intergovernmental Affairs, 325, 490n
Nebraska AppleSeed Center for Law in the Public Interest, 413
Nebraska Commission on the Status of Women, 413
Nebraska Community Foundation, 413, 498–99n
Nebraska Department on Aging, 48, 50, 399–401
neighborhood redevelopment, 74, 123, 133, 166–68, 209, 246, 289, 358, 458n, 469n; and Community Development Block Grants, 321; and Comprehensive Plan, 156, 276; as issue, 63, 147; legacy, 376; and U.S. Conference of Mayors, 312
neighborhood groups, 85, 123–24, 167, 261–62, 284, 368, 379
Nellas, Betty Flogeras (HB's aunt), 175, 178, 182–83, 204
Nellas, JoAnne and Tom, 204
Nelson, Ben: co-chair for Carter campaign, 5, 316; elected governor, 394; governor's race co-chair, 5, 134–35, 304, 345, 390; on HB, 258, 259
Nelson, Don, 153, 346
Netsch, Dawn Clark, 142–43, 485n
Netsch, Walter, 142
new federalism. *See* federalism, new
"New Pols," 261
Northeast Radial project, 213, 260, 283–86, 288, 482
nuclear power plants, 151–52, 275

Obama, Barack, 440n
oil embargo (1973), 119, 147–49
"Old Pols," 261–62
Omaha Public Power District (OPPD), 151–52
O'Neill, Tip, 334
Orme, Fern Hubbard, 25
Orr, Kay, *91, 305*; absence of tax plan, 302, 483–84n; ads on taxes in gubernatorial campaign, 294–99, 300–303, 305; anti-business accusations against HB, 343; background, 49; campaign's own poll, 483n; comparisons with HB, 252–53, 345; endorsements, 386; fiscal record of, 346–47; fundraising, 136, 349, 496n; and gubernatorial election results, 505n; image of, 253, 345; loses governorship to Nelson, 394; position on corporate farming, 341; position on LB662, 298, 344, 385, 393, 505n; position on tax increases, 293–97, 483–84n; positions on ERA and abortion, 96, 393; Reagan campaigning for, 51, 52, 136, 301, 341; in Republican gubernatorial primary, 3, 4, 5, 7, 43, 46, 49; summer campaign strategy, 257–58; tax increases as governor, 506n; ties to Thone, 49, 345, 346
"O Street gang," 85, 440–41n
ostrich race, 350, 364, *365*
Oxman, Neil, 1, 7–11, 134, 297–98, 303, 383–84, 506n

parking downtown, 164–65, 210
Parks and Recreation Department, 353–55, 459n
Pelosi, Nancy, 60
"people's mayor," 380, 503
Peterson, Betty, 226, 506–7n
Peterson, Dean, 38, 101, 235
Peterson, Glenda, 413, 475n

Petr, Jerry L., 146
Pfeifer, Betty, 15, 26, 164
Pfeifer, Ronnie, 13–15
Pfeifer family, 25, 26
Phillips, Ted, 187
Pierce, Samuel, 333
Planning Commission, City-County. *See* Lincoln–Lancaster County Planning Commission
Planning Department, 217–18, 246, 278. *See also* Brogden, Doug
poetry book, HB's lost, 461
poker game, 187, 414–15
police chief controversy, 103–14, 147, 208, 358, 445n, 446n, 447n
police chief finalist selection committee, 105, 107, 111, 112
Police Review Board, 106, 113, 126, 358
police union, 107, 108, 113, 282
Porter, Helen, 25
Potter, Jan, 498–99n
"poverty, pockets of," 269, 315, 474n
Powell, Richard, 172. *See also* Human Rights Commission
President's Commission on the Status of Women, 55
Pritchard, Marty, 455
private sector. *See* public-private partnerships
Private Sector Initiatives Task Force, 331–32, 405
program budgeting, introduction of, 117–18
public-private partnerships: Centrum Project, 164–65, 264–65; Cornhusker Square, 268–70; Kawasaki employees, 332; promoted by HB, 239, 375, 491n; and Reagan administration, 331–32, 491n; and U.S. Conference of Mayors, 312, 338–39
Public Works Department, 115–16, 459n

Radial. *See* Northeast Radial

Ray, Dixie Lee, 88

Reagan, Ronald, *324*, 503n; effect of administration on cities, 320–27, 491n; and Kay Orr, 49, 51, 52, 136, 341. *See also* federalism, new

Reed, Christie, 38

revenue sharing, federal, 121, 313, 459n; cuts in, 321, 326–27, 333

ride-sharing carpool/van-pool program, 149, 247, 273

Riley, Joe, 339

ring, stolen, 409–10

Robb, Charles, 139

Robinson, John: on 1975–77 city council, 101, 106, 110, 124–25, 129, 151, 154; on 1977–79 city council, 160, 169; and 1977 city council election, 157; on 1979–81 city council, 243; and decision not to run for reelection (1981), 286, 287; and Joe Hampton, 172–73, 460n

Rockefeller, David, 120

Rockefeller, Nelson, 121

Rockey, Brian, 249

Roeser, Tom, 140–41, 143

Roe v. Wade decision, 62

Rooney, Andy, 375

Roosevelt, Franklin and Eleanor, 24, 55, 186, 203, 423

Rosenow, John, 212, 377, 410–11, 491n

Ross, Nellie Tayloe, 88

Royer, Charles, 315

Royko, Mike, 97

Rutledge, Kathleen, 96, 212, 295, 345–46, 386

sales tax increase request to state legislature, 352–53, 476n, 496n. *See also* LB662 referendum (school consolidation and sales tax for education)

San Francisco Gay Men's Chorus, 357–58

Sankey, Stevie, 14

Sarbanes, Paul, 141, 142, 174, 322

Sater, Ione Geankoplis (HB's sister), 177, 179, 191, 204, 336

Savery, Gil, 381

Scanlon, Bob, 210–11, 463n

Scheibel, Jim, 416

Scherer, Leo: on 1977–79 city council, 162, 208, 209; in 1977 city council election, 157–59; on 1979–81 city council, 260, 262–63; and 1979 city council election, 223, 224, 243, 244; and 1979 mayoral campaign, 213–14; and decision not to run for reelection (1981), 286–87, 481n; on police chief controversy, 109, 208

Schlaebitz, Bill, 323

Schlafly, Phyllis, 361

school consolidation referendum. *See* LB662 referendum (school consolidation and sales tax for education)

Schrepf, Bob, 215, 441

Schroeder, Pat, 361, 436n

Schwartzkopf, Christie, 288, 435n

Schwartzkopf, Sam, 71; in 1975 mayoral race, 60, 64–66, 68–69, 73–79, 82, 84–85, 439–40n; and 1979 mayoral race, 207; and city council, 101, 159, 160, 172; as mayor, 39; and police chief, 103–4

Seacrest, Mike, 415

Seng, Coleen, 78, 280, 379, 503n

senior center downtown, 164

seniors and citizen involvement, 400, 408

Seventh Day Adventists, 221–22, 231, 465n

Shackelford, Louis, 288, 482n

Shanks, Hughes, 104, 126–27

Shanks, Lela, 104–5

Shelley, Nancy, 16

Shelley, Sue, 15–16, 164, 413

Shelley family, 14, 15, 25, 26

Shrier, Howard, 303

Shugrue, Richard, 297, 345, 348

Sikyta, Bob: on 1975–77 city council, 101, 108, 109, 115, 117, 124–25; on 1977–79 city council, 159, 161–63, 167, 170–71, 208, 216–17, 235; in 1979 city council election, 223–25, 238; and 1979 mayoral campaign, 213–14; in 1981–83 city council, 279; and appointment to Lincoln General Hospital, 127–28; on city council with HB, 39; criticism of HB, 102, 117, 125, 129, 130, 212; defeat of (1979), 243, 244; on HB, 376; on Goals and Policies monitoring board, 279; proposed run for mayor, 209, 211–12

Sileven, Everett, 97

Simon, Paul, 502

Simpson, Alan, 407

Sittig, Robert, 50, 59, 68–69, 158–59, 254, 343, 345

Smith, Margaret Chase, 442n

Snelling, Richard, 330

snow-removal policy as issue in 1979 election, 218, 229

Soglin, Paul, 77, 84

solar energy, 151

"Sound Off to City Hall" forums, 123, 283

Southeast Community College and Comprehensive Plan, 154–55, 277

Southeast Nebraska Cancer Foundation, 413

Starkweather, Charles, 14

state legislators, women as, 56–57, 89

Steinman, Mike, 224, 243, 245, 261, 286, 357

Stevens Creek development: in 1975 mayoral campaign, 74; and 1977–79 city council, 153–56, 157, 162–63, 457n; in 1979 mayoral term, 278–79; as campaign issue (1983), 369; and zoning code, 469n

Stockman, David, 326–27, 333

strong-mayor form of government in Lincoln, 20–22, 37, 61, 101–2, 172, 440n, 445n

Suffrage Movement, 56, 441n

Sun Yun-suan, 318

superwoman myth, 360–61

Swartzlander, David, 378

Swift, Dean, 140

Switt, Jane, 441–42n

swimming pools, 34–35

Taiwan, mayors' delegation to, 318, 489n

tax increases: as issue in governor's race, 291–306, 344–46, 393–94, 483–84, 494–95n, 505n; under Orr's governorship, 394, 506n

tax increment financing, 268–69, 473n

tax swap plans (Illinois, Michigan), 485n

telemarketing fraud, 407

"The Home Energy (T.H.E.) Audit" program, 275

Thompson, Jack, 24

Thone, Charles, 49, 135, 322, 325, 384, 490n, 501n

Tiemann, Nobby, 6

Townsend, Kathleen Kennedy, 442

transit. *See* mass transit

transportation department, 161. *See also* Lincoln Transportation System (LTS)

Truman Presidential Museum and Library, 396

Tupper, Gail, 38

Tyrrell, Del, 30, 32, 34, 37

UDAG (Urban Development Action Grant) program. *See* Urban Development Action Grant (UDAG) program

"ultra-liberal," accusations of, 65, 75–79, 84

UMTA grants. *See* Urban Mass Transit Administration (UMTA)

unemployment: in Lincoln, 313, 315, 375, 487–88n; and Reagan administration, 331, 333–34, 492n

University of Nebraska–Lincoln Osher Lifelong Learning Institute, 413

Urban Development Action Grant (UDAG) program, 269, 315, 321, 333, 474n, 491n

Urban Development Department, 115, 123, 166–68

Urban Mass Transit Administration (UMTA), grants, 321–22

urban policy: Carter administration, 309–13; Reagan administration, 320–21, 337–38

Urbom, Warren and Joyce, 415

U.S. Conference of Mayors: fiftieth anniversary of, 336; HB as president, 322–39; HB as president-elect, 314–18; HB joins, 119–21, 449n; HB's early leadership roles in, 307–14; history of, 313, 486n; Human Development Standing Committee, 312–13, 330, 487n, 502n; international visits representing, 320–38; and Reagan administration, 320–36; seventy-fifth anniversary of, 493n; and U.S. Department of Education hearings, 358–59

U.S. Congress, women in (1986), 56, 88

U.S. Department of Transportation ridesharing grants, 273

USSR, mayors' delegation to, 318–19, 493

Vatz, Joan and Ken, 417

Vavoulis, George, 417

Vavoulis, Tina Geankoplis (HB's sister), 177, 179, 179, 185, 189, 193, 204, 336, 392

V.I.P. program, 354–56

Voinovich, George, 174, 339, 377

volunteers: citizen advisory groups, 122–29; HB as, 12–25, 396; and reduced park services, 353–56. *See also* citizen involvement

voter education, and AARP, 403

Wallace, Lurleen, 88

Walton, Don, 49, 164, 295, 300, 348, 349, 394–95, 396–97, 444n

Warner, Carolyn, 89

waste-burning plant: 150–51, 453n, 476n; in 1979 mayoral term, 274. *See also* garbage-fueled generation of electricity

Water Advisory Board, 127

water policy, 116, 447n

water resources, 152–53

Watson, Steve, 165, 264

Waxman, Laura DeKoven, 487n

Weber, Warren, 75, 171

Welch, Susan, 211

Wells, Jack, 24

White, Dick, 165, 458n

White, Kevin, 449n

White, Tom, 374

Whitmore, Bee, 299

Whitmire, Kathy, 339

Wiese, David, 349

Williamson, Rich, 324, 337

Wilson, Marie, 59–60

Wilson, Ted, 339

Winter, A. B., 85

Winters, Gordon, 159

Wolf, Alice, 416

women's commissions: Lincoln-Lan-

caster Commission on the Status of Women, 131–32, 359, *414*; Nebraska Commission on the Status of Women, 413, 498–99n; President's Commission on the Status of Women, 55
Women Executives in State Government (WESG), 52
women in the political arena: background, 55–57, 90, 435n; elected officials, 56, 88–89, 435n; first woman president of U.S. Conference of Mayors, 314, 323; first two-woman race for governor, 45–46, 87–98, 252, 442n; HB's support for, 132, 361–62, 363, 498n; HB's view of, 63, 92–93; history, 88–90, 132–33, 471n; as issue in 1975 mayoral election, 61–63; as issue in 1979 mayoral campaign, 210–11, 229; opposition to HB in, 67; perceptions of women candidates, 59–60, 62, 89–90; prejudice against, 29, 96–97; reactions to HB during first term on city council, 36–37; in U.S. Conference of Mayors, 314
Women's Campaign Fund, 96
women's activism for social change, 56, 435n

women's rights: in governor's race, 94–95, 345; HB's concerns for, 131–32, 359–63
Women's Rights Movement, 56–57, 363
Wood, Dick, 109
Woodcock, Leonard, 120
Woolman, Clancy, 354
Wright, Judy, 38, 67

yard signs in HB's campaigns, 29–30, 72
Yates, Burnham, 269
"The Year of the Woman," 87–88
Young, Coleman, 139, 339, 449
Youngberg, Eric, 224, 243, 261, 274, 286, 357

Zerschling, Lynn, 76
zoning: in 1975 mayoral campaign, 63; in 1975 mayoral term, 162–63; in 1979 mayoral campaign, 210, 213, 216–18, 222; in 1979 mayoral term, 276–80, 342; adoption of zoning code, 246–47, 469n. *See also* Comprehensive Plan
Zorinsky, Ed, 135, 390